RENAISSANCE HISTORICISM

Renaissance Historicism

SELECTIONS FROM

English Literary Renaissance

EDITED BY

Arthur F. Kinney

AND

Dan S. Collins

THE UNIVERSITY OF MASSACHUSETTS PRESS

AMHERST

1987

Library of Congress Cataloging-in-Publication Data

Renaissance historicism.

Includes index.

1. English literature—Early modern, 1500–1700—
History and criticism. 2. Renaissance—England.
3. Literature and history—England. 4. Historical
criticism (Literature). 5. Historicism. I. Kinney,
Arthur F., 1933–   . II. Collins, Dan S.
III. English literary renaissance.
PR423.R46   1987   820′.9′003   87–6052
ISBN 0–87023–598–2 (pbk.: alk. paper)

British Library Cataloguing in Publication data are available

Acknowledgments on Illustrations: Reproductions from Sebastian Brant's edition of Vergil (p. 85) and from Spenser's *Shepheardes Calendar* (p. 86) are reprinted here courtesy of the Library of Congress, Washington, D.C.; the Dutch broadside *The Kingly Cock* (p. 272) is reproduced by courtesy of the Trustees of the British Museum; the illustrations from the works of George Wither, Geffrey Whitney, and Hans Holbein (pp. 331–32) are reprinted with permission of the Beinecke Rare Book and Manuscript Library, Yale University; illustrations from the works of Thomas Browne, Cesariano, and Agrippa (pp. 373, 376) are reprinted with permission of The Huntington Library, San Marino, California; and the fold-out table from a work by John Wilkins (pp. 374–75) is reproduced by permission of Hamilton College.

Contents

Preface
ARTHUR F. KINNEY   vii

The New Historicism in Renaissance Studies
JEAN E. HOWARD   3

"Eliza, Queene of shepheardes," and the Pastoral of Power
LOUIS ADRIAN MONTROSE   34

Re-opening the Green Cabinet: Clément Marot and Edmund Spenser
ANNABEL PATTERSON   64

The Hegemonic Theater of George Puttenham
JONATHAN V. CREWE   93

Senecan and Vergilian Perspectives in *The Spanish Tragedy*
EUGENE D. HILL   108

Renaissance Family Politics and Shakespeare's
The Taming of the Shrew
KAREN NEWMAN   131

Francis Bacon and the Style of Politics
F. J. LEVY   146

"Best Men are Molded out of Faults": Marrying the Rapist
in Jacobean Drama
SUZANNE GOSSETT   168

"The Comedians' Liberty": Censorship of the Jacobean Stage
Reconsidered
PHILIP J. FINKELPEARL   191

The Nature of Jonson's Roman History
PHILIP J. AYRES   207

Women in Men's Clothing: Apparel and Social Stability in
  The Roaring Girl
  MARY BETH ROSE   223

Embarrassing Ben: The Masques for Frances Howard
  DAVID LINDLEY   248

Entertaining the Palatine Prince: Plays on Foreign Affairs 1635–1637
  MARTIN BUTLER   265

The Politics of Allusion: The Gentry and Shirley's
  The Triumph of Peace
  LAWRENCE VENUTI   293

New Science and the Georgic Revolution in Seventeenth-Century
  English Literature
  ANTHONY LOW   317

"Wee feaste in our Defense": Patrician Carnival in Early
  Modern England and Robert Herrick's "Hesperides"
  PETER STALLYBRASS   348

Sir Thomas Browne's *The Garden of Cyrus* and the Real Character
  JANET E. HALLEY   367

Notes on Contributors   393

Index   397

Preface

Every modern literary text is composed in, and so constitutes part of, some moment in history, but the very possibility of a disjunction between creation and participation of a text *in* history shows how problematic, or various, the relationships between historical moments and literary texts can be. This is, in the present crisis of literary theory and analysis, nowhere more evident than in our perception and examination of the English Renaissance.

Traditionally, scholars and critics have studied the relationship between history and literature by recovering historical facts and formative ideas (as well as the historical forces, attitudes, and events), textual resources, and traditions that have inspired, initiated, or directed the form and content of literary texts. Such an approach "privileges" the work of literature when it sees that work not only as a repository of cultural and historical values and beliefs, but also as the best and most complete—even the most moving and significant—record of an age; indeed, when it sees that as *written* records, works of literature also appear to many to be more central, more stable, and more permanent. The focus, the very centrality, they have been awarded by such examinations and analyses therefore seems to such critics not only deserved but natural and necessary.

There is some indication that the age itself would have agreed with such an attitude. Sir Thomas North's 1579 translation of Jacques Amyot's French *Preface* to Plutarch's Greek *Lives of Noble Greeks and Romans* remarks decisively that literary history "helpeth not itself with any other thing than with the plain truth." This appears generally to have been the accepted Tudor definition, but always with varying shades and distinctions of meaning or emphasis. Just ten years later, for example, in 1589, George Puttenham tells us in *The Arte of English Poesie* that there "was nothing committed to history, but matters of great and excellent persons and things that the same by imitation of good courages (such as emulation causeth) might work more effectually." It is the poetics here of an avowed humanist, the writer working by *imitatio,* the reader instructed by *mimesis.* A slight turn of phrase makes all writing, contrarily, hegemonic, applying the principle of emulation by sharply narrowing it. Thus Thomas Heywood argues as part of *An Apology for Actors* (1612) that the "true use" of history is "to teach the subjects obedience to their king, to shew the people the untimely ends of such as have moved tumults, commotions and insurrections, to present them with the flourishing estate of such as live in obedience, exhorting them to allegiance, dehorting them from all trayterous and fellonious stratagems." When Patricia Parker and others write of "the static conservatism of Tillyard's long-influential *Elizabethan World Picture,*" then, she is also commenting on ideas and images deeply and frequently rooted in Renaissance thought and writing itself. But this world picture is *interpretive* history, nonetheless, and William Camden's doctrine in his *Britannia* (1586) that only history can "recall home Verity" is already ambiguous and debatable.

Tillyard's sense of a cohesive world view as a stabilizing historical context for the literature of the English Renaissance—one drawn from Ptolemaic cosmology and Galenic chemistry and psychology, in part propagated by classical texts newly discovered and widely taught, and frequently illustrated in political pamphlets, social commentary, and religious tracts and homilies of the period—may thus be viewed as a culture protesting too much. Don E. Wayne writes of us too that "tradition is invoked most often in order to preserve a static image of culture. Such an image has the power of eliciting from us a strong emotional commitment because it fulfills, however temporarily, our desire to escape that palpable sense of discontinuity which has marked our social and personal experience for more than a century." But such discontinuity has also marked recent histories of the English Renaissance. Studies by political and social historians such as G. R. Elton, Wallace MacCaffrey, Christopher Hill, and Lawrence Stone suggest that we should call into question any monolithic way of thinking about, classifying, or interpreting historical events or the works that arise from them. So a literary critic such as Frank Whigham can say conversely that "the court was simultaneously an arena of conflict and a mart of opportunity as well as a radiant center of order." Some time ago Earl Miner showed us how Cavalier poets displaced political anxieties into metaphor; more recently, Richard Helgerson has traced the distinctive autobiographical (and fictional) demands that vary the trope of the prodigal son in popular romances and chapbooks as well as the individual jockeying of more sophisticated writers to fashion themselves as poets laureate. In such cases language is seen not as a fixed text where each word has a single meaning, but as a medium that catches kaleidoscopically events and behavior from disparate and perhaps fragmentary points of view. For the late Paul de Man, language becomes mobile. It also becomes fluid and polysemous. Moreover, we are led to realize that to study a text we must understand the occasion that prompts it, while noting that the text itself also forms an occasion from which other matters arise in turn. The range, then, between writing and interpretation, between intention and reception, widens enormously, allowing Jonathan Goldberg, for instance, to argue in *Voice Terminal Echo* for "reengagement with the materiality of texts in all their historical contingency." He goes on:

In such a reading, every page trembles, vulnerable to manifold incursions—of prior texts, of future accidents, of reading and writing. To write now, then, open to the historicity of Renaissance texts and to the historicity of criticism invites (demands) a style assaultive in its refusals of the tactics of making sense, yet this is not (as is sometimes claimed) simply a practice of reversal or a pursuit of a *via negativa,* transcendent in its own fashion. Reinscribing loss, facing annihilation, texts lose their monumental status, and regain it—as memorial stones, implacable in their refusals as much as in their recording. The value of texts lies in their contingency, not in some security or consolation they may offer.

Such infinite possibilities, however, have led some past writers as well as present critics to entertain what Paul Riceour has called "the hermeneutics of suspicion."

In such a multivalent—or ambiguous or equivocal—environment, writers are thus led to a new sense of "invention" in which premises or "finding places" of literature are not, as the humanists had taught, copious reconfigurations of received sayings but also phrases and observations newly coined: *making* as *making up.* This is further compounded, as Ralegh confesses at the start of his *History of the World* (1614), by "Informations [which] are often false, records not always true, and notorious actions commonly insufficient to discover the passions, which did set them first on foot." There has been in Renaissance literary criticism of the past two decades, then, a marked shift from a reliance on such fixed, stabilizing nouns as *order, degree, hierarchy, integration,* and *equilibrium* to a reliance on more dynamic, unstabilizing (if often specialized) verbs as *appropriate, situate, inscribe,* and *subvert.* Indeed, renewed study of the rhetorical basis for much of the thinking, writing, and theorizing about writing that went on in England during the sixteenth and seventeenth centuries has often led critics to see texts as socially and politically generated and contingent in their meaning; they refuse closure because they depend, as all rhetoric does, on interaction with and the participation of the audience or reader. What first appears linear or sequential may instead be dialectic. There is, therefore, an increased interest in language patterns (and conceptual patterns) in historical and literary texts that deal with synchronicity in language: with puns, parody, dislocation, structural disjunction, metaphysical imagery. Postmodernist and deconstructionist critics have been further concerned with the fragmentation of texts, questioning how any verbal system can convey, even partially, an event of which it is also a part.

Such new critical developments give fresh contexts for viewing and re-viewing specific sources for texts, traditions of belief or genre apparently imitated by texts, or conventions constituting texts when they are seen arising from a society of various competing systems of attitudes and purposes—but as a number of literary historians in this collection who practice more traditional methods of analysis demonstrate, older approaches are neither outmoded nor irrelevant. At the same time, these newer examinations of history suggest that older methods may not now be the only ways to "situate" literary texts. While most critics hold to a fundamental, shared understanding of periodization as one possible definition of the subject—not unlike the identifiable collocations of distinguishing forces that Michel Foucault has called an "episteme"—many recent thinkers, drawing on cultural semiotics, see literary texts as sets of signs, signs of no greater or lesser importance than political events, social customs, or public gestures. Thus, while critics of the newer methods still keep both history and literature in play, they deny the primacy of literature (or the isolation of it).

The relationship between history and literature—not to say the validity and reliability of texts—has been further challenged by a new interest in a revised marxism that has questioned the static model of base and superstructure. Critics are now able to draw on such diverse figures as Raymond Williams and Louis Althusser to provide more sophisticated analyses of how literature relates to a period's modes of production. Moreover, what can be established as a pattern of dominant and institutionalized belief—such as the Tudor myth or the Elizabethan world picture, say—may create a marginalization that is available for exploitation. Texts may contain subversive gestures to demystify or expose such exploitation. But the same texts may also be structured eventually to reinforce the dominant ideology either appropriating the activity of subversion or containing it. Current marxist approaches to Renaissance history and literature have awakened us to all these possibilities.

Equally important, however, has been Foucault's challenge to marxism. Foucault asks that we see literature as a discursive practice fully implicated within a culture's distribution of power. Mikhail Bakhtin's study of carnivalesque tradition in European cultures has also brought into question the usefulness of studying high art exclusively by emphasizing the study of popular culture. "Carnival is put into operation as resistance to any tendency to authority," Michael D. Bristol writes, "and to the disruptive radicalizations of social life proposed and implemented by powerful ruling elites." Recent anthropological theory also bears on such a position. Clifford Geertz argues that there is no human nature independent of culture but that cultural patterns are not "complexes of concrete behavior patterns—customs, usages, traditions, habit clusters"—but rather "a set of control mechanisms—plans, recipes, rules, instructions." By such prescriptions, then, a culture "inscribes" individual personalities and postures.

Social history has also made us much more keenly aware of the patriarchal inflections of the English Renaissance; even Elizabeth I's stress on her gender in the mythology developed at court and for progresses and pageants makes her a female *prince* who is still a *ruler*. Her frequent speeches about being married to the nation, wedded to power because mothering her people, were inherently patriarchal too—so much so that, as Goldberg comments, James I had little trouble taking up the same posture as husband and father to England. Beginning with the studies of Alice Clark, Joan Kelly-Gadol, and Natalie Zemon Davis, however, scholars are investigating how the marginalization of women—into a subsidiary population urged to be chaste, silent, and obedient—buries their significant activity in writing texts, in serving as patrons for texts, and in becoming a discriminating audience. Indeed, some of the most imaginative work of the period—we need only think of transvestism on the stage or of the changing morality regarding rape—shows that gender itself was becoming a central and problematic concern.

In such an unsettled view of history and such a propositional view of literary texts, we can see how Rosalie L. Colie's understanding of Renaissance genres—what she calls resources of kind—can be liberating rather than repressive refigurations and redistributions of materials, concerns, and styles: the culture that has found the sacred and secular concurrent and indivisible in *The Second Shepherds Play* has no difficulty, in *The Comedy of Errors,* staging in a single work such competing frames of reference as Roman satire, Hellenic romance, and Christian rebirth and baptism. For the men and women of the Renaissance, like the characters portrayed in their literature, are, as Claude Lévi-Strauss has taught us, concerned to view the self "more and more as a construct, the result of systems of conventions." Stephen Greenblatt has seen the lives of the Renaissance as self-fashionings that result from the two processes of absorption and displacement: "the process whereby a symbolic structure is taken into the ego so completely that it ceases to exist as an external phenomenon" and "the process whereby a prior symbolic structure is compelled to coexist with other centers of attention in its gravitational pull." In his preface to *Allegory and Representation* he further refines acts of representation that result:

All discourse is improvisation, both an entry into and a deflection of existing strategies of representation. The improvisor never encounters the theoretical origins of signification, whether they lie in pure presence or absence. All artists enter into representations that are already under way and make a place for themselves in relation to these representations which are, we might add, never fully coordinated. Even in the most oppressive or, alternatively, the most happily unified of cultures, there are always conflicts of interest, strategy, and desire, so that the artist's task includes a substantial element of choice or tact or struggle. This task is shaped by the fact that the improvisor is himself in part the product of these prior representations. But only in part, for were there a perfect fit, there would no longer be that craving for reality that forever generates ironic submission and disguised revolt.

Historical representation, then, like literary representation, like literary re-presentation, is a partial, unstable, contingent activity, a fluctuating series of becomings rather than a singular being.

All of this is not removed from how the Renaissance saw itself: we have only to recall Bacon's distrust of an inherited and fixed language, his hatred of codified figures of rhetoric, and his insistence on empiricism. Foucault's contention that we as readers and critics, as scholars and interpreters, bring our historical biases to bear on texts themselves biased by their own cultural positionings was also recognized by the age. "The human understanding is like a false mirror which, receiving rays irregularly, distorts and discolours the name of things by mingling its own nature with it," Bacon writes; and Ralegh concurs: "Every understanding hath a peculiar judgment, by which it both censureth other men, and valueth itself." Just as there is no singularly valid and reliable perspective in the Renaissance writing on the Renaissance—all the writers including Hall, Holinshed, Camden, and Stow are prone to selectivity, disposition, imagination, and bias—so we too are always multiple. According to Marjorie Garber, "what is recognized (or re-cognized) in the Renaissance itself is then a construction projected from and by the wishes and fears—as well as the presuppositions—of critics and scholars inevitably reading its cultural codes in relation to their own." To begin to determine the Renaissance, then, we must first determine ourselves (to note what is self-imposed) and to see what is different about that age (that is, what is remote, oppositional, even alien). Here too, reading history and reading literature, we, like the Tudors and Stuarts before us, are engaged in a dialectical process.

There is still a quite different view of history as hermeneutics proposed in 1960 by Hans-Georg Gadamer in his dense but provocative study *Truth and Method*. According to Gadamer, what is historical truth is not what truth is located in the past but, rather, what past truth is still presently true and therefore historically truthful. Indeed, it is only the bridge between past and present that makes the past accessible to the present at all. Moreover, according to Gadamer, if the truth we learn from the past is necessarily something that concerns us now—if in fact it is something we *have* to learn—then any suspension or repression of the present is finally a denial of the past's claim to be true. It follows, then, for Gadamer, although it may surprise us, that any reconstruction of the past which fails to incorporate the present as well is a falsification of history.

All of these possible relationships between literature and history, history and literature, inform the essays in this present collection, and each relationship serves as the basis for one or more essays here. The use of literary tradition, literary history, literary convention, intertextuality, and specific literary or political sources are examined in relationship to literary texts and subtexts as well as extraliterary texts, and such concerns as ideology, gender, authority, and occasion are considered by one or more of the contributors. Perhaps this variety, however, only illustrates in still another way a culture in which rhetorical *copia* seem always to have been available as a resource and technique. Rhetoric, we remember, was philosophical for Plato and Aristotle, sophistic for Cicero and Quintilian—and both for the Renaissance. For Plato and Aristotle, rhetoric is an act of invention by tropes, seeking out the best concrete or particularized expression for the Idea or Form, or the action being imitated by way of *mimesis*. For Cicero and Quintilian, rhetoric was a manipulation of language for the ends of persuasion, in contexts that were as often political and judicial—as Kathy Eden suggests in her incisive new study of *Poetic and Legal Fictions in the Aristotelian Tradition*—as literary. So the ideas presented here are inherently not only as old as the period they examine; they go back beyond that to the classical heritage of ancient Greece and Rome, to the age recorded by Plutarch. Nor is the variety of new perspectives itself a new awareness. Jacob Burckhardt is universally credited with reawakening our interest in the Renaissance and first making it an identifiable period worthy of advanced study. He is frequently coupled with Tillyard these days, yet it is Burckhardt who said, in 1860, that "To each eye, perhaps, the outlines of a given civilization present a different picture; and in treating of a civilization which is the mother of our own, and whose influence is still at work among us, it is unavoidable that individual judgment and feeling should tell every moment both on the writer and on the reader." To Burckhardt this remained a fundamental obligation of historian and literary scholar alike. That obligation is also inescapably ours just as it has been, and is, inescapably that of all the writers whose work appears here.

The present volume began with the need to keep in print the most widely read and widely discussed issue of *English Literary Renaissance* (16:1 [Winter 1986]), an issue that was sold out a few months after it was first published. But the present collection, while keeping most of the work of that issue, adds a number of other essays from the past six years of *ELR* that raise still other necessary dimensions, in theory and practice, of the relationships between history and literature. All of the essays published here, representing traditional methods of historical scholarship as well as newer methods, were originally submissions to the journal and, like all submissions to *ELR,* were read by three or more editors and specialists before they were discussed at board meetings and accepted for publication. But *ELR* has been, from the beginning, a broad-based, communal enterprise. The editors of *ELR* are also grateful to the Graduate School, the Dean of the Faculty of Humanities and Fine Arts, and the Department of English at the University of Massachusetts, Amherst, who have subsidized the original publication of these works, and to the Director and staff of the University of Massachusetts Press for producing this volume.

Amherst, Massachusetts   ARTHUR F. KINNEY,
February 1987   *for the editors*

RENAISSANCE HISTORICISM

The New Historicism in Renaissance Studies

JEAN E. HOWARD

A new kind of activity is gaining prominence in Renaissance studies: a sustained attempt to read literary texts of the English Renaissance in relationship to other aspects of the social formation in the sixteenth and early seventeenth centuries. This development, loosely called the "new history" and flourishing both in Europe and America, involves figures such as Stephen Greenblatt, Jonathan Dollimore, Alan Sinfield, Kiernan Ryan, Lisa Jardine, Leah Marcus, Louis Montrose, Jonathan Goldberg, Stephen Orgel, Steven Mullaney, Don E. Wayne, Leonard Tennenhouse, Arthur Marotti, and others.[1] Journals such as *ELH, English Literary Renaissance, Representations,* and *LTP: Journal of Literature Teaching Politics* regularly publish "new history" pieces. In short, a critical movement is emerging, and in this essay I want to look at the new historicism both to account for its popularity and to try to define what, if anything, is new about its approach to the historical study of texts and then to examine some instances of new historical criticism.

1. Stephen Greenblatt is perhaps the central figure in the American branch of this movement; see *Renaissance Self-Fashioning: From More to Shakespeare* (Chicago, 1980). In his introduction to a volume entitled *The Forms of Power and the Power of Forms in the Renaissance* (*Genre* 15 [1982], 3–6), he outlines what he sees as a few of the distinguishing features of the "new historicism." I will discuss at length the work of Greenblatt and Montrose and their contributions to the new historical criticism in a later section of this essay. For representative works, see Jonathan Dollimore, *Radical Tragedy: Religion, Ideology and Power in the Drama of Shakespeare and His Contemporaries* (Chicago, 1984); Alan Sinfield, *Literature in Protestant England 1560–1660* (London, 1982); Kiernan Ryan, "Towards a Socialist Criticism: Reclaiming the Canon," *LTP: Journal of Literature Teaching Politics* 3 (1984), 4–17; Lisa Jardine, *Still Harping on Daughters: Women and Drama in the Age of Shakespeare* (New York, 1983): Leah Marcus, *Childhood and Cultural Despair: A Theme and Variations in Seventeenth-Century Literature* (Pittsburgh, 1978) and "'Present Occasions' and the Shaping of Ben Jonson's Masques," *ELH* 45 (1978), 201–25; Jonathan Goldberg, *James I and the Politics of Literature: Jonson, Shakespeare, Donne, and Their Contemporaries* (Baltimore, 1983); Stephen Orgel, *The Illusion of Power: Political Theater in the English Renaissance* (Berkeley, Cal., 1975); Steven Mullaney, "Strange Things, Gross Terms, Curious Customs: The Rehearsal of Cultures in the Late Renaissance," *Representations* 3

I

Historical scholarship linking Renaissance literary works to various non-literary historical contexts is not, of course, in and of itself, new, although in the last thirty years in particular, formalist approaches have been in the ascendency in some quarters of Renaissance studies. This is partly due to the importance of the lyric and partly due to the importance of Shakespeare in the English curriculum. For quite different reasons, formalism has dominated the study of both. In America, the lyric poems of the Renaissance provided many of the set texts, the verbal icons, used by New Critics to demonstrate their critical methods, and several generations of students trained in the New Criticism now teach today's students. And in both England and America, the plays of Shakespeare have often been treated not as products of a particular moment but as works for and of all times: universal masterpieces.[2] Consequently, until quite recently formalist studies of theme, genre, and structure dominated the criticism of these texts. History, when broached at all, usually meant the history of ideas, as in E. M. W. Tillyard's famous study of the importance to Renaissance literature of the "Elizabethan world picture."[3] In part, then, the new historicism is a reaction against formalism, though one must note that certain very contemporary formalisms—particularly structuralism and deconstruction—have not been enor-

---

(1983), 40–67; Don E. Wayne, "Drama and Society in the Age of Jonson: An Alternative View," *Renaissance Drama* XIII (1982), 103–29 and *Penshurst: The Semiotics of Place and the Poetics of History* (Madison, Wis., 1984); Leonard Tennenhouse, "The Counterfeit Order of *The Merchant of Venice*," in *Representing Shakespeare: New Psychoanalytic Essays,* ed. Murray M. Schwartz and Coppélia Kahn (Baltimore, Md., 1980), pp. 54–69 and "Representing Power: *Measure for Measure* in its Time," in *The Forms of Power,* ed. Greenblatt, pp. 139–56; and Arthur Marotti, "'Love is not love': Elizabethan Sonnet Sequences and the Social Order," *ELH* 49 (1982), 396–428. I do not mean the foregoing list to be inclusive or to suggest that the concerns of these critics are monolithic. Many of them employ quite different methodological and theoretical perspectives, and the significance of the differences between the cultural materialism of many of the English critics and the kind of historical work being done by a figure such as Greenblatt is only becoming clear with the publication of volumes such as *Political Shakespeare: New Essays in Cultural Materialism,* ed. Jonathan Dollimore and Alan Sinfield (Ithaca, N.Y., 1985). This essay is primarily concerned with what motivates the turn to history and with the theoretical problems posed by such a move, rather than with defining what are clearly emerging as differences among those now doing historical criticism.

2. For a provocative discussion of the way Shakespeare has been constructed in twentieth-century British culture as the writer who best reveals the timeless elements of the human condition see Derek Longhurst, "'Not for all time, but for an Age'; an approach to Shakespeare studies," in *Re-Reading English,* ed. Peter Widdowson (New York, 1982), pp. 150–63.

3. E. M. W. Tillyard, *The Elizabethan World Picture: A Study of the Idea of Order in the Age of Shakespeare, Donne and Milton* (London, 1943).

mously influential in Renaissance studies. The novel and the Romantic and modern periods have more often provided the exemplary texts for these movements. By contrast, the new historicism has been taken up with particular intensity, in part has been created, by Renaissance scholars.[4]

Why is this so? In part, I believe, many teachers of Renaissance literature simply have grown weary, as I have, of teaching texts as ethereal entities floating above the urgencies and contradictions of history and of seeking in such texts the disinterested expression of a unified truth rather than some articulation of the discontinuities underlying any construction of reality. Yet a purely formalist pedagogy should be debilitating for those who teach *any* literature, not just that of the Renaissance. Why, then, is it critics of Renaissance texts who have found in a new historicism an answer to their dissatisfaction?

The answer, I believe, lies partly in the uncanny way in which, at *this* historical moment, an analysis of Renaissance culture can be made to speak to the concerns of late twentieth-century culture. For a long time the Renaissance as cultural epoch was constructed in the terms set forth by Jacob Burckhardt; it was the age of the discovery of man the individual, the age of the revival of classical culture, the age of the secularization of life.[5] How enmeshed this picture was in nineteenth-century ideology is now clear, but it may be less clear what the *current* revival of interest in the Renaissance may have to do with twentieth-century concerns. Consider, for example, the work of Jonathan Dollimore, who is particularly interested in the way in which what he calls essentialist humanism has both dominated the study of English literature in the twentieth century and also has prevented recognition of the fact that man is not so much possessed of an essential nature as constructed by social and historical forces. Looking back at the seventeenth century, Dollimore sees it as a sort of privileged era lying between the Christian essentialism of the Middle Ages—which saw man as a unitary being who

---

4. I do not mean to suggest that *only* Renaissance scholars are interested in historical approaches to texts. At the 1983 MLA convention Jonathan Culler devoted a major presentation to an attack, by way of Terry Eagleton, on the reification of history in much contemporary criticism. Culler's attention to this issue I take as an indication of the crucial professional space historical studies are now assuming in many quarters of the discipline. Critics as diverse as Eagleton in *Literary Theory: An Introduction* (Minneapolis, Minn., 1983) and Frank Lentricchia in *After the New Criticism* (Chicago, 1980) have led the way in arguing that the most serious flaw of the major critical movements of the last several decades has been their failure to acknowledge history, and it is that failure which is now being redressed.

5. Jacob Burckhardt, *The Civilization of the Renaissance in Italy* (New York, 1958).

took his essence from God—and Enlightenment humanism—which first promulgated the idea of man the individual: a unified, separate, and whole entity with a core of identity emanating from within. For Dollimore, the late Renaissance was the age of skepticism in which in the drama in particular one finds recorded a recognition of the discontinuous nature of human identity and its social construction.[6] It is not hard to see affinities between this picture of the Renaissance and certain contemporary understandings of our own historical moment as the post-humanist epoch in which essentialist notions of selfhood are no longer viable.

I will return later to the theoretical issues raised by the fact that when a new historian looks at the past he or she is as likely as an old historian to see an image of the seeing self, not an image of the other. But for the moment I want to continue to pursue further the way in which "the Renaissance" is being reunderstood within that configuration of periods which constitutes the framework by which literary historians make the past intelligible. Within this framework the Renaissance has usually been assigned a transitional position between the Middle Ages—held to be encumbered with a monolithic Christian ideology and a static and essentially unhistorical view of itself—and the modern era—marked by the rise of capitalism with its attendant bourgeois ideology of humanism, progress and the all-important interiority and self-presence of the individual. Almost inevitably, this construction of the past has produced the question: just *how* modern and *how* medieval was this transitional period?[7] Burckhardt, looking back at Renaissance Italy from mid-nineteenth century Germany, stressed the modernity of the Renaissance, its sense of itself as definitively different from prior periods of history. Others have insisted on the fundamental continuity between the Renaissance and the Middle Ages. But now, as critics and historians sense the modern era slipping away and a new episteme inchoately emerging, the Renaissance is being appropriated in slightly different terms: as *neither* modern nor medieval, but as a boundary or liminal space between two more monolithic periods where one can see acted out a clash of paradigms and ideologies, a playfulness with signifying systems, a self-reflexivity, and a self-consciousness about the tenuous solidity of human identity which

6. Jonathan Dollimore, *Radical Tragedy*, esp. Chap. 10, "Subjectivity and Social Process," pp. 153–81.

7. Consider, for example, the lengthy debate surrounding Sir Thomas More and whether or not his *Utopia* reflects an essentially Medieval and monastic conception of life (see R. W. Chambers, *Thomas More* [London, 1935]) or an enlightened anticipation of modern socialism (see Karl Kautsky, *Thomas More and His Utopia,* trans. H. J. Stenning [1888; rpt. New York, 1927]).

resonate with some of the dominant elements of postmodern culture.

In short, I would argue that the Renaissance, seen as the last refuge of preindustrial man, is of such interest to scholars of the postindustrial era because these scholars construe the period in terms reflecting their own sense of the exhilaration and fearfulness of living inside a gap in history, when the paradigms that structured the past seem facile and new paradigms uncertain. Clearly this emerging reading of the Renaissance is made possible by the traditional emphasis on the Renaissance as an age of transition. Previously critical emphasis was on continuity—on the way the period linked to the past or anticipated the future. Now the emphasis is on *dis*continuity, seen most clearly perhaps in Dollimore's insistence on the early seventeenth century as a kind of interperiod standing free of the orthodoxies of the Middle Ages and the Enlightenment. But the difference between prior and past conceptions of the Renaissance is also clear in the way the new historical critics so often make the period intelligible by narratives of rupture, tension, and contradiction, as, for example, when Greenblatt talks about the gap between the Renaissance ideology of human freedom and the actuality of Renaissance man as the subject of determining power relations[8] or, as we shall see, when Louis Montrose stresses the enormous contradictions in the social formation which Renaissance literature attempted to mediate.[9] And, as I have been hinting, these narratives of discontinuity and contradiction are narratives which owe much to the way late twentieth-century man construes his own historical condition.

Having said this much, I hope it is clear that I don't find it odd or arbitrary that the new historical criticism has taken the Renaissance as one of its primary objects of study. And I hope it is also clear that at least in one respect I find the "new history" resembling older forms of historical inquiry in that both see the past at least in part through the terms made available by the present. This observation, moreover, raises a more fundamental question: in just what ways is the "new" historical criticism new? Does its newness consist simply in its break with the formalism that has long been prominent in the study of Renaissance literature? Is its newness due mainly to the way it draws a somewhat different picture of the Renaissance than Burckhardt drew? Or are its methods and its understanding of what constitutes the historical investi-

---

8. Greenblatt, *Renaissance Self-Fashioning,* esp. pp. 1–9.

9. This idea is present in many of Montrose's early essays. See, in particular, "'The Place of a Brother' in *As You Like It:* Social Process and Comic Form," *Shakespeare Quarterly* 32 (1981), 28–54.

gation of texts in some fundamental way different from those which enabled an earlier historical criticism?

To answer these questions, I want to sketch what must of necessity be a simplified picture of some of the assumptions underlying the historical criticism of a figure such as Tillyard. These assumptions include the following: that history is knowable; that literature mirrors or at least by indirection reflects historical reality; and that historians and critics can see the facts of history objectively. (This last assumption is particularly paradoxical since it rests on the premise that while literature is implicated in history, historians and critics are not.)[10] The criticism resulting from these premises often led to the trivialization of literature: to its reduction to a mere reflection of something extrinsic to itself, and to the trivialization of criticism: its reduction to a mode for explaining (not reading) texts in terms of their relationship to a fixed ground, such as James I's monarchical practices, English imperialism, or Puritan theology. At its worst, such criticism reduced literary study to the search for topical references; at its best it illuminated particular texts in relationship to great men or events or ideas of a period, but its distinguishing mark was always the assumption that literature was a mirror reflecting something more real and more important than itself.[11]

Contemporary theoretical work, it seems to me, has seriously put in question a number of these assumptions. For example, much reception and reader-response criticism has directly challenged the idea that a reader/interpreter can ever escape his or her own historicity in order to encounter objectively the historical difference encoded in texts. Consequently, one must question the status of that "knowledge" about the past produced either by the historian or the historically minded critic. Similarly, Saussurian linguistics has challenged the premise that language functions referentially. One mode of historical criticism assumes that literature is connected to history in that its representations are direct reflections of historical reality, but one must ask what happens to that assumption when the referentiality of language itself is questioned. If

10. For a useful critique of naive historicism see David Carroll's essay, "Mimesis Reconsidered: Literature, History, Ideology," *Diacritics* 5 (1975), 5–12.

11. Perhaps the most notorious example of a critic reducing a Renaissance text to the contours of its supposed historical referent is Josephine Waters Bennett's *Measure for Measure as Royal Entertainment* (New York, 1966). But even in a work as recent—and as interesting—as Philip Edwards' *Threshold of a Nation: A Study in English and Irish Drama* (Cambridge, 1979), one can still see operating the idea that literature is the mirror reflecting the social realm and that an historical approach to literature means retrieving that social ground.

literature refers to no ground extrinsic to itself, what can be the nature of its relationship to an historical context or to material reality? In fact, if one accepts certain tendencies in poststructuralist thought, is the possibility of an historical criticism even conceivable?

It is only by addressing these and a number of other equally urgent theoretical issues that a new historical criticism can distinguish itself from an older, more positivistic critical practice. The new historicism may well turn out to be an important extension of the theoretical ferment of the past two decades, a movement which will fundamentally rethink how we study texts in history. On the other hand, there is a real danger that the emerging interest in history will be appropriated by those wishing to suppress or erase the theoretical revolution that has gone on in the last several decades. Ironically, the "new history" may well turn out to be a backlash phenomenon: a flight from theory or simply a program for producing more "new readings" suited to the twenty-five-page article and the sixty-minute class.[12] Readings remain, after all, the dominant form of scholarly production in the discipline, and as many are discovering, a cursory journey through Lawrence Stone or Keith Thomas can open up numerous possibilities for new readings based on the ostensible family structure, economic dilemmas, or political upheavals of the sixteenth and seventeenth centuries. There is nothing inherently wrong with doing readings, but if those readings are based on untenable or unexamined assumptions about literature and history, then they are merely a form of nostalgia and not a serious attempt to explore what it means to attempt an historical criticism in a postmodern era.

In order to evaluate just how new the historical work being done in regard to Renaissance literature really is, I want to do two things. First, I wish to examine in much greater detail some of the theoretical issues facing any historical criticism today and, second, to examine in some detail the work of two of the best practitioners of the new history—Stephen Greenblatt and Louis Montrose—in order to see how they engage or ignore the problematics of their undertaking. From this double examination I hope it will be possible to suggest some of the directions in which such criticism must move if its newness is to be fundamental and not cosmetic.

---

12. For a provocative discussion of the dominance and the conventions of "the reading" as a mode of criticism see Richard Levin's *New Readings vs. Old Plays: Recent Trends in the Reinterpretation of English Renaissance Drama* (Chicago, 1979).

II

In order to understand what does, or might, constitute the core of a truly new historical criticism one must begin, I believe, with the basic issue of what one assumes to be the nature of man, the creature whose works, thought, and culture have been the focus of most historical inquiry. One of the most striking developments of contemporary thought is the widespread attack on the notion that man possesses a transhistorical core of being. Rather, everything from maternal "instinct" to conceptions of the self are now seen to be the products of specific discourses and social processes.[13] This is a much more radical view of just how thoroughly man is a creature of history than has obtained in the past. It is quite different to argue that man has no essential being and to argue that, while in different periods people display different customs and social arrangements, they nonetheless possess an unchanging core of human traits that makes them all part of "the family of man."[14]

One can see the idea of a transhistorical human essence in Jonas Barish's very fine study of what he calls "the anti-theatrical prejudice" in Western culture. For him, the prejudice, while taking slightly different forms from antiquity to the present, nonetheless reflects a fear or a distrust innate to or inherent in the human mind.[15] Barish does not really entertain the possibility that a phenomenon in one period, which *seems* analogous to a phenomenon in another, may arise amid such different social conditions and play such a different role in a culture's power relations and discursive systems that the two phenomena cannot be seen as continuous with one another or as the products of an underlying human nature.

13. See, for example, Nancy Chodorow's *The Reproduction of Mothering: Psychoanalysis and the Sociology of Gender* (Berkeley, 1978) which argues that "mothering" is not innate or physiological, but a product of socially structured psychological mechanisms transmitted by culture. For a striking investigation of the relatively late emergence of the concept of "man" as a self-sufficient, autonomous being possessed of interiority and self-presence see Michel Foucault, *The Order of Things: An Archaeology of the Human Sciences* (1966; New York, 1970), esp. Chap. 9, "Man and His Doubles," pp. 303–43 and Chap. 10, "The Human Sciences," pp. 344–87. For an important attempt to theorize the social and linguistic production of subjectivity see Julian Henriques, Wendy Hollway, Cathy Urwin, Couze Venn, Valerie Walkerdine, *Changing the Subject: Psychology, Social Regulation, and Subjectivity* (London, 1984).

14. On the sentimental and antihistorical uses of the concept of "the family of man" see Roland Barthes' essay, "The Great Family of Man," in *Mythologies,* trans. Annette Lavers (1957; rpt. New York, 1972).

15. Jonas Barish, *The Anti-Theatrical Prejudice* (Berkeley, 1981), esp. p. 2.

By contrast, Jonathan Dollimore, in his study of seventeenth-century tragedy, takes as his point of departure the idea—which he sees inscribed within Renaissance texts—that man has no essential nature, no traits not the product of social forces at a particular historical juncture.[16] Consequently, while Barish assumes an essential core of humanness which history can modify or shape in various ways, Dollimore assumes that nothing exists before the human subject is *created* by history. Consequently, an historical criticism working from Dollimore's premises will find an enormous range of new topics open for historical investigation; topics such as the way emotions and what we call instincts—and not just economic structures or political beliefs—are produced in a particular, historically specific social formation, and the way, of course, in which literature variously participates in this process of construction.

While one may accept in theory that there is no shared human essence linking contemporary man to Renaissance man, however, that does not solve the problem of how one is to acknowledge or recognize the radical otherness of the past. As I suggested earlier, there is a powerful tendency to appropriate the past in terms of the present, and contemporary reader-response theorists have acutely drawn the attention of literary critics to the extent to which the interpreter and his or her historical moment are present in their interpretations of earlier literary works.[17] Hayden White has been perhaps the most eloquent spokesperson for the view that the same is true for historians. For White, interpretation is a key part of each historian's work and consists largely of providing a "plot structure for a sequence of events so that their nature as a comprehensible process is revealed by their figuration *as a story of a particular kind,*" that is, as a narrative intelligible to the readers of a particular age.[18] White stresses how thoroughly the historical discipline differs from a pure descriptive science and how much it owes to literary art, as, through its

16. Dollimore, *Radical Tragedy,* pp. 17–19.

17. This perception is articulated in a variety of ways. Norman Holland, for example, writing from the perspective of American ego psychology, sees the reader constantly projecting his or her identity theme onto the work of art ("Unity Identity Text Self," *PMLA* 90 [1975], 813–22). In his latest work Stanley Fish sees both the properties of texts and their meanings as produced by the conventions of the historically-specific interpretive community to which the reader belongs (*Is There A Text in This Class? The Authority of Interpretive Communities* [Cambridge, 1980]). And Hans Robert Jauss argues that the meaning of a work of art will depend in large measure upon the different "horizons of reading" which in each era determine the reader's access to the text (*Towards an Aesthetic of Reception,* trans. Timothy Bahti. Theory and History of Literature, 2 [Minneapolis, Minn., 1982]).

18. Hayden White, *Tropics of Discourse: Essays in Cultural Criticism* (Baltimore, Md., 1978), p. 58.

dominant tropes and narrative structures, it gives to "history" a shape owing as much to the patterns of intelligibility available to the historian from his own culture as to those that may have informed a prior age.

Similarly, Tzvetan Todorov in his new book on the Spanish conquest of Central America takes as his primary concern the way the Spanish dealt with the otherness of the American Indians, either by construing them as nonhuman or bestial and, as such, fair game for any kind of genocidal treatment, or by construing them as embryonic Europeans needing only the help of a Spanish education and a Spanish religion to make them mirrors of their white "brothers." In neither case was the *difference* of the Indian tolerated or allowed to interrogate European ways. Instead, the Indians were either denied inclusion within the category of the human or assimilated utterly into the Spanish idea of what the human was.[19]

Recognizing in a fresh way the difficulty of escaping the prison of the present moment and present culture to realize historical and cultural otherness, how is a contemporary historical criticism to proceed? One of Michel Foucault's central contributions to contemporary historical studies has been to recognize and strive against the tendency to project the present into the past and so to construct narratives of continuity. He counters this tendency by postulating the notion of radical breaks between historical epistemes. He refuses to look for continuities, for precursors of one era in former eras, but by a massive study of the situated discourses of particular disciplines he attempts to let their strangeness, their difference, speak.[20] Foucault's is a procedure of vigilance, and it produces some remarkable results. But it does not erase the fact that there is no transcendent space from which one can perceive the past "objectively." Our view is always informed by our present position; the objects we view available only in the slipperiness of their textualization. That does not seem to me to negate the project of historical investigation, but it does mandate a transformed attitude toward it. First of all, it seems necessary to abandon the myth of

19. Tzvetan Todorov, *The Conquest of America: The Question of The Other*, trans. Richard Howard (New York, 1984).

20. For an introduction to Foucault's idea of discontinuous history see "Nietzsche, Genealogy, History," in *Language, Counter-Memory, Practice*, ed. Donald Bouchard (Ithaca, N.Y., 1977), pp. 139–64. For a much fuller account of the episteme see Foucault's *The Order of Things*. As an overview of Foucault's contribution to historical study I have found useful Mark Poster's "The Future According to Foucault: The Archaeology of Knowledge and Intellectual History," in *Modern European Intellectual History: Reappraisals and New Perspectives*, ed. Dominick LaCapra and Steven L. Kaplan (Ithaca, 1982), pp. 111–52.

objectivity and to acknowledge that all historical knowledge is produced from a partial and a positioned vantage point. Further, instead of evoking a monolithic and repressive "history," one must acknowledge the existence of "histories" produced by subjects variously positioned within the present social formation and motivated by quite different senses of the *present* needs and *present* problems which it is hoped will be clarified or reconfigured through the study of the past.[21]

The intellectual historian Dominick LaCapra captures something of the difficulty of contemporary historical criticism when he speaks of establishing a self-conscious "dialogue" with the past. By using this term, he wishes to acknowledge, on the one hand, the impossibility of retrieving the "objective facts" of history, and, on the other hand, the undesirability of a "'presentist' quest for liberation from the 'burden' of history through unrestrained fictionalizing and mythologizing."[22] LaCapra deliberately evokes the language of psychoanalysis to explain his idea of this process of transference, a process in which past and present remain separate and yet merged, an understanding of the one proceeding only from self-conscious entanglement with the other. The goal of such a dialogue is not, certainly, the willful reproduction of the present in the mirror of the past, but it involves a steady acknowledgement that the past is not transparent and that the pursuit of history is neither objective nor disinterested.

I take, then, that as starting points a new historical literary criticism assumes two things: (1) the notion that man is a construct, not an essence; (2) that the historical investigator is likewise a product of his history and never able to recognize otherness in its pure form, but always in part through the framework of the present. This last point leads one to what is perhaps the crux of any "new" historical criticism, and that is to the issue of what one conceives history to be: a realm of retrievable fact or a *construct* made up of textualized traces assembled in various configura-

21. Terry Eagleton, writing of Walter Benjamin, sees Benjamin anticipating Foucault's emphasis on the need for discontinuous history which will shatter narratives of continuity through which the heterogeneity of the past is constantly suppressed. Yet Benjamin insists more strikingly than Foucault that the critic's intervention—by which traces of the past are liberated from a repressive historicism of continuity to interrogate the present ideological formation—is a political and of necessity an urgent intervention since the pressures of the capitalist system to produce monolithic, continuous history are enormous and their disruption extremely difficult. See Terry Eagleton, *Walter Benjamin, or Towards a Revolutionary Criticism* (London, 1981), esp. ch. 3, "History, Tradition and Revolution," pp. 43–78.

22. LaCapra, "Rethinking Intellectual History and Reading Texts," in *Rethinking Intellectual History: Texts, Contexts, Language* (Ithaca, N.Y., 1983), p. 63.

tions by the historian/interpreter. Hayden White points to the central question in dispute when he argues that history is produced, not discovered, and when he shows how those synthesizing histories which attempt to describe a period are *someone's* historically-conditioned constructs. In doing so, he calls in question one of the ways literary critics have often used "history," that is, as the realm of fact which can ground the seeming multiplicity or polysemous nature of the literary artifact. White writes: "Nor is it unusual for literary theorists, when they are speaking about the 'context' of a literary work, to suppose that this context—the 'historical milieu'—has a concreteness and an accessibility that the work itself can never have, as if it were easier to perceive the reality of a past world put together from a thousand historical documents than it is to probe the depths of a single literary work that is present to the critics studying it."[23]

More is at stake here, I think, than a simple naivete on the part of literature professors about what historians do. Rather, the notion of history as transparent and objectively knowable is *useful* to the literary critics, for it can serve as a means of unclouding the stubborn and troubling opacity of the literary text and of stabilizing its decentered language. A common way of speaking about literature and history is just that way: literature *and* history, text *and* context. In these binary oppositions, if one term is stable and transparent and the other in some way mirrors it, then that other term can be stabilized and clarified, too. This is particularly crucial at a time when the notion of textuality has challenged traditional ideas about a literary work's communicative clarity and mimetic nature. By explaining literature by a ground extrinsic to itself, the ground of history, which literature supposedly reflects, the critic makes the problem of opacity disappear. But at a price. One result of seeing literature and history in this particular way is the inevitable "flattening" of the literary work. It is emptied of its rich signifying potentiality by being used as a springboard to something else, a mere pointer back to extratextual reality, as when Duke Vincentio is read simply as a representation of James I and the whole of *Measure for Measure* reduced to a comment on this monarch's beliefs and practices. Literature thus becomes, not something to be *read,* but to be *explained.* Second, such a procedure seldom stops to question why a particular historical context has been selected to align with the literary text, as if such choices were not often arbitrary in the extreme and inimical to seeing the full intertextual network in which a literary work exists. Third, the practice

---

23. White, *Tropics of Discourse,* p. 89.

reduces literature to a merely mimetic object. I don't think any serious historical criticism can dodge the fact that undertaking such criticism raises the questions of some relationship between literature and what may be considered external to itself. The key question is: what is the nature of that relationship? Does the text absorb history into itself? Does it reflect an external reality? Does it produce the real?

It increasingly seems that in confronting these issues a new historical criticism has to accept, first, that "history" is not objective, transparent, unified, or easily knowable and consequently is extremely problematic as a concept for grounding the meaning of a literary text; second, that the very binarism we casually reinforce every time we speak of literature and history, text and context, is unproductive and misleading. Literature is *part* of history, the literary text as much a context for other aspects of cultural and material life as they are for it. Rather than erasing the problem of textuality, one must enlarge it in order to see that *both* social and literary texts are opaque, self-divided, and porous, that is, open to the mutual intertextual influences of one another. This move means according literature real power. Rather than passively reflecting an external reality, literature is an agent in constructing a culture's sense of reality. It is part of a much larger symbolic order through which the world at a particular historical moment is conceptualized and through which a culture imagines its relationship to the actual conditions of its existence. In short, instead of a hierarchical relationship in which literature figures as the parasitic reflector of historical fact, one imagines a complex textualized universe in which literature participates in historical processes and in the political management of reality.

I take as an exemplary brief example of these assumptions Don Wayne's work on the way Ben Jonson's plays help to produce an ideology for a pre-capitalist age. Wayne argues that while Jonson seemingly remained an apologist for an older feudal ideology which stressed the importance of the social collectivity over the individual, plays such as *The Alchemist and Bartholomew Fair* find him paradoxically promulgating contractual rights by which the prerogatives of the individual are secured, including the rights of individual authorship.[24] Clearly Jonson is responding to something in the social formation around him—to the emerging possibilities for printing texts as individual enterprises, to the breakdown of a national sense of community under the Stuarts, to the allure of the entrepreneurial spirit released by Puritanism

24. Wayne, "Drama and Society in the Age of Jonson," pp. 103–29.

and by the growth of the London merchant and professional class. Yet Wayne's chief point is that Jonson is also—through his dramatic texts—*producing* the modes of thought that encouraged and to some extent created these other changes so that it becomes nearly impossible to pinpoint an origin or single cause for social change. Many aspects of the social formation, including literary texts, work in a variety of ways and at a variety of speeds to produce the variegated entity we call history.

A major feature of a new historical criticism, therefore, must be a suspicion about an unproblematic binarism between literature and history and a willingness to explore the ways in which literature does more than reflect a context outside itself and instead constitutes one of the creative forces of history. In fact, until one truly banishes a mimetic theory of literature, several problems which have characteristically bedeviled the historical study of literature will continue to rear their heads. It is always interesting, for example, to watch what happens when people read Lawrence Stone on the Renaissance family and then try to relate what they find there to, say, Shakespeare's romantic comedies. Stone argues that marriages, at least among the middle and upper classes, were made late, were arranged by parents, were made largely for economic convenience, not love, and resulted in conjugal and parent-child relationships often lacking in warmth and intimacy.[25] What has all this to do with the picture of romantic love and rebellion against parental authority we see in Shakespeare's comedies? On the surface, not much; but what does this discrepancy mean: that Stone got things wrong? that literature is autonomous from the social realm? that Shakespeare is a universal genius who got at the enduring truths of life rather than at the anomalies of a particular historical moment? that literature is, after all, something to be read on a bus, a pure escape from the real? It is when faced with just these sorts of problems that one realizes the need for more than a simple mimetic theory of literature. A culture's discourse about love and the family need not, and probably seldom does, correspond exactly to how people live. (One could say the same about politics, economics, or personal identity.) One of the great strengths of Foucault, in my view, is his recognition that the discursive practices of an age, while producing or enabling certain behaviors, never coincide with them exactly. There is always some gap between what discourse authorizes and what people do, though "history" may never be able to disclose that gap precisely. What is important is how and why cultures produce and

25. Lawrence Stone, *The Family, Sex and Marriage in England 1500–1800* (New York, 1977).

naturalize particular constructions of reality: what contradictions such constructions neutralize or expose, what economic and political ends they advance, what kinds of power relations they display. Literature is one of many elements participating in a culture's representation of reality to itself, helping to form its discourse on the family, the state, the individual, helping to make the world intelligible, though not necessarily helping to represent it "accurately."

In any particular instance, to see how a text functions in the construal of reality means seeing it in an intertextual network of considerable historical specificity. For example, to understand how women were made intelligible in the Renaissance, one cannot look only to social "facts," such as how many children they had, or of what diseases and at what ages they died. One must also consider how the medical, legal, and religious spheres functioned to provide a discourse about women which may have represented them in ways quite at odds with what *we* see as the apparent "facts" of their situation. The whole point is to grasp the terms of the discourse which made it possible to see the "facts" in a particular way—indeed, made it possible to see certain phenomena *as* facts at all. Only then will we begin to grasp how another period shaped individuals as historical subjects; and to see literature's role in this process one must place literary representations in a much broader differential field in which *how* they correspond to or challenge other constructions of reality and *how* they take their place in a particular configuration of discursive practices and power relations can be observed.

In this rethinking of the place of literature *in* history, it seems to me that much of the historically-based literary criticism can benefit from recent developments in Marxist thought. It used to be that Marxism, while providing one of the few theoretically coherent approaches to an historical criticism, suffered from its own version of the history/literature binarism in that it saw in literature and other elements of "the superstructure" a reflection of the dominant economic mode of production and of the class struggle it spawned. In other words, a particular privilege was given to the economic realm as the determining factor in every sort of cultural production and in the shaping of human consciousness. This assumption has been challenged, perhaps most influentially, by Louis Althusser, who argues for the *relative* autonomy of the superstructure from the material base and for the importance of the educational apparatus, the institution of literature, and other factors, in the shaping of human consciousness. In short, he acknowledges that there is not an homologous relationship between all levels of culture such that the ideologies of the superstructure can in any simple way be related to an economic base. Consequently, one finds the question of cause and effect relationship more complicated than was formerly thought, as I have already noted in regard to Wayne's work on Jonson; and one must take more seriously than before the role of literature in changing human consciousness and so, eventually, in affecting other material practices—not merely being affected by them.[26]

Furthermore, while it has always been Marxist criticism which has most insistently probed the question of literature's relationship to ideology, contemporary Marxism has developed more complex ways of approaching that question than it formerly possessed. While ideology is a vexed term with a complex history, it may be useful to distinguish two of its most common definitions: first, as the false consciousness foisted on the working classes by a dominant class; second, as any of those practices by which one imagines one's relations to the actual conditions of one's existence.[27] This second, Althusserian definition of ideology denies that the ideological is simply the product of a conspiratorial power group. Rather, the ideological is omnipresent; it inheres in every representation of reality and every social practice, as all of these inevitably confirm or naturalize a particular construction(s) of reality. Consequently, there is no way in which ideology can ever be absent from literature, any more than it can be absent from *any* discursive practice. Jonathan Dollimore argues, and I agree with him, that it may be useful to retain both understandings of ideology: to retain the option of seeing some literature as the conscious and direct product of one power group or class's attempts to control another group or class by the misrepresentation of their historical condition; and at the same time to recognize that in most instances power groups or classes are both less self-conscious and less monolithic than such a formulation implies and that a more complex approach to the problem of ideology requires a recognition of the pervasive, masterless (in the sense of acknowledging no one origin), and often heterogeneous nature of the ideological.

This being so, that the ideological is everywhere and traverses literature as surely as other modes of representation, the question becomes: does literature have a special way of treating the ideological? This, of

26. See, in particular, Althusser's key essay, "Ideology and Ideological State Apparatuses" in *Lenin and Philosophy and Other Essays* (New York, 1971), pp. 127–86.

27. For the first understanding of ideology see Karl Marx, *The German Ideology* (London, 1965); for the second understanding see Althusser, "Ideology and Ideological State Apparatuses."

course, has been an issue that has bedeviled Marxism for some time. In the 1960's Pierre Machery contended that literature, separate both from science and ideology, inevitably produced a *parody* of ideology, a treatment of it which inevitably distanced the reader from the ideological matter being treated, exposing its contradictions and laying bare the artifice surrounding its production.[28] But does literature really handle the ideological in this way? I think not, at least not in every instance. First, as Tony Bennett has recently shown, such a view rests on the premise (deriving most centrally in the twentieth century from Russian Formalism) that literature is a special and unique form of writing with its own inherent and universal properties, one of which is the way it acquires internal distance from the ideological material which traverses it.[29] But as any historian of literature can show, the literary canon is a social construct, not an empirical given. As a number of boundary cases make clear today, some texts are regularly treated as literature and as something else. For example, are Bacon's essays literature or philosophy? Are diaries literature or something else? Is travel literature really literature or history or even philosophy? While it is quite possible in practical terms to speak of a literary canon, it seems quite another matter to assume that the texts in that canon are there by virtue of some mysterious inner property which they all share. They are all there for a variety of reasons having to do with the privileging of certain artifacts by powerful groups, and their "properties" are in large measure the result of the operations performed upon them by generations of critics.[30] Hence, while it may be useful for strategic or practical purposes to retain the category "literature," it seems wrong to assign to the texts gathered under that rubric a single, universal stance toward the ideological.

In fact, I would argue that a new historical criticism attempting to talk about the ideological function of literature in a specific period can most usefully do so only by seeing a specific work relationally—that is, by seeing how its representations stand in regard to those of other specific works and discourses. A work can only be said to contest, subvert, recuperate, or reproduce dominant ideologies (and it may do any of these) if one can place the work—at least provisionally and strategi-

28. Pierre Macherey, *A Theory of Literary Production,* trans. Geoffrey Wall (London, 1978), esp. pp. 51–65.

29. Tony Bennett, *Formalism and Marxism* (London, 1979), esp. ch. 2, "Formalism and Marxism," pp. 18–43.

30. Bennett, p. 9 and Terry Eagleton, *An Introduction to Literary Theory,* esp. "Introduction: What is Literature?", pp. 1–16.

cally—in relation to others. And, as I have argued above, the most illuminating field of reference may not be just other literary works. To return to the example of the representation of women: in order to understand the ideological function of, say, certain plays for the public theater, it may be important to see their representations of women in the light of the representations offered in masques, in conduct manuals, in medical treatises, and in Puritan polemics all written at approximately the same time.

Moreover, it seems important to entertain the possibility that neither literary texts nor other cultural productions are monologic, organically unified wholes. Only when their heterogeneity is suppressed by a criticism committed to the idea of organic unity do they seem to reveal a unitary ideological perspective or generic code. It may be more productive to see them as sites where many voices of culture and many systems of intelligibility interact. Dominick La Capra makes this point, and in doing so he draws both on the work of Jacques Derrida and on that of Mikhail Bakhtin, thus uniting deconstruction and Marxist demystification in the project of fracturing the unified surface of the text to let the multiplicity of its social voices be heard. In this project he finds two of Bakhtin's concepts, *heteroglossia* and *carnivalization* (in Michael Holquist's translation), to be particularly useful in that the first suggests that novelized discourse is polyvalent, riddled with "unofficial" voices contesting, subverting, and parodying dominant discourses, while the second suggests that the emergence in writing of these "unofficial" voices has the revolutionary potential to expose the arbitrary nature of official constructions of the real.[31] But it is important to remember that for Bakhtin not all literature performs a carnivalizing function or is dialogic and polyvalent. There are no inherent laws governing the functioning of those texts we call literature. Consequently, one of the greatest challenges facing a new historical criticism is to find a way to talk about and discriminate among the many *different* ways in which literature is traversed by—and produces—the ideologies of its time.

III

What I have proposed so far are some of the principles contributing to an historical criticism which would not simply recapitulate the positivis-

31. For LaCapra's view of the multiplicity and self-divisions of texts see "Rethinking Intellectual History and Reading Texts," esp. pp. 52–55 and 58–61. M. Bakhtin's work on *heteroglossia* and *carnivalization* can be found in *The Dialogic Imagination: Four Essays*, ed. Michael Holquist, trans. Caryl Emerson and Michael Holquist (Austin, 1981), pp. 259–422.

tic work of the early part of this century. Some of these ideas already inform the practice of certain of the new historical critics of Renaissance literature. I would like to end this essay by looking at some of the actual work which makes it possible to speak of a new historicism in Renaissance studies, in order both to acknowledge the importance of this work, in part as it spurs further theoretical speculation and inquiry, and to tease from it an exact sense of the theoretical and methodological issues it has not yet resolved or, in some cases, even faced.

My main reservation about much of this work is its failure to reflect on itself. Taking the form of the reading, a good deal of this criticism suppresses any discussion of its own methodology and assumptions. It assumes answers to the very questions that should be open to debate: questions such as why a particular context should have privilege over another in discussing a text, whether a work of art merely reflects or in some fundamental sense reworks, remakes, or even produces the ideologies and social texts it supposedly represents, and whether the social contexts used to approach literary texts have themselves more than the status of fictions. The practical mind may shrink from such questions as merely impeding real work, the commonsense business of doing what one obviously can do, which is taking some historical source, George Puttenham's *Arte of English Poesie,* for example, or the Elizabethan homily on obedience, and relating these in some way to literary works written during the reigns of Elizabeth I and James I. Such work can be done, and it may be rich and provocative. But I would argue that the best criticism performs two tasks at once: the practical business of reading another text and the critical business of explaining the terms of that reading. Especially when one is attempting a new sort of critical undertaking, it is important to explain the problematics and the promise of that undertaking and to show that one is not merely reinscribing old practices and assumptions under the guise of new terms. A good reading can be a masterpiece, but it usually has the status of an isolated event. Essays which explain how and why one does and should read in a particular way are both more generous and more risky since they do not try to seal themselves off from what is polemical by aspiring to a timeless commonsense, but expose what is difficult and what is at stake in "making knowledge" at *this* historical moment.

As examples of two of the best historical critics working in the Renaissance at the moment, I want to look at the work of Louis Montrose and Stephen Greenblatt, both of whom combine a degree of methodological self-consciousness with an obvious delight in the careful reading of complex texts. My purpose is not to provide a thorough review of the work of either, but to gather from their practice a sense of both the varying possibilities and the limitations of historical approaches to Renaissance texts.

Louis Montrose has written a series of excellent essays in which, from a loosely Marxist and anthropological perspective, he relates the literary texts of Sidney, Spenser, and Shakespeare to social phenomena in the late sixteenth and early seventeenth centuries. Some of the early essays, in particular, provide relatively local readings of specific texts in specific social contexts. For example, in one he examines Sidney's pastoral entertainment, *The Lady of May,* produced at Wanstead in 1578 or 1579.[32] Montrose reads the entertainment as Sidney's sophisticated comment on Elizabeth's courtier system and on his own place within it. Two figures, forester and shepherd, represent two types of courtiership. The forester, resembling Sidney, is audacious, self-reliant, and aggressive. The shepherd, really a voluptuary masking as a contemplative, is used subtly to demean the overly compliant courtier whom Sidney feels Elizabeth favors over his own more independent, ardently Protestant stance. The essay is a subtle reading of a complex social interaction between Elizabeth I and Sidney at a time when their relations are strained; it also shows how a stylized form of pastoral entertainment can intervene in real-life situations and social relations.

But in my view such an essay does not represent Montrose's most important work. Court masques and courtly entertainments, being designed for an extremely particularized audience, easily reveal topical meaning and invite readings in terms of local situations. More crucial is Montrose's insistence that particular works of art, and even whole genres such as Elizabethan pastoral, perform more far-reaching acts of social mediation. He makes an argument, for example, elaborated through a number of essays, that "the symbolic mediation of social relationships was a central function of Elizabethan pastoral forms; and that social relationships are, intrinsically, relationships of power."[33] He adds: "They [pastorals] are symbolic instruments for coping with the goddess Fortune, with the endemic anxieties and frustrations of life in an ambitious and competitive society. Pastorals that celebrate the ideal of content

---

32. Louis Adrian Montrose, "Celebration and Insinuation: Sir Philip Sidney and the Motives of Elizabethan Courtship," *Renaissance Drama* N.S. 8 (1977), pp. 3–35.

33. Montrose, "'Eliza, Queene of shepheardes,' and the Pastoral of Power," *English Literary Renaissance* 10 (1980), 153–82 at 153.

function to articulate—and thereby, perhaps, to assuage—*discontent*" (155). In other words, he sees such pastoral literature as a way of managing the anxiety and contradictions caused by a particular social formation. Thus, for example, he argues that *As You Like It* deals with the anxiety caused among younger sons by the fact that in England, much more strongly than on the Continent, primogeniture was a nearly universal fact, a way of preserving intact an accumulation of property and so of enhancing a family's prestige, even though, ironically, the result of so doing was to pauperize some elements of that family.[34] In *As You Like It,* while the principle of primogeniture remains untouched, the Utopian impulse of pastoral miraculously leads the younger son, Orlando, to find in Duke Senior a second and loving Father who bestows upon him the prizes (wife, fortune, and favor) befitting the eldest offspring. Moreover, Duke Senior's own natural rights as elder brother are confirmed, without violence, by his younger brother's sudden abdication of his usurped throne.

In such essays, Montrose implicitly assumes that literature performs the ideological work of obscuring the contradictions of a particular social formation and of helping to naturalize arbitrary social arrangements which work to the benefit of particular groups and classes. In the case of *As You Like It,* for example, primogeniture is presented, not as an arbitrary social arrangement, but as a "natural force" sanctioned by God. When usurping brothers are touched by divine truth, they see the selfishness of their former acts. Moreover, the pain such a social arrangement causes to younger brothers, while firmly articulated by Orlando as the play begins, by play's end is suppressed. The deserving younger son finds a place, a wife, a second father, and his alienation is erased. At other times, Montrose suggests, pastoral works allay the pain caused by the inequalities of a strenuously hierarchical social system by indicating that the duties of obedience and subservience will be well rewarded by the gifts, patronage, and favor of a benevolent monarch.[35] In other words, appropriate rewards flow from obedient subservience, rewards which supposedly redress inequalities of power and prestige.

This view of literary forms as mediating the tensions and contradictions caused by particular economic and political institutions is vaguely Marxist. I say vaguely because Montrose is a remarkably undoctrinaire

34. Montrose, "'The Place of a Brother'," pp. 28–54.

35. Montrose, "Gifts and Reasons: The Contexts of Peele's *Araygnment of Paris,*" *ELH* 47 (1980), 433–61, esp. 454, where Montrose argues that for Peele "hierarchical social relationships are ritually defined and affirmed in the offering and acceptance of gifts."

critic, and only in his most recent essays does he lay out a specific explanatory model by which he approaches the question of literature's function in history. The Marxist flavor in his early work is largely conveyed by certain key terms, such as *mediation,* which he favors, and by his tendency to privilege as the explanatory context for literature the economic structures and the class and status systems of the period. Montrose's work is strong in dealing skillfully with the details of specific texts, in acknowledging the important differences which distinguish works in a particular genre from one another, and in keeping delicate hold on the ideological project that informs them all. The early essays, however, often lack a sustained consideration of his fundamental assumptions about the role of literature in history and a sustained consideration of ideology *per se*: what it is, how it is produced, whether or not literary texts ever elude its grasp or at least contest its authority. I question, for example, whether *As You Like It* does quite the work Montrose assigns to it; that is, whether by the exaggerated nature of the conversions and abdications which mark the play's final acts the play does not in large part undo the very work Montrose says it does in naturalizing the custom of primogeniture and effacing its arbitrary and unjust aspects. In essence, Montrose sees the comic form as a vehicle for articulating, only to erase, the contradictions of a particular social formation. I would simply argue that a text such as *As You Like It* is more subversive of formulations of reconciliation than Montrose's reading allows and that this may have implications for other texts which on the surface perform clear acts of social mediation.

Others of Montrose's essays raise further questions of this sort. In "The Purpose of Playing: Reflections on a Shakespearean Anthropology," Montrose shows the strong influence on his work of cultural anthropologists such as Victor Turner and Clifford Geertz and social historians such as Keith Thomas. What he argues is that Shakespearean drama (drama for the public stage) filled a void left in Elizabethan social life by the suppression of Catholic ritual and folk custom. Magic, as Thomas has argued, partly filled this void, but so, according to Montrose, did the public stage on which was enacted, in the persons of Prince Hal or Rosalind or Lear, those "rites of passage which give a social shape, order, and sanction to human existence. By means of transition rites, social boundaries are symbolically imposed upon the life cycle and can be safely crossed; these rites mediate the discontinuities they themselves create."[36]

36. Montrose, "The Purpose of Playing: Reflections on a Shakespearean Anthropology,"

Superficially, it looks as if Montrose's view of drama remains the same: it mediates social problems, papers over discontinuities. And yet, to see drama as enacting rites of passage in the life cycle can remove it from history altogether if, as Montrose seems at times to imply, these transition points are seen as a universal and timeless aspect of human nature and not as products of particular cultural formations. In other words, Montrose verges on an idealist perspective in which timeless and universal problems are what literature handles, rather than those of a particular historical era and material organization. But the countermove in the essay is the suggestion that, specifically in the Elizabethan period, the public stage became the site for challenges to traditional orthodoxies. Borrowing a term from Victor Turner, Montrose speaks of Elizabethan plays as "antistructures" which free the viewer from ordinary structures of cognition and make cultural innovation possible.

What is needed, clearly, is an extended discussion of subversion and contestation. In much of Montrose's work he suggests that literature participates in the circulation and confirmation of dominant ideologies. But the essay on the anthropology of the stage suggests that drama, at least, could contest dominant ideologies. Is it only drama that has this potential? And where does the contestatory impulse come from? From language itself? From contradictions in the social formation that inevitably surface in writing and resist a final resolution? From the marginality of certain groups whose voices are inscribed in dominant modes of expression? From the marginality of the theater as an institution? Moreover, one needs to ask to what extent works which *seem* to break with dominant orthodoxies actually engage in subtle acts of recuperation by which a dominant ideology transmutes itself just enough to insure its own essential reproduction.[37]

What I like in all of Montrose's essays is their steady assumption that literature or dramatic texts always do social *work*. And in his recent pieces, especially "Of Gentlemen and Shepherds: The Politics of Elizabethan Pastoral form," "'Shaping Fantasies': Figurations of Gender and Power in Elizabethan Culture," and "The Elizabethan Subject and the Spenserian Text," he has more clearly theorized his critical practice and to some extent modified its thrust.[38] I see three especially important

Helios 7 (1980), pp. 51–74 at 63.

37. See the work of Pierre Bourdieu and Jean-Claude Passeron, esp. *Reproduction in Education, Society and Culture,* trans. Richard Nice (London, 1977).

38. "Of Gentlemen and Shepherds: The Politics of Elizabethan Pastoral Form," *ELH* 50

theoretical developments in these more recent pieces. First, Montrose increasingly emphasizes the relative autonomy of cultural productions. In "Of Gentlemen and Shepherds" he specifically shows how his work relates to the later work of Raymond Williams who, repudiating a model of culture seen "as a superstructural reflection of an economic base," embraces a model in which "culture is represented as at once more autonomous in its processes and more material in its means and relations of production" (p. 419). If Montrose's early essays move rather insistently from world to literary text and so, however obliquely, suggest that literary writing is primarily a *reaction* to the extraliterary world, his later work does indeed begin to stress the relative autonomy of culture and its *productive* role within the social formation. This means that more attention gets paid to the way in which, by shaping a culture's discourse about "real life," literature is one of the many discursive practices defining the conditions of possibility for thought and action within Renaissance culture.[39] Second, Montrose's essays increasingly emphasize the implication of the historian in the knowledge he/she produces and of criticism in constructing what, supposedly, it merely transcribes.[40] This acknowledgement must, I feel, temper Montrose's earlier somewhat unproblematic reliance on the synthesizing histories of such scholars as Christopher Hill, Stone, and Thomas, to provide an adequate or objective account of the social text of Renaissance England. Third, in these more recent essays, Montrose increasingly moves to theorize the problems of agency and freedom. While acknowledging the enormous extent to which subjects are created by the discourses of their culture, he wants, as well, to explore the ways they preserve some degree of autonomy within these discourses, using them for their purposes even as they are used by them. Thus, in discussing Spenser's apparent submission to political

---

(1983), 415–59; "'Shaping Fantasies': Figurations of Gender and Power in Elizabethan Culture," *Representations* 2 (1983), 61–94. Professor Montrose was kind enough to send me the essay "The Elizabethan Subject and the Spenserian Text" in typescript. It is forthcoming in *Critical Theory and Renaissance Texts* to be published by Johns Hopkins University Press.

39. In "'Shaping Fantasies'," p. 62, Montrose writes: "whether or not Queen Elizabeth was physically present at the first performance of *A Midsummer Night's Dream,* her pervasive *cultural presence* was a condition of the play's imaginative possibility. This is not to imply that *A Midsummer Night's Dream* is merely an inert 'product' of Elizabethan culture. The play is rather a new *production* in Elizabethan culture enlarging the dimensions of the cultural field and altering the lines of force within it. Thus, in the sense that the royal presence was itself represented within the play, it may be said that the play henceforth conditioned the imaginative possibility of the Queen."

40. "The Elizabethan Subject," esp. pp. 4–5.

authority, Montrose writes: "In the Spenserian text, and elsewhere, we can observe a mode of contestation at work within the Elizabethan subject's very gestures of submission to the official fictions. We might call this mode of contestation appropriative, for it does not repudiate the given fictions of power but rather works within and through them, reinscribing them in the culture as the fictions of the speaking or writing subject."[41] In attempting to argue for a circumscribed but real role for human agency, Montrose is at once contesting Greenblatt's more pessimistic views of the possibility of human autonomy and opening important new territory for further discussion. In short, in Montrose's work one can see a relatively untheoretical critical practice becoming increasingly methodologically self-reflexive and moving, I would argue, steadily away from an "old" historicism to something which is more deservedly given the label "new."

In the work of Stephen Greenblatt one can find a somewhat different and more varied historical criticism than one finds in Montrose's work, but Greenblatt's recent writings also lead one, ultimately, to a consideration of the subversive or contestatory role which literature plays in culture. Up through his important book *Renaissance Self-Fashioning,* Greenblatt's main concern was identity formation. In that book he showed how the historical moment defined the conditions of possibility for constituting selves in sixteenth-century England. In a series of careful analyses he examined how selves took shape in the sixteenth century in relationship to specific authorities and their culturally-derived antitheses or demonic others.[42] Among the many influences on the book is Lacan's neo-Freudian psychology with its assumption, not of a unified and autonomous self, but of a provisional and contradictory self which is the product of discourse. Consequently, the book repudiates the humanist notion that man, the protean actor, is in control of his own identity formation; rather, he is presented in Greenblatt's work as the product of impersonal historical forces largely inimical to individual control.

One remarkable aspect of the book is the way it employs a contemporary theory of identity formation with something approaching reluctance. There is a lingering nostalgia for studying individual lives, for mystifying the idea of personal autonomy, even after Greenblatt has directly discarded notions of autonomy and the organically unified self. However, more important for present purposes is the way Greenblatt

---

41. "The Elizabethan Subject," p. 48.
42. Greenblatt, *Renaissance Self-Fashioning,* esp. p. 9.

moves between analyses of the lives of historical figures (such as More and Spenser) and analyses of literary "people" (Othello, Tamburlaine). Greenblatt appears unwilling to hold the two realms in an antithetical relationship or to talk about one as the ground for the other. Rather, he seems to suggest that discourse about the self has no single point of origin but constantly evolves in response to various forms of cultural authority, manifesting itself both in literary paradigms and in the construction of actual lives. In short, by stressing that he wishes to "investigate both the social presence to the world of the literary text and the social presence of the world in the literary text" (p. 5), Greenblatt moves to replace metaphors of mirrors and grounds with an interactive model of how the literary and social texts relate.

Productive as I find this aspect of his methodology, I find problematic another dimension of his practice: namely, his use of the illustrative example. Repeatedly, he presents historical figures and incidents as representations of large groups of people, actions, or mental sets. But how does one establish that Shakespeare was representative of a number of people in the late Renaissance in England whose characteristic stance toward authority was submissive subversiveness?[43] Is one going to make the case statistically? by citing a range of examples that *suggest* the pervasiveness of the tactic? by admitting that one cannot or does not know how representative a strategy this was, but by arguing that one's reading of Shakespeare—enabled by a theory of how people respond to authority—can give us a new and important way to understand the possibilities for self-definition in the later Renaissance? Greenblatt is evasive when it comes to defining his own attitude toward this problem. He continues to use the language of representativeness and to speak of certain figures (those people, inevitably male, upon whom a great deal of critical attention has already been focused) as epitomizing or crystalizing the period's characteristic strategies for self-fashioning. Yet he does not really question whether his perception of the centrality of these figures is an effect of the critical attention they have historically received or if it stems from some essential quality they inherently possess; nor does he make any serious attempt to prove their representativeness in the statistical terms likely to satisfy the empiricist nor argue for the irrelevance of such criteria in ways likely to satisfy those who see the "facts" of history largely produced by the operations of a particular discourse or act of theoretical intervention. In short, Greenblatt makes the issue of repre-

43. Greenblatt, pp. 222–54.

sentativeness a nonproblem, while I see it as a crucial issue. Such has been the influence of Greenblatt's practice, however, that there is now a spate of essays which begin with the painstaking description of a particular historical event, place, or experience and from that supposedly paradigmatic moment sketch a cultural law. It is a procedure which bears an anthropological stamp, but there is often no observation or consideration of a culture's whole system of signifying practices which would allow one to assess, relationally, the importance and function of the particular event described. In short, neither the rationale for the method nor the status of the knowledge produced is made an issue; and it is this sort of theoretical aporia which requires some redress by the new historical critics.

Greenblatt has now, however, moved to a set of problems slightly different from those which concerned him in his earlier book. Now he is investigating subversion: how and why a culture produces and deals with challenges to its dominant ideologies. Increasingly, Foucault seems an important influence, for this work takes Greenblatt deep into the territory of how a culture maintains itself by excluding, exorcising, or banishing challenges to its dominant ideologies or forms of knowledge. It is his thesis that such literature of the Renaissance period, particularly literature meant for the public theater, deliberately produces subversion in order to contain it.[44] He argues that this particular way of producing and containing subversion "is not a theoretical necessity of theatrical power in general but an historical phenomenon, the particular mode of this particular culture" (p. 57) which does not have a highly developed apparatus for repression and surveillance, such as one sees in the nineteenth century, but instead depends on "a ruler whose power is constituted in theatrical celebrations of royal glory and theatrical violence visited upon enemies of that glory" (p. 57). This proposal strikes me as an important insight into the way sixteenth-century texts often serve the larger interests of ideological domination. And it has affinities with Greenblatt's earlier assertion that authority maintains itself by the existence—or production—of a demonic other. One question, however, is how monolithic this practice of producing and demonizing alien ideologies really is in the Renaissance. For example, there seem to be a number of Renaissance texts in which ideological orthodoxies maintain themselves, not simply by producing and exorcising their subversive

44. Greenblatt, "Invisible Bullets: Renaissance Authority and Its Subversion," *Glyph* 8 (1981), 40–61, esp. 50–53.

opposites, but by recuperating them—that is, by domesticating and incorporating alien elements which thereby lose their subversive power. I think, for example, of the way in which a play such as *A Woman Killed with Kindness* handles the threat of the sexually eager, nonmonogamous wife, Anne Frankford. Potentially, she represents a challenge to patriarchy and to the whole ideology of a man's ownership of his wife's sexuality and thereby his exclusive ownership of the children produced by her. But, of course, she does not end up serving this function. She repents her "crime," dies of a broken heart at her husband's sadistic "kindness" and becomes a testament to the rightness of male rule. In short, the subversive elements of her sexuality are recuperated by a Christian ideology in the service of patriarchy which interprets a woman's sexual independence as a sin and a violation of natural order. And the woman is represented, finally, as concurring.

A further issue Greenblatt has not yet fully addressed is the question of whether Renaissance literature always, or even usually, controls—reins in—the subversive elements it supposedly produces or whether there are works which genuinely challenge orthodox constructions or attain a space outside of ideology altogether. This last possibility seems to be the burden of Greenblatt's final sentence in a brief essay in which he discusses *King Lear* and Harsnett's treatise on exorcism. He argues that while the play is fully implicated in the "network of social conditions, paradigms, and practices" of Shakespeare's age, nonetheless "the ideological and historical situation of *King Lear* produces the oscillation, the simultaneous affirmation and negation, the constant undermining of its own assertions and questioning of its own practices—in short, the supreme aesthetic self-consciousness—that lead us to celebrate its universality, its literariness, and its transcendence of all ideology."[45] But what we need to know are the exact conditions under which a work traversed by ideology can transcend it. Is this a quality of a few great texts? Is it a result of the special nature of literary language, defined as somehow different from other uses of language? Is it a result of the material or institutional context for the text's production? In a later, expanded version of the *Lear* essay, Greenblatt goes somewhat further in answering these questions and in explaining how the play, as a work for the public stage, serves different interests than those served by Harsnett's violently anti-Catholic polemic.[46] While both reveal the empty theatricality of exorcism, *Lear*

45. Greenblatt, "*King Lear* and Harsnett's 'Devil-Fiction,'" *Genre* 15 (1982), 239, 242.
46. Greenblatt, "Shakespeare and the Exorcists," in *After Strange Texts: The Role of Theory in the*

does so within the sphere of the theater itself where not only the ritual of exorcism is emptied of its significance, but also all gestures of faith in the "clear gods." Consequently, while Shakespeare loyally reiterates the official position on exorcism, he does so in a context which makes it something other than an apology for triumphant Protestantism. In my view such a reading of *Lear* does not place the play *above* ideology, but simply in an ambivalent or contestatory relationship to the ideology of the "source" with which it is being compared. Greenblatt seems, however, to be moving away from the position that in Elizabethan culture subversion is inevitably contained, to a position which acknowledges that through certain cultural practices, such as the production of plays on the public stage, a space for more than compliance with dominant ideologies may be opened. This is a position that clearly invites further elaboration. Is *Lear* a special instance, or is it typical of the way plays for the Elizabethan public stage empty ideological positions from the center of the culture of their efficacy?

As Greenblatt develops his work on subversion, moreover, he also seems to be developing a way of establishing the historical situation of a given literary text by locating it directly in relationship to other types of cultural texts, rather than locating it by means of secondary histories of the period. Regularly, he talks about one cultural text, such as Dürer's sketches, in direct juxtaposition to another, such as Sidney's *Arcadia,* as both help to produce a culture's discourse on a particular subject and to enact certain strategies of containment.[47] The method brings great immediacy to the study of disparate cultural texts. They can hardly be reduced to illustrations of the historical "background" when they are offered as the primary documents of a history to be constructed. But again, as with Greenblatt's use of the illustrative example, one wants to know more about the process by which disparate phenomena are chosen for juxtaposition and discussion; the juxtaposition can seem arbitrary to those reared on the notion of "coverage," that is, on the idea that all the texts and all the documents need to be surveyed before one can say with confidence that any two stand in a pivotal cultural position. Greenblatt's practice implicitly challenges this mode of thinking, but one wishes for an overt articulation of his oppositional point of view.

Study of Literature, ed. Gregory S. Jay and David L. Miller (University, Alabama, 1985), pp. 101–23.

47. Greenblatt, "Murdering Peasants: Status, Genre, and the Representation of Rebellion," *Representations* 1 (1983), 1–29.

IV

I have examined aspects of the work of Montrose and Greenblatt because each seems, through practical work with texts, to be pushing the historical study of literature in new directions, though it is also clear that these two types of historical practice are different from one another and that each raises theoretical problems not yet fully explored and resolved. Each critic strikes me as typically American in his reticence to discuss the theory that informs his practice. Each, at times, naturalizes his critical practice and so obscures the many crucial theoretical questions being engaged or ignored at every stage. This makes it difficult always to discern what is new in this work, other than its insistence that a purely formalist approach to Renaissance texts is insufficient. That there *are* genuinely new assumptions informing the work of both critics is clear, but the hesitancy in foregrounding these differences diminishes their potential to alter ways of thinking about what we mean to do when we say we wish, in a poststructuralist age, to study literature historically.

My own sense is that to represent anything like a genuinely poststructuralist criticism, the new work in the historical critique of Renaissance texts needs to take several steps. First, it must grow increasingly less literature-centered both as a way of acknowledging the arbitrary nature of the designation, "literature," and also because it is clear that the ideological significance and the historical situation of those representations we label literary can only be understood when looked at in relation to other sorts of contemporaneous representations and discursive practices.

Second, it seems necessary that some of the critical skills literary critics have brought to the study of literary texts be applied both to aspects of the social text and to what we designate as non-literary forms of writing. These skills include the techniques of deconstructive reading by which the self-divisions of the text are revealed and by Marxist techniques of demystification by which the social and ideological elements of these divisions are revealed. Doing so will help to topple the assumption that the texts—social and written—which we read to acquire our sense of the past, of history, are either transparent, organically unified, or outside of ideology and the network of power relations.

Third, the new historicism needs at every point to be more overtly self-conscious of its methods and its theoretical assumptions, since what one discovers about the historical place and function of literary texts is in large measure a function of the angle from which one looks and the assumptions that enable the investigation. This means examining overtly and directly a number of the questions raised in the second and third parts of this essay, questions such as whether or not literature reflects or produces our understanding of the real, how literature can best be related to other aspects of the social formation, and what status one gives to the isolated text or artifact when what occupies categories such as the "representative" and the "important" is itself a product of a particular political history of canon formation.

Finally, it seems to me that the historically-minded critic must increasingly be willing to acknowledge the non-objectivity of his or her own stance and the inevitably political nature of interpretive and even descriptive acts. Self-effacement, neutrality, disinterestedness—these are the characteristics privileged in the Academy, but are claims to possess them more than a disingenuous way of obscuring how one's own criticism is non-objective, interested and political? I am not suggesting that it is desirable to look at the past with the willful intention of seeing one's own prejudices and concerns. Nonetheless, since objectivity is not in any pure form a possibility, let us acknowledge that fact and acknowledge as well that any move into history is an *intervention,* an attempt to reach from the present moment into the past to rescue both from meaningless banality. One hopes that from the encounter, more urgent, perhaps, than LaCapra's notion of "dialogue" will admit, can come revisioning of both the past and the present. But such encounters start somewhere, and that is with the active intervention of the historically constituted critic. That accepted, it may be more possible to break free from the other positivistic assumptions that still inhibit the "newness" of the new history.

"Eliza, Queene of shepheardes," and the Pastoral of Power

PASTORAL POWER might seem an ox moronic notion, for pastoral literature is ostensibly a discourse of the powerless in dispraise of power. In his study of Elizabethan poetic kinds, Hallett Smith characterizes "the central meaning" of Elizabethan pastorals as "the rejection of the aspiring mind. The shepherd demonstrates that true content is to be found in this renunciation."[1] Smith's perspective on pastoral equates "theme" with "meaning"; my perspective distinguishes "form" from "function." The repertoire of pastoral forms includes images and metaphors; conventions of person, place, and diction; and distinctive generic features and their combinations. This repertoire was exploited and elaborated by Elizabethan poets and politicians, by sycophants and ideologues, by the Queen herself. My argument is that the symbolic mediation of social relationships was a central function of Elizabethan pastoral forms; and that social relationships are, intrinsically, relationships of power.[2]

The Arte of English Poesie, a guide to the practice of courtship and courtly poetry that was dedicated to Queen Elizabeth, claims that modern poets have devised pastoral poetry, "not of purpose to counterfait or represent the rustical manner of loves and communication: but under the vaile of homely persons, and in rude speeches to insinuate and glaunce at greater matters and such as perchance had not bene safe to

---

1. *Elizabethan Poetry* (1952; rpt. Ann Arbor, 1968), p. 10.

2. In this essay, I construe "power" and "politics" in broadly social terms. See Abner Cohen, *Two-Dimensional Man: An Essay on the Anthropology of Power and Symbolism in Complex Societies* (1974; rpt. Berkeley, 1976), p. xi: "'Power' is taken to be an aspect of nearly all social relationships, and 'politics' to be referring to the processes involved in the distribution, maintenance, exercise and struggle for power. . . . Power does not exist in a 'pure form' but is always inherent in social relationships."

have been disclosed in any other sort."[3] Puttenham suggestively describes a verbal complex that is literally pastoral in form, pervasively amorous in content, and intrinsically political in purpose. Puttenham calls allegory both "the figure of false semblant" and "the Courtier": "the Courtly figure *Allegoria,* is . . . when we speake one thing, and thinke another, and that our wordes and our meanings meete not" (p. 186). In his peroration, Puttenham tells the Queen—"if it please your Majestie"—that her courtier should "dissemble his conceits as well as his countenances, so as he never speake as he thinkes, or think as he speaks, and that in any matter of importance his words and his meaning very seldome meete"; and that "our courtly Poet" should "dissemble not only his countenances & conceits, but also all his ordinary actions of behaviour, or the most part of them, whereby the better to winne his purposes & good advantages" (pp. 299-300). In Puttenham's own courtly discourse, the courtly poet and the courtier finally merge. Within this context of socio-literary analogies and ironies, Puttenham's own version of pastoral exemplifies his version of allegory. The otiose love-talk of the shepherd masks the busy negotiation of the courtier; the shepherd is a courtly poet prosecuting his courtship in pastoral forms.

In pastoral forms, Queen Elizabeth and her subjects could pursue their mutual courtship subtly and gracefully; they could perform a wide range of symbolic operations upon the network of social relationships at whose center was the sovereign. Queen Elizabeth is the cynosure of my essay as she was of Elizabethan pastoralism. But if the poet's task was to celebrate, the critic's task is to understand the uses of celebration. My purpose is to explore the range of motives in pastorals whose subject, audience, or performer was the Queen, and to situate this Elizabethan flowering of royal pastoral forms within the historical process of which it was a part.[4]

I Princess and Milkmaid

If Elizabeth's most memorable pastoral persona is to be a resplendent queen of shepherds, her quaintest is to be a humble milkmaid. In those

3. Ed. Gladys D. Willcock and Alice Walker (Cambridge, Eng., 1936), p. 38. (Subsequent page references will be to this edition.) I accept the ascription of this work to George Puttenham. In quotations from this and other Elizabethan texts, I have modified obsolete typographical conventions.

4. My own selective and speculative study is indebted to the comprehensive survey of royal pastorals in Elkin Calhoun Wilson, *England's Eliza* (1939; rpt. London, 1966), pp. 126–66.

anxious years under the rule of her Catholic half-sister Mary, Elizabeth seems already to have created for herself a rustic, "mere English" version of pastoral; it complements that which was to be created for her by her poets. Holinshed reports an incident that took place while Princess Elizabeth was under house-arrest at Woodstock (1554-1555):

Thus this woorthie ladie oppressed with continuall sorrow, could not be permitted to have recourse to anie friends she had; but still in the hands of hir enimies was left desolate, and utterlie destitute of all that might refresh a dolfull hart, fraught full of terror and thraldome. Whereupon no marvell, if she hearing upon a time out of hir garden at Woodstocke, a certeine milkmaid singing pleasantlie, wished hir selfe to be a milkemaid as she was, saieng that hir case was better, and life more merier than was hirs in that state as she was.[5]

The episode is perhaps apocryphal but nevertheless attractive and in-structive. The rejection of aspiration and the celebration of *otium* ex-pressed here and in so many Elizabethan pastorals exemplifies what Puttenham characterizes as the recreative function of poetry: "the common solace of mankind in all his travails and cares of this transitory life" (p. 24). When they fulfill this function, pastorals and other imag-inative forms are (in Kenneth Burke's fine phrase) "equipment for living." They are symbolic instruments for coping with the goddess Fortuna, with the endemic anxieties and frustrations of life in an am-bitious and competitive society. Pastorals that celebrate the ideal of content function to articulate—and thereby, perhaps, to assuage—*dis*content. Elizabeth's pastoral impulse juxtaposes her experience of contingency and personal danger in a violent, deceptive world with an idealized lowly life in a world of unalienated labor synchronized with the orderly cycles of nature—the diurnal and seasonal rounds and the productivity of domesticated animals. Leisure and labor, aspiration and content, interact ambiguously in an hierarchical political context. A princess caught in a position of impotence and constraint projects herself into a lowly milkmaid. The subject is not the simple milkmaid but the complex princess-as-milkmaid; through Elizabeth's perspective, the actual powerlessness and compulsory physical labor of the peasant are transformed into a paradoxical experience of power, freedom, and ease. It was only society's elite, like Princess Elizabeth, who were in a position to be tragic actors upon the world-stage of history. The operations of pastoral forms may have provided them with a symbolic

5. *Holinshed's Chronicles of England, Scotland, and Ireland*, 6 vols. (1808; rpt. New York, 1965), IV, 133.

means to express and manage the threats and fears of living at or near the apex of the hierarchy, the center of power. But for the great, the material reality of a peasant's life can hardly have been a desirable or even a feasible option.

While a captive princess, Elizabeth might give pastoral form to a sentimental fantasy; as a queen regnant, she used pastoral forms as instruments of policy. In her speech to Parliament in 1576, in another response to the constant urging by the many men around her that she marry, Elizabeth wrote: "If I were a milkmaid with a pail on my arm, whereby my private person might be little set by, I would not forsake that poor state to match with the greatest monarch."[6] Elizabeth's rhetoric builds subtly upon an analogy of sexual and social hierarchies: a milkmaid is both a maiden and a peasant, both sexually and socially inferior to "the greatest monarch," the powerful male whom she would spurn. Elizabeth's hyperbole renders the marginal states of virginity and poverty as sources of power. The rhetorical point of the hypothesis, however, is that she herself is *not* a milkmaid, not a mere private woman but a great monarch in her own right. And if, as a poor and private milkmaid, she might eschew marriage on personal grounds, so much the more must she do so on political grounds: to marry would be to relinquish the anomalous but very real power that she enjoys as a maiden queen in a masculine and patriarchal world. She puts her policy succinctly in a remark to the earl of Leicester: "I will have here but one Mistress, and no Master."[7]

Elizabeth was fond of saying that she was married to her people, and she assured the Commons "that, though after my death you may have many stepdames, yet shall you never have a more natural mother than I mean to be unto you all."[8] As virgin, spouse, and mother, Elizabeth gathered unto herself all the Marian attributes. It was left to her preachers, propagandists, and poets to isolate the remaining female archetype—the whore—in the Catholic Mass, the Papacy, and the Queen of Scots. For purposes of public relations, however, Elizabeth might cast even Mary Stuart as a milkmaid. In the interval between Mary's trial and her execution, Elizabeth worked hard on speeches to Parliament, intended for publication and popular consumption, in which she reluctantly justified her government's proceedings:

6. Quoted in J. E. Neale, *Elizabeth I and Her Parliaments 1559–1581* (New York, 1958), p. 366.

7. Sir Robert Naunton, *Fragmenta Regalia* (written circa 1630; printed 1641), ed. Edward Arber (London, 1870), p. 17.

8. Parliament of 1563. Quoted in Neale, *Elizabeth I and Her Parliaments 1559–1581*, p. 109.

And if, even yet, now the matter is made but too apparent, I thought she truly would repent—as perhaps she would easily appear in outward show to do—and that for her none other would take the matter upon them; or that we were but as two milk-maids, with pails upon our arms; or that there were no more dependency upon us, but mine own life were only in danger, and not the whole estate of your religion and well doings; I protest . . . I would most willingly pardon and remit this offence.[9]

The royal rhetorician consistently invokes the pastoral contrast not as a desired escape from the burdens of *negotium* but as a foil for the exercise of power, not as a rejection of aspiration but as an assertion of authority.

According to William Empson, pastoral's characteristic operation is to put "the complex into the simple"; its characteristic effect is "to imply a beautiful relation between rich and poor" in which "the best parts of both [are] used."[10] His formulations are pertinent to some Elizabethan versions of pastoral. The pastoralization of the Elizabethan body politic puts the complex into the simple and puts public relationships of power into intimate relationships of love—a love that is variously spiritual, maternal, and erotic. It creates beautiful and benevolent relationships between the royal shepherdess and her flock, and between the queen of shepherds and the spiritual and temporal pastors who guard her flock: that is, between the sovereign and the whole people, and between the sovereign and the political nation, the elite through whom she governs her people. The gentleman lawyers of Gray's Inn, a nursery of the political nation, celebrated these relationships in the spectacular court revels of Shrovetide 1595.[11] The central device, Proteus's Adamantine Rock, splits open in the Queen's presence and the liberated masquers dance forth, drawn by the "trew adamant of Hartes" (l. 197) which is both England and England's Queen:

> Under the shadow of this blessed rock
> In Britton land while tempests beat abroade,
> The lordly and the lowly Shepheard both
> In plenteous peace have fedd their happy flockes. (ll. 246-49)

Characteristic examples of each of these pastoral forms of political relationship are to be found in the work of George Peele, one of the most assiduous and able of Elizabethan mythmakers. In *Descensus Astraea* (1591), a city pageant for the installation of the new Lord Mayor of

9. Quoted in J. E. Neale, *Elizabeth I and Her Parliaments 1584–1601* (New York, 1958), p. 117.
10. *Some Versions of Pastoral* (1936; rpt. New York, 1968), pp. 22 and 11-12.
11. The text is preserved in BL MS Harley 541; I quote from the excerpts printed in Marie Axton, *The Queen's Two Bodies* (London, 1977), pp. 85–87.

London, the Queen is identified with the pagan virgin goddess of Justice. This identification was a popular one in the later part of the reign; Peele's innovation is to make his Eliza-Astraea a shepherdess, a "Celestiall sacred Nymph, that tendes her flocke / With watchfull eyes, and keeps this fount in peace."[12] Peele's pageant is part of an annual rite renewing the special relationship between the sovereign and the citizens of London; the pageant symbolizes that relationship as one between a shepherdess and her flock. "Astraea with hir sheep-hook on the top of the pageant" speaks reassuringly to her sheep and to her audience: "Feed on my flocke among the gladsome greene / Where heavenly Nectar flowes above the banckes" (ll. 54-55). Astraea dwelt on earth during the Golden Age; a Golden Age of peace, pros-perity, and Protestantism has descended upon England with the advent of "Our faire Astraea, our Pandora faire, / Our Eliza, or Zabeta faire" (ll. 40-41). Peele expresses in delicate pastoral form the vital and wary economic relationship between the crown and the companies of London merchants, tradesmen, and artisans; he sublimates the expanding market economy of an age of gold into the maternal plenitude of a Golden Age.

One of Peele's numerous bids for aristocratic patronage was "An Eclogue Gratulatorie entituled to the right honorable, and renowned Shepheard of Albions Arcadia: Robert Earl of Essex and Ewe" (1589). In this Spenserian mixture of encomium and complaint, Peele elaborates the relationship of Essex and his forces to their royal mistress by a rather precious pastoral allegory. Essex "is a great Herdgroome, certes, but no swaine, / Save hers that is the Flowre of Phaebes plaine" (ll. 48-49); "He waits where our great Shepherdesse doth wunne, / . . . his lustie flocke him by" (ll. 56, 58). Peele includes a memorable contribution to the pas-toral mythologizing of Sidney as "that great Shepherd good Philisides" (l. 62), and of Essex as Sidney's spiritual and ideological heir:

> With him he serv'd, and watcht and waited fate,
> To keepe the grim Wolfe from Elizaes gate:
> And for their Mistresse thoughten these two swains,
> They moughten never take too mickle paines.   (ll. 66-69)

Peele's sentiment notwithstanding, Eliza often found such pains reckless and self-serving.[13] Indeed, she herself might use Peele's pastoral meta-

---

12. Lines 20-21. All quotations are from *The Life and Minor Works of George Peele*, ed. David H. Horne (New Haven, 1952). Further line references will be noted parenthetically in the text.

13. See my study of the politics of Sidney's royal entertainments: "Celebration and Insinua-

phor as an instrument of instruction and chastisement. When Thomas Arundell of Wardour returned from the Continent in 1596 an "Earl of the Holy Empire," the Queen of England expressed her displeasure in a pointed pastoral: "Betweene Princes and their Subjects there is a most straight tye of affections. As chaste women ought not to cast their eye upon any other than their husbands, so neither ought subjects to cast their eyes upon any other Prince, than him whom *God* hath given them. I would not have my sheepe branded with another mans marke; I would not they should follow the whistle of a strange Shepherd."[14] Prince, Husband, and Shepherd are analogized as superior terms in hierarchical opposition to Subject, Wife, and Sheep. The virgin Queen must have relished thoroughly her own paradoxical analogy.

Elizabeth enthusiastically adopted into her discourse the splendid pastoral persona given her by her poets. And her poets managed to find their own encomiastic uses for the rustic pastoral persona recurrently invoked by the Queen. When she entered the estate of the Countess of Derby at Harefield in the summer of 1602, Elizabeth was confronted by a dairymaid named Joan. Joan invited Elizabeth to spend the night in her dairy house and told her she would be better accommodated there than at the great house. Here at last, on what was to be her final progress, the aged queen had her opportunity to experience the life of a milkmaid. Joan went on to tell the visitors quite candidly that the intent of her hospitality was to oblige them to work at the harvest: "to carry them into the fields; and make them earne their entertaynment well and thriftily; and to that end I have heere a *Rake* and *Forke*, to deliver to the best Huswife in all this company." [15] The note in the printed text informs us that at this point the Queen was presented with "2 Juells." The episode has no more intrinsic dramatic or poetic merit than most Elizabethan royal entertainments. But the fascination and the power of such multi-media happenings lie elsewhere, in their facile deployment of the whole range

---

tion: Sir Philip Sidney and the Motives of Elizabethan Courtship," *Renaissance Drama*, N.S. 8 (1977), 3–35.

14. William Camden, *Annales or, the History of the most Renowned and Victorious Princesse Elizabeth*, trans. R. N., 3rd ed. (London, 1635), p. 469; quoted in Wilson, *England's Eliza*, p. 212. Elizabeth's pastoral metaphor could also be beneficent. For example, she nicknamed Sir Christopher Hatton her "Bell-wether" and her "Mutton"; Sir Thomas Heneage wrote to Hatton (July 1581) that the Queen "willed me to send you word, with her commendations, that you should remember she was a Shepherd, and then you might think how dear her Sheep was unto her" (see Eric St. John Brooks, *Sir Christopher Hatton* [London, 1946], pp. 99-100, 302-03).

15. The text is printed from MS in John Nichols, *The Progresses and Public Processions of Queen Elizabeth*, 3 vols. (1823; rpt. New York, 1966), III, 586–95; I quote from p. 588.

of Elizabethan encomiastic strategies in a melding of life with art. A rake and a pitchfork for the best of huswives are also jewels in the shapes of a rake and a pitchfork for the best of queens. Like the entertainment of which they are a part, the jewels are both tangible and symbolic offerings in a transaction between giver and recipient. The pert dairymaid's allegorical gifts make a striking emblem for Elizabethan pastoral itself: objects and relations in the material world of peasant labor are sublimated into forms of lordly splendor. Like the poet's figuratively ornamented pastorals, the dairymaid's bejewelled rake and pitchfork "counterfait or represent the rustical manner of loves and communication" so as "to insinuate and glaunce at greater matters." It is to the sources and the substance of those matters that I now turn.

II Body Politic and *Corpus Christi*

Michael Drayton rephrases a commonplace of Renaissance poetics when he writes that "pastorals, as they are a Species of Poesie, signifie fained Dialogues, or other speeches in Verse, fathered upon Heardsmen . . . who are ordinarie persons in this kind of Poeme, worthily therefore to be called base, or low. . . . The subject of Pastorals, as the language of it ought to be poor, silly, & of the coursest Woofe in appearance." The interrelated principles of hierarchy, analogy, and decorum produce a literary kind that is base in style, in subject, and in its status within a system of literary forms, within a verbal body politic. In his next sentence, however, Drayton reveals the inherent paradox of this pseudo-simple form: "Neverthelesse, the most High, and most Noble Matters of the World may be shaddowed in them, and for certaine sometimes are." Drayton's qualification alludes to the pastorals of Saint Luke's Gospel and Vergil's fourth eclogue: "The Blessing which came . . . to the testimonial Majestie of the Christian Name, out of *Sibyls* Moniments, cited before *Christ's* Birth, must ever make *Virgil* venerable with me; and in the *Angels* Song to Shepheards at our Saviours Nativitie Pastoral Poesie seemes consecrated." [16] Vergil's fourth eclogue celebrates an unborn child who will make time run back to the Golden Age. Christian exegetes accommodate Vergil's oracular and encomiastic Roman mythmaking by a creative misreading: the eclogue is an inspired nativity hymn, a prophecy of the advent of Christ and the Christian dispensation.

The amorous lyric—invitational, celebratory, or plaintive, Petrar-

16. "To the Reader of His Pastorals" (1619), in *The Works of Michael Drayton*, ed. William Hebel *et al.*, 5 vols. (Oxford, 1961), II, 517.

chan, mythological, or rustic—is characteristic of the great Elizabethan pastoral anthology, *Englands Helicon* (1600), and of Elizabethan pastoral poetry in general. But the Christological reading of Vergil's Golden Age eclogue and the pastoral imagery of the nativity and ministry of Christ may occasionally infuse the landscape of Elizabethan pastorals with an aura of religious mystery. *Englands Helicon* contains an example in E.B.'s "Sheepheards Song: A Caroll or Himme for Christmas." [17] Here the paradoxical languages of pastoral and religion merge: "For loe the worlds great Sheepheard now is borne / A blessed Babe, an Infant full of power" (ll. 33-34); "Sprung is the mirthful May, / Which Winter cannot marre" (ll. 39-40). Edmund Bolton, who is presumably the "E.B." of "The Sheepheards Song," also contributed to *Englands Helicon* "A Canzon Pastorall in honour of her Majestie" (p. 17). This lyric fuses pastoral's spiritual and amorous strains into a royal encomium alluding to the month of the Queen's own nativity: "With us as May September hath a prime" (l. 8). Bolton's pastoral song for a national goddess appropriates the language of the shepherd's Christmas hymn: "Winter though every where / Hath no abiding heere: / . . . The Sunne which lights our world is always one" (ll. 25-26, 28). Implicit in the juxtaposition of these two lyrics is the whole complex of verbal strategies I have called the Elizabethan pastoral of power.

The grounding of pastoral's power in the conjunction of classical and biblical mysteries, so eloquently described by Drayton, is better exemplified in the early fifteenth-century Nativity pageants of the Wakefield Master than in almost any Elizabethan pastorals. In the *Prima Pastorum*, in fact, one of the shepherds quotes and interprets the Vergilian prophecy at the dramatic moment of its fulfillment, at the birth of Christ. The events dramatized in these plays make spiritual love and power immanent in a world that is not allegorically but literally humble and pastoral. This quality fuses the sacred and the profane, the mysterious and the naturalistic, the biblical and the contemporary, in a popular and collective art form which exploits—as Renaissance texts rarely do—the radical social implications of pastoral's Christian context. Most Elizabethan pastorals were produced by poets and scholars under the patronage or influence of court and aristocracy or by gentleman amateurs; the social milieu and informing spirit of the Nativity pageants are alien to Elizabethan pastorals.

---

17. *Englands Helicon*, ed. Hugh Macdonald (1949; rpt. Cambridge, Mass., 1962), pp. 135-36. Further quotations are from this edition.

The religious mystery of Christ's double nature generates the pastoral paradox that Christ is both the Lamb of God and the Good Shepherd. In relationship to Christ, to a transcendent Lord metaphorized as a Pastor, *all* human creatures belong to a single flock of sheep. But among themselves, within the political domain, human creatures are most rigorously classified and stratified. The "Exhortation, concerning good order and obedience, to rulers and magistrates" (1559) is an authoritative exposition of Tudor ideology: "Everye degre of people, in theyr vocation, callyng, and office hath appointed to them, theyr duety and ordre. Some are in hyghe degree, some in lowe, some kynges and prynces, some inferiors and subjectes, priestes, and layemenne, Maysters and Servauntes, Fathers and chyldren, husbandes and wives, riche and poore." [18] To translate into the discourse of pastoral: some are shepherds and some are sheep—some are the shearers and some are the shorn. A tension between temporal hierarchy and spiritual communion was woven into the fabric of traditional Europe's Christian culture; in pastoral forms, this tension might combine with a tension between literal and metaphorical shepherds, between peasants and lords. Such tensions are expressed and contained at the end of the Nativity pageant of the Chester cycle, when the three naturalistically presented shepherds who have witnessed the first Christmas resolve to become preachers of the Gospel; as V. A. Kolve puts it, "these shepherds of sheep have become shepherds of men." [19]

The verse from the Gospel of Luke (1:52) that was used as the Canticle for Vespers—"He hath put down the mighty from their seat, and hath exalted the humble"—was in daily use before the Reformation of the English Church. But, as Kolve writes,

the text came into special prominence . . . during the Christmas season at the feast of the Innocents, when the custom grew up of electing from the choir a Boy Bishop for the day and allowing the boys to sit in the seats of their elders and superiors and to conduct certain of the divine offices. The truth enshrined in that custom was felt to be a part of the deepest significance of the Incarnation. England took the festival to its heart; it seems to have been more common there than anywhere else in Europe. And thus, this theme of the exaltation of the humble had a particular Nativity reference. Though it originally concerned the Virgin, it came to apply to the Innocents slaughtered by Herod, and directly to Jesus Himself: on Christmas a babe is born in a mean stable who will displace the powerful and privileged . . . . We see here wedded the two ideas: the

18. *Elizabethan Backgrounds*, ed. Arthur F. Kinney (Hamden, Conn., 1975), p. 60. This homily was first printed in 1547.

19. *The Play Called Corpus Christi* (Stanford, 1966), p. 154.

humble overthrowing the mighty; the young overthrowing the old. It is a profound part of the meaning of the Nativity, and no Corpus Christi cycle neglects it. (pp. 156-57)

In the apocalyptic perspective of the cycle plays, the only true king is the King of Kings; even Christian rulers might be contaminated by Herod's image.[20] Elements of the inversion and levelling that were explicit in the divine pastoral of the Nativity texts might subtly infiltrate other pastoral forms. This context had to be expunged or transformed if pastoral metaphors were to function effectively as benign images of the stable and rigorously hierarchical social order which Tudor governments sought to establish and preserve.

The sixteenth-century movement toward the centralization of nation-states under the rule of dynastic monarchs proceeded internally against the power of local magnates and regional loyalties, and internationally against Reformation religious crises, political instability, and armed conflict. Changes in the nature and location of power and authority are inseparable from changes in the structure and function of the symbolic forms in which power and authority are expressed, controlled, and enhanced. In regard to royal ceremonial, Roy Strong points out that

the medieval heritage of festival was basically ecclesiastical, celebrating the prince in relation to Holy Church, his sacred anointing at his coronation, his presentation of myrrh, frankincense, and gold at Epiphany or the washing of the feet of the poor on Maundy Thursday. These occasions were inherited by the great dynasties of Europe in the sixteenth century but extended and overlaid by what might be described as a liturgy of State. This can be followed in its most extreme form in Protestant countries, where the splendours of Catholic liturgical spectacle were banished at the Reformation along with the old medieval saints' days. To replace these came State-promoted festivals.[21]

The Henrician regime abolished the rite of the Boy Bishop by royal proclamation and enacted statutes forbidding possession of the English Bible to anyone below the status of gentleman. A copy of Thomas Langley's *Abridgement of Polydore Vergil* bears this telling inscription: "I bout this boke when the Testament was obberagatyd [abrogated], that shepeherdys myght not red hit. I prey God amende that blyndnes. Wryt by Robert Wyllyams keppynge shepe upon Seynbury hill 1546." [22] The Catechism in *The Book of Common Prayer* (1559), which all English chil-

---

20. See Kolve, pp. 104-05 and 143.

21. *Splendour at Court: Renaissance Spectacle and Illusion* (London, 1973), pp. 21-22.

22. Quoted in A. G. Dickens, *The English Reformation* (New York, 1964), p. 191.

dren were supposed to know by heart, included a version of the pastoral "rejection of the aspiring mind"; it was a personal acknowledgement of the duty "to submit myself to all my governors, teachers, spiritual Pastors and masters. To order myself lowly and reverently to all my betters."[23] The monumental Statute of Artificers (1563) was notably concerned with the regulation of agrarian laborers and youths. Within the analogical system of thought that sanctioned social hierarchy, pastoral mystifications of relations between the humble and the mighty, the young and the old, were reinforced by examples of benevolent relationships between superiors and inferiors that were literally pastoral (the shepherd and his flock) and spiritually pastoral (Christ and humanity).

Power relationships might be metaphorized as pastoral relationships in various aspects of social life. But the pastoral analogy was a particularly apt ideological instrument for a government trying to subordinate the wills of all subjects to the will of their Queen, a government which had promulgated royal supremacy and popular uniformity in religion. References to the Virgin were excised from the English translation of the liturgy, and the pageants involving the Virgin were excised from the Corpus Christi plays. The process of suppressing the plays was virtually complete by 1580.[24] By that time, a professional city drama and amateur courtly poetry had begun to flourish. They were fostered by the Crown and employed in the creation of a syncretic Elizabethan mythology, iconography, and ritual. The Elizabethan suppression of the cult of the Virgin Mary, of the craft cycles, and of medieval spirituality and much of its related folk culture, inevitably involved the suppression of the popular and vital version of pastoral that was expressed in Nativity pageants.

These suppressions were in fact only a stage in a larger process of appropriation and transformation. A virgin Queen who united church and state, brought relative peace and security to her people, and secured the triumph of the reformed religion attracted to herself the feminine symbolism of the Virgin Mary as well as the pastoral symbolism of Christ's Nativity and the Church's ministry. The custom of celebrating the Queen's accession day began to flourish following the suppression of the northern rebellion and the York Corpus Christi play in 1569, and the promulgation of the Papal Bull excommunicating Elizabeth on Corpus

23. Rpt. in *Liturgies and Occasional Forms of Prayer Set Forth in the Reign of Queen Elizabeth*, ed. W. K. Clay (1847; rpt. New York, 1968), p. 213.

24. See Harold C. Gardiner, S. J., *Mysteries' End* (New Haven, 1946).

Christi Day 1570. Roy Strong suggests that "Accession Day represented a development of the medieval tradition of combining a feast day of the Church with secular rejoicing. The Reformation had swept away many important Catholic feast days, above all Corpus Christi. . . . The rise of the Queen's Day festivities enabled these energies to be concentrated into a stream designed to glorify the monarchy and its policies."[25] In 1576, the Elizabethan Church made the Queen's accession day one of its very few official holy days; it became known as "The Birthday of the Gospel." And the Queen's own birthday, which happened to fall on the eve of the Virgin's Nativity, also came to be celebrated as a national holiday. It is no wonder that Catholic propagandists attacked the cult of the Queen as an abominable blasphemy, and that Puritans occasionally made so bold as to denounce it as idolatry. These dissenting voices of reaction and revolution frame what was an extraordinary transformation of cultural symbols—a transformation partly spontaneous and popular, partly calculated and official. It seems to have worked to various ends: to the emotional benefit of the populace, the political benefit of the government, and the economic benefit of the artists and craftsmen, performers and patrons, who helped to body it forth.

Yates and Strong have argued persuasively that there must have been a collective *psychological* need for rites and images to replace those obliterated in the Reformation. I would add that rulers and poets also had a vital "professional" need for them. The iconoclastic tendencies of reform threatened both the monarchy and the arts in which it symbolized itself. Eventually, the threat was realized in the Puritan revolution against the ideology of Stuart court culture—a revolution epitomized in Milton's response to the royalist "idolatry" of *Eikon-Basilike* with a tract entitled *Eikonoklastes* (1649). The Elizabethan government had to find ways to channel and delimit iconoclasm and to check the momentum of reform if the symbols through which its power was manifested were to remain untainted and efficacious.[26] This process of containment and decontamination was relatively successful in the short run, in part because "symbolic formations and patterns of action tend to persist longer

25. *The Cult of Elizabeth: Elizabethan Portraiture and Pageantry* (London, 1977), p. 119. On Accession Day rites, see J. E. Neale, *Essays in Elizabethan History* (London, 1958), pp. 9–20; Frances A. Yates, *Astraea: The Imperial Theme in the Sixteenth Century* (London, 1975), pp. 88–111; and Strong, *The Cult of Elizabeth*, pp. 117–62.

26. On iconoclasm, see John Phillips, *The Reformation of Images: Destruction of Art in England, 1535–1660* (Berkeley, 1973); on the production, distribution, and desecration of the royal image, see Roy C. Strong, *Portraits of Queen Elizabeth I* (Oxford, 1963).

than power relationships in changing socio-cultural systems" (Cohen, *Two-Dimensional Man*, p. 36). As Cohen explains, the ambiguity, flexibility, and multivocality characteristic of symbolic forms provide a measure of continuity in social change:

Social life is highly dynamic, continuously changing, and if the symbols associated with these relations change erratically there will be no order, and life will be chaotic and impossible. . . . Symbols are continuously interpreted and reinterpreted. . . . It is this very "conservative" characteristic of theirs that makes symbolic formations so fundamental for the establishment and continuity of social order. One of the contradictions of social change is that it is effected through continuities. (pp. 37-38)

The pastoral images, motifs, and stylistic conventions of Elizabethan culture were grounded not only in literary history but also in contemporary religious and socio-economic experience; they constitute one of the "symbolic formations" contributing to the establishment and continuity of the Elizabethan regime in a period of religious and socio-economic upheaval. Elizabethan culture inherited and imported a richly heterogeneous pastoral tradition: pagan and biblical, satiric and romantic, rustic and courtly, religious and erotic. The makers of Elizabethan culture exploited an affinity between pastoral form and the feminine symbolism that mixed Marian and Petrarchan elements with a Neoplatonic mythography of love. Such a combination of symbolic formations was perfectly suited to the unique character of this ruler: a womanl a virgin, an anointed sovereign, and the governor of a reformed Christian church. Royal pastoral was developed into a remarkably flexible cultural instrument for the mediation of power relations between Queen and subjects.

One of the richest literary realizations of this symbolic complex is also one of the earliest: Colin Clout's "laye of fayre *Elisa*, Queene of shepheardes all," in *The Shepheardes Calender* (1579).[27] By placing his pastoral encomium of Elizabeth in the fourth eclogue, Spenser was challenging comparison with Vergil's "messianic eclogue." Colin, Spenser's pastoral persona, metamorphoses an Ovidian aetiological myth into a Tudor genealogical myth:

> For shee is *Syrinx* daughter without spotte,
> Which *Pan* the shepheards God of her begot:

27. The lay was reprinted separately in *Englands Helicon*. References are to the often reprinted one-volume Oxford Standard Authors edition of Spenser's *Poetical Works*, ed. J. C. Smith and E. de Selincourt. In the following discussion, I borrow some phrases from my longer study of the *Calender*: "'The perfecte paterne of a Poete': The Poetics of Courtship in *The Shepheardes Calender*," *Texas Studies in Literature and Language*, 21 (Spring 1979), 34–67.

> So sprong her grace
> Of heavenly race,
> No mortall blemishe may her blotte. (ll. 50-54)

In the learned commentary pretentiously published with the *Calender*, E. K. glosses Pan both as Christ and as Henry VIII. The genealogy alludes to the immaculate conception of a blessed virgin, cleverly countering Catholic insinuations of Elizabeth's bastardy with an insinuation of her divinity. It also echoes the Anglican apologetics that justified the Queen's claim to be God's heir to the spiritual and temporal sovereignty of England. If we follow out the Ovidian logic of the myth, which E. K. retells concisely in his gloss, we see that Elisa is also the personification of pastoral poetry: the "offspring" of the love chase and the nymph's transformation were the reeds from which Pan created his pipe. Spenser's treatment of the symbolic union of Pan and Syrinx suggests three successive dimensions of meaning: in the simple allegorical correspondence that E. K. gives us, Elisa is Elizabeth Tudor, daughter of Henry and Anne and supreme governor of the English church and state; the Elisa of *Aprill* is also the idealized personification of the body politic, created by the Queen's poets, artisans, preachers, and councillors to focus the collective energies and emotions of her subjects and to harness and direct their diverse and potentially dangerous personal aspirations; finally, Elisa is the re-creation of the various accretions of Elizabethan symbolism into a new and complex image within Spenser's text. The first and second Elisas are subsumed by the third, who is engendered by the poet and his muse.

The genealogical myth is repeated at the center of the encomium. The pastoral poet now includes himself within the frame of the image that he is creating; the overworked and sunburned shepherd is present at a Nativity scene:

> *Pan* may be proud, that ever he begot
>   such a Bellibone,
> And *Syrinx* rejoyse, that ever was her lot
>   to bear such an one.
> Soone as my younglings cryen for the dam,
> To her will I offer a milkwhite Lamb;
>   Shee is my goddesse plaine,
>   And I her shepherds swayne,
> Albee forswonck and forswatt I am. (ll. 91-99)

"This our new Poete" (as E. K. calls him) has seized upon the combination of sources in which "Pastorall Poesie seemes consecrated" and has transformed them into a pastoral consecration of the English, Protestant, and Tudor present. Spenser's *Aprill* brilliantly epitomizes the synthetic achievement of the English literary Renaissance that it inaugurates. It fuses Vergilian imperial pastoral, Gospel nativity pastoral, and Arcadian erotic pastoral; eclogue, hymn, and love song. Elizabeth achieves an ideological fusion of classical *imperium* and Christian reform; Spenser's Elizabethan celebration achieves a poetic fusion of classical and humanist with medieval and native literary traditions.

The shepherd's *gift*—both his *talent* and his *offering*—is the power to create symbolic forms, to create illusions which sanctify political power; his expectation is a reciprocal, material benefit. At the center of the idealizing pastoral form within which the poet has created Elisa, the humble shepherd-courtier worships her. The adoring shepherd offers a milk-white lamb to his goddess; the ambitious young poet offers an encomiastic pastoral to his Queen. The poet who fathers Elisa is Elizabeth's subject and her suppliant. The eclogue thus suggests the dialectic by which poetic power helps to create and sustain the political power to which it is subservient. Spenser's *Aprill* is more than a brilliant and influential example of Elizabethan pastoral celebration. Its very subject is the paradoxical artistic and social process by which Elizabethan pastoral celebration comes into being.

III Court and Country

The popular and medieval pastoral of the craft cycles was being weeded out at the same time that the elite and Renaissance pastoral of the lyric, romance, and masque was being cultivated. In the stylistic and thematic juxtapositions of *The Shepheardes Calender*'s moral, plaintive, and recreative eclogues, Spenser seems to strive for a synthesis of old and new. But most of the pastoral entertainments devised for presentation to the Queen in court and on progress strive to replace the old with the new. These occasional, celebratory, and ritualistic creations exemplify the dialectic between enduring symbolic forms and the flux of social relations. Although some of the entertainments performed on progress were more explicitly pastoral than others, the very institution of the progress had strong affinities with Elizabethan pastoral forms and thematics. The progress was, after all, a movement from the court and the city to the country, from Westminster and London to aristocratic estates, royal hunting lodges, and provincial towns. Temporarily removing from the physical center of power and trade, population and plague, the Queen on progress was living a pastoral romance. If the progress had the pastoral function of periodically renewing court and monarch by immersion in things healthy and natural, simple and traditional, it was also eminently pastoral in that it insinuated and glanced at matters greater than rustic bride-ales and mythological fantasies. It was a paradoxical fusion of *otium* and *negotium*, holiday and policy.

Elizabeth's summer progresses began with the reign and were an almost annual occasion for two decades. From the end of the 1570s until the beginning of the 1590s, Queen and government were preoccupied by diplomacy and warfare; progresses diminished while drama and masquing flourished in the court. Then, at the beginning of the 1590s, the Queen started travelling again and continued to do so until almost the end of her life. Plans were made but never realized that would have taken her as far as Shrewsbury and York, where the Councils of the Marches and the North administered the remoter regions of her island realm. Over the years, however, she did manage to see and be seen by great numbers of her subjects in the most populous, prosperous, and loyal regions of England. One of her recent biographers suggests that "over a large part of south-east and central England Elizabeth was a known, if not quite a familiar figure; there can have been few people in these areas who did not get a chance to see her."[28] In addition to the orations and debates, pageants and fireworks, dances and dramas that regularly entertained her, there were rituals of greeting and parting and of gift-giving by the local hosts at the boundaries of every shire, town, and estate. The Queen travelled in an entourage sometimes numbering upwards of five hundred. From her itinerant court emanated an aura of splendor and an illusion of authority that far belied the limits of her government's police power, administrative efficiency, and fiscal resources. Thus the progress was more than an instrument of public relations and a refreshing change of scene; it was an extraordinarily elaborate and extended periodic ritual drama, in which the monarch physically and symbolically took possession of her domains.

Elizabethan progresses and pageants and other public spectacles ranging from Garter rites to executions may usefully be thought of as examples of what social anthropologists call "social dramas." These are collective temporal forms, characteristic of all societies,

28. Paul Johnson, *Elizabeth I: A Study in Power and Intellect* (London, 1974), p. 226.

in which the political and the symbolic orders interpenetrate and affect one another. Each drama tries to effect a transformation in the psyches of the participants, conditioning their attitudes and sentiments, repetitively renewing beliefs, values and norms and thereby creating and recreating the basic categorical imperatives on which the group depends for its existence. At the same time, some or many of the participants may attempt to manipulate, modify or change, the symbols of the drama to articulate minor or major changes in the "message." (Cohen, *Two Dimensional Man*, p. 132)

This concept illuminates a basic feature of state spectacles: their various entertainments are framed within a larger social drama; performers, writers and artisans, sponsors, the Queen and her entourage, spectators—*all* are encompassed as participants within the social drama. The entertainments performed during a progress are plays-within-a-play. Of course, the entertainments acknowledge this fusion of art and life quite explicitly and in various ways: the Queen is directly addressed or she is included within the fictions; debates are referred to her wise judgment; conflicts are resolved, savage men are civilized, virgins escape defilement, blind men regain their sight simply by virtue of her magical presence. Elizabeth did not need to be provided with acting parts—she merely played herself. And she did so consummately well, as a dispatch from an attentive Spanish ambassador testifies: "She was received everywhere with great acclamations and signs of joy, as is customary in this country, whereat she was exceedingly pleased and told me so, giving me to understand how beloved she was of her subjects and how highly she esteemed this. . . . She would order her carriage sometimes to be taken where the crowd seemed thickest, and stood up and thanked the people."[29] Of Elizabeth's own performances on progress, Sir John Neale observed half a century ago that "the supreme moments of her genius were these, and if with their masques and verses her progresses belong to the history of the drama, they are no less part of the unwritten story of government propaganda."[30] To this I would add that the progresses and their entertainments did not serve the interests of the Queen and her government exclusively; they also proffered occasions and instruments to those in pursuit of offices and honors, gifts and pensions, influence and power. In other words, the symbols of celebration could be manipulated to serve simultaneously a variety of mutual interests and self-interests. They might influence

29. *Calendar of State Papers, Spanish* (1568–1579), pp. 50-51, quoted in Neville Williams, *Elizabeth, Queen of England* (London, 1967), p. 233.
30. "The Sayings of Queen Elizabeth" (1926), rpt. in *Essays in Elizabethan History*, p. 96.

the attitudes and sentiments of the royal actress herself, as well as those of her audience and her fellow performers.

Re-creating a text in the context of its performance will add substance to the preceding generalizations. My text is that of the scenarios, speeches, and songs intended for performance before the Queen at Sudeley during the progress of 1591.[31] The Sudeley entertainment has received little critical attention; admittedly, its literary merits are relatively slight. Such entertainments, however, have a significance that is genuinely historical *and* literary. They exhibit particularly well the social instrumentality of figurative language, the dialectic between power relations and symbolic forms.

Let us begin at the front door. "At her Majesties entrance into the Castle, an olde Shepheard spake this saying":

Vouchsafe to heare a simple shephard: shephards and simplicity cannot part. Your Highnes is come into Cotshold, an uneven country, but a people that carry their thoughts, levell with their fortunes; low spirites, but true harts; using plaine dealing, once counted a jewell, nowe beggary. These hills afoorde nothing but cottages, and nothing can we present to your Highnes but shephards. The country healthy and harmeles; a fresh aier, where there are noe dampes, and where a black sheepe is a perilous beast; no monsters; we carry our harts at our tongues ends, being as far from dissembling as our sheepe from fiercenesse; and if in anything we shall chance to discover our lewdnes, it will be in over boldnesse, in gazinge at you, who fils our harts with joye, and our eies with wonder. As for the honoreble Lord and Lady of the Castle, what happines they conceive, I would it were possible for themselves to expresse. . . . This lock of wooll, Cotsholdes best fruite, and my poor gifte, I offer to your Highnes; in which nothing is to be esteemed, but the whitenes, virginities colour; nor to be expected but duetye, shephards religion. (p. 477)

A pastoral "rejection of the aspiring mind" and a beautiful relationship between peasantry, aristocracy, and sovereign are expressed in the elegant and fashionable courtly rhetoric of a shepherd too simple to be anything but honest and plain. We are plunged immediately into the paradox—or the duplicity—of the pastoral style. The secular religion of devotion to a mistress that is the theme of so many Elizabethan pastorals appears here in its undisplaced political form, as duty to a social superior.

The old shepherd's vision of life in the Cotswolds idealizes the remnants of a feudal agrarian society. In fact, the English countryside was

31. Printed in *Speeches Delivered to Her Majestie this Last Progresse*, etc. (Oxford, 1592); rpt. in *The Complete Works of John Lyly*, ed. R. Warwick Bond, 3 vols. (Oxford, 1902), I, 477–84. Parenthetical citations in my text will be to volume one of this edition. Bond's ascription of the work to Lyly on stylistic grounds has received no substantiation. I have chosen this entertainment for detailed study because it is pastoral, short, and skillful in its rhetorical strategies.

being profoundly transformed by the centralizing efforts of the Elizabethan regime, great advances in farming and husbandry techniques,
demographic growth, and the expansion of a market economy.[32] Sheep
were vital to the economy and society of the Cotswolds, and to the
complex relations of production and distribution affecting the welfare
of the whole nation.[33] Thus it was particularly appropriate that the
Queen meet a shepherd in this part of Gloucestershire. The topography
of the Cotswolds was ideally suited to the sheep-raising that flourished
there, and the physical details of landscape and population are accurately reflected in the shepherd's speech. But the economic significance
of animal husbandry, farming, and wool industries disappears into
encomiastic iconography: in wool, "nothing is to be esteemed, but
whitenes, virginities colour." Here pastoral's metaphorizing process
is quite explicitly a process of purification. The shepherd's assertion
demonstrates that the creation of figurative pastoral discourse involves
a distortion, a selective exclusion, of the material pastoral world. One
of the most remarkable features of this appropriation of pastoral forms
by Renaissance court culture is its transformation of what in other
contexts was a vehicle of agrarian complaint, rustic celebration, and
popular religion into a vehicle of social mystification.

On the second day of the Sudeley entertainments, the pastoral style
and setting change from rustic and local to learned and mythological.
But the scenario continues to develop its royal theme: a celebration
of the power of virginity and the virginity of power. The scenario
enacts an episode from the first book of Ovid's *Metamorphoses* and then,
in effect, metamorphoses it: Daphne, pursued by Apollo, is changed
into a tree; Apollo's song concludes that "neither men nor gods, can
force affection." "The song ended, the tree rived, and DAPHNE issued
out, APOLLO ranne after," himself apparently quite unregenerate.
"DAPHNE running to her Majestie uttred this": "I stay, for whether
should chastety fly for succour, but to the Queene of chastety." Daphne

---

32. *The Agrarian History of England and Wales, Volume IV, 1500–1640*, ed. Joan Thirsk (Cambridge, Eng., 1967), is comprehensive and technical. There are concise surveys in Christopher
Hill, *Reformation to Industrial Revolution*, rev. ed., The Pelican Economic History of Britain, Volume
2, 1530–1780 (Harmondsworth, 1969), pp. 61–71; and D. C. Coleman, *The Economy of England
1450–1750* (New York, 1977), pp. 31–47.

33. See Peter J. Bowden, *The Wool Trade in Tudor and Stuart England* (London, 1962), p. xv:
"Wool was, without question, the most important raw material in the English economic system.
. . . Every class in the community, whether landlord, farmer, merchant, industrial capitalist or
artisan, had an interest in wool, and it was the subject of endless economic controversy." On
Cotswold ecology, see Thirsk, *Agrarian History*, pp. 64–66.

is retrieved from the effects of Apollo's lust and craft by the power of Elizabeth's presence, "that by vertue, there might be assurance in honor" (pp. 479-80). Cotswold has become Arcadia. Elizabeth is the queen of this pastoral and sylvan domain; she incarnates Diana, to whom Ovid's Daphne is votary. When Ovid's Daphne cries to her father Peneus to help her, she is changed into the laurel. At Sudeley, Daphne's metamorphosis is less an escape than a demonic imprisonment from which she must be liberated. The Queen's virtuous magic derives from a kind of matriarchal virginity; her powers transcend those of the lustful and paternal pagan gods.

Daphne makes an offering to her savior: "these tables, to set downe your prayses, long since, *Sibillas* prophesies, I humbly present to your Majesty, not thinking, that your vertues can be deciphered in so slight a volume, but noted" (p. 480). She alludes to the oracular source of Vergil's "messianic" eclogue and to the sense of strain that arises when "the most high and noble matters of the world" are confined within poor and silly pastoral forms. The logic of combining Vergilian imperial pastoral with Ovidian erotic pastoral lies in the aetiological character of the Daphne myth as it is treated in the *Metamorphoses*. Apollo establishes the laurel as his tree and institutes the triumph:

> Thou shalt adorne the valiant knyghts and royall Emperours:
> When for their noble feates of armes like mightie conquerours,
> Triumphantly with stately pompe up to the Capitoll,
> They shall ascende with solemne traine that doe their deedes
> extoll.[34]

Such allusions deftly link the Sudeley entertainment to an ingenious political myth that claimed the spiritual and temporal authority of the primitive church and the Empire of Constantine as the inheritance of the Elizabethan regime. Frances Yates interprets this aspect of the Elizabeth cult in terms of an international policy:

By claiming for the national church that it was a reform executed by the sacred imperial power as represented in the sacred English monarchy, the Elizabeth symbol drew to itself a tradition which also made a total, a universal claim—the tradition of sacred empire. . . . The arguments for sacred empire—that the world is at its best and

34. *Ovid's Metamorphoses: The Arthur Golding Translation* (1567), ed. John Frederick Nims (New York, 1965), I, 687-90. Like Golding's translation, the Sudeley pageant is considerably more pastoral in its treatment of the Daphne myth than is Ovid's original. In Spenser's *Aprill*, the Muses bring bay branches to adorn Elisa; E. K. glosses them as "the signe of honor and victory, and therefore of myghty Conquerors worn in theyr triumphes, and eke of famous Poets" (*Poetical Works*, p. 434).

most peaceful under one ruler and that then justice is most powerful—are used to buttress her religious rights as an individual monarch. The monarch who is One and sovereign within his own domains has imperial religious rights, and he can achieve the imperial reform independently of the Pope. (*Astraea*, pp. 58-59)

This remarkably allusive entertainment weaves together Ovidian mythology, Vergilian and Sybilline prophecy, and Imperial policy with an iconography of virtuous desire adapted from Petrarch's *Canzoniere* and *Trionfi*. Petrarch wrote of Laura as another Daphne, the inspiration of his laureate verse; Elizabethan courtier-poets worshiped their royal mistress as another Laura.[35] At Sudeley, Daphne is liberated from her Ovidian arboreal form, and the triumph of heroic warfare is modulated into a Triumph of Chastity befitting a virgin empress.

The resonant complex of associations that unfolds during the entertainments of the first and second days at Sudeley is brought to a climax and conclusion on the third day. The festivities were in fact spoiled by bad weather but the intended scenario is preserved. "This it should have beene, one clothed all in sheepe-skins, face & all, spake this by his interpreter":

May it please your highnes, this is the great Constable and commandadore of Cotsholde; he speaks no language, but the Rammish tongue; such sheepishe governours there are, that can say no more to a messenger than he, ([*here the* Constable *utters*] Bea!) this therfore, as signifying his duety to your Majestye, and al our desires, I am commanded to be his interpreter. Our shepheards starre, pointing directly to Cotshold, and in Cotshold, to Sudley, made us expect some wonder, and of the eldest, aske some counsel: it was resolved by the ancientst, that such a one should come, by whome all the shepheards should have their flocks in astonishment: our Constable commaunds this day to be kept holliday, all our shepheards are assembled, and if shepheards pastimes may please, how joyful would they be if it would please you to see them. (p. 481)

Royal compliment is leavened by rustic comedy. The combination of Ovidian metamorphosis and pastoral metaphor is consummated in the presentation of the high constable of Cotswold—a shepherd of shepherds—actually transformed into a sheep.

Although we have returned from Arcadia to the rustic here-and-now of the Cotswolds the place and time are irradiated by the Queen's coming. "Her Majesty was to be brought amonge the shepheards amonge whome was a King and a Queene to be chosen" (p. 481). The scene would have introduced quite artfully the reversals appropriate to an apocalyptic moment. The pretty trifles performed by the shep-

35. See Wilson, *England's Eliza*, pp. 230-72; Yates, *Astraea*, pp. 112-20.

herds and shepherdesses include a squabble over mastery between shepherd king and queen. Elizabeth is set apart from the kings of the earth when the shepherdess triumphantly concludes that "the Queene shall and must commaunde, for I have often heard of a King that could not commaunde his subjects, and of a Queene that hath commaunded Kings" (p. 482). When the shepherds consult their almanac regarding "the starr, that directs us hither" (p. 483), their eyes fall on the Queen's birthday, which had passed a few days before: "The seventh of September, happines was borne into the world." The prognostication which follows brings the pageant to its consummation in the here-and-now, in a mutual transformation of life and art: "At foure of the clocke this day, shal appeare the worldes wonder that leades England into every land, and brings all lands into England" (p. 484). The pastoral show has shifted from the metamorphosis of Daphne to the apotheosis of Elizabeth. The shepherds discover that the Queen is already in their midst; "espying her Majesty," they kneel and worship. It is a rare instance of prophecy's immediate fulfillment:

This is the day, this the houre, this the starre: pardon dread Soveraigne, poor shepheards pastimes, and bolde shepheardes presumtions. We call our selves Kings and Queenes to make mirth; but when we see a King or Queene, we stand amazed. . . . For our boldnes in borrowing their names, and in not seeing your Majesty for our blindnes, we offer these shepheards weedes, which, if your Majestye vouchsafe at any time to weare, it shall bring to our hearts comfort, and happines to our labours. (p. 484)

So concludes the printed text of Her Majesty's entertainment at Sudeley. Poor shepherds playing kings adore their authentic sovereign lady. Celebrating the anniversary of her nativity, they laud the preaching of her gospel and the advent of a national and Protestant *imperium*.

   Half a century earlier, the Protestant Princess Elizabeth had been living under constant threat and suspicion, a rural exile from her Catholic half-sister's court. Now she is the governor of state and church, the cynosure of court and country; she is moving through her land on a royal progress, in the procession of a blessed virgin. In entertainments like this, we find a confluence of the varied resources of national, religious, and personal symbolism that goes beyond appropriation of the Marian cult to associate the advent of Elizabeth with the Advent of Christ. The arrival of the Queen in this notable sheep-farming area at a time just after her birthday provides the circumstances for a metamorphosis of the scene that was acted in the pastoral Nativity pageants of the Corpus Christi plays. Thematically unified though loosely episodic in form, the cycle of pageants at Sudeley is given a kind of closure by its final offering. At her entry, the Queen receives a lock of wool; at the conclusion of the festivities, she receives what is presumably some rich garment made from Cotswold wool. During the entertainment's performance, wool is transformed into apparel; rural society is transformed into a pastoral playground; the Queen's visit is transformed into a theophany. The final gift offering to the Queen, from rustics who have played kings, conflates the adoration of the Magi and the adoration of the Shepherds with a felicitous economy typical of the humble form, "poor, silly, & of the coursest Woofe in appearance," in which, "neverthelesse, the most High, and most Noble Matters of the World may bee shaddowed." Vergilian eclogue and evangelical narrative, the two great traditions in which "Pastorall Poesie seemes consecrated," have been skillfully combined. The shepherds' final act of homage and offering combines intimacy and awe; it is a synecdoche for the social drama in pastoral form that the Queen and her hosts have performed. An eminently political occasion has been elevated into a spiritual mystery.

Reflecting on the Elizabethan iconography of empire, Frances Yates writes suggestively that "the lengths to which the cult of Elizabeth went are a measure of the sense of isolation which had at all costs to find a symbol strong enough to provide a feeling of spiritual security in face of the break with the rest of Christendom" (*Astraea,* p. 59). Yates implies that the cult is not only an instrument of foreign policy but also a source of strength, perseverance, and legitimation for the Queen personally and for the nation collectively. I would add that the persistence and elaboration of this cult during the reign undoubtedly served collaterally as an instrument of domestic policy, as another symbolic means by which the crown might procure the loyalty, obedience, and service of both the unenfranchised masses and the political nation. I have suggested that the Sudeley pageantry creates a complex and hyperbolic role for the Queen and a simple, collective, and idealized relationship between the Queen and her subjects. To specify the functions of this entertainment requires speculation about the motives and interests of its sponsor. My speculations proceed on the principles that human motives are complex, that the interest groups in Elizabethan society are heterogeneous, and that a multiplicity of meanings and functions can be articulated in the same symbolic form.

Sudeley Castle had been built during the troubled reign of Henry

VI, in a period of great civil discord and dynastic power struggles among the nobility. In order to endure, the Tudor dynasty had to check such baronial disorder. But without its prior existence, Elizabeth's grandfather would probably not have been able to prosecute successfully his own relatively weak claim to the throne. Lawrence Stone stresses that

the greatest triumph of the Tudors was the ultimately successful assertion of a royal monopoly of violence both public and private. . . . The first task of the Tudors was to rid the country of the overmighty subject whose military potential came not far short of the monarchy itself. . . . This was a task which could only be achieved by a hundred years of patient endeavour on a broad front using a wide diversity of weapons. It called for a social transformation of extreme complexity, involving issues of power, technology, landholding, economic structure, education, status symbols, and concepts of honour and loyalty.[36]

It is precisely within this context of social transformation that the apparently frivolous Sudeley entertainment should be understood. It is a minor but not insignificant event in the Elizabethan social process; it figures and manipulates relations of domination and subordination in cultural forms. Both the royal visitor and her baronial host are playing their parts in another of those continuous acts of reciprocal courtship, display, and conciliation by which Elizabeth and the English peerage managed with relative success to maintain the stability of their caste and a consensus of interests throughout the reign.

Giles Brydges, Queen Elizabeth's host, was third Lord Chandos and one of some sixty peers of the realm. The Brydges were a long established gentle house that produced notable servants and soldiers for the Tudor dynasty; they had been raised to the peerage by Mary. According to Stone, the titular peerage "comprised the most important element in a status group, a power *elite,* a Court, a class of very rich landlords, an association of the well-born"; the peerage should be viewed as "the only common factor in a whole series of overlapping ranking variables in a hierarchical society" (*Crisis of the Aristocracy,* p. 64). Stone cites Lord Chandos as one of the great landowners who at Court "were less influential and less respected than a mere favourite like Ralegh, and of negligible consequence in comparison with a powerful official like Sackville or Egerton" (p. 63). Giles Brydges may have lacked influence at Queen Elizabeth's court, but at the local level his power rivaled hers. "In the late sixteenth century," notes Stone, "Lord Chandos was known as 'King of the Cotswolds'."

36. *The Crisis of the Aristocracy 1558–1641* (Oxford, 1965), pp. 200-01.

In Gloucestershire in the 1570's, Giles Lord Chandos used armed retainers with guns at the ready to frighten off the under-sheriff, protected servants of his who robbed men on the highway near Sudeley Castle, so that the inhabitants dared not arrest the thieves nor the victims prosecute their assailants, rigged juries, and put in a high constable of the shire who used his office to levy blackmail on the peasantry. When summoned to the Council of Wales he did not deign to come, retorting loftily that "I had thought that a nobleman might have found more favor in your Courte, then thus to be delt with (as I am) lyke a common subjecte." (*Crisis of the Aristocracy*, pp. 229-30)

Such facts help us imaginatively to return a now-lifeless Elizabethan text to its living context in the material relations of Elizabethan people.

By his actions and by his words, Lord Chandos exemplifies the exploitative rural elite who were traditional targets of agrarian satire and protest of the kind that could be heard at the opening of the *Secunda Pastorum.* The version of life in the Cotswolds presented to the Queen under this lord's auspices, however, has been metamorphosed into an extravagant but benign pastoral pageant of holiday games, presentations, and celebrations. The welcome, the gifts, and the acts of homage made by the shepherds to the Queen are presented on behalf of "the honoreble Lord and Lady of the Castle" (p. 477); presumably, the Queen's lordly host hopes to insure a reciprocal flow of the perquisites, honors and offices, and grossly undervalued tax assessments that the aristocracy considered its due. The shepherds' prominence in the entertainments and in exchanges with the Queen is deceptive. The essential trick of this version of pastoral is to appropriate shepherd figures as mediators of a beautiful relationship between peer and monarch in which the best parts of both are used. The scenarios of the Sudeley festivities suggest a remarkable sublimation of the local conditions and events described by Stone: a terrorized and exploited peasantry are presented as happy shepherds and shepherdesses at play; a predatory high constable is replaced by "one clothed all in sheepeskins, face & all," who merely "baa's" meekly, in what seems a grimly comic miming of pastoral satire's "wolf-in-sheep's clothing" motif; a truculent and obstreperous magnate ("the King of the Cotswolds") turns Sudeley into Bethlehem in a show of love and fealty to "a Queene that hath commaunded Kings."

The social functions of the Sudeley entertainment and other such public spectacles are multiple and diverse. Yates suggests a collective psycho-social function for the Eliza cult, benefitting the Queen and the nation in terms of international politics and religious conflict; and I have suggested a supplementary socio-political function, benefitting the monarchy and the Elizabethan regime in terms of the loyalties of the English people. More particularly, in a context in which the commons were actually present as performers or as spectators, pageants like the one at Sudeley might fortify loyalty toward the crown among those whose relationship to the landlords who were their immediate and tangible superiors was one of endemic suspicion or resentment. "In the sixteenth century," writes Christopher Hill, "the threat to the unprivileged came not so much from the central government as from the local feudal lord, against whom the monarchy might be conceived as a protector. This was often found to be an illusion . . . the king's interests were inseparably bound up with those of the landed ruling class. Yet he *had* an interest in preventing the grosser forms of injustice, and in the maintenance of law and order" (*Reformation to Industrial Revolution,* p. 55). Thus the pastoral pageants at Sudeley and others like them might affirm a benign relationship of mutual interest between the Queen and the lowly, between the Queen and the great, and among them all.[37]

This complex and convenient ambiguity was produced by the interaction of *segmentary* power relations with *multivocal* symbolic forms:

All politics, all struggle for power, is segmentary. This means that enemies at one level must be allies at a different level. . . . It is mainly through the "mystification" generated by symbolism that these contradictions are repetitively faced and temporarily resolved. . . . The degree of "mystification," and of the potency of the dominant symbols that are employed to create it, mounts as the conflict, contradiction, or inequality between people who should identify in communion increases. . . . It is indeed in the very essence of the symbolic process to perform a multiplicity of functions with economy of symbolic formation. (Cohen, *Two-Dimensional Man,* p. 32)

There can be several dimensions to the political dynamic of Elizabethan pastoral forms such as those of the Sudeley entertainment: they may function to transcend socio-economic stratification in "a beautiful relation between rich and poor," to atone the commons, the gentles,

---

37. Compare Joel Hurstfield, *Freedom, Corruption and Government in Elizabethan England* (London, 1973), p. 46: "To understand the relationship between the Tudor people and their governments, it is essential to take into account that this was minority rule, an uneasy and unstable distribution of power between the Crown and a social elite in both the capital and the shires, and that this governing class, this elite, itself played a double role. It was under pressure to conform and was at the same time the channel of communication for a vast mass of propaganda in defense of the existing order, pumped out through press and pulpit, through preambles to Acts and through proclamations read out in the market-place, through addresses to high court judges in Star Chamber and by high court judges at the assizes, through all the pageantry and symbolism of royal progresses."

and the Queen of England; they may function to assert a bond of reciprocal devotion and charity between lowly subjects and sovereign, perhaps strengthened by the implication of a common interest opposed to the aristocracy; and they may function to confirm and preserve the delicate balance of interests between the crown and the political nation, so that power, wealth, and prestige will continue to be shared exclusively among the shepherds of men. In the first instance, the whole people is united against a foreign threat; in the second, the crown and the commons are united against a baronial threat; in the third, the crown and the social elite are united against a popular threat. From every angle, the political dynamic was advantageous to Eliza, Queen of shepherds.

What is most impressive about Elizabethan pastorals of power is how successful they really are at combining intimacy and benignity with authoritarianism. This success must be attributed in large part to the fact of the monarch's sex and to the extraordinary skill with which she and her courtier-poets turned that potential liability to advantage. Sir John Hayward, who had been imprisoned by the Queen for his *History of Henry IV,* ungrudgingly admired her mastery of the royal role: "Now, if ever any persone had eyther the gift or the stile to winne the hearts of people, it was this Queene . . . in coupling mildnesse with majesty as shee did, and in stately stouping to the meanest sort."[38] "Coupling mildnesse with majesty" describes perfectly the paradoxical effect and the particular utility of royal pastoral—of putting the complex into the simple, of placing Eliza among her shepherds and among her sheep. The "symbolic formation" of pastoral provided an ideal meeting ground for Queen and subjects, a mediation of her greatness and their lowness; it fostered the illusion that she was approachable and knowable, lovable and loving, to lords and peasants, courtiers and citizens alike. What was ostensibly the most modest and humble of poetic kinds lent itself effortlessly to the most fulsome of royal encomia. The charisma of Queen Elizabeth was not compromised but rather was enhanced by royal pastoral's awesome intimacy, its sophisticated quaintness. Such pastorals were minor masterpieces of a poetics of power.

IV Epilogue

In the speech which opened his first English Parliament (1603), King James lectured the assembled lords, gentlemen, and citizens on the

---

38. Hayward, *Annals,* ed. John Bruce (London, 1840), pp. 6-7, quoted in Neale, *Essays in Elizabethan History,* p. 92.

analogies of power: "I am the Husband, and all the whole Isle is my lawful Wife; I am the Head, and it is my Body; I am the Shepherd, and it is my Flocke."[39] Elizabeth's political predilection was as absolutist as James's but her own pastoral strategies were usually subtler, especially when she was playing to Parliament or the populace. Her performances were graced by a sure sense of public relations that her successors lacked or disdained. But there was more at work than the accidents of royal personality in the fragmentation and polarization of a national, Protestant, and humanist English culture during the Jacobean and Caroline reigns. P. W. Thomas suggests that

there were it seems two warring cultures. But it is more accurate to talk of a breakdown of the national culture, an erosion through the 1630's of a middle ground that men of moderation and good will had once occupied. . . .

The Civil War was about the whole condition of a society threatened by a failure of the ruling caste both to uphold traditional national aims and values, and to adapt itself to a rapidly changing world.[40]

In the 1630s, in the isolated splendor of the Caroline court, Queen Henrietta Maria sponsored and performed in Neoplatonic pastoral fantasies like *The Shepherd's Paradise* (1630) and *Florimène* (1635); while in *Lycidas* (1638), Milton was giving new force to Spenser's earlier pastoral attacks on a derelict and corrupt church hierarchy: "Blind mouths! that scarce themselves know how to hold / A Sheep-hook" (ll. 119-20).[41]

It was at the Hampton Court Conference (1604), when a Puritan divine mentioned presbytery, that King James remarked angrily, "no Bishop, no King."[42] His quip was to prove an ironic history lesson. When *Poems of Mr. John Milton* was registered for publication by the Puritan polemicist in 1645, he superscribed to *Lycidas* (first printed 1638) a note that it "By occasion foretells the ruin of our corrupted Clergy then in their height"; now Milton could claim membership in a tradition of vatic poets. First among the English poems in his 1645 collection, Milton placed "On the Morning of Christ's Nativity" (written 1629). In the ode's harmonious incorporation of Vergilian Golden Age eclogue and naive Christmas carol, in Drayton's words "Pastorall Poesie seemes consecrated." And in the political context of the mid 1640s, Milton's first

39. *The Political Works of James I*, ed. C. H. McIlwain (1918; rpt. New York, 1965), p. 272.

40. "Two Cultures? Court and Country under Charles I," in *The Origins of the English Civil War*, ed. Conrad Russell (London, 1973), pp. 184 and 193.

41. Texts and parenthetical line numbers follow John Milton, *Complete Poems and Major Prose*, ed. Merritt Y. Hughes (New York, 1957).

42. See David Harris Willson, *King James VI & I* (1956; rpt. New York, 1967), p. 207.

publication of his youthful work takes on added resonance. For the poem's energy is not focused on ingeniously paradoxical descriptions of the Incarnation or on homely details of the Nativity, but on the intense imagining of a revolutionary moment:

> And Kings sat still with awful eye,
> As if they surely knew their sovran Lord was by.   (ll. 59-60)

> Th'old Dragon under ground,
> In straiter limits bound,
>   Not half so far casts his usurped sway,
> And wroth to see his Kingdom fail,
> Swinges the scaly Horror of his folded tail.   (ll. 168-72)

> In Urns and Altars round,
> A drear and dying sound
>   Affrights the *Flamens* at their service quaint;
> And the chill Marble seems to sweat,
> While each peculiar power forgoes his wonted seat.   (ll. 192-96)

For Milton, spiritual revolution is also historical revolution; it demands a revival and completion of the English Reformation. This implies a transformation of polity and of culture, a recovery of the authentic sources and forms of pastoral power.

Re-opening the Green Cabinet: Clément Marot and Edmund Spenser

ANNABEL PATTERSON

THE "green cabinet" of my title is surely the most celebrated of the quotations from Clément Marot that Edmund Spenser built into *The Shepheardes Calender* (1579). Its presence in the "December" eclogue signifies that his closing poem is largely a paraphrase of Marot's *Eglogue au roy, soubz les noms de Pan & Robin,* where Marot, as Robin, addresses Pan, or Francis I, in his "vert cabinet." Now *The Shepheardes Calendar* is the single book that in English literary history most clearly resembles Vergil's *Eclogues.* Its presentation as a coherent "eclogue-book," its elaborate provision of glosses by a certain E. K., and its woodcuts at the head of each of the twelve eclogues all suggest a holistic attempt to replicate in English the cultural phenomenon that Vergil's text had become, a phenomenon that combined the aesthetics of book production, the politics of self-representation, and a historically-constituted system of textual exegesis. Clément Marot left no such structure. Yet the poem that had pride of place in his first collection of poems was his translation of Vergil's first eclogue; and the echo of his "vert cabinet" is only one of many indications in the *Calender* that Marot stood for Spenser as an intermediary between himself and Vergil. As E. K. puts it in a characteristically obfuscating gloss to "January," even Spenser's pastoral pseudonym Colin Clout has a complicated precedent that includes Marot along with the native Skelton:

> But indeede the word Colin is Frenche, and used of the French Poete Marot (if he be worthy of the name of a Poete) in a certein AEglogue. Under which name this Poete secretly shadoweth himself, as sometime did Virgil under the name of Tityrus.[1]

---

1. *The Poetical Works of Edmund Spenser,* ed. J. C. Smith and E. de Selincourt (Oxford, 1912), p. 422.

In this essay I propose to reconsider the Vergilianism of Marot and Spenser, for several reasons. First, they each and together represent a version of Renaissance humanism that would have been inconceivable and unnecessary without the Reformation, and which shows how elastic our conception of humanism in the sixteenth century must necessarily be. Second, the connection between them has not been interrogated hitherto with any persistence, in part because Marot's English reputation has been regarded as insignificant, as accurately reflected in E. K.'s condition, "if he be worthy of the name of a Poete."[2]Instead, I shall argue, Marot's status as an early supporter of the Reformation in France virtually guaranteed him Spenser's admiration, whether for his verse paraphrases of the Psalms for the Geneva psalter or for his personal history as a Lutheran exile. But beyond this, it was the connection made by Marot between his Protestantism and his reinterpretations of Vergil that made him for Spenser a challenging and provocative model, one that affected the whole emotional tone of the *Calender*, and gave it its melancholy and wintry aspect. And third, as my readers will no doubt already be wondering what relation such an argument might bear to Thomas Rosenmeyer's *The Green Cabinet*,[3] this essay will finally come to terms both with Rosenmeyer's essentially Modernist and idealist position, and with its most strenuous competitor in post-modernist theory of pastoral, that of Louis Adrian Montrose.[4] For both of these powerful critics have produced a view of the *Shepheardes Calender* that will have to be adjusted in the light of the series Vergil-Marot-Spenser.

I

I begin with a contention: that the power of Vergil's *Eclogues* over the humanist imagination during the Renaissance resided primarily in the first eclogue, because it provided in effect a poetics. Thanks to the life of Vergil by Donatus and the commentary of Servius,[5] the confrontation

2. See Anne Lake Prescott, *French Poets and the English Renaissance* (New Haven and London, 1978), pp. 1–36. Being dependent on actual references to Marot in England, Prescott's careful influence study did not report inferences, and she therefore concluded that his "reputed Protestantism" failed to win him sympathy in England. Such analysis as there is of Spenser's debt to Marot is perhaps typified by Nancy Jo Hoffman, *Spenser's Pastorals* (Baltimore, Md., 1977), who argued that Marot only understood Vergil "remotely," and that Spenser echoed Marot only to dissociate himself from the pastoral of state (pp. 34–40).

3. Thomas Rosenmeyer, *The Green Cabinet: Theocritus and the European Pastoral Lyric* (Berkeley and Los Angeles, 1969).

4. See notes 42 and 43 below.

5. Maurus Servius Honoratus, grammarian and teacher of rhetoric at the end of the fourth

between Tityrus and Meliboeus in that poem was recognized as the contrast between a poet who had successfully accommodated himself to the sources of power in his culture and one who had not, one who had achieved a protected leisure and a space in which to write, and one whose exile from his patrimonial estate—a consequence of the unjust expropriations after Philippi—must result in his abandonment of poetry ("Carmina nulla canam"). If Vergil primarily represented himself as Tityrus, the fortunate shepherd, Servian commentary indicated, he had at the same time through Meliboeus suggested obliquely ("latenter") his criticisms of Octavian's policy,[6] and more subtly, perhaps, the ethical ambivalence with which Vergil viewed his own position of privilege.

To what extent did Marot and Spenser endorse the Servian reading of Vergil? We might begin by noting that our key-term, "cabinet," is a word by no means innocent or transparent, despite E. K.'s (dis)ingenuous gloss to the effect that it is merely the diminutive of "cabin." One of its connotations was, certainly, a rustic summer-house or bower, as in Spenser's own designation of Guyon's mission against the Bower of Bliss: "their cabinets suppresse."[7] Yet even here there is a trace of contamination by other meanings, senses in which artfulness, privacy or secrecy may be present, separately or together. As a private chamber of the privileged, for reading, writing or keeping one's treasures, we find it in Rabelais' *Gargantua* (1532) in a context suggestive of the artful confusion of art and nature, inside and outside, "Toutes les salles, chambres et cabinetz, estoient tapissez en diverses sortes, *selon les saisons de l'année.* Tout le pavé estoit couvert de *drap verd*,"[8] (Chapter 55; italics added). These green cabinets are recreational; but as a private place for conducting business, especially of state, "cabinet" could acquire a more tendentious meaning. In Francis Bacon's essay "Of Counsels" we find a critique of "the doctrine of Italy, and practice of France in some Kings' times," the introduction of "cabinet councils" for the sake of secrecy, a remedy, Bacon added in 1627, "worse than the disease."[9] Yet for Agrippa

---

century A.D., whose commentary on Vergil was standard equipment in almost all Renaissance editions. The definitive edition is by Georg Thilo and Hermann Hagen, *Servii Grammatici qui feruntur in Vergilii carmina commentarii*, 3 vols. (Leipzig, 1878).

6. Servius, ed. Thilo and Hagen, III, 8, "Sicut nunc Vergilius sub Persona Tityri dicit se amore libertatis Romam venire compulsum, item latenter carpit tempora, quibus non nisi in urbe Roma erat." See also the gloss on "solacia," III, 112.

7. Spenser, *The Faerie Queen*, II.xii.83. Note that Spenser's victim of the Bower is named Verdant.

8. Rabelais, *Gargantua*, in *Oeuvres Complétes*, ed. Jean Plattard, 4 vols. (Paris, 1955), I, 185.

9. Bacon, *Essays*, ed. S. H. Reynolds (Oxford, 1890), p. 148.

d'Aubigné, one generation younger than Marot, the word could also stand for human mental space:

> La memoyr heureuse qui leur faict
> Ses contemplations metre en son cabinet
> Leurs resolutions, chose qui rend facile
> Pour mediter souvent la chose difficile.[10]

I have selected these instances of polysemy, not only to show how exclusive was E. K.'s gloss, but also because this is a plausible collocation of meanings in which pastoral already had a special interest. Indeed, in d'Aubigné's configuration of terms—memory, contemplation, meditate—as operations which define the human mental cabinet, we see something of the semantic potency that resides in Vergil's *umbra, meditaris, resonare,* thoughts, echoes, figures, shadows, all of the lexical apparatus by which we try to catch the mind at work: "souvent la chose difficile."

II

How much of this was conceivable to Marot in 1538, when he addressed his *Eglogue au roy* to Francis I, with the salient request

> Escoute ung peu, de ton vert cabinet,
> Le chant rural du petit Robinet?[11]

is unclear. Indeed, the clearest, if not necessarily the most direct, route to an answer is by way of Marot's biography, from the moment in 1519 that he entered the household of Francis' sister, Margaret of Angoulême, later queen of Navarre, to the period of his second exile when he fled to the protection of Calvin in Geneva. For what marks the career of Marot as a writer, what gives his Vergilianism its resonance, is the way in which circumstances and his own behavior shuffled him from one side to another of the Vergilian pattern of "lots," fortunate and unfortunate shepherd, protection and exile. In many ways his career strikingly predicted that of d'Aubigné, who narrowly escaped the massacre of Protestants on St. Bartholomew's Day, 1572, and who in 1620 also fled to Geneva for protection from the consequences of his publications. While Marot never achieved the range and power of d'Aubigné as an analyst and critic of the French wars of religion, his eclogues do have a sociopolitical cause and the color, however cautious, of dissent.

10. D'Aubigné, *Oeuvres Complétes,* ed. E. Reaume and F. de Caussaude, 6 vols. (Paris, 1873), III, 440.

11. C. A. Mayer, ed. *Clément Marot: Oeuvres Lyriques* (London, 1964), p. 343.

As a member of Marguerite's staff, Marot began his career in the protection of an educated woman known to be sympathetic to the reformist, if not to the schismatic elements of Lutheranism.[12] But in 1525 the new pope, Clement VII, addressed a letter to the Parlement of Paris, urging them to combat the spreading heresy, and the queen mother, Louise of Savoy, ordered the papal bull to be put into execution. In March 1526 Marot was arrested and imprisoned, perhaps on the pretext that he had eaten meat during Lent, a gesture perceivable as symbolic defiance of the Catholic church and support for the anti-ritualist preacher Aimé Maigret.[13] This experience produced his first major critique of the ecclesiastical establishment, *L'Enfer,* in which Marot represented himself as a prisoner at the bar in the underworld and presenting, in self-defense, an account of himself and his beliefs. Central to this credo was wordplay on his own name. Marot explored ironically the relationship between the name Clement, which he shared with the persecuting pope, and its latinate meaning, clemency; and as for his surname:

> Il tire à cil du Poete Vergille,
> Jadis chery de Mecenas à Romme:
> Maro s'appelle, & Marot je me nomme,
> Marot je suis, & Maro ne suis pas;
> Il n'en fut oncq' depuis le sien trespas;
> Mais puis qu'avons ung vray Mecenas ores,
> Quelcque Maro nous pourrons veoir encores.[14]

> [It derives from the poet Vergil, whom Maecenas cherished in Rome: Maro he was called, and I am named Marot: Marot I am, and Maro I am not: after death he was no more; but since we have now a true Maecenas, we may hope to see again some other Maro.]

We should not underestimate the importance for Marot of this symbolic nominalism, this recognition of a patronymy, in both senses, that is embedded genetically in the structure of his language, in what French culture has inherited from Roman culture.[15] In his dazzling study of onomastics in the French Renaissance, François Rigolot remarked that

12. See P. Jourda, *Marguerite d'Angoulême* (Paris, 1930); and P. M. Smith, *Clément Marot: Poet of the French Renaissance* (London, 1970), pp. 49-51.

13. See C. A. Mayer, *Clément Marot,* (Paris, 1972), pp. 83-131, esp. p. 130; P. M. Smith, pp. 71-73.

14. C. A. Mayer, ed., *Clément Marot: L'Enfer, Les Coq-à-L'Âne, Les Élégies* (Paris, 1977), p. 16.

15. Clearly I dissent from the view of Robert Griffin, *Clément Marot and the Inflections of Poetic*

"La duplicité marotique trouve dans la similarité des noms une *syntaxe* dont elle prétend faire la norme du monde."[16] But while he applauded the panache of the gesture, Rigolot, from the perspective of a post-Saussurian critic, declared it a sign of a tension in Marot's mind between words and things, "une querelle entre le nominaliste et le réaliste qui se déroule au gré des exigences textuelles" (p. 67). I believe it to have been, rather, a sign of the special character of Marot's humanism, in which his budding Protestantism, his ideals of learning and respect for antiquity, his interest in interpretation that would eventually lead him to translate the Psalms, and his commitment to the French language, all coalesce in an intense focus on words, a textuality that is never oppressed by the incapacity of words to mean, even though, with the help of "la duplicité marotique," they may mean more than one thing at a time. And in a present tense that assumed what he desired, Marot appealed to Francis I to reincarnate Augustus: "O Roy heureux, soubs lequel sont entres / (Presque periz) les lettres & Lettrés!" ["O happy king, under whom are returned (almost eradicated) both letters and lettered men!"]

Released from prison through the influence of Marguerite, Marot succeeded to his father's place in the King's own household, to enter on a period of royal favor such as he had proleptically described in *L'Enfer,* which was in the meantime discreetly withheld from publication. It was from this secure position that he launched his first collected edition of poems, the *Adolescence Clementine,* precisely dated 12 August 1532. The first item in this volume was Marot's translation of Vergil's first eclogue, stated in the author's preface to have been "translatée (certes) en grande jeunesse,"[17] an assertion that has been taken at face value by subsequent readers. Yet if we wonder why Marot seems so insistent ("certes") upon the youthfulness of his translation, the answer may be that he had come to see it, whenever produced, as having a special pertinence to his situation in 1532; for Marot's situation now resembled that of Tityrus, while others suspected of Lutheranism, such as Jacques Le Fèvre, were already in exile. Moreover, in March 1532 Marot had again been charged by the ecclesiastical authorities with eating meat during Lent, and again

---

Voice (Berkeley and Los Angeles, 1974), that "aside from a superficial resemblance in the names Marot-Maro on which he occasionally played with skill, Marot seems not to have had with Vergil the consanguinity of parallel careers and emotional isolation he had with Ovid" (p. 181). Griffin's position, however, is based on the fact that Marot never wrote an epic. And he later (p. 196) admits that the homonymy could be used seriously.

16. François Rigolot, *Poétique et Onomastique* (Geneva, 1977), p. 66.

17. *Adolescence Clementine,* ed. V. L. Saulnier (Paris, 1958), p. 14.

been saved from prison by Marguerite's intervention. As one of the lucky ones, Marot must have known that he held his security precariously; and with a peculiar mixture of bravado and caution, a mixture apparent also in his social behavior, he published the eclogue and held back *L'Enfer*. "Amour de liberté," that which had propelled his Tityrus to Rome, restricted Marot to protest by allusion, while the trope of juvenilia, of pre-maturity, was invoked to give him another kind of protection.

III

Yet the volume clearly contained poems that no stretching of the term of adolescence could contain. His elegy for Louise of Savoy, who died in 1531, when Marot was thirty-four, was the first formal eclogue in French literature; and everything about it registers it as an expression of French vernacular humanism, including the strenuous wordplay by which the Arcadian landscape and topoi are literally translated into France. Thus the "francs Bergers, sur franche herbe marchans"[18] are free/French shepherds who walk on fresh/French grass, a statement which was not intended to be merely playful. The two pastoral speakers named in the eclogue's elaborate title are "Colin d'Anjou & Thenot de Poictou"; and it is worth noticing that Colin (whom E. K. assumed to be Marot's own persona) lists his own place of origin among the French locales whose response to the death of Louise is expressed in terms of puns on their names. Amboise, the King's residence, "en boyt une amertume extreme" (l. 161), but Anjou, oddly, "faict jou," as does Angoulême, birthplace of Marguerite. The play on names, crucial to French national-ism in the same sense that Francis I signifies his country, permits the expression of local divisions of feeling. "Jouer sur les mots" means to equivocate. As premier poet of the French court, Marot was now in a situation of having to formalize the lament for a woman who had been largely responsible for the persecution of himself and his fellows. Anjou plays games indeed, using the convenience of a ready-made system of reference in which ideals of liberty were culturally embedded, alongside and perhaps in tension with ideals of peace. The real claim of Louise to Marot's regard was that she had negotiated the "paix de Dames," the treaty of Cambrai that concluded the Hapsburg-Valois wars over Italy, and permitted her description, in Augustan terms, as "la Bergère de Paix" (l. 240); but in the tradition of writing "latenter" about Octavian's

18. *Oeuvres Lyriques*, p. 329.

justices Marot played also on the right of the French to freedom, a right built into the very structure of their name as a nation.

According to Mayer, Marot's elegy for Louise went directly back to the Greek sources of the pastoral elegy, and from Vergil "il n'a pris en somme que des détails beaucoup moins important," (p. 26). One of these details, however, is an unmistakable quotation from Vergil's first eclogue, which may be more important than it seems. When Colin speaks of the portents that should have warned him of the Queen's death, he speaks in the superstitious voice of Meliboeus:

> Ha, quand j'ouy l'autrhyer (il me souvient)
> Si fort crier la Corneille en ung Chesne,
> C'est ung grand cas (dis je lors) s'il n'advient
> Quelcque meschef bien tost en cestuy Regne. (ll. 181–84)
>
> [Ah! now I remember how I heard the other day the
> raven crying so loudly in an oak; it will be by great luck
> (I said then) if we don't have some mischance, very
> soon, in this kingdom.]

On the one hand, to recall the voice of Meliboeus was to invoke the Lutheran exiles like Jacques Le Fevre; on the other, it was to quote his own Vergilian translation, and hence to reveal, not its naiveté, but its cultural self-consciousness:

> Ha Tityrus (si j'eusse esté bien sage)
> Il me souvient que souvent, par presage,
> Chesnes frappez de la fouldre des cieulx
> Me predisoient ce mal pernicieux:
> Semblablement la sinistre corneille
> Me disoit bien la fortune pareille.[19]

The very question of priority and origin is here literally inscribed, in the relation between "sage" and "présage," "dire" and "prédire," along with the dependence of a sense of origin on an act of memory ("Il me souvient"); but what this chain of linguistic echoes also tells us is that not only texts but *fortunae*—career-patterns and real experience—often recall ("souvent/souvient") each other. In the mirror of the translation, the elegy for Louise intensifies its relationship to Vergilian tradition, and permits a more complicated meditation on the cultural effects of her death.

19. *Adolescence Clementine*, p. 18. I find the translation much more interesting than did Alice Hulubei, *L'Eglogue en France au seizième siècle* (Paris, 1938), p. 50; despite her immense authority, it is unfortunate that Mayer, who grouped together all the other eclogues in his edition of the *Oeuvres Lyriques*, should not have included the translation among them.

As it turned out, the intermittent campaign against the Lutheranists was not coterminous with Louise, in part because the more extremist reformers seemed determined to provoke confrontation. In October 1534, pamphlets were distributed in the streets of Paris and Amboise, where the king resided, attacking the Mass. The enraged Francis was easily persuaded to take extreme measures against any and all suspects. Officers were sent to Marot's home at Blois; he escaped to Navarre; but his books and papers were seized, and in January 1535 his name was listed in a royal proclamation of those condemned to banishment from French territory. He did not return to Paris until 1537, having finally taken advantage of the general amnesty offered by Francis to all who would formally abjure their Protestantism and promise to live in future "comme bons & vrays catholiques." And Marot's formal adjuration has, of course, considerably obscured his ideological trail.

Meanwhile, a new edition of the *Adolescence Clementine* had appeared in 1536, an exile's edition, published in Antwerp, and containing an outspoken *Epistre au Roy, du temps de son exil a Ferrare*. In this poem, our key term, "cabinet," appears as the meeting-place of two concepts which, we may infer, had governed his poetics hitherto: the idea of poetic immunity from censorship, and the ideal of intellectual liberty of interpretation, a direct consequence of the Lutheran approach to scriptural exegesis. Marot complained to the King about the seizure of his books and papers at Blois:

> . . . o juge sacrilege,
> Qui t'a donné ne loy ne privileige
> D'aller toucher & faire tes massacres
> Au cabinet des sainctes Muses sacres?
> Bien est il vray que livres de deffence
> On y trouva; mais cela n'est offence
> A ung poëte, a qui on doibt lascher
> La bride longue, & rien ne luy cacher,
> Soit d'art magicq, nygromance ou caballe;
> Et n'est doctrine escripte ne verballe
> Qu'ung vray Poëte au chef ne deust avoir
> Pour faire bien d'escripre son debvoir.[20]

> [O sacrilegious judge, who gave you the legal right
> or privilege to go tampering and wrecking in the
> cabinet of the sacred Muses? It is true that they found
> forbidden books there; but that is no offence in a poet,

---

20. *Epitres*, pp. 202-03.

who should be allowed a long rein, and have nothing
hidden from him, whether it be magic, necromancy or
cabbalism; there is no doctrine, written or spoken, that
a true poet should not understand in order to do his
duty as a writer.]

The cabinet sacred to the Muses, therefore, is a symbol simultaneously of
intellectual privacy and artistic liberty. For General Chambor, who
wrote his own epistle in response, Marot's defence of "la liberté de
scavoir" was tantamount to an admission of heresy;[21] and indeed it was
immediately followed, in the *Epistre au Roy,* by an argument for the right
of the Christian intellectual to choose for himself between good and bad
books, true and false doctrine, by testing his "sens d'eslire" against the
"sacre sens" of "l'escripture."

But the enclosure of these statements in a poem seems partially to have
gained Marot's point about poetic immunity; for he received back his
place as the king's *valet de chambre,* and was once again recognized as the
official poet of the French court. The most palpable signs of his acceptance were a new edition of his *Oeuvres* published in 1538 by special royal
privilege, and the royal gift of a house near St. Germain. It was in
response to this royal generosity that Marot composed the *Eglogue au Roy,
soubz les noms de Pan & Robin,* his third French eclogue,[22] and the one in
which the cabinet reappears with a different coloring (green), defined
now as the pastoral center, or shrine of Pan; that is to say, the court, or
perhaps the privy chamber, of Francis I.

IV

Like the pastoral elegy for Louise of Savoy, the *Eglogue au Roy* is an
anthology of pastoral quotations; but in selecting his pretexts Marot was
once again going beyond mere textual archaeology. It opens with a
subtle synthesis of Vergil's first and second eclogues.

> Ung pastoureau qui Robin s'appelloit
> Tout à par[t] soy nagueres s'en alloit
> Parmy fousteaulx (arbres qui font umbraige);
> Et là tout seul faisoit, de grand couraige,
> Hault retentir les boys & l'air serain,
> Chantant ainsi: O Pan dieu souverain,

21. *Epistre de general Chambor, Le Printemps de l'humble esperant* (Paris, 1536), cited by Mayer, ed.
Epitres, p. 203.
22. He had written an intermediate pastoral to celebrate the birth of Renée de France's third
child in 1535.

Qui de garder ne fuz oncq paresseux
Parcs & brebis & les maistres d'iceulx. (*O.L.*, p. 343)

The setting in the shade ("umbraige") of beech trees and the song that makes the woods echo identify the speaker as Tityrus; his isolation, signalled by repetition ("Tout à part . . . tout seul"), aligns him also with Corydon, while the address to Pan as "he who guards folds and flocks and those in charge of them" is a direct translation of 2:33 ("Pan curat ovis oviumque magistros"). Such echoes are appropriate to a poem whose first level of significance (which is already a second level) is an expression of gratitude to a royal patron. But this does not remain a poem of security unquestioned. Transforming the seasonal structure of Mantuan's sixth eclogue into a sociopolitical argument for change, rather than a metaphor for the natural unavoidability of sorrow, Robin appeals to Pan to protect him from the coming of a winter of discontent. Birds of harsh voice now threaten the approach of the cold season, "triste yver, qui la terre desnue," (l. 222); his flocks huddle together, and seem to beg the poet to appeal to Pan on their behalf; and if he will continue his protection, promises the poet, his pipe which has been hung up on an oak ("à ung chesne pendue") will be taken down again, and he will sing again, in security ("à seureté"). For poetry's continuance the poet needs to be assured that the favor he now enjoys will not be taken from him.

Marot's response to the Vergilian dialectic, in other words, was sufficiently alert to its cultural transferability to produce a new story, in which the lots of the fortunate and unfortunate shepherd might alternate in a single life (or the life of a nation, perhaps). And on the basis of this perception we can better understand the function of his other major quotation from Vergil in the *Eglogue au Roy*. In the center of his paraphrase from Jean Lemaire de Belges,[23] and in the process of merging the paternal shepherd with old Janot (his real father, Jean Marot), Clément Marot inserted his own version of the Vergilian idyll in its purest and only possible form, hypothesis. Vergil made this the most poignant contribution of Meliboeus—the capacity to describe for all time the value of what one cannot have. In Marot's poem, this responsibility is transferred to the father-figure, who proposes that idyll is possessible, again under certain conditions. Worship Pan, so went the paternal advice, and teach the landscape to echo ("rechanter") his name:

23. Jean Lemaire de Belges, *Oeuvres*, ed. J. Stecher, 4 vols. (Louvain, 1882), I, 133–52. This discovery was made simultaneously by J. Bayet, "La source principale de l'eglogue de Marot," and G. Charlier, "Sur l'enfance de Marot," *Revue d'Histoire Littéraire de la France*, 34 (1927), 567-71.

Car c'est celluy par qui foisonnera
Ton champ, ta vigne, & qui te donnera
Plaisante loge entre sacrez ruisseaulx
Encourtinez de flairans arbrisseaulx.
La, d'ung costé, auras la grande closture
De saulx espes, ou, pour prendre pasture,
Mousches a miel le fleur sucer iront,
Et d'ung doulx bruit souvent t'endormiront:
. . . .
T' esveillera aussi la colombelle,
Pour rechanter encores de plus belle. (ll. 85–102)

[For it is he who will make your field, your vine,
bear harvest, and who will give you a pleasant dwell-
ing among the sacred streams surrounded by sweet-
smelling shrubs. On the one side you will have the
great enclosure of thick willows, where the bees go to
suck the flowers, and with their sweet noise often lull
you to sleep . . . and you will also hear the dove, for
singing again all the more sweetly.]

One could argue that by framing this passage as a promise of goods within the tactful poet's reach Marot had eliminated (or failed to understand) the ironies of its presentation in the original. But in fact the language of his translation suggests the opposite. "La grande closture" is his addition, a phrase which illuminates the enclosed status of the passage as a premise, rather than a promise; while the repetition of "rechanter" at beginning and end also bespeaks both boundaries and echoes. These elegant lexical adjustments (no translation can do justice to the syntactical ambiguity of that "encores") suggest that classical imitation has become its own theme; and the Vergilian echo is itself doubly nested in French culture, within the remembered speech of Marot's father inside a quotation from Jean Lemaire de Belges.

This reading of the *Eglogue au Roy* must be strengthened by the fact that after Marot's death there was discovered among his papers its companion piece. *La Complaincte d'un Pastoureau Chrestien,* published in Rouen in 1549,[24] announces in the remainder of its title that the Pan of this poem is God himself. Its opening lines, however, establish a clear intertextual relationship to the *Eglogue au Roy:*

Un pastoreau n'agueres je escoutois,
Qui s'en alloit complaignant par les boys,

24. *Oeuvres Lyriques,* p. 56. It was first attributed to Marot in a Paris edition of 1558.

Seul, & privé de compagnie toute,
N'ayant en luy de plaisir une goute.[25]

The sad shepherd in this poem, totally deprived of pleasure as of company, has therefore to be understood in terms of Marot's habit of self-quotation; but he is also to be seen as a correction of Vergil's. However initially solitary, he laments primarily on behalf of others, his "compaings," unmistakably the Lutheran exiles, who have suffered "pareille amertume," (ll. 220–23) and who are now "peregrins en region loingtaine" (l. 49); while his references to his own exile, leaving behind his wife and infant child ("ton humble bergerette, / Et du petit bergeret qu'elle alaicte," ll. 103–04) are offered in order to establish his claim to the role of witness. The poem's object is to enable Pan to observe the injustices taking place in his realm; and then, promises the complaining shepherd, "Mon flageolet, à un chesne pendu, / Sera aussi proprement despendu," (ll. 295–96).

The opening and closing connections between the *Complaincte* and the *Eglogue* would seem to settle the question of Marot's authorship of both.[26] It follows that, whenever the *Complaincte* was written, the period of exile referred to was that of 1534, when Marot did leave behind a newly-married wife. If he wrote it in 1534, and withheld it, its quotation in the *Eglogue* has the effect of making that already subtle construct more subtle still, giving body to those premonitions of a winter of discontent, and explaining his most significant change in its Vergilian opening: for "umbraige," as a rhyme, was there significantly modified by "couraige," the solitary voice in the shade of the pastoral metaphor daring to speak out, but only so far as the convention of literariness will permit.

If, however, the *Complaincte* was written after the *Eglogue,* the most likely date for its composition was during Marot's third and final exile. In August 1542, Francis sent out letters patent for the searching out of Lutheranists. Marot's *Trente Pseaulmes* had actually been authorized for publication by the Sorbonne; but in early 1542, Étienne Dolet, perhaps overconfident, had issued the first French edition of *L'Enfer*. Whether or not this was the cause, by the end of that year Marot had taken refuge in Geneva under the protection of Calvin; and the next edition of his Psalms carried a preface by Calvin himself. From that moment, Marot's identi-

---

25. *Oeuvres Lyriques*, p. 390–91. Mayer, however, separates the poems by consigning the *Complaincte* to an appendix.

26. Mayer declared that "Il est impossible de prouver son authenticité; il est tout aussi impossible de prouver que la pièce soit apocryphe," *Oeuvres Lyriques*, p. 57.

fication with radical Protestantism was unavoidable; and when he wrote from exile an adaptation of Vergil's fourth eclogue on the birth of the Dauphin, he represented himself explicitly as "l'infortuné Berger," the only excluded celebrant at an occasion "dont la Gaule est si gaye."[27]

For Marot, then, the eclogue was an ambiguous vehicle, capable of promoting a new French Augustanism while annotating, through textual and intertextual nuance, its deficiencies. What distinguishes his reading of Vergil is his subtle and continuous meditation on the first eclogue, with its opportunities for insight into the ethical problems of dependency and privilege. His grasp of pastoral as the language of exile he shared with Petrarch and Sannazaro, but added to it a personal gloss on the inevitable predicament of the intellectual, the problem of mediation between the self, "tout seule," and the community, particularly the community at risk. And he especially exceeded his Italian predecessors by his fix on the ontology of imitation itself, his sense of the memorial and reflective function of quotation as echo.

V

What, then, did Marot as a model mean to Spenser, when not only the "vert cabinet" but the whole of the *Eglogue au roy* attracted his attention? It is not always noted that "January" as well as "December" bears the imprint of Robin's address to Pan, framing the poem in a cold wind blowing from the Continent. References to Marot also figure prominently in E. K.'s commentary, which despite the fact that they are not always correct suggest a larger influence still. Marot is the only French poet mentioned in E. K.'s epistle, along with Theocritus, Vergil, Mantuan, Petrarch and Sannazaro. The "November" elegy for Dido is stated to be an "imitation of Marot his song, which he made upon the death of Loys the frenche Queene," although the textual resemblance there is marginal when compared to that between "December" and the *Eglogue au roy,* about which E. K. says nothing at all. No mention is made of the fact that the emblem of this poem, "La mort ny mord," was the motto under which Marot published his *Oeuvres* of 1539. And the use of the name "Roffy" in "September" is explained as "the name of a

27. *Oeuvres Lyriques*, p. 354. Georges Guiffrey suggested that the prophetic text so resecularized concealed an ironic subtext supporting the claim of his Genevan psalter to be restoring the golden age of *sacred* verse, and that he had chosen the Vergilian model precisely because its interpretive history could suggest such a critique while protecting him from its consequences: "la pensée de poete française se dissimulait habilement sous l'imitation du poete latin." See his *Les Oeuvres de Clément Marot*, 5 vols. (Paris, 1876-1911), I, 546.

shepehearde in Marot his AEglogue of Robin and the Kinge," when in fact it occurred in the elegy for Louise. At the very least, this unreliable commentary seems designed to drive the reader back to Marot's work, where a certain initial puzzlement might have led to further inquiry.

We can safely assume that Spenser accepted Marot as a model for how to proceed in writing the pastoral of state, or, more precisely, in adapting to the needs of a modern European nation the Vergilian strategy of address to those in power. So the "Romish Tityrus", as E. K. himself put it, "by Mecaenas means was brought into the favour of the Emperor Augustus," (p. 459). But we must also now recognize that Marot represented a more problematic example of that process than even Vergil himself, one that considerably extended the terms of confrontation within the forms of accommodation. Spenser would certainly have been informed of Marot's reputation as a figure of embattled Protestantism by virtue of his own involvement in Van der Noot's *Theatre for Worldlings,* his first literary venture.[28] Another crucial historical ingredient in this relationship would have been the tone of English-French relations at this time; a question to which another of E. K.'s glosses gives at least a partial answer. In commenting on the fable of the fox and the kid in "May," E. K. underlined the topical meaning of its anti-catholic satire: "the morall of the whole tale . . . is to warne the protestaunt beware, howe he geveth credit to the unfaythfull Catholique: whereof we have dayly proofes suficient, but one most famous of all, practised of Late yeares in Fraunce, by Charles the nynth." He spoke, of course, of the massacre of the Huguenots on St. Bartholomew's Day in 1572, that hideous breach of contract for which the French house of Valois, and specifically Charles IX, under the influence of his mother, Catherine de Medici, was held responsible. In 1562 the English had signed the treaty of Hampton Court with the Huguenot rebels, and had themselves been driven out of Le Havre a year later; yet at the time Spenser was constructing *The Shepheardes Calender* Elizabeth was planning her marriage to a member of that fatal dynasty, Francis, duke of Alençon, Charles IX's brother. It would be fair to say that these negotiations were creating the first major rift between Elizabeth and her public. Sir Philip Sidney, to whom the *Calender* was dedicated, wrote a bold letter to the

---

28. Six of the sonnets that Spenser contributed to Van der Noot's *Theatre for Worldlings* (1569) were translations of Marot's translations from Petrarch. On Van der Noot's Protestantism, see Carl Rasmussen, "'Quietnesse of Minde': *A Theatre for Worldlings* as Protestant Poetics," *Spenser Studies* 1 (1980), 3–27.

Queen advising against the match;[29] and even as the *Calender* was being completed, the country saw a striking example of what happened to those who spoke out publicly against the French connection. On October 13, 1579, John Stubbs, author of *The Gaping Gulf, whereinunto England is like to be swallowed by another French marriage,* his publisher and printer, were all tried for seditious libel and sentenced to lose their right hands. The printer, who somehow escaped this punishment, was Hugh Singleton, who then proceeded to publish the *Calender*. By citing a French poet as one of his major models, then, but by choosing one whose ideology set him retroactively more clearly among the victims than the protégés of the French monarchy, Spenser placed himself in a position with respect to the pastoral of state that was not uncomplicated, but consistent with his own choice of patron (Sidney) and his connections (through Singleton) with the oppositionist press.

The precise nature of that stance was to be primarily defined by the complex structure of the *Calender* itself, in which the contrasting eclogues, the pseudo-Servian commentary, the woodcuts, the seasonal structure, all played a part. The reader who opened *The Shepheardes Calender* in 1579 would have known instantly that the strange composite work he held in his hand, whatever it was,[30] was ideologically complex. E. K.'s opening epistle seems to address both international humanists and linguistic nationalists, courtiers and the general public. The new poet's persona, as defined in the opening gloss to "January," also looked two ways; for if Marot was an authority in the new genre of Protestant poetry, the "ragged" rhymes of Skelton's *Colin Clout* had served, among other clerkly purposes, to defend the Catholic church against the invasions of Lutheranism.[31] And the very structure of the *Calender* was presented, from the first, as something about which rational persons could have different positions, the debate on the January versus the March opening of the year serving, among other things, to alert the

---

29. *A Discourse of Syr Ph. S. To The Queenes Majesty Touching Hir Marriage With Monsieur* survives in a number of manuscripts but was first published in 1663. See *The Complete Works of Sir Philip Sidney,* ed. A. Feuillerat, 4 vols. (Cambridge, 1912; rpt. 1969), III, 51–60.

30. Ruth Samson Luborsky, in "The Allusive Presentation of *The Shepheardes Calender,*" *Spenser Studies* 1 (1980), 29–68, sees it as alluding to the mixed precedents of Renaissance editions of Vergil, Aesop's fables, and the *Kalendar and Compost of Shepherds*. Bruce R. Smith, "On Reading *The Shepheardes Calender,*" *Spenser Studies* 1 (1980), 69–93, sees it as a merger of classical eclogue, medieval almanac and Renaissance pastoral romance.

31. Skelton attacked those members of the clergy who were "somewhat suspect / In Luther's sect," or who talk of that "heresiarch / Called Wicliffista." See *Complete Poems of John Skelton Laureate,* ed. Philip Henderson (London, 1931: rev. 1948), p. 266.

reader to the choice here made, and its historical and aesthetic consequences.

A similar but more exacting balance appears to have been struck in the *Calender* between two versions of nationalism, that which could be expressed in whole-hearted appreciation of Elizabeth I and that which admitted the anxieties of the Protestant activists grouped around Sidney, Leicester and Walsingham, whose power at court and even whose access to Elizabeth had been severely encroached upon by the French marriage negotiations. Spenser's response to this division in his loyalties is articulated in the symmetrical relationship between the "April" and "November" eclogues, the first a simple eulogy to Elizabeth, unmistakably glossed as such by the woodcut, which showed the Queen, surrounded by ladies of her court playing musical instruments, an identification further confirmed by the poem's "argument." On the other hand, the elegy for Dido in "November" is presented by E. K. as the most enigmatic and profound poem in the series: "he bewayleth the death of some mayden of great bloud, whom he calleth Dido. The personage is secrete, and to me altogether unknowne, albe of him selfe I often required the same." And, while remarking that this poem is an imitation of Marot's elegy for Louise of Savoy, E. K. added that it is "farre passing his reache, and in myne opinion all other the Eglogues of this book." The suggestion implicit in this comment is that "November" concerns the death of a queen; and in 1961 it was in fact so interpreted. In a systematic attempt to uncover the topical significance of the *Calender*, to which E. K.'s comments give such provocative presence, Paul McLane read "November" as an allegorical expression of grief at the prospect of the French marriage, by which, it was argued, the Queen would be to all intents and purposes dead to the nation. McLane adduced in support of his hypothesis the Vergilian equation between the names Dido/Elissa, suggesting that the "April" and "November" eclogues were the two sides of Spenser's ambivalent view of his sovereign.[32]

From the perspective of Spenser's Vergilianism, McLane's hypothesis deserves more respect than it has generally achieved. For it is only if we consider Dido as a dark prognosis of what Elizabeth might become that the formal structure of the *Calender*, and indeed the entire project that it

---

32. Paul E. McLane, *Spenser's Shepheardes Calender: A Study in Elizabethan Allegory* (Notre Dame, Ind., 1961), pp. 27–60. The contemporary identification of Dido with Elizabeth I was confirmed at her death by John Lane, whose pastoral *Elegie upon the death of the high renowned Princesse, our late Souveraigne Elizabeth* combined obvious quotations from both "April" and "November." See Helen Cooper, *Pastoral: Mediaeval into Renaissance* (Ipswich and Totowa, N.J.), p. 209.

represents, becomes fully intelligible. That is to say, the contrast between "April" and "November" represents two views of the English cultural situation, with the more sombre one, given the circumstances of 1579, prevailing. For Spenser to function as the second English Tityrus (with Chaucer as the first) he needs not only a Maecenas but an Augusta; and in the "April" eclogue (significantly the fourth in the series, in imitation of Vergil's "Pollio") Elizabeth is given the primary qualification for that role, namely that she has brought her country peace, symbolized by her crown, not of flowers, but of olives: "Olives bene for peace, / When wars doe surcease: / Such for a Princesse bene principall," Spenser commented. And for good measure E. K. added his own version of the Servian gloss on Georgic I, 11–13:

> The Olive was wont to be the ensigne of Peace and quietnesse, eyther for that it cannot be planted and pruned, and so carefully looked to, as it ought, but in time of peace: or els for that the Olive tree, they say, will not growe neare the Firre tree, which is dedicate to Mars the god of battaile, and used most for speares and other instruments of warre. Whereupon it is finely feigned, that when Neptune and Minerva strove for the naming of the citie of Athens, Neptune striking the ground with his mace, caused a horse to come forth, that importeth warre, but at Minervaes stroke sprong out an Olive to note that it should be a nurse of learning, and such peaceable studies.[33]

Yet as the *Calender* moves on through the seasonal cycle, this spring-like optimism is replaced by an increasingly gloomy cultural prognosis. The "October" eclogue which presents to Cuddie, as "the perfecte patterne of a Poete," the stages of Vergil's model career for him to follow, also declares that such a career cannot be replicated:

> But ah Mecaenas is yclad in claye,
> And great Augustus long ygoe is dead:
> And all the worthies liggen wrapt in leade,
> That matter made for Poets on to play. (ll. 61–64)

"November" offers an example of one such "worthy," whose formal relationship to Eliza is marked by the substitution of a different kind of wreath: "The water Nymphs, that wont with her to sing and daunce, / And for her girlond Olive braunches beare, / Now balefull boughes of Cypres doen advaunce," (ll. 142–44). And "December" closes down the cycle by returning to Marot's *Eglogue au Roy*, and accepting from it only

---

33. Servius, III, 133: "fabula talis est: cum Neptunus et Minerva de Athenarum nomine contenderent, placuit diis, ut eius nomine civitas appellaretur, qui munus melius mortalibus obtulisset. tunc Neptunus percusso litore equum, animal bellis aptum, produxit; Minerva iacta hasta olivam creavit, que res est melior conprobata et pacis insigne."

what is unrelievedly depressing. In "January" Colin breaks his pipe; in "December" he hangs it upon a tree, unconditionally. And at precisely the point where Marot had incorporated into his conditional praise of Francis/Pan an echo, suitably ironized, of Tityrus' idyll as conceived by Meliboeus, including the hypothesis that *otium* will be accompanied by nature's lullabies, Spenser translates the dream into nightmare:

> Where as I was wont to seeke the honey Bee,
> Working her formall rowmes in Wexen frame;
> The grieslie Todestoole growne there moght I see
> And loathed Paddocks lording on the same.
> And where the chaunting birds luld me a sleepe,
> The ghastlie Owle her grievous ynne doth keepe. (ll. 67–72).

In the English winter, poetry is effectively discontinued.

Here again the woodcuts contribute to the argument, directly but subtly. It has been recognized for some time that the woodcuts for the *Shepheardes Calender* must owe something to earlier traditions of Vergilian illustration,[34] and specifically to the great series of woodcuts by Sebastian Brant,[35] first published in the Grüninger edition of 1502. Brant's design for the first eclogue (Plate I) set up a visual antithesis which would remain virtually unchanged long after his late-medieval techniques had been replaced by true perspective and Renaissance naturalism. The contrast between the fortunate and the unfortunate shepherd is represented first and foremost by their posture, the one in repose under a tree, the other conceived as in transit, his exile's lot signified by the walking staff. Note the particular instrument given to Tityrus—not the panpipes or the flute—but the bagpipes; which would reappear in the *Calender* as the broken instrument at the feet of January's Colin Clout (Plate II). Behind the protagonists in Brant's version are two other symbolic alternatives, the rustic city of Mantua behind Meliboeus, the towered city of Rome behind Tityrus; and between them, the peculiar image of a woodcutter with lifted axe about to cut down a leafless tree.

And in Spenser's "January," also, there are versions of the two cities, Rome represented in shorthand by two of its pointed towers but also having gained, unmistakably, a section of the Colosseum; but the myste-

---

34. Smith, "On reading *The Shepheardes Calender*," pp. 80–84.

35. On Brant, see Theodore K. Rabb, "Sebastian Brant and the First Illustrated Edition of Vergil," *Princeton Library Chronicle* 21 (1960), 187-99; and Eleanor Winsor Leach, "Illustration as Interpretation in Brant's and Dryden's Editions of Vergil," in *The early illustrated book: essays in honor of Lessing J. Rosenwald*, ed. Sandra Hindman, (Washington, D.C., 1982).

rious woodcutter has disappeared, only to reappear in a slightly different posture, in "February" (Plate III). While this visual quotation is not without significance for Spenser's fable of the oak and the briar, its chief importance for this argument is in showing how closely, indeed, Spenser too was working with the dialectical structure of Vergil's first eclogue; and while his Colin is identified as Tityrus by virtue of his possession of the broken bagpipes, his *stance* in "January" *also* identifies him as Meliboeus: upright, leaning on a crook which resembles the exile's walking staff, beneath a leafless tree which can afford him no protection, Spenser's shepherd is one whose happy days are over, whose journey is about to begin. To recognize the sources of this design is to confirm, from another perspective, the argument of this essay. Poised uncertainly between Tityrus and Meliboeus, between the poetics of accommodation and the poetics of dissent, Spenser presented himself (anonymously) to the English public as a mutant in the Vergilian tradition mediated by Marot; and in self-fulfilling prophecy he predicted the great paradox of his later career—that the greatest representation of Elizabethanism as a national ideology should be offered to the country by the exile who had promised to sing no more.

VI

As Spenser's Augusta, Elizabeth's beneficent influence is limited in the *Calender*, partly because she must reincarnate both Caesars, the rising star of Eclogue 4 and the dead shepherd, however apotheosized, of Eclogue 5; but also because her relationship to English culture must be inferred from the relationship of Spenser's pastoral practice to Marot's. By choosing Marot's *Eglogue au roy* as his *frame*, Spenser demanded from his readers an ability to translate one metaphorical system into another, a personal explanation of Colin's melancholy into a national one. By going significantly beyond his French model in pessimism, Spenser also showed how well he understood the special character of Marot's Vergilianism, its network of internal pressures and anxieties that were specific to French culture at the very beginning of the Reformation. And in his later knowledge of Marot's own career and his sense of how that career fitted into the recent history of French/English relations, Spenser proceeded in his rewriting of Vergil still further in the direction that Marot has showed him. It may be true that "La mort ny mord," and that the meaning of Colin's missing emblem (why is it missing?) in "December" is that "all thinges perish and come to theyr last end, but workes of learned wits and monuments of Poetry abide for ever." But it is also true that the first significant English pastoral of state (for that is what the *Calender* surely was) is unmistakably dominated by the unhappy, and not the fortunate shepherd.

But the French marriage question was not the only issue on which the *Calender* might seem to have been taking a dangerous position, however cautiously. Spenser's position on the character and government of the English church is also, unmistakably, part of his subtext, and goes considerably beyond the generalized anti-catholic satire of "May," disclosing itself in "August" as a marked sympathy for the reformist and radical wing of English Protestantism. In "May," "July," and "August" the authority deferred to is no longer either the Romish Tityrus or the English one, but the figure of Algrind, whom Thomalin cites as a major critic of worldly and ambitious ecclesiastics. It has been long recognized that Algrind is a barely-concealed representation of Edmund Grindal, Archbishop of Canterbury, and that his alarming fate, when an eagle drops a shellfish on his head, so that "now astonied with the stroke, / he lyes in lingring payne," (ll. 227–28) refers to his punishment by Elizabeth for refusing to suppress the radical "prophesyings" or unauthorized meetings of ministers to discuss the interpretation of biblical texts. In other words, by keying his anticlerical eclogues, "May," "July," and "September," into a local confrontation between Elizabeth and her senior bishop, Spenser provided a contemporary and national equivalent to both the pre-reformation critiques of the Roman church by Petrarch, Boccaccio and Mantuan, and the early embattled Protestantism of Marot.

For the purposes of this argument, the most salient detail of Grindal's biography is the fact that his refusal to suppress the prophesyings was expressed in a letter to the Queen, dated 20 December 1576, a striking parallel to Sidney's letter against the French marriage, the cause of *his* temporary disgrace and rustication. Grindal's letter had, moreover, been carried to the Queen by Leicester, who was by now Spenser's patron. In the letter, Grindal defended the prophesyings as an essential tool in creating a learned clergy; reminded Elizabeth that widespread preaching was an important instrument of hegemonic control, instancing the loyalty of the Londoners to the Queen as compared to the recently rebellious northern counties; and assured her that there would be no confusion between matters of church and state at the public meetings: "No Controversie of this present Time and State shall be moved or dealt

The labels within the image read: MELIBEVS, TITYRVS

PLATE I. Vergil, "Eclogue I" from *Opera,* ed. Sebastian Brant. Strasbourg: J. Grüninger (1502), Sig. A1v. Reprinted from the copy at the Library of Congress, Washington, D.C.

Ianuarye.

Ægloga prima.

PLATE II. "Ianuarye" from Edmund Spenser, *The Shepheardes Calender*. London: Hugh Singleton (1579), fol.1. Reprinted from the copy at the Library of Congress, Washington, D.C.

Februarie.

Ægloga Secunda.

PLATE III. "Februarie" from Edmund Spenser, *The Shepheardes Calender*. London: Hugh Singleton (1579), fol.3. Reprinted from the copy at the Library of Congress, Washington, D.C.

withal. . . . None is suffered to glaunce openly or covertly at Persons publick or private." And perhaps most significantly, he defended the principle of freedom of interpretation: "Neither is there any just Cause of Offence to be taken, yf divers Men make divers Senses of one Sentence of Scripture; so that all the Senses be good and agreeable to the Analogie and Proportion of Faith."[36] The Queen was unimpressed by these arguments and angered by his challenge to her supremacy over the church. In June 1577 Grindal was sequestered from his office by order of the House of Lords, and the six months' sentence was later extended indefinitely.

VII

Spenser's representation of Grindal was, however, scarcely more transpicuous than the biblical texts. Although he introduces unassailable pastoral models of unworldliness, Abel, the first shepherd, and Moses, the patriarchal one, Grindal himself is described as coming to grief as a result of imprudent exposure "upon a hyll," the symbol of ambition and one which Morell himself plans to climb. But Thomalin declares himself "taught by Algrins ill, / to love the lowe degree." There is, therefore, a true Vergilian ambiguity built into the value structure of this dialogue. Was Grindal's error in standing up to the Queen, or in holding high ecclesiastical office in the first place? Such questions become still further complicated the more one knows of Grindal's biography; for he walked a narrow line of ecclesiastical policy, parallel to but slightly to the left of the Elizabethan settlement itself, and was far from being an advocate of free discussion. One wonders whether Spenser knew that, under pressure from the Privy Council, Grindal had forbidden the ministers in his diocese from discussing in their pulpits the secular or religious implications of John Stubbs's *The Gaping Gulf.*[37]

The first Elizabethan pastoral of both church and state, then, was distinctly equivocal in structure and expression; and it was precisely this quality of enigma and lack of transparency that is emphasized in Elizabethan pastoral theory (such as it is) that followed the *Shepheardes Calender*.

36. John Strype, *The History of the Life and Acts of . . . Edmund Grindal* (London, 1710), Appendix 3, pp. 74–85.

37. Strype, pp. 242–43. Strype's emphasis on Grindal's severity against the Puritan activists should, however, be read in the light of his explicit project, to recuperate Grindal from overemphasis on his suspension from office, and a subsequent assumption of an "Inclination in him towards a Discipline in this Church different to what was established," (iii). Compare Patrick Collinson, *Archbishop Grindal 1519–1583: The Struggle for a Reformed Church* (Berkeley and Los Angeles, 1979), pp. 18–19, for Strype's own political contexts, and the connection of his biography to the notorious Sacheverell trial, in June 1710.

The earliest comments came from a person with an obvious interest in the *Calender*, Sir Philip Sidney himself. In his *Defence of Poesie*, probably written in 1580, Sidney built into his cumulative defense of the poetic genres an account of pastoral that was not only Vergilian in focus and political in inference, but peculiarly limited to the first eclogue and its dialectical structure:

> Is the poor pipe disdained, which sometimes out of Meliboeus' mouth can show the misery of people under hard lords or ravening soldiers? and again, by Tityrus, what blessedness is derived to them that lie lowest from the goodness of them that sit highest; sometimes, under the pretty tales of wolves and sheep, can include the whole considera-tion of wrongdoing and patience.[38]

The sociopolitical force of this passage resides in the connection between living "under hard lords" and writing *under* a pastoral veil, a less benign explanation for the pastoral of state than is found in contemporary French criticism.[39] So too the primary emphasis on Meliboeus suggests repression; and even the elliptical account given of Tityrus suspiciously connects his "blessedness" to his capacity to keep a low profile.

A decade after the *Calender* was published, when the vogue for Elizabethan pastoral of all kinds was at its height, an *Arte of English Poesie* was published by an anonymous author, later agreed to be George Puttenham. He offered a definition of pastoral that was clearly, even more than Sidney's, an updating of the Servian hermeneutic:

> the poet devised the Eglogue . . . not of purpose to counterfait or represent the rusticall manner of loves and communication; but under the vaile of homely persons, and in rude speeches to insinuate and glaunce at greater matters, and such as perchance had not bene safe to have disclosed in any other sort, which may be perceived in the Eglogues of Virgill, in which are treated by figure matters of greater importance then the loves of Titirus and Corydon.[40]

---

38. *An Apology for Poetry*, ed. Geoffrey Shepherd (London, 1965), p. 116.

39. Compare Thomas Sebillet, *L'Art poétique francoys*, ed. Felix Gaiffe (Paris, 1932), pp. 159–61, where the eclogue is defined as that which treats "under a pastoral premise and language deaths of princes, calamities of the times, alterations of republics, happy successes and events of fortune . . . under so clear an allegory that the designs . . . are made clearly visible, as a painting is perceived under its glass" ("soubz propos et termes pastoraus, mortz de Princes, calamitez de temps, mutations de Republiques, joyeus succés et evenements de fortune . . . soubz allégorie tant clére, que lés desseins . . . lés facent voir clérement, comme s'appercoit la peinture soubz le verre"). As the Servian veil of political allegory has been made perspicuous, crystallizing to a "verre" that needs no withdrawal, we can infer that for Sebillet (who derives his pastoral theory entirely from Vergil and Marot), a political subtext is not seen as threatening to the system or the poet.

40. George Puttenham, *The Arte of English Poesie* (1589), ed. G. D. Willcock and A. Walker (Cambridge, 1936), pp. 38–39.

Puttenham's emphasis on what "had not bene safe" is threatening from the point of view of both the poet and the state, suggesting that the political subtexts of Elizabethan pastoral were more likely to be seen as subversive than as legitimating.

Reinforced by these *de post facto* reports of the anxiety quotient in *English* pastoral, we may return to the *Calender* and consider again the function of E. K.'s commentary, proposed as an instrument of clarification. In fact, if we look in E. K. for a full equivalent of Servian commentary, what is most conspicuous by its absence is any satisfactory account of the meaning of the different eclogues, or of the intentions of the work as a whole. The epistle to the reader characteristically presents its comments in the form of a series of competing hypotheses as to what this mysterious, anonymous poet is up to; and on the central point of motive E. K. is deliberately evasive: "Now as touching the generall dryft and purpose of his AEglogues, I mind not to say much, him selfe labouring to conceale it"(p. 418). In his account of the "generall argument of the whole booke," E. K. follows his famous classification of the poems into plaintive, moral and recreative by the statement that "to this division may every thing herein be reasonably applyed: A few onely except, whose speciall purpose and meaning I am not privie to." Comments of the same provocative kind appear throughout the *Calender* in both glosses and arguments, climaxing in the already-cited argument to "November," and augmented by a gloss which insists again that Dido's identity, as that of the "great shepheard" who chiefly mourns her, are "unknowen and closely buried in the Authors conceipt." It need hardly be said that these are the strategies of a discourse that cannot risk either full transparency or incomprehensibility; and that the new function of the commentator in the native pastoral of state is *not* to explain, but on the contrary to incite the reader to interpretive speculation.

VIII

This account of the *Shepheardes Calender*, it will by now be apparent, runs considerably athwart of two other powerful impulses in the pastoral theory of our own century. The first is Modernism, which has been on the whole hostile to, or at least depreciatory of, any version of pastoral that takes valence from sociopolitical cause and content. Which brings me back to Thomas Rosenmeyer, one of the most influential exponents of a Modernist theory of pastoral. In his preface to *The Green Cabinet* Rosenmeyer explained the origins of his title:

Theocritus does not, as a rule, call his pleasance green, nor does he think of it as an enclosure. But "green cabinet" caught my eye when I read it in Spenser's "December," as *"vert cabinet"* had caught Spenser's eye when he found it in Marot's "Eglogue au Roy." It is the sort of phrase which is at home on a title page. And, with a bit of squeezing, it can be made to fit the *locus amoenus* of Greek pastoral poetry.[41]

It is perhaps unfair to catch a critic in a confidential moment and hold him to its consequences. Yet this accidental catching of the eye is revealing, connecting the green cabinets of Marot and Spenser with an account of pastoral tradition dominated by the concept of "green thought" or world-avoidance, as Marvell encapsulated that concept in *The Garden*. And in fact the squeezing that goes on in *The Green Cabinet* extends beyond the choice of title; for Theocritus is made the norm of pastoral theory, and all non-Theocritean pastoralists, especially Vergil, moved as far as possible by redescription in the direction of that norm. It is stated in the final chapter that *both* Theocritus and Vergil are alike in avoiding allegory, in avoiding any form of representation that has designs on the reader. "Neither the poet nor the poem is in the business of therapy, or social adjustment or ideological conversion" (p. 280).

This credo produces, on the one hand, negative evaluations of early Renaissance pastoral, of Petrarch, Boccaccio and Mantuan, for creating "closet poetry, esoteric and inbred, a development . . . which makes a sham of the original mandate of the genre," (p. 274); and, on the other, wishful thinking. The writers of the High Renaissance, according to Rosenmeyer, "went back to the pre-Virgilian writers and discovered Theocritus' combination of detachment and immediacy. Sannazaro, Montemayor, Sidney, even Spenser, yearn for the pure air of pastoral innocence, doctrinal or ideological innocence, that is. In spite of the satire of the church in 'May,' 'July' and 'September,' the pastoral art of the *Calender* is relatively free of the pervasive symbolisms that we associate with the Middle Ages" (p. 273). Wherever ideological innocence may reside, it is not here, in these statements. And if we squeeze firmly in the other direction, by putting less emphasis on the significance of "green" and more on the semantics of "cabinet," we can come closer to the actual texture of the *Calender* as I have described it. "How our Poete is seene," E. K. reminds us, depends on whether the reader is "privie to his study" (p. 466). And the cabinet, in one sense, is Spenser's study, the space filled with books, the place pastoral as he understood it could be written. The *Calender* and its glosses are the record of a

41. Rosenmeyer, *The Green Cabinet*, p. vii.

considerable education. But the second meaning of the cabinet is, surely, that it is "privie," a place of secrets. The function of E. K.'s apparatus is not only to present the English *Eclogue-book* and its producers as "the equal to the learned of other nations" (p. 418), but also to reveal *by failing to reveal* the mysteries of the text. A Modernist reading can take no notice of such strategies, lest attention is drawn thereby to another structure of meaning less innocent of ideological commitment.

But there is a third meaning of "cabinet" relevant to this argument, one conveniently suggested by Puttenham's *Arte*. For in discussing successful relationships between poets and monarchs Puttenham mentioned not only Vergil and Augustus, but how "Frauncis the Frenche king made . . . Clement Marot of his privy Chamber for [his] excellent skill in vulgare . . . Poesie" (p. 16). Here is the cultural space to which any serious poet might aspire, the place of "cabinet councils," though not quite in the Baconian sense. And it is this space which has been most interesting to the criticism that followed Modernism, a criticism which sees pastoral, once again, as primarily a discourse of the relations of power. In the case of Elizabethan pastoral, the leading exponent of this position has been Louis Adrian Montrose, who fastened upon the *Arte of English Poesie* as the key. For Montrose, working out of, but beyond, the Marxist premises of Raymond Williams in *The Country and the City*, the meaning of Elizabethan pastoral begins with the conspicuous irrelevance to it of all genuinely rural or agricultural concerns, despite the fact that statistically England was still a country of sheep-farmers. The result of this exclusion was a striking social and formal paradox, by which "agrarian social relations are inscribed within an ideology of the country but also . . . appropriated, transformed, and reinscribed within an ideology of the court."[42] Connecting Puttenham's emphasis on the "vaile" of pastoral to his peculiarly institutionalized definition of allegory as "the Courtly figure . . . when we speake one thing, and thinke another," Montrose elevated the *Arte of English Poesie* to the status of a complete semantics of power relations in the last quarter of the sixteenth century. And because Elizabeth herself happily embraced the pastoral metaphor as one element of her personal mythography and iconography, and enjoyed such social rituals as the Sudeley entertainment of 1591, which featured shepherd speakers and allusions to Vergil's fourth eclogue, Montrose concluded that "in pastoral forms, Queen Elizabeth

---

42. Louis Adrian Montrose, "Of Gentlemen and Shepherds: The Politics of Elizabethan Pastoral Form," *ELH* 50 (1983), 429.

and her subjects could pursue their mutual courtship subtly and gracefully; they could perform a wide range of symbolic operations upon the network of social relationships at whose center was the sovereign."[43]

From my own perspective, which is certainly no less historically and socially conditioned than any described here, Montrose's position seems considerably nearer the mark than the Modernist one, at least as a description of Elizabethan pastoral in general. Yet the essay from which my last quotation from Montrose was taken is entitled, "'Eliza, Queene of shepheardes,' and the Pastoral of Power," a strategy which makes Spenser's "April" eclogue both the center of the argument and definitive of the *Shepheardes Calender* as a whole. Such a reading, it should now be clear, can be at best only a partial one; and it does in a curious way reinstate the idealism of the earlier twentieth-century criticism, by suggesting that the heart of the *Calender* is a rewriting of the messianic eclogue to the poet's and the monarch's mutual benefit. While it is certainly true that the *Calender*, as the first systematic reinterpretation of Vergil's *Eclogues* in England, has as one of its subjects the poet's power "to create illusions which sanctify political power,"[44] and his natural ambition to be rewarded for doing so, its *other* subject, to which Spenser gave more than equal time, is the poet's responsibility to suggest *latenter* what is wrong with the system, and the dangers he may incur by doing so. Marot's appeal to Pan in his green cabinet was a form of advice to his monarch that drew much of its strength from that statement from Marot's other life, the withheld and only posthumously published *Complaincte* of the poet of exile. It is a tribute to Spenser's intelligence and his courage that he conceived a way to say, as it were, both things at once, to publish the unspeakable criticism alongside the celebration; and although he did not exactly get away with it (spending the rest of his life in cultural exile in Ireland), the product was a text so peculiarly equivocal that even now it remains possible for readers to see in the *Calender* only what they choose.

43. Montrose, "'Eliza, Queene of shepheardes,' and the Pastoral of Power," *English Literary Renaissance* 10 (1980), 154.

44. Montrose, "Eliza, Queene of Sheapheardes," p. 168.

The Hegemonic Theater of George Puttenham

JONATHAN V. CREWE

I N *Homo Ludens,* Johan Huizinga practically dismissed the Renaissance notion of the theater of the world as an effete topos of neoplatonism—as, implicitly, a debilitated metaphysics even in its most worldly guise as political theater.[1] In doing so, he opened the way to his own quasi-anthropological treatment of play as a phenomenon no longer theatrically determined in the first instance. Whatever we may think of the outcome, his restoration of theater to a place *in* the world may prompt us to reconsider the extent to which we, by contrast—even in our most apparently unrelenting analyses of the Elizabethan and Jacobean political scenes—have again become prisoners of the topos. Do we, on one hand, exaggerate the explanatory power of the theatrical metaphor, and on the other effect a totalizing assimilation of the political order to the theatrical one—virtually to that of court theater—and in doing so suppress other categories of political interpretation? Or do we simply lose sight of everything that courtly "theater" fails to include?

If George Puttenham, nominal author of *The Arte of English Poesie* (1589), enables us to pursue such reflections as these, he does so in a very limited and paradoxical way. His own *Arte* testifies as strongly as any document of its time to the intense theatricality of Elizabethan courtly-political life,[2] and hence to the possible constitutiveness of the theatrical "metaphor." Yet Puttenham doesn't lose sight of the phenomenon of theater as one material institution among others in the world. Nor does he evade recognition of what, with glancing reference to the terminol-

---

1. Johan Huizinga, *Homo Ludens* (Boston, 1955) p. 5.
2. This is an aspect of the work extensively explored since Daniel Javitch's seminal *Poetry and Courtliness in Renaissance England* (Princeton, N.J., 1976). See also Louis Adrian Montrose, "Of Gentlemen and Shepherds: The Politics of Elizabethan Pastoral Form," *ELH* 50 (Fall, 1983), 415-60. Montrose correctly suggests that pastoral poetry, which implies a theory of origins other than that governing Puttenham's narrative in general, threatens to disrupt Puttenham's account of generic succession.

ogy of Antonio Gramsci,[3] we might call the hegemonic *necessity* inherent in any enduring situation of political inequality or class antagonism, a necessity by no means fully discharged by public spectacle and the opulent theatricalization of royal power.

To say this is not to claim Puttenham, of all people, as a Gramscian before his time, nor is it to suggest that we will find in Puttenham's work any full-scale anticipation of Gramsci's conception of hegemony. It is only to suggest that Puttenham's account—which is also categorically an account of theater *in* the world—implies a view of theater as a major hegemonic institution of the state; as one more important, in a sense, than the state's formal apparatus of legal, educational and bureaucratic institutions. The arresting implication arising from Puttenham's history of the dramatic forms is that public drama—and hence public theater—alone possesses the ability to institute hegemonic control in a situation otherwise insusceptible to "enlightened" or "lawful" rule, albeit rule in the manifest interests of a ruling *class*.[4] By dramatic, and hence theatrical, means alone can the otherwise ungovernable populace be persuaded to relinquish its own desires, to suppress its antagonism to its self-elected rulers, and to become essentially self-regulating.

Puttenham's discussion of drama is of course only a part (even a small part, though that isn't without significance) of a larger discussion of poetry in the world. This discussion is informed at every point by commonplace Renaissance-neoclassical conceptions of poetic form and function, and the affinities between Puttenham's conceptions and those of Sidney, for example, are obvious.[5] But the value of Puttenham's discussion from my point of view arises from his narrative rearticulation of these commonplaces in such a way as to present a unified theory of cultural politics, and it is in the course of that rearticulation that his conception of an "hegemonic theater" emerges. After attempting a critical rehearsal of Puttenham's exposition, I shall try to suggest some ways in which Puttenham's account may inform if not form our own conceptions.

3. Antonio Gramsci, *Prison Notebooks*, ed. and tr. Quintin Hoare and Geoffrey Nowell Smith (London, 1973), pp. 210-75.

4. To the extent that a political theory informs the *Arte* it is evidently that of broadly monarchical "good government," in which no real distinction exists between political and moral versions of good order. The prompting, however, of Sir Thomas Elyot's *The Boke Named the Gouernour* (1531) is apparent, as no doubt is that of *The Mirrour of Magistrates* (1559). Note in this context Elyot's dictum that the effect of reading tragedies is to make men "execrate and abhor the intollerable life of tyrants." (*Gouernour*, 2 vols., ed. H.H.S. Croft [London, 1883] I, 71.)

5. Some of Puttenham's sources and affinities are traced in *The Arte of English Poesie*, ed.

I

The Arte of English Poesie begins, as readers will recall, by narrating the origin and succession of the poetic genres. This narrative of origin also discloses the logical necessity under which the poetic forms subsist in the world, and is thus capable of being described, albeit erroneously, as an evolutionary narrative by Puttenham's modern editors. As Puttenham conceives them, the poetic forms (such as hymn, epic, or pastoral) are transcendentally founded, and they persist culturally in the context of certain timeless occasions—such as those of heroic action, love, marriage, and death—to each of which a proper decorum corresponds. The dramatic genres, in contrast to the poetic ones, are *politically* instituted from the beginning. The standard dramatic genres, which, for Puttenham, are those of satire [*sic*], comedy and tragedy, originate in typical, successive phases of communal development leading from the most primitive to the most sophisticated of human polities. Not only does a particular dramatic form correspond to each phase of development, but each form arises only in reaction to a radical threat to the maintenance of "good order" in the particular community. By implication, the persistence of any dramatic form is not the result of its ontologically determined necessity, but of the persistence of typical threats to good order. There is thus fundamental difference in the character and status of the poetic and dramatic genres. This difference remains ineffaceable despite Puttenham's attempt to incorporate both within the same history and despite his characterization of authentic dramatic forms as those of dramatic *poesie*, thus bringing them under a general poetics.

For Puttenham, as for many of his humanist contemporaries, "poesie" originates in the creative will and/or inspiring presence of the divine Mind:

A Poet is as much to say as a maker . . . Such as (by way of resemblance and reuerently) we may say of God: who without any trauell [work; movement away from itself into the temporal spacing of *representation*] to his diuine imagination made all the world of nought . . . Euen so the very Poet makes and contriues out of his owne braine, both the verse and matter of his poeme, and not by any foreine copie or example. . . . If they do it by some instinct diuine or naturall, then surely much fauored from aboue (pp. 3-4).

Whether this "poesie" manifests itself as vatic utterance or through the faculty of the poetic "maker," its good origin secures it in its essence throughout its subsequent history. But the same does not apply to drama,

Gladys Doidge Willcock and Alice Walker (Cambridge, 1936). Although cited here, this edition can no longer be considered definitive.

not even in its guise as dramatic poetry. In the beginning, there is no drama. What first constitutes the human polity (if polity is the word for it at this stage) is an essentially pure force of poetic persuasion. Puttenham tells us how it is "fayned," albeit authoritatively, that Amphion and Orpheus were the poets of "the first aige" (p. 6). It is also "written" (by Ovid among others, though Puttenham hardly needs to tell his audience so) that "Poesie was th'originall cause and occasion of the first assemblies, when before the people remained in the woods and mountains, vagrant and dispersed like the wilde beastes, lawlesse and naked . . . " (p. 6). While Amphion "builded vp cities, and reared walles with the stones that came in heapes to the sounde of his harpe," Orpheus instituted civility in the wilderness by his "discreete and wholesome lessons vttered in harmonie with melodious instruments." In the state of civility and humane rule thus established, the poets remained, again by virtue of their God-given faculty, the first systematic observers of the natural order, the first prophets, priests and lawgivers, the first "Philosophers, Astronomers, Historiographers Oratours and Musitians" (p. 8). Neither drama nor theater is yet in evidence, the malign necessity under which both emerge not yet having disclosed itself.

So the familiar story goes in a canonical humanist poetics to the persistent cultural authority of which Rilke among others still testifies in the twentieth century in his "Sonnets to Orpheus." "In the beginning," the poet is the universal man, at once the founder and acknowledged legislator of human society. But what is true in the beginning is implicitly *always* true, and the original condition of human civility remains throughout Puttenham's account the ideal condition, one never to be superseded in the course of time. More than this, it remains the permanent if subsequently *recessive* (unacknowledged?) condition of any community that can lay claim to lawfulness or civility, and the founding poetic priesthood continues, any appearances to the contrary, to retain its prerogatives and functions even when a recognizably political order has supervened.

Immediately after Puttenham's opening exposition, a break threatens to disclose itself in the narrative. It does so when Puttenham has to negotiate the transition from authoritatively "fayned" preliterate antiquity to written history; from the world of the poetic founders to that of political record. The poetic form that Puttenham situates on the threshold between two worlds is the archaic hymn sung by the primitive community to its god(s). This form is before writing; it is also written down rather than written ("always and already") in such poems as the psalms and Homeric hymns. Implicitly, poetry "enters history" without compromising itself, while the archaic poetic theocracy remains, as one might say, proximate to the society of the poetic founders. But the narrative rupture is only briefly postponed, although Puttenham finesses both it and its possible implications.

"Some," writes Puttenham, "perchance would thinke that next after the praise and honoring of the gods, should commence the worshippings and praise of good men" (p. 30), but this step, which might seem to be called for by the logic of poetic development, has to be postponed on account of an unforeseen contingency. What has immediately to be reckoned with, both in the history of literary forms and in the world fashioned by the poetic priesthood, is the unaccountable manifestation of communal "vice" and "idleness."

Even if Puttenham writes as a Christian in a postlapsarian world, and even if a Fall predating the foundation of the poetic community would have been taken for granted by Puttenham's readers (it is explicitly invoked by Thomas Wilson in his *Arte of Rhetorike*),[6] we as readers have been led to suspect no failure or *lack* in the ideal community of the poetic founding fathers. Suddenly, and perhaps catastrophically in both senses of the word, that community is one in which authority is challenged and vice threatens virtue: " . . . before that came to passe [i.e. the praising of famous men], the Poets or Holy Priests, chiefly studied the rebuke of vice, and to carpe at the common abuses, such as were most offensiue to the publique and priuate, for as yet for lacke of good ciuilitie and wholesome doctrines there was greater store of lewde lourdaines then of wise and learned Lords, or of noble and vertuous Princes and gouernors" (p. 30). Here we manifestly enter a new, bad economy, or an economy *per se*, in which a "lacke" of civility produces an unwanted surplus of "lewde lourdaines." This economy of imbalance is also a *political* economy in which distinctions have appeared between the realms of public and private interest and to which the notion of the unitary "commonwealth" no longer seems to apply.

If we can perceive the moment of awkwardness for Puttenham, we can by the same token "appreciate" his finessing of it. He implies that no problem exists except in the mind of a reader capable of being surprised by the mere local contingency of vice or disorder in the ideal poetic commonwealth. For Puttenham, only a minor deviation in the no doubt wrongly expected course of the master-narrative is required to accommodate this contingency. It is, however, in response to *that* contingency,

6. Thomas Wilson, *The Arte of Rhetorike* (1560), facs. ed. G.H. Mair (Oxford, 1909), sig. A8.

and within a bad political economy of lack and surplus, that drama is somewhat inauspiciously born.

Confronted by an unpersuaded and unmollified (unpropertied?) mob, the "priests" invent the first form of dramatic "reprehension," in doing so constituting drama as "reprehensive" in principle. In their attempt to curb "vice," the priests at first devise only the satirical diatribe in "plaine meetres, more like to sermons or preachings then otherwise" (p. 30), but the ineffectiveness—the lack of *authority*—of this form is almost immediately evident. It is in recognition of this lack that a theatrical supplement fatefully gets introduced. "The hallowed places dedicate to their gods," in which the people had assembled "because they had yet no large halles or places of conuenticle" (pp. 30-31) are implicitly transformed into theaters in which the poets—or a new class of functionaries known as "reciters"—can appear masked and amplify the power of the invective:

> . . . the first and most bitter inuective against vice and vicious men, was the Satyre: which to the intent that their bitterness should breede none ill will, either to the Poets, or to the recitours, (which could not haue been chosen if they had been openly knowen) and besides to make their admonitions and reproofs seeme grauer and of more efficacie, they made wise as if the gods of the woods, whom they called *Satyres* or *Siluanes*, should appeare and recite those verses of rebuke, whereas indeed they were but disguised persons vnder the shape of Satyres, as who would say, these terrene and base gods being conuersant with mans affaires and spiers out of all their secret faults (p. 31).

In what is, for Puttenham's narrative, the unacknowledged moment of truly *political* inception, the place of communal devotion in which the people are present to themselves, their fathers, and their gods is transformed into the site of a theatrical masquerade. The moment in which the priests or their surrogates become maskers is also the one in which they decisively alienate themselves as a ruling class from the community, irrevocably politicize their own existence, and substitute the power of theatrical artifice for the primordial authority of the word. The transparency and immediacy of "good government" are simultaneously lost, and representation is inaugurated as misrepresentation.

Theatricality, as well as the originary dramatic form of "satyre," begins in the moment of this fall into politics (the occurrence of which it also signifies) and it remains wholly excluded from the "fayned" condition of true civility. To say now that drama is born as the hegemonic instrument of the ruling caste in Puttenham's account is to draw attention to its unique capacity to induce consent, or at least to institute effective control short of direct violence. The intense hostility of the populace to their self-elected rulers—a hostility that Puttenham attributes to the power of vice—necessitates the use of the mask in the first instance as a means of self-protection, shielding the "reciters" from identification, but the mask is then also found to invest the reproofs of the rulers with a "grauetie" and "efficicie" otherwise unattainable. The impersonation of the "Satyr" invests the players (as well as the puppet-masters) with a supernatural authority to which they cannot presume in their own persons, and it invests the wearers with a semblance of worldly omniscience as "spiers out" of mortal transgressions.

If Puttenham can silently approve the tactics of the rulers, it is partly because of his access to moral categories under which idleness and rebellion are *ipso facto* vicious, and partly because the political order in the process of being constituted—or hegemonically reconstituted—remains contained in its own inferior sphere, its own narrative loop. The entire history of the dramatic forms, and of everything that they imply, is encapsulated within the history of poetic forms, the integrity and magisterial succession of which it is not allowed to disturb. No "other" origin of drama, and hence no radically other way of comprehending the history of literary forms, is acknowledged by Puttenham; no doubt such possibilities are unthinkable by him, although not undreamt of by some of his contemporaries.[7]

Drama thus remains a form of convenience in more ways than one: politically convenient, too, in that certain embarrassments are averted in Puttenham's own history of the poetic forms. Both the poetic persona and the phenomenon of (mis)representation enter the history of "poesie" only by way of the dramatic back door; to the extent that performativeness, deception or even "reprehension" might also manifest themselves in poetry, they would do so only after they had been inaugurated as phenomena of outsidedness and fallen secondarity. They would not be part of the original constitution of the poetic, nor would they ever be of the poetic essence. The integrity of poetic forms, and the integrity of the true civility that they reciprocally guarantee, remains inviolate.

As a form of convenience, drama remains bound, as one might say, to the original sin that elicits it. It remains not only bound to the forms of evil that it combats, but becomes increasingly bound to *represent* the evils

7. It is a commonplace that a demonic theatricality and/or origin of theater is assumed by many Elizabethan antitheatricalists, and is also frequently imagined in Elizabethan drama. Puttenham's rationalization and containment of drama depends on his ability to construe its forms as those of dramatic *poesie*, on his silent disqualification of the "unlawful" forms of native drama, and on his placing of the "primitive" form of tragedy last, not first, in his line of succession.

that it seeks to overcome. As its forms develop beyond that of "satyre" (satire/satyr play) the "good" of drama, unlike that of poetry, comes to consist in its conquest of the evil that is present within it from the start. The defense of drama, which is never capable of embodying ideal forms for emulation,[8] accordingly becomes a more sophisticated undertaking than the defense of poetry, since it must concede the claim of Elizabethan antitheatricalists that drama is an "infectious"[9] staging of vice and promiscuity. Puttenham's implicit defense of drama concedes, in effect, that vice is always the thing represented, but it locates the salutary effect of the representation in an audience-response that becomes predictable and hence capable of being engineered. This response is one in which the audience, far from being seduced by the appeal of staged vice, will imaginatively reconstitute the *law* under which criminal licentiousness remains effectively prohibited.

But this is to anticipate: such sophistications as these are latter-day ones, not foreseen in the phase of "satire." The second phase in dramatic "history" begins when the priesthood recognizes the relative ineffectiveness of satire as a form of control. Drama thus progresses, just as it originates, only when a particular lack has disclosed itself. The section on comedy (in which Puttenham distinguishes between Old and New) is introduced by the heading: "How vice was afterward reproued by two other manner of poems, better reformed then the Satyre, whereof the first was Comedy, and the second Tragedie" (p. 31). It is only after recognition of an insufficiency has occurred that it becomes possible to inaugurate the more sophisticated (better reformed) comedy. Yet this development does not simply occur as a technical adjustment. What renders satire ineffective, and at the same time creates a situation favorable to the emergence of comedy, is an advance in the form of society itself.

No longer does an embattled "priesthood" confront an unruly populace; division of labor manifests itself in the stereotypical characters of comedy that Puttenham enumerates, and a world of trade and industry has silently been inaugurated. (Apparently, too, a parasitic class of petty criminals has also arisen; Puttenham mentions, in addition to legitimate

---

8. This is seen in the iconic poetics of Sidney, for example, in which the image of the epic hero (notably Aeneas) remains constant throughout the endless vicissitudes of the narrative in which he is represented. This image of virtue as perfect constancy (a virtue reaffirmed rather than negated by Aeneas' desertion of Dido) becomes the fixed point toward which epic poetry ostensibly draws the reader.

9. The subtitle of William Rankins' antitheatrical pamphlet, *A mirrour of Monsters* (1589), refers to the "infectious" sight of plays.

"marchants, souldiers [and] artificers," whole classes of "bawds, brokers [and] ruffians" [p. 32].) Perhaps the satyr-hegemony has made this social advance possible, but if so it has rendered itself obsolete. In the newly advanced society that manifests itself, "rebuke, vttered by the rural gods out of bushes and briers" (p. 31) understandably produces little effect. Something more urbane is called for, and the "finer heads" as Puttenham now calls his poet-priest-politicians (or perhaps only an inner cabinet) invent comedy: "The Poets deuised to haue many parts played at once by two or three or foure persons that debated matters of the world . . . but neuer medling with Princes matters nor such high personages." (p. 32). Recognizing not only the inadequacies of the undivided satirical persona and rustic *mise-en-scène*, but also of the reprehensive dramatic monologue as a form (which is "not so popular as if it were reduced into action . . . or by many voices liuely represented" [p. 31]), the plotters of public restraint *devise* comedy as a dialogic and fully representational form, one so naturalistic that "a man might thinke it were euen now a doing" (p. 31). Accompanying the emergence of comedy, pleasure and profit make their first separate appearance among the categories of Puttenham's discussion. The desired *utile* comes paradoxically to depend on *dulce* instead of remaining hopelessly at odds with it: "It was also much for the solace & recreation of the common people by reason of the pageants and shewes" (p. 32).

What has happened is that an irrevocable concession has been made to "popularity"—to the populace, to the "vicious" popular demand for pleasure—and the regulative power of drama must now be detoured through the process of gratification. Yet this concession is highly productive; it not only attenuates an unconquerable antagonism, but allows for far more sophisticated control. The ventriloquism of the rulers is more effectively camouflaged than it can be in the satirical masquerade, and the audience is solicited to engage itself in the issue debated in the onstage dialogue—issues that are of course presented as debatable, but of which the dramatized resolution remains under the control of the "finer heads." Finally, the audience is invited to see its own image(s) rather than those of dubious authority in the ludicrous representations of comedy; the application is left to the audience, as is the internalization of the law and of the forms of "perfection" under which vice remains effectively prohibited.

In the moment in which the audience succumbs to comedy, the hegemonic institution of theater is apparently perfected—yet this appearance is premature, since perfectedness would also imply a termination in the process of social change. What can apparently never be foreseen at any one stage is simply the next stage, the beginning of which will be marked by an unexpected deficiency. The insufficiency of comedy is discovered when, for no apparent reason, certain individuals acquire fame and hence power (forms of excess) beyond the limits of the still implicitly local or organic community; the individual as a new and paradoxical *type* also emerges to supersede the castes and classes that have hitherto been in evidence. This acquisition of individual eminence turns out to be nothing more than a prelude to the indulgence of "lusts and licentiousness" of hitherto unprecedented magnitude—ones manifestly beyond any power of comic containment. The political form of tyranny rather than of popular misrule threatens by the same token to gain possession in place of any "lawful" form of government including that of the priestly caste.

Before considering the tragic response devised to meet this new contingency—one so drastic and disorienting as to threaten the "composure" of Puttenham's narrative of succession—we must recall that the "priesthood" now coexists with a latter-day state apparatus comprising kings, titular lords and governors, and preachers and educators of the professional rather than poetic variety. Indeed, as Puttenham dutifully proclaims, "princes and gouernors of the earth [possess] a souereignty and function next unto the gods" (p. 30), and the poetic priesthood as a now unacknowledged legislature has receded from the forefront. Yet even if the priesthood has effaced itself (been effaced) and the nominal divinity of kings *does* require acknowledgement, the exercise of its hegemony remains compatible with the existence of a legitimate state apparatus. But the rise of the lawless individual to eminence and even "soueraignetie" (p. 30)[10] is perceived as a greater threat to this hegemony than even popular misrule would be. It is as if the dispersed power and desire of the populace were concentrated, and thus rendered effective, in the person of the individual tyrant, a being capable either of living beyond the law or of becoming a law unto himself.

By the logic of Puttenham's argument, it is necessary that this lawless individualism rising to the power of tyranny should fully manifest itself before the dramatic response can be fashioned. So Puttenham rather bleakly acknowledges that during the ascendancy of the tyrant nothing

10. Since sovereignty emerges as the common property of lawful kings and illegitimate tyrants in Puttenham's account, it may seem as if we are always confronting a distinction without a difference. The best gloss of which I am aware on the indistinguishable sovereign/tyrant in Elizabethan political life and drama is Franco Moretti's "The Great Eclipse" in *Signs Taken for Wonders*, tr. Susan Fisher, David Forgacs and David Miller (London, 1983), pp. 42-82.

can be done to restore either civility or legitimacy. The tyrannical individual simply exerts a power beyond the control of any law or hegemonic device. During the reign of the tyrant, the poets themselves are silenced (or implicitly reduced to flattery) while in his "great prosperitee" the tyrant will be "feared and reuerenced in the highest degree" (p. 33). Only posthumously can tyrants' "infamous life and tyrannies" be "layd open to all the world, their wickedness reproached, their follies and extreme insolencies derided, and their miserable ends painted out in playes and pageants" (p. 33). Lacking the power to oppose entrenched tyrannies, the poets can only (and quite literally) re-present the career of the dead tyrant in such a way as to make it exemplary and odious. Tragedy is always thus a "revisionist" portrayal of an ostensibly prosperous career (now a career finished and cast in definitive form by its providential ending) and it always anatomizes (lays open) an evil formerly hidden by good appearances. Tragedy comes after the event of tyranny, and the repetition of tragedy in the theater seeks to forestall the repetition in political reality of tyrannical rule.

Readers familiar with sixteenth-century poetics will not of course be surprised at this iconoclastic treatment of the tragic protagonist—by Puttenham's denial to that figure of any pathos, nobility or serious ability to contest either the decrees of fate or the laws of god. It will also surprise no informed reader that Puttenham is more indebted to medieval "tragic" notions of Fortune's Wheel and the Fall of Princes than to classical conceptions. Even by the standards of his contemporaries, however, Puttenham's account of tragedy may seem reductive. Sidney, for example, includes "wonder" among the appropriate responses to tragedy, and seemingly tries to conceive of tragedy as therapeutic as well as exemplary spectacle. A *pathology* of the tragic protagonist as well as of the spectators is implicit in Sidney's reference to "the high and excellent Tragedy, that openeth the greatest wounds, and showeth forth the ulcers that are covered with tissue."[11] Cauterization vies with anatomization as a possible aim of tragedy, and the recuperability of the patient(s) seems to be envisaged. But in his relentlessly monocular account of tragedy—the form of which remains strictly related to the *function* of demystifying the tyrant—Puttenham conceives of a spectacle that will unequivocally cut the protagonist down to size. No sympathetic appeal, no countercurrents, and no superfluous effects are admitted within the tragic experience.

In presenting his necessarily reductive, consistently functionalist,

11. Sir Philip Sidney, *An Apology for Poetry*, ed. Geoffrey Shepherd (London, 1965), p. 117.

account of tragedy, an account focused exclusively on the tragic protagonist, Puttenham cannot but betray his consciousness of a contest for
power and legitimacy occurring between the idealized ruling caste and
the sovereign tyranny that at once mirrors and opposes it; that is, of a
division and contest for priority *within* the symbiosis of the "ruling class."
Abruptly, the designated audience is no longer necessarily popular,
although the upstart character of the tyrant means that his career is
implicitly open to anyone at all, and a timely warning need not be lost on
any member of the audience. But the critical tradition Puttenham shares
with Sidney, as well as the actuality of Elizabethan playgoing, makes the
sovereign himself (herself) the proper witness of tragedy: "Tragedy . . .
that maketh kings fear to be tyrants, and tyrants manifest their tyrannical
humours" (*Apology*, p. 118).[12]

As the form of last resort and of veiled political contestation within
the "ruling class," however, Puttenham's "tragedy" understandably
lacks the full rationale, corresponding to a transcendent intention, that
can be imputed to comedy in his account. Indeed, Puttenham's account
makes tragedy seem almost like a crude regression to farce, an "evolutionary" throwback unaccountably occurring at the end of the succession. Denied any capacity to excite pity or terror, the protagonist is
exposed and even pilloried before a vulgar audience seemingly afforded
no interpretive latitude about the laws that apply in this case. Yet
countering this movement of degradation, a marked elevation of decorum also occurs: "the Poets stile was also higher and more loftie, the
prouision greater, the place more magnificent" (p. 34) than they had
hitherto been. Paradoxically justified by the bad eminence of the principal character, the entire representation becomes almost literally more
stilted: "These matters of great Princes [*sic*] were played vpon loftie
stages, & the actors thereof ware vpon their legges buskins of leather
called *Cothurni*, and other solemne habits, & for the speciall prehemi-
nence did walke vpon . . . high corked shoes" (p. 34).

Contradictory and even bizarre as this form may appear, one thing
that seems clear is that the demystification of the "tyrant" is accompanied by an elevating mystification of theatrical representation itself; of the
institution that has acquired its own cultural place and relative political
autonomy. Yet even this "positive" development—representing, no
doubt, the developing institutionalization of the public theater in Eliz-

12. Although a conception of English tragic drama as "the defense of the commonwealth" is
suggested by Joyce E. Peterson, for example, in *Curs'd Example: "The Duchess of Malfi" and
Commonweal Tragedy* (Columbia, Mo., 1978), Puttenham's narrative makes perspicuous the fact
that "commonwealth" is a name under which limited interests are served.

abethan England—is not enough, since the tragic performance still cannot be staged at all without revealing the impotence of any *human* law to contain the passion of the tyrant. What apparently has still to be risked in the last resort is the audience's identification with represented unpunishable "lusts and licentiousness" (their own writ large) and hence with the tyrant-sovereign.[13] The very coarseness and violence of the tyrant's exposure seem designed to break this romantic identification, arising from his ability to act out the prohibited grand desires of those who observe him. All that tragedy can do is to capitalize on the end of the tyrant's career and allude to interpretive schemata under which that ending is to be understood as providentially "bad"; it remains for the audience to make the leap of faith that will reaffirm the providential necessity to which the tyrant succumbs, and to which it implicitly remains subject.

II

It goes almost without saying that Puttenham's attempt to tell the whole story of drama in a particular temporal order—whatever its interest in comparison with subsequent attempts, including our own—is a conceptual spacing and hence representation of a single phenomenon (drama) that cannot be "thought" all at once. A comparable spacing of the cultural and political orders is also evident in the *Arte* as a whole. If this attempt is manifestly problematical—or manifestly "ideological"— it also reveals the difficulty of fully rationalizing dramatic forms in which archaic and ritualistic "survivals" remain incorporated: satyr-play, ritual regicide, scapegoating. My point, however, is that the *consistent* claim throughout Puttenham's account of drama is that its function is hegemonic, and what does evolve smoothly in his narrative, emerging finally into prominence in its own right, is the physical institution of theater. Following the "conversion" of rustic places of devotion into impromptu theaters-in-the-round, *ad hoc* "floores" and "scaffolds" emerge as the settings of comedy, while these in turn are superseded by the permanent "loftie stages" and magnificent "place" of tragedy. A progressively evolving institution of theater remains, in Puttenham's account, both the instrument and the sign of effective hegemonic rule. Nothing, it seems, compromises that success.

I began by suggesting that Puttenham restores the perspective of a theater *in* the world, and in doing so going somewhat against the grain of

13. Anxiety about the popularity of a theatricalized monarchy and the corresponding unpopularity of an hegemonic enlightenment is apparent in Rankins' *Mirrour*, as it may be in Puttenham's *Arte*.

our own criticism as well as against that of Elizabethan plays (notably Shakespeare's, of course) in which an attempt is made to think through the implications of imagining that all the world *is* a stage. I also suggested that Puttenham allows us to consider from the outside, so to speak, the character of theater as an institution within the political domain rather than as one encompassing it. Yet the attractions of this approach are not obvious. Puttenham might be called crudely reductive in ways that prevent him from doing justice to English Renaissance drama. A more serious objection concerns Puttenham's qualifications to interpret the Elizabethan theater at all. *The Arte of English Poesie* postdates the establishment of the public theater in 1576, but its own appearance in 1589 makes it virtually coincide with the first performances of Marlowe's work; Puttenham does not therefore write as a witness to the Elizabethan drama that we now designate major; he does not write as a witness to the peculiarly Elizabethan mutant of "revenge tragedy"; he does not write as a witness to the increasingly complicated involvement of the players in court life; and, even more disastrously than the maligned Sidney, he remains a prisoner of his own neoclassical categories in approaching such native or romantic drama as he might have been able to witness. Significantly, Puttenham cannot name a single English dramatist or "dramatic poem" worthy of the name, while even Sidney can acknowledge the propriety of *Gorboduc*. As a commentator before the event on both the dramatic forms and the institution of theater after 1590, Puttenham seems positively to disqualify himself.

Yet the hypothesis offered by Puttenham, in the teeth of the facts to come, is that public or communal theater, insofar as it exists at all as an institution in the world, can *only* function in the hegemonic way I have outlined. While it would not be necessary for that theater to represent any particular form of government as good, it would be bound to the task of representing—and of inviting spectators to participate in the defeat of—threats to the hegemonic *status quo*. The audience is invited not merely to acknowledge but imaginatively to embody the law of which *it* is the ultimate subject. In Puttenham's terms, an unbreakable reciprocity exists between the public institution of theater and the possibility of "good government," and no other theoretical or practical possibility exists for that theater. The consistency and intransigence of this implicit claim constitute its force, and the claim itself might be read as a prophecy of what occurs when, under Jacobean and Caroline rule, an hegemonic public theater is weakened and partly appropriated for the purposes of the sovereign-tyrant.[14] In Puttenham's terms the institution of drama (and of theater) is essentially denatured or radically misconceived in becoming the mirror of a wished-for tyranny, while the hegemonic principle is also fatally betrayed.

From our own standpoint, of course, Puttenham's claim has to be reinterpreted and perhaps "corrected," yet the utility of considering his thesis may be somewhat heightened by the fact that the role of theater in *Elizabethan* society is manifestly at issue in his "history." Although his history moves by implication from "fayned" antiquity by the way of Greece to Rome, it reveals itself in its many anachronisms as a history of the present and future; it also emphasizes the development of the theatrical institution accompanying or subtending the succession of dramatic forms. The three phases of social and dramatic development projected into the past coincide in the present in which Puttenham writes, just as the three dramatic forms—satire, comedy, tragedy— coexist and retain their functions in the stratified society Puttenham inhabits. The point is that the institutional apparatus of the state alone remains, in Puttenham's view, insufficient to establish effective control of a divided society or to hold it together as a community; what is called for, either in fact or in principle, is the powerful hegemonic institution of theater as a political "conventicle." The history of the dramatic forms thus doubles as an explanation of successful rule in general and of an always possible "good government" of the Tudors in particular; the phenomenon of theater as a major public institution carries with it this one inescapable meaning for Puttenham.

No doubt it is possible for us to think otherwise, particularly in a Gramscian framework in which theater might be reconceived (some modern commentators have done so)[15] as a site in which contestation of the dominant ideology is capable of occurring, and in which forms of cultural and political transgression may be staged to subversive effect. Yet in a sense it is *this* claim that Puttenham anticipates and, perhaps heuristically from our standpoint, rewrites as an hegemonic one, implying that such stagings can only, in the last resort, reinstate the law that is transgressed.

14. See Stephen Orgel's *The Illusion of Power* (Berkeley, 1978) for possible confirmation.

15. Jonathan Dollimore, *Radical Tragedy: Religion, Ideology and Power in the Drama of Shakespeare and his Contemporaries* (Chicago, 1984).

Senecan and Vergilian Perspectives in
The Spanish Tragedy

EUGENE D. HILL

I N an article published in 1935, Howard Baker sought to diminish the Senecan influence on Thomas Kyd's *Spanish Tragedy*. Baker's findings have not been generally accepted, but in large measure, I think, they have set the terms of scholarly discussion for almost two generations. Focusing his attention quite properly on the Induction to Kyd's play, Baker chose "to emphasize the Virgilian rather than the Senecan element" of *The Spanish Tragedy*.[1] Oddly, however, Baker thought that Kyd's Vergilian materials came, not from the *Aeneid*, but mainly from metrical tragedies like Sackville's "Induction" in *The mirror for magistrates*. Later scholars have had little difficulty in showing the major influence of Senecan forms and themes in the Induction (and in the play as a whole).[2] But Baker's appeal to the metrical tragedies has, I fear, proved misleading: his paper diverted attention from that very "Vergilian element" to which he sought to alert us. Kyd's use of the *Aeneid*, although noted long ago by Boas,[3] has gone unexplored. No critic has addressed what in my view is the real problem (and the theatrical heart) of Kyd's Induction, and of the play as a whole: the relation between Senecan and Vergilian forms and themes.

---

1. Howard Baker, "Ghosts and Guides: Kyd's *Spanish Tragedy* and the Medieval Tragedy," *Modern Philology*, 33 (1935), 29. Baker incorporated this article into his larger study, *Induction to Tragedy* (Baton Rouge, La., 1939).
2. See Arthur Freeman, *Thomas Kyd: Facts and Problems* (Oxford, 1967), pp. 65–66. For helpful surveys of scholarship on Seneca and English drama, consult Raimund Borgmeier's essay (with full bibliography) on "Die englische Literatur" in *Der Einfluss Senecas auf das europäische Drama,* ed. Eckard Lefèvre (Darmstadt, 1978), pp. 276–323; and Frederick Kiefer, "Seneca's Influence on Elizabethan Tragedy: An Annotated Bibliography," *Research Opportunities in Renaissance Drama,* 21 (1978), 17–34.
3. Frederick S. Boas, ed., *The Works of Thomas Kyd* (Oxford, 1901), pp. xvii–xviii, xxxii.

In reopening the debate on Kyd's classical sources, I am mindful of a warning issued by G. K. Hunter: "The danger of *Quellenforschung* is that it tends to treat as *passive* a situation in which good work is essentially active, creative and to this extent unique."[4] I contend that Thomas Kyd's was such an active intelligence, and that his canny operations on his transmitted sources demand scrutiny if we are to get at his play's Elizabethan significance. To be sure, the study of sources must not be limited to the compilation of parallel passages; such study must expand its purview to include the study of transmission, of how one author's text is rearticulated into another's. For it is from the play of sameness and difference that Kyd generates meaning. What matters most, accordingly, is not the analogy or the genealogy of passages, but the dynamics of passage from one text to another.

My language here may sound out of place to readers for whom Kyd remains the vigorous naif portrayed in much of the scholarship. But I hope to show that Kyd's text plays knowingly with issues of transmission from passage to passage, text to text, language to language. Properly read, *The Spanish Tragedy* evokes, foregrounds, and enacts a *translatio studii*, an historical rearticulation of privileged cultural models. So from readers who hold (with no less gifted a critic of Renaissance drama than Robert Heilman) that *The Spanish Tragedy* is "merely an accumulation of spectacular happenings" with no "coherent pattern of meaning,"[5] I can only beg for a brief suspension of disesteem. Jonson called this playwright "sporting Kyd," and I invite the reader to enter into his play of meaning where the text does—with Seneca and Vergil.

The Spanish Tragedy[6] opens with an Induction: the deceased warrior and lover Don Andrea recounts his search for his proper place in the realm of the dead, a search which takes him first to the three judges (Aeacus, Rhadamanth and Minos), who cannot agree on his due place; then to Pluto and Proserpine; and finally, at Proserpine's bidding, to Revenge, who leads Don Andrea "through the gates of horn" and bids him "see the mystery" unfold in the body of the play. The ascent of a ghost accompanied by a personification allegory represents a schema derived from the Senecan prologue; in the *Thyestes* the ghost of Tantalus

4. G. K. Hunter, "Seneca and the Elizabethans: A Case-study in 'Influence,'" *Shakespeare Survey*, 20 (1967), 18.

5. Robert Heilman, ed., *An Anthology of English Drama Before Shakespeare* (New York, 1962), p. xii.

6. I cite throughout from the Revels edition of *The Spanish Tragedy,* ed. Philip Edwards (1959; London, 1969).

is driven by a Fury to return to earth and goad his descendants to mad and murderous actions. But into this Senecan framework Kyd has fitted Vergilian material: the moral topography of the underworld in Andrea's speech derives from the Sixth book of the *Aeneid*. Like Aeneas, Andrea crosses Avernus, placates Cerberus, goes through a crossroads on his way to the Elysian green, presents something to Proserpine, and passes through a mysterious gate.

Baker rightly notes the differences between Seneca's prologue and Kyd's Induction. The terrified Tantalus knowingly embodies "a family curse of long duration"; only under severe compulsion will he return to his sinful house. But Andrea bears no such burden. An "amazed specta- tor," he only gradually becomes caught up in the stage action. In Baker's view, Andrea is above all "the most curious member of the audience"; he leads and exemplifies the audience's response to the events on stage. And his tone of address in the Induction, unlike Senecan horror, sounds almost jaunty; as Baker rightly says, "Andrea's tale is an astonishing, almost gay, narrative."[7]

In his misguided attempt to minimize the Senecan element of the play, Baker neglects to offer an interpretation that would account for Kyd's divergence from Seneca. Hardly un-Senecan, the Induction transforms Seneca in specifiable and deeply motivated ways. And these will emerge if we stand back for a moment to view the relationship between Kyd's sources for the Induction—a typical Senecan play like the *Thyestes* and the Sixth Book of Vergil's *Aeneid*.

At its peak in the Renaissance, Seneca's reputation plummeted when the Greek tragedians became accessible to a wide readership. Seneca seemed a luridly rhetorical debaser of his Attic models, an author whom only Latinists and the occasional student of Renaissance rhetoric need bother reading. But recent American criticism has restored Seneca to his place as an independent master and enabled us, I think, to see him much as the Elizabethans did, for whom he was the prime exemplar of classical tragedy. As C. J. Herington remarks (speaking of Seneca's *Oedipus*), a Senecan play should be approached as a "Neronian Fantasia on a Theme by Sophocles." His plays are "violent impressionist canvases" which represent moral and political corruption with "the immediate impact of nightmare." "A Senecan tragedy . . . tells what evil feels like to an acutely sensitive mind under abnormally evil conditions." And those conditions were not only elements of a fiction: as Herington reminds us,

7. Baker, "Ghosts and Guides," 32–34.

there are few if any horrors in Seneca's plays that lack analogues in Neronian Rome.[8] Indeed, W. M. Calder argues that Seneca was a "realist," whose "transcendental tyrants" have been rendered credible for us by Hitler and Stalin.[9] Critics like Herington and Calder insist that we misread Seneca if we see him as a mere purveyor of rhetorical horrors; and Thomas Newton made a similar point in his dedicatory preface to *Seneca His Tenne Tragedies* (1581), distinguishing the shocking words and acts in the play from Seneca's virtuous moral teaching ("the dryft, whereunto he leueleth the whole yssue of ech one of his Tragedies").[10] I suspect that Newton and Kyd would have recognized the author whom I would summarize in these words: the master of the anti-tyrant play, Seneca has no peer among classical poets in conveying the texture of evil in a hopelessly corrupt polity. His tragedies typically enact the bursting forth of malign forces (Herington speaks of a Cloud of Evil) from the underworld, forces which, in the course of the play, infest and destroy a royal house.

If in a typical Senecan play hell claims earth and devastates a kingdom, in the Sixth Aeneid an earthling visits the underworld and uses the buried forces (of the personal and racial past, of anger and mourning) to found an enduring kingdom. Bearing with him the Golden Bough—traditionally interpreted as wisdom—Aeneas confronts and overcomes the burdens of the past: the personal, familial and historical past. He buries a forgotten corpse, and solaces the ghosts of a fallen helmsman and a mutilated Trojan. And, having allayed the ghosts of the past, Aeneas is granted insight into the real story in which, up to this middle point of the epic, he has been an uncomprehending and at times reluctant participant. As Servius explains in his commentary (which appeared in most sixteenth-century editions of the *Aeneid*), "These are the causes for which Aeneas descends to the underworld: recognition of his *genus* [origin, race, descendants] and the name of his city, which nobody has predicted to him—only his father makes it known. For the true name of the city lies hidden; wherefore his father says to him as if it were a mystery (*quasi pro*

8. C. J. Herington, "Senecan Tragedy," in *Essays on Classical Literature,* ed. Niall Rudd (Cambridge, Eng., 1972), pp. 195, 196, 208, 196, 178; the essay is reprinted from *Arion,* 5 (1966), 422–71.

9. William M. Calder, "Seneca: Tragedian of Imperial Rome," *The Classical Journal,* 72 (1976), 2.

10. *Seneca His Tenne Tragedies,* ed. Thomas Newton, anno 1581 (1927; Bloomington and London, 1966), p. 5.

mysterio) 'that glorious Rome' (*illa inclita Roma*; VI.781)."[11]

In the Senecan and Vergilian texts, read not as repositories of motifs but as dynamic enactments of patterns of rise and fall, we see the same story running in opposite directions. In Seneca we observe with horror a hell-bent royal house, foundering in corruption. In Vergil we participate with wonderment in a rite of passage which inaugurates a new era of history. In both texts the personal and the historical are inextricably interwoven. And in each, a movement upward provokes a movement downward: the Senecan ascent of the underworld to destroy the present, the Vergilian *descensus* which grounds and enables the Roman future. And this inverted mirroring of Vergilian in Senecan text must be borne in mind if we are to solve the "mystery" embodied in the Induction to Kyd's *Spanish Tragedy*.

In the concluding lines of that Induction, Revenge says, "Here sit we down to see the mystery, / And serve for Chorus in this tragedy." As the editor of the Revels edition notes, "mystery" appears here in "an unusual sense" (p. 8). No critic has explained what the mystery is. William Empson tried: he argued that behind the play lies the unstated fact that the Spanish and Portuguese courts had conspired to effect the murder of Don Andrea, the proud lover of the Spanish princess Bel-Imperia.[12] But if *this* is the play's secret, it seems incomprehensible that at the end of the play Don Andrea gives no sign of having learned it. Nor is the audience in any way let in on this "mystery." Surely Empson was right in thinking that the Induction prepares the audience for some secret, but it must be something that the poet Kyd could rightly hide from his infernal revenant Don Andrea.

The opening lines of Kyd's Induction provoked many parodies over the next decades.[13] To understand why, we must, I suggest, imagine the moment when the actor faced the Elizabethan audience and spoke with pride mingled with perplexity:

> When this eternal substance of my soul
> Did live imprison'd in my wanton flesh,
> Each in their function serving other's need,
> I was a courtier in the Spanish court.

11. My translation of Servius' comment on *Aeneid* V. 737 from *Servianorum in Vergilii Carmina Commentariorum . . . Volumen III,* eds. A. F. Stocker and A. H. Travis (Oxford, 1965), 573.

12. William Empson, "*The Spanish Tragedy,*" in *Elizabethan Drama: Modern Essays in Criticism,* ed. Ralph J. Kaufman (New York, 1961), pp. 60–80.

13. Claude Dudrap, "La 'Tragédie Espagnole' face à la critique élisabéthaine et jacobéenne," in *Dramaturgie et Société,* ed. Jean Jacquot (Paris, 1968), II, 628–30.

> My name was Don Andrea, my descent,
> Though not ignoble, yet inferior far
> To gracious fortunes of my tender youth:
> For there in prime and pride of all my years,
> By duteous service and deserving love,
> In secret I possess'd a worthy dame, (1.1.1–10)

That first line hisses at the audience, and the pious hierarchical formulas of ll. 1–3 ("eternal substance," "wanton flesh") are undermined by the asserted reciprocity of l. 3. The fourth line, delivered with the proper curt stresses on the hard initial *c*'s and a suitably villainous flourish on the adjective, would elicit no little scorn from an English audience in the late 1580s; and the arrogantly false modesty of ll. 5–7 would not raise Andrea in the audience's esteem. In the following lines the Spaniard specifies the kind of "service" he most avidly pursued, slickly sliding from "service" to "deserving" in a sound figure that mimes the speaker's self-regard. And here the remembered pleasures of love provoke Andrea to the first rhyme of the play, a rhyme that draws attention to the "name" of his beloved: Bel-Imperia. What we have here, clearly, is no virtuously mourning ghost, but a slick Spanish Don[14] boasting of his amorous prowess.

With Andrea's character established, Kyd lets him speak of his bewildering experiences in the underworld. "For in the late conflict with Portingale / My valour drew me into danger's mouth, / Till life to death made passage through my wounds" (15–17). Line 17 seems an oddly mannered way of describing a death; but the phrasing introduces the motif of *passage* which will come to dominate the Induction. Charon, Andrea tells us, would not allow his ghost to cross "the flowing stream of Acheron" (19) until Don Horatio had performed the funeral rites— much as Aeneas did for Misenus in *Aeneid* VI. "Then was the ferryman of hell content," Andrea reports, "To pass me over to the slimy strond" (27–28). Pleasing Cerberus, Andrea "pass'd the perils of the foremost porch" (30–31). Next he approaches the judges of Hell "To crave a passport for my wand'ring ghost" (35).

---

14. Compare the language of a contemporary pamphlet, in which the English people are exhorted "to despise those magnificent *Dom Diegos* and *Spanish Cavalieros,* whose doughtiest deedes are bragges and boastinges, and themselves (for the most part) shadowes without substaunce: whose affected *Monarchie,* is like to proove a confounded *Anarchie.*" The passage is from Robert Ashley's dedicatory epistle to his translation (from an anonymous French original) of *A Comparison of the English and Spanish Nation* (1589), sig. A3; I have eliminated the long "s" and normalized the use of u/v. See Virgil B. Heltzel, "Robert Ashley: Elizabethan Man of Letters," *Huntington Library Quarterly,* 10 (1947), 349–63.

But the judges prove little less bewildered than Andrea himself, and Kyd delights in the comedy of their pronouncements:

> But Minos, in graven leaves of lottery,
> Drew forth the manner of my life and death.
> "This Knight," quoth he, "both liv'd and died in love,
> And for his love tried fortune of the wars,
> And by war's fortune lost both love and life."
> "Why then," said Aeacus, "convey him hence,
> To walk with lovers in our fields of love,
> And spend the course of everlasting time
> Under green myrtle trees and cypress shades."
> "No, no," said Rhadamanth, "it were not well
> With loving souls to place a martialist,
> He died in war, and must to martial fields." (36–47)

The prissy pedantry of these judges, finely evoked in the rhythm of lines like 38 and 45, cannot resolve the case. The divisions that the judges invoke somehow fail to fit the particulars of Andrea's life, so they send him on to a higher (in hell, of course, this also means a lower) authority. Minos has a "passport" (54) drawn up that will take Andrea to Pluto's court, on the way to which Andrea pursues Aeneas' path:

> Three ways there were: that on the right-hand side
> Was ready way unto the foresaid fields,
> Where lovers live, and bloody martialists,
> But either sort contain'd within his bounds.
> The left-hand path, declining fearfully,
> Was ready downfall to the deepest hell. (59–64)
>
> 'Twixt these two ways, I trod the middle path,
> Which brought me to the fair Elysian green. (72–73)

Here again we note the oddities of phrasing—the seemingly pointless insistence on division in line 62.

At last Andrea presents his passport to Proserpine—to whom Aeneas had offered the Golden Bough, which had served as his passport through the underworld.

> Here finding Pluto with his Proserpine,
> I show'd my passport humbled on my knee:
> Whereat fair Proserpine began to smile,
> And begg'd that only she might give my doom.
> Pluto was pleas'd and seal'd it with a kiss.
> Forthwith, Revenge, she rounded thee in th'ear,
> And bade thee lead me through the gates of horn,

Where dreams have passage in the silent night.
No sooner had she spoke but we were here,
I wot not how, in twinkling of an eye. (76–85)

Andrea's long speech rightly leads to the lame jangle of "I wot not how,"
for throughout the passage Andrea has been an Aeneas deprived of
insight. Repeatedly Kyd's language here does what Proserpine does: it
teases Andrea with a secret which it refuses to yield up. Like Proserpine's
enigmatic smile, Kyd's text suggests a meaning but veils that meaning, at
least from Andrea.

I have, I trust, established the comic elements of Andrea's speech; no
wonder Renaissance authors delighted in parodying the arrogant Spaniard's words (the surprise is that modern critics have evidently missed the
tone of the scene). Andrea's issueless quest for his proper place in the
underworld, his vain effort "to end the difference," yields him only
deferral. The distinctions he draws, the symmetries he sets up—all fail
him, leaving Andrea in a middle ground without content or definition.[15]

But the unsatisfied Andrea has emerged before us, the audience, and
he has come (as he reports) "through the gates of horn"—the gates of
true dreams. Kyd inverts the concluding action of *Aeneid* VI, in which
Aeneas, in a famously difficult passage, exits from the underworld
through the gates of ivory, the gates of false dreams. And the reversal of
the gates is by no means Kyd's only change here from his Vergilian
source. Indeed, and this is my central contention, Kyd has taken the
Senecan prologue and rewritten it as an *inversion* of Book Six of the
Aeneid. In systematic fashion, Kyd inverts the motifs of Vergil's marvel-
ous *katabasis*. Thus, in place of *pius* Aeneas, who seeks counsel in living his
life and fulfilling his role in history, Kyd gives us proud Andrea, who
seeks his place in the realm of the dead. Aeneas is led into the underworld
by the ever-vigilant Sybil, who hurries him along when he delays;
Andrea is taken from the underworld by Revenge, who falls asleep.
Aeneas learns the glorious destiny of his Trojan line and sees the future
Emperor of Rome; Andrea watches the downfall of the Spanish royal
house, "the whole succeeding hope" of Spain (4.4.203).

---

15. What I want to call the empty center was important to Kyd. As Boas noted long ago (p.
394), in ll. 72–73 of the Induction Kyd modifies his Vergilian source: in *Aeneid* VI. 540–43 there are
two ways, not three—one to Elysium, one to "pitiless Tartarus" (Fairclough's Loeb rendering).
Kyd revises Vergil to produce a structure of ineffectively mediated symmetry. The same
structure holds the center of Andrea's speech (41–53). And cf. in the next scene the dispute over
the captured Prince, which repeats the structure of would-be mediation, even echoing some of
the words of the Induction, e.g. "difference," "doom."

Another of Kyd's revisions of Vergil is particularly telling. At a gateway where the two roads converge, Aeneas presents to Proserpine the Golden Bough; having done so, he is free to enter the Blessed Groves. The Bough is the operator of mediation in the *Aeneid*; both metallic and vegetable-like,[16] it links the two halves of Aeneas' story, Old Troy and New Troy, the dead past and the sprouting future. In many senses it serves, as a modern critic remarks, as Aeneas' "passport" through the underworld.[17] In place of the Golden Bough, Kyd has Andrea present Proserpine with a literal passport; and this provides no aureate insight but literally passes Andrea on, defers him. Again, Kyd offers us inversion: in Vergil the Bough functions as a facilitator of transmission, authorizing an insight-producing movement downward to ground a glorious future; in Kyd the literal passport initiates a bewildered movement upward to observe a foundering present.

Andrea of course understands none of this. Oblivious of the Vergilian linkage of the personal and the political, he takes personally all the events described in the Induction; even the name of the former mistress he recalls with longing (Bel-Imperia—the beauty, the glory of empire) sparks no insight in this counter-Aeneas. Tracking the inversions of Vergil, however, we understand Kyd's "mystery." The secret of *Aeneid* VI—what Anchises (in Servius' words already quoted) tells Aeneas *quasi pro mysterio*—is the name of empire: the people to whom *imperium* is to be transmitted.

The Vergilian material in the Induction to *The Spanish Tragedy* hints at something that can be stated (as we shall see) only indirectly and in passing in the Spanish setting, but that lies at the heart of the play's Elizabethan significance. This is a providential tragedy, one in which Vergilian prophecy counterpoises Senecan horror. And the tragedy is providential in that it is a *Spanish* tragedy that implies an English comedy, the Spanish counter-*Aeneid* hinting at the real Rome-like future of England. The Induction sets Seneca against Vergil to provoke us to juggle with, to articulate, the Senecan and Vergilian futures of the two rival powers. Coming to us through the gates of true dreams, Don Andrea embodies (unbeknownst to him) *our* dreams of Empire—a vision of England's destiny that was already being articulated when Kyd wrote

16. Charles Paul Segal, "*Aeternum per saecula nomen*: The Golden Bough and the Tragedy of History, Part Two," *Arion*, 5 (1966), 39–43.

17. Mario A. Di Cesare, *The Altar and the City: A Reading of Vergil's "Aeneid"* (New York, 1974), p. 102.

the play, probably sometime between 1585 and 1589.[18] The rupture of Andrea's body and soul implies the impending dissolution of the imperial body politic of Spain which expansion-minded English observers were already predicting in Kyd's day.

II

A good part of the history of English foreign policy in Elizabeth's long reign centers upon what R. B. Wernham calls "a remarkable reversal of alliances": as Lord Burghley remarked in 1589, "The state of the world is marvellously changed when we true Englishmen have cause for our own quietness to wish good success to a French King" and the opposite to a King of Spain.[19] The movement that put the long-time allies England and Spain at odds was a gradual one; but if we wish to put a date on the reversal, it would be 1585, when Elizabeth sent an army under the Earl of Leicester to support the rebels in the Low Countries. This step was a serious provocation, much greater than the privateering against their Empire which had long been a sore point with the Spanish. But the plight of the Dutch, weakened by the assassination of the Prince of Orange in 1584, demanded action on the part of the British; if the Dutch collapsed, Spain would emerge as an intercontinental power of menacing proportions. Now accepted as patron by the Catholic League in France, and King of Portugal as well since 1580, Philip of Spain would be free to employ the strong Portuguese fleet against the English. Indeed, as early as March 1579/80 one Englishman warned that "if King Philip have Portugal, with his West Indies and with their East Indies, he might . . . embrace and crush the world: Therefore it behoveth his equals to lame him of one of those arms."[20]

Elizabeth had maneuvered as long as she possibly could to avoid a Continental war, and Burghley too had shown caution. But a group led by Leicester and Walsingham had for years favored vigorous support of

---

18. For a summary of the debate on dating *The Spanish Tragedy*, see Dickie Spurgeon's bibliographical essay on Kyd in *The Predecessors of Shakespeare*, eds. Terence P. Logan and Denzell S. Smith (Lincoln, Neb., 1973), pp. 100–01. (And see *n.* 25 below.)

19. R. B. Wernham, *The Making of Elizabethan Foreign Policy 1558–1603* (Berkeley and Los Angeles, Cal., 1980), p. 1. On political and military history I follow Wernham's book and Wallace T. MacCaffrey, *Queen Elizabeth and the Making of Policy, 1572–1588* (Princeton, 1981).

20. Richard Topclyffe to the Earl of Shrewsbury, 16 March 1579/80; Talbot MSS. F. f. 377. I take the passage from E. M. Tenison, *Elizabethan England*, IV (Royal Leamington Spa, Warwick: Issued for the Author, 1933), 63. Tenison's twelve-volume work, subtitled *the History of this Country "In Relation to all Foreign Princes,"* offers excellent documentation of English views of Spain and Portugal in the 1580s. See especially volume IV, passim.

Continental Protestantism and a veritable crusade against a Spanish King who in their eyes was a tyrant and a Popish tool, if not worse. Thus, looking back years later at the political career of Sir Philip Sidney (d. 1586), Walsingham's son-in-law and a leading proponent of action against Spain, Fulke Greville calls Sidney "our unbelieved Cassandra," who urged a dangerously overcautious Queen to move before it was too late.[21] A good part of Greville's *Life of Sidney* is devoted to the Spanish menace. Now Greville's book (published in 1652, probably written c. 1612) may be suspected of tendentious distortion of events a generation past. So it is particularly welcome that we have a treatise written in 1584 by Richard Hakluyt, an associate of Walsingham and of Ralegh, which makes substantially the same case that Greville makes. This is the *Discourse on Western Planting.*[22] Hakluyt's work is both a careful account of the geopolitical situation of the 1580s and a charter for a British Empire. In whatever year Kyd composed *The Spanish Tragedy,* an aggressive anti-Spanish policy was being propounded by an influential group of courtiers and soldiers. This is obvious for the Armada year of 1588 and thereafter; but Hakluyt's treatise shows the same forces at work before the middle of the decade.

Hakluyt's position can be summarized in this way:

Basing England's prior claim on the Cabots' work, Hakluyt argued that it was England's duty to bring the glories of civilization and Christianity to North America. Strategically, English settlements would be of great value as bases of operation against Spanish and Portuguese fishing fleets on the Newfoundland banks and especially against the treasure fleets of Spain in the West Indies. By hitting at Spain in the New World and at the source of her wealth, the English could overthrow her empire and relieve England and Europe of Spanish intimidation. Furthermore, England would acquire from her settlements products which she could not herself produce and which she had at present to import from the Continent; her trade could thus be free from many tariffs and taxes. In addition, the colonists and Indians would furnish a lively market for manufactured commodities.[23]

What especially concerns us is the tone of voice Hakluyt adopts: he has many fine ways of sneering at Spain. For example, he asserts that, if England pursues the course of action propounded in the *Discourse,*

---

21. *Sir Fulke Greville's Life of Sir Philip Sidney,* ed. Nowell Smith (Oxford, 1907), p. 115.

22. Composed at Ralegh's request in the summer of 1584 and presented to the Queen later that year, the *Discourse on Western Planting* did not reach print for almost three hundred years. References in my text are to the *editio princeps,* published as volume II of the *Documentary History of the State of Maine,* ed. Charles Deane (Cambridge, Mass., 1877). For the connections between Hakluyt and Ralegh, see the Introduction by Leonard Woods.

23. Willard M. Wallace, *Sir Walter Raleigh* (Princeton, 1959), p. 37.

no doubte but the Spanishe empire falles to the grounde, and the Spanishe kinge shall be lefte bare as Aesops proude crowe; the peacocke, the perot, the pye, and the popingey, and every other birde havinge taken home from him his gorgeous fethers, he will, in shorte space, become a laughinge stocke for all the worlde; with such a mayme to the Pope and to that side, as never hapned to the sea of Rome by the practise of the late Kinge of famous memory, her Majesties father, or by all the former practises of all the Protestant princes of Germanie, or by any other advise layde down by Monsieur de Aldegond, here after by them to be put in execution. If you touche him in the Indies, you touche the apple of his eye; for take away his treasure, which is *neruus belli,* and which he hath almoste oute of his West Indies, his olde bandes of souldiers will soone be dissolved, his purposes defeated, his power and strengthe diminished, his pride abated, and his tyranie utterly suppressed. (p. 59)

Similarly, Hakluyt takes pleasure in

comparinge the Spaniardes unto a drone, or an emptie vessell, which when it is smitten upon yeldeth a great and terrible sounde, and that afarr of; but come nere and looke into them, there ys nothinge in them; or rather like unto the asse which wrapte himselfe in a lyons skynne, and marched farr of to strike terror into the hartes of the other beastes, but when the foxe drewe nere he perceaved his longe eares, and made him a jeste unto all the beastes of the forrest. In like manner wee (upon perill of my life) shall make the Spaniarde ridiculous to all Europe, if with percinge eyes wee see into his contemptible weakenes in the West Indies, and with true stile painte hym oute *ad vivum* unto the worlde in his fainte colours. (p. 69)

Hakluyt also calls upon history to guy the Spaniards: "surely the more I thinke of the Spanishe monarchie, the more me thinketh it is like the empire of Alexander the Greate, which grewe upp sooddenly, and sooddenly upon his deathe was rente and dissolved for fault of lawfull yssue. In like manner the Kinge of Spaine" will by his death provoke the collapse of his Empire (pp. 80–81). For "ys it not likely," Hakluyt asks, "that every province will seke their libertie? And, to say the truthe, what nation, I pray you, of all Christendome loveth the Spaniarde, the scourge of the world,[24] but from the teethe forwarde, and for advauntage?" (p. 81). Hakluyt has one nation in particular in mind: "The poore oppressed prince and people of Portingale doe watche nighte and day when to finde a convenient occasion of defection" (p. 82).[25] Evidently, the union of the

24. This view (which modern historians have come to call the Black Legend) of Spain and the Spaniards as the scourge of history arose in the sixteenth century and was familiar throughout the Western world. See Charles Gibson, ed., *The Black Legend* (New York, 1971) and William S. Maltby, *The Black Legend in England* (Durham, N.C., 1971).

25. Hakluyt's evident sympathy for the Portuguese typifies English sentiment for most of the decade. But things changed rapidly in mid-1589 when the Portuguese failed to rise (as they had

two Iberian kingdoms cannot long endure, as is true in *The Spanish Tragedy*.

Hakluyt's humor is at its broadest when (in the longest chapter of the *Discourse*) he attacks the attempt on the part of the Spanish and Portuguese to divide, by treaty and papal action, the New World between them. Looking back to 1493/94 and the Pontificate of Alexander VI, Hakluyt asks,

Why, then, doth the Pope, that woulde be Christes servaunte, take upon him the devision of so many kingdomes of the worlde? If he had but remembred that which he hath inserted in the ende of his owne Bull, to witt, that God is the disposer and distributer of kingdomes and empires, he woulde never have taken upon him the devidinge of them with his line of partition from one ende of the heavens to the other. The historie of the poore boye whome God stirred upp to confounde and deride the Spaniardes and Portingales, when they were devidinge the worlde betwene themselves alone, is so well knowen as I nede not stande to repeate it. But it is the Popes manner alwayes to meddle. (p. 130)

The reader's appetite thus whetted, Hakluyt will, of course, retell the good story (however familiar) a few pages later. When the Pope made

his generall and universall donation of all the West Indies to the Kinges of Spaine, by drawinge a lyne of partition from one pole unto another, passinge a hundred leagues westwarde of the Iles of Azores; which division, howe God caused to be deryded by the mouthe of a poor, simple childe, Fraunces Lopez de Gomera, one of the Spaniardes owne historiographers, dothe specially note in manner following: Before I finishe this chapter (saieth he), I will recite, to recreate the reader, that which happened, upon this partition, to the Portingales. As Fraunces de Melo, Diego Lopes of Sequeria, and others, came to this assembly, and passed the river by Quidiana, a little infant that kepte his

---

promised to) in support of Drake's mission to reestablish King António at Lisbon. As H. V. Livermore writes in *A New History of Portugal* (Cambridge, Eng., 1966; rpt. 1969), "António's supporters were cowed by a few acts of terrorism, and gave no response as [Drake] approached" (p. 165). The English view of this abortive expedition is clear from *A true coppie of a discourse written by a gentleman, employed in the late voyage of Spaine and Portingale* (1589), an anonymous work which Hakluyt (reprinting it in his *Voyages,* 1599) attributed to Anthony Wingfield (consult the DNB entry). Defending the English generals' conduct of the Iberian expedition, the gentleman author bitterly laments the cowardice and "infidelitie" of the Portuguese: "what Countrey living in slaverie under a stranger whom they naturally hate: having an Armie in the Field to fight for them & their libertie, would lie still with the yoke upon their neckes, attending if anie strangers would unburthen them, without so much as rousing themselves under it but they"? (p. 38; spelling normalized). In Kyd's play I find a comparable stress on Portuguese weakness: the first time we see him (1.3) the Portuguese King falls to the ground and removes his crown; and one of the play's running jokes is the habit the Portuguese Prince has of getting lost in his own verbiage. I am, accordingly, inclined to date *The Spanish Tragedy* no earlier than mid-1589; but my interpretation of the play does not depend upon this argument for a late date.

mothers clothes, which she had washt and honge abroade to drye, demaunded of them, whether they were those that shoulde come to devide the worlde with the Emperour; and as they answered yea, he tooke up his shirte behinde and shewed them his buttocks, sayenge unto them: Drawe your lyne throughe the middest of this place. This, saieth the author, was published in contempte all abroade, bothe in the town of Badayos and also in the assemblye of these committies. The Portingales were greately angrie therewith-all, but the rest turned yt to a jest and laughed yt oute.

But what wise man seeth not that God by that childe laughed them to scorne, and made them ridiculous and their partition in the eyes of the worlde and in their owne consciences, and caused the childe to reprove them, even as the dombe beaste, speakinge with mans voyce, reproved the foolishnes of Balam the Prophett! (pp. 141–42)

The vain partitions that pervade Kyd's Induction have, it would appear, their historic point to make—the very one that Hakluyt asserts toward the end of his chapter on the Donation:

God that sitteth in heaven laugheth them and their partitions to scorne, and he will abase and bringe downe their proude lookes, and humble their faces to the duste; yea, he will make them, at his goodd time and pleasure, to confesse that the earthe was not made for them onely; as he hath already shewed unto the Portingales, which, not longe since, takinge upon them to devide the worlde with lynes, doe nowe beholde the line of Gods juste judgemente drawen over themselves and their owne kingdome and posses-sions. And nowe, no doubte, many of them remember that the threateninge of the prophet hath taken holde upon them, whoe pronounceth an heavie woe against all such as spoile, because they themselves shall at length be spoiled. (p. 150)

Although Hakluyt's text was not printed until the nineteenth century, there can be no doubt that it speaks for a significant body of advanced Elizabethan opinion on the most pressing issue of the day. With the vigor and clarity of an adept pamphleteer, Hakluyt defines for us the thematic core of *The Spanish Tragedy,* which the playwright, with Spenserian canniness, has veiled in a "mystery," a poetic fiction that demands interpretation. Like Hakluyt, Kyd presents a Spain too arrogant to note that it is ripe for downfall—due to be replaced as a leading imperial power by the lowly English.

But one other current of thought must be adduced before we return to the play. If Hakluyt expounds the geopolitics of Empire, there was no shortage of comment on the political symbols of Tudor Empire. And that strand of thought, too, underlies a play much of whose intrigue deals with the question, Who shall possess Bel-Imperia, the glory of empire?

The Imperialist elements of Elizabethan thought have been brought to prominence by the late Frances Yates. In the essays collected under the title *Astraea: The Imperial Theme in the Sixteenth Century* (1975), Yates showed how commonly the monarchies of the period adapted the universalist ideology of Empire to their particular national purposes. Thus Henry VIII's Act of Restraint of Appeals (1533) opened with the phrase "This Realm of England is an Empire." The formula was a familiar medieval one (*rex in regno suo est imperator*) based on late Roman law, but the use to which the phrase is put is sharply new: Henry is claiming to wield the Constantinean power of the Roman Emperor over the governance of the Church. Henry had for years shown interest in the notion of *imperium,* as Richard Koebner demonstrates in an important article; but it was the break with Rome which provoked him to apply "this interest . . . originated in dreams of self-glorification . . . to avert religious misgivings which Henry's revolutionary step might arouse in his catholic subjects."[26]

Henry's imperial claims survived even Mary's reign,[27] and they were revived and systematized under Elizabeth. The English viewed themselves as New Romans; London, like Rome, was a New Troy. As Frank Kermode crisply summarizes Yates' findings, "The Empire was founded in Troy, and the Tudor dynasty partook of it from the beginning. The *renovatio* of English Church and Empire found its Eusebius in Foxe, its Virgil in Spenser." And Elizabeth's "artist-propagandists, beneficiaries of the *translatio studii* which accompanied the renovation, took every opportunity to domesticate the *imperium.*"[28] Indeed, the very phrase "British Empire" first appears in the late 1570s, from the pen of John Dee.[29] And a decade later, "the first vital tragedy in our language"[30]—as Schelling properly labels Kyd's masterwork—adopted this notion that the English were the New Romans as the figure in its carpet, the "mystery" of its Induction.

III

Before summarizing my argument, I want to comment briefly on some passages and scenes from the body of Kyd's play to show how they

---

26. Richard Koebner, "'The Imperial Crown of this Realm': Henry VIII, Constantine the Great, and Polydore Vergil," *Bulletin of the Institute of Historical Research,* 26 (1953), 42. See also Walter Ullmann, "'This Realm of England is an Empire,'" *Journal of Ecclesiastical History,* 30 (1979), 175–203. For a general treatment of British imperial thought and its sources, consult the opening chapters of Koebner's book *Empire* (1961; New York, 1965).

27. Koebner, "Imperial Crown," 48.

28. Frank Kermode, *The Classic* (New York, 1975), p. 58.

29. Koebner, "Imperial Crown," 50n.

30. Felix E. Schelling, *Foreign Influences in Elizabethan Plays* (New York, 1923), pp. 16–17.

fit into, and contribute to, the interpretation advanced in this essay. I also want to refer to some of the stronger critical essays to date on *The Spanish Tragedy* to show how they, too, fit into the present argument; I do so not in the spirit that Richard Levin aptly mocked with the formulation "My Theme Can Lick Your Theme,"[31] but in the hope of synthesizing some valuable work that has appeared in the last half-generation.

Scholarship has not located a source for the main action of *The Spanish Tragedy,*[32] and critics have often seen it as a melodramatic succession of plots and murders in which Kyd "has no purpose much deeper than making our hair stand on end."[33] But in view of the Induction as we now understand it, as a counter-*Aeneid,* the body of the play takes on a different light. The ghosts that return to watch the earthly action, the corpses that litter the stage, demanding vengeance: these are not merely the devices of "Senecan" horror. They are motifs from Book Six of the *Aeneid*: Hieronimo, like Aeneas before he reaches Elysium and his prophetic father, is confronted by the dead, who solicit burial and vengeance. But, unlike Aeneas, Hieronimo cannot find a passport to knowledge and action. Like Andrea in the Induction, Hieronimo is arrested in his passage toward a future he cannot grasp. He is tormented by the unburied and unavenged corpse of his murdered son Don Horatio—as Aeneas is troubled by the unburied Palinurus and the unavenged Deiphobus.

Hieronimo's soliloquies are forced out of him by the horror of stasis; the heavens, he laments, yield no passage to his words, no guide to his action. Thus Pedringano is executed for murder, and the Deputy commands: "let his body be unburied. / Let not the earth be choked or infect / With that which heaven contemns and men neglect" (3.6.106–08). And with these words the executioners leave the corpse on stage, and Hieronimo enters, complaining of how *he* has been contemned and neglected (the staging here brilliantly identifies Hieronimo with the corpse):

> Where shall I run to breathe abroad my woes,
> My woes, whose weight hath wearied the earth?
> Or mine exclaims, that have surcharg'd the air
> With ceaseless plaints for my deceased son?

31. Richard Levin, *New Readings vs. Old Plays* (Chicago, Ill., 1979), p. 28.
32. See Edwards ed., pp. xlviii–xlix.
33. The phrase is Gāmiṅi Salgādo's in the Introduction to his Penguin *Three Jacobean Tragedies* (Harmondsworth, Eng., 1965), p. 13.

The blust'ring winds, conspiring with my words,
At my lament have mov'd the leaveless trees,
Disrob'd the meadows of their flower'd green,
Made mountains marsh with spring-tides of my tears,
And broken through the brazen gates of hell.
Yet still tormented is my tortur'd soul
With broken sighs and restless passions,
That winged mount, and, hovering in the air,
Beat at the windows of the brightest heavens,
Soliciting for justice and Revenge:
But they are plac'd in those empyreal[34] heights
Where, countermur'd with walls of diamond,
I find the place impregnable, and they
Resist my woes, and give my words no way. (3.7.1–18)

This is what happens to Hieronimo repeatedly in the play: passage arrested yields passion. And when passion becomes excessive it turns to murderous rage. What Hieronimo says of the killer Pedringano a minute or two before the soliloquy will soon be true of him:

O monstrous times, where murder's set so light,
And where the soul, that should be shrin'd in heaven,
Solely delights in interdicted things,
Still wand'ring in the thorny passages
That intercepts itself of happiness. (3.6.90–94)

Lost in these "thorny passages," Hieronimo, like most of the characters of the tragedy, becomes prey to—or an avatar of—Senecan horror. Kyd's counter-*Aeneid* releases and authorizes all the blood-curdling horrors of Roman tragedy. But here they are not simply the moralistic formulae of earlier rhetorical Tudor tragedy. Kyd's play shows uncommon insight into the nature of Senecan drama, which enacts the eruption of infernal passions into the world of men. Seneca's tragedies repeatedly break the boundary between the underworld and the world of man: they give passion its way, its passport. And they do so, not merely to revel in horror, but to make a political point: the nightmarish inferno of Senecan tragedy cunningly reflects the doomed Neronic tyranny in which the playwright lived. Using his parodic Vergilian framework and identifying Seneca's nightmarish realm of political tragedy with the Spain of the

---

34. It is worth noting that "empyreal" is Schick's conjecture (1892). The early editions read "imperiall."

Black Legend, Kyd has made the *energies* and the *implications* of Senecan tragedy available to the English popular stage.

But in *The Spanish Tragedy* Senecan energy is always qualified by the ironic perspective of Vergilian prophecy. Not only Hieronimo, but all of Kyd's characters act in ignorance of their place in the movement of history—not least Andrea, who is given what seems to him a privileged position to follow the play's action. He is, however, privy only to the Senecan element and entirely misses the Vergilian. That is available to the audience in a number of ways.

Consider, for example, the penultimate scene of Act One, in which the Portuguese Prince and Ambassador and the Spanish King and his court celebrate the overcoming of the opposition between their two countries. "Spain is Portugal, / And Portugal is Spain" (1.4.132–33), says the King, who calls upon Hieronimo "To grace our banquet with some pompous jest" (137). In a dumb show three Knights capture three Kings. The Spanish King asks Hieronimo for an explanation of the "mystery," echoing a term from the end of the Induction. Hieronimo identifies the three Knights as three Englishmen, and the three Kings as two Portuguese and a Spaniard. The King and the Ambassador interpret the "pompous jest" as a reminder of the need for humility, since both states have been "Enforc'd . . . / To bear the yoke of the English monarchy" (145–46). The party then proceed with their drinking.

The illogic of the Spanish King's explanation is patent, although it goes unremarked amid the carousing. England has compelled one Portuguese King "To bear the yoke of the English monarchy" and captured, on another occasion, a second "King of Portingale"; the English have also taken a King of Spain prisoner; *therefore* (!) the Portuguese should be less discomforted by their loss to the Spaniards, while the Spaniards should not boast too much. The King's fatuous misreading of the dumb show serves as a warning to Kyd's audience. For the Spanish King, "little England" (as he calls it; 1.4.160) is peripheral to the meaning of the dumb show; but for the English audience it is the central agent of the dumb show—and of *The Spanish Tragedy* as a whole. The three captive Kings of the dumb show—which recall the three paths and three judges of the Induction—represent two countries (Portugal and Spain), but one fate: submission to English power. Hieronimo with his playlet reminds the onstage audience of past defeats at the hand of (as it happens) the English; Kyd with that same playlet hints at the return of English dominance. For the true mediator between Spain and Portugal will be England, "little

England," which will humble them both.[35]

For, as the play shows us, neither the Spanish nor the Portuguese suitor will possess Bel-Imperia on earth. Rather, what that somewhat tarnished Spanish virgin (see 2.3.43) represents—the glory of Empire—will be transmitted to another and truer imperial virgin. I mean to Elizabeth, who from captive Princess (the parallel with Bel-Imperia's plight is, I think, intended) had become an adept juggler of suitors, a skillful wielder of Empire. Elizabeth will rule on an island at the end of the world, an island which her countrymen—following an ancient tradition—identified with the Elysian Fields.[36] And that, of course, was the destination of Aeneas, which he reaches at the center of Vergil's poem. The depths of Kydian implication here are Spenserian indeed.

---

35. The dumb show of 1.4 offers a good example of what Sacvan Bercovitch in an excellent article ("Love and Strife in Kyd's *Spanish Tragedy,*" *Studies in English Literature,* 9 [1969], 215–29) sees as the play's central theme: the Empedoclean conflict of love and strife. Hieronimo uses the dumb show of warfare to enact the loving union of Spain and Portugal, and Bercovitch shows how much of the play can be interpreted in terms of love and strife. But the philosophical notion that Bercovitch finds in Kyd and attributes to Empedocles—the claim that all things exist by the interplay of contraries—could derive from other sources; thus Louis le Roy in his *De la vicissitude ou variété des choses en l'univers* (1575; I cite from a 1584 Paris reprint) adduces in this connection Heraclitus, Homer and Plato, as well as Empedocles (fol. 10–12v). Second, by pressing the case for his pre-Socratic source, Bercovitch misses the contemporary political import of Kyd's dialectic of contraries. Sixteenth-century political writers saw the hand of providence in the reciprocal interchange of political ascendancy between states established (in their view) by God as contraries. Philippe de Commynes argues this position in Book V of his *Mémoires,* citing, for example, Venice and Florence, Spain and Portugal. Le Roy, too, asserts that like everything else in the universe, politics rests upon the interplay, the concordant discord, of opposites. God wants the world, Le Roy writes, to be "temperé par changemens alternatifs, & maintenu par contraires" (fol. 1). So too in politics, Le Roy argues: all rests on opposites, of which he cites examples ancient (Romans and Carthaginians, for example) and modern (English and French—this is from the 1570s; French and Italians, etc.); see Le Roy, fol. 12. On Le Roy see Werner L. Gundersheimer, *The Life and Works of Louis le Roy* (Geneva, 1966), esp. pp. 96–97 and 104–07; and G. W. Trompf, *The Idea of Historical Recurrence in Western Thought* (Berkeley and Los Angeles, Cal., 1979), pp. 280–81 and passim. Trompf discusses theories of beneficial rivalry in the Renaissance; see esp. p. 290, from which I have borrowed the above reference to Commynes. Trompf explains why Commynes held that "God had provided each ruler and state with 'its contrary' (*Mém.* V, 18, 19)." "On his reading of historical tendencies, men are continually inclined to do violence to each other, so that God provides constraints through both his retributive justice and the contraries, the presence of these reciprocal principles being illustrated by the events of European history. . . . Although the ancient Greek idea of change into contraries may have influenced Commynes' position, he nevertheless modified that idea quite radically and integrated it with Christian providentialism" (pp. 290–91).

36. See Josephine Waters Bennett, "Britain among the Fortunate Isles," *Studies in Philology* 53 (1956), 121, 124.

IV

Having looked so closely at the opening scene of Act One, we should not leave unexamined the brief scene that concludes the Act. Revenge and Andrea step forward to center stage, and Andrea voices his outrage at what he has just witnessed:

> Come we for this from depth of underground,
> To see him feast that gave me my death's wound?
> These pleasant sights are sorrow to my soul,
> Nothing but league, and love, and banqueting!
>
> (1.5.1–4)

Here Andrea echoes a motif of Senecan tragedy, in which infernal revenants ask, "Have I come back on earth for *this*?," the very opposite of what I desired to see (cf. *Hippolytus*, l. 1213: "In hoc redimus?"). Revenge calms Andrea by promising to destroy the happiness of the Spanish and the Portuguese. The audience shares Andrea's distaste for the fatuous complacency of the banqueters, but they will have noticed what both the Portuguese and·the Spaniards (including Don Andrea) miss, that England will be the true Revenger.[37]

Another passage that would have carried a deeper meaning for Kyd's audience than for his characters comes, significantly, at the very center of the play.[38] I refer to the business with the empty box, a motif whose sources have been studied by Frank Ardolino in a valuable recent article.

---

37. Ronald Broude has commented perceptively on connections between Kyd's play as a revenge tragedy and the providential comeuppance which the British saw themselves administering to the supposedly depraved Spaniards. It is no coincidence that "in 1588 the flagship of the force led by Drake against the Armada was named the *Revenge*"; see "*Vindicta Filia Temporis*: Three English Forerunners of the Elizabethan Revenge Play," *Journal of English and Germanic Philology* 72 (1973), 502; and the same author's "Time, Truth and Right in *The Spanish Tragedy*," *Studies in Philology* 68 (1971), 130–45. Broude neglects to discuss the Induction, so he misses a good deal of the wit and poetic cunning of Kyd's fiction. A similar failing mars another of the best studies of the play, S. F. Johnson's "*The Spanish Tragedy*, or Babylon Revisited," in *Essays on Shakespeare and Elizabethan Drama*, ed. Richard Hosley (1962; London, 1963), 23–36. Johnson keenly notes elements in the play that foreshadow the fall of Spain, such elements as the garden that Hieronimo's wife destroys and the polylingual, Babel-like playlet. But Johnson misreads the tone of Kyd's work: he can even write that "Hieronimo has created in Spain a situation like that of Elizabethan England: the nation has an aging sovereign, but that sovereign has no direct heir, and the question of the succession is cause for real anxiety" (p. 36).

38. "Enter *Boy* with the Boxe." is line 1440 of the Malone Society Facsimile of the 1592 quarto, eds. W. W. Greg and D. Nichol Smith (Oxford, 1948); and the box is discussed by Pedringano and the Hangman in lines 1529–42. The play has a total of 2967 lines.

Pedringano (the name, Ardolino notes, can mean "the wandering or morally errant one")[39] jests himself to death, relying all the while on the empty box to which the mugging juvenile points with the broadest of comic gestures. The boy has shared his secret with the audience in the only extended prose passage in the play (3.5, the fifteenth of thirty scenes in the—to be sure, modern—division of the play). Hardly able to repress his chuckling, the boy expounds the horrible comedy of the scene he is about to play through:

> I cannot choose but smile to think how the villain will flout the gallows, scorn the audience, and descant on the hangman, and all presuming of his pardon from hence. Will't not be an odd jest, for me to stand and grace every jest he makes, pointing my finger at this box, as who would say, "Mock on, here's thy warrant." Is't not a scurvy jest, that a man should jest himself to death? Alas, poor Pedringano, I am in a sort sorry for thee, but if I should be hanged with thee, I cannot weep. (3.5.13–19)

For a moment we seem to be in a different play: the vigorous prose here has the rhythms of Elizabethan coney-catching, not of what Hieronimo will call "stately-written tragedy, / *Tragedia cothurnata*" (4.1.159–60). But, as in a Shakespeare play, the comic prose literalizes and makes more explicit the poet's major theme. For the central passage of Kyd's play defines, I suggest, our attitude toward all the Iberian courtiers—whose hopes (Kyd implies) have as little substance as Pedringano's. The Spaniards' triumphal center is an empty box.

Several disputed elements of the play's final act carry the same implication. Hieronimo—whose name is that of the greatest of transmitters, of passage-makers, Jerome—finds a way to make tragedy live again. Hieronimo's heretofore "fruitless poetry" (4.1.72) can now serve for "the passing of the first night's sport" (64), and Hieronimo promises that "it will prove most passing strange" (84). The polyglot playlet—Hieronimo promises Latin, Greek, Italian and French—is of course actually given in English. Critics who have worried about what they take to be an anomaly have, I fear, missed the point: the medium (English) here is the message. The playlet is an enacted pun on translation in different senses and different media. The real "passing" involved is the *translatio imperii*—to England, to English. That is the *translation* that matters to Kyd.

So too with the celebrated autoglossotomy, in which, again, Kyd plays with different registers and channels of communication, at once to

---

39. Frank Ardolino, "The Hangman's Noose and the Empty Box: Kyd's Use of Dramatic and Mythological Sources in *The Spanish Tragedy* (3.4–7)," *Renaissance Quarterly* 30 (1977), 339.

conceal and reveal his point. Hieronimo bites out his tongue rather than reveal a secret, although critics cannot agree on what secret he can retain, having told the royal audience everything he knows. Here again, as with the "mystery" of the Induction, Kyd is playing with the problematics of transmission. Hieronimo cannot speak what he does not know, so Kyd switches the medium here and effects a further metonymic conversion. Without a voice, Hieronimo can use a pen, and with the penknife he stabs the Duke and himself, taking with him into death "the whole succeeding hope / That Spain expected after my decease" (4.4.203–04), as the Spanish King laments. And that Spanish hopelessness is (unbeknownst to him) the point of Hieronimo's insane actions.

The play concludes as it began, with an exchange between Andrea and Revenge. And if the opening of the play dealt with problematic partitions, the conclusion offers clear-cut substitutions: Andrea replaces the tortured villains of mythology with his own enemies ("Place Don Lorenzo on Ixion's wheel"). The *topos* is a familiar one from Senecan tragedy (see *Medea,* 740ff.; *Hippolytus,* 1229ff.). But Andrea, still reading everything personally, misses the real substitution that has dominated Kyd's play from its tantalizing Induction to its "passing strange" conclusion, the emergence of England as the New Empire. For in the Senecan framework of the drama, the "endless tragedy" (the last words of the play) to which Andrea would condemn his enemies represents the impending decline of Spain and rise of England on the next cycle of history; and in the Vergilian framework the emergence of an enduring tragic drama which will celebrate that Empire.

V

My argument has been this. Far from being a naive potboiler, *The Spanish Tragedy* is a deeply self-conscious work, one of whose major concerns is with the problematic passage between Senecan and modern tragedy. Dilemmas of transition dominate the play from the opening scene, in which the image of the "passport" is so oddly stressed. And while the Induction introduces Seneca's notion of tragedy as the passage of passion on its obstructed path to infernal vengeance, it also presents Vergilian material that places the Senecan elements in an ironic light. Kyd's borrowings from and transformations of Vergil's Sixth Aeneid systematically define Andrea's voyage as the inverse of Aeneas'; thus the Vergilian material hints to the audience at something none of the characters is able to see: the transmission of Empire can happen again. It is "little England" that will *debellare superbos.*

Correct appraisal of Kyd's use of Vergil to unlock (as it were) the emotional riches of Seneca's tragedies reveals a poet closer in his meaningful playfulness to Spenser than to the crowd-pleasing hack for which critics have so often mistaken him. If Kyd knew Sidney's *Defence of Poesie* in manuscript, he might have taken particular pleasure in Sidney's remark that "truly neither philosopher nor historiographer could at the first have entered into the gates of popular judgments, if they had not taken a great passport of Poetry."[40]

---

40. Sir Philip Sidney, *An Apology for Poetry,* ed. Geoffrey Shepherd (London, 1965), p. 97.

Renaissance Family Politics and Shakespeare's
The Taming of the Shrew

KAREN NEWMAN

ETHERDEN, *Suffolk. Plough Monday, 1604.* A drunken tanner, Nicholas Rosyer, staggers home from the alehouse. On arriving at his door, he is greeted by his wife with "dronken dogg, pisspott and other unseemly names." When Rosyer tried to come to bed to her, she "still raged against him and badd him out dronken dogg dronken pisspott." She struck him several times, clawed his face and arms, spit at him and beat him out of bed. Rosyer retreated, returned to the alehouse, and drank until he could hardly stand up. Shortly thereafter, Thomas Quarry and others met and "agreed amongest themselfs that the said Thomas Quarry who dwelt at the next howse . . . should . . . ryde abowt the towne upon a cowlestaff whereby not onley the woman which had offended might be shunned for her misdemeanors towards her husband but other women also by her shame might be admonished to offence in like sort."[1] Domestic violence, far from being contained in the family, spills out into the neighborhood, and the response of the community is an "old country ceremony used in merriment upon such accidents."

Quarry, wearing a kirtle or gown and apron, "was carryed to diverse places and as he rode did admonishe all wiefs to take heede how they did beate their husbands." The Rosyers' neighbors re-enacted their troubled gender relations: the beating was repeated with Quarry in woman's clothes playing Rosyer's wife, the neighbors standing in for the "abused" husband, and a rough music procession to the house of the transgressors. The result of this "merriment" suggests its darker purpose and the anxiety about gender relations it displays: the offending couple left the village in shame. The skimmington, as it was sometimes called, served its

---

1. This would seem to be Rosyer's neighbor's duty. The OED cites Lupton's *Sivgila,* p. 50 (1580) as an early use of *cowlstaff*: "If a woman beat hir husbande, the man that dwelleth next unto hir sha ride on a cowlstaffe."

purpose by its ritual scapegoating of the tanner, and more particularly, his wife. Rosyer vented his anger by bringing charges against his neighbors in which he complained not only of scandal and disgrace to himself, "his wief and kyndred," but also of seditious "tumult and discention in the said towne."[2]

The entire incident figures the social anxiety about gender and power which characterizes Elizabethan culture. Like Simon Forman's dream of wish-fulfillment with Queen Elizabeth, this incident, in Louis Montrose's words, "epitomizes the indissoluably political and sexual character of the cultural forms in which [such] tensions might be represented and addressed."[3] The community's ritual action against the couple who transgress prevailing codes of gender behavior seeks to re-establish those conventional modes of behavior—it seeks to sanction patriarchal order. But at the same time, this "old country ceremony" subverts, by its re-presentation, its masquerade of the very events it criticizes by forcing the offending couple to recognize their transgression through its dramatic enactment. The skimmington seeks "in merriment" to reassert traditional gender behaviors which are naturalized in Elizabethan culture as divinely ordained; but it also deconstructs that "naturalization" by its foregrounding of what is a humanly constructed cultural product—the displacement of gender roles in a dramatic representation.[4]

II. *Family Politics*

The events of Plough Monday 1604 have an uncanny relation to Shakespeare's *The Taming of the Shrew* which might well be read as a theatrical realization of such a community fantasy, the shaming and subjection of a shrewish wife. The so-called induction opens with the hostess railing at the drunken tinker Sly, and their interchange figures him as the inebriated tanner from Wetherden.[5] Sly is presented with two "dreams," the dream he is a lord, a fantasy which enacts traditional

2. PRO STAC 8, 249/19. I am grateful to Susan Amussen for sharing her transcription of this case, and to David Underdown for the original reference. We do not know the result of Rosyer's complaint since only the testimony, not the judgment, is preserved.

3. Louis Montrose, "'Shaping Fantasies': Gender and Power in Elizabethan Culture," *Representations* 1 (1983), 61–94.

4. See Natalie Z. Davis, "Women on Top" in *Society and Culture in Early Modern France* (Stanford, Cal., 1975); E. P. Thompson, "Rough Music: 'le Charivari Anglais'" *Annales ESC* 27 (1972), 285–312.

5. In *The Taming of a Shrew*, the frame tale closes the action; Sly must return home after his "bravest dreame" to a wife who "will course you for dreaming here tonight," but he claims: "Ile to my/Wife presently and tame her too." See Geoffrey Bullough, *Narrative and Dramatic Sources of Shakespeare* (London, 1957), I, 108.

Elizabethan hierarchical and gender relations, and the "dream" of Petruchio taming Kate. The first fantasy is a series of artificially constructed power relationships figured first in class relations, then in terms of gender. The lord exhorts his servingmen to offer Sly "low submissive reverence" and traditional lordly prerogatives and pursuits—music, painting, handwashing, rich apparel, hunting, and finally a theatrical entertainment. In the longer, more detailed speech which follows at Ind., 1. 100 ff., he exhorts his page to "bear himself with honourable action/ Such as he hath observ'd in noble ladies/ Unto their lords." Significantly, Sly is only convinced of his lordly identity when he is told of his "wife." His realization of this newly discovered self involves calling for the lady, demanding from her submission to his authority, and finally seeking to exert his new power through his husbandly sexual prerogative: "Madam, undress you and come now to bed" (Ind., 2.118). By enacting Sly's identity as a lord through his wife's social and sexual, if deferred, submission, the Induction suggests ironically how in this androcentric culture men depended on women to authorize their sexual and social masculine identities.[6] The Lord's fantasy takes the drunken Sly who brawls with the hostess, and by means of a "play" brings him into line with traditional conceptions of gender relations. But in the Induction, these relationships of power and gender, which in Elizabethan treatises, sermons and homilies, and behavioral handbooks and the like were figured as natural and divinely ordained, are subverted by the metatheatrical foregrounding of such roles and relations as culturally constructed.

The analogy between the events at Wetherden and Shakespeare's play suggests a tempting homology between history and cultural artifacts. It figures patriarchy as a master narrative, the key to understanding certain historic events and dramatic plots. But as Louis Althusser's critique of historicism epigrammatically has it, "history is a process without a *telos* or a subject."[7] This Althusserian dictum repudiates such master narratives, but as Frederic Jameson points out, "What Althusser's own insistence on history as an absent cause makes clear, but what is missing from the formula as it is canonically worded, is that he does not at all draw the fashionable conclusion that because history is a text, the 'referent' does not exist . . . history is *not* a narrative, master or otherwise, but that, as an absent cause, it is inaccessible to us except in textual form, and that our approach to it and to the Real itself necessarily passes through its prior

6. See Montrose's discussion of the Amazonian myth, "'Shaping Fantasies,'" pp. 66–67.
7. *Réponse à John Lewis* (Paris, 1973), pp. 91–98.

textualization, its narrativization in the political unconscious."[8] If we return to Nicholas Rosyer's complaint against his neighbors and consider its textualization, how it is made accessible to us through narrative, we can make several observations. We notice immediately that Rosyer's wife, the subject of the complaint, lacks the status of a subject. She is unnamed and referred to only as the "wief." Rosyer's testimony, in fact, begins with a defense not of his wife, but of his patrimony, an account of his background and history in the village in terms of male lineage. His wife has no voice; she never speaks in the complaint at all. Her husband brings charges against his neighbors presumably to clear his name and to affirm his identity as patriarch which the incident itself, from his wife's "abuse" to the transvestite skimmington, endangers.

From the account of this case, we also get a powerful sense of life in early modern England, the close proximity of neighbors and the way in which intimate sexual relations present a scene before an audience. Quarry and the neighbors recount Rosyer's attempted assertion of his sexual "prerogatives" over his wife, and her vehement refusal: "she struck him several times, clawed his face and arms, spit at him and beat him out of bed." There is evidently no place in the late Elizabethan "sex/gender system"[9] for Rosyer's wife to complain of her husband's mistreatment, drunkenness and abuse, or even give voice to her point of view, her side of the story. The binary opposition between male and female in the Wetherden case and its figuration of patriarchy in early modern England generates the possible contradictions logically available to both terms: Rosyer speaks, his wife is silent; Rosyer is recognized as a subject before the law, his wife is solely its object; Rosyer's family must be defended against the insults of his neighbors, his wife has no family, but has become merely a part of his. In turning to *The Taming of the Shrew*, our task is to articulate the particular sexual/political fantasy or, in Jameson's Althusserian formulation, the "libidinal apparatus" that the play projects as an imaginary resolution of contradictions which are never resolved in the Wetherden case, but which the formal structures of dramatic plot and character in Shakespeare's play present as seemingly reconciled.

II. *A Shrew's History*

Many readers of Shakespeare's *Shrew* have noted that both in the induction and the play language is an index of identity. Sly is convinced

8. Frederic Jameson, *The Political Unconscious* (Ithaca, N.Y., 1981), p. 35.
9. Montrose, p. 62, after Gayle Rubin.

of his lordly identity by language, by the lord's obsequious words and recital of his false history. Significantly, when he believes himself a lord, his language changes and he begins to speak the blank verse of his retainers. But in the opening scene of the play proper, Shakespeare emphasizes not just the relationship between language and identity, but between women and language, and between control over language and patriarchal power. Kate's linguistic protest is against the role in patriarchal culture to which women are assigned, that of wife and object of exchange in the circulation of male desire. Her very first words make this point aggressively: she asks of her father "I pray you, sir, is it your will / To make a stale of me amongst these mates?"[10] Punning on the meaning of stale as laughing stock and prostitute, on "stalemate," and on mate as husband, Kate refuses her erotic destiny by exercising her linguistic willfulness. Her shrewishness, always associated with women's revolt in words, testifies to her exclusion from social and political power. Bianca, by contrast, is throughout the play associated with silence (1.1.70-71).[11]

Kate's prayer to her father is motivated by Gremio's threat "To cart her rather. She's too rough for me" (1.1.55). Although this line is usually glossed as "drive around in an open cart (a punishment for prostitutes)," the case of Nicholas Rosyer and his unnamed wife provides a more complex commentary. During the period from 1560 until the English Civil War, in which many historians have recognized a "crisis of order," the fear that women were rebelling against their traditional subservient role in patriarchal culture was widespread.[12] Popular works such as *The Two Angry Women of Abington* (1598), Middleton's *The Roaring Girl* (1611), *Hic Mulier*, or *The Man-Woman* (1620), and Joseph Swetnam's *Arraignment of lewd, idle, froward and inconstant women*, which went through ten editions between 1616 and 1634, all testify to a preoccupation with rebellious women.[13]

10. (1.1.57-58); all references are to the New Arden edition, ed. Brian Morris (London, 1981).
11. See, for example, Robert Greene's *Penelope's Web* (1587) which presents the Renaissance ideal of womanhood—chastity, obedience and silence—through a series of exemplary tales; see also Ruth Kelso, *Doctrine for the Lady of the Renaissance* (Urbana, 1956); Linda T. Fitz, "'What says the Married Woman?': Marriage Theory and Feminism in the English Renaissance," *Mosaic* 13 (1980), 1–22; the books Suzanne Hull examines in her *Chaste, Silent and Obedient: English Books for Women, 1475-1640* (San Marino, 1982); and most recently Lisa Jardine, *Still Harping on Daughters* (Sussex, Eng., 1983), 103–140.
12. See, among others, Lawrence Stone's *The Crisis of the Aristocracy 1558-1641* (Oxford, 1965) and Keith Wrightson's *English Society 1580-1680* (New Brunswick, N.J., 1982), esp. chs. 5 and 6. I am grateful to David Underdown for referring me to Wrightson.

What literary historians have recognized in late Elizabethan and Jacobean writers as a preoccupation with female rebellion and independence, social historians have also observed in historical records. The period was fraught with anxiety about rebellious women. David Underdown observes that "Women scolding and brawling with their neighbours, single women refusing to enter service, wives dominating or even beating their husbands: all seem to surface more frequently than in the periods immediately before or afterwards. It will not go unnoticed that this is also the period during which witchcraft accusations reach their peak."[14]   Underdown's account points out a preoccupation with women's rebellion through language. Although men were occasionally charged with scolding, it was predominantly a female offence usually associated with class as well as gender issues and revolt: "women who were poor, social outcasts, widows or otherwise lacking in the protection of a family . . . were the most common offenders."[15] Underdown points out that in the few examples after the restoration, social disapproval shifts to "mismatched couples, sexual offenders, and eventually . . . husbands who beat their wives."[16] Punishment for such offences and related ones involving "domineering" wives who "beat" or "abused" their husbands often involved public shaming or charivari of the sort employed at Wetherden. The accused woman or her surrogate was put in a scold's collar or ridden in a cart accompanied by a rough musical procession of villagers banging pots and pans.

Louis Montrose attributes the incidence of troubled gender relations to female rule since "all forms of public and domestic authority in Elizabethan England were vested in men: in fathers, husbands, masters, teachers, magistrates, lords. It was inevitable that the rule of a woman would generate peculiar tensions within such a 'patriarchal' society."[17] Instead of assigning the causes of such rebellion to the "pervasive cultural presence" of the Queen, historians point to the social and economic factors which contributed to these troubled gender relations. Underdown observes a breakdown of community in fast-growing urban centers and scattered pasture/dairy parishes where effective means of social

13. Stone cites Swetnam, *Family*, p. 137; for references to *Hic Mulier*, see David Underdown, "The Taming of the Scold: the enforcement of patriarchal authority in Early Modern England," in *Order and Disorder in Early Modern England*, ed. by Anthony Fletcher and John Stevenson (Cambridge, 1985), 116–36.
    14. Underdown, p. 119.
    15. Underdown, p. 120.
    16. Underdown, p. 121, citing E. P. Thompson.
    17. Montrose, pp. 64–65.

control such as compact nucleated village centers, resident squires, and strong manorial institutions were weak or non-existent. He observes the higher incidence of troubled gender relations in such communities as opposed to the arable parishes which "tended to retain strong habits of neighborhood and cooperation." Both Montrose's reading of the Elizabethan sex-gender system in terms of "female rule" and Underdown's explanation for this proliferation of accusations of witchcraft, shrewishness and husband domination are less important here than the clear connection between women's independent appropriation of discourse and a conceived threat to patriarchal authority contained through public shaming or spectacle—the ducking stool, usually called the cucking stool, or carting.[18]

From the outset of Shakespeare's play, Katherine's threat to male authority is posed through language; it is perceived as such by others and is linked to a claim larger than shrewishness—witchcraft—through the constant allusions to Katherine's kinship with the devil.[19] Control of women and particularly of Kate's revolt is from the outset attempted by inscribing women in a scopic economy.[20] Woman is represented as spectacle (Kate) or object to be desired and admired, a vision of beauty (Bianca). She is the site of visual pleasure, whether on the public stage, the village green, or the fantasy "cart" with which Hortensio threatens Kate. The threat of being made a spectacle, here by carting, or later in the wedding scene by Petruchio's "mad-brain rudesby," is an important aspect of shrew-taming.[21] Given the evidence of social history and of the play itself, discourse is power, both in Elizabethan and Jacobean England and in the fictional space of the *Shrew*.

The *Shrew* both demonstrated and produced the social facts of the patriarchal ideology which characterized Elizabethan England, but *representation* gives us a perspective on that patriarchal system which

18. Montrose, pp. 64–65. See also Davis and Thompson, cited above.

19. See, for example, 1.1.65, 105, 121, 123; 2.1, 26, 151; for the social context of witchcraft in England, see Alan Macfarlane, *Witchcraft in Tudor and Stuart England* (New York, 1970) and Keith Thomas, *Religion and the Decline of Magic* (London, 1971).

20. On the importance of the gaze in managing human behavior, see Michel Foucault, *Surveiller et Punir* (Paris, 1975); see also Laura Mulvey's discussion of scopophilia in "Visual Pleasure and Narrative Cinema," *Screen* 16 (1975), 6-18, and Luce Irigaray's more philosophical *Speculum de l'autre femme* (Paris, 1974).

21. Kate's speech at 3.2.8, 18–20 makes clear this function of his lateness and his "mad-brain rudesby." She recognizes that this shame falls not on her family, but on her alone: "No shame but mine . . . Now must the world point at poor Katherine/'Lo, there is made Petruchio's wife, If it would please him come and marry her'" (3.2.8,18–20). Although Katherine to herself, she recognizes that for others she will be "Petruchio's wife."

subverts its status as natural. The theatrically constructed frame in which Sly exercises patriarchal power and the dream in which Kate is tamed undermine the seemingly eternal nature of those structures by calling attention to the constructed character of the representation rather than veiling it through mimesis. The foregrounded female protagonist of the action and her powerful annexation of the traditionally male domain of discourse distances us from that system by exposing and displaying its contradictions. Representation undermines the ideology about women which the play presents and produces, both in the Induction and in the Kate/Petruchio plot: Sly disappears as lord, but Kate keeps talking.

III. *The Price of Silence*

At 2.1, in the spat between Bianca and Kate, the relationship between silence and women's place in the marriage market is made clear. Kate questions Bianca about her suitors, inquiring as to her preferences. Some critics have read her questions and her abuse of Bianca (in less than thirty lines, Kate binds her sister's hands behind her back, strikes her and chases after her calling for revenge) as revealing her secret desire for marriage and for the praise and recognition afforded her sister. Kate's behavior may invite such an interpretation, but another view persistently presents itself as well. In her questions and badgering, Kate makes clear the relationship between Bianca's sweet sobriety and her success with men. Kate's abuse may begin as a jest, but her feelings are aroused to a different and more serious pitch when her father enters, taking as usual Bianca's part against her sister.[22] Baptista emphasizes both Bianca's silence, "When did she cross thee with a bitter word?" and Katherine's link with the devil, "thou hilding of a devilish spirit" (2.1.28, 26). We should bear in mind here Underdown's observation that shrewishness is a class as well as gender issue—that women "lacking in the protection of a family . . . were the most common offenders."[23] Kate is motherless, and to some degree fatherless as well, for Baptista consistently rejects her and favors her obedient sister. Kate's threat which follows, "Her silence flouts me, and I'll be reveng'd" (2.1.29) is truer than we have heretofore recognized, for it is that silence which has insured Bianca's place in the male economy of desire and exchange to which Kate pointedly refers in her last lines:

> What, will you not suffer me? Nay, now I see

22. See Marianne Novy's discussion of the importance of the father and paternity in her essay "Patriarchy and Play in *The Taming of the Shrew*," *English Literary Renaissance* 9 (1979), 273–74.

23. Underdown, p. 120.

She is your treasure, she must have a husband,
I must dance barefoot on her wedding day,
And, for your love to her lead apes in hell. (2.1.31-34)

Here we recognize the relationship between father and husband, in which woman is the mediating third term, a treasure the exchange of which assures patriarchal hegemony. Throughout the play Bianca is a treasure, a jewel, an object of desire and possession. Although much has been made of the animal analogies between Kate and beasts, the metaphorical death of the courtly imagery associated with Bianca has been ignored as too conventional, if not natural, to warrant comment.[24] What seems at issue here is not so much Kate's lack of a husband, or indeed her desire for a marriage partner, but rather her distaste at those folk customs which make her otherness, her place outside that patriarchal system, a public fact, a spectacle for all to see and mock.

In the battle of words between Kate and Petruchio at 2.1.182ff., it is Kate who gets the best of her suitor. She takes the lead through puns which allow her to criticize Petruchio and the patriarchal system of wooing and marriage. Her sexual puns make explicit to the audience not so much her secret preoccupation with sex and marriage, but what is implicit in Petruchio's wooing—that marriage is a sexual exchange in which women are exploited for their use-value as producers. Significantly, Petruchio's language is linguistically similar to Kate's in its puns and wordplay. He also presents her, as many commentators have noted, with an imagined vision which makes her conform to the very order against which she rebels—he makes her a Bianca with words, shaping an identity for her which confirms the social expectations of the sex/gender system which informs the play. Their wooing can be interestingly compared with the next scene, also a wooing, between Bianca and her two suitors. Far from the imaginative use of language and linguistic play we find in Kate, Bianca repeats verbatim the Latin words Lucentio "construes" to reveal his identity and his love. Her revelation of her feelings through a repetition of the Latin lines he quotes from Ovid are as close as possible to the silence we have come to expect from her.

In the altercation over staying for the wedding feast after their marriage, Kate again claims the importance of language and her use of it to women's place and independence in the world. But here it is Petruchio

24. See Novy's detailed discussion of Kate's puns, animal imagery and sexual innuendoes in this scene, p. 264, and Martha Andreson-Thom's "Shrew-taming and other rituals of aggression: Baiting and bonding on the stage and in the wild," *Women's Studies* 9 (1982), 121-43.

who controls language, who has the final word, for he creates through words a situation to justify his actions—he claims to be rescuing Kate from thieves. More precisely, he claims she asks for that rescue. Kate's annexation of language does not work unless her audience, and particularly her husband, accepts what she says as independent rebellion. By deliberately misunderstanding and reinterpreting her words to suit his own ends, Petruchio effectively refuses her the freedom of speech identified in the play with women's independence. Such is his strategy throughout this central portion of the action, in their arrival at his house and in the interchange with the tailor. Kate is figuratively killed with kin-dness, by her husband's rule over her not so much in material terms—the withholding of food, clothing and sleep—but the withholding of linguistic understanding. As the receiver of her messages, he simply refuses their meaning; since he also has material power to enforce his interpretations, it is his power over language that wins.

In the exchange between Petruchio and Kate with the tailor, Kate makes her strongest bid yet for linguistic freedom:

> Why, sir, I trust I may have leave to speak,
> And speak I will. I am no child, no babe.
> Your betters have endur'd me say my mind,
> And if you cannot, best you stop your ears.
> My tongue will tell the anger of my heart,
> Or else my heart concealing it will break,
> And rather than it shall, I will be free
> Even to the uttermost, as I please, in words. (4.3.73–80)

When we next encounter Kate, however, on the journey to Padua, she finally admits to Petruchio: "What you will have it nam'd, even that it is, / And so it shall be so for Katherine" (4.5.21–22). On this journey Kate calls the sun the moon, an old man a budding virgin, and makes the world conform to the topsy-turvy of Petruchio's patriarchal whimsy. But we should look carefully at this scene before acquiescing in too easy a view of Kate's submission. Certainly she gives in to Petruchio's demands literally; but her playfulness and irony here are indisputable. As she says at 4.5.44–48:

> Pardon, old father, my mistaking eyes,
> That have been so bedazzled with the sun
> That everything I look on seemeth green.
> Now I perceive thou art a reverend father.
> Pardon, I pray thee, for my mad mistaking.

Given Kate's talent for puns, we must understand her line, "bedazzled with the sun," as a pun on son and play with Petruchio's line earlier in the scene "Now by my mother's son, and that's myself, / It shall be moon, or star, or what I list" (4.5.6–7). "Petruchio's bedazzlement" is exactly that, and Kate here makes clear the playfulness of their linguistic games.

In his paper "Hysterical Phantasies and their Relation to Bi-Sexuality" (1908), Sigmund Freud observes that neurotic symptoms, particularly the hysterical symptom, have their origins in the daydreams of adolescence.[25] "In girls and women," Freud claims, "they are invariably of an erotic nature, in men they may be either erotic or ambitious."[26] A feminist characterological re-reading of Freud might suggest that Kate's ambitious fantasies, which her culture allows her to express only in erotic directions, motivate her shrewishness.[27] Such behavior, which in a man would not be problematic, her family and peers interpret as "hysterical" and/or diabolic. Her "masculine" behavior saves her, at least for a time, from her feminine erotic destiny.

Freud goes on to claim that hysterical symptoms are always bi-sexual, "the expression of both a masculine and a feminine unconscious sexual phantasy."[28] The example he gives is a patient who "pressed her dress to her body with one hand (as the woman) while trying to tear it off with the other (as the man)."[29] To continue our "analysis" in the scene we are considering, we might claim that Kate's female masquerade obscures her continuing ambitious fantasies, now only manifest in her puns and ironic wordplay which suggest the distance between her character and the role she plays.[30] Even though she gives up her shrewishness and acquiesces to Petruchio's whims, she persists in her characteristic "masculine" linguistic exuberance while masquerading as an obedient wife.[31]

Instead of using Freud to analyze Kate's character, a critical move of debatable interpretive power, we might consider the Freudian text

25. *Collected Papers*, tr. Joan Riviere (London, 1948), II, pp. 51–59.

26. *Collected Papers*, II, p. 51.

27. For a discussion of female fantasy, see Nancy K. Miller, "Emphasis Added: Plots and Plausibilities in Women's Fiction," *PMLA* 97 (1981), 36–48.

28. *Collected Papers*, p. 57.

29. *Collected Papers*, p. 58.

30. See Joan Riviere's essay on female masquerade in *Psychoanalysis and Female Sexuality*, ed. H. Ruitenbeek (New Haven, 1966); also of interest is Sir Thomas Elyot's *Defense of Good Women* in which Zenobia is allowed autonomy in relation to her husband, but exhorted to dissemble her disobedience. See Constance Jordan, "Feminism and the Humanists: The Case of Thomas Elyot's *Defense of Good Women*," *Renaissance Quarterly* 36 (1983), 195.

31. Freud describes a similar strategy of evasion in his essay, *Collected Papers*, II, p. 58.

instead as a reading of ideological or cultural patterns. The process Freud describes is suggestive for analyzing the workings not of character, but of Shakespeare's text itself. No speech in the play has been more variously interpreted than Kate's final speech of women's submission. In a recent essay on the *Shrew*, John Bean has conveniently assigned to the two prevailing views the terms "revisionist" for those who would take Kate's speech as ironic and her subservience as pretense, a way of living peaceably in patriarchal culture but with an unregenerate spirit, and the "anti-revisionists" who argue that farce is the play's governing genre and that Kate's response to Petruchio's taming is that of an animal responding to "the devices of a skilled trainer."[32] Bean himself argues convincingly for a compromise position which admits the "background of depersonalizing farce unassimilated from the play's fabliau sources," but suggests that Kate's taming needs to be seen in terms of romantic comedy, as a spontaneous change of heart such as those of the later romantic comedies "where characters lose themselves in chaos and emerge, as if from a dream, liberated into the bonds of love."[33] Bean rightly points out the liberal elements of the final speech in which marriage is seen as a partnership as well as a hierarchy, citing the humanist writers on marriage and juxtaposing Kate's speech with the corresponding, and remarkably more mysogynist, lines in *The Taming of a Shrew* and other taming tales.[34]

Keeping in mind Bean's arguments for the content of the speech and its place in the intersection of farce and romantic love plot, I would like to turn instead to its significance as representation. What we find is Katherine as a strong, energetic female protagonist represented before us addressing not the onstage male audience, only too aware of its articulation of patriarchal power, but Bianca and the Widow, associated with silence throughout the play and finally arriving by means, as Petruchio calls it, of Kate's "womanly persuasion"(5.2.120).

Unlike any other of Shakespeare's comedies, we have here represented not simply marriage, with the final curtain a veiled mystification

32. "Comic Structure and the Humanizing of Kate in *The Taming of the Shrew*," *The Woman's Part,* ed. Carolyn Ruth Swift Lenz, Grayle Greene, and Carol Thomas Neely (Urbana, Ill., 1980). Bean quotes the "anti-revisionist" Robert Heilbrun, "The *Taming* Untamed, or, the Return of the Shrew," *Modern Language Quarterly* 27 (1966), 147-61. For the revisionist view, see Coppélia Kahn's *The Taming of the Shrew*: Shakespeare's Mirror of Marriage," *Modern Language Studies* 5 (1975), 88-102.

33. Bean, p. 66.

34. Bean, pp. 67-70.

of the sexual and social results of that ritual, but a view, however brief and condensed, of that marriage over time.[35] And what we see is not a quiet and submissive Kate, but the same energetic and linguistically powerful Kate with which the play began. We know, then, in a way we never know about the other comedies, except perhaps *The Merchant of Venice*, and there our knowledge is complicated by Portia's male disguise, that Kate has continued to speak. She has not, of course, continued to speak her earlier language of revolt and anger. Instead she has adopted another strategy, a strategy which the French psychoanalyst Luce Irigaray calls mimeticism.[36] Irigaray argues that women are cut off from language by the patriarchal order in which they live, by their entry into the Symbolic which the Father represents in a Freudian/Lacanian model.[37] Women's only possible relation to the dominant discourse is mimetic:

> To play with mimesis is . . . for a woman to try to recover the place of her exploitation by language, without allowing herself to be simply reduced to it. It is to resubmit herself . . . to ideas—notably about her—elaborated in and through a masculine logic, but to "bring out" by an effect of playful repetition what was to remain hidden: the recovery of a possible operation of the feminine in language. It is also to unveil the fact that if women mime so well they are not simply reabsorbed in this function. *They also remain elsewhere.*[38]

Whereas Irigaray goes on to locate this "elsewhere" in sexual pleasure (*jouissance*), Nancy Miller has elaborated on this notion of "mimeticism," describing it as a "form of emphasis: an italicized version of what passes for the neutral . . . Spoken or written, italics are a modality of intensity and stress; a way of marking what has already been said, of making a common text one's own."[39]

Joel Fineman has recently observed the difficulty in distinguishing between man's and woman's speech in the *Shrew* by demonstrating how the rhetorical strategies Kate deploys are like Petruchio's.[40] But Kate's

---

35. See Nancy K. Miller's discussion of the mystification of defloration and marriage in "Writing (from) the Feminine: George Sand and the Novel of Female Pastoral," *The Representation of Women, English Institute Essays* (Cambridge, 1983).

36. *Ce sexe qui n'en est pas un* (Paris, 1977), pp. 134ff.

37. *Speculum de L'autre femme*, particularly pp. 282–98. Contemporary handbooks often seem an uncanny description of woman as Other: the popular preacher Henry Smith, whose *Preparative to Marriage* was published in 1591, suggests that marriage is an equal partnership, but goes on to declare that "the ornament of women is silence; and therefore the Law was given to the man rather than to the woman, to shewe that he shoulde be the teacher, and she the hearer" (quoted in Novy, p. 278).

38. Irigaray, p. 74, quoted and translated by Nancy Miller, "Emphasis Added:" cited above, p. 38.

39. Miller, p. 38.

self-consciousness about the power of discourse, her punning and irony, and her techniques of linguistic masquerade, are strategies of italics, mimetic strategies, in Irigaray's sense of mimeticism. Instead of figuring a gender-marked woman's speech, they deform language by sub-verting it, that is, by turning it inside out so that metaphors, puns and other forms of wordplay manifest their veiled equivalences: the meaning of woman as treasure, of wooing as a civilized and acceptable disguise for sexual exploitation, of the objectification and exchange of women. Kate's having the last word contradicts the very sentiments she speaks; rather than resolve the play's action, her monologue simply displays the fundamental contradiction presented by a female dramatic protagonist, between woman as a sexually desirable, silent object and women of words, women with power over language who disrupt, or at least italicize, women's place and part in culture.

To dramatize action involving linguistically powerful women characters militates against patriarchal structures and evaluations of women in which their silence is most highly prized—which is why so many of Shakespeare's heroines, in order to maintain their status as desirable, must don male attire in order to speak: Rosalind, Portia, even the passive Viola. The conflict between the explicitly repressive content of Kate's speech and the implicit message of independence communicated by representing a powerful female protagonist speaking the play's longest speech at a moment of emphatic suspense is not unlike Freud's female patient who "pressed her dress to her body with one hand (as the woman) while trying to tear it off with the other (as the man)." We might even say that this conflict shares the bi-sexuality Freud claims for the hysterical symptom, that the text itself is sexually ambivalent, a view in keeping with the opposed readings of the play in which it is either conservative farce or subversive irony. Such a representation of gender, what I will call the "female dramatizable,"[41] is always at once patriarchally suspect and sexually ambivalent, clinging to Elizabethan patriarchal ideology and at the same time tearing it away by foregrounding or italicizing its constructed character.

IV. *Missing Frames and Female Spectacles*

Kate's final speech is "an imaginary or formal solution to unresolvable

40. Joel Fineman, "The Turn of the *Shrew*," in *Shakespeare and the Question of Theory,* eds. Patricia Parker and Geoffrey Hartman (London, 1985), pp. 141–144.

41. See D. A. Miller's discussion of the "narratable" in *Narrative and its Discontents* (Princeton, 1981), especially the chapter on Austen.

social contradictions," but that appearance of resolution is an "ideological mirage."[42] On the level of plot, as many readers have noted, if one shrew is tamed two more reveal themselves. Bianca and the widow refuse to do their husbands' bidding, thereby undoing the sense of closure Kate's "acquiescence" produces. By articulating the contradiction manifested in the scene's formal organization and its social "content"— between the "headstrong women," now Bianca and the widow who refuse their duty, and Kate and her praise of women's submission—the seeming resolution of the play's ending is exploded and its *heterogeneity* rather than its unity is foregrounded. But can transgression of the law of women's silence be subversive? It has become a theoretical commonplace to argue that transgression presupposes norms or taboos. Therefore, the "female dramatizable" is perhaps no more than a release mechanism, a means of managing troubled gender relations. By transgressing the law of women's silence, but far from subverting it, the *Shrew* reconfirms the law, if we remember that Kate, Bianca and the widow remain the object of the audience's gaze, specular images, represented female bodies on display, as on the cucking stool or in the cart, the traditional punishments for prostitutes and scolds. Representation contains female rebellion. And because the play has no final framing scene, no return to Sly, it could be argued that its artifice is relaxed, that the final scene is experienced naturalistically. The missing frame allows the audience to forget that Petruchio's taming of Kate is presented as a fiction.

Yet even with its missing frame and containment of woman through spectacle, the *Shrew* finally deconstructs its own mimetic effect if we remember the bisexual aspect of the representation of women on the Elizabethan and Jacobean stage. Kate would have been played by a boy whose transvestism, like Thomas Quarry's in the Wetherden skimmington, emblematically embodied the sexual contradictions manifest both in the play and Elizabethan culture. The very indeterminateness of the actor's sexuality, of the woman/man's body, the supplementarity of its titillating homoerotic play (Sly's desire for the page boy disguised as a woman, Petruchio's "Come Kate, we'll to bed"), foregrounds its artifice and therefore subverts the play's patriarchal master narrative by exposing it as neither natural nor divinely ordained, but culturally constructed.

42. Jameson, pp. 79, 56.

Francis Bacon and the Style of Politics

F . J . L E V Y

EARLY in 1597, there came from the press a small book entitled *Essayes. Religious Meditations. Places of perswasion and disswasion*, by a middle-aged lawyer and place-hunter named Francis Bacon, best known to his contemporaries as an author of slightly ponderous government propaganda who occasionally turned his hand to the lighter task of writing entertainments for his patron, the Earl of Essex.[1] The *Essayes* were composed in a novel style, full of short, sharp sentences, with the connections between sentences so delicately indicated as to force the reader to struggle to comprehend the author's entire meaning. That difficulty in reading, however, was part of the author's intent, as it was that of others who were adapting the prose style of Silver Age Latin to English: *difficilia quae pulchra*.[2] Analyses of politics, of patron-client relations, of the tricks of language—the sorts of things to be found in the *Essayes*—were not to be revealed to the mass of humanity. Only a select readership was to understand Bacon's aphoristic and rather disjointed prose, and the mysteries hidden within it, and this would largely consist of those contemporaries who, like Bacon himself, had passed through the Elizabethan political system.[3]

Bacon's later revisions of his text, which turned it into something very

1. Bacon's career is best followed in James Spedding, *The Letters and the Life of Francis Bacon*, 7 vols. (London, 1861-74), here abbreviated as Spedding. Joel J. Epstein, *Francis Bacon: A Political Biography* (Athens, 1977), adds little to Spedding. I have looked at Bacon from a different point of view in the introduction to my edition of his *The History of the Reign of King Henry the Seventh* (Indianapolis, 1972).

2. Tacitus, *The Ende of Nero and the Beginning of Galba*, trans. H. Savile (Oxford, 1591), A. B. to the Reader. See also Daniel Javitch, *Poetry and Courtliness in Renaissance England* (Princeton, 1978), pp. 65-66, and note 13 below.

3. Anthony Esler, *The Aspiring Mind of the Elizabethan Younger Generation* (Durham, 1966) is an interesting if not wholly convincing generational portrait of Bacon and his contemporaries. The political world of the nineties and the patronage system on which it rested have been described by

different—and much grander—hinder our efforts at understanding his original intentions.[4] The editions of 1612 and 1625 were no longer the work of a man trying desperately to put his foot on the lowest rung of the ladder of advancement. For us to understand the original *Essayes* as first issued in 1597, we must see the book as a response to a crisis in English politics which, amidst a more general reorientation of thought, caused Bacon to engage in an examination of his political role. To do that, we must first look at the general situation of the well-born and humanistically educated gentleman, then at the events of the 1590s and Bacon's part in them, and conclude with a careful examination of his book in the light of what we know of the circumstances of its writing.

I

The decade of the 1590s saw the first questioning of that doctrine of "political humanism" which itself had only just achieved the status of an orthodoxy. Political humanism may be described as an amalgam of an Italian-based "new philosophy of political engagement and active life" with older chivalric ideas about the relationship between a monarch and the aristocracy.[5] It had always been a lord's duty to give counsel to his king. Now, added to that, was the strong conviction that it was a citizen's duty to serve his common weal. Any Elizabethan schoolboy would have absorbed that sense of duty from his reading of Cicero, amidst much encouragement from schoolmasters who had been taught the same thing by such philosophers of education as Erasmus and Vives.[6] So everyone sought to serve their country—and of course themselves. Queen Elizabeth herself encouraged them. In a famous speech to the students of Cambridge, she told them to continue as they had begun and

Sir John Neale, "The Elizabethan Political Scene," in his *Essays in Elizabethan History* (London, 1958), pp. 59-84, and Wallace MacCaffrey, "Place and Patronage in Elizabethan Politics," in *Elizabethan Government and Society*, eds. S. T. Bindoff, J. Hurstfield and C. H. Williams (London, 1961), pp. 95-126.

4. R. S. Crane, "The Relation of Bacon's Essays to his Program for the Advancement of Learning," in *Schelling Anniversary Papers*, ed. A. H. Quinn (New York, 1923), pp. 87-105.

5. Hans Baron, *The Crisis of the Early Italian Renaissance*, rev. ed. (Princeton, 1966), p. 459 and passim; see also the same author's "Cicero and the Roman Civil Spirit in the Middle Ages and the Early Renaissance," *Bulletin of the John Rylands Library*, 22 (1938), 72-97, and Lauro Martines, *The Social World of the Florentine Humanists* (Princeton, 1963). For the connection to England, see Arthur B. Ferguson, *The Articulate Citizen and the English Renaissance* (Durham, 1965), which discusses the combination of medieval and civic humanist ideals in great detail.

6. Daniel Javitch, *Poetry and Courtliness* (Princeton, 1978), ch. I; Hugh Kearney, *Scholars and Gentlemen* (London, 1970), pp. 37-38.

preferment would surely follow.[7] The gentlemen crowding the universities were evidence that the Queen's advice was being followed. Nor was all this merely a matter of ambition and selfishness, for many were convinced that birth and training had to be completed by some form of action benefiting the realm.

Yet the English context was very different from that in which the philosophy of political engagement was born. Originally it had been designed for a republic, where participation meant seeking elective office or taking part in great assemblies—the picture of Cicero attacking Catiline in the Roman Senate was intended to come to mind. But what use was such an ideology at the court of an absolute prince, where few if any elective offices existed and where most debates were conducted before an audience of one? That problem was already evident in Castiglione's *Courtier* and was to become more so in Tudor England.[8]

The situation of these well-born and humanistically-educated men was exacerbated by the fact that the Roman concept of the orator, from which Renaissance ideals of education were adapted, emphasized the combination of virtue with rhetoric. Indeed, the adaptation made the point even more strongly than the original, for to Stoic virtue was added Christian. The Christian orator, or statesman, was a virtuous man able to speak well. But was such an ideal compatible with the highly competitive reality of the courtier's world? In order to promote his ideals, the courtier had first to achieve office; to achieve office, he frequently had to compromise his ideals. Thomas More had posed the problem eloquently in *Utopia*—and had chosen office. In the mid-century rush for office which followed, his doubts were forgotten. But, toward the end of Elizabeth's reign, as the flow of offices slackened and the competition became ever more intense, the same problems re-emerged.

Bacon's career exemplified this general pattern. As early as 1580, in the first of a long series of appeals for help addressed to his uncle, Lord Burghley, the young Francis revealed his hope to emulate his recently

7. The Queen's speech was quoted by Mark H. Curtis, *Oxford and Cambridge in Transition, 1558–1642* (Oxford, 1959), p. 7, who discusses its implications there and in "The Alienated Intellectuals of Early Stuart England," *Past and Present* 23 (1962), 25-43. I have investigated individual cases in "Fulke Greville: The Courtier as Philosophic Poet," *Modern Language Quarterly* 33 (1972), 433-48 and in "Philip Sidney Reconsidered," *English Literary Renaissance* 2 (1972), 5-18.

8. On this, see J. G. A. Pocock, *The Machiavellian Moment* (Princeton, 1975), esp. ch. X. For Italy, see also Lauro Martines, *Power and Imagination* (New York, 1979), pp. 328-31; and for England, G. K. Hunter, *John Lyly: The Humanist as Courtier* (Cambridge, Mass., 1962), ch. 1. Javitch's *Poetry and Courtliness* is concerned specifically with the translation of the courtier to England; however, he sees court culture more positively than I do.

deceased father and dedicate his life to her Majesty's service. Admittedly, he was not yet prepared for this high vocation, "but calling to mind how diversly and in what particular providence God hath declared himself to tender the estate of her Majesty's affairs, I conceive and gather hope that those whom he hath in a manner pressed for her Majesty's service, by working and imprinting in them a single and zealous mind to bestow their days therein, he will see them accordingly appointed of sufficiency convenient for the rank and standing where they shall be employed."[9] This was to make political humanism a part of the divine purpose, and to dignify the search for office by associating it with God's evident desire to help his chosen people survive and prosper. A dozen years later, still searching for employment suitable to his skills and ambitions, still anxious to labor for Queen and commonwealth, he wrote Burghley once more: "I ever bare a mind (in some middle place that I could discharge) to serve her Majesty; not as a man born under Sol, that loveth honour; nor under Jupiter, that loveth business (for the contemplative planet carrieth me away wholly); but as a man born under an excellent Sovereign, that deserveth the dedication of all men's abilities."[10] Moreover, for Bacon, the situation was intensified by a strong personal conviction that the high birth, great abilities, and careful training given him by God's grace and his father's love had to be completed by the action to which these same qualities had destined him. His humanist training had prepared him for a world of political activity, and even if his personal inclination were toward contemplation, acceding to the pull of an ivory tower was to reject all the values instilled in him by years of education. But, unfortunately for Bacon, by the time his training had been completed, the demand for classically-educated gentlemen was slackening. More of them sought public office than there were offices to fill. A sense of frustration beset the losers, revealing itself in the fashionable disease of melancholy or leaving them subject to the temptations of rebellion.[11] So Bacon's career under Queen Elizabeth exemplified not only the ideology of political engagement but also its failure in practice.

The general crisis of English political humanism, which began in the last two decades of Elizabeth's reign and which lasted at least to the

9. Spedding, I, 14.

10. Spedding, I, 108.

11. Bacon noted this himself, and described these frustrated gentlemen as *materia rerum novarum*, fuel for revolution: Spedding, IV, 253.

outbreak of civil war, was entangled in the 1590s with a much more specific "external" crisis. The war with Spain had been fought openly since 1585, and the fighting now extended to the Netherlands, France, Ireland, and the open sea. Occasionally, war touched Spain herself and might, at any moment, reach England as well. Moreover, in the minds of many, vastly more was involved than opposition to Spain's imperialism and aggression: this was a war for the preservation of Protestantism, a crusade undertaken at God's behest, to be shirked only at imminent danger to one's very soul. England's role, as the chief Protestant power, was not only to defend herself but to come to the aid of all others of the reformed faith. But such a role was difficult to act, partly because English resources were inadequate to the task, but more especially because of the uncertainty of the succession to Queen Elizabeth. The good queen resolutely refused to designate an heir, leaving the field open to claimants of all persuasions. Most men tended toward the claim of the Protestant King James of Scotland. But Philip of Spain argued that his daughter had the best title, and some English Catholics were inclined to agree. And Philip was likely to assert his claim with considerable force, as he had already demonstrated when, in a similar situation, he had seized Portugal. Besides these, there were some home-grown candidates as well. Most important for judging the temper of the times, however, is the fact of uncertainty. With the Queen noticeably aging, with the power of Spain as enormous as ever, no man could be sure who his next ruler might be, nor of the religion that ruler might bring with him to impose upon possibly unwilling subjects.[12]

The question of the preservation of Protestantism had of course engaged men's minds for all of Elizabeth's reign, and few had been more eager in their efforts to assist their co-religionists than Sir Philip Sidney and his uncle, the Earl of Leicester. These men, and those allied with them, had consistently argued in favor of war with Spain, wherever and whenever necessary to preserve the reformed faith. When war came at last, Leicester went to the Low Countries as commander of the English forces, and Sidney, at the head of a troop of horse, was permitted to follow him. Within the year Sidney lay dead at Zutphen, leaving his best sword to be inherited by his young friend and spiritual heir, Robert Devereux, Earl of Essex. By the time that Leicester passed from the scene, Essex was already established as the Queen's new favorite. The

12. Joel Hurstfield, "The Succession Struggle in late Elizabethan England," in his *Freedom, Corruption and Government in Elizabethan England* (London, 1973), pp. 104-34.

old group of adherents surrounding Sidney—his brother Robert, his friend Fulke Greville among them—transferred their allegiance to their leader's designated successor, and continued the old policy. Essex signalled his agreement by marrying Sidney's widow, Frances Walsingham, daughter of Leicester's ally, the warlike Principal Secretary, Sir Francis Walsingham. Bacon, his appeals to his uncle unheard, and office still eluding him, now turned to the new power at court for help, and thus allied himself with the war party.

Essex held some of the most important offices at court and, since the war continued and he had had more military experience than any other courtier, his opinion counted for much. But that was not enough to give him preeminence. Baron Burghley, the Lord Treasurer, and his son, Sir Robert Cecil, in practice Principal Secretary, dominated both the Council and the patronage system by which effective factions were built up. Furthermore, the Queen, who had never shared the extreme Protestant view that it was England's duty to aid any and all opponents of Catholicism, trusted the Cecils more than she did the war party. The "temporizers" stayed firmly in control of policy, to the frustration of those who came gradually to think of accommodation as akin to treason.

For the Essex group and its sympathizers, all this posed a problem of understanding. What they sought was some method by which to analyze and comprehend a crisis of so great a magnitude, a crisis in which the Queen, led astray (as they believed) by a group of self-interested courtiers, was taking the commonwealth down a road leading toward destruction and rejecting the offers of service from those most capable of saving the situation, such as Essex and Greville and Francis Bacon. These, and others associated with them, experimented with new modes of political analysis. Greville, still under the literary influence of Sidney, developed a species of tragedy through which he could express his views on the effects of favorites on weak monarchs. Henry Savile and John Hayward, on the fringes of the Essex circle, saw the writings of Tacitus as offering guidance on how men might survive under the rule of tyrants. Bacon himself at one time believed that the appropriate mode for such analysis was discourses on history, in the style of Machiavelli. And these men brought their questioning down to the basic problem of language itself. They came gradually to distrust the open and flowing Ciceronian style, redolent of the Roman republic, with its overtones of civic humanism, and to replace it with a sharper and more secretive style, abrupt and appropriate to tyranny, that of Seneca and Tacitus.[13] Thus matters of literary form and style became connected, in their minds, with matters of morality, with the result that changes in one reflected changes in the other. Bacon, Greville, and the rest were raising questions about the validity of the ethic of political humanism, and in so doing were questioning the bases of political morality as well. They did so under the pressure of the events of the 1590s.

II

Even for one so well-connected as Bacon, whose father had been Queen Elizabeth's first Lord Keeper and whose uncle was the great Lord Burghley, entry into court politics was by no means automatic.[14] Bacon assumed that family loyalty would force his uncle to do something for him; after all, one test of a patron's power was his ability to find places for his relations. But that reasoning neglected one crucial fact: Burghley's determination to see his younger son placed as his successor. The old Lord Treasurer would help his nephew a little, but he would not set up possible rivals to Robert Cecil. For years Bacon appealed to Burghley; then, when bitter disillusionment finally set in, he turned instead to Burghley's greatest enemy, the young Earl of Essex. Essex, as we have seen, was the leader of the old Leicester-Sidney connection, to which Bacon had no personal or ideological ties. But Essex was also the perfect courtier in the humanist mold. Well-educated, something of an intellectual, Essex resembled Sidney in his insistence on combining the active, military life with the contemplative, but far exceeded him in the amount of political patronage at his disposal. Here, then, was an opportunity for both men to use the patronage system for idealistic ends.

In a sense, Bacon and Essex were exactly complementary. That

13. The "new" style was first analyzed in a series of essays by Morris W. Croll, gathered and edited by J. Max Patrick and Robert O. Evans in *Style, Rhetoric, and Rhythm* (Princeton, 1966); the discussion was elaborated by George Williamson, *The Senecan Amble* (Chicago, 1951), esp. pp. 122-25, 191-93 and much modified by Brian Vickers, *Francis Bacon and Renaissance Prose* (Cambridge, 1968). On the interest in Tacitus, see also J. H. Whitfield, "Livy > Tacitus," in *Classical Influences on European Culture, A. D. 1500–1700*, ed. R. R. Bolgar (Cambridge, 1976), pp. 281-93; Peter Burke, "Tacitism," in *Tacitus. Studies in Latin Literature and its Influence*, ed. T. A. Dorey (London, 1969), pp. 149-71; Edwin B. Benjamin, "Bacon and Tacitus," *Classical Philology*, 60 (1965), 102-10; and most recently, Kenneth C. Schellhase, *Tacitus in Renaissance Political Thought* (Chicago, 1976), esp. pp. 157ff. and Alan T. Bradford, "Stuart Absolutism and the 'Utility' of Tacitus," *Huntington Library Quarterly* 46 (1983), 127-55.

14. There is a good account of this portion of Bacon's life in Jonathan L. Marwil, *The Trials of Counsel* (Detroit, 1976), ch. 2, though Marwil takes a more cynical view of Bacon than I do; see also Paul H. Kocher, "Francis Bacon and His Father," *Huntington Library Quarterly* 21 (1958), 133-58.

Bacon needed a patron was clear enough. Essex, for his part, also required a great deal of assistance. Any councillor who was also leader of a faction had to have staff support. For example, the Principal Secretary received his foreign information from the Queen's ambassadors and agents; Essex, his political opponent, anxious to pursue a very different foreign policy, had to find and coordinate his own sources of information. Francis Bacon solved that problem for him by persuading his brother, Anthony, to return from France (where he had been resident for many years) and act as Essex's "foreign secretary." Francis himself offered advice on domestic matters. More than that, he helped to manage the Earl's affairs during Essex's frequent absences on service abroad or on the high seas. Indeed, Bacon later said, for years "I applied myself to him. . . . For I did not only labour carefully and industriously in that he set me about, whether it were matter of advice, or otherwise, but neglecting the queen's service, mine own fortune, and in a sort my vocation, I did nothing but devise and ruminate with myself to the best of my under-standing, propositions and memorials of any thing that might concern his Lordship's honour, fortune, or service."[15] Bacon's further argument, that he did all this only for the good of the commonwealth, is perhaps a little disingenuous; he anticipated, quite rightly, that Essex would work equally hard to help Bacon gain the public office he so desperately sought.

That, in the end, Bacon failed to gain office was more his fault than his patron's. In 1593, at a time when the relations between the two men were as close as they were ever to be, Bacon, as a member of the House of Commons, rose to resist the Queen's appeal for extraordinary taxation. It was not that he found the amount of money called for so appalling; instead, he believed that the way in which it was to be collected was of dubious legality and would set an unfortunate precedent. Precisely why Bacon made so unpolitic a speech is now impossible to determine. That he spoke at Essex's behest or in his interest is unlikely, since one of his principal opponents in the debate was Fulke Greville, another of the Earl's men. Perhaps we may believe his own statement that his interven-tion was "in discharge of my conscience and duty to God, her Majesty and my country," especially as he then went on

If my heart be misjudged by imputation of popularity or opposition by any envious or officious informer, I have great wrong; and the greater, because the manner of my

15. *Sir Francis Bacon His Apologie* (1604), Spedding, III, 143.

speech did most evidently show that I spake simply and only to satisfy my conscience, and not with any advantage or policy to sway the cause; and my terms carried all signification of duty and zeal towards her Majesty and her service. It is true that from the beginning, whatsoever was above a double subsidy, I did wish might (for precedent's sake) appear to be extraordinary, and (for discontent's sake) mought not have been levied upon the poorer sort; though otherwise I wished it as rising as I think this will prove, and more.[16]

Such letters, sent broadside to anyone who might possibly help, not only did Bacon no good, but revealed a fundamental misunderstanding of the workings of the Elizabethan patronage system. After all, Essex did not himself grant appointments to public office; his contribution was his free access to the Queen, in whose sole gift such appointments lay. But the Queen did not allow open opposition, least of all from suppliants for her favor. Once the fatal speech had been uttered and reported to her Majesty, there was only one way for Bacon to regain the lost ground: he needed to apologize, as quickly and abjectly as possible, and he had to accept the inevitable fall from favor. Then, over time, his friends' efforts and his own would reinstate him in the Queen's good graces. This scenario had been played out at Court many times; there was no reason why Bacon should not have been familiar with the stage directions. Instead, he made excuses, offered interpretations of his words, and worst of all, pleaded conscience and duty. Such language might be appropriate for a civic humanist living in a republic, but it was not politic for an aspiring courtier. In essence, Bacon had set himself, and his private conscience, as equal to the Queen. That was what Elizabeth found unforgivable. She required royal servants, not equals.

Yet, it was at precisely this moment that Essex tried to place his friend in the post of Attorney-General and, when that failed, in the subordinate post of Solicitor-General. The effort was genuine enough, although Essex probably misjudged the Queen's obduracy or over-estimated his own ability to change her mind. "Your access," she said of Bacon, "is as much as you can look for. If it had been in the King her father's time, a less offence than that would have made a man be banished his presence for ever."[17] Despite the fact that Essex and Bacon were able for once to enroll the Cecils on their side, despite the concurrence of Lord Keeper Puckering, the most that Bacon's friends could achieve was to delay the appointment of some rival. Bacon himself grew more and more des-

16. Spedding, I, 234.
17. Spedding, I, 254.

pondent, and by 1594 had plunged into melancholy. "No man," he wrote
Essex, "ever received a more exquisite disgrace. And therefore truly, my
Lord, I was determined, and am determined, if her Majesty reject me,
this to do. My nature can take no evil ply; but I will by God's assistance,
with this disgrace of my fortune, and yet with that comfort of the good
opinion of so many honourable and worthy persons, retire myself with a
couple of men to Cambridge, and there spend my life in my studies and
contemplations, without looking back."[18] But this was to threaten Essex,
not the Queen, with withdrawal of service, and Essex already was doing
his uttermost. And, in fact, the failure of the effort was a direct result of
the extreme pressure exerted by Essex and Bacon and their allies. They
left the Queen with no avenue of escape, a situation in
which she always hated to find herself, with the result that "she did in
this as she useth in all, went from a denial to a delay" until, in the end, she
felt the time ripe to appoint Serjeant Fleming.[19]

The whole business showed Bacon at his worst. He was unable to
adopt the cool stance recommended by his cousin, Robert Cecil, who
himself had suffered by having to spend years doing the work of the
Principal Secretary without receiving either the title or the emoluments.
Bacon made enemies with hasty and sharp letters, and then had no idea
how to apologize. At one point, on the basis of an unconfirmed rumor
that Lord Keeper Puckering had defected from the Bacon-Essex camp,
he wrote him "there hath nothing happened to me in the course of my
business more contrary to my expectation, than your Lordship's failing
me and crossing me now in the conclusion, when friends are best tried."
Puckering endorsed this "Mr. Bacon wronging me."[20] Calming Puckering was extremely difficult. It was also vital, because the Queen was
most unlikely to appoint a Solicitor-General over the considered opposition of the head of the legal system. Since Bacon's apology (predictably)
failed to mollify, Essex ultimately had to intervene by writing to the
Lord Keeper himself:

I told your Lordship when I last saw you, that this manner of his [Bacon's] was only a
natural freedom and plainness, which he had used with me, and in my knowledge with
some other of his best friends, than any want of reverence towards your Lordship; and
therefore I was more curious to look into the moving cause of this style, than into the

18. Spedding, I, 291.
19. Thomas Birch, *Memoirs of the Reign of Queen Elizabeth from the Year 1581 till her Death*, 2 vols.
(London, 1754), I, 172.
20. Spedding, I, 364-65.

form of it; which now I find to be only a diffidence of your Lordship's favour and love towards him, and no alienation of that dutiful mind which he hath borne towards your Lordship.[21]

There is more than a little irony in Essex's placing the blame for Bacon's predicament on his style.

No wonder, then, that Bacon too considered his problem to be a matter of language. The language of truth, and of conscience, having failed him, he determined to examine the reverse, the language of seeming. The manuscript entitled *Promus of Formularies,* dated 1594-95, contains lists of phrases which seem intended to be used in such letters as he was writing at the time—"The matter goeth so slowly forward that I haue almost forgott it my self so as I maruaile not if my frendes forgett"—as well as long lists of proverbs and aphorisms. Some of these last are familiar enough to readers of Bacon's later works: "Faber quisque fortunae suae;" "It is in action as it is in wayes; comonly the nearest is the fowlest." Toward the end of the manuscript, the random lists give way to structures ordered by political questions: "Vpon Impatience of Audience," "Vpon question to reward evill wth. evill," "Vpon question whether a man should speak or forbear speach," each with appropriate adages. *Promus* represents the beginning of a study of political language, completed two years later in the *Essayes*.[22]

When finally the episode of the Solicitor-Generalship ended, Essex, conscious that he had failed in his role of patron, alleviated Bacon's notorious financial difficulties with the splendid gift of a manor; and Bacon, despite his continuing inability to secure office, retained his position as one of the Earl's advisers. Only a few years later, when Essex's headlong rashness had almost drowned him in innumerable difficulties, Bacon had the pleasure of suggesting that the way to regain the Queen's favor was "by obsequiesness and observance," not by the "kind of necessity and authority" which, when the Earl put it into practice, finally led him to the block.[23]

III

The 1597 edition of the *Essayes* was a small octavo of seven sheets,

---

21. Spedding, I, 366.

22. The text of *Promus* is in B. L., Harl. MS. 7017, ff. 83-132; it was printed in an appendix to Sir Edwin Durning-Lawrence, *Bacon is Shake-Speare* (London, 1910), pp. 185-286; my quotations may be found on pp. 201, 212, 220, 251. The beginning of a discussion of the "colors of good and euill" occurs on p. 275. Two leaves of the MS are dated: 5 December 1594 and 27 January 1595.

23. Spedding, III, 144.

containing ten Essays, a dozen Religious Meditations (in Latin; they were translated into English in the edition of 1598), and a fragment variously described as "Of the Colors of Good and Evil" or as "Places of Persuasion and Dissuasion." The book's dedication to the writer's brother, Anthony Bacon, made the usual excuses for publication: the manuscript had been circulating, a printer had gotten hold of it and was threatening to publish an unauthorized version, and the author had no choice but to protect himself and his text by publishing first. Moreover, Bacon went on to say, he had himself played the part of official censor, only to "find nothing to my understanding in them contrarie or infectious to the state of Religion, or manners, but rater (as I suppose) medicinable."[24]

The *Essayes* then may be seen as a corrective, as well to a way of behavior as to a point of view. A contemporary reader might, at first glance, have considered the book as an idiosyncratic version of that typical Renaissance product, the "institute," an ideal portrait of an institution, society, or occupation along the lines of Thomas Elyot's *The Book called the Governour* or Sir Thomas More's *Utopia*. Such an "institute" could be descriptive, as More's was, or prescriptive, as Elyot's. In the latter case, the reader was offered a model to imitate, together with a series of formulae to help achieve a species of self-fashioning.[25] Now, Bacon certainly understood the art of the "institute" and had, in his letter on travel to the Earl of Rutland of 1595, sketched his own, straightforward picture of "*cultum animi*, the tilling and manuring of your own mind."[26]

The purpose of travel, he said, as well as of education more generally, was to increase the Beauty, Health, and Strength of the mind. However, Bacon conceived of these three mental qualities in political terms. For example, beauty of mind was shown in sweetness of behavior, "and they that have that gift cause those to whom they deny anything to go better contented away, than men of contrary disposition do them to whom they grant."[27] Health was constancy, freedom from passions, a Stoic detach-

24. *The Works of Francis Bacon*, eds. James Spedding, R. L. Ellis and D. D. Heath, 7 vols. (London, 1857-59), VI, 523. This will be cited hereafter as *Works*. On the dedication, see also W. W. Greg, *Some Aspects and Problems of London Publishing between 1550 and 1650* (Oxford, 1956), pp. 56-58, 76, and Marwil, *Trials of Counsel*, 87-88.

25. Thomas Greene, "The Flexibility of the Self in Renaissance Literature," in *The Disciplines of Criticism*, ed. Peter Demetz, Thomas Greene, and Lowry Nelson, Jr. (New Haven, Conn., 1968), pp. 241-64. "Self-fashioning" comes from Stephen Greenblatt, *Renaissance Self-Fashioning* (Chicago, 1980), who applies the term primarily to middle-class writers; but see pp. 161ff.

26. Spedding, II, 6-15; the quotation is on p. 7.

ment, while Strength was the ability to perform good and great things. Of these three qualities, Beauty (behavior) was the one most susceptible to education; thus civil knowledge, a kind of behavior, could be acquired by study, by conference and, as here (in a tractate on travel) by observation at home and abroad, especially by observation of cause-and-effect, of counsels given and of the events which followed. Such political education, Bacon reminded Rutland, was intended for action, not for table-talk, for use rather than for ostentation. The letter can be read as a partial program for the *Essayes*, except that as, in the intervening years, Bacon's own opportunities for "action" receded, the tone became increasingly ironic.

In comparison to the Letter to Rutland, the 1597 *Essayes* mark a change from *Faber quisque ingenii sui*, Man is the maker of his own talents, to *Faber quisque fortunae suae*, "The Mould of a Mans fortune is in himself." The latter phrase, a version of which Francis' father, Sir Nicholas, often quoted and ultimately had painted on the walls of his long gallery, could easily be misinterpreted. "Sir Nicholas liked to observe that 'though he knew that *unusquisque suae fortunae faber* was a true and good principle, yet the most in number were those that marred themselves.'"[28] Francis at first agreed, and thought the adage insolent and unlucky. Gradually, however, he changed his mind, and came eventually to think of the public man as one "politic for his own fortune." Bacon shifted his emphasis from man's ability to train and control himself to resist the onslaughts of fortune to man's ability to control fortune herself, to be the architect of fortune.[29] That shift was heralded by replacing the effort of *cultum animi* by an examination of the arts of rising at court, that is, by replacing how to "be" with how to "seem." Thus, in the first of the essays, "Of Studies," Bacon said, "Reading maketh a full man, conference a readye man, and writing an exacte man. And therefore if a man write little, he had neede haue a great memorie, if he conferre little, he had neede haue a present wit, and if he reade little, hee had neede haue much cunning, to *seeme* to know that he doth not," and he took up the

---

27. Spedding, II, 7.

28. *Sir Nicholas Bacon's Great House Sententiae*, ed. Elizabeth McCutcheon, *English Literary Renaissance* Supplement #3 (1977), 32, quoting Sir Robert Naunton; the earliest discussion of this is in "A Letter and Discourse to Sir Henry Savill, touching helps for the intellectual powers," *Works*, VII, 98.

29. *Advancement of Learning*, *Works*, III, 469ff. This discussion owes much to Rexmond C. Cochrane, "Francis Bacon and the Architect of Fortune," *Studies in the Renaissance*, V (1958), 176-95.

point again in the following essay, "Of Discourse," in such sentences as "If you dissemble sometimes your knowledge of that you are thought to knowe, you shall bee thought another time to know that you know not."[30] Thus the result of the new emphasis on man's ability to control his own fortune was a concentration on means rather than ends, for the only end was success, a variable which altered according to circumstance. This, in turn, explains the linking of the *Essayes* with the *Colours of Good and Evil*, for the former constituted an analysis of how action might be used to manipulate men, while the latter demonstrated how language could be used to the same end.

The question remains, however, why Bacon should have chosen to investigate political action, and political language, by way of the essay form. Bacon was not only the first Englishman to use "essay" as a title but appears as well to have been the first actually to write in the new genre. Whether he learned of Montaigne's *Essaies* directly, or from Montaigne's translator, John Florio, or (most likely) through his brother Anthony, who during his long stay in Bordeaux became friendly with the Frenchman, it is impossible now to determine. In any event, as Bacon pointed out, "the word is late, but the thing is ancient."[31] Both men began with commonplace-books, large collections of maxims and sayings drawn largely from their reading in the classics. And Bacon would have agreed with Montaigne's use of the word "essay" as meaning "to test," provided that what was being tested was experience, either that of the author himself or that which the author had derived from his reading in the ancients. Thereafter, though, the points being made by the two essayists were fundamentally different. Montaigne's subject was himself, a particular man

> very ill-formed, whom I should really make very different from what he is if I had to fashion him over again. . . . I cannot keep my subject still. It goes along befuddled and staggering, with a natural drunkenness. I take it in this condition, just as it is at the moment I give my attention to it. I do not portray being: I portray passing. . . . This is a

30. *Works*, VI, 525 (my emphasis); 526.

31. Spedding, IV, 340-41; for relations to Montaigne, see Jacob Zeitlin, "The Development of Bacon's Essays—with special reference to the question of Montaigne's influence upon them," *JEGP* 27 (1928), 496-519; A. M. Boase, "The Early History of the *Essai* Title in France and Britain," in *Studies in French Literature presented to H. W. Lawton*, ed. J. C. Ireson, I. D. McFarlane and Garnet Rees (Manchester, 1968), pp. 67-73; Ted-Larry Pebworth, "Jonson's *Timber* and the Essay Tradition," in *Essays in Honor of Esmond Linworth Marilla*, ed. Thomas Austin Kirby and William John Olive (Baton Rouge, 1970), pp. 115-26; and more generally, Elbert N. S. Thompson, *The Seventeenth-Century English Essay*, University of Iowa Studies, Humanistic Studies, III (1926).

record of various and changeable occurrences, and of irresolute, and when it so befalls, contradictory ideas . . . If my mind could gain a firm footing, I would not make essays, I would make decisions; but it is always in apprenticeship and on trial.[32]

Thus, Montaigne tried to capture each fleeting mood or thought, in the hope that those who followed him down that road of self-examination would, in the end, be the wiser for it: "I do not correct my first imaginings by my second. . . . I want to represent the course of my humors, and I want people to see each part at its birth."[33] Bacon's essays, on the other hand, explored a topic rather than himself, with the result that they were much more straightforward in organization, and much less introspective, than those of Montaigne. Furthermore, Bacon's style was very different from Montaigne's, in accordance with the vast difference in their subject-matter. For while Montaigne's style projected a series of snapshots of a human spirit constantly in motion, Bacon's, in the 1597 *Essayes*, consisted of linked aphorisms, whose purpose was not to draw a picture, or to make a case, but to raise a question in the mind of the reader.[34]

Bacon's intention was to refashion political thinking, and the use of aphorisms seemed to offer the most hope for accomplishing this. Collections of adages, even of political adages, were nothing new. The Italian historian, Francesco Guicciardini, had himself compiled a volume of *Ricordi,* based on the same experiences that were the basis of his history of Italy. Later, other writers went to Guicciardini's works, and to Machiavelli's, and derived the maxims from the text.[35] But these maxims offered summaries drawn from the events described, conclusions in the form of precepts for future political behavior; and, as Bacon noted when collecting them, it was an easy matter to find pairs of plausible maxims which directly contradicted each other. Other handbooks of politics limited themselves to moral imperatives. Bacon's view was entirely different. "Aphorisms, representing a knowledge broken, do invite men to enquire farther; whereas Methods, carrying the shew of a total, do secure men, as if they were at furthest."[36] What Bacon seems to have had

32. *The Complete Works of Montaigne*, trans. Donald M. Frame (Stanford, Cal., 1957), pp. 610-11 ("Of Repentance").

33. *The Complete Works of Montaigne*, p. 574 ("Of the Resemblance of Children to Fathers").

34. Bacon's method is best discussed by Vickers, *Francis Bacon and Renaissance Prose*, and by Lisa Jardine, *Francis Bacon: Discovery and the Art of Discourse* (Cambridge, 1974), esp. ch. 13.

35. On this, see my *Tudor Historical Thought* (San Marino, 1967), pp. 239-40, and Vickers, pp. 68-70.

36. *The Advancement of Learning, Works*, III, 405; on aphorisms and their uses, the best discussion is in Jardine, pp. 176-78.

in mind was this: in a subject which, like political thought, was so immersed in the everyday details of action that it had not yet reached full development, it was too soon for the production of a formal treatise, for such a treatise would obstruct future work by implying that the subject was much more developed than in fact it was. What was needed was a method of presentation which would advance thought rather than retard it. One possibility here would be a commentary on matters of fact, in the style of Machiavelli's *Discourses on Livy*, for "history of Times is the best ground for discourse of government."[37] That would work well if one were interested in the behavior of states, less well if one's concern were with "negotiation," the political behavior of individuals. Unfortunately, this study was "of a nature whereof a man shall find much in experience, and little in books."[38] Here was no place for the method of axiom and deduction, which promised a certainty belied by the intractable materials of politics. Instead, the broken method of aphorism would be the more fruitful way. Here, by the artful juxtaposition of words, of maxims, of paragraphs, even of essays, the author could encourage his reader to construct his own provisional manual of politics. When this had been done enough times, these "manuals" could be combined, and an inductive science of politics be derived from them. But that was still far in the future.

In the meantime, the aphoristic method was inherently ambiguous, as indeed it had to be if Bacon were not to seize the initiative from his reader. Anne Righter has put the point very neatly: "It is the nature of the aphorism to mean more than one thing. In the words themselves, not merely in the progression of the sentences, Bacon contrives to gather together a whole series of different and sometimes contradictory meanings and emotions; to hold them in suspension in such a way that they react upon one another; and to explore without dictating."[39] The ambiguity of the *Essayes*, which is most noticeable in the edition of 1597, is thus to be taken positively, as a virtue; but that ambiguity also reflects Bacon's own doubts about the political situation of the mid-1590s. It is never easy to discover how much of what Bacon says is mockery or satire, intended to expose rather than to propose. But it does appear to be true that, by 1597, he had come to adopt Machiavelli's view that it was more impor-

---

37. *The Advancement of Learning, Works*, III, 453.

38. Spedding, IV, 340 [manuscript draft of a preface to the second edition of the *Essays*].

39. Anne Righter, "Francis Bacon," in *The English Mind*, ed. Hugh Sykes Davies and George Watson (Cambridge, 1964), p. 28.

tant to study what men do rather than what they ought to do, and to guide one's own actions by the conclusions deriving from such study. Only thus might a man be *Faber quisque fortunae suae.*

IV

The political uses of ambiguity and the method of the *Essayes* may be illustrated in the resounding opening sentence of the second of them, "Of Discourse:"

Some in their discourse desire rather commendation of wit in being able to holde all arguments, then of iudgement in discerning what is true as if it were a praise to know what might be said, and not what shoulde be thought. .

Long habit, developed through reading some of the countless "institutes" in which Renaissance England abounded. would make the reader take this as a prelude to some sort of moral imperative, to some elevation of truth above wit. The next sentence would begin to dispel the illusion, for Bacon went on to disparage those who had only a few themes, who lacked variety and thus were tedious, even (occasionally) ridiculous. The sentence following clinched the matter: "The honourablest part of talke is to guide the occasion, and againe to moderate and passe to somewhat else." The reader, taken aback, came to the realization that, far from condemning wit, Bacon was making suggestions on how to seem more witty than one was. The art of making a good impression consisted of steering the conversation toward one's best subject. The remainder of the essay was devoted to the details of using discourse to seem wise, and it ended with the simple dictum "To vse too many circumstances ere one come to the matter is wearisome, to use none at all is blunt."[40]

What Bacon had done was to open with a most grandiloquent sentence, the parts so carefully balanced as to make the whole appear ambiguous, and then follow it with a series of detailed statements which did not so much illustrate the principal, orthodox point as to raise doubts about it. The idea may have come from Machiavelli, whose *Prince* borrowed its (Latin) headings from the older moral treatises and then placed beneath them an (Italian) text based on entirely different premises. The purpose of all this was to foil the reader's expectations, not for the sake of clever trickery but to force him to think the issue through.

40. *Works*, VI, 526. My reading of Bacon owes a great deal to Stanley E. Fish, *Self-Consuming Artifacts* (Berkeley, 1972), ch. II: "Georgics of the Mind: The Experience of Bacon's *Essays*." Fish's admirable and exciting essay, however, studies the changes in the text over the three editions (1597, 1612, 1625) rather than examining any one edition in its totality.

Moreover, Bacon's art of juxtaposition was not limited to single essays. "Of Discourse" was an elaboration of a single clause in the opening part of the preceding essay, "Of Studies," in which we had been told that studies served for pastimes, ornaments and abilities, and that the chief use for ornament was in discourse. Discourse, then, had no virtue of its own, but was entirely instrumental; it was a way of seeming great, and wise, without necessarily being so. But even virtue did not escape unscathed. The immediately succeeding essay "Of Ceremonies and Respectes" opened once more with a morally dubious generalization—"He that is onely reall had need haue exceeding great parts of vertue, as the stone had neede be rich that is set without foyle"—which suggests that seeming virtue can replace real virtue, and then twisted its way down once more to a specific conclusion, returning to matters of discourse: "It is a good precept generally in seconding another: yet to adde somewhat of ones owne; as if you will graunt his opinion, let it be with some distinction, if you wil follow his motion, let it be with condition; if you allow his counsell, let it be with alleadging further reason."[41]

Similarly, in "Of Faction," Bacon began by denying the opinion of Machiavellian politicians that a wise prince ruled through the manipulation of factions. Quite the reverse, he said; the prince's time was better spent in dealing with individuals, and in seeing to it that factions agreed on the most important things and limited their squabbling to the trivial. Once more, Bacon opened with an orthodox opinion, obliquely expressed; this time, however, he issued a warning: "But I say not that the consideration of Factions is to be neglected." Nor was it. In the ensuing paragraph, Bacon switched the focus from the prince to the subjects, and in doing so shifted from the ideal to the real. For in a real world, factions existed, and the question thus became how subjects could make the best use of them. Thus Bacon differentiated between the roles of great men and lesser, between new men and old; he examined what happened to factions over time, and what happened to politic men who had succeeded in using factions to gain their ends. Slowly, he worked his way down the scale of faction-bound politicians until he reached the lowest of them all, "the traitor in Factions"—who, contrary to expectation, was commonly not punished for his sins, but "lightly goeth away with it . . . and getteth al the thankes."[42] So Bacon moved from the very general, the theory of how a prince should handle factions, to the very

41. *Works*, VI, 527.
42. *Works*, VI, 532-33.

specific and individual, and in the succeeding essay, "Of Negociating," analyzed the ways by which negotiation between competing entities— great men at court—might be carried out.

Factions were made up of followers, of men who "follow not vpon affection to him with whome they raunge themselues, but vpon discont- entment conceiued against some other," and it was this fact that led to the ill-will so common between the great men at court. Such followers were to be eschewed, along with those whose costs, in money and prestige, were too high. Indeed, the only sort of follower worth having was one who joined himself to you because you advanced the virtuous. Nor should the leader promote men too quickly, for fear of raising higher expectations than could be met. Indeed, in the distribution of favors, the leader should resemble a Calvinist deity, using men "with much differ- ence and election," which makes those preferred grateful and the rest more eager to please. Such were Bacon's comments in an essay entitled "Of followers and friends," in which friendship was not mentioned until a few lines from the end, and then was introduced in most ambiguous fashion:

> To be gouerned by one [follower] is not good, and to be distracted with many is worse; but to take aduise of friends is ever honorable: *For lookers on many times see more than gamesters, And the vale best discouereth the hill.* There is little friendship in the worlde, and least of all betweene equals; which was wont to bee magnified. That that is, is betweene superiour and inferiour, whose fortunes may comprehend the one the other.[43]

Thus Bacon explicitly defeated the reader's expectation: instead of building up to the anticipated high praise of true friendship, in the familiar style of Damon and Pythias, there was leader and follower, master and servant, whose "friendship" was a matter of utility only. And what did Bacon intend here by "fortunes?" Money was one possibility, influence and the power to wield it another. Or he may have meant that the good or ill fortune of one of these unequal partners would raise or lower the other. What is certain is that Bacon equated friendship with dependency, with the corollary that such friendship was inevitably ephemeral, lasting only so long as their common bonds and aspirations united the friends. The reader, by now accustomed to Bacon's method, could not have been too surprised to find, on the next page, "Of Sutes."[44]

---

43. *Works*, VI, 527-28.

44. "Of Sutes" was probably a typographical error; in the list of essays prefixed to the collection, this was called "Sutors," and it retained that title in later editions. Bacon intended the emphasis on the person of the suitor.

In "Of Honour and reputation" Bacon varied the pattern only slightly. Once more, the reader's expectations go unfulfilled, for the author does not contrast honor to reputation, but instead contrasts both to virtue. Honor, it turned out, was virtue's public reputation and as such could and should be augmented. In practice, that meant a wise man would exercise his virtue where it was most noticeable. Originality mattered. "If a man performe that which hath not beene attempted before . . . he shall *purchase* more Honour, then by effecting a matter of greater difficulty or vertue, wherein he is but a follower."[45] The word "purchase" was ambiguous in Bacon's time, meaning both "acquire" and "buy," and Bacon surely relished the ambiguity. But his meaning was not in doubt, for he had already said that "Riches are for spending, and spending for honour and good actions."[46] Honor, once a matter of high praise, had been reduced to the mercenary, and Bacon, again using familiar vocabulary in a novel way, had cast doubt not only on the word but on the thing.

So honor, like other erstwhile virtues, was turned into a matter of politics, a weapon in the hands of the courtier anxious to get ahead. In the realm of politics, Bacon argued, it was more important to seem to have a virtue than really to have it. In politics, all men wore masks. The man of judgment, the friend of the great, could offer two sorts of advice: how best to wear a mask, and how to discover the reality behind the masks of others. Much of the *Essayes* was devoted to the first of these, but Bacon concluded with the second, which was especially important in "negotiating," for "if you would worke any man, you must either know his nature and fashions and so leade him, or his ends, and so winne him, or his weaknesses or disaduantages, and so awe him, or those that haue interest in him and so gouerne him." The same methods were essential "in dealing with cunning persons," for to strip away their masks "we must euer consider their endes to interpret their speeches."[47]

To aid in the same work, Bacon appended the fragmentary "Colors of Good and Evil." To "color" an argument was to embellish it in such a way as to make it persuasive, so that the audience would be moved to a particular course of action. The aspiring courtier needed to be able to "sway the ordinary judgment either of a weak man, or of a wise man not

45. *Works*, VI, 531 [my emphasis].
46. In "Of Expense," *Works*, VI, 530.
47. *Works*, VI, 534.

fully and considerately attending and pondering the matter."[48] Bacon's text shows how, by the use of examples, plausibly drawn from history or fable or parable, the argument might be augmented so that the careless listener might find himself drawn to actions unprofitable to his cause. But since, for Bacon, the use of "colors" was not ethically neutral, he also saw it as his duty to protect the courtier against this dangerous weapon by illustrating, in each case, the "fallax" in the argument. These places of persuasion and dissuasion were thus an elaboration on the art of "negotiating" so necessary to success at court.

V

So the *Essayes* of 1597, and the "Colors of Good and Evil" associated with them, represented the culmination of that study of political language which Bacon had begun in the aftermath of his rejection by the Queen four years earlier. In 1593 he had convinced himself that his motives, and those of men like him, had been misconstrued, and he tried to explain them. At that point, he continued to believe in the doctrine of political humanism which, as he understood it, was intended to produce an ethical courtier, one who sought patronage as a means to approach the seat of power in order to influence the monarch to govern well. The great Protestant hero, Sir Philip Sidney, had pursued that goal. So now did the Earl of Essex, Sidney's political heir and Bacon's patron. They had failed. Sidney, and Essex after him, could not persuade Elizabeth to become the champion of European Protestantism, and each had to suffer periods of political banishment as punishment for their fervor. So Bacon, in his own turn, having taken what he considered to be the ethical line about taxes in the 1593 Parliament, could not convince the Queen of the rightness of his position.

At first, Bacon believed that his fault lay in his words, and he responded—as the notes in his *Promus* indicate—with a thorough-going analysis of the arts of persuasion in general, and of political persuasion specifically. That study seems to have been responsible for his growing doubts about the necessity of the link between patronage and humanism, the link which had produced the idea of the ethical courtier in the handbooks from Castiglione onwards. Instead, Bacon concluded, the ethical courtier had failed precisely because of his ethics.

Bacon's analysis of the language of politics enabled him to separate the

---

48. *Works*, VII, 77. See Jardine, *Francis Bacon: Discovery and the Art of Discourse*, pp. 219-24.

pursuit of power from its ethical moorings. The *Essayes*, in which that analysis first appeared publicly, represented his way of dealing with the question of political patronage, which he now defined entirely as an art of self-advancement. Where earlier treatises, the "institutes" of human-ist education, had tried to fashion the perfect courtier, laboring to elevate him to the heights of Christian morality, Bacon responded by seeing the whole enterprise as a sham. "Studies," as he conceived them, might serve as the amusement of the retired, or to ornament discourse, or they might serve to improve the mind. But such studies might easily be overdone. Sloth or affectation could result. And even the truly learned were better fitted to pronounce judgments than to perform great deeds. Studies held, at best, an intermediate position: "They perfect *Nature*, and are perfected by experience." Moreover, studies "teach not their owne vse, but that is a wisedome without them: and aboue them wonne by observation."[49] However, in the traditional institutes, studies *did* teach "their own use," for the purpose of study had been to inculcate the virtue thought to be necessary for the perfect courtier. Bacon now denied it. Studies might still improve a man's untutored nature and hone his judgment, but the experience of courts and politics mattered more. Guided by that expe-rience, the courtier living in the bleak world of Elizabethan politics learned that the political humanism he had been taught served best as a mask, to be put on when it could be advantageous to him.

49. *Works*, VI, 525.

"Best Men are Molded out of Faults": Marrying the Rapist in Jacobean Drama

SUZANNE GOSSETT

HISTORICAL sources agree that after 1612, with the deaths of Prince Henry and Salisbury, and especially after 1616, with the fall of Somerset and the rise of Buckingham, sexual vice was increasingly conspicuous at the Jacobean court. Whitehall was a "constant round of dissipation and libertinism,"[1] scandals touched the greatest in the land, and the King was sinking "into physical decay and into premature senility."[2] At the same time the drama had moved—decayed, some would say—into tragicomedy, a form well-adapted to titillation and suggestiveness. One little-remarked result of this combination of changing social mores and changing dramatic form was an abrupt departure from the previously stereotyped rape plot. From 1594 to 1624 the depiction of rape on the English stage went through a series of alterations. Following nearly twenty years of plays based on classical models and influenced by English law and traditional morality, four plays of the late Jacobean period abandon the usual story in ways which undermine the force in any verbal strictures against rape. Then, just before the court atmosphere changes again with the coronation of Charles I, Massinger takes the new plot structures and demonstrates that the conventional moral order can be imposed upon them.

Although many plays contain intended or attempted rapes, there are only four plays in the period 1594–1612 in which rape actually occurs and in which the victim and her attacker must therefore confront the

---

1. The phrase is Thomas Longueville's in *The Curious Case of Lady Purbeck* (London, 1901), p. 66. There is a discussion of the sexual vices of the court in G.P.V. Akrigg, *Jacobean Pageant* (New York, 1967), pp. 240ff.
2. D. Harris Willson, *King James VI and I* (London, 1956), p. 378.

consequences and choose future courses of actions.[3] The four plays, *Titus Andronicus, The Revenger's Tragedy,* Heywood's *The Rape of Lucrece,* and Fletcher's *Valentinian,* demonstrate the existence of a norm for the dramatic depiction of rape. In all four plays the raped woman is married, virtuous, chaste, and religious. All four plays follow one of the two classical models, the stories of Lucrece or of Procne and Philomel. *Titus,* which recalls the Philomel story, has numerous references to Lucrece, as well as a married heroine like Lucrece herself. The raped woman is avenged by her husband or her father. The rapist or rapists are regarded as unforgiveable, and must be executed in the play: "Base rape shall bleed" (*Lucrece* 5.1.216).[4] All four heroines also die, Lavinia of necessity by her father's hand, the others by their own. The plays are all tragedies despite the positive political changes which occur as incidental effects in three of them.

The moral condemnation of rape is constant and unambiguous. Only a villain like Aruns could suggest of Lucrece "was she not a woman? Ay, and perhaps was willing to be forced" (5.2.22). Each rape is simply presented as a wicked attack on virtue. The women are physically overcome and, in the cases of Lucrece and Lucina, tricked. The men's motives are primarily sexual, although several times tinged with political antagonism toward the woman's family. In *Titus Andronicus* Demetrius

3. Of course there may have been rapes in plays which are not extant. Intended or attempted but unsuccessful rapes occur in *Lust's Dominion* (Day, Dekker, and Haughton, 1600); *The Wonder of Women or the Tragedy of Sophonisba* (Marston, 1605); *Volpone* (Jonson, 1606); *Pericles* (Shakespeare, 1608); *Cymbeline* (Shakespeare, 1609); *The Atheist's Tragedy* (Tourneur, 1609); *The Second Maiden's Tragedy* (Anonymous, 1611). The manuscript play *The Fatal Marriage or a Second Lucretia,* which may be the same as the *Galiaso* mentioned by Henslowe in 1594, contains an abduction but no rape. In *Bonduca* (Fletcher, 1611–1614) the rape of the Queen's daughters is part of the prehistory of the play. No details are given of the attack, which occurred during an earlier war between the Britons and the Romans. The daughters do ultimately commit suicide, but their reason is to avoid capture by the victorious Romans and to save their patriotic honor as British princesses.

4. References in the text are to *Thomas Heywood,* ed. A. Wilson Verity (London, n.d.); to *The Complete Works of Shakespeare,* ed. David Bevington, Third Edition (Glenview, Ill., 1980); to John Fletcher, *The Queen of Corinth,* in *The Works of Francis Beaumont and John Fletcher,* eds. Arnold Glover and A. R. Waller (Cambridge, Eng., 1904–1910); to Fletcher, Massinger, and Field, *The Tragedy of Valentinian,* ed. Robert K. Turner, Jr., in *The Dramatic Works in the Beaumont and Fletcher Canon,* ed. Fredson Bowers, Vol. 4 (Cambridge, Eng., 1979); to Cyril Tourneur, *The Revenger's Tragedy,* ed. Lawrence J. Ross (Lincoln, Neb., 1966); to William Rowley, *All's Lost by Lust,* ed. Charles Wharton Stork (Philadelphia: *University of Pennsylvania Publications in Philology and Literature,* Vol. 13, 1910); to *The Plays and Poems of Philip Massinger,* eds. Philip Edwards and Colin Gibson (Oxford, 1976); to Thomas Middleton, *Women Beware Women,* ed. J. R. Mulryne (London, 1975); and to Thomas Middleton, *The Spanish Gypsy,* in *The Works of Thomas Middleton,* ed. A. H. Bullen (Boston, 1885).

and Chiron both "love" Lavinia but are content with "some certain snatch" (2.1.95); only Aaron sees how their lust can be used to further Tamora's revenge on the Andronici. Valentinian is lustful and "must have women" (3.1.10). Sextus "cannot rest / Till our hot lust embosom in thy breast" (3.4.164–65), and Youngest Son says he was moved to Antonio's wife by "flesh and blood" (1.2.47). The women's very chastity is an incentive to violation: in *Titus* Lavinia is raped partly because she "stood upon her chastity" (2.3.124); Lord Antonio's wife is "that religious lady" (1.1.111); and when the rape is over Valentinian tells Lucina not to curse him but "her that drew me . . . Curse those faire eyes, and curse that heavenly beauty, / And curse your being good too" (3.1.54–57).

The women invariably accept the patriarchal value system and the inevitability of their own deaths. Although there is usually some explicit statement that the raped woman is not guilty but a victim, she must "die . . . and [her] shame with [her]" (*Titus,* 5.3.46), because as Lucrece explains, "though my thoughts be white as innocence, / Yet is my body soiled with lust-burnt sin" (5.1.98–99).[5]

By the time of *Valentinian,* the last of these plays,[6] certain of the norms are reduced to outline form, suggesting that the audience response could be taken for granted. Lucina, Maximus' wife, has a "God of vertue" (1.1.73) in her which tempts the emperor Valentinian: "she is such a pleasure, being good, / That though I were a god, she would fire my bloud" (1.3.249–50). Valentinian himself is a compendium of sins as spelled out by his loyal general Aecius. In a variation of the Lucrece story, Valentinian wins Maximus' ring at dice, sends for Lucina, and rapes her in the palace. Fletcher invokes the classical precedents to insure our response. Earlier, when asked what she would do if the emperor forced her, Lucina "pointed to a *Lucrece*" (1.1.92), and in upbraiding

5. The value system operative here is explored more fully by Catharine R. Stimpson, "Shakespeare and the Soil of Rape," in *The Woman's Part: Feminist Criticism of Shakespeare,* ed. Carolyn Ruth Swift Lenz, Gayle Greene, and Carol Thomas Neely (Urbana, Ill., 1980), pp. 56–64, and by Coppélia Kahn, "The Rape in Shakespeare's *Lucrece,"* *Shakespeare Studies,* 9 (1976), 45–72.

6. *Valentinian* has traditionally been dated between 1610, when its source was published, and December 1614, when William Ostler, who appears in the F2 actors list, died. R. K. Turner, Jr. has recently suggested that the song "Care charming sleep" (5.2.13ff.) was adapted by the death of Prince Henry and that the play therefore dates before 6 November 1612. (Turner, *Valentinian,* pp. 263, 389–90.) The two-year difference does not affect the argument, but there is a nice parallel if the last exemplar of the traditional model does coincide with Prince Henry's death. There are no further rapes in extant plays until 1616–17 (see below).

Valentinian after the rape, she calls down curses "Even those the *Sabines* sent, when *Romulus, /* (As thou hast me) ravish'd their noble Maydes." She adds, "The sins of *Tarquin* be rememberd in thee" (3.1.88–91).

When Maximus and Aecius come upon Lucina weeping they recognize what has happened without any explanation. Her husband says:

> Oh my best friend, I am ruind; goe *Lucina,*
> Already in thy teares, I have read thy wrongs,
> Already found a *Cesar;* go thou Lilly,
> Thou sweetly drooping floure: go silver Swan,
> And sing thine owne sad requiem: goe *Lucina,*
> And if thou dar'st, out live this wrong. (3.1.156–61)

Lucina replies simply, "I dare not." No fewer than six times does Maximus urge her to suicide and bid her farewell. Aecius feebly encourages her to live, using three standard arguments: she might draw Valentinian to repentance, the deed is not hers, and "such deaths are superstitious" (3.1.246). None of these arguments has any weight against Maximus' traditional patriarchal explanation of why she must die:

> If she were any thing to me but honour . . .
> Or could the wrongs be hers alone, or mine,
> Or both our wrongs, not tide to after issues . . .
>   [But] our names must find it,
> Even those to come; and when they read, she livd,
> Must they not aske how often she was ravishd,
> And make a doubt she lov'd that more then Wedlock?
> Therefore she must not live. (3.1.232–45)

In complete accord with these values Lucina leaves. Fletcher is so entrenched within the convention that he does not bother to create a mechanism for her death. Instead her woman simply reports that, entering the house weeping and blushing, "Dare I, said she, defile this house with whore, / In which his noble family has flourish'd? / At which she fel, and stird no more" (3.1.366–68). The very silence reveals that the method of death is insignificant.

At this point it becomes Maximus' duty to revenge his wife's rape and death, and here Fletcher complicates the plot by introducing the conflict between two kinds of honor—absolute loyalty to sovereign, and loyalty to self and family. It is too simple to dismiss the result as *servile de jure* royalism; in fact, Maximus' failure to revenge the rape straightforwardly reveals the deep flaws in his character. To reach Valentinian he basely causes the death of his best friend, Aecius, who has urged him not to kill the emperor. Yet once the way is cleared, Valentinian is murdered not by Maximus but by Aecius' eunuchs, whose loyalty to their master implicitly criticizes Maximus. Finally, while relishing the removal of Valentinian, Maximus completes the process of self-condemnation by the comment, "Why may not I be *Caesar* . . . If I rise, / My wife was ravish'd well" (5.3.26, 38–39). Apparently he convinces the widowed empress that he did everything, even "make the rape," to gain her, but she is not fooled and in a final surprise kills Maximus at the coronation. Despite the complications *Valentinian* adheres to the same values as the earlier plays. Lucina must die, and Valentinian cannot live, having raped her. Though Maximus, like Antonio in *The Revenger's Tragedy,* might have acceptably become ruler as an accidental result of the revenge, his wickedness is confirmed by his attempt to profit from the rape, and he must also die. *Valentinian* is very poorly constructed—Maximus decides he wants to be emperor in the fifth act—but by 1612 Fletcher had not changed the assessment either of rape or of its perpetrators.

II

A few years later, in *The Queen of Corinth,* Fletcher, along with Massinger and Field, initiates a dramatically different handling of the rape plot. This is the first of four plays, *The Queen of Corinth, All's Lost by Lust, Women Beware Women,* and *The Spanish Gypsy,* which in the seven years 1617–1623 abandon the established model in striking ways. *All's Lost by Lust,* the only one which attempts the traditional plot, is inconsistent in its treatment of key elements. The other three form a pattern. None of the plots is based on Lucrece or Philomel. In all three plays the heroine survives the rape and marries the rapist. Twice the ravisher is not recognized by the victim, although he is known to the audience, and the plot focuses as much on finding him as on revenge. Most surprising of all, two of these plays have happy, or at least tragicomic, endings.[7]

To understand how shocking these innovations were it is helpful to examine the law and the reality of rape in Jacobean times. Law is an

7. A partial model for the situation in these plays is found in Terence's comedy *Hecyra* or *The Mother-in-Law.* However, the Roman play differs radically in mores and in atmosphere from the Jacobean plays. In *Hecyra* the rape has occurred before the play, which begins when the victim, who never appears, has been married to her attacker for seven months. The two mothers-in-law and the husband's former mistress are important characters. There is no repentance, merely a sorting out of facts when the victim delivers the child she conceived during the rape. The Renaissance plays have no equivalent to the young man's relationship with the courtesan or his attitude toward the child; in fact, there was a common superstition that rape could not lead to conception.

embodiment of the social and moral attitudes of a society, and although the Elizabethan legal system discountenanced revenge, it was almost as harsh as the classical legends in dealing with rape. As summarized by W. S. Holdsworth, "Rape from the earliest times was remedied by the appeal of the injured woman. . . . If prosecuted by the woman by way of appeal it was a felony, and the penalty was loss of limb; but the appeal might be compromised, and sometimes was compromised, on the basis of marriage. If the woman brought no appeal and the ravisher was indicted [i.e., prosecuted by the crown], the crime was not regarded as a felony, and could be expiated by fine and imprisonment."[8]

There had been some changes in the law in the fourteenth century. The statute of Westminster I, 1375, while it lengthened the time in which a woman could appeal, attempted to lessen the punishment for rape to fine and imprisonment. But, Edward Coke writes, "it is not credible what ill successe this act, that mitigated the former punishment, had; for many ill disposed persons taking . . . encouragement to follow the heat of lust, did many shamelesse and shamefull rapes in barbarous and inhumane manner. . . . This crying sin daily increasing, our noble king, ten yeares after this act, made rape by authority of parliament felony [i.e., in Westminster II, 1385.]"[9]

As part of its increased rigor the new law specifically reduced the possibility of expiating rape through marriage. Coke says that before Westminster I, the rapist "should lose his eyes and his privy members, unlesse she that was ravished before judgement demaunded him for her husband; for that was onely in the will of the woman and not of the man." But Westminster II provided that "if a man . . . do ravish a woman . . . where she did not consent, neither before nor after, he shall have judgement of life and of member. And likewise where a man ravisheth a woman . . . although she consent after, he shall have such judgement as before is said, if he be attainted at the king's suit." Coke comments, "hereby the auncient law concerning the election given to her that is ravished is taken away . . . Afterwards by the statute of R. 2. a greater punishment is inflicted upon the party ravished, if she after consent to the ravisher, *viz.* that as well the ravished as the ravisher should be disabled to challenge inheritance, dower, or joynt-feoffement."[10] The law was

---

8. Holdsworth, *A History of English Law,* 3rd Ed., III (Boston, 1923), p. 316.

9. *The Second Part of the Institutes of the Laws of England* (1797), I, 181.

10. Coke, I, 180; II, 432–33. Of course if there was no indictment, the victim could marry her ravisher without penalty. Sir William Blackstone comments that "even now marriage closes the

particularly concerned to protect property. Holdsworth explains, "in 1557–1558 the abduction of heiresses, being minors under sixteen, without their parents' consent, was made punishable with fine or imprisonment; and a long term of imprisonment was imposed on those who in addition violated or married such heiresses. If the heiress consented, her next of kin were to enjoy the profits of her land during her life."[11] These laws remained in effect throughout the Elizabethan and Jacobean period—even in the eighteenth century stealing an heiress was a felony regardless of her eventual consent.[12] No change in the law accounts for the change in the drama in the later years of James. Were it not that the plays we shall examine are set in far away Corinth or Spain, their tragicomic conclusions would be vitiated by the audience's knowledge that a raped girl who agrees to marry her violator loses her inheritance and, it appears, any presumption of innocence.

Turning from law to historical fact, we find that rape was either rare or, more probably, poorly reported. In J. S. Cockburn's study of the nature and incidence of crime in England from 1559 to 1625, only 50 of 7544 indictments at Assizes in several test counties were for rape.[13] Bridenbaugh claims that sexual laxity was on the increase in the years prior to 1640, but in one of his sample years in Middlesex (1624), only two of 250 true bills found for crimes before the Court of Quarter Sessions were for rape.[14] In Essex, the most closely studied county, "somewhat unexpectedly, the Assize records . . . yield very few charges. In contrast, twenty-three cases came up at the archdeacons' courts, of which seventeen were for attempted rape."[15]

Information in Emmison's studies of Elizabethan life suggests that reporting may have been uncommon because it was not always useful. For instance, in three early accusations of what must have been a

---

mouth of the principal witness, and thus practically operates as a condonation of the offense." *Sir William Blackstone, Commentaries on the Laws of England, Book the Fourth,* ed. William G. Hammond, (San Francisco, Cal. 1890), p. 269n.

11. Holdsworth, *A History of English Law,* 3rd Ed., IV (1924; rpt. London, 1966), p. 514.

12. Blackstone, pp. 265–66.

13. Cockburn, "The Nature and Incidence of Crime in England 1559–1625," in *Crime in England 1550–1800,* ed. J. S. Cockburn (Princeton, N.J., 1977), p. 58.

14. Carl Bridenbaugh, *Vexed and Troubled Englishmen* (New York, 1968), p. 367, p. 388.

15. F. G. Emmison, *Elizabethan Life: Morals and the Church Courts* (Chelmsford, Eng., 1973), p. 44. In *Law and Order in Historical Perspective, The Case of Elizabethan Essex* (New York and London, 1974), p. 20, Joel Samaha has a table of crimes by years. Except for a sudden increase in rapes between 1580 and 1583 (seven in 1581) his figures are very low, frequently zero.

common occurrence, the rape of a servant girl by her master, the defendants were all acquitted.[16] The results of three other cases reveal a tendency to blame the victim: repeatedly women did penance when men were accused of adultery. Joan Somers accused Rice Evans of violently abusing her body: "strangely enough, the presentment lay against her— for fornication—and this was her defence." Although John Robinson was accused of adultery with Jasper Cole's wife, it was she who "should have done penance," and when Katherine Lee, taken in bed with one Robert Wrignelles, claimed he provoked her, partly by force, "she (not he) was ordered full penance." If the findings of the church courts were similar to these of the Assizes, we cannot agree with F. G. Emmison that "the small number of prosecutions for alleged violent assaults on virgins' chastity or wives' virtue . . . is somewhat unexpected." He is more probably correct that "perhaps females' fear of court proceedings induced inaction until pregnancy was realized, when it was probably too late to accuse the assailant."[17] The evidence suggests that a girl might consider herself lucky to marry her rapist, especially if she was pregnant. Because of the burden placed on the community, bastardy was severely treated.

At court no single notorious case of rape accounts for the change of dramatic treatment starting around 1617. But it was at this time that, as Lawrence Stone writes, "public attention was finally riveted on the sexual behavior of the aristocracy by a series of sensational scandals which found their way into the law courts."[18] Trouble began with the 1613 annulment of the marriage of Frances Howard and the Earl of Essex; by 1615 the complicity of this lady and possibly her new husband, the royal favorite Somerset, in the Overbury murder was discovered. In 1617 the notorious treatment of Frances Coke, abducted first by her mother and then by her father for the purposes of different marriages, mocked any pretense that marriage was not a property arrangement; in 1618 there was the Roos incest scandal. Apparently the new favorite, Buckingham, did not take rape seriously; although one Dr. Lambe, whom Chamberlain called a "notorious old rascall," was found guilty of

16. F. G. Emmison, *Elizabethan Life: Disorder* (Chelmsford, Eng., 1970), p. 196.

17. Emmison, *Morals and the Church Courts*, pp. 44–47. Samaha, p. 46, writes, "The records are virtually bulging with examinations laying out in the minutest detail the acts leading up to sexual intercourse that resulted in the birth of illegitimate children in Elizabethan Essex, and there is not a single one in which the woman's contention that she was forced into the sexual act was taken seriously. . . . few accused rapists [were] ever convicted."

18. *The Crisis of the Aristocracy, 1558–1641*, Abridged Edition (New York, 1967), p. 300.

rape at the King's Bench in the summer of 1624, he escaped punishment because he was favored at court by Buckingham and his mother.[19]

Two cases from the early 1630s show the extremes with which rape could be treated, while also revealing how far sexual laxity might go. Among the Ellesmere papers in the Huntington Library is a group of letters and testimonials to the Earl of Bridgewater about the alleged rape of one Margery Evans by Philbert Burghill. Margery, a servant girl, was only fourteen; she met Burghill on the road, and later claimed that he had raped and robbed her. According to her aunt she raised hue and cry as required and found the man in the house of the bailiff. She wanted him carried before the justice of the peace, but instead she was herself committed to jail for almost a month. Finally, after one assize court had refused to indict, "at the Last Assizes at Herefford Philbert Burghill gent. and one Williams his man were indicted for a rape and felonie. . . . The matter appeared soe odious to Baron Trevor Judg there that hee caused Burghill to bee taken from the barr to the Gaole and in open Assizes said hee should not come thence till hee came to bee hanged yet Neverthelesse the Jury upon life and death acquited him to the admiration of the Judg and the whole Court." Two of Bridgewater's informants reveal what the local attitude was. One notes the inequality between a "woman poore and frendlesse" and a "man famed to be wicked yet having many frends of power." Another writes that "I finde none there willing to examine a rape against Burghill; the man as I heare is reputed to be of evill behavior but not of soe highe a straine as felony unlesse he may come somewhat neere a rape."[20] We cannot know whether Margery was raped, but the correspondence suggests that her social status, her age, and her lack of powerful friends were more important in the final decision than was the truth.[21]

On the other hand, the Earl of Castlehaven was actually beheaded for sexual crimes in 1631. Once he had been accused by his son of assisting in the rape both of his own second wife and of his son's twelve-year-old wife, the charges could not be ignored. The Earl was tried by a jury of his peers and he and the actual rapists, his servants, were executed. The

19. Longueville, p. 97; Chamberlain letter in *Calendar of State Papers Domestic*, 184, p. 98. The *Calendar of State Papers Domestic* records a pardon for rape March 22, 1616.

20. Huntington Library, Ellesmere MSS. 7403, 7399, 7394.

21. The case is discussed at length in Leah Sinanoglou Marcus, "The Milieu of Milton's *Comus*: Judicial Reform at Ludlow and the Problem of Sexual Assault," *Criticism* 25 (1983), pp. 293–327. I would like to thank Dr. Marcus for alerting me to these materials in the Ellesmere papers.

raped women were mother and daughter, and apparently there was a presumption that they must have been at least partially guilty. There was a lengthy delay before they were pardoned, for reasons probably best revealed in the attitude of the Countess of Castlehaven's mother. She, the Countess Dowager of Derby, was "by no means willing to forgive her daughter and granddaughter as being merely the victims of Castlehaven's lascivious designs," and would not have them in her house until they had received the King's pardon. The Countess of Castlehaven testified that following the first rape she "would have killed herself afterwards with a knife, but that hee tooke it from her."[22] One wonders whether her failure to commit suicide was considered a sign of her inherent corruption. If she had succeeded, her behavior would have come much closer to the expectations aroused by the earlier literature. Well before 1631, though, these norms had been abandoned on the stage, and perhaps they never existed in real life.

III

It was probably a combination of the changing social climate and the growing vogue for tragicomedy which permitted experimentation with the standard rape plot. Tragicomedy led dramatists into a constant search for situations which "want deaths . . . yet bring some near it," as Fletcher puts it. Rape was a good example. Additionally, the atmosphere of never-never land in tragicomedy meant that an audience could be asked temporarily to suspend its knowledge of the unchanging law. Finally, in a period of rampant literary imitation, once Fletcher had adapted his classical source for the plot of *The Queen of Corinth,* other writers were free to follow, adding developments or complications as they saw fit.

Eugene Waith discovered that *The Queen of Corinth* is based on the Senecan *Controversia,* "The Man who Raped Two Women." The situation, given to young lawyers as an exercise in argumentation, is this: "A woman who has been raped may choose whether her seducer shall be executed or shall marry her without a dowry. In one night a man raped two women; one chooses his death, the other chooses to be married."[23] By emphasizing only the ingenious rhetoric this situation allows, Waith

---

22. Barbara Breasted, "*Comus* and the Castlehaven Scandal," *Milton Studies* 3 (1971), pp. 212–14.

23. Eugene M. Waith, *The Pattern of Tragicomedy in Beaumont and Fletcher* (New Haven, 1952), p. 89.

obscures the extent to which *The Queen of Corinth* deviates from the rape story previously conventional on the English stage. He does not analyze the content, the characters, or the total emotional impact of the play, writing that "in none of the Beaumont and Fletcher plays does plot dominate more completely. . . . In the play as in the school of declamation the real object is not to convince anyone of anything and not to move the passions violently but to provide a certain emotional thrill and to delight by means of virtuosity."[24] Yet when we examine the play against the background of expectations established by the earlier drama, it becomes clear that the audience would have been passionately surprised by the characterization, dilemma, and solution presented here.

Assuming that Fletcher and his collaborators were attracted first by the Senecan plot and its possibilities for a stunning final trial, their problem was to make the prior history plausible and the conclusion acceptable.[25] To allow for the tragicomic ending, they introduce one radical change into their material: Prince Theanor only thinks he has raped two women. In fact, his first victim was substituted for the second woman when the second rape was anticipated. Thus the paradox of the plot will be solved when the woman pleading for his death admits that she was never raped.[26]

The greater difficulty lay in the characters—the woman who does not commit suicide and the rapist who will not be executed. To excuse Theanor, the prince, Fletcher gives him a political motive and an evil advisor. As the play opens, the Queen of Corinth, Theanor's mother, has just awarded Merione to Prince Agenor of Argos as part of a general peace settlement. The gentlemen who discuss the matter in the first scene are taken aback: "Nor was her Highness ignorant, that her Son / The Prince *Theanor* made love to this Lady, / And in the noblest way." The Queen is a "*Spartan* Lady" whose concern for the "common good" incites her not only to "subdue / Her own affections, but command her

24. Waith, p. 136, pp. 190–91.

25. The play is by Fletcher, Field, and Massinger. Massinger wrote Acts 1 and 5, Fletcher Act 2, and Field Acts 3 and 4. Cyrus Hoy, "The Shares of Fletcher and His Collaborators in the Beaumont and Fletcher Canon, (IV)," *Studies in Bibliography* 12 (1959), pp. 98–100. The collaborators' attitudes toward rape may have varied—I shall argue below that Massinger writing alone was or became conventional—but they wrote as part of Fletcher's atelier and he was their leader.

26. Coke was aware of the Roman case and his comment reveals that this change was essential: "[in Seneca] the case is largely and doubtfully disputed, which in our law would make but little question; for though the one for the offence done to her might take him to her husband, yet shall he suffer death according to the law for the offence done to the other" (I, 180).

Sons." The gentlemen are dubious that the prince can or should "sit down with this wrong" (1.1.29–31, 41–44, 50).

Theanor is led astray by the villain, Crates. At first Theanor is uncertain about the proposed rape:

> And yet the desperate cure that we must practice
> Is in it self so foul, and full of danger,
> That I stand doubtful whether 'twere more manly
> To dye not seeking help, or that help being
> So deadly, to pursue it. (1.1.72–76)

The prince chooses wrong and repeated comments stress his loss of manliness. Merione, raped, asks him to marry her; when he turns away in scorn she calls his behavior "a more unmanly violence than the other" (2.1.24). He treacherously tries to have the rape blamed on the Queen's favorite, and when that fails and the favorite is to marry Beliza, he tells Crates, "I long to have the first touch of her too, / That will a little quiet me." Even Crates is shocked: "You'll be the Tyrant to Virginity; / To fall but once is manly, to persevere / Beastly" (4.3.191–96).

In the last act the Prince is captured and becomes contrite. His mother's speeches emphasize his degeneration: "Thy lust hath alter'd so thy former Being, / By Heaven I know thee not. . . . My Son was born a Free-man, this a Slave / To beastly passions" (5.2.95–122). In his repentance the prince seems to "suffer like a Woman" but really "consideration of what's past, more frights him / Than any other punishment" (5.4.16–20). He offers to marry Merione to save her honor before dying; when he learns that he was tricked to "work in him compunction" his silence may reveal a new, better man or may merely reveal Fletcher's inability to imagine what a reformed and pardoned rapist would say (5.4.249ff).

The treatment of Merione is less consistent. There were models of repentant villains in the drama, but none for women who had survived rape. The problem is exacerbated because although Merione herself accepts all the patriarchal values, the plot requires her to live. Since a woman should belong to the man who first has sexual relations with her, Merione immediately begs her attacker, "You have had your foul will; make it yet fair with marriage" (2.1.37). Instead he drugs her and vanishes. Awakening, she tells Agenor she cannot marry him because she is no longer "unspotted, / Pure and unblasted" (2.3.121–22). He urges the usual excuse: "The stain was forc'd upon ye / None of your wills, nor yours," and she gives the standard reply: although her will is "still a Virgin" her body is "corrupt" (2.3.193–94, 199–203). The outcome of such a belief has always been suicide. For Merione not to kill herself is to prove the truth of Crates' contemptuous reassurance to the Prince: "Nay, forget it, / The woman is no *Lucrece*" (2.3.24–25). Merione herself asks for the company of those who have "Despis'd their honours; those that have been Virgins / Ravish'd and wrong'd, and yet dare live to tell it" (2.3.131–32). Again she comments "I have read . . . of such an injury / Done to a Lady: and how she durst dye" (3.2.154–56). The implication is that remaining alive is a failure of the will to suicide.

In the conclusion Massinger tried to fall back on *Measure for Measure* for assistance. Mariana's belief that "best men are molded out of faults" presumably answers Beliza's—and the modern audience's—query about "what joys thou canst expect from such a Husband" (5.4.114). Apparently we are also meant to be assuaged by Crates' explanation that "she was his Wife before the face of Heaven, / Although some ceremonious forms were wanting" (5.4.224–25). This excuse is not justified by the preceding events; it bypasses the moral issue and eliminates the legal one, since the law did not recognize that a man could rape his wife. There is a considerable difference between Mariana's consent beforehand to be substituted in Angelo's bed, and Merione's abduction in the street on her return from Vesta's temple, assault with drugs, rape, and abandonment. We are left with an uncomfortable sense that Theanor is getting away without proper punishment, and that the play has not resolved the issue of rape.[27]

In 1619 Rowley attempted to revive the tragic plot of rape and revenge. *All's Lost by Lust,* with its Moors and mutilations, is a hodge-podge of motifs going back to *Titus Andronicus.* However, Rowley also introduced modifications which weaken the clear logic and morality of the older plays. Most important, he carried over from *The Queen of Corinth* the unmarried heroine, apparently not realizing that this removed a critical part of the usual justification for suicide following rape.

Iacinta is surrounded by references to Lucrece. Like Lucina, she is

---

27. Nancy Cotton Pearse, *John Fletcher's Chastity Plays* (Lewisburg, Pa., 1973), has a very different interpretation. She calls Merione a "Christianized Lucrece" (p. 163) and since she thinks the rape is "a secondary issue . . . a test not of chastity but of mercy" (p. 160) she finds the forgiveness of Theanor acceptable.

pursued by the King; when she tells her father "There hast bin ravishers, remember Tarquin," he replies, "There has bin chast Ladies, remember Lucres" (1.2.97–98). The King sends her father away as general in his battle against the Moors, and then rapes Iacinta. She escapes in disguise to the battlefield where her father hears her complaint, asking "Rodoricke a Tarquin?" "Yes," she replies, "and thy daughter (had she done her part) / Should be the second Lucrece: view me well / I am Iacinta" (4.1.98–101). Yet Iacinta, unlike Lucrece, does not commit suicide. She also has no husband the purity of whose line she must maintain. Her father speaks briefly of her "forced stain of lust" but when the Moorish King, with whom the general now allies himself in revenge, offers to marry "thy ravisht daughter," the father urges him to "wooe, win, and wed her" (4.1.134, 181, 185). Once again the possibility of marriage rather than death for the rape victim appears. Both the Moor and the Spanish general seem to consider Iacinta available for marriage, even though another man has already had sexual possession of her. And offended as Iacinta is at the potential violation of her religious loyalties— "O my second hell, / A Christians armes embrace an infidell" (4.1.183–84)—she does not assert that she cannot marry anyone because she is soiled. Eventually the Moor, angered by her refusal, cuts out her tongue, blinds her father, and arranges a duel so that the father will accidentally kill her.

Rowley provides no clear account of the philosophical motivations for Iacinta's actions. Neither the father nor the daughter invokes the Christian prohibition against suicide, nor argues either the inevitable corruption or the inherent innocence of the rape victim. "Had she done her part" may imply the same self-criticism from Iacinta that we heard from Merione. Her father's last words to her are "Thinke of Cleopatra and Brutus wife, / There's many wayes to end a weary life" (5.5.173–74), but the mention of women who committed suicide for reasons other than rape merely confuses the question, especially after the father had agreed to Iacinta's marriage. The plot developments obscure the issue of the rape victim's future. Iacinta dies because of the wickedness of the Moor rather than specifically because of the rape, and oddly enough at the end of the play both the deposed King who raped her and the Moor who pursued and mutilated her are alive. Apparently Rowley disapproved of the tragicomic solution proposed in *The Queen of Corinth,* but because he does not justify the necessity of Iacinta's death after the rape, nor confront the full implications of having an unmarried heroine, the play does not succeed in re-establishing the earlier paradigm and the experiments continue.

The next attempt to defy the conventional treatment was made by Middleton in *Women Beware Women,* where he turns his intense realism upon the traditional situation. As in the earlier plays, a married woman is raped by the state's most powerful man, in this case the Duke of Florence. Critics who have treated Bianca's fall as a seduction are wrong. Bianca was seduced by Leantio; rather like Desdemona, she consented to her lover's arguments and ran away from home, family, and state to be with him. This constituted theft, as Leantio repeatedly says; the law would call it abduction. But the situation in Livia's house is entirely different. Confronted in a private gallery by the Duke, Bianca is in precisely the same situation as Lucina in *Valentinian,* also tricked to the palace and suddenly confronted by the Emperor. Irving Ribner objects that Bianca's seduction, with her "feeble attempts at resistance, is an elaborate game," yet it is only a game for the Duke.[28] He makes clear both what he wants and Bianca's lack of options: "I am not here in vain . . . Take warning I beseech thee . . . I should be sorry the least force should lay / An unkind touch upon thee . . . I . . . never pitied any . . . That will not pity me. I can command, / Think upon that" (2.2.334–63). If this is not rape, it is certainly sexual mastery rather than sexual persuasion.

The innovations begin not in the rape scene but thereafter, when none of the principals behaves according to the pattern. Bianca, although angry at Livia and Guardiano, makes only the most oblique reference to the possibility of suicide:

> The weather of a doomsday dwells upon him.
> Yet since mine honour's leprous, why should I
> Preserve that fair that caused the leprosy?
> Come poison all at once. (2.2.423–26)

She immediately turns to the attack on Guardiano, telling him that he is guilty of "off'ring the first-fruits to sin" (2.2.434). From this point she seems to think of herself as a strumpet, a term other characters repeatedly apply to her. Her psychological development is fascinating. Critics have emphasized her moral deterioration, which climaxes in the attempt

---

28. Irving Ribner, *Jacobean Tragedy* (London, 1962), p. 144.

to murder the Cardinal.[29] However, the most remarkable of Middleton's changes from the standard rape plot—and from *The Queen of Corinth*—is that Bianca comes to love her attacker. Once again the audience must consider what joys she can expect. In a play constantly concerned with money Bianca is obviously attracted to the Duke's wealth and position. But there seems to be more. One popular theory has always held that women enjoy fantasies of being sexually overpowered, and Bianca is drawn by the very power which the Duke has expressed through rape. The duality of love and destruction which the rape therefore necessarily generates culminates in the final scene, which parodies *Romeo and Juliet*. Bianca swallows the remains of the poison which she had prepared for the Cardinal, but which was given to the Duke. She kisses his body saying, "Thus, thus reward thy murderer, and turn death / Into a parting kiss" (5.2.195–96). Her final image is of "tasting the same death in a cup of love" (5.2.221). And the audience cannot simply condemn her, since it also recognizes the Duke's superiority to Leantio and so becomes complicit in Bianca's attraction to him. Both rapist and victim die, as usual, but not because the victim's honor automatically demands it; rather, rape is seen to lead inevitably to other crimes involving both victim and attacker.

Middleton also reshapes the role of the husband. Leantio is no Collatine or Maximus; instead he is a simple factor, lascivious and self-satisfied when we first see him, appalled and offended by Bianca's change, and arrogant and angry in his brief glory as Livia's lover. He never contemplates revenge on the Duke; how could he? In a patriarchal society the husband owns the wife, but Bianca was stolen goods to begin with, and simply passes to the stronger man. Indeed, Leantio briefly inverts the usual pattern following a rape by wishing for his own death: "Methinks by right, I should not now be living, / And then 'twere all well" (3.3.322–23).

Middleton's plot can be seen as a response to *The Queen of Corinth*. Having promised his brother to end his adulterous relationship with Bianca, the Duke has Leantio killed so that he may marry her, and his casuistry is only more overt and deadly than the casuistry in the earlier play. Bianca does willingly what Merione obscures by her virtuous

---

29. A good recent discussion is Verna Ann Foster, "The Deed's Creature: The Tragedy of Bianca in *Women Beware Women*," *Journal of English and Germanic Philology* 78 (1979), pp. 508–21. Foster, however, refers to Bianca's "deed" as a seduction and thus attributes blame to Bianca for what happens to her.

rhetoric. The inherent destructiveness of the marriage between rapist and victim is vividly displayed; no happy ending is possible. The play does not accept the conventions of the earlier tragedies, or of the innovative tragicomedy.

If *The Spanish Gypsy* is by Middleton and Rowley as traditionally argued, then both men were returning to the subject of rape after only a short interval.[30] Middleton was again faced with a plot where the victim marries her rapist, one where he could re-explore the psychological and personal circumstances which might make this conclusion acceptable. Just a few months earlier Rowley had collaborated with Fletcher on *The Maid in the Mill.* In this comedy an attempted rape is defeated by the young woman's cleverness, and in a conclusion not usually found in the earlier plays about attempted rape, she is rewarded with marriage to her noble abductor. But any other author writing in the small world of the London theater would also have known the earlier plays about rape. *The Spanish Gypsy* is the first play to put the issue into a Christian context and to consider seriously the implications of the tragicomic ending pioneered in *The Queen of Corinth.* Furthermore, comparison with the source, Cervantes' *La Fuerza de la Sangue,* reveals that while the Spanish story provides a strong Catholic background, it is significantly different from the play, whose tone is the creation of its English dramatists.[31]

The opening of the play is startling. Roderigo and his friends, a group of young Spanish noblemen, capture Clara and her parents; Roderigo hurries Clara away and rapes her. Despite protestations that they will only do what is "fit for gentlemen," "anything in the way of honour," the friends accept Roderigo's assurance that "For a wench, man, any course is honourable" (1.1.11, 33–34). These young noblemen are a pack of hoodlums, and the sole motive for the rape is sexual infatuation. For the first time in all of these plays, neither party knows the other, going the plot of the "unknown ravisher" one better. Much later in the play Clara's parents regret that they had covetously considered matching Clara to their foolish ward, but Roderigo, unlike Theanor, cannot plead that he was intending to interrupt this inappropriate marriage.

30. The play was attributed to Middleton and Rowley in the 1653 quarto. Many modern critics see the hand of Ford, at least in the revisions.

31. Cervantes' tale is more lighthearted. Some of the differences include the departure of the hero for Italy immediately after the rape, his lack of penitence, the long period of time which elapses, allowing for the birth and growth of a child from the rape, and the grandparents' recognition of their grandchild. The story does not focus as intently on the characters of rapist and victim.

Left alone for a moment in her ravisher's room, Clara steals a crucifix which will later lead to Roderigo's discovery. This object emphasizes the Christian background, and Clara's holiness, unlike the purity of the other heroines which merely served to titillate the rapist, truly supports her in her trial.[32] Although she at first asks Roderigo to kill her, and later wonders if she should be alive—"do not wonder that I live to suffer / Such a full weight of wrongs, but wonder rather / That I have liv'd to speak them" (3.3.55–57)—Clara does not contemplate suicide. Both she and her parents rely on a providential heaven for assistance. The moon rises at Clara's behest to show the chamber (1.3), and her parents feel assured that when "mischief hath wound up . . . the ravisher's foul life" the poise will "sink down his soul . . . Darkness itself / Will change night's sable brow into a sunbeam / For a discovery" (2.2.10–17). Clearly Providence brings Clara accidentally back to Roderigo's house. Belief in heaven-dealt justice is also present in Roderigo's father Ferdinand, who arranges for Roderigo to marry Clara without recognizing her and then tricks him into confessing the rape by telling him that his new wife is wanton, certainly the punishment for some sin of his: "Else heaven is not so wrathful to pour on thee / A misery so full of bitterness. . . . Impossible that justice should rain down / In such a frightful horror without cause" (5.1.15–21). Clara has the summary comment, "Heaven is gracious" (3.3.104).

One reason why Clara does not kill herself is that she is the first heroine to be genuinely uncertain that she is stained. St. Augustine long ago argued that if Lucrece's will did not consent, she remained chaste and ought not to have killed herself.[33] The authors of *The Spanish Gypsy* divide the stain between Roderigo and Clara, and she is the first to be cleansed. After her immediate reaction, asking him to let out her "blood which is infected now / By your soul-staining lust," she prays for assistance to the powers "that guard the innocent" and announces that she has "washed off the leprosy that cleaves / To my just shame in true and honest tears" (1.3.12–13, 51, 63–64). Later she seems less certain, saying "I have offended. . . . I have fallen," (2.2.1–4) and refers to her shame when she finds herself with Ferdinand. Although the handling is somewhat inconsistent, the usual emphasis on pollution and loss of honor is omitted, and

32. A. L. and M. K. Kistner, *"The Spanish Gypsy,"* *Humanities Association Review* 25 (1974), pp. 211–24, discuss the pattern of sin, repentance, and rebirth which underlies several plots of the play.

33. Kahn, p. 63.

Clara does not suffer Merione's feelings of self-contempt. She even agrees to see her noble suitor Louis briefly, although the effort proves too much for her. Unlike Fletcher, the authors here are trying to give a context to the heroine's failure to commit suicide; they also create some hope that the marriage of Roderigo and Clara might be happy.

The most striking change is in the development of the rapist. Roderigo begins as lustful and heedless, unaware that the girl he proposes to abduct is his friend Louis' beloved. He overrules his companions' objection that the unknown girl's father might be noble by protesting that he is "as noble." Louis drily rejoins, "would the adventure were so!" (1.1.37–38). After the rape Roderigo's first reaction is to try to deny the nature of the incident and turn Clara into a strumpet by offering her money; she indignantly refuses. The significant innovations begin when Roderigo, unlike Theanor, experiences guilt and repentance before he is found out. Clara's cry that her blood is infected "by your soul-staining lust" is ambiguous; his soul is stained by lust as well as hers. The third act opens with a soliloquy in which Roderigo berates himself in conventional religious terms. He meditates on the commonplace, "what vild prisons / Make we our bodies to our immortal souls" (3.1.1–2). When informed of the rape, his father Ferdinand thinks of the male family line as corrupted, for he pleads for "pity / To my till now untainted blood and honour" (3.3.86–87). This is quite different from the taint which adheres through a wife's pollution. Ferdinand is concerned about Roderigo's sinfulness. He is prepared for his son to die "basely and cursedly," although delighted that Clara will settle for a "balm / To heal a wounded name" (3.3.86, 97–98). Roderigo's weakest moment comes when he ignores his feelings of guilt and marries Clara without knowing who she is. Then Ferdinand plays his trick, extracts the confession, tells Roderigo "young man, thou shouldst have married her," and brings him to agree that this would have made him "the happiest man alive" (5.1.34–38). The marriage is thus the desire of both parties. The happy ending has been carefully prepared. A contrite Roderigo is perhaps reformed enough to deserve Clara, and the stain on both will be eradicated by marriage.

Modern readers remain uneasy, and so, I suspect, were at least some members of the Jacobean audience. Our discomfort has several sources. Our natural inclination is not to accept this very vivid rape as the foundation of a marriage. In English law, as we saw above, the abduction of an heiress was a felony even if she consented afterwards and married the man. Finally, the psychological implications of the two tragicomedies are disturbingly similar despite their different treatments. The audience watches the fulfillment of a fantasy of rape and yet the guilt attached to the fantasy—and the act—is removed by the final marriage. The fantasy is both permitted and denied, which may account for the appeal of the plot but leaves us feeling that we have been in forbidden territory.

Furthermore, these plays are not merely tragicomic because they "want deaths." Rape itself undergoes a reevaluation because of this plot treatment. While rape is verbally condemned when it occurs, the structure of the plays identifies rape with all sexual impulse as it is treated in comedy. It becomes a natural instinct which must be brought under social control by marriage. In Touchstone's words explaining his marriage to Audrey, "we must be married, or we must live in bawdry" (*As You Like It,* 3.3.88–89). Rather than being a tragic crime rape becomes a comic error cured by being brought into the social order.

The new ending also implies different judgments about the worth of men and women. More and more these plays suggest that rape is just an unfortunate side effect of that valuable commodity, manliness. Although Crates, who bluntly calls one rape "manly," is a villain, Bianca apparently arrives at a similar view of the Duke's action, and Roderigo is the hero of *The Spanish Gypsy.* Rape must still be expiated by marriage, but the unspoken conclusion is that the men have proved their manhood in the process and will be desirable husbands. Women, however, do not gain in value when they enter into marriages with their rapists instead of dying. On the contrary, the classic patriarchal ending, while it protected the male line from pollution, at least implied that women have a personal integrity which cannot survive violation. The ostensible happy ending retains the notion that a woman is marked as the property of a man who has sexual relations with her, but it does not confront her feelings as she enters the marriage. Both Middleton, who tries to account for Bianca's love in terms of her attraction to money and power, and the authors of *The Spanish Gypsy,* who show Clara submitting to the will of heaven, try to get around this problem, but unsuccessfully.

Such objections may seem anachronistic. However, the appearance of Massinger's play, *The Unnatural Combat,* within two years of *The Spanish Gypsy* suggests that Massinger too was no longer willing to accept a tragicomic marriage ending to a story of rape. While Rowley had moved away from the tragic *All's Lost by Lust* to the tragicomic conclusion of *The Spanish Gypsy,* Massinger went in the reverse direction. He had written the trial scene of *The Queen of Corinth,* where Merione and Beliza debate death or marriage for Theanor. He had next taken up the subject of rape in *The Bondman* (1623). The plot of that play centers on a slave revolt in which the hero Pisander displays his concealed nobility by refusing the opportunity to rape Cleora. Since the 1624 quarto of *The Bondman* contains a poem referring to *The Spanish Gypsy,* licensed five months earlier to the same company, Massinger may have intended Pisander as a contrast to Roderigo.[34] Tragicomedy in *The Bondman* comes from the danger, not the act, of rape. Finally Massinger returned directly to the rape plot he had helped to launch. The result was tragedy of the traditional kind.

According to Philip Edwards and Colin Gibson, Massinger found the inspiration for *The Unnatural Combat* in some lines of Jonson's *Catiline* (1611) which describe Catiline's misdeeds as "incests, murders, rapes . . . forcing first a *Vestall* nunne . . . parricide . . . thy incestuous life."[35] Most of these sins occur in the play, and the line about the vestal nun may also have inspired events in *The Queen of Corinth,* where Merione is raped as she leaves Vesta's temple. However, the actual plot of rape in *The Unnatural Combat* is apparently Massinger's own, an intentional modification of the tragicomedies of the preceding years. Like Rowley in *All's Lost by Lust,* Massinger borrows their main innovation, the unmarried heroine. But he then deliberately and coherently reimposes the traditional pattern, in which rape leads immediately and inevitably to death for both victim and attacker. This play completes the cycle which began in 1594.

Montrevile, the rapist of *The Unnatural Combat,* cannot be remolded into a hero. He echoes *The Queen of Corinth* in excusing his attack on the heroine, Theocrine—"she being in a kinde contracted to me, / The fact may challenge some qualification" (5.2.249–50)—but in this play moral judgments are absolute, not qualified. Massinger is willing to titillate the audience with Malefort's incestuous contemplations of his daughter's beauty, but sees to it that Malefort is struck by lightning at the end. Rape is one of a long series of horrors and must lead to tragedy.

One result is a renewed simplification of the heroine. Theocrine is seen exclusively as a sexual object, easily victimized. In the first scene Montrevile suggests that she can free her father from imprisonment by

34. Gerald Eades Bentley, *The Jacobean and Caroline Drama* (Oxford, 1941–1968), IV, 770.
35. Edwards and Gibson, *Massinger,* II, 184.

offering sexual favors to the governor. Her father loves her incestuously and sends her to Montreville's fort to protect her from himself. Although presumably virtuous, her lover Beaufort thinks only of engrossing "those favours . . . which are not to be nam'd" (3.4.33–34). Finally she is raped. Her father's speech in 4.1, blaming her virtue, beauty, duty, and intelligence as temptations to him, epitomizes her situation. She is never a person but, like Lucrece, an object of competition between men. Indeed, she has so little individuality that part of Montrevile's desire comes from Theocrine's likeness to her dead mother, whom he also loved. The only suspense in the plot is whether Theocrine can be given to "lawful" desires before illicit ones overwhelm her.

Once Theocrine is raped there is no possibility of reconciliation; she is dishonored and Montrevile a villain. She is thrust forth, "*her garments loose, her haire disheveld,*" asking "Hath he rob'd me of / Mine honour, and denies me now a roome / To hide my shame?" Her stain is actualized: her father hardly recognizes her. "Who is this? how alter'd! how deform'd!" She tells him, "I am dead indeed to all but misery / O come not neere me sir, I am infectious" (5.2.186–88, 190, 197–98). The second line, which recalls Beatrice-Joanna's speech at the end of *The Changeling,* is an example of rape transferring guilt to the victim. For while Beatrice-Joanna has initiated much of the evil in her story, Theocrine has done nothing.

Theocrine's fate is inevitable and automatic:

> [Montrevile] Abus'd me sir by violence, and this told
> I cannot live to speake more; may the cause
> In you finde pardon, but the speeding curse
> Of a ravish'd maid fall heavie, heavie on him.
> *Beaufort* my lawfull love, farewell for ever. *She dies.* (5.2.212–16)

In this instant death, with no cause alleged beyond the rape itself, Massinger returns to the pattern of *Valentinian.* Theocrine, like Lucina, cannot live "infectious . . . altered . . . deformed." Neither can Montrevile, who will be sentenced by the King. In the last lines of the play Beaufort looks at the dead Theocrine and says, "Here's one retaines / Her native innocence" (5.2.336–37). She has proved it in the traditional way, by her death.

Massinger thus deliberately rejects the tragicomic solution which makes rape ultimately inconsequential. We cannot be satisfied with either outcome, the woman who must die once she is raped or the woman "happily" married to her attacker. Paradoxically, the plays which assume that rape victims must die may imply a concern and respect for women in general which is missing from the plays which do not automatically condemn the heroine to death. The heroines who survive are much more individualized, and interesting, but the authors never quite convince us that they are not also compromised. *The Unnatural Combat,* which restores the traditional pattern, appeared shortly before the accession of Charles and Henrietta Maria, whose taste in both court morals and in drama was for the pure and the platonic. The decadent Jacobean exploration of rape, with its heretical suggestion that rapists may be heroes and that women may love their attackers, vanished.

"The Comedians' Liberty": Censorship of the Jacobean Stage Reconsidered

PHILIP J. FINKELPEARL

T HE legal term for the crime of speaking too freely about persons or state affairs is "libel." Since libel was regarded in Renaissance England as deserving of the "greatest punishment nexte to treason,"[1] it was administered primarily by the King's Privy Council—called, when sitting in a judicial capacity, the Star Chamber. Punishment for libel was severe: "fine, imprisonment, loss of ears or nailing to the pillory, slitting the nose, branding the forehead, whipping . . . , wearing of papers [i.e., signs descriptive of the offense] in public places, or any punishment but death."[2] The Star Chamber was not bound by the constraints of the common law; its procedures were "designed not for the protection of the innocent but for the conviction of the guilty."[3] It operated swiftly, its celerity often aided by torture.

The most potent libel statutes, collectively known as *Scandalum Magnatum*, were framed to suppress rumors regarding the sovereign and great men of the realm; from 1606 it became a crime to speak against dignitaries even if the libel were true. Two notorious Jacobean cases will illustrate the kinds of libel that most exercised the Star Chamber. In 1605 one Pickering pinned scandalous verses to the hearse of Archbishop Whitgift, attacking him, Queen Elizabeth, and others. For this he was severely punished.[4] Another great libel case concerned the erratic but probably harmless ravings of an elderly Puritan clergyman named Edmund Peacham. His sermons against King James and his court were so offensive that his house was raided and treasonous writings discovered.

---

1. *Les Reportes del Cases in Camera Stellata (1593–1609)*, ed. William Paley Baildon (London, 1894), p. 188.

2. William Hudson, "A Treatise on the Court of Star Chamber" in *Collectanea Juridica*, ed. Francis Hargrave (1792), p. 224.

3. Fredrick S. Siebert, *Freedom of the Press in England, 1476–1776* (Urbana, Ill., 1952), p. 120.

4. *Les Reportes*, p. 225.

After extended torture which produced no confession, Peacham died in prison in 1616.[5] Despite the fearsome penalties and the assiduity of authorities in employing poursuivants and informers to ferret out libel, the Jacobean period was, as Lord Chancellor Ellesmere lamented, "a lybellinge time."[6] Between 1603 and 1625 libel was a significant element in no fewer than 577 Star Chamber cases.[7] This figure is not all-inclusive since Star Chamber records are incomplete and other lower courts would also occasionally handle libel. As for their frequency, libel cases seem to have been spaced evenly throughout the reign.

Yet the fact remains that during King James's reign as in Elizabeth's not one prominent poet or playwright was punished for libel. Most scholars who have dealt with this subject would take this for granted. They would ascribe it to the efficient, carefully supervised system of control whose severe penalties deterred writers and acting companies from speaking too freely. Before a book could be printed, approval was required by an agent of the Stationers' Company and by an official licenser: for medical books, a medical authority; for heraldic books, the Earl Marshall; for plays, the Master of the Revels; for law books, a judicial officer; for politics, one of the secretaries of state; for religious and all other works including poetry, an ecclesiastical officer. The actual performance of plays was also, of course, subject to the approval of the Master of the Revels.[8]

This system of surveillance and control worked fairly well under Elizabeth I. Most scholars believe that under James I it was even more efficient once the royal family made the various acting companies its personal servants. Glynn Wickham's view is representative in seeing the Stuarts' vigorous oversight of the theaters as having far-reaching consequences:

A control of the drama so absolute as that exercised by James, his family and his immediate Court advisers could not but serve to divorce the theatre from the popular audience on which it had previously been based and from which it had drawn its vigour. The actors and their playmakers, as royal servants, could scarcely avoid aligning the subject matter of their plays in future to suit the tastes of their patrons and protectors in preference to that of humbler citizens: just as relevant, the most topical of all subject

5. Samuel Gardiner, *History of England from the Accession of James I to the Outbreak of the Civil War, 1603–1642*, 10 vols. (London, 1895), II, 272–83.

6. *Les Reportes*, p. 230.

7. I have computed this from *List and Index to the Proceedings in Star Chamber for the Reign of James I (1603–1625) in the Public Record Office London, Class STAC 8*, ed. Thomas Barnes (Chicago, 1975).

8. Siebert, p. 143.

matter, the relationship between Church, State and individual being—the topic that had kept English drama so vividly in touch with life in the Tudor era—was the very subject matter which the whole machinery of censorship and control had been devised to license and suppress. And suppressed it most surely was. The decadence in Jacobean and Caroline dramatic writing which has so frequently been remarked and debated by literary critics is thus, in my view, due in far greater measure to the censorship (in the widest sense of that word) as exercised by early Stuart governments than to any particular failing in the writers themselves.[9]

Whether viewing Jacobean censorship from the stance of G. E. Bentley studying the functioning of the office of the Master of the Revels, or of Fredrick S. Siebert discussing freedom of the press in England, or of Russell Fraser analyzing attacks on verse and theater in the sixteenth and seventeenth centuries, some version of Wickham's view of the influence of Jacobean censorship prevails.[10] I do not propose to dispute the general conclusion of these eminent scholars: that, on the whole, the system worked well and dampened down the powerful urge felt across the whole range of society to express some measure of criticism of England's rulers and their manner of governance.

However, I do want to suggest that the orthodox view of the system, at least during the Jacobean period, as a smooth-running, terrifying mechanism which efficiently controlled dissident expression oversimplifies a complicated and often confusing situation. In fact, confining this discussion primarily to the drama, evidence survives that violations of nearly unbelievable magnitude occurred throughout the Jacobean period. Possibly the implications of this evidence have been slighted because much of it exists in the form of allusions to and accounts of plays that have not survived.[11] But there is no reason to doubt the accuracy of the evidence, much of it the personal testimony of the French and Venetian ambassadors or of English eyewitnesses with no particular axe to grind.

It is out of such material that E. K. Chambers constructs a picture of the occasionally anarchic state of the stage early in James's reign:

For some years after the coming of James, the freedom of speech adopted by the stage, in a London much inclined to be critical of the alien King and his retinue of hungry Scots, was far beyond anything that would have been tolerated by Elizabeth. The

9. Glynn Wickham, *Early English Stages 1300–1600*, 4 vols. (London, 1959-), II, part 1, p. 94.

10. Gerald E. Bentley, *The Profession of Dramatist in Shakespeare's Time* (Princeton, 1971); Siebert, *Freeedom of the Press in England*; Russell Fraser, *The War against Poetry* (Princeton, 1970).

11. That the texts of so many of these extreme examples have not survived suggests effective *ex post facto* censorship. But that does not confute my claim that a theatrical company willing to take chances could almost always stage a play, at least briefly.

uncouth speech of the Sovereign, his intemperance, his gusts of passion, his inordinate devotion to the chase, were caricatured with what appears incredible audacity, before audiences of his new subjects. "Consider for pity's sake," writes Beaumont, the French ambassador on June 14, 1604, "what must be the state and condition of a prince, whom the preachers publicly from the pulpit assail, whom the comedians of the metropolis bring upon the stage, whose wife attends these representations in order to enjoy the laugh against her husband." Beaumont's evidence is confirmed by a letter of 28 March 1605 from Samuel Calvert to Ralph Winwood in which he writes that "the play[er]s do not forbear to represent upon their stage the whole course of this present time, not sparing either King, state, or religion, in so great absurdity, and with such liberty, that any would be afraid to hear them."[12]

We do not know what plays are being referred to here, but for my purposes the important point is not only that these prodigious violations of the *Scandalum Magnatum* statutes are reported by unimpeachable sources, but that as far as we know they went unpunished.[13]

These plays were presented early in James's reign; their allowance might be explained as the inevitable outcome of disorganization in a new administration. But the staunchest defender of the efficiency and integrity of the censorship system, G. E. Bentley, concedes that the years immediately after those Chambers described, that is, the period between 1606 and 1610, were also fraught with violations:

Anyone conversant with the history of the Jacobean stage has probably observed that . . . the standards and regulations of the Master of the Revels and the Privy Council appear to have been violated with excessive frequency by the boy companies in the first decade of the reign of James I. Of course we may be misled by the comparative paucity of direct theatre records in the absence of Henslowe's diary and Herbert's office book in these years, but Heywood's statement in his *An Apology for Actors*, published in 1612 [but probably written in 1607], suggests that the impression is false.

Bentley quotes Heywood as lamenting the "abuse lately crept into the quality [i.e., the acting profession], as an inveighing against the State, the Court, the Law, the City and their governments, with the particularizing of private men's humors (yet alive) Noblemen and others."[14]

Again we would expect to find evidence of reprisals for such activities, but nothing of the sort seems to have happened. Instead, we have clear confirmation of Heywood's picture of uncontrolled, irreverent

12. *The Elizabethan Stage,* ed. E. K. Chambers (Oxford, 1923), I, 325.

13. The evidence of onstage attacks on the King before 1605 for his inordinate devotion to hunting is particularly vivid in British Museum Sloane MS3543 from which Edward J. L. Scott quotes in *Athenaeum* 1 (1896), 756 and Richard Simpson in *N.S.S. Transactions,* Series I, Part II (1875), 375.

14. *The Profession,* p. 166. Evidence for the earlier date of composition is given by Chambers, *Elizabethan Stage,* IV, 250.

satire. William Crashaw (the Puritan preacher and father of the poet Richard) in a sermon of 1607 attacks the players who "grow worse and worse, for now they bring religion and holy things upon the stage: no marvel though the worthiest and mightiest men escape not."[15] In 1609 John Melton, a lawyer at the Inns of Court, suggests that the current *Scandalum Magnatum* statutes are not restraining the players and that "some severe law might be enacted, for the punishing of such scandalous libelling as is, or may be at any time coloured under the name of poetising, and playmaking."[16] And in 1610 the epilogue to *Mucedorus* speaks of the propensity of the boy actors to compose "dark sentences, / Pleasing to factious brains; / And every other where place me a jest, / Whose high abuse shall more torment than blows."[17]

Even after the childrens' companies faded as a significant part of the London theatrical scene around 1612, we can discern occasional violations of the libel laws as extreme as any discussed thus far. On or around 1617 a publicly performed play (unidentifiable but mentioned in a lawsuit) represented the sport-obsessed, peace-loving King James as a huntsman who says that he had rather hear a dog bark than a cannon roar.[18] Even more surprising was the play Prince Charles had his own players produce at court before his father in 1620. Again the text has not survived, but it is described by the Venetian ambassador in a letter to the Doge:

The comedians of the prince, in the presence of the king his father, played a drama the other day in which a king with his two sons has one of them put to death, simply upon suspicion that he wished to deprive him of his crown, and the other son actually did deprive him of it afterwards. This moved the king in an extraordinary manner, both inwardly and outwardly.

It is impossible to reconstruct the intent of the play or the motives of the Prince in presenting it, but this remarkable near-reenactment of the play scene of *Hamlet* inspired the ambassador to the most extreme statement extant about freedom of speech on the Jacobean stage:

In this country however the comedians have absolute liberty to say whatever they wish against any one soever, so the only demonstration [i.e., punishment] against them [for presenting this play] will be the words [the reprimand] spoken by the king.[19]

15. *The Sermon Preached at the Crosse*, Feb. 14, 1607 (London, 1608), p. 171.

16. *A Sixe-folde Politician* (London, 1609), pp. 41–42.

17. *Drama of the English Renaissance*, ed. Russell Fraser and Norman Rabkin, 2 vols. (New York, 1976), I, 480, ll. 40–43.

18. *State Papers Domestic, 1611–18*, vol. XC, art. 66. The suit is dated 14 February 1617.

19. *State Papers, Venetian, 1619–21*, p. 111.

In fact, the ambassador's comment conforms to what we know about the general state of affairs in the closing years of James's reign. Libelling became so widespread that the King was impelled to issue a proclamation in 1620 and a nearly-identical one a year later against "excess of lavish and licentious speech of matters of state."[20] Nonetheless, Middleton's anti-Spanish *Game at Chess* (1624) with its unmistakable representation of the entire court (including once again the King) became a nine days' wonder in London. By whatever means permission to perform was obtained—it has recently been argued that the anti-Spanish faction at court led by Pembroke engineered it[21]—the *drame à clef* plainly violated all notions of what was permissible expression. If we are to believe one observer of precisely this moment, there was nothing extraordinary about Middleton's audacity. Such licentious expression sprang naturally from James's policies:

Peace begot Plenty, and Plenty begot Ease and Wantonness, and Ease and Wantonness begot Poetry, and Poetry swelled to that Bulk in his time, that it begot strange Monstrous Satyrs against the King's own Person, that haunted both Court and Country, which express'd would be too bitter to leave a sweet Perfume behind him.[22]

The French ambassador saw where all these libels were leading: "It is a strange thing, the hatred in which this King is held, in free speaking, cartoons, defamatory libels—the ordinary precursors of civil war."[23]

When we turn to the few surviving pieces of evidence of punishment for violation of the libel statutes, the results are not what one would expect. Chapman, Jonson, and possibly Marston were briefly imprisoned for their joint authorship of *Eastward Ho* in 1605, a play that took some hard shots at the Scots. Jonson told Drummond that the collaborators fully expected the normal punishment for libel, "ears cut and noses."[24] Instead, they were swiftly released from jail unpunished. Similarly, John Day for his part in *The Isle of Gulls* (1606), a play that caused a great stir for its depiction of "two divers nations"[25] (the Scots and the English) in a

20. "A Proclamation against excess of Lavish and Licentious Speech of Matters of State," 24 December 1620 in *Stuart Royal Proclamations*, ed. James F. Larkin and Paul L. Hughes (Oxford, 1973), p. 495.

21. Margot Heinemann, *Puritanism and Theatre* (Cambridge, 1980), pp. 166-69.

22. Arthur Wilson, "The Life and Reign of James I" in *A Complete History of England*, 2 vols. (London, 1719), II, 792.

23. *Stuart Royal Proclamations*, p. 496n.

24. *The Elizabethan Stage*, III, p. 254.

25. The phrase is from a letter by Sir Edward Hoby to Sir Thomas Edmunds, quoted by Chambers, *Elizabethan Stage*, III, 286.

state of friction, was temporarily committed to Bridewell but released unscathed.

There is, however, one exception that severely tests my view that libelous activity in the Jacobean theater was treated with remarkable leniency. I refer to a play once again known only through a letter, in this case by the French ambassador de la Boderie in 1608. It displayed James in unmistakable and unflattering terms. Speaking of the acting company known as the Children of the Blackfriars, the ambassador said,

Un jour ou deux devant ilz avoient dépêché leur Roi, sa mine d'Escosse, et tous ses favorits d'une estrange sorte; car aprés luy avoir fait depiter le ciel sur le vol d'un oyseau, et faict battre un gentilhomme pour avoir rompu ses chiens, ils le dépeignoient ivre pour le moins une fois le jour.[26]

To this extreme public indignity James finally reacted as a Renaissance prince should. According to Sir Thomas Lake, James "vowed they should never play more, but should first begg their bred and he wold have his vow performed."[27] It was ordered that the company be dissolved; if Chambers' conjecture is correct that Marston was the author of the play, his nearly simultaneous imprisonment may be ascribed to this offense. Marston seems to have acted under some kind of compulsion at this time for he suddenly sold his interest in the Blackfriars company, abandoned playwriting, disappeared from London, and made an utterly implausible vocational shift to the clergy. But instead of the expected bread-begging and mutilations, the children's company resumed its activities within the year. And Marston, unlike poor Peacham and Pickering, received as his severe punishment a living at the magnificent church in Christchurch, Hampshire. James's bark was worse than his bite.

Another point about the "Scots' Mine" play needs to be stressed. It is unthinkable that such a play could have passed the official review process which required both perusal of the text and a dress rehearsal in the presence of the Master of the Revels or one of his deputies. Yet somehow the play was acted in public, however briefly. In fact, there were many loopholes in the system for the clever to exploit. A play could be altered after approval by the Master by adding offensive material in the live performance or by the players' tonal emphases or impromptu gestures. (One recalls Cleopatra's fear that "the quick comedians / Extemporally

26. Chambers, III, 53.
27. Chambers, III, 54.

will stage us.") With printed texts, a license to print might conform completely to the version submitted to the authorities, and when reprinted (without permission required) new and offensive material might be inserted. Or the text might be completely inoffensive, and illegal material inserted into a dedication never seen by the authorities. Moreover, some works received approval by careless or inconsistent application of the rules. None of these tricks or defects was exploited with any consistency, but it is important to realize that in practice the system was far from foolproof.[28]

The situation in the office of the Master of the Revels in the first decade of James's reign may in part account for this relatively lax state of affairs. Since 1578 Edmund Tilney had been serving as Master; he remained at least nominally in charge until his death in 1610. Sir George Buc (a very distant relative but not, as the DNB claims, a nephew of Tilney's) was granted the position in reversion in 1597, but it is unclear when he actually took charge as Master. Some evidence points to 1603, and certainly by 1606 he was doing work in that capacity. On the other hand Tilney remained actively involved in the office as late as 1608. Moreover, while Buc performed the important role of "corrector" of printed texts of plays in 1607, Buc's Deputy, Sir George Segar, along with Tilney and someone named Wilson, also "corrected" certain plays after 1607. Two of the years from October 1608 we know from Buc's biographer, Mark Eccles, were for him a "tyme . . . of long sicknesse & adversity." Nor, according to Eccles, were relations between Buc and Tilney always harmonious. In the best Jacobean manner they seem to have been adversaries in a complex legal battle about an inheritance.[29]

There was a further complication in the administration of the Revels Office. In 1604 Samuel Daniel was appointed special licenser of plays produced by one of the acting companies, the Children of the Queen's Revels. It is not clear how long he retained this authority. To compound the confusion, in the spring of 1608 when the Children of the Chapel were performing their most libelous plays, the Revels Office was moving from the quarters it had occupied at St. John's Gate for nearly a century. Tilney old but hanging on, Buc sometimes seriously ill, both intermit-

---

28. Siebert, pp. 143-44.

29. The discussion of Buc is based largely on Mark Eccles, "Sir George Buc, Master of the Revels" in *Thomas Lodge and Other Elizabethans*, ed. Charles J. Sisson (Cambridge, Mass., 1933), pp. 409-506. For Buc's period of illness, see p. 462; for his legal battle with Tilney, pp. 416-17 and p. 445.

tently acting as Master while involved in a serious legal squabble, Daniel and others also responsible for surveillance of some plays, the office in physical disarray: this confluence of factors may account for the acting companies' audacity during the first (and for the drama, most important) decade of the seventeenth century.

But chaos in the Revels Office does not explain occasional outbreaks of libelous activity—admittedly much less frequent—after Tilney died in 1610 and Buc was in sole command. We have already heard about the play of 1617 in which the King was portrayed as a huntsman and the play of 1620 by Prince Charles's Company which caused the King such consternation. We know nothing of Buc's role in these; but in the handling of Fletcher's (and possibly Massinger's) *Sir John van Olden Barnavelt* (1619) we once more encounter a situation of conflicting authority and a sense that the regulatory agencies could be circumvented, at least for awhile. Buc did censor this politically sensitive play; there is no evidence that he licensed it. At one point the Bishop of London prohibited its production. But we hear from a contemporary that the "Players . . . had bestowed a great deale of money" on it, and so in the mysterious manner such things were effected, "Our players . . . fownd the meanes to goe through with the play."[30] We will probably never know whether it was the players' unwillingness to lose their investment or someone else's desire to have the recently-executed Barnavelt portrayed on the London stage which frustrated the Bishop of London's wishes. What is clear in this case, at least, is the relative impotence of the regulators.

We have further and, considering the source, absolute corroboration of the view that the Revels Office—at least until 1623—had not been enforcing the libel laws with as much rigor as it might. It comes from Sir Henry Herbert who, upon becoming Master of the Revels in 1623 (a position he held at least nominally for fifty years), issued a directive that "all ould plays" receive a new seal of approval, the reason being that such plays "may be full of offensive things against church and state, the rather that in former time the poetts tooke greater liberty than is allowed them by mee."[31] Herbert certainly ranks as the most responsible, efficient, and rigorous of the holders of his office. (Incidentally, he devised means to exploit it for the most financial benefit.) But even he was unable to prevent the presentation of one of the most scandalous of Jacobean plays,

30. Gerald E. Bentley, *The Jacobean and Caroline Stage*, 7 vols. (Oxford, 1941-68), III, p. 415.
31. *Dramatic Records of Sir Henry Herbert*, ed. J. Q. Adams (New Haven, Conn., 1917), p. 21.

The Game at Chess, when other powers wanted it presented. Nor was Herbert always aware of the dangerous implications of some of the plays he licensed. One instance (which must serve for many) is his licensing in 1632 of Fulke Greville's posthumously published *Mustapha.* Its anti-monarchical sentiments must have sounded enticingly timely: "No People, No. Question these Thrones of Tyrants."[32] As Edwin H. Miller has pointed out in discussing Elizabethan censors in general and Herbert in particular, "Fortunately for posterity, censors have generally been more concerned with the words than with the implications of subject matter. . . . Herbert thought he was protecting the nation's youth when he altered 'by Jesu' to 'believe me.'"[33]

Perhaps the censors performed inconsistently because they received confusing signals from their superiors. At the top sat that "misshapen chaos of well-seeming forms," King James, who numbered among the many discordant elements in his makeup a curiously modern-sounding, if inconsistent, respect for the freedom of speech. It is hard to imagine a true despot like Henry VIII issuing a proclamation that could say,

in Our owne Nature, and Judgement, Wee doe well allow of convenient freedome of speech, esteeming any over curious or restrained hand carried in that kind, rather as a weaknesse, or else over much severitie of Government, then otherwise.[34]

A cynic could legitimately object that this passage appears within a proclamation "against excesse of Lavish and Licentious Speech of matters of State."[35] But we do have reliable eyewitness testimony to James's amazingly tolerant response to an extreme assault on the *Scandalum Magnatum* statutes. In the early 1620s one of the King's chaplains delivered in his presence at Greenwich a sermon that developed the conceit that all of the leading officers in the government were servants of the devil,

running through the Body of the Court; discovering the Correspondencies with Jesuits; secret Pensions from Foreign Princes; betraying their Masters Counsels to deserve their rewards, working and combining to the Prejudice of God's People. And when he came to describe the Devil's Treasurers Exactions and Gripings, to get Money, he fix'd his eye upon Cranfield, then Lord Treasurer . . . and pointing at him with his Hand, said

32. "Mustapha" in *Poems and Dramas of Fulke Greville,* ed. Geoffrey Bullough, 2 vols. (New York, 1945), II, 131, l.92.

33. *The Professional Writer in Elizabethan England* (Cambridge, Mass., 1959), p. 197.

34. *Stuart Royal Proclamations,* p. 495. In fact, Bacon drafted this proclamation, but Buckingham wrote to Bacon, "His Majesty liketh [it] in every point so well both in matter and form, that he findeth no cause to alter a word in it" (p. 495n).

35. *Stuart Royal Proclamations,* p. 495.

with an emphasis, *That Man* (reiterating it) *That Man, that makes himself rich and his Master poor, he is a fit Treasurer for the Devil.* This the Author heard, and saw, whilst *Cranfield* sat with his Hat pulled down over his Eyes, asham'd to look up, lest he should find all Mens Eyes fix'd upon him; the King who sat just over him, smiling at the quaint Satyr so handsomely coloured over.[36]

James's sophisticated amusement at this public humiliation of one of the highest and (at the time) most trusted officers in the land was not an isolated occurrence. He could and often did laugh at himself and at subjects close to his heart, as we hear in a letter of James Howell. Recalling a time when he was in the King's presence,

as the passages . . . of very abusive Satire in Verse . . . were a-reading before him he often said, That if there were no more men in England, the Rogue should hang for it; At last being come to the Conclusion, which was (after all his Railing)—
> Now God preserve the King, the Queen, the Peers,
> And grant the Author long may wear his ears;
this pleas'd his Majesty so well, that he broke into a laughter, and said, By my sol, so shalt for me: thou art a bitter, but thou art a witty knave.[37]

As the "Scots' Mine" episode demonstrated, it was part of James's nature eventually to forgive and forget. He reacted in a similar way when faced with the question of how severely to punish those involved in the *Game at Chess* scandal of 1624. He decreed harsh penalties (apparently never carried out) for those directly responsible for the composition and production of the play, but not for the whole company: "His Majestie beinge unwillinge for ones sake, and only fault to punish the innocent or utterly ruine the Companie."[38] It was surely an exaggeration by the Venetian ambassador to say (as we have heard) that "the comedians have absolute liberty to say whatever they wish against anyone whatsoever." They might be forced to close up shop after an indiscretion, but eventually the King's anger melted away. I do not propose James for honorary membership in the Civil Liberties Union, but among the many traits he displayed—along with a drunkard's indifference—was an intermittent predilection for tolerance and even compassion.

Just below James the signals to the censors sounded even more

36. Wilson, "The Life and Reign of James I," p. 729.

37. Quoted by Evelyn M. Albright, *Dramatic Publication in England, 1580–1640* (New York, 1927), p. 156n. There is much valuable material in this remarkably unfocused book. Bentley, *Jacobean and Caroline Stage*, IV, 876 quotes some verses apparently written by Middleton during the *Game at Chess* imbroglio which plead for forgiveness in much the same witty manner as in Howell's story and apparently with similar success.

38. *A Game at Chesse*, ed. R. C. Bald (Cambridge, 1929), p. 164.

confusing. An efficient system of censorship depends upon a monolithic government with a clear sense of purpose, hence a sharp definition of what is permissible and impermissible. The latest historians of the Jacobean period caution us against describing the obvious dissidence at James's court as evidence of a nascent "Oppositionist" party which would eventually become the anti-royalist rebels of the Civil War. But we are permitted to speak of "factions," various groups of nobles and other courtiers ruthlessly jockeying for power and influence and differing on the key issues of the day: how to treat Catholics, Puritans, Spain, Favorites, Parliament, the Common Law, and the Monarchy. The many members of the House of Howard were for years as close to the King as anyone but the reigning Favorite, but even one of them might sympathize with the anti-Scots sentiments of undeniably libellous playwrights on the verge of mutilation by the Star Chamber. I refer here to Thomas Howard, Earl of Suffolk, who was involved in the rescue of Jonson and Chapman from prison for their part in the *Eastward Ho* scandal of 1605.[39] The grounds of Suffolk's interest in this case are unclear. What is important for my argument is the power such a courtier had in a situation of this sort—enough to prevail against a prosecutor enforcing the libel laws. Similarly, Alfred Harbage quite plausibly ascribes to noble protectors the privileged position of the perpetually outrageous children's companies.[40] We may never discover its precise makeup, but it is not idle to hypothesize the existence of a faction of nobles eager to employ the children to satirize aspects of the court.

Pembroke's role in the production of *A Game at Chess* remains the outstanding instance of the blunting of the powers of the Master of the Revels by a politically-committed, powerful noble. As Lord Chamberlain he was the immediate superior of the Revels' Master; in addition, Pembroke was Sir Henry Herbert's patron and a distant kinsman. While we do not have documentation of how *A Game* was licensed, we do possess a letter in which Pembroke interceded with the King in behalf of the errant acting company, the King's Men.[41] One of the most widespread misapprehensions about James's court is that it had anything like a "courtly" aesthetic or a "courtly" politics. The make-up of the court—that conglomeration of Scots and English, old and new nobility, learned and unlearned, Catholics, Puritan sympathizers and Established

---

39. See Chambers, *Elizabethan Stage*, III, p. 255.
40. Alfred Harbage, *Shakespeare and the Rival Traditions* (New York, 1952), p. 80.
41. *A Game at Chesse*, pp. 164-65.

Churchmen, sophisticates and provincials—formed far too diverse a group for any unity of attitude to exist. What would have seemed scandalous to one would have sounded like legitimate criticism to another.[42] In any case the purveyors of scandal were merely players, hence the ideal currency for *quid pro quo* deals between more or less corrupt power brokers: "Leave my company of players alone in this instance, and I won't contest your petition to the King."

Modern readers tend to forget that drunken kings and power-and money-hungry courtiers may not have taken very seriously the gibes and japes of rogues, vagabonds, sturdy beggars, and young boys. I don't deny that in Jacobean London there were many who believed in the centrality and power of art and the theater: writers, serious readers, aesthetes, what would now be called the intelligentsia. But to those in power or lusting for power, it may be doubted whether words or actions on a stage would have seemed more important than they did to the condescending, time-killing courtiers in the final scene of *A Midsummer Night's Dream*. Would not the Carrs, the Buckinghams, the Howards, not to mention the King have regarded players as all-licensed fools? James's vast disdain of "the quality" is evident in his warning to Prince Henry in *Basilikon Doron* to "delight not to keepe ordinarily in your companie, Comoedians or Balladines"[43] (OED: "A theatrical dancer; mountebank, buffoon"). From his own court fool, Archie Armstrong, James was willing to accept public abuse.[44] His forbearance toward the Children of Blackfriars would seem to have emanated from the same general attitude. The tendency to treat players as privileged creatures, outside the laws that bound other citizens, is what particularly galled William Crashaw in 1610:

they play with *Princes* and *Potentates*, Magistrates and Ministers, nay with *God* and *Religion*, and all *holy things*: nothing that is good, excellent or holy can escape them: how then can this action [the colonizing of Virginia]? But this may suffice, that they are *Players*: they abuse *Virginia*, but they are Players: they disgrace it: true, but they are but players, and they have played with better things, and such as for which, if they speedily repent not, I dare say, vengeance waites for them.[45]

For an important courtier like Fulke Greville, rightly suspected by

42. I argue this point at some length in "The Role of the Court in the Development of Jacobean Drama," *Criticism*, 24 (1982), 138-58.

43. *The Political Works of James I*, ed. Charles H. McIlwain (Cambridge, Mass., 1918), p. 50.

44. See Enid Welsford, *The Fool* (London, 1935), pp. 171-81.

45. *A Sermon Preached in London before the . . . Captain General of Virginia* (London, 1610), sigs. H3v-H4.

Cecil of harboring sympathies for the shattered Essex faction, the writing of a political play was an altogether more dangerous matter. In his *Life of Sidney* he reveals that he "sacrificed to the fire" a play on Antony and Cleopatra which, he concedes, could have been "construed or strained to personating of vices in the present Governors, and government."[46] This action was neither paranoid nor cowardly. Even without such evidence, Greville's former allegiances made him so suspect that for a decade he held no significant position at court. Had his play been discovered by the wrong people, Greville might well have become an intimate of such long-term residents of the Tower as Ralegh and the "wizard" Earl of Northumberland.

It was not merely the writings of important public figures that were subjected to careful scrutiny and severe penalties. Any serious study of the law, of theology, or of history could endanger the author if it seemed to smack of the heretical or unconventional. Even a work like Dr. John Cowell's *The Interpreter* (1607), a legal dictionary felt to be immoderately supportive of the King's prerogative, caused that distinguished civil lawyer serious trouble with parliamentary supporters of the common law; the book was burned publicly.[47]

In 1599 the Bishop of London and the Archbishop of Canterbury ordered the mass burning of books, largely satiric in nature, at Stationers' Hall. No primarily "literary" writing suffered such a fate under James. In 1607, the same year Cowell's book was burned, Francis Beaumont published his most overtly political play, *The Woman Hater*. It included a Prologue which slyly mocks the libel laws and demonstrates how difficult it was to enforce them. Beaumont claims that the laws have made him careful not to supply material to government informers in the audience who jot into their "Table bookes . . . fit matter to feede his mallice on." (The missing word is probably "Majesty's.") Beaumont asserts that fear of the penalty has made him careful not to write libelously: "he that made this Play, meanes to please Auditors so, as hee may be an Auditor himselfe hereafter, and not purchase them with the deare losse of his eares." Then he saucily exposes the impotence of the law by concluding with the sort of negative-enwrapped double entendre no censor could quite punish him for: "hee did never thinke, but that a Lorde borne might bee a wise man, and a Courtier an honest

---

46. *Life of Sir Philip Sidney* (Oxford, 1907), pp. 155, 156.

47. See Wallace Notestein, *The House of Commons, 1604–1610* (New Haven, Conn., 1971), pp. 293-97.

man."[48] *The Woman Hater* shows no wise lords or honest courtiers: quite the contrary. Moreover, the stupid favorites, unequal justice, lavish expenditures, and hints of homosexuality in the title figure might have made it possible for a malign interpreter to ferret out dangerous implications, but the Italianate setting and generalized humors characters made censorship, much less the snipping of Beaumont's ears, nearly impossible.

Occasionally writers went further than Beaumont in flouting the laws in order to speak their minds. Bacon described Coke as having a "perpetual turbulent carriage."[49] The same may be said of Marston. As early as 1599 in his verse satire *The Scourge of Villainy* (one of the volumes burned) he proclaimed that he would denounce vice wherever he saw it, come what may. His "satyrick vaine," he says, won't be "muzled": "No gloomy Juvenall, / Though to thy fortunes I disastrous fall."[50] As we have seen, this bit of youthful bravado proved to be eerily prophetic. Marston was not the only playwright to take what must surely have been regarded as clearly defined, conscious risks. Day, Sharpham, Jonson, Chapman, and Middleton also committed more or less flagrant violations of the libel laws. Since nothing like the brutal mutilation of Stubbes under Elizabeth I or Pyrnne under Charles was ever meted out despite extreme provocation, I would conclude that it was almost impossible for a Jacobean dramatist to become a martyr for free speech.

My argument leads to two conclusions. The first is that it is unjustifiable to dispose *a priori* of a political interpretation of a Jacobean play. I refer to the manner in which, for example, G. K. Hunter dismisses the hypothesis that Marston's *The Fawn* might contain a character representing the King: "the date when the play was printed (1606) does not seem to me a time when anti-royalist publication would have been allowed."[51] There was never a time when antiroyalist publication would have been allowed, but there was never a time when it would have been impossible to produce or to publish such a play. In his authoritative work *The Profession of Dramatist in Shakespeare's Time* G. E. Bentley goes even further in this *a priori* direction:

The hypotheses so often and so solemnly advanced by many critics and readers of Tudor

48. *The Dramatic Works in the Beaumont and Fletcher Canon*, ed. Fredson Bowers (Cambridge, 1966), I, p. 157.

49. Quoted by Christopher Hill, *Intellectual Origins of the English Revolution* (Oxford, 1965), p. 247.

50. *The Poems of John Marston*, ed. Arnold Davenport (Liverpool, 1961), p. 117, ll. 193-96 passim.

51. *MLQ*, 31 (1970), 377.

and Stuart plays about the dramatist's "advice to the Queen" or "protests against the law" or "assertions of his religious dissent" must be made either in ignorance of the powers of the Master of the Revels or in assumption of his incompetence or venality.[52]

I would argue that Professor Bentley's assertion describes the situation more or less accurately depending upon who the Master of the Revels was, how competent and venal he was, how daring the author was, what courtiers the author was connected with, and how tolerant (or sober) the Monarch at that moment was. My second, more important conclusion concerns the creative atmosphere in which Jacobean drama developed. If the mechanisms of censorship had been as effective as Wickham claims, dramatists would have been prevented from depicting, as they so often did, the central public concern of the period, the tension in society between Court and Country (to adopt a brief formulation with an honorable lineage). Rather than an errorless, mechanistic monster like Nazi Germany, Jacobean England more nearly resembles such inefficient authoritarian regimes as those in present-day Hungary or (some years ago) Poland and Czechoslovakia. There, in films at least, much is allowed and more slips by through artistic cunning and the employment of arcane codes mastered by the cognoscenti.[53] Only such a model can account for the production, from James's accession in 1603 until at least 1622 (the date of Middleton and Rowley's *The Changeling*), of a body of drama which with unparalleled richness portrayed the entire range of human experience, political as well as personal.

---

52. P. 149.

53. See Annabel Patterson, *Censorship and Interpretation: The Conditions of Writing and Reading in Early Modern England* (Madison, Wis., 1984) for a pioneering, if not always persuasive, effort to describe such codes in seventeenth-century England.

The Nature of Jonson's Roman History

IT is a critical commonplace that in *Sejanus* and *Catiline* Jonson assumes the dual offices of poet and historian. In affirming the supreme importance of "truth of Argument,"[1] we are told, he took upon himself the functions of the historian, and gave us in these plays "a great poet's illumination of two important segments of Roman history."[2] So extensive, detailed, and precise is Jonson's scholarship that most readers who approach them require "diligent preparation for the experience of *Sejanus* and *Catiline*"—only in this way can we, like the learned historians Camden, Speed, and Selden, whose friendship and esteem Jonson sought and presumably enjoyed, properly appreciate the fidelity to historical truth these plays manifest.[3] Certain minor qualifications are admitted: careful attention has been paid to the ways in which the dramatist deliberately introduced subtle and not so subtle changes into the historical narrative, enhancing the effectiveness of his Roman plays.[4] "With few and trifling exceptions," however, "the plot of *Sejanus* is built with severe conformity to the historical record," and the same could be said of *Catiline*.[5] Jonson may have put aside the historian's recognition of the complexities of human nature in a Catiline and "taken the poet's role by detracting from Catiline's reforming fervor—his populism becomes merely the revolt of a degenerate aristocrat against a degenerate society,"[6] as Jonson had previously put it aside in radically simplifying

---

1. *Sejanus*, "To the Readers," ll. 18-19. All quotations from Jonson are taken from C. H. Herford and P. Simpson, *Ben Jonson*, 11 vols. (Oxford, 1925-1952).
2. Joseph Allen Bryant, "The Significance of Ben Jonson's First Requirement for Tragedy: 'Truth of Argument,'" *Studies in Philology* 49 (1952), 213.
3. Bryant, pp. 212, 206.
4. Herford and Simpson, *Ben Jonson*, I, 11-15.
5. *Ben Jonson*, I, 15, 116.
6. W. F. Bolton and Jane F. Gardner, eds., *Catiline* (London, 1973), Introduction, p. xv.

the complex and tortured personality of Tacitus's Tiberius into the scheming Machiavellian tyrant of *Sejanus*.[7] But this, it is implied, is simply a question of characterization and takes nothing away from the claim that *Catiline* "asserts the transcendental unity of the historian's private study with the poet's public stage" or that this play and *Sejanus* everywhere reveal "their concern for Roman history, their careful and rational buttressing with historical fact."[8] It is taken as self-evident that, in the words of Jonas Barish, to the writing of *Sejanus* "Jonson brought a scholar's command of the historical materials, and a scholar's conscience in dealing with them," so that the play "constitutes in itself a piece of historiography. It offers something like an archaeological reconstruction of the epoch it deals with, and a fully worked out interpretation of its subject, arrived at through a consideration of all relevant evidence," it marries "moral truth" to "historical truth," and it shows Jonson "fulfilling the offices of historian and poet simultaneously."[9]

This generally-held assumption that the Roman plays everywhere reveal a "concern for Roman history" emerging out of a "consideration of all relevant evidence" is in need of qualification of a sort it has never received. In most important ways, Jonson displays very little interest in or concern for the larger processes of Roman history in the periods his plays animate. It is curious, for example, that one can ask the most fundamental questions about Jonson the historian's treatment of Roman history and, in the very process of asking them, become aware that they are somehow not the right questions. What is Jonson's position on the respective claims of the senatorial oligarchy and the *populares*? If Jonson is a Pompeian—as he clearly is—then is it not logical to expect him to be more interesting on the character of Sulla? After all, Sulla restored the Republic, and even his enemies respected his achievements, allowing him to live unthreatened among them after his voluntary surrender of the dictatorship. Sulla's mantle passed to Pompey. Should not Jonson, as a Pompeian Republican, at least distinguish between the Senate's ruthless champion Sulla and the ruthless *popularis* Marius? For Marius foreshad-

---

7. On the simplification of major characters in *Catiline* and *Sejanus*, see K. M. Burton, "The Political Tragedies of Chapman and Ben Jonson," *Essays in Criticism* 2 (1952), 403-04; K. W. Evans, "*Sejanus* and the Ideal Prince Tradition," *Studies in English Literature 1500-1900*, 11 (1971), 249; and A. R. Dutton, "The Sources, Text, and Readers of *Sejanus*: Jonson's 'integrity in the story,'" *Studies in Philology* 75 (1978), 185-87.

8. Bolton and Gardner, p. xxiv; and Ralph Nash, "Ben Jonson's Tragic Poems," *Studies in Philology* 55 (1958), 185.

9. Jonas Barish, ed., *Sejanus* (London, 1965), Introduction, pp. 4-5.

ows the anti-Republican *popularis* Caesar, a monster in Jonson's eyes, while Sulla was at least on the right side. How significant were the Gracchi in the processes that led to the death of the Republic? Does Jonson have any qualms on the use of the *senatus consultum ultimum*—the emergency decree of a state of siege that empowered the consul Opimius to order the execution without trial of Caius Gracchus and the consul Cicero similarly to order the deaths of the disarmed Catilinarian conspirators? What were the underlying causes of the conspiracy? Is there not some disproportion in Jonson's presentation of a divine Augustus Caesar and a demonic Julius Caesar? Does Jonson accept the Roman Revolution of Augustus, and if so, with what reservations? If it was noble and valiant of "the constant BRVTVS" to "strike / So braue a blow into the monsters heart" (*Sejanus*, 1.93-95), can we find reasons in Jonson's *Sejanus* for the dramatist's refusal to endorse such an action if it were to be carried out against the monster Tiberius?—or is this an unaccountable inconsistency? If each play had indeed offered us "a fully worked out interpretation of its subject, arrived at through a consideration of all relevant evidence," we might expect answers to such questions. In fact, however, most of them are "the wrong questions," though they are certainly the historical questions, and to only two or three can any straightforward answer be given.

Jonson's classical scholarship issues in meticulously transcribed, literally translated passages of Sallust, Tacitus, and the rest, and is at its best in the re-creation of the "accidentals" of Roman history—the minutiae of topography, customs, religion, the formulae of senatorial procedure—all resulting in a great deal of Roman "atmosphere." The texts of historians, the phrases of orations and the echoes of the lines of a wide range of poets and philosophers, familiar to many in Jonson's audience from their labors at school, are vivified, and the impression created that the dramatic poet Jonson is not only a very fine classical scholar but a fine historian to boot, offering us a more convincing re-creation of the Roman world than Shakespeare, with his "small Latin and less Greek," could ever have hoped to do. The truth, however, is that to the materials of history he has so carefully sifted and assembled Jonson brings not the subtly discriminating mind of an historian but that same critical, simplifying eye of the moralist that critics have detected in his handling of the central "tragic" characters, particularly Tiberius and Sejanus (there are admitted ambiguities about Cicero). His Roman plays may be "archaeologically" unexceptionable, but in the final analysis they are not, by Roman or for that matter Elizabethan standards, good history. If one is interested in the general causes of Rome's moral decline one will read these tragedies with interest, but if one's fascination is with the play of complex historical forces and personalities, *Catiline* and *Sejanus* will not cater to it. Much better to go to *Coriolanus, Antony and Cleopatra, Julius Caesar*, or even to Thomas Lodge's *Wounds of Civil War.*

It may be instructive, therefore, to inquire into the ways in which Jonson does characterize late-Republican and early-Imperial history, comparing his views at certain points with the views of Elizabethan historians of Rome, and to give a summary of his "position" in these plays on the decline and death of the Republic. My focus here will not be upon the central characters of Catiline, Cicero, Tiberius and Sejanus, since there is some critical agreement that in his characterization of them Jonson at least modified the historical record, but upon the historical contexts Jonson has incorporated into the plays. By examining these we can clarify for ourselves the nature of Jonson's "historiography," using that term in a broader sense than critics generally do when they meticulously trace the facts, features and language of his plays to their sources and assume that in so doing they have demonstrated Jonson's qualifications as an historian. At the same time we may usefully circumscribe the term "historian" as (and if) it can be applied to Jonson by directing a tighter and more accurate, if less fulsome, praise to this side of the dramatist's achievement since, as Jonson himself observed in "To the Reader in Ordinarie" prefixed to *Catiline*, "nothing is more dangerous then a foolish prayse." For purposes of historico-chronological sense I will treat the plays as though they were two parts of a sustained analysis of Roman history—a justifiable approach, since they embrace, in their subjects and their references to events beyond those subjects, Roman history from the Gracchi to Caligula.

I

Jonson, in common with historians since Polybius, traces the causes of the Republic's sickness to the second century B.C. and the increasing wealth and openness to outside (particularly Greek) influences that followed success in the Second Punic War. This process was accelerated in the first century B.C. and it constitutes the theme of the Chorus that closes the first Act of *Catiline* ("Can nothing great, and at the height / Remaine so long?"). It is on this theme that Jonson is, as we might expect, most comfortable in the role of historian. Poverty made virtue before, but now Rome "doth joy / So much in plentie, wealth, and ease, / As, now, th'excesse is her disease" (1.548-50). Wealth has corrupted her women (1.555-59) and her men (1.560-64). Their tastes are now unnatural (1.563-64) and only novelties are in demand (1.569-72).

> Hence comes that wild, and vast expence,
> That hath enforc'd *Romes* vertue, thence,
> Which simple pouerty first made:
> And, now, ambition doth inuade
> Her state, with eating auarice,
> Riot, and euery other vice.
> Decrees are bought, and lawes are sold,
> Honors, and offices for gold;
> The peoples voyces: and the free
> Tongues, in the *Senate*, bribed bee. (1.573-82)

Rome has become "her owne spoiler, and owne prey" (1.586), and having conquered Asia, she finds herself conquered by Asia's vices (1.587-90)—and, it is implied, by the similar ones of Greece. Jonson is at one with Cato the Censor: outside influences are generally harmful. The plotter Sempronia, "a great states-woman" who is "both a mistris of the *latine* tongue, / And of the *greeke*" (2.38-41), is disinclined at first to see the Allobrogian ambassadors on account of their primitiveness: "Are they any schollers?" "Ha' they no *greeke*?" "Fie, what doe I here, wayting on 'hem then? / If they be nothing but meere states-men" (4.708-11). There are good things to be had from Greece (Cicero "suck'd at *Athens*," 2.137), but the stress is on the bad things like "licence" and "lust" (*Sejanus*, 3.442-43). Graecinus Laco, whose name gives him away, is even less trustworthy than "*Greeke*-SINON" (*Sejanus*, 4.360). In his tastes, Tiberius, who is fond of dropping phrases in Greek (2.330), rejects Rome, preferring to spend his time on Rhodes or Capreae, surrounding himself with his "rout" of Chaldeans. Domitius Afer the orator, one of the least savory characters in *Sejanus*, is, like Laco, given away by his name: historically, he came from Nemausus in Narbonensian Gaul, but Jonson suspects an African connection and has Arruntius call Afer "The Crocodile of *Tyber*" (2.424), an apt pun on his name (which means African) since crocodiles come from Africa.

Already by Cicero's time we find "*Romes* faultes" "now growne her Fate" (*Catiline*, 3.847), and Tiberius and Sejanus represent a part of Rome's punishment for those faults (she "felt her faults, before her punishment," *Catiline*, 3.875). Of these faults, the worst is ambition (*Catiline*, 3.860-71). With a few exceptions like Cicero and Cato, gone are the men who would count their gain "the republiques, not their owne" (*Catiline*, 2.390), "the old BRVTI, DECII . . . / The CIPI, CVRTII, . . . the great CAMILLI, too; / The FABII, SCIPIO'S" (2.391-96). Here we come right down, in effect, to Publius Cornelius Scipio Aemilianus, an adopted Scipio, strangled 128 B.C., perhaps by Caius Gracchus.

Jonson's attitude to the Gracchi accords with that of Elizabethan historians only because the historians choose unanimously in this instance not to present a balanced argument. They do this, in the face of the far more balanced (though never thoroughly sympathetic) discussions of the Gracchi by Plutarch and other Roman historians, because to them, as good Elizabethans, the attempted reforms of Tiberius and Caius Gracchus are seditious not only in the violent and unconstitutional manner of their introduction—one could agree with them there—but in their substance, particularly land reform. For these reasons William Fulbecke endorses the murder of Tiberius Gracchus by the consul Publius Scipio Nasica who, "thogh he were nearly linked in kindred to Tiberius Gracchus, yet [preferred] his countrey before his kindred."[10] Tiberius Gracchus "fell from vertue to vice, and extreme villanie: and hauing promised vpon a dissolute fancie, that he would enfranchise and receiue into the Citie anie Italian whosoeuer, turned all things into a contrarie state, mingled vertues with vice, lawes with lust, and brought the common-weale into a headlong and hideous danger" in "the first conspiracy in which ciuil bloud was shed, and the first dispensation of drawing swordes within the walles: after that time right was oppressed by violence, and the mightier man was accompted the better." There is no suggestion that the Agrarian Law might have been defensible—indeed, it is the radical reforms themselves, rather than their unconstitutional introduction, that are the most worrying: "to be briefe, [Caius] left almost nothing vnaltered or vndisturbed."[11] Jonson endorses this view because it is politically germane to him and because it accords with his clear-cut ethical approach to history. In *Catiline*, the dead Gracchi inhabit the same hell as Sulla, Cinna, and Marius.

It is in the period following the death of Caius Gracchus that Jonson parts company with the historians, who on subsequent events and personalities (Catiline excepted) generally prefer the complex truth to the poet's simplification—in Sidney's words, "what is" to "what shoulde bee."[12] They know, as William Cornwallis knew, that "to acknowledge the vertues of the vicious, is such a right, that what *Historian* willingly omitteth them, therin becommeth vicious himselfe."[13] The first Roman civil war was caused by Marius' challenging Sulla's command of the expedition against Mithridates, given to Sulla by the Senate. After returning to Rome, forcing Marius out of the city and temporarily settling affairs there, Sulla left Rome to its fate and pursued the war against Mithridates. In his absence Marius entered Rome where he and Cinna ruthlessly slew thousands of their opponents, including many senators. The authority of the Senate now counting for nothing, the Republic was effectively dead. Sulla, after negotiating a peace with Mithridates, returned to Italy in 83 B.C., defeated the dead Marius' son at Praeneste and the Samnites outside the Colline gate, and entered Rome, where he revenged the massacres carried out by Marius' party and introduced reforms that included the reduction of the tribunician power and a return of authority to the Senate. After only two years in his role as perpetual dictator, having restored and settled the Republic, he resigned the dictatorship, challenged a critical examination of his administration, and retired to live in peace unmolested by his surprised and admiring fellow Romans.

All historians acknowledge his enigmatic character, and in the Elizabethan histories of Rome one finds a diversity of views on him, none of them simply condemnatory. In N. Haward's translation of Eutropius we learn that "the residue of the Senate, leauing the city of their own accord, fled to Sylla into Greece: and besoughte him, that he woulde without farther delaye succoure his countrye." Sulla returns to Italy, but there is no mention of his proscriptions. All we are told of his subsequent actions in Rome is that he "appeased and sette in order the weal publique."[14] William Fulbecke argues that Sulla's "medicine was worse than the maladie it selfe,"[15] but he leaves no doubt in our minds that the responsibility for the bloodshed of the first civil war belongs primarily with Marius. In Sulla's absence, Marius and Cinna had behaved like "wolues" and "bloudhounds" in their slaughters at Rome, "euery good and discrete Italian making recourse vnto [Sulla]" who provides "an

12. *An Apology for Poetry*, in G. Gregory Smith, ed., *Elizabethan Critical Essays* (Oxford, 1964), p. 164.

13. *Essayes of Certaine Paradoxes* (1616), sig. C2.

14. *A Briefe Chronicle* (1564), sigs. I4v, I6.

15. *An Historicall Collection*, sig. C4v.

example of a double and diuerse mind in one man": merciful in war, cruel in peace, Sulla Felix was a man of "vexed soul" who lacked "true felicitie."[16] These historians follow Sallust in his general revulsion at the behavior of both sides, but not in his political sympathy with the policies of Marius.

Jonson takes over from Sallust the moral revulsion, but unlike Sallust and the Elizabethan historians he is not interested in the political causes and consequences of the civil war, at least within the "political" framework of *Catiline*, because the points of reference in that play are historical only insofar as they relate to moral decline. The idea, expressed in Tacitus, that Caligula could have "all the vices of Sulla with none of the Sullan virtues"[17] is incomprehensible in the context of *Catiline*, where Sulla, like Marius, Cinna, and the Gracchi, has no virtues, only vices. Sulla is a "pestilence" "sent from the *Stygian* sound" who allies himself, quite incredibly, with the other side—with the Gracchi, Cinna, and Marius (1.14,11,21). Historically pro-Senatorial in outlook, in this play he gleefully encourages a Catiline who intends the liquidation of the Senate. Jonson could elsewhere echo Plutarch's praise of the Sulla who "inforced frugality by the Lawes,"[18] but the Sulla of *Catiline* who introduces us to his protégé is not out of Plutarch. Perfectly unhistorical, his origins, like those of the Machiavel who introduces us to his pupil Barabas in Marlowe's *Jew of Malta*, lie in the morality tradition. Each is essentially a Vice figure. Had there not been such critical unanimity about Jonson's adoption of the "office of historian" in these plays, it would hardly have been necessary to make the point. By contrast with Jonson, Thomas Lodge, in dealing with the same period in *The Wounds of Civil War* (c. 1588), gives us all the historical points of reference. His Scilla aims to "Banish the name of tribune out of town" (2.1.194), his Cinna follows Marius in seeking "to unite the old citizens [*Optimates*] with the new [*Equites*]" (2.3.82) and in his support for the "Italian freeman" (3.1.59).[19] Scilla, after his second triumphant entry into Rome, gesturing to the "mangled members, streaming blood," points out to the crowd that "The reasons of this ruthful wrack / Are your seditious innovations, / Your fickle minds inclin'd to foolish change" (5.1.7-10). Pompey's words on "this trophy of renown" close the play: "What

16. *An Historicall Collection*, sigs. K1, K3v, L2.
17. Tacitus, *Annals*, ed. John Jackson, Loeb edn. (London, 1956), VI. xlvi.
18. *Discoveries*, l. 1009.
19. Quotations are from the Regents edn. of Joseph W. Houppert (London, 1970).

Roman ever was / That merited so high a name as he?" (5.5.403, 391-92). For all Lodge's wrenching of our moral sympathies in regard to this character, it has to be said that his play has at least got its historical bearings right. Historical cause and effect, the policies of the opposing sides, are of some interest to him. Jonson is interested solely in getting his moral bearings "right."

By contrast with his mentor Sulla, Gnaeus Pompey, the high-handed demolisher of Sulla's work in shoring up the Senatorial authority against consuls-turned-*imperatores*, emerges from Jonson's plays a paragon of republican virtue. In *Catiline* he is an unseen presence, commanding the Senate's army in Asia, but about to return. For that reason, Catiline must act quickly (3.554-56), or be destroyed by Pompey. Jonson is a Pompeian because Pompey supported the Senate (without indulging in Sulla's scale of bloodletting) in opposition to Caesar who, like Crassus, is a seditious *popularis*. It is that simple. In *Sejanus*, Pompey, seventy years dead, still has followers: the Germanicans bemoan the fact that Pompey's theater has been defiled by the setting up within it of a statue of Sejanus, and the historian Cremutius Cordus is, like Livy, a Pompeian, although one would hope a more balanced one than Jonson. On the Senate, Jonson wants it both ways: he appears to endorse the Allobroges in the contempt they feel for all its members with the exception of Cato, Cicero, and Catulus ("these men / Seeme of another race," 4.35-36) while he supports its authority literally to the hilt with regard to its right to invoke the *senatus consultum ultimum*, which allowed the consul, in an emergency, to take without trial the lives of Romans who threatened the state. Jonson thinks it was correctly employed not only after the discovery of the Catilinarian conspiracy, but by the consul Opimius in 121 B.C. against Caius Gracchus (*Catiline*, 4.197-201, 5.247-51). He believes it was wrongly invoked in the prosecution of Caius Silius in A.D. 24 (*Sejanus*, 3.201-09), or at least its phraseology—that the consul see to it "that the Commonwealth receive no loss"—was used misleadingly by Tiberius during the trial. Jonson's position on the Senate of the Empire, however, is much less clear-cut because, as we shall see, he locates the authority of the divine Augustus and his less divine successors in a social compact which permanently changed the constitution of the state.

When presenting him as the Senate's most dangerous enemy, Jonson is not especially interested in Julius Caesar as a representative of a political or philosophical tendency. His Caesar is a Machiavellian cynic who can derisively refer to Cicero as one of the "popular men" as if he were not one himself (*Catiline*, 3.93-98). His advice to Catiline regarding the conspiracy is to "Let 'hem call it mischiefe; / When it is past, and prosper'd, 'twill be vertue" (3.504-05). Ends justify means, and in his words to Catiline he forewarns us of his own future methods: the way to "any great thing" is through "violence" and "fraud" (3.515-16). In *Sejanus* he is a "monster" (1.95), albeit a "spirited" one (1.151). The best that Jonson can say for Caesar in these plays is said by the Pompeian Cremutius Cordus in *Sejanus*: Caesar chose not to punish Cicero for his *Cato* but to reply in kind with his *Anticato* (3.427-30). Brutus was entirely in the right in his conspiracy, if Arruntius speaks for Jonson, for "the constant BRVTVS

> (being proofe
> Against all charme of benefits) did strike
> So braue a blow into the monsters heart
> That sought vnkindly to captiue his countrie. (1.93-96)

Cordus, in referring to Brutus and Cassius as "the last of the Romans," underlines the point.

Yet this view of Caesar, more poetic than historical, does not represent Jonson's considered verdict on the man. It is, in fact, a deliberate de-historicizing of the character for the plays. Elsewhere, in the *Discoveries* and the *Epigrams*, he chooses the approach of the historian in his remarks on Caesar, emphasizing for us the fact that in his tragedies, where he was using but not presenting history, he simplified a character he himself knew to be complex. In the *Discoveries* Caesar is praised for his patriotic, statesmanlike, and unselfish care of the state.

> *I have* ever observ'd it, to have beene the office of a
> wise Patriot, among the greatest affaires of the *State*, to
> take care of the *Common-wealth* of Learning. For Schooles,
> they are the *Seminaries* of State: and nothing is worthier
> the study of a States-man, then that part of the
> *Republicke*, which wee call the *advancement* of Letters.
> Witnesse the care of *Iulius Caesar*; who, in the heat of
> the civill warre, writ his bookes of *Analogie*, and
> dedicated them to *Tully*. (ll. 924–31)

An equally revealing contrast with the Caesar of the plays is provided by Epigrams cx and cxi, "To Clement Edmonds, on his *Caesar's Commentaries obserued, and translated*" and "To the Same; on the Same." In the first of these, Caesar, though he caused "*Rome*, and her libertie" to yield to him, is seen as ennobled by the opposition of Pompey and Cato, and partly excused as one who lived "midst enuy' and parts [factions]; then fell by rage" (ll. 3–5, 14). "He wrote, with the same spirit that he fought" (l. 8), and in Edmond's book he is so restored "that he can dye no more" (l. 22). In the second, Jonson speaks for Caesar in a telling metaphor: to Edmond's critics

> CAESAR stands vp, as from his vrne late rose,
> By thy great helpe: and doth proclaime by mee,
> They murder him again, that enuie thee. (ll. 12-14)

There is no single "position" on Caesar adopted in Elizabethan histories of Rome. Richard Reynolds in his *Chronicle* judges Caesar and Pompey equally harshly: both were overly ambitious and both were cast down, their aspirations confounded by the will of God;[20] but this is an early history along the lines of *A Mirror for Magistrates*. William Fulbecke takes his stand against the assassination of Caesar: it was unlawful according to Roman law on several counts, but more to the point, "Surely they that will end tumult with tumult, can neuer be seized of good successe or fortunate euent."[21] He puts the question, "But was Iulius Caesar a tyrant? Surely there was more tyrannie in the slaughter then in the man slaine."[22] W. Traheron's translation of Pedro Mexia, *The Historie of all the Romane Emperors* (1604) presents Caesar as "the most mightie, the most worthie, valiant, wise and fortunate Prince and captaine," who "had fewer imperfections and vices then any other": even his ambition "he held for no vice, and might alleadge that he was compelled thereto," and as for anything else held against him, "it doth rather appeare to be the murmuring and slandering of his adversaries, then any truth."[23] Cornwallis, like Mexia, was an unabashed Caesarian: the great man was not only "worthy of an eternall memory, and of neuer ending praises;" he is Cornwallis' own greatest inspiration.[24] It would appear that Jonson's considered position on Caesar was mid-way between the extremes of Reynolds on the one hand and Mexia and Cornwallis on the other, but the Caesar of the plays is little more than an emblem of future tyranny in *Catiline* and of past tyranny in *Sejanus,* held, like the main characters in these works, in the frame of a distorting

---

20. *A Chronicle of all the noble Emperours of the Romaines, from Iulius Caesar* (1571), sig. B7v.
21. *An Historicall Collection*, sigs. Z1, Z1v.
22. *An Historicall Collection*, sig. Z2v.
23. *The Historie of all the Romane Emperors* (1604), sig. C6v.
24. *Essayes* (1601), part 1, sig. L7.

"mirror for magistrates" in which the subtle images of history are transformed into the starkest of contrasts.

II

From it, the picture of Augustus emerges as Caesar's antithesis. This might be expected, given the uncritical view of him already presented in *Poetaster* two years before *Sejanus* appeared, and considering the generally favorable view Elizabethan historians take of Augustus.[25] That is not to say there were no demurrers: Fulbecke argues that had Julius Caesar not been assassinated, "though there had bene a Caesar, yet should there neuer haue bene an Augustus," without whom the Republic might still have been preserved.[26] What is so interesting about the Augustus Jonson evokes in *Sejanus* is that his system, which Tiberius has inherited, was, it is implied, made permanent by being founded in a social contract whose theoretical basis is Elizabethan rather than Roman.

As Jonson sees it, Augustus changed the old constitution, in effect dissolved in civil war, with the blessing of the Roman people, and in such a way that the kind of action Brutus took against Caesar is no longer justifiable against a Tiberius. The rules have been permanently changed. Under the Republic supreme authority rested with the Senate, and it might be argued that Brutus simply defended it against Caesar's attempt to usurp its authority; under the Principate, however, final authority rests with the *princeps*, whose *tribunicia potestas* effectively makes him supreme. The Germanicans recognize this; republican in their sympathies, they accept nevertheless that they live under a different and properly constituted dispensation emerging out of, and finally putting an end to, a state of civil war. The "old liberty" has been lost for good. The crucial lines are Sabinus':

> A good man should, and must
> Sit rather downe with losse, then rise vniust.
> Though, when the *Romanes* first did yeeld themselues
> To one mans power, they did not meane their liues,
> Their fortunes, and their liberties, should be
> His absolute spoile, as purchas'd by the sword. (4.165-70)

Jonson's conception of the Augustan "constitution" is that it was based in the consent of the governed—though Tiberius behaves as if it had been

25. As opposed to Octavius. See Robert P. Kalmey, "Shakespeare's Octavius and Elizabethan Roman History," *Studies in English Literature 1500–1900* 18 (1978), 275-87.

26. *An Historicall Collection*, sig. Z2.

"purchas'd by the sword" that is not in fact how it was established by Augustus.[27] Tiberius does not act according to the rules of the compact, but that fact can never justify rebellion on the part of the citizens. Jonson very seriously endorses what Coleridge called the "James-and-Charles-the-First zeal for legitimacy of descent"[28] in Arruntius' lines:

> The name TIBERIVS
> I hope, will keepe; how ere he hath fore-gone
> The dignitie, and power. SIL. Sure, while he liues.
>   ARR. And dead, it comes to DRVSVS. Should he fayle,
> To the braue issue of GERMANICVS. (1.244-48).

In Tacitus, however, the Principate does not work in quite this way. While Tacitus does imply (what Sejanus assumes) that in A.D. 23 the logical "line of succession" ran as Arruntius has it,[29] it need not do so. Augustus, Tacitus has earlier informed us, considered Lucius Arruntius himself for the "succession," which did not have to be a matter of lineal descent at all. This question is particularly important, for it concerns the man Jonson chose as the chief commentator on the action in *Sejanus*. In the last few years it has been claimed that Arruntius "did not appear on the scene till two years after Sejanus's death,"[30] and that Arruntius does not exist in Tacitus "in Sejanus's lifetime,"[31] statements which, while startling errors, are not surprising in a period when there has been much bold talk about how "the Germanicans contribute directly to the decline of their civilization"[32] and demonstrate "the failure of virtuous men to construct a viable alternative."[33] In fact Arruntius does appear on Tacitus' "scene" "in Sejanus's lifetime." He was consul in A.D. 6, his connections were Sullan and Pompeian, and according to Tacitus he was a senator of great wealth, talent, integrity, and public spirit. It is

27. Compare the lines of Sabinus above, especially the crucial third and fourth lines, with the phraseology of Hooker on the original social contract in *Of the Laws of Ecclesiastical Polity*, ed. Christopher Morris (London, 1907), vol. 1, I.x.4: "To take away all such mutual grievances, injuries, and wrongs, there was no way but only by growing unto composition and agreement amongst themselves, by ordaining some kind of government public, and by yielding themselves subject thereunto; that unto whom they granted authority to rule and govern, by them the peace, tranquillity, and happy estate of the rest might be procured."

28. *Lectures and Notes on Shakespeare* (London, 1914), p. 413.

29. *Annals*, IV. iii.

30. Gary D. Hamilton, "Irony and Fortune in *Sejanus*," *Studies in English Literature 1500–1900* 11 (1971), 278.

31. Dutton, p. 187.

32. Marvin L. Vawter, "The Seeds of Virtue: Political Imperatives in Jonson's *Sejanus*," *Studies in the Literary Imagination* 6 (1973), 46.

33. Dutton, p. 189.

therefore not surprising that, as Tacitus informs us,

> Augustus, in his last conversations, when discussing possible holders of the principate—those who were competent and disinclined, who were inadequate and willing, or who were at once able and desirous—had described Manius Lepidus as capable but disdainful, Asinius Gallus as eager and unfit, Lucius Arruntius as not undeserving and bold enough to venture, should the opportunity arise. The first two names are not disputed; in some versions Arruntius is replaced by Gnaeus Piso: all concerned, apart from Lepidus, were soon entrapped on one charge or another, promoted by Tiberius. (*Annals*, I, xiii)

There are quite a few other appearances of Arruntius in Tacitus during Sejanus' lifetime, but this one is crucial. Jonson chooses to neglect a passage in Tacitus that is supremely flattering to his chief commentator, and for a very good reason: the passage contradicts Jonson's neat concept of lineal descent which he makes Arruntius, of all people, proclaim. Like all of Jonson's simplifications of historical truth, this one—legitimacy of descent—promotes the didactic function that is so proper to literature, for it gives Jonson an easy way out of the problem of how to account for the lack of what the spy Latiaris calls "active valor" in the Germanicans by turning it into civic virtue. Jonson could not tamper with the historical fact that during the reign of Tiberius the Germanicans did not marry this sort of active *virtus* to their moral opposition to Tiberius. What he could and did do was complicate and justify the fatalism which in Tacitus the Germanicans share with the author. Jonson combined this fatalism with an orthodox Elizabethan attitude toward "legitimate," "lineal" tyranny: "A good man should, and must / Sit rather down with losse, then rise vniust," but Jonson did so by contradicting an intractable passage in Tacitus unsuitable to his purposes. If Jonson had wanted to present the passive stoicism of the Germanicans critically he would have hardly bothered to take such pains and liberties to "establish" that in a tyranny-by-lineal-descent founded on good Hookerian contract theory they could not justifiably do otherwise than watch and condemn.

There is another problem with the "irresponsible Germanicans" theory: it asks us to accept that in their case Jonson has blurred the moral blacks and whites he otherwise shows such fondness for, and to which he deliberately and habitually reduces the complex colorations of history. This is his way with practically every historical reference contained in *Sejanus* and *Catiline*, which are profoundly moral essays on civic virtue and civic vice and in which little is allowed to spoil the clarity of the contrasts (even Cicero, perhaps, was for Jonson more clear-cut than most critics would want to admit). Thus the violent Drusus of history, since he is an opponent of Sejanus, has perforce to be whitewashed—to this end, Sabinus and Silius immediately "correct" with ringing praises (1.106-16) the historically valid description Arruntius gives of him ("a riotous youth")—while one would never guess the Germanican Caligula of this play had any connection with the emperor of that name. (The worst to be said of him is said by Pomponius, a confederate of Sejanus, "the young Prince" has an "appetite" for Macro's wife [4.516-17].)

There are few plays in the corpus of English Renaissance drama whose exemplars of civic virtue and civic vice are less accessible to ironic interpretation than those in *Sejanus*, a fact well worth emphasizing when one considers that the propensity to read everything ironically has never been as great as it is today, when one expects, any time now, the appearance of an ironic reading of Spenser's Red Crosse Knight. Jonson is no more interested in presenting irresponsible Germanicans than he is in the positive view of Sejanus offered in Velleius Paterculus' history of Rome, written a year before Sejanus fell. His purpose is rather to create, out of what Sidney calls the "what is" of history, the dramatic embodiment of "what should be." As we have seen, in respect to practically every detail of the historical contexts which these plays create in their references to character and event from the Gracchi to Caligula, Jonson follows Sidney's prescription for the poet rather than the historian. And the reason he follows Sidney is because Jonson, like that critic, accepts Aristotle's argument that (in Sidney's words)

Poetry is *Philosophoteron* and *Spoudaioteron*, that is to say, it is more Philosophicall and more studiously serious then history. His reason is, because Poesie dealeth with *Katholou*, that is to say, with the vniuersall consideration; and the history with *Kathekaston*, the perticuler: 'nowe,' sayth he, 'the vniuersall wayes what is fit to bee sayd or done, eyther in likelihood or necessity, (which the Poesie considereth in his imposed names), and the perticuler onely marks whether *Alcibiades* did, or suffered, this or that.' Thus farre *Aristotle*: which reason of his (as all his) is most full of reason. For indeed, if the question were whether it were better to haue a perticular acte truly or falsly set downe, there is no doubt which is to be chosen, no more then whether you had rather haue *Vespasians* picture right as hee was, or at the Painters pleasure nothing resembling. But if the question be for your owne vse and learning, whether it be better to haue it set downe as it should be, or as it was, then certainly is more doctrinable the fained *Cirus* in *Xenophon* then the true *Cyrus* in *Iustine*, and the fayned *Aeneas* in *Virgil* then the right *Aeneas* in *Dares Phrigius*.[34]

34. *An Apology for Poetry*, pp. 167-68.

When Jonson speaks in his address "To the Readers," prefixed to *Sejanus*, of his "truth of Argument," he ought not to be taken too literally, for much of the strictly particular (historical) truth has been shaped and simplified in the interests of universal (philosophical) truth. He is not taking on the role of historian but that of a poet who turns the materials of history into poetry, and his plays do not reveal "a transfer to drama of the traditional function of history."[35] There is no conflict between Jonson and Sidney on the function of poetry, because Sidney's comments on the poet's way with the materials of history apply in a quite precise way to Jonson's tragedies, in which "the fained *Cirus* in *Xenophon*" is inevitably preferred to "the true *Cyrus* in *Iustine*."

---

35. Bryant, p. 204.

Women in Men's Clothing: Apparel and Social Stability in The Roaring Girl

MARY BETH ROSE

THE CENTRAL figure in Thomas Middleton and Thomas Dekker's city comedy *The Roaring Girl* (c. 1608–1611) is a woman named Moll Frith, whose distinguishing feature is that she walks around Jacobean London dressed in male clothing.[1] It should be stressed that Moll is not in disguise: she is neither a disguised player, a man pretending to be a woman; nor is she a disguised character, whose role requires a woman pretending to be a man. Unlike the disguised heroines of romantic comedy, Moll seeks not to conceal her sexual identity, but rather to display it. Although certain of the *Dramatis Personae* in *The Roaring Girl* occasionally fail to recognize her immediately, the fact that Moll is a woman is well known to every character in the play. She simply presents herself in society as a woman wearing men's clothes. Demanding merely by her presence that people reconcile her apparent sexual contradictions, she arouses unspeakable social and sexual anxieties in the established society of the play. Indeed Middleton and Dekker create Moll as the fulcrum of *The Roaring Girl*, and the other characters' reactions to her tend to define them as social and moral beings. As a result, society's effort to assess the identity of this female figure in male attire becomes the central dramatic and symbolic issue of the play.

Recognizing the title figure's assumption of male attire as the symbolic focus of social and moral concern in *The Roaring Girl* allows us to connect the play with the intense, often bitterly funny debate about women wearing men's clothes that was taking place in contemporary moral and religious writing, and which came to a head in 1620 with a pair of pamphlets entitled, respectively, *Hic Mulier: Or, The Man-Woman,* and

---

1. I would like to acknowledge my gratitude to the Monticello College Foundation and The Newberry Library, whose generous support made possible the research for this essay.

Haec-Vir: Or The Womanish-Man.[2] Indeed the figure of the female in male apparel emerges from the documents of this controversy much as Moll Frith does from the text of *The Roaring Girl:* an embodiment of female independence boldly challenging established social and sexual values and, by the fact of her existence, requiring evaluation and response. Although historians of Renaissance conduct literature as well as more recent literary critics have discussed the *Hic Mulier / Haec-Vir* controversy,[3] no attempt has been made to view *The Roaring Girl,* with its "man-woman" heroine, in the context of this debate. Both because the controversial issue involved has an ongoing importance in Renaissance England and because I am not seeking to establish a direct influence between documents and play, the small chronological discrepancy between the performance and publication of *The Roaring Girl* (c. 1608–1611) and the high point of the debate (1620) is not relevant to my purposes here; rather I am interested in exploring the fact that the figure of the female in male attire is portrayed in both dramatic and social contexts with simultaneous admiration, desire, abhorrence, and fear. The following essay attempts to demonstrate the ways in which parallel treatments of women in men's clothing in the drama and the debate illuminate this phenomenon of fashion as the focus of considerable moral and social anxiety aroused by changing sexual values in Jacobean England; and to show that, taken together, artistic representation and social commentary suggest a deep cultural ambivalence in the British Renaissance about female independence and equality between the sexes.

I

Elizabethan and Jacobean sermons and conduct books continually castigate the fickleness of fashion and the vanity of sumptuous apparel. To cite one very typical example, the writer of the sermon "Against

---

2. The full names of these colorful pamphlets are as follows: *Hic Mulier: Or, The Man-Woman: Being a Medicine to cure the Coltish Disease of the Staggers in the Masculine-Feminines of our Times* and *Haec-Vir: Or The Womanish-Man: Being an Answer to a late Booke intituled Hic-Mulier.* All citations from the pamphlets are taken from the edition published by *The Rota* at the University of Exeter, 1973.

3. See Louis B. Wright, *Middle-Class Culture in Elizabethan England* (Chapel Hill, N.C., 1935), pp. 494–97; Carroll Camden, *The Elizabethan Woman* (New York, 1952), pp. 263–67; Juliet Dusinberre, *Shakespeare and the Nature of Women* (London, 1975), pp. 231–71; Linda T. Fitz, "What Says the Married Woman: Marriage Theory and Feminism in the English Renaissance," *Mosaic,* 13 (Winter, 1980), 1–22; and Linda Woodbridge, *Women and the English Renaissance: Literature and the Nature of Womankind, 1540–1620* (Urbana, 1984), pp. 139–51.

Excess of Apparel" in *Homilies Appointed to be Read in the Time of Queen Elizabeth* sees the English preoccupation with the novelties of fashion as a futile expenditure of energy, indicating an endlessly detrimental spiritual restlessness: "We are never contented, and therefore we prosper not."[4] Furthermore the conservative spirit frequently links propriety of dress with the coherence of society and views as a threat to social stability the tendency of the pretentious or the newly prosperous to dress so elegantly that it was becoming increasingly difficult to distinguish among social classes by the varied attire of their members.[5] Along with the upwardly mobile and the fop, women were singled out as creators of chaos for seeking to seduce men other than their husbands by wearing enticing clothes and for being generally disobedient, disrespectful, shallow, demonic, and extravagant in their preoccupation with fashion.[6]

From these characteristic themes the phenomenon of women dressing in male clothing begins gradually to assume a distinct identity as a separate issue; or, more accurately, as an issue that, in its symbolic significance, articulates a variety of social and moral concerns. The few available references to the phenomenon in the 1500s are largely paren-thetical. In the early part of the sixteenth century, the idea of women wearing men's clothes apparently seemed too appalling even to be feared. Ever zealous of female virtue, John Louis Vives, for example, issues an ultimatum on the subject in *Instruction of a Christian Woman* (c. 1529) only as a last line in his chapter on feminine dress, a mere after-thought to the more important prohibitions against brazenness and extravagance in female attire. Citing Deuteronomy 22.5, he writes, "A woman shall use no mannes raymente, elles lette hir thinke she hath the mans stomacke, but take hede to the woordes of our Lorde: sayinge, a woman shall not put on mans apparell: for so to do is abhominable afore God. But I truste no woman will do it, excepte she be paste both honestee and shame."[7] Vives' confidence in womanly docility was, however,

---

4. Quoted from *Certain Sermons or Homilies Appointed to be Read in Churches in the Time of Queen Elizabeth* (London: Society for Promoting Christian Knowledge, 1908), p. 327.

5. See, for example, "Against Excess of Apparel" in *Homilies*; Thomas Nashe, *Christs Teares over Jerusalem*, 1593, in John Dover Wilson, *Life in Shakespeare's England* (Cambridge, 1920), p. 125; and Phillip Stubbes, *Anatomy of Abuses*, 1583, ed. Frederick J. Furnivall, The New Shakespeare Society (London, 1877–1879), pp. 33–34.

6. See, for example, William Harrison, *Description of England, 1587* in Wilson, pp. 124–25. Cf. Wright, p. 493; Camden, pp. 257–67; and Fitz.

7. John Louis Vives, "Of raiments," in *Instruction of a Christian Woman*, trans. Richard Hyrde (1557), Book II, Chap. VIII. Deuteronomy 22.5 reads: "The Woman shall not wear that which

misplaced. In George Gascoigne's satire *The Steele Glas* (1576), complaints about women in male attire, although still relegated to the status of an epilogue, are nevertheless becoming decidedly more pointed and vociferous:

> "What be they? women? masking in mens weedes?
> With dutchkin dublets, . . . and with Jerkins jaggde?
> With high copt hattes and fethers flaunt a flaunt?
> They be so sure even *Wo* to *Men* in dede."[8]

The astonished despair of female modesty expressed in Gascoigne's mournful pun takes the form of accusations of sexual and, by clear inference, social, moral, and cosmic perversion in the rhetoric of Phillip Stubbes. Writing in 1583, in the midst of a general denunciation of the apparel of both sexes, Stubbes mentions women with "dublets and Jerkins as men have heer, buttoned up the brest, and made with wings, welts, and pinions on the shoulder points, as mans apparel is."[9] Stubbes lucidly states his indignant alarm at the possibility of not being able to distinguish between the sexes: "Our Apparell was given us as a signe distinctive to discern betwixt sex and sex, and therefore one to weare the Apparel of another sex is to . . . adulterate the veritie of his owne kinde. Wherefore these Women may not improperly be called *Hermaphroditi,* that is, Monsters of bothe kindes, half women, half men."[10]

While Stubbes' rhetoric is always colorfully extravagant, the topic of women in male attire continued to elicit highly emotional reactions at a growing rate, particularly in the second decade of the seventeenth century when, amidst a marked increase in satiric attacks upon women in general, references to the "monstrous . . . *Woman* of the *Masculine Gender*" multiplied notably.[11] As Louis B. Wright has demonstrated, this expansion in both the volume and hostility of satire against women represented the misogynistic, ultra-conservative voice in the lively debate about

---

pertaineth unto a man, neither shall a man put on a woman's garment: for all that do so *are* abomination unto the Lord thy God."

8. George Gascoigne, *The Steele Glas,* 1576, in ed. Edward Arber, *English Reprints,* V (London, 1868), pp. 82–83.

9. Stubbes, p. 73.

10. Stubbes, p. 73. Cf. Harrison, in Wilson, pp. 124–25.

11. Henry Fitzgeffrey, *Notes from Black-fryers,* 1617. Cited by Wright, p. 492. See Wright, pp. 483–94 for other references to the "man-woman," including Barnabe Rich, in *The Honestie of this Age* (1614); Alexander Niccoles, in *A Discourse of Marriage And Wiving* (ed. of 1620); and Thomas Adams, in *Mystical Bedlam* (1615).

woman's nature, behavior, and role that was taking place in the moral and religious writing of the early decades of the century.[12] According to Wright and other critics, the content of this conduct literature can be distinguished roughly along class lines: where "learned and courtly" works tended to discuss women in the abstract and spiritualized terms of neoplatonic philosophy, middle-class tracts disputed more practical and social issues, such as the appropriateness of female apparel.[13] While the documents in the controversy surrounding women in male attire indicate that both upper- and middle-class females followed the fashion, they are much too partisan and factually imprecise to convey the actual extent to which the style was adopted.[14]

Nevertheless by 1620 the phenomenon of women in men's clothing had become prominent enough to evoke an outraged protest from King James, recorded in a letter of J. Chamberlain to Sir D. Carleton, dated January 15, 1620:

Yesterday the bishop of London called together all his clergie about this towne, and told them he had expressed commandment from the King to will them to inveigh vehemently against the insolencie of our women, and theyre wearing of brode brimed hats, pointed dublets, theyre haire cut short or shorne, and some of them stilettoes or poinards, and such other trinckets of like moment; adding that if pulpit admonitions will not reform them he would proceed by another course; the truth is the world is very much out of order.

On February 12, Chamberlain adds the following: "Our pulpits ring continually of the insolence and impudence of women, and to helpe the matter forward the players have likewise taken them to taske, and so to the ballades and ballad-singers, so that they can come nowhere but theyre eares tingle; and if all this will not serve, the King threatens to fall upon theyre husbands, parents, or frends that have or shold have power

12. Wright, p. 490. Anger against women reached its zenith in Joseph Swetnam's misogynistic tract, *The Araignment of Lewd, Idle, Froward, and unconstant Women* (1615), which had ten printings by 1634 and inspired several responses (see Wright, pp. 486–93), including a stage-play, *Swetnam, the Woman-hater, Arraigned by Women*, (1620).

13. Wright, p. 507 and Fitz, pp. 2–3.

14. Along with the numerous isolated references to the *Hic Mulier* phenomenon cited in Wright, these documents include the *Hic Mulier* and *Haec-Vir* pamphlets, noted above, and another pamphlet, *Mulde Sacke: Or The Apologie of Hic Mulier: To the late Declamation against her* (1620). By referring to the *Hic Mulier* phenomenon as a "transvestite movement," or even as a "rough-and-ready unisex movement" (p. 15), Fitz implies more coherence and range to the fashion than these pamphlets can document. Cf. Woodbridge, pp. 139–51.

over them, and make them pay for it."[15] The King's protest amounted
to a declaration of war. While undoubtedly resulting in part from James'
considerable misogyny,[16] the actions following his protest also revealed
that, among all the satiric targets on the subject of female fashion,
women in men's clothing had assumed threatening enough proportions
in the conservative mind to be singled out in a conscientious and
thorough attempt to eliminate the style from social life. In February,
1620 the pamphlets *Hic Mulier,* which represented the conservative
viewpoint, and *Haec-Vir,* which defended the practice of women wearing male attire, appeared. Because the pamphlets are anonymous, it is
impossible to link their opinions to the gender of their author or authors.
More importantly, the subject of the unconventional "man-woman" had
evolved into a full-fledged debate, in which conservative and liberal
positions are clearly and elaborately defined.

Wright believes the hostile conservative response to women in men's
clothing was a defensive reaction against an increasingly successful
demand both for moral and spiritual equality between the sexes and for
greater social freedom for women: freedom, for example, from con-
finement to the home, from the double standard of sexual morality, from
wife-beating and from forced marriage. "The average [i.e., middle-
class] woman," Wright concludes, "was becoming articulate in her own
defense and . . . was demanding social independence unknown in
previous generations."[17] According to Wright, the female adoption of
male apparel aggressively and visibly dramatized a bid for social independence, which comprised a largely successful and coherent challenge
to existing sexual values that is reflected in *Haec-Vir,* a pamphlet Wright
believes to be "the *Areopagitica* of the London woman, a woman who had
attained greater freedom than any of her predecessors or than any of her
European contemporaries."[18] It is true that the challenge that women in

15. Edward Phillips Statham, *A Jacobean Letter-Writer: The Life and Times of John Chamberlain*
(London, 1920), pp. 182–83.

16. We should not, I think, take for granted that misogynistic and feminist attitudes can be
aligned neatly with gender in the Renaissance. The relative paucity of literature in the early 1600s
in which women are clearly speaking for themselves makes specifically female attitudes
extremely difficult to distinguish and assess. Resolving the problem of the correlation between
gender and attitude is not, however, prerequisite to the present analysis, which seeks to compare
the sexual values clearly articulated in the *Hic Mulier/Haec-Vir* debate with the artistic conception
of a *Hic Mulier* figure in *The Roaring Girl.*

17. Wright, p. 490.

18. Wright, p. 497.

male attire presented to the existing imbalance of power between the sexes can be discerned in the vindictive bitterness of the opposition to the androgynous style. Yet Linda T. Fitz has recently provided a useful and fascinating corrective to the hopeful interpretation of the extent and coherence of Jacobean feminism advanced by Wright and critics like Juliet Dusinberre by stressing the restrictiveness, rather than the liberating potential, of middle-class conduct literature. In her discussion of the controversy surrounding women in men's clothing, Fitz points out some serious oversights in Wright's optimistic view of the *Hic Mulier/Haec-Vir* debate; nevertheless Fitz ends by conceding that "Wright is quite justified in his . . . assessment" of a resounding victory for female freedom articulated in this controversy.[19] My own analysis of the debate suggests an attitude toward the *Hic Mulier* phenomenon and the sexual freedom it represented which is more complex than either Wright perceives or Fitz explores, an attitude that both acknowledges injustice and fears change, that wants sexual freedom yet perceives its attainment as conflicting with an equally desirable social stability.

II

After an introductory lament that "since the daies of *Adam* women were never so Masculine" (sig. A3), the pamphlet *Hic Mulier* or *The Man-Woman* begins by propounding a familiar Renaissance ideal of woman as chaste, maternal, compassionate, discreet, and obedient, a model of behavior and sentiment from which the notorious "man-woman" is believed to depart "with a deformitie never before dream'd of" (sig. A3v).[20] In contrast to this modestly attired paragon, the *Hic Mulier* figure, sporting a "cloudy Ruffianly broad-brim'd Hatte, and wanton Feather . . . the loose, lascivious civill embracement of a French doublet . . . most ruffianly short lockes . . . for Needles, Swords . . . and for Prayer bookes, bawdy Jigs" is "not halfe man, halfe woman . . . but all Odyous, all Divell" (sigs. A4–A4v). In elaborating the polemical

19. Fitz, pp. 16–17. Fitz, for example, sees as unfortunate the argument in *Haec-Vir* (sig. C2v) that it is a law of nature that differences between the sexes be preserved by designated dress and behavior. She also remarks that "Renaissance women so far accepted the masculine rules of the game that they felt they had to adopt the clothing and external attributes of the male sex in order to be 'free.' This was true in drama as in life: witness the transvestite heroines of Shakespeare's romantic comedies." See also Woodbridge, pp. 148–49.

20. See Suzanne W. Hull, *Chaste Silent & Obedient: English Books for Women 1475–1640* (San Marino, Cal, 1982). Hull provides an ample bibliography of documents that articulate the Renaissance ideal of womanhood.

intention of this pamphlet—to eliminate the heinous fashion by demonizing its proponents—the author builds a case around two major arguments.

As might be expected, the first group of arguments centers on the dangerous sexual chaos which the author assumes will result from the breakdown of rigid gender distinctions symbolized by the "man-woman's" attire. The writer perceives in *Hic Mulier's* choice of male clothes unconventional sexual behavior; therefore she automatically becomes a whore, who inspires by her lewd example a pernicious illicit sexuality in others. As implied in the description of her "loose, lascivious civill embracement of a French doublet, being all unbutton'd to entice" (sig. A4v), she will allow, even invite, "a shameless libertie to every loose passion" (sig. C2). Despite—indeed because of—her mannishness, then, *Hic Mulier* displays and encourages a free-floating sexuality, a possibility which the author views as socially destabilizing and therefore disastrous, "most pernicious to the common-wealth" (sig. C2). As we will see, this interesting association between socially threatening female sexiness and the breakdown of polarized gender identities and sexual roles becomes very important in *The Roaring Girl*. The fear seems to be that without rigidly assigned, gender-linked roles and behavior, legitimate, faithful erotic relations between the sexes will become impossible and the integrity of the family will consequently disintegrate: "they [i.e., the "men-women"] are neither men, nor women, but just good for nothing . . . they care not into what dangers they plunge either their Fortunes or Reputations, the disgrace of the whole Sexe, or the blot and obloquy of their private Families" (sigs. B2, C2).

However ominous, the unleashing of Eros and the breakdown of sexual polarization do not preoccupy the author as much as do questions of social status and hierarchy. The implied norm behind the satire in the pamphlet is a stable society which derives its coherence from the strict preservation of such essential distinctions as class, fortune, and rank. Not only do women in men's clothing come from various classes in society; they also have the unfortunate habit of dressing alike, obscuring not only the clarity of their gender, but the badge of their social status as well, and thereby endangering critically the predictable orderliness of social relations. To convey the seriousness of this offense, the author employs the rhetorical device of associating the hated style by turns with decaying aristocrats and gentry ("the adulterate branches of rich stocks" [sig. B1]), women of base birth ("stinking vapours drawne from dunghils" [sig. B1]), females of the upper classes "knowne great" ("no more shall their greatness or wealth save them from one particle of disgrace" [sigs. B1v, B2v]), and middle-class wives (tailors have "metamorphosed more modest old garments . . . for the use of Freemens wives than hath been worne in Court, Suburbs, or Countrey" [sig. C1v]), all of which leads to the indignant outburst: "It is an infection that emulates the plague, and throwes itselfe amongst women of all degrees . . . Shall we all be co-heires of one honor, one estate, and one habit?" (sigs. B1v, B4v). Like death and disease, then, the female in male attire serves as a leveler; and, just as such issues as the inflated sale of honors by the Crown seemed to the conservative mind to be undermining social coherence by threatening the traditional prestige of inherited nobility, so the phenomenon of women of different social positions dressing in similar male clothing appeared intolerably chaotic. As Fitz has shown, English Renaissance women, particularly in the middle classes, used their apparel as a showpiece to advertise the prosperity of their fathers and husbands.[21] That women should perversely refuse, by donning look-alike male clothes, to serve their crucial function as bearers of social class status and distinction is the issue that arouses the author's most vindictive antipathy: "Let . . . the powerfull Statute of apparell but lift up his Battle-Axe, so as every one may bee knowne by the true badge of their bloud, or Fortune: and then these *Chymera's* of deformitie will bee sent backe to hell, and there burne to Cynders in the flames of their owne malice" (sig. C1v).

The pamphlet *Hic Mulier* ends with an invective against all social change (sig. C3). Given the hectic violence of this author's conservatism, it is not surprising that the rebuttal in the pamphlet *Haec-Vir: Or The Womanish-Man,* which appeared seven days later, would dwell on the folly of thoughtlessly adhering to social custom. Interestingly, the *Haec-Vir* pamphlet ignores the issue of whether women of different social categories dressing alike as men disrupt the alignment of social classes; instead the second pamphlet argues solely in terms of gender and sexual roles. Rather than appearing as the product of a single mind, *Haec-Vir* is presented as a dialogue between two characters, the *Hic Mulier* and the *Haec-Vir* figures, suggesting by its very form and by the introduction of a new figure, the womanish man, to whom I will return, a greater openness to discussion and to cooperation between the sexes. The irrationality of the author of the first pamphlet is also clarified and

---

21. Fitz, pp. 9–10. Also see Wright, pp. 490–91. See also Dusinberre, pp. 234–35.

undercut at the beginning of the second when the two figures conduct a witty exchange about their mutual inability to identify one another's gender. Thus a tolerant and urbane tone is set in which *Hic Mulier* (now a sympathetic figure) can defend her behavior.

Hic Mulier's defense elaborates in positive terms the fact that her attire symbolizes a demand for recognition of spiritual and moral equality between the sexes, a recognition which she regards as her birthright: "We are free-borne as Men, have as free election, and as free spirits, we are compounded of like parts, and may with like liberty make benefit of our Creations" (sig. B3). Consequently she counters *Haec-Vir's* charge that assuming male apparel makes her a mere slave to the novelties of fashion both by defining her outfit as symbolizing her freedom of choice and by redefining slavery as *Haec-Vir's* mindless submission to the tyranny of pointless custom, "for then custome, nothing is more absurd, nothing more foolish" (sig. B2). The customs she resents as most false and destructive to female freedom and equality are those gender-linked stereotypes which constrain female behavior to compliance, subordination, pathos, and passivity:

But you say wee are barbarous and shameless and cast off all softness, to runne wilde through a wildernesse of opinions. In this you express more cruelty then in all the rest, because I stand not with my hands on my belly like a baby at *Bartholomew Fayre* . . . that am not dumbe when wantons court mee, as if Asse-like I were ready for all burthens, or because I weepe not when injury gripes me, like a woorried Deere in the fangs of many Curres: am I therefore barbarous or shamelesse? (sig. B3)

"*I stand not with my hands on my belly like a baby at* Bartholomew Fayre . . . *as if Asse-like I were ready for all burthens.*" *Hic Mulier* argues that to reduce woman to the position of static icon, allegedly "so much better in that she is something purer" (sig. B1v) than man, is actually to infantilize and dehumanize her by denying her full participation in adult reality, which she optimistically defines as a world of creative movement and change, in which man can "alter, frame, and fashion, according as his will and delight shall rule him" (sig. B1v). This conception, which locates adult reality in the creative opportunities provided by public life, recognizes that women are unjustly confined by tradition to perpetual fantasy and immaturity. It therefore forms the most strikingly modern of *Hic Mulier's* arguments.

The eloquence and clarity with which these convictions are expressed make the retrenchment that occurs in the pamphlet's conclusion all the more startling. Having established herself as the rational contender in the debate, the "man-woman" suddenly withdraws before the irrational onslaught of *Haec-Vir,* the womanish man who ignores her arguments, rather than systematically rebutting them. Suddenly the focus shifts to the way that *Haec-Vir* (who, it has been suggested, represents the homosexuality of the Jacobean court)[22] has relinquished his manhood and become a fop, aberrant male behavior which is now viewed as the sole reason for the existence of the notorious "man-woman." In an astonishing abandonment of her considerable powers of logic, *Hic Mulier* nostalgically evokes chivalric gallantry, recalling the bygone days when men were men:

Hence we have preserved (though to our owne shames) those manly things which you have forsaken, which would you againe accept, and restore to us the Blushes we lay'd by, when first wee put on your Masculine garments; doubt not but chaste thoughts and bashfulnesse will againe dwell in us . . . then will we love and serve you; then will we heare and obey you; then will wee like rich Jewels hang at your eares to take our Instructions. (sigs. C2v, C3v)

It is a bargain, an offer he can't refuse; the dialogue concludes with *Haec-Vir* having the last word, just as he had had the first, and the entire phenomenon of women in men's clothing is rationalized, not as an attempt to achieve unrealized social freedom for women, but rather to return society to the idealized sexual norm of gender polarization and male dominance. As in King James' protest and the end of the *Hic Mulier* pamphlet, responsibility for the unconventional style of female dress, now recognized by all as deformed, is seen to rest with men because power does.[23]

Although the concluding section of the *Haec-Vir* pamphlet articulates this drastic shift in perspective, it is nevertheless short, and it fails to cancel or even to qualify the dominant logic of *Hic Mulier's* stirring defense of her freedom, a speech which remains the focus of the second pamphlet. We are therefore left with a disjunction between the stubbornly rebellious, salient content of the second pamphlet and the conservative structure of the debate as a whole. On the one hand, the dominant

22. Dusinberre, pp. 234–35, 239.
23. See *Hic Mulier* (sig. C2v): "To you . . . that are Fathers, Husbands, or Sustainers of these new *Hermaphrodites,* belongs the cure of this Impostume; it is you that give fuell to the flames of their wilde indiscretion." Cf. J. Chamberlain, in Statham, pp. 182–83: "A tax upon unruly female relatives! . . . the King threatens to fall upon theyre husbands, parents or frends that have or shold have power over them, and make them pay for it."

content of the *Haec-Vir* pamphlet convincingly challenges the justice and reality of the existing sexual power structure by enumerating the illusory, sentimental, and destructive premises on which it is based. On the other, the form of the debate as a whole perpetuates the status quo by attempting to absorb this cogent demand for change into a larger movement of re-aligning the established society into conformity with an old ideal, a rhetorical endeavor that does not, however, entirely succeed in quelling the vigor of the opposition. As a result of this disjunction between content and form, female independence and equality between the sexes are depicted in the debate as desirable and just, but also as impossible for a hierarchical society to absorb without unacceptable disruption.

III

A pronounced ambivalence toward sexual equality as represented by the *Hic Mulier* figure is discernible in the *Hic Mulier/Haec-Vir* debate, then, and this attitude can be viewed in aesthetic terms as a disjunction between content and form. In *The Roaring Girl* a similar dislocation between thematic content and dramatic form can be perceived in the representation of the title character, Moll Frith, a point to which I will return. Middleton and Dekker modeled their unusual central figure after a real-life "roaring girl," popularly known in Jacobean London as "Moll Cutpurse." As this name implies, the real Moll was an underworld figure, notorious as a thief, whore, brawler, and bawd. Much of the reliable evidence we have about her exists in the court records made after her several arrests for offenses that included a scandalous appearance at the Fortune Theater, where she "sat there upon the stage in the publique viewe of all the people there p[rese]nte in mans apparrell & playd upon her lute & sange a songe."[24] Most of the existing criticism of *The Roaring Girl* attempts to date the play with reference to this incident.[25]

Whatever the precise connections between the events in the life of the

---

24. Cited in P. A. Mulholland, "*The Date of The Roaring Girl,*" *Review of English Studies,* 28 (1977), 22, 30–31. See also Andor Gomme, Introd., *The Roaring Girl,* by Thomas Middleton and Thomas Dekker, (London, 1976), pp. xiii–xix, and Margaret Dowling, "A Note on Moll Cutpurse—'The Roaring Girl,'" *Review of English Studies,* 10 (1934), 67–71. There is a pamphlet called *The Life and Death of Mrs. Mary Frith,* published in 1662, but it is not thought to be reliable. For a review of the play's dramatic and non-dramatic sources, as well as references to the real Moll Frith, see Gomme, pp. xiii–xix, and Mulholland, pp. 18–31.

25. Mulholland, pp. 18–31, is the most recent example. Gomme, pp. xiii–xix, also sums up the attempts to date the play.

actual Mary Frith and the performance and publication of *The Roaring Girl,* the court records show that the playwrights drew heavily on the habits and physical appearance of the real-life Moll, with her brawling, singing, and smoking, her lute, her boots, her sword, and, above all, her breeches; as has been suggested, it is also probable that Middleton and Dekker were attempting to benefit from the *au courant* notoriety of the actual Moll in the timing of their play.[26] Nevertheless in his address to the reader attached to the 1611 quarto, Middleton takes pains to distinguish the created character from the real person, hinting that the play will present an idealized .interpretation of this odd figure: "'Tis the excellency of a writer to leave things better than he finds 'em."[27] In fact the playwrights maintain an ambivalent attitude toward the outlaw status of their central character, in whom courageous moral and sexual principles combine with a marginal social identity, both of which are symbolized in the play by her male attire.

The address to the reader and ensuing prologue clarify the controversial nature of the title character and emphasize the importance of assessing her identity:

> Thus her character lies—
> Yet what need characters, when to give a guess
> Is better than the person to express?
> But would you know who 'tis? Would you hear her name?
> She's called mad Moll; her life our acts proclaim.
>
> (Prologue, 26–30)

In their introduction of Moll Frith, the playwrights evoke themes identical to those surrounding the *Hic Mulier* figure in the *Hic Mulier/Haec-Vir* debate. First, they associate Moll's male apparel with erotic appeal and illicit sexuality.

> For venery, you shall find enough for sixpence, but well couched and you mark it; for Venus being a woman passes through the play in doublet and breeches; a brave disguise and a safe one, if the statute untie not her codpiece point.
>
> ("To the Comic Play-Readers")

26. Mulholland, 18–19. As Mulholland observes (pp. 20–21), the *Consistory of London Correction Book* record concerning Mary Frith, which he cites at length on pp. 30–31, provides an extraordinary account both of the actual Moll and of the vehement opposition in Jacobean society to women wearing male attire, which is one offense of hers that is reiterated in the *Correction Book* entry.

27. Thomas Middleton, "To the Comic Play-Readers, Venery and Laughter," in Thomas Dekker and Thomas Middleton, *The Roaring Girl.* All citations from the play are taken from *Drama of the English Renaissance,* eds. Russell A. Fraser and Norman Rabkin (New York, 1976), II, 334–38.

Secondly, as in the debate, erotic questions are less preoccupying than social ones: the entire prologue attempts to assign Moll a specific class and rank, "to know what girl this roaring girl should be / For of that tribe are many" (Prologue, 15–16). While the dramatists assure us that their Moll is neither criminal, brawler, whore, nor city wife, the question of her actual social status is left unanswered. As the action unfolds, the playwrights' vision of the controversial "roaring girl's" exact position in the Jacobean social hierarchy gradually assumes its distinct and complicated shape; and other characters are defined as social and moral beings according to their responses to her.

The play has a traditional New Comedy plot in which a young man, Sebastian Wengrave, outwits his snobbish, greedy father, Sir Alexander Wengrave, who has threatened to disinherit Sebastian if he marries the woman he loves, all because of her relatively meager dowry. The subplot involves a theme equally characteristic of the Jacobean dramatic satirist: the attempt of lazy, poor, arrogant, upper-class "gallants" to cheat and seduce the wives of middle-class shopkeepers. Like the prologue and the *Hic Mulier/Haec-Vir* debate, the main plot stresses social issues while the secondary plot focuses on erotic complications. The conservative faction in the play is most strikingly represented by the father, Sir Alexander, and the lecherous, misogynistic gallant, Laxton, both of whose negative attitudes toward Moll resemble those of the author of the *Hic Mulier* pamphlet toward women in men's clothing.

Moll enters the play for the first time during the subplot, as Laxton and his cohorts are busily seeking to form illicit liaisons with shopkeepers' wives, chuckling privately over their erotic cunning and prowess. In this Renaissance equivalent of the locker room, Moll, who will smoke and swear, is greeted enthusiastically by the men, although with considerably less relish by the women, one of whom screams, "Get you from my shop!" (2.1.248). Both men and women, however, associate her mannishness with deformed and illicit sexuality:

> *Mrs. G.*   Some will not stick to say she is a man, and
> some, both man and woman.
> *Lax.*   That were excellent: she might first cuckold
> the husband, and then make him do as much for the wife.
> (2.1.219–22)

Like the author of the *Hic Mulier* pamphlet, Laxton finds this mannish woman sexy ("Heart, I would give but too much money to be nibbling with that wench") (2.1.193–94); he also automatically assumes from her unconventional sexual behavior that she is a whore: "I'll lay hard siege to her; money is that aqua fortis that eats into many a maidenhead; where the walls are flesh and blood, I'll ever pierce through with a golden augur" (2.1.203–05). Complacently, Laxton secures an assignation with Moll, to which he travels overcome with self-pleasure and a thrilling sense of his own power in arranging a forbidden encounter.

Laxton is unpleasantly surprised. In his confrontation with Moll, which takes the appropriate form of a duel, Moll emerges as a defiant champion of female freedom from male sexual dominion, a role symbolized by her male attire. When Laxton arrives on the scene searching for a woman in a "shag ruff, a frieze jerkin, a short sword, and a safeguard [i.e., a petticoat]" (3.1.34–35), Moll appears instead in male clothes, the significance of which she underscores: when Laxton, who takes a few moments to recognize her, remarks, "I'll swear I knew thee not," Moll replies meaningfully, "I'll swear you did not; but you shall know me now." Laxton, who is not at all clever, mistakes this response for an erotic overture: "No, not here; we shall be spied" (3.1.58–61). Discarding subtlety as hopeless, Moll beats up Laxton while delivering a stirring oration on the sexual injustices suffered by women at the hands of arrogant, slanderous men:

> Thou'rt one of those
> That thinks each woman thy fond flexible whore . . .
> How many of our sex, by such as thou,
> Have their good thoughts paid with a blasted name
> That never deserved loosely . . .
> There is no mercy in't.
>
> (3.1.77–93)

Furthermore, Moll attributes female sexual vulnerability specifically to the superior social power of male seducers, which she defies:

> In thee I defy all men, their worst hates
> And their best flatteries, all their golden witchcrafts,
> With which they entangle the poor spirits of fools,
> Distressed needle-women and tradefallen wives;
> Fish that must needs bite, or themselves be bitten.
> Such hungry things as these may soon be took
> With a worm fastened on a golden hook.
> Those are the lecher's food, his prey; he watches
> For quarreling wedlocks and poor shifting sisters.
>
> (3.1.97–105)

Finally, she does not simply dwell on female victimization, but asserts positively the capacity of women for full sexual responsibility, authority, and independence:

> I scorn to prostitute myself to a man,
> I that can prostitute a man to me . . .
> She that has wit and spirit,
> May scorn to live beholding to her body for meat;
> Or for apparel, like your common dame,
> That makes shame get her clothes to cover shame.
>
> (3.1.116–46)

Like the sympathetic *Hic Mulier* figure in the debate, Moll takes upon herself the defense of all women. Indeed Laxton's attempted violation of Moll's chastity connects her with, rather than distinguishes her from, the shopkeepers' wives, most of whom are willingly engaged in sexual collusion with the gallants when the play begins. As a result, we perceive that the "man-clothed" Moll,[28] the notorious roaring girl and *Hic Mulier*, is actually a sexual innocent compared to the conventional middle-class wives. More important than the wives' hypocrisy, however, is their eventual reform; at the end of the play they see through the schemes of their would-be seducers and choose to reject them in favor of their husbands, just as Moll's defeat of Laxton has portended that they would. The seducing gallants, who represent illicit sexuality, therefore turn out not to constitute a real threat to the social order at all. Moll herself recognizes this fact immediately: "Oh, the gallants of these times are shallow lechers . . . 'Tis impossible to know what woman is throughly honest, because she's ne'er throughly tried" (2.1.336–40).

As Moll's defeat of Laxton makes clear, free-floating, amoral eros is stripped of its socially destructive power when women decide to take responsibility for themselves. The aborted sexual encounter between Moll and Laxton also dramatizes the specious logic involved in connecting Moll's unconventional male attire automatically with whorish behavior. In their depiction of Laxton's complacence, the playwrights clearly associate lechery and misogyny with obtuse, unobservant social conformity.[29] As we have seen, the idea of mindlessly adhering to social custom is the principal target of the sympathetic *Hic Mulier* figure when

28. The phrase is from Fitz, p. 16.

29. Laxton expresses his general view of women in 3.2.266–69: "That wile / By which the serpent did the first woman beguile / Did ever since all women's bosoms fill; / You're apple-eaters all, deceivers still."

she defends her freedom in the debate. In *The Roaring Girl* this theme is amplified in the main plot through the representation of the censorious attitudes and actions which Sir Alexander Wengrave takes toward Moll Frith.

In his self-righteousness, self-deception, and self-pity, Sir Alexander is all self, incapable of distinguishing his emotional attachments from virtue. Proud of what he thinks is his shrewd observation of social life, trying to conform to a preconceived ideal, he continually misapprehends the realities which confront him. Sebastian recognizes that his father's vulnerability to the opinion of others exceeds even his greed, and he forms a plan to gain both his inheritance and his true love, Mary Fitzallard, by telling his father that he plans to marry Moll Frith, the outrageous roaring girl who fights, smokes, swears, and wears men's clothes. Like Laxton, Sir Alexander assumes from Moll's masculine attire that she is both a whore and a thief, who can be entrapped into stealing money, exposed, and safely removed from the proximity of his son. Like Laxton, he fails repeatedly in his assaults on her integrity.

Sir Alexander inveighs against Moll as a monster (1.2.130–36; 2.2.81–83), a siren (2.1.219–20), a thief (1.2.175; 4.1.201–06; 2.2.139), and a whore (1.2.137; 2.2.160). One funny scene shows him spying on her, appalled, as her tailor fits her for breeches. Like the conservative author of the *Hic Mulier* pamphlet, Sir Alexander perceives in Moll's male clothing a symbol not only of perverse sexuality, but also of the inevitable disintegration of stable marital relations: "Hoyda, breeches? What, will he marry a monster with two trinkets [i.e., testicles]? What age is this? If the wife go in breeches, the man must wear long coats, like a fool." (2.2.81–84). At the end of the play, before a nearly-reformed Sir Alexander has discovered his son's true marital intentions, Moll's urbane teasing exposes his desire to maintain rigid gender roles as a regressive anxiety:

> *Moll:* (referring to herself) Methinks you should be
>   proud of such a daughter,
>   As good a man as your son . . .
>   You do not know what benefits I bring with me;
>   No cheat dares work upon you with thumb or knife,
>   While you've a roaring girl to your son's wife.
>   (5.2.153–62)

More than any of the specific evils he attributes to her, Sir Alexander fears Moll's conspicuousness, her unconventionality, her social aberrance; the sheer embarrassment of having such a daughter-in-law is equivalent to ruin. "Why wouldst thou fain marry to be pointed at?" he asks his son. "Why, as good marry a beacon on a hill, / Which all the country fix their eyes upon, / As her thy folly dotes on" (2.2.142–46). It is Sir Alexander's shallow, malicious willingness to accept received opinion without observing for himself, his bourgeois horror of nonconformity, that moves Sebastian to a rousing defense of Moll, the clearest articulation of her honesty in the play:

> He hates unworthily that by rote contemns . . .
>   Here's her worst,
> Sh'as a bold spirit that mingles with mankind,
> But nothing else comes near it; and often times
> Through her apparel somewhat shames her birth;
> But she is loose in nothing but in mirth.
> Would all Molls were no worse!
>
>   (2.2.176–86)

And it is precisely this thoughtless social conformity, dramatized by his malignant intolerance of Moll, that Sir Alexander abjures at the end, thereby making possible the formation of a new comic society which will be both flexible and just:

> Forgive me; now I cast the world's eyes from me,
> And look upon thee [i.e., Moll] freely with mine own . . .
>   I'll never more
> Condemn by common voice, for that's the whore,
> That deceives man's opinion, mocks his trust,
> Cozens his love, and makes his heart unjust.
>
>   (5.2.244–51)

In "The Place of Laughter in Tudor and Stuart England," Keith Thomas analyzes the ways in which comedy conservatively affirms the status quo by revealing, mocking, and containing social tensions; yet, Thomas points out, "There was also a current of radical, critical laughter which, instead of reinforcing accepted norms, sought to give the world a nudge in a new direction."[30] Given the heavy emphasis which the majority of English Renaissance society placed on gender-polarized sexual decorum and subdued, modest female behavior, it is evident that, with their idealized comic portrait of the *Hic Mulier* figure Moll Frith, Dekker and Middleton were joining those who, like the author of the

---

30. Keith Thomas, "The Place of Laughter in Tudor and Stuart England," *Times Literary Supplement* (January 21, 1977), 78.

Haec-Vir pamphlet, were beginning to call for greater freedom for women and equality between the sexes. As we have seen, serious opposition to Moll is represented in the play as mindless conformity. Not only do the playwrights decline to link Moll's freewheeling, immodest habits and appearance with perverse or dishonest behavior, but they also give her ample opportunity to acquit herself from her reputation as a criminal (5.1.323–73). Furthermore, Dekker and Middleton portray as noble Moll's integrity in refusing Sebastian Wengrave's proposal of marriage, made before she knows it is only a sham to deceive his father. Like the sympathetic, eloquent *Hic Mulier* figure, Moll refuses the conventional subordination required of a wife:

I have no humor to marry . . . I have the head now of myself, and am man enough for a woman. Marriage is but a chopping and changing, where a maiden loses one head, and has a worse i' th' place.

(2.2.38–48)

Moll's virginity represents the particular condition of independence which Carolyn Heilbrun defines as "that fierce autonomy which separates the individual from the literal history of his sexual acts":[31] "Base is that mind that kneels unto her body . . . / My spirit shall be mistress of this house / As long as I have time in't" (3.1.149–52).

How far does *The Roaring Girl* go in its sympathetic imaginative vision of sexual nonconformity, female independence, and equality between the sexes, all conditions embodied in the title character? Clearly Laxton's humorous stupidity and Sir Alexander's petty malice are no match for Moll's integrity, vitality, intelligence, and courage. Yet a more subtle counter-movement in the play resists the absorption of Moll into the tolerant new society which forms in the final scene.

Far from direct disapproval, this strand of qualified feeling can be discerned as an ambiguous undercurrent in the primarily positive attitude with which Moll is regarded by Sebastian and his fiancée, Mary Fitzallard, the couple whose relationship and opinions represent the desirable social norm in the play. For example, when Sebastian reveals to Mary his scheme of pretending to court Moll, he describes the roaring girl as "a creature / so strange in quality" (1.1.100–01) that Mary could not possibly doubt his love. As noted, Sebastian provides the major defense of Moll in the play; but the defense, while eloquent and just, is

31. Carolyn G. Heilbrun, *Toward a Recognition of Androgyny* (New York, 1973), p. 39.

delivered to his father in the course of a deception and is couched entirely in terms of existing standards of sexual decorum, the basis of which Sebastian never questions: "and oftentimes / Through her apparel [she] somewhat shames her birth; / But she is loose in nothing but in mirth" (2.2.183–85). Is Sebastian referring to Moll's gender, social status, or both in his reference to her birth? This point is never clarified, nor is the rather odd remark which Mary makes when Sebastian introduces her to Moll:

Seb.	This is the roaring wench must do us good.
Mary.	No poison, sir, but serves us for some use;
	Which is confirmed in her.

(4.1.148–50)

Furthermore, Moll herself seems to acquiesce in the view which regards her as aberrant, thereby indirectly affirming existing sexual values: when Sebastian proposes to her she responds, "A wife you know ought to be obedient, but I fear me I am too headstrong to obey . . . You see sir, I speak against myself" (2.2.40–41, 62). These and similar remarks are too infrequent and undeveloped to undercut the predominant theme of approval and admiration which surrounds Moll in the play; but they do qualify the potential for any radical change in sexual values implicit in the full social acceptance of Moll Frith.

The play makes clear that, if the stifling, malignant conformity which unjustly opposes Moll is one thing, incorporation of her into society is quite another. Full social acceptance is no more the destiny of the *Hic Mulier* figure in this play, no matter how benevolent, than it is the fate of the sympathetic *Hic Mulier* in the debate, no matter how reasonable, eloquent, or bold. Earlier I observed that the playwrights' ambivalence toward Moll can be discerned as a disjunction between thematic content and dramatic form. While the dominant content of *The Roaring Girl* elicits but does not clarify this issue, formal analysis makes its subtlety more readily perceptible. A brief discussion of the function of disguise in the play should help to clarify the point.

Although Moll Frith wears male clothing, she makes no attempt to conceal her identity and all the other characters know she is a woman: in short, she is not in disguise. When used simply to denote a costume, worn in a play or festival for example, "disguise" could be used as a morally neutral term in Jacobean England. But discussions of apparel in the moral and religious literature more often use "disguise" as an inclusive censorious term meaning, roughly, "deformity of nature" and comprehending in the range of disapproval not only the player, but the fop, dandy, overdressed woman and, of course, the *Hic Mulier*.[32] According to this conservative mentality, the roaring girl would be in "disguise"; but, as we have seen, the play rejects precisely this negative interpretation of Moll's apparel. More illuminating for present purposes is a brief comparison between Moll and the disguised heroines of Shakespearean romantic comedy.

In contrast to Moll, who insists on being recognized as a woman, heroines like Rosalind and Viola seek to conceal their identities and to protect themselves by masquerading as men. Modern criticism has been particularly adept at recognizing the symbolic, structural, and psychological functions of these romantic disguises. On the psychological level, the male disguise allows the Shakespearean heroine the social freedom to extend her personality and expand her identity by exploring the possibilities inherent in male sexual roles.[33] This opportunity for heightened awareness and personal growth incorporates into the desirable comic society formed at the end of the play an androgynous vision, recently defined as "a psychic striving for an ideal state of personal wholeness, a microcosmic attempt to imitate a mythic macrocosm," in which "being a human being entails more than one's sex identification and attendant gender development"[34]

The romantic comic form, however, represents neither a mythical nor a revolutionary society, but a renewed traditional society, whose stability and coherence is symbolized by marriage and is based on the maintenance of traditional sexual roles.[35] It is the temporary nature of the heroine's male disguise which contains the formal solution to the poten-

---

32. See, for example, *Hic Mulier*, sig. C3: "Doe you make it the utter losse of your favour and bounty to have brought into your Family, any new fashion or disguise, that might either deforme Nature, or bee an injury to modestie." Cf. Harrison, in Wilson, p. 123: "You shall not see any so disguised as are my countrymen of England," and Nashe, in Wilson, p. 125: "England, the players' stage of gorgeous attire, the ape of all nations' superfluities, the continual masquer in outlandish habiliments, great plenty-scanting calamities art thou to await, for wanton disguising thyself against kind; and digressing from the plainness of thy ancestors."

33. See Alexander Leggatt, *Shakespeare's Comedy of Love* (London, 1974), p. 202; Helen Gardner, "*As You Like It*," in *Modern Shakespearean Criticism*, ed. Alvin B. Kernan (New York, 1970), pp. 199, 202; Helene Moglen, "Disguise and Development: The Self and Society in *Twelfth Night*," *Literature and Psychology*, 23 (1973), 13–19; and Dusinberre, p. 257.

34. Robert Kimbrough, "Androgyny Seen Through Shakespeare's Disguise," *Shakespeare Quarterly*, 33 (Spring, 1982), 20, 19. Cf. Margaret Boerner Beckman, "The Figure of Rosalind in *As You Like It*," *Shakespeare Quarterly*, 29 (Winter, 1978), 44–51.

35. Cf. Gardner, pp. 190–203 and Northrop Frye, "The Argument of Comedy," in ed. Kernan, pp. 165–73.

tial psychological and social problems it raises: that is, the heroine gladly sheds her disguise with its accompanying freedoms at the end of the play, in order to accept the customary social role of wife, thereby allowing the play's androgynous vision to remain spiritual and symbolic without awakening the audience's dissatisfaction or desire for social change.[36] Northrop Frye has shown that the resolution of comedy, which is usually erotic, is often brought about by a bisexual Eros figure who, like Puck, "is in himself sexually self-contained, being in a sense both male and female, and needing no expression of love beyond himself." In Shakespeare's later comedies, this structural role is taken over by the disguised female; but when the Eros figure is no longer supernatural, "his" character must break down, as Viola's does into Viola and Sebastian in *Twelfth Night,* or be superseded, as Rosalind's is, by the figure of Hymen in *As You Like It.*[37] As another critic puts it, "The temporary nature of the male disguise is of course essential, since the very nature of Shakespearean comedy is to affirm that disruption is temporary, that what has been turned topsy-turvy will be restored."[38]

Like Shakespearean comedy, *The Roaring Girl* concludes festively with the re-formation of a flexible and tolerant society, whose stability and integration are symbolized in marriage. But in *The Roaring Girl* the functions performed by the disguised heroine in Shakespeare are structurally divided and displaced. Moll clearly answers to much of Frye's analysis of the comic Eros figure: first, with her self-imposed virginity, refusal to marry, and men's clothes, she is "in a sense both male and female" and needs "no expression of love beyond [her] self"; secondly, it is she who brings about the benevolent and satisfactory resolution of the action when she actively helps Sebastian to gain Mary. Sebastian recognizes her function as the play's Eros figure when he says, "Twixt lovers' hearts she's a fit instrument / And has the art to help them to their own" (2.2.204–05). In Frye's terms, Moll is a figure in whom Eros "is a

---

36. Cf. C. L. Barber, *Shakespeare's Festive Comedy: A Study of Dramatic Form and its Relation to Social Custom* (Princeton, N.J., 1959), pp. 245–47; Leggatt, p. 211; F. H. Mares, "Viola and other Transvestist Heroines in Shakespeare's Comedies," in ed. B. A. W. Jackson, *Stratford Papers on Shakespeare* (McMaster University Library Press, 1969 for 1965–1967), pp. 96–109; and Nancy K. Hayles, "Sexual Disguise in *As You Like It* and *Twelfth Night,*" *Shakespeare Survey,* 32 (1979), 63–72.

37. Northrop Frye, *A Natural Perspective* (New York, 1965), pp. 82–83.

38. Clara Claiborne Park, "As We Like It: How a Girl Can be Smart and Still Popular," in *The Woman's Part,* eds. Carolyn Ruth Swift Lenz, Gayle Greene, and Carol Thomas Neely (Urbana, Ill., 1980), p. 108.

condition, not a desire."[39] But unlike Puck, Moll is not supernatural; she is human and will not disappear from social life. She is neither on an odyssey toward sexual and social integration, as Rosalind and Viola are, nor can she be said to grow psychologically, happily internalizing the discovery of love and freedom in the way that they do. She has no intention of marrying, no intention of relinquishing either her outfit or the unconventional principles and behavior it represents. She therefore assumes the social and psychological freedom of the traditional disguised heroine without providing the corresponding reassurance implicit in that heroine's eventual erotic transformation. These functions are instead displaced onto Mary Fitzallard, who, disguised as a page, joyously sheds the disguise to take her place as Sebastian's wife in the final scene. Moll, on the other hand, having served as the instrument who brings about the happy ending, is nevertheless excluded from the renewed comic society of married couples which forms on the stage at the end of the play. Sir Alexander makes this clear when he defines the new society by addressing "You kind gentlewomen, whose sparkling presence / Are glories set in marriage, beams of society / For all your loves give luster to my joys" (5.2.260–62). The playwrights conclude *The Roaring Girl* with an epilogue in which they emphasize the strangeness of the fictional, and the criminality of the real, Moll Frith.

In a sense the dramatists call attention to both a structural and social ambiguity in the world of the play by refusing to conflate Moll and Mary into a single figure.[40] By excluding Moll from the traditional, rejuvenated society demanded by the comic form, Middleton and Dekker never quite succeed in separating her from her outlaw status, despite the approval and admiration with which her integrity, courage, and freedom are depicted in the play. It is true that Moll herself displays nothing but a benign indifference toward acceptance by established society: "I pursue no pity; / Follow the law and you can cuck me, spare not; / Hang up my viol by me, and I care not." (5.2.253–55). Moll's good-natured indifference allows the predominant tone of the ending of the play to remain festive. Yet her definition of herself as anti-social (5.1.362–63) and her exclusion by others combine to render unsettling the fact that her sexual independence has left her isolated from the very social structure which

39. Frye, p. 83.

40. See Gomme, p. xxiii, who points out that Mary and Moll have the same name, and that Moll "impersonates" Mary in the final scene "in order to complete the trick which secures Mary's happiness."

her courage and vitality have done so much to enliven and renew. The question of her social identity, raised at the beginning of the play, therefore remains unresolved at the end. It is because she has helped to create a society from which she is both excluded and excludes herself that Moll's status remains unclear; insofar as it is ambiguous, marginal, and problematic, Moll's social identity can be seen as a metaphor for the changing condition of women in early modern England.

IV

Both *The Roaring Girl* and the *Hic Mulier/Haec-Vir* debate represent the figure of the woman in men's clothing as the symbolic focus of concern about sexual freedom and equality in Jacobean society. Each text depicts this unconventional figure as attractive and virtuous, while those who regard her as socially and sexually disruptive are represented in contrast as hostile, anxious, and self-deceived. When confronting the irrationality of her enemies, the *Hic Mulier* figure emerges as the voice of reason and common sense. In both play and debate it is she who possesses imagination, insight, and courage; it is she who embodies the promise of freedom and even of happiness. Nevertheless this hopeful, likeable figure fails in each context to gain full social acceptance; not only is she excluded by others, but she herself acquiesces in her own defeat: in the debate she retreats completely, surrendering to the very values she had arisen to oppose; in the play she remains pleasantly isolated from society, a loveable outlaw whose eccentricity insures that she will not constitute a social threat. But while these formal resolutions of debate and play are both agreeably festive in tone, neither effort to adhere to the comic purpose of reconciling social tensions is entirely convincing. The powerfully rendered figure of *Hic Mulier* continues in each case to tower over the less compelling society that endeavors unsuccessfully to absorb her; viewed in terms of aesthetic logic, the *Hic Mulier* figure becomes content that cannot (illogically) be contained by form.

With their similarly ambivalent visions of *Hic Mulier* and Moll Frith as necessary but disruptive, benevolent but anti-social, both the debate and the play present an image of Jacobean society as unable to absorb one of its most vital and complex creations into the existing social and sexual hierarchies. The mixed approval and exclusion of the *Hic Mulier* figure evident in artistic representation and social commentary indicate a simultaneous search for and rejection of greater flexibility in sexual values. The parallel treatments of the controversy surrounding women in men's clothing in the dramatic and moral literature therefore combine to illuminate a particularly heightened time of groping for resolutions: in both *The Roaring Girl* and the *Hic Mulier/Haec-Vir* debate, the moral ambiguity and social challenge of sexual identity and equality as they were perceived in Renaissance England stand sharply before us.

Embarrassing Ben: The Masques for Frances Howard

DAVID LINDLEY

AFTER the failure of *The New Inn* in 1629 Ben Jonson wrote his angry "Ode to Himself." In it he berates the ignorance of theater audiences, sideswipes at other dramatists, and exhorts himself to

> Leaue things so prostitute,
> And take the *Alcaick* lute;
> Or thine owne *Horace,* or *Anacreons* lyre;
> Warme thee, by *Pindares* fire:
> And though they nerues be shrunke, and blood be cold,
> Ere yeares have made thee old;
> Strike that disdaine-full heate
> Throughout, to their defeate.[1]

The tone of arrogant defiance is characteristically Jonsonian; so too is his turning to classical authors as comfort and inspiration. Equally characteristic, though to modern readers much less comfortable, is the use to which he proposes to put his poetry:

> But, when they heare thee sing
> The glories of thy *King,*
> His zeale to *God,* and his iust awe o're men;
> They may, blood-shaken, then,
> Feele such a flesh-quake to possesse their powers;
> As they shall cry, like ours
> In sound of peace, or warres,
> No harpe ere hit the starres;
> In tuning forth the acts of his sweet raigne:
> And raising *Charles* his chariot 'boue his *Waine.*

---

1. C. H. Herford, Percy and Evelyn Simpson, eds., *Ben Jonson,* 11 vols., (Oxford, 1925–1951), VI, pp. 493–94. All subsequent references are to this edition, and are given in the text after each quotation.

A modern reader is probably much less at ease with Jonson's presentation of panegyric as his true poetic role than with the Stoic retreat to private, inner virtue that we find elsewhere in his work. Nowhere is such unease more clearly felt than in contemplating the flattery of monarch and court exhibited in Jonson's masques.

In the well-known preface to *Hymenaei* Jonson offers his most substantial defense of the masque, articulating its duty to "sound to present occasions" while at the same time laying hold "on more remou'd *mysteries*" (VII, p. 209). *Hymenaei* therefore works by seeing through the marriage for which it was commissioned to the general truths of which it could be made to function as an image.

It is a work aggressively crammed with Jonson's classical learning, and builds toward the signifying emblem of the dance where the participants first trace the letters of the Bridegroom's name and then form a chain whose significance Reason explains:

> Svch was the *Golden Chaine* let downe from *Heauen;*
>   And not those linkes more euen,
> Then these: so sweetly temper'd, so combin'd
>   By VNION, and refin'd.
> Here no *contention, enuy, griefe, deceit,*
>   *Feare, iealousie* haue weight;
> But all is *peace,* and *loue,* and *faith,* and *blisse:*
>   What *harmony* like this? (VII, p. 221)

The ambiguity of the deictics in this speech, pointing both to the dance and to the previous devices of the masque itself, as well as outwards to the married couple sitting in the audience, blends present occasion and Platonic mystery with serene confidence. Furthermore, the idealized image of the masque as a whole represents allegorically the Union between England and Scotland which was then James's pet project, and alludes to the truth of the Anglican settlement, as D. J. Gordon and Leah Marcus have shown.[2]

Whatever one's view might be of a work of art designed specifically to endorse and sustain royalist ideology and James's particular policies, one would have to accept that Jonson manifests considerable dexterity in prosecuting his commisson, and converting mundane reality into transcendent image. Nonetheless, problems obstinately remain. For in a later

2. See D. J. Gordon, "*Hymenaei:* Ben Jonson's Masque of Union," in *The Renaissance Imagination,* ed. Stephen Orgel (Berkeley and London, 1975), pp. 157–84, and Leah Sinanoglou Marcus, "Masquing Occasion and Masque Structure," *Research Opportunities in Renaissance Drama,* 24 (1981), 7–16.

masque, *Love's Triumph Through Callipolis,* Jonson claims that "publique Spectacles, eyther have bene, or ought to be the mirror of man's life" (VII, p. 735).

The occasion of this masque was the wedding of Frances Howard, daughter of Thomas Howard, Earl of Suffolk, to the Earl of Essex. The bride was thirteen, the groom fifteen, and it was already agreed (in a customary fashion) that the marriage would not be consummated until both were of age. What kind of "mirror," then, is offered by the epithalamic ending of the masque which calls on Hymen to "Cheere vp the faint, and trembling *Bride,* / That quakes to touch her *Bridegroom's* side" (VII, p. 224)? It would seem that Jonson has conveniently forgotten "present occasions" in his zeal to demonstrate his command of classical epithalamic form.

Whether Frances and her husband were embarrassed is not recorded (though the fact that only the first stanza of the concluding epithalamion was actually performed on the night seems to indicate that someone exercised a modicum of tact, rather to Jonson's annoyance). Ten years later, however, Jonson himself was to be embarrassed by this masque when, in a fashion to be more fully described shortly, Frances Howard was disgraced. When *Hymenaei* was published in the Folio of 1616 all mention of its specific occasion was deleted. It was subtitled only "The solemnities of Masque and Barriers at a Marriage."

The suppression of the occasion is significant, for it emphasizes, even as it attempts to obscure, Jonson's sense of the uncomfortable disparity between the idealized vision his work attempted to create, and the stubborn intractability of the real world. In the same way, a modern reading which rests content with explication of the masque's iconology, while it may soften our contemporary discomfort with panegyric, ignores the problematic nature of individual works, and of the genre as a whole.

I

The embarrassments of *Hymenaei* are, however, less extreme than those which surround the two later masques which are now to be considered. For in 1613 Jonson agreed to the composition of two masques for the celebrations which attended Frances Howard's second marriage, to Robert Carr, Earl of Somerset. This occasion focuses the problems of panegyric with unusual clarity, and in order to separate the multiple layers of embarrassment which attend these texts, it is necessary briefly to sketch in the circumstances.[3]

After the 1606 marriage, Essex was dispatched on foreign travels, returning to claim his bride in 1609. He got a dusty welcome, and for the next three years the marriage remained unconsummated, no doubt because Frances had, during her husband's absence, become enamored of Robert Carr, the rising favorite of the King. In 1613 Frances sued for divorce, on the grounds that her husband was impotent toward her. The case was tried before commissioners appointed by James I. When they divided evenly, he promptly nominated two more commissioners sure to vote in favor. The divorce was duly granted, and Frances was free to marry Carr. The whole episode was attended with a great deal of scandalized comment, the product largely of a fear that to grant such a divorce would open the floodgates for disappointed women to secure their freedom. Unsavory gossip proliferated, suggesting, for example, that Frances was anything but the virgin she claimed to be, and that the examination she endured to test her virginity was 'fixed' by substituting another girl in her place. Many felt that the affair was symptomatic of the decay and moral corruption of court society.[4]

Modern commentators on the affair have reacted with uniform distaste. Philip Edwards, for example, speaks of a "sordid divorce" and "this repellent intrigue and divorce, which disgusted all decent men and women."[5] It is vital, however, to recognize that this sort of vituperation derives principally from the fact that it was revealed in 1615 that before their marriage took place Frances Howard and Robert Carr were implicated in the murder of Thomas Overbury in the Tower. While there can be no excusing their conduct, there is no evidence that anyone entertained suspicions of murder at the time of the divorce and re-marriage. Indeed, it is proper to argue that writers such as Campion, Chapman, Donne, and Jonson, as well as the commissioners who voted in favor of the divorce were not motivated solely by a time-serving self-interest.[6]

3. For a full account, see Beatrice White, *Cast of Ravens* (London, 1965).

4. Against this sort of rumor Chapman wrote his *Andromeda Liberata,* and Campion confronted it directly in his masque for the occasion. (For an extended discussion of Campion's work see David Lindley, *Thomas Campion* [Leiden, 1986], and for Chapman's poem, see Raymond B. Waddington, "Chapman's *Andromeda Liberata:* Mythology and Meaning," *PMLA* 81 [1966], 34–44).

5. In *Threshold of a Nation* (Cambridge, 1979), p. 168.

6. There is some evidence that Frances was indeed the virgin she claimed to be in the letters of the Earl of Northampton to Robert Carr contained in Cambridge Univeristy Library MS

Indeed, moral indignation stirred by the later revelations has cast up a fog which has prevented the circumstances within which Jonson's masques were written from being accurately described. For this marriage, like the marriage to Essex, had a political content. Carr was the King's favorite, and by the second decade of the century he who had access to Carr had access to the King. All court factions therefore made every effort to secure his interest on their behalf. The Howard family would have been foolish not to capitalize upon the possibilities that Frances' attachment to Carr offered them. The match was a triumph for the Howard clan, and a significant set-back for the more bellicose, pro-Protestant faction that sided with Essex. Traditional history, operating with hindsight and fortified by a general distaste for the Howards, has misrepresented the political intentions of the marriage. For although it was a triumph, Thomas Howard seems to have hoped that in circumstances where an earlier attempt to heal factional division by the marriage with Essex failed, this new match might help to bring together discordant parties. So at least it appeared to John More when he wrote that "Here is a general reconcilement made between my ld. of Howard and my lords of Pembroke, Southampton etc. in this conjuncture."[7] Be that as it may, once the marriage was an unavoidable fact of life almost all the courtiers hastened to ingratiate themselves with the newly-married couple. Chamberlain comments that: "The presents indeed were more in number and value, than ever I thincke were given to any subject in the land."[8]

The marriage took place on 26 December 1613, and was attended with a number of entertainments. On the evening of the marriage, Campion's *The Somerset Masque* was performed. On the 27th two Cupids, scripted by Jonson, issued *A Challenge at Tilt*. Two days later Jonson's *Irish Masque at Court* occupied the evening, and on 1 January the challenge of the Cupids was taken up in a tilting. On 3 January Jonson's *Irish Masque*

Dd.3.63. A rather touching picture of the way Frances may have been regarded by those not determined to do her ill is to be found in the testimony recorded by Sir Simonds D'Ewes of one Captain Field, that she was "of the best nature, and the sweetest disposition of all her father's children; exceeding them also in the delicacy and comeliness of her person."(*The Autobiography of Simonds D'Ewes,* ed. J. O. Halliwell [London, 1845], p. 74).

7. In *HMC Downshire MSS,* IV, p. 252. (It is perhaps also significant that the Earls of Southampton, Pembroke and Montgomery, as well as their "opponents," the Earls of Northampton and Suffolk, were involved in the ceremonies for the investiture of Robert Carr as Earl of Somerset).

8. N. E. McClure, ed., *The Letters of John Chamberlain* (Philadelphia, 1939), I, p. 456.

was given again, by popular demand, and the following night the couple, attended by a huge troop, set off for the Merchant Taylor's Hall where the Lord Mayor entertained them with a feast, two masques (including Middleton's lost *Masque of Cupid*), a play, and a banquet. (The Mayor had initially refused to offer any celebration, but submitted to the King's bullying.) Finally, 6 January saw the performance by gentlemen of Gray's Inn of the anonymous *Masque of Flowers,* for which Francis Bacon footed the bill.

What of Jonson's attitude toward the marriage? He must have been aware of the irony that Chamberlain noted in his comment that "The Deane of the chapell coupled them, which fell out somwhat straungely that the same man shold marrie the same person, in the same place, upon the self-same day (after sixe or seven yeares, I know not whether) the former partie yet living" (p. 495). But he certainly had no inkling of the darker deeds that were later to become public knowledge, for in a poem to Robert Carr he wrote, "May shee, whome thou for spouse, to day, dost take, / Out-bee y^t *Wife,* in worth, thy freind did make" (VIII, p. 384). The "freind" is Thomas Overbury, and the allusion is to his well-known *Characters.* Even in a panegyric poem, Jonson could scarcely have referred to him if he thought that Carr was implicated in Overbury's death.

The same poem indicates that Jonson, like Campion and the rest, was prepared to endorse the divorce itself, as he urges Carr to "exalt / Hymens amends, to make it worth his fault." Later he refers to the hope of offspring from the marriage, thus concurring with the grounds for the divorce that other writers (notably Chapman) also emphasized as the strongest justification for Frances' actions.

Outwardly at least, Jonson seems to have registered little embarrassment at prosecuting this commission, and it would be wrong simply to condemn him for it. Nonetheless the two masques he provided for the celebration do, in their very different ways, expose the deep-seated problems of panegyric or epideictic art, and confront us directly with the problems of the modern reader in coming to terms with it.

II

A Challenge at Tilt is perhaps the less problematical of Jonson's two contributions to the occasion. The challenge arises out of a contention between two Cupids—pages of the bride and groom—each claiming to be the "true" Cupid. Mainly their quarrel stays at the level of generalities, avoiding the kind of direct engagement with the scandalous and rumor-ridden nature of the divorce that marks Campion's masque. (The allusions to the wedding night, however, with their implication of the bride's virginity, would no doubt have registered upon the audience with the same sort of frisson as the fact that Frances defiantly wore her hair loose at the wedding ceremony.) After the elaborately staged tilting Hymen adjudicates their quarrel by explaining that the two Cupids were equals, representing Eros and Anteros, *both* born of Venus and Mars. He narrates the story of their birth, and rises to an eloquent conclusion:

> This is the loue, that *Hymen* requires, without which no marriage is happie: when the contention is not, who is the true loue, but (beeing both true) who loues most; cleauing the bough betweene you, and diuiding the Palme; This is a strife, wherein you both winne, and begets a concord worthy all married mindes emulation, when the louer transformes himselfe into the person of his belou'd, as you two doe now; By whose example, let your Knights (all honourable friends and seruants of loue) affect the like peace, and depart the lists equall in their friendships for euer, as to day they haue bene in their fortunes. And may this royall court neuer know more difference in humours; or these well-grac'd nuptials more discord in affections, then what they presently feele, and may euer auoid (VII, p. 395).

The allusions to the circumstances of the marriage are clear. This is to be a marriage *without* strife (unlike the last). More pointed is the way Jonson makes this hoped-for marital harmony stand as an image for harmony in the court as a whole (an idea also present in Campion's and Chapman's works). The fact that this entertainment is a tilt, rather than a masque, means that the contest which the spectators witness is directly translatable into a image of jarring factions within the court. It would seem that Jonson designed it specifically to enact the hope that the marriage would lead to the kind of concord that, it was earlier suggested, formed a part of the Earl of Suffolk's hopes for the marriage.

The contention was made even more directly applicable to the particular circumstances of this marriage, by dividing the combatants into two groups, one wearing the colors of the bride, the other of the groom. The Howard family and clients fought in the colors of the *groom,* while among the *bride's* supporters were the Earls of Pembroke and Montgomery, noted opponents of the Howards and of the match itself. Thus the political hopes of the Howards were vividly embodied in the actuality of the mythologized tournament.

It must be doubted, however, whether the presentation was unambiguously successful. The Agent of Savoy reported that "Many lords have been invited to a certain tilt, but many of them have refused because they are relatives of the Earl of Essex, and others have excused themselves, not being part of this [Howard] faction."[9] The harmonious surface of the printed text, then, conceals a dissonance that would have been sharply apparent to the original spectators who were as aware of who was not there as of those who were present. The Earl of Suffolk must have been embarrassed by this conspicuous failure, and even though we might claim that Jonson responded to his commission with some integrity, celebrating hopes which were not in themselves ignoble, his work was sabotaged by the evident failure of reality and myth to coincide. For the work's optimistic didacticism was subverted even as it was offered. He must, therefore, have been implicated in the factional politics of the occasion, and he must have laid himself open to disapproval from those who distanced themselves from the Howard clan.

III

The *Irish Masque at Court* is altogether more complex a case. Before discussing it in detail, it is necessary to give a brief outline of its device. The bulk of the text is taken up by an antimasque of four comic Irish servants who embark upon a circuitous explanation of the fact that twelve of their Lords had set out to honor the marriage but had lost all their fine masquing clothes in a tempest in the Irish sea. When the Lords finally arrive, they are forced to perform their dance in their cloaks. But, with promise of their obedience and loyalty to James I, a Gentleman appears, accompanied by a Bard. He praises James's efforts to settle Irish problems, and suggests that if the Lords "will stoupe but to the musique of his peace" they will "come forth new-borne creatures all." This is duly symbolized as the masquers drop their cloaks and discover their masquing apparel. The work is rounded out by a song from the Bard celebrating the delights of peaceful obedience and praising James.

The work is clearly and emphatically structured to embody and celebrate James's desire to bring unity to disunited Ireland. In this respect its message has some similarity to that contained in the earlier *Hymenaei*. But where in the earlier masque the harmonizing power of the King is perceived *through* the "present occasion" of the marriage of Frances and Essex, here the marriage, although the ostensible occasion of the Lords' journey in the first place, is scarcely mentioned in the course of the work.

9. See John Orrell, "The London Court Stage in the Savoy Correspondence, 1613–1675," *Theatre Research International* 4 (1979), 80.

However one might wish to claim that the absence of much direct reference to the marriage figures some buried discomfort with the circumstances (and it is always possible that Jonson edited the masque before he published it in 1616, after the disgrace of Frances made him again remove reference to the occasion from the title-page), it is obvious enough that this work, commissioned directly by the King and performed by his servants, was primarily concerned with a different political circumstance. And it is in relation to its Irish subject, rather than to the marriage which was its pretext, that the problems of the work are generated. For at the precise moment of the masque's performance, problems in Ireland were at a head. The Plantation of Ulster had been proceeding apace for the previous few years. In 1612 it was decided to call a Parliament and, in order to guarantee a majority in favor of the King's policies, many new seats had been created which were certain to return Protestant members.

On 30 December 1612, Sir Arthur Chichester had written optimistically that: "The House of Parliament is now like to be compounded of all the parts of the Realm vnited, and to be much better tempered by the access of the new Corporations of the province of Vlster, and others now erected, which we presume will be the greatest strength of the house."[10] But even as soon as 4 January he was anxious that "most mens hearts" were "bent to withstand and oppose the passing of the Acts to be propounded" (p. 74). And when the Irish Parliament was finally summoned, his fears were justified, for the Catholic "Old English" members refused to accept the nomination as speaker of the Protestant Sir John Davies, and, amid unruly scenes, attempted to install their own candidate in the speaker's chair. When the attempt failed, the Catholics withdrew from the Parliament and refused to take any further part in its deliberations, complaining at the "fixing" of the new seats but primarily concerned to resist the legislative attempts to impose religious conformity upon them. By 26 May, Chichester was writing in a very different tone to the King: "This is such an affront and blow giuen vnto your Majesties sacred Rule and Authoritie here as we for the discharge of our dutys, may neither hide nor dissemble from you, being so greatly perplexed as we are, with the consideration of their contempts and insolencies, and of the events which they may haplie bring forth" (p. 102).

Throughout the summer of 1613 fears grew that the failure of the Parliament would be but the beginning of more serious rebellion. During

10. "The Letter-Book of Sir Arthur Chichester," *Analecta Hibernica* 8 (1938), 71.

that time a number of the Irish came over to England to put their case before the King. As Aidan Clarke expresses it, "A major part of the delegation's task had been to convince the King of the opposition's sincere loyalty to the crown. The members attempted to do this repeatedly, with prolix fervour."[11]

But James, in receiving the delegation, had "probed the attitudes of the principal members of the delegation, forcing them to face the ultimate dilemma of the loyal catholic and declare for pope or king in his presence."[12] And Chichester, in June, had advised: "The chief labour and industry must be how to free our selves from scorn and to bring them to an orderly Parliament with vs, by all possible means, and whereas they now neither fear nor revere his Majesties Laws and mild Government, now that duty may be timely begotten in them. This will require great prudence and some royal animositie. I fear it cannot be but with demonstration of force. Their nature is so malignant and crooked, as benefits cannot lenifie, but doth rather exasperate them" (p. 106). In the event, James did visit some of his anger on twc of the delegation who refused to declare for the King—Sir William Talbot and Thomas Luttrell. Three months in the Fleet prison brought Luttrell to obedience, but Talbot refused to bend, and was prosecuted in Star Chamber shortly after the performance of the *Irish Masque*.

At the time of the masque, then, the political situation was highly fraught, and Jonson's work had an obvious topicality. In general, Jonson's masque employs much of the standard rhetoric of Elizabethan and Jacobean discussion of Ireland, both in its verbal detail and in the outline of its dramatic structure. By far the commonest opposition in all such discussion is that between English "civility" and Irish "barbarism." Barnaby Rich, for example, asserted that the Irish "had rather stil retaine themselues in their sluttishnesse, in their vncleanlinesse, in their rudeness, and in their inhumane loathsomnes, then they would take any example from the English, either of *ciuility, humanity,* or any manner of *Decencie.*"[13] The response of the English was to hope, like all imperialists, that, in Sir John Davies' words, "the next generation will in tongue and heart and every way else become English, so there will be no difference or

11. Aidan Clarke with R. Dudley Edwards, "Pacification, Plantation and the Catholic Question, 1603–1623," in *A New History of Ireland,* ed. J. W. Moody, F. X. Martin and F. J. Byrne, (Oxford, 1976) III, p. 217.

12. Clarke, p. 216.

13. Barnaby Rich, *A New Description of Ireland,* (London, 1610), p. 16.

distinction but the Irish Sea betwixt us."[14]

The whole movement of Jonson's masque dramatizes these precon-
ceptions and hopes. The comic indecorum of the four servants, which
represents the standard view of Irish rudeness and incivility, reaches its
height when Dermock confidentially leans toward the King as the
Gentlemen dance and asks "How like tow tish, YAMISH?" (VII, p. 403).
They are dismissed by one described, significantly, as "a ciuill gentleman
of the nation," who berates them:

> Hold your tongues.
> And let your courser manners seeke some place,
> Fit for their wildnesse. This is none, be gone. (pp. 303–04)

The assertion of civility is symbolized by the movement from servant
to gentleman; prose to verse; dialect to "standard" English; and, of
course, antimasque to masque. Furthermore, the transformation of the
masquers itself works within these assumptions. They are forced at first
to dance in their "Irish mantles," since their finery is lost, but the promise
of obedience clothes them in English garb. There is, to us, a certain
amusement at the presentation of James's transforming power as that of
a kind of magic tailor, but at the time the mantle was a particularly
potent symbol of Irishness. Sir John Davies, indeed, in expressing his
hopes for the future, comments that "these ciuil assemblies and assizes
and sessions haue reclaimed the Irish from their wildness, caused them to
cut off their glibs and long hair, *to conuert their mantles into cloaks,* to
conform themselves to the manner of England in all their behaviour and
outward form."[15] Perhaps this work, published in 1612, actually inspired
Jonson's device, but in any case it makes clear the force of the central
symbol of *The Irish Masque.*

The complacency of this picture of Irish submission to English culture
is further supported by the generally reassuring tone of the work. Early
on, the servants assure the court:

> *Dermock.* Vee be Irish men, and't pleash tee.
> *Donnell.* Ty good shubshects of Ireland, an't pleash ty mayesty.
> (p. 400)

---

14. Sir John Davies, *A Discovery of the True Causes why Ireland was never entirely Subdued . . .* , in
Ireland Under Elizabeth and James the First, ed. Henry Morley, (London, 1890), pp. 335–36.

15. Davies, (my italics). Spenser has a long disquisition on the mantle, which he sees as symbol
for everything deceptive and dangerous in the Irish character. See David Beers Quinn, *The
Elizabethans and the Irish* (Ithaca & New York, 1966), Plates 2–8 for illustrations. This work is
generally very useful for its collection of Elizabethan and early Jacobean comments on the Irish.

And later they speak of their masters:

Donnell.	Tey be honesht men.
Patrick.	And goot men: tine owne subshects.
Dermock.	Tou hasht very goot shubshects in Ireland.
Dennise.	A great goot many, o' great goot shubshects.
Donnell.	Tat loue ty mayesty heartily.
. . . .	
Donnell.	Be not angry vit te honesh <t> men, for te few
Patrick.	rebelsh, & knauesh.
Dermock.	Nor beleeue no tayles, king YAMISH.
	For, by got, tey loue tee in Ireland. (p. 402)

This insistent reassurance is obvious enough. But the choice of a Bard to sing the final songs of obedience and love in the masque is itself also symptomatic of the work's general tendency to anaesthetize anxieties. Philip Edwards had commented on the absurdity of the picture of the Bard singing to two harps, symbolizing the union of English and Irish culture, for, as he says, "when the Gaelic way of life went, the bards went too. There was no possibility that with the social and political system—of which they were so integral a part—in ruins, *they* should survive and serve an English polity."[16] But Jonson's real address here is to the anxieties that Spenser and Rich had expressed. In Spenser's *View of the Present State of Ireland,* Ireneus argues for the suppression of the bards because they are

so farre from instructing yong men in morall discipline, that they themselves doe more deserve to bee sharpely disciplined; for they seldom use to choose unto themselves the doings of good men for the arguments of their poems, but whomsoever they find to be most licentious of life, most bolde and lawlesse in his doings, most dangerous and desperate in all parts of disobedience and rebellious disposition, him they set up and glorifie in their rithmes.[17]

Rich makes a similar point, when claiming

there is nothing that hath more led the Irish into error, then lying Historiographers, their *Chroniclers,* their *Bardes,* their *Rhythmers,* and such other their lying Poetes; in whose writinges they do more relie, then they do in the holy Scriptures."[18]

In this attitudinal context, Jonson's presentation of a dutiful Bard takes on the character of complacent reassurance, as all customary fears are simply suppressed, and the Bard stands as a figure more akin to the author

16. Edwards, *Threshold of a Nation,* p. 13.
17. In Morley, p. 121.
18. Rich, p. 3.

of the masque himself than to the potentially dangerous bogey of contemporary polemic.

The masque, of course, places James at the center of the civilizing enterprise. The Gentleman praises his love of peace, and claims that he comes in fulfillment of old prophecies. It is precisely this kind of rhetoric that sustains Sir John Davies' treatise, which also presents the king as a Messianic figure long desired and foretold. (Interestingly enough, it links with the characteristic propaganda employed in supporting James's earlier project of uniting England and Scotland.)[19]

If the masque has much in common with the general line of Jacobean attitudes toward Ireland, so too it seems to reflect directly upon the particular circumstances of its historical moment. In the early part of the masque, the footmen engage in a comic competition concerning who is to speak first—surely a version of the disorderly Parliamentary proceedings, especially as Dennise threatens, like the Old English of that Parliament, to withdraw without speaking. Certainly the tendency of the masque as a whole is to prefigure James's own judgement upon the Catholics, when he declared "that you have carried yourselves tumultuously, and that your proceedings have been rude, disorderly and worthy of severe judgement."[20] It is perhaps no wonder that the masque was called for again, when it so complacently endorsed and confirmed both official policy and inbred attitudes. Yet even at the time Chamberlain reported that "the device (which was a mimicall imitation of the Irish) was not so pleasing to many, which thincke it no time (as the case stands) to exasperate that nation by making it ridiculous."[21]

Perhaps the strongest case against the masque, however, is the way its presentation of political attitudes threatens to undercut the very processes by which the masque should, according to Jonson's own prescription, work. The collusion between the masque and the anaesthetic of official propaganda is strongly marked by the basis of its fiction. At the time real Irishmen were anxiously awaiting the outcome of their real embassy about important political issues, including the right of the King to rig a Parliament. The masque's fiction suggests that the Irish embassy is occasioned by nothing more significant than the marriage of the King's

19. See, for example, the epigram Campion prefixed to his *Lord Hay's Masque* (*The Works of Thomas Campion,* ed. Walter R. Davies, [London, 1969], p. 207). For further use of the prophecies of Merlin in political propaganda see Keith Thomas, *Religion and the Decline of Magic,* (Harmondsworth, Eng., 1973), pp. 494–96.

20. In *CSP (Carew), 1603–1624,* p. 290.

21. Quoted in Herford and Simpson, X, p. 510.

favorite. This transposition carefully obscures the true seriousness of the matters it claims to be addressing, and moves the work as a whole into a fundamentally complacent posture. The work *seems* to reflect present occasions, but in subordinating Irish matters to the celebration of a marriage, the masque so falsifies them that it is difficult to take the comment on either seriously. This complacency enters into every detail of the work's construction.

The antimasque contains a number of references to the white stick of the Lord Chamberlain, employed in trying to debar the footmen from entering the Hall. At one level this allusion to the circumstances of masque performance is no more than a joke—for the Chamberlain was Thomas Howard, father of the bride, and his stick had, some eight years previously, been employed in ejecting Jonson himself from Daniel's *Vision of Twelve Goddesses*. Two years earlier, in *Love Restored,* the antimasque figure of Robin Goodfellow also complained of hindrance in getting in to the masque. There he stood for the kind of vanity that *should* be excluded from court performance. In the later work, the justice of the complaint of the Irish is difficult to resist.

But something rather more sinister is going on. The reducing of the Irish to comic figures, sneered at for their lower-class indecorum, enables the "white stick" to be used as an acceptable manifestation of royal power, obscuring and rendering comfortable the real force that James was prepared to excercise, for example, in his imprisonment of Talbot and Luttrell, of which the Spanish Ambassador wrote: "The king was very angry insomuch as he commanded him to be returned to the Tower, and it was thought he should have been hanged, and sure he was in very nigh it. . . . But it seems that all these threats were used only to reduce him."[22]

Nothing could indicate more clearly the complicity of the masque-maker in concealing the true nature of political power than this conversion. And nothing more clearly demonstrates the moral complacency that Jonson shows in the masque than the way he separates the exercise of power in the antimasque from the submission of the Gentlemen in the masque itself. The "disobedience" of the Irish Parliamentarians is diminished by its presentation as the rude unmannerliness of servants, while the Gentlemen "naturally" and spontaneously proffer obedience. It is conveniently then forgotten that it was the Gentlemen from Ireland, the "ringleaders" of the revolt, upon whom royal power was, in reality,

22. In *CSP (Irish), 1611–14,* p. 543.

exercised, not upon their comic servants.

One's disquiet with this masque is further compounded by the dubious nature of the transformation which is its central symbol. After the masquers' first dance (which they perform in their Irish mantles), Dermock wishes "tey had fine cloyshs now, and liueries, like tine owne men, and't bee" (p. 403). We have seen how this agrees with the political stance toward the Irish problem, but at the same time it was, for the audience present at the performance, a joke—for the masque was performed, at James's request, by his "own men" indeed, the "Gentlemen the King's Servants" mentioned in the work's published title. Far from insisting upon the power of masques to *transform* the masquers, to image their ideal potential, everything in this masque points toward the *fiction* of the masque, the fact that it is merely a dressing up for a party. The Gentlemen are not Irish at all; they have themselves learned nothing from the experience, and for the audience the revelation that is offered by their "transformation" is only to confirm that they are what we knew they were all along, the English servants of the King. The message of the masque is therefore directed *at* the benighted and comic Irish from the point of view of secure and self-satisfied English and Scottish masquers.

This complacent correspondence between the masquers' real selves and the roles they play is perhaps the most insidious devaluation of the high theory of the masque. For the form characteristically entertains a dialectical relationship between the courtiers and their roles, enabling the beholder, in perceiving the discrepancy, to grasp the possibility of aspiring to the presented ideal. Here the obliteration of that gap signals only the underlying assertion of the masque that to be Irish is essentially and inevitably to be inferior.

The sense that Jonson is running dangerously close to sabotaging the theory of the masque he himself did so much to promulgate is further intensified by the fact that part of the comedy of *The Irish Masque* derives from its inclusion of detailed parody of the elements of Campion's *Somerset Masque,* his entertainment for the occasion. Specifically, in presenting twelve masquers hindered from arriving at the celebrations, Jonson adopts the same fiction that Campion employed. He then contrasts his "realistically" naked masquers with those in Campion's work who had the benefit of "a deuoish vit a clowd to fesh 'hem out o' te bottome o'te vayter" (p. 401). In the dispute regarding who is to speak first he also pokes fun at Campion's masque, as he does in allusions to the symbolic use of the number four.

No doubt this reflects Jonson's arrogant sense of his own superiority as a writer of masques; perhaps it also witnesses to a sense of pique that Campion, who provided the main masque for Princess Elizabeth's marriage earlier in 1613 when Jonson was away, should be rewarded with the marriage-night masque for this Howard triumph. But if so, the ridicule of the machinery of the masque, and especially of symbolic number, comes somewhat dangerously from the poet who validated his own symbolic gestures in *Hymenaei* and other masques by their capacity to image divine harmonies. It makes of *The Irish Masque* a work confined to its purely literary space, as one of a series of mere entertainments offered before a knowing audience.

The rejection of a high style, and the pretended realism of the masque in contrast to Campion's work, is in a paradoxical way symptomatic of Jonson allowing to the surface a fundamental unease with the whole business of courtly mythmaking, a practice which Philip Edwards has pointed to in a number of Jonson's works. (pp. 149–71).[23]

When Jonson published these two masques in 1616 the revelation of the Overbury murder meant that he again felt compelled to remove the record of their specific occasion, as he did for *Hymenaei*. In 1614 he wrote, in "An Epistle to Master John Selden," of his sense that he had "too oft preferr'd Men past their termes, and prais'd some names too much" (VIII, p. 159). That awareness, and the embarrassment that accompanied it can only have been intensified by the case of Frances Howard. But Jonson's own unease is only a symptomatic part of the story. For in their different ways each of these masques raises for the modern reader substantial questions of how to read and respond to a panegyric art. It is too simple to concur with the idealizing ambition of the masques, and mistaken to lift them out of their particular social and political context, since to do so is to falsify their contemporary aim and effect. The reader must register and deal with a modern embarrassment when faced with the masque, and with the specific ideological tendency of a work like *The Irish Masque at Court,* since it is only by such precise and detailed location that the nature of its conspiracy with the prevailing direction of Stuart politics will emerge. But, on the other hand, it would be equally misguided to dismiss Jonson's intellectual effort and didactic aspiration as superficial flattery and time-serving. For it is precisely in registering the complexity of the struggle within the poet's work to sustain the transmutation of the circumstances of the Jacobean court and its politics into

23. See also David Norbrook, *Poetry and Politics* (London, 1984), ch. 7.

self-sufficient myth that the true fascination of the genre lies. We perceive Jonson's own embarrassments; we recognize also the complacencies that engender our own discomfort; and in the gaps and discontinuities between the two, we comprehend the complexities involved in decoding this panegyric art.

Entertaining the Palatine Prince: Plays on Foreign Affairs 1635–1637

MARTIN BUTLER

THE arrival in London of Charles Louis, exiled Count Palatine of the Rhine and Prince Elector of the Holy Roman Empire, on November 21, 1635,[1] was calculated to provoke his uncle and godfather, Charles I, into offering active support on his behalf on the Continent. About to enter on his majority, Charles Louis hoped to regain the lands and dignities lost by his father, Frederick, through his rash and ill-fortuned defiance of the Habsburg Emperor Ferdinand II in 1618. Frederick had plunged the divided German states into a prolonged and complex war which saw in 1635 a loosely Protestant alliance, between France and Sweden, fighting the Catholic powers, Spain and Austria, on German soil. However, the Protestant cause was going badly, having lost its champion, Gustavus of Sweden, in 1632, and subsequently suffering several bad defeats. By the Peace of Prague (1635), Ferdinand drew the non-aligned German states into closer dependence on him, while excluding Charles Louis' claims, and he was planning an electoral meeting (to which Charles Louis was not invited) to confirm Habsburg succession to the imperial throne for autumn 1636. James and Charles had always regarded the European conflict with some aversion; but at this juncture a declaration of family obligation would have been timely.[2]

The Prince was received at Whitehall with "a great deale of state in generall, wch hath given the worlde much satisfaction, & makes all men

I am grateful to the British Academy for a "Thank-Offering to Britain" Research Fellowship that has enabled me to research and write this paper.

1. W. Laud, *The Autobiography* (Oxford, 1839), p. 160.
2. C. V. Wedgwood, *The Thirty Years' War* (London, 1938), *passim*; F. C. Springell, *Connoisseur and Diplomat* (London, 1963), pp. 1–3.

think that this journey will conduce much to the good of his affaiers."
Commentators noted the enthusiasm of his welcome "by the general,
with whom he is very popular, because of his mother [Princess Eliza-
beth]."[3] To the broad militant wing of English Protestantism, the
Palatine exiles were shameful examples of England's failure to meet her
traditional religious and political loyalties. In the unstable years
1623–1625, radical writers had looked back to England's national greatness under Queen Elizabeth and ascribed it, somewhat unhistorically, to
a consistent commitment to England's Protestant alliances and to aggression towards Spain, policies that James and Charles were allowing to
lapse. The dispossession of Princess Elizabeth was cited as a leading
instance to prove the implacable hatred that Spain and the Pope had for
Protestantism in general, and England in particular; her plight prompted
the puritan pamphleteer John Reynolds to evoke the glorious days of her
namesake: "Shee inheriteth the Name and Vertues, the Majestie and
generositie of our Immortall Queen *Elizabeth,* and is a Princess of such
excellent hoapes and exquisite perfections, that I cannot speak of her
without prayse, nor prayse her without admiration, sith shee can be
immytated by none, nor parraleld by anie but by herselfe; And yet will
your Majestie neglect her, and will you not drawe your Sworde in her
just Quarrell, whose Fame and Vertues hath drawne most hartes to
adore, all to admyre her."[4] Reynolds' conclusion is "Our famous *Elizabeth* did beate *Spayne,* and shall our Royall and Potent King JAMES feare
it."[5] In the following decade, such plain speaking was prohibited, but it
was still possible to admonish England that Antichrist was making
"havocke in the florishing Churches of *Bohemia,* the *Palatinate,* and other
parts of Germany," and that "they pray, and call upon us, as farre as
Prague, as farre as Heidelberg, as farre as France, that we would take
notice of their afflictions."[6] In the distress of Charles' kin was figured the
dishonor of the English church and people; Milton later accused the
bishops of leaving England "naked of our firmest and faithfullest neighbours abroad, by disparaging and alienating from us all Protestant
princes and commonwealths."[7] Consequently, Charles Louis' visit resur-

---

3. J. Cornwallis, *The Private Correspondence* (1842), p. 281; *Calendar of State Papers, Venetian*
[hereafter *CSPV*], 1632–1636, p. 468.

4. "S.R.N.I.," *Votivae Angliae* (Utrecht, 1624), sig.D3.

5. *Votivae Angliae,* sig.E2.

6. T. Taylor, *Christ's Victory over the Dragon* (1633), p. 721; C. Hill, *Puritanism and Revolution*
(London, 1958), pp. 124–25.

7. Hill, *Puritanism and Revolution,* p. 129.

rected fierce expectations of a return to an old-style anti-Spanish policy based patriotically on England's national and naval supremacy and reminiscent of her Elizabethan greatness: "The news was received with more pleasure by those who fervently desire a parliament than by any others. They build the most solid hopes upon it, as it is practically certain that the king will not refuse to assume openly the protection of his nephew, when he comes to ask it in person." In early 1636 the recall of Parliament and intervention in Europe were strongly canvassed. "These ideas are occasionally maintained before the king and are constantly dinned into the Palatine's ears."[8]

The King, however, had no intention of allowing either. He treated the Palatinate as a single issue which could be resolved by diplomacy. In addition, he had a temperamental leaning towards Spain, with whom he was already negotiating when Charles Louis arrived. The following months held only frustration for the Prince as his uncle hesitated between French offers of an alliance and Spanish proposals to restore Charles Louis if he made a proper submission to the Emperor. In the summer ambassadors were sent simultaneously to Paris and Vienna, but each was hamstrung by Charles' reluctance to make openly any positive proposals and by his fear of offending the opposite party. Both returned empty-handed, one, the Earl of Arundel, warning Charles not to let himself be "despised by his enemies for inactivity and remain exposed to scorn."[9] In 1637 another French alliance was proposed, broken off, and Spanish negotiations re-opened. In February Charles accepted a privateering scheme against Spanish shipping, but only secretly "because he will not yet break with Spain." Anyway, the Venetian ambassador reflected, the Spanish "really desire nothing in this matter except that nothing shall be concluded."[10]

Nevertheless, Charles Louis had powerful sympathizers among the aristocracy. In January 1636 "mighty Feasting of the Prince *Elector*; since his coming into *England*" was reported, "both in the Court and out of it."[11] He received gestures of support from the Earls of Bedford, Essex,

8. *CSPV*, 1632–1636, pp. 469, 500, 511.

9. Springell, *Connoisseur and Diplomat*, p. 37; cf. S. R. Gardiner, *History of England . . . 1603–42*, 10 vols. (London, 1883–1884), VIII, 97–98, 159–63; *CSPV*, 1632–1636, p. 471.

10. Gardiner, *History*, VIII, 204, 217; *Calendar of State Papers, Domestic* [hereafter *CSPD*], 1636–1637, p. 422; *CSPV*, 1632–1636, p. 490.

11. *The Earl of Strafford's Letters and Dispatches*, ed. W. Knowler, 2 vols. (1739), I, 506.

Northumberland, and Warwick, all prominent noblemen of "country" or "puritanical" leanings, who favored a more vigorous foreign policy.[12] The Papal legate described the Countess of Arundel as "most charming, but such a partisan of the Prince Palatine that it is a shame."[13] The Earl of Craven, who had fought on the Continent, offered prodigal financial help.[14] At court Princess Elizabeth's campaign was coordinated by the diplomat Sir Thomas Roe, who argued her case before the King (that he must "do something, for . . . a thousand ciphers added make but one nothing"), communicated with ministers, and got the Earl of Holland to "disperse transcripts [of her proposals] to those who have power and will to use them, especially to the Lord Keeper [Coventry], who is a most worthy man, most faithful to the religion, and most affectionate to her service."[15]

In the unfocused and intrigue-ridden Caroline court, an important figure was Queen Henrietta Maria herself. Naturally inclined to the pro-French position, she also had strong links with several courtiers (such as Holland) who wished to push Charles towards a Spanish war. They seem to have manipulated her discreetly, realizing her potential as a lever by which "opposition" pressure could be brought against Charles.[16] In 1635, through her they were urging Charles to reconvene parliament and make war; a connection was established with Roe; and in October French military defeats caused "a great Sense of Sorrow on the Queen's side."[17] Charles Louis and his brother Rupert, who joined him in February 1636, one "a very handsome young Prince, modest, very bashful," the other "full of spirit and action, full of observation and judgment," were just the romantic types to attract the young Queen's attention, and she embraced their cause. The French position was impeded in December 1635 by the ambassador's reluctance to give the Prince his electoral title, while the Spaniard, "having lately much mended his Pace herein," leaped into Charles' favor by addressing his nephew as his

12. Knowler, *Strafford Letters*, I, 504; S. D'Ewes, *The Autobiography and Correspondence*, ed. J. O. Halliwell, II (1845), 138; A. Collins, *Letters and Memorials of State*, II (1746), 472; *CSPD*, 1637, p. 251.

13. M. F. S. Hervey, *The Life, Correspondence and Collections of Thomas Howard, Earl of Arundel* (Cambridge, Eng., 1921), p. 398.

14. Knowler, *Strafford Letters*, II, 49.

15. *CSPD*, 1635–1636, p. 243; 1636–1637, p. 99.

16. D. Mathew, *The Age of Charles I* (London, 1951), p. 57; R. M. Smuts, "The Puritan Followers of Henrietta Maria in the 1630s," *The English Historical Review*, 93 (1978), 26–45, *passim*.

17. Smuts, "The Puritan Followers," pp. 36–37; Knowler, *Strafford Letters*, I, 474.

"Electoral Highness." The Queen however found the French "an expedient which will prove very opportune for them in time; that is, when they meet him in the queen's chamber, where they both have occasion to go almost every day, they have already had more than one colloquy with him, without a formal visit and merely as private courtiers." Thereafter French negotiations proceeded under her sponsorship, for in February meetings were still being arranged in her rooms. Later that month, the Privy Council debated the French proposals.[18]

Moreover, Henrietta Maria was also a patron of the drama, and I propose now to show in detail how the contemporary stage engaged in the debate of these issues. Far too simplified assumptions about the workings of Caroline politics and the dependence of the dramatists on royal favor have produced a picture of the Caroline stage as invariably expressing, monolithically and uncritically, the point of view of the King and his court. The reality was much more complex, and much more interesting.

II

Charles Louis was welcomed with great magnificence. "Comedies, festivities and balls are the order of the day here, and are indulged in every day at Court for the prince's sake, while all the greatest lords vie with each other in entertaining him at noble and sumptuous banquets"; the Earl of Essex, for example, presented him "with a play, & dancing, & a supper that cost 200*ll*."[19] English plays were mixed with French and Spanish performances by visiting foreign troupes,[20] and in December he saw the Queen's pastoral, *Florimène,* acted in French by her maids, with elaborate scenery by Inigo Jones, and songs and dances. The Venetian ambassador noted that "The Court has never been so frequented and they say it has not been in such a state for any one for many years past."[21]

This "Royall Entertainment" was celebrated in a doggerel "Poem of Joy" presented to the Prince on his arrival.[22] Addressing him as a young

18. Knowler, *Strafford Letters,* I, 489, 504; *CSPD,* 1636–1637, p. 71; *CSPV,* 1632–1636, pp. 491, 516, 523.

19. *CSPV,* 1632–1636, p. 491; Bodleian MS. North c.4, fol.7.

20. G. E. Bentley, *The Jacobean and Caroline Stage* [hereafter *JCS*], 7 vols. (Oxford, 1941–1968), VII, 100.

21. *CSPV,* 1632–1636, p. 486.

22. Public Record Office, S. P. 302/141. The author, who describes himself as having been loved by King James, may have been the Earl of Holland, who is said (in 1637) to have written

branch of the British tree, "A stock Hew'd out from Cedar James," the author attributed his welcome to the popularity of his mother:

> For's Lady mothers sake, Elizabeth of Grace
> Princess pallatine, like Queen El'abeths fface
> Her Godmother, Englands Glory shynd wth ffame
> As Royall Charles and James, possest y^{e} same.

The rebirth of Queen Elizabeth in her goddaughter prompts the reminder that the English monarchs should be Defenders of the Faith:

> In Hebrew El=isha=beth (woman of gods house) was shee
> As James and Charles, for gods house Kings they bee
> Th'one in heav'n, Thother Bryttaines glory
> Lives for us and you, a Heav'nly story
> Though Elizas troubles as the name doth, beare
> Was like Eliza=Queen (wth Greefes and feare)

"Elizas troubles" were the persecutions of the future Queen by her Catholic sister Mary, which John Foxe narrated in his *Book of Martyrs* as the sufferings of a Protestant saint. The poet implies that, like her, Princess Elizabeth suffers for the sake of her faith, and he anticipates the inevitable defeat of the Catholic menace by the true "heav'nly Hope" of "Christ & Charles, Great Kings bove Pope":

> Though Pope and's Kings Raigne . . .
> T'imbroyle ye world wth blood, and wrongfull Action
> yet heere set rest in both, wth Comforts Heare
> Christ and high Charles, will still be brothers Deare
> And wth true patience, yett you doe endure
> Heav'n and Earths Parlymentes can make ytt sure.

The reference to "Earths Parlymentes" indicates clearly the means through which he expects this to happen.

The same ideas were voiced from the stage in a special prologue and epilogue written to greet the Prince at court by Thomas Heywood,[23] a dramatist of the older generation who had recently produced his own prose account of Queen Elizabeth's persecution, *England's Eliza* (1631). He welcomed the Palsgrave as an auspicious "bright hayr'd Comet," or as

---

verses, "the worst that ever wear seene" (Historical Manuscripts Commission, *Report* [hereafter HMC] 77 [De Lisle and Dudley MSS], vi, p. 94).

23. T. Heywood, *Pleasant Dialogues and Dramas* (1637), pp. 250–51.

> a glorious thinge
> As if the Eagle from her spatious wing
> Had her prime feather dropt, which to regaine,
> She (almost) would give *Almaigne, Rome,* and *Spaine.*

This is the imperial eagle, Ferdinand himself, or simply "the Empire," whose first prince Charles Louis is:

> may your fame flie
> Mounted upon those plumes that soare most hie:
> Of which, make two rare presidents, We intreat,
> One of *Charles* little, th'other *Charles* the Great.

"*Charles* the Great" is evidently Charlemagne, the ideal ruler, but also the first post-classical western emperor, a champion of the faith under whom all Christendom was united and the Roman empire of justice and world rule reborn. Queen Elizabeth was held to have reasserted the imperial authority of Constantine and Charlemagne against the Pope's corruptions;[24] linking Charles Louis with his homonymous predecessor, Heywood indicates the future European role he envisages for him. The epilogue, opening with the same image as the "Poem of Joy," is more explicit:

> A numerous fruit, sprung from a golden Tree,
> Such (as old Atlas, was ne're seene by thee
> In thine *Hesperian* orchard) long t'indure
> And prosper in the world: now growes mature.
> And the faire blossoms ready even to spread
> Their leaves abroad, and top the *Eagles* Head
> (The Roote still safe) where-ever shall bee seene
> Scient, transplanted, may it still grow greene,
> So may none issuing from King *James* his Stemme,
> But be thought fit to weare a Diadem

These unambiguous words were addressed to the Palsgrave, but are clearly also an indirect admonition to the King concerning his lineal duty. Heywood belonged to the Queen's Men and had earned Henrietta Maria's favor with his complimentary *Love's Mistress, or the Queen's Masque* (1634). His sentiments echo her opinions rather than the "official" attitudes of the King; perhaps the play the Palsgrave saw was

---

24. F. Kermode, *Renaissance Essays*, 2nd ed. (London, 1973), pp. 17–21; F. Yates, *Astraea*, 2nd ed. (Harmondsworth, 1977), pp. 2–5, 29–47.

A NOTE ON THE ILLUSTRATION

Crispin de Passe, *The Kingly Cock* (second state, 1637)

In this Dutch broadside, evidently designed for circulation in England in conjunction with the agitation over foreign policy, King Charles sits asleep in the chair of state, his sword unbuckled, while the Spanish ambassador plays soothing tunes on his flute and offers him a chest of treasure and a basket of child's toys. On the other side, the King of France, sword in hand, tries to waken Charles and is seconded by Charles Louis and Rupert, whose brothers and sisters present him with a victor's garland. The "Hispaniolized Courtier" (probably Cottington) attempts to prevent him. On the right, Arundel returns from the Emperor bearing a packet marked "Nihil ope Requ est." Through the window, the fleet waits ready at Dover.

In the verses which accompany the engraving, the French King calls on Charles to awaken to his danger and to Spain's treachery, and to join him in arms against Spain: "Looke on your owne deare blood, these branches faire / Who through this tirants rage as exiles are, / And never more shal repossess their land / By peace, as you doe dreame, but by strong hand." The unheroic courtier retorts "'t Is better dance, be merrie, joviall still, / With Spanish Pistolets our purses fill, / Better with pictures gaie to feed our sight / Than naked corpses gor'd with blood in fight." The Spaniard admits that should Charles awake, Spain's conquests may be lost again, but if his tunes keep him asleep, Spain may yet overrun France and England too. Bristling with indignation at the Emperor's scorn, Arundel recommends a practical course of action: "It is our Cannon and the martiall wight / That exercis'd in warre is . . . that must get / Better content than any Legate yet. / Take out of every towne one man of ten / And with those well train'd well arm'd English men / Invade we Flanders, this is the way I tender / To make them on good termes the Paltz surrender." One wonders who the poet was that dared to write such lines.

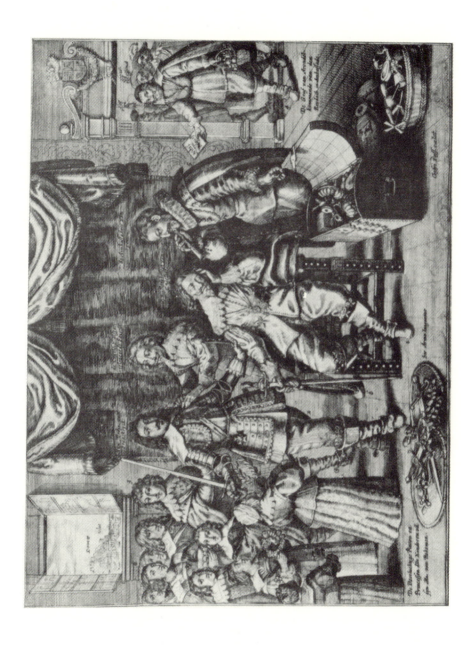

Heywood's own dramatization of Elizabeth's accession and the Armada victory, thirty years old yet still in his company's repertoire.[25]

In January 1636 the Prince left Whitehall for "Feasting and Comedies" at Cambridge.[26] Here he was made an honorary Master of Arts, and heard orations and a Latin play, probably the anonymous *Senilis Amor*.[27] He could have found little enjoyment in this confused comedy of intriguing lovers interspersed with farcical low-life slapstick, but one joke was tailored to his interests, deliberately it seems. A drunken sailor finds two coins left in his purse: "The head of Ferdinand! Hail, Caesar! Certainly you are rich, Tytubus; this gold takes pride in bearing the image of Adolphus; if the Roman eagles should flee, it certainly would not be strange for they have always hated the Suevi. But let me offer a tithe as soon as I have found a comrade. Caesar, you shall go first, for always the Suevi came out second."[28] Tytubus's two coins are imperial and Swedish (with the head of Gustavus Adolphus, Ferdinand's enemy), and their jangling suggests to him the conflicts of Ferdinand's predecessor as Roman imperial head, Julius Caesar,[29] with the Suevi, a Germanic tribe whose defeat is told in the *Gallic War* (I,54; IV, 1–3; VI, 9–10). The Suevi, however, belonged to the Rhinelands; probably the author knew that the Palsgrave's authority (in his own words) extended "over all the Countries of the Rhine, Suevia and Franconia."[30] Charles Louis would have been gratified to see the Roman eagles flying from the Suevi, if only in emblem.

III

The Inns of Court had given the Prince a supper in December, but the Middle Temple had had additional plans for "a Royal Entertainment with Masks, Dancings, and some other Exercises of Wit, in Orations or Arraignments" for some weeks.[31] Dramatic exercises were a traditional element in the legal curriculum, and the Inns had once been important literary centers whose Christmas revels were substantial occasions.[32]

25. See Heywood's *If You Know Not Me*, Pt. 1, ed. M. Doran (Oxford, 1935), pp. xiv–xv.

26. Knowler, *Strafford Letters*, I, 510.

27. Bentley, *JCS*, V, 1408.

28. *Senilis Amor*, ed. L. J. Mills (Bloomington, Ind., 1952), pp. 89–91.

29. Ferdinand is "Caesar" throughout V. a Frubach, *The Evaporation of the Apple of Palestine* (1637), and Henry Glapthorne, *Albertus Wallenstein* (1635?).

30. Charles Louis, *The Manifest of the Most Illustrious Prince* (1637), sig.Q3v.

31. Knowler, *Strafford Letters*, I, 504, 507.

32. See P. J. Finkelpearl, *John Marston of the Middle Temple* (Cambridge, Mass., 1969), pp. 18–44.

However, no masque was written by a termer after 1615, and apart from Shirley's *Triumph of Peace,* produced in special circumstances in 1634, no Inn had mounted a masque for fifteen years. In general, the authorities (the Benchers) at the Caroline Inns tried to prevent extravagant Christmas feasting and revelling; consequently, the revival of the revels on a large, Elizabethan scale in 1635–1636 was all the more remarkable an event.

The Middle Temple in particular had a strong tradition of festive controversy. A "Christmas Game" of 1627 had developed into a street battle between their Christmas prince and the city watch. In 1630 the Benchers were scandalized by a group of students who defied their orders against holding Christmas commons and, "on pretence of their liberties (as they termed it) being infringed," assembled a mock parliament, passed sentence on the Steward and forcibly set him in the stocks, "which they call their Tower."[33] The following Christmas, despite dire warnings, another revolt occurred and a festive parliament was again created which "made an order . . . to drink healths in Hall with loud music."[34] There were further "insufferable enormities" in 1638, and in 1639 swords were drawn when the termers again set up illegal Christmas commons, constituted a mock Bench, and elected officers. This time the King was drawn in, and the students were warned by the Lord Chief Justice, at "his Majesty's special direction, to break up their commons and conform to order."[35] In these conflicts jest and earnest blur ambiguously; festive freedoms were producing quasi-serious challenges to authority.

The tendency in these incidents towards parody of authority's forms reiterates a traditional element in the Elizabethan revels, which had given the Christmas prince a temporary court over which he really ruled like his Whitehall counterpart, maintaining state, receiving ambassadors, choosing councillors, arraigning criminals, and issuing edicts. Such serious sports were educative, providing aspiring statesmen with opportunities to rehearse the roles they naturally anticipated playing in real life, but they were also vehicles of argument. Imitation served the lawyers' political interests by raising questions of state on which in their

---

33. H. L'Estrange, *The Reign of King Charles,* 2nd ed. (1656), p. 70; C. T. Martin, ed., *Minutes of Parliament of the Middle Temple,* II (London, 1904), 771–73.

34. Martin, *Minutes of Parliament,* p. 791.

35. Martin, *Minutes of Parliament,* pp. 876–77, 888–89.

professional capacity they had been silenced.[36] The revellers of 1636 were certainly men who expected to make significant and varied contributions to state affairs. One masquer was a nephew of Sir Humphrey May (d. 1630), the Surveyor of the Court of Wards and Chancellor of the Duchy of Lancaster; he later became a Baron of the Exchequer. Another was son of Sir Nicholas Hyde (d. 1631), Chief Justice of the King's Bench, and cousin of Edward Hyde (later Earl of Clarendon), then resident at the Middle Temple. Another was Clarendon's friend, John Bramston, the son of a judge who in the following year gave judgment against the Crown in the Ship Money case. A fourth was brother of the regicide John Lisle (also in residence at the Middle Temple); a fifth was cousin of Sir Henry Spelman, the antiquary, MP, and constitutionalist.[37] Several others were lawyers of ten years' standing or more. Most interesting of all, the Christmas prince himself was the son of a Cornish knight, Sir Francis Vivian, who in 1632 had been trounced in the Star Chamber over irregularities in his captaincy of St. Mawes castle and had received an expensive and humiliating sentence.[38] An entertainment by such men would carry no little weight.

Contemporaries particularly noted the splendor of the 1636 revels. To James Howell, the mock king was "Our famous Prince *d'Amour*," and another reported "his Court and retinue in transcripts [were] published from hand to hand."[39] George Garrard wrote a complete account:

> The *Middle-Temple-House* have set up a Prince, who carries himself in great State, one Mr. *Vivian* a *Cornish* Gentleman . . . He hath all his great Officers attending him, Lord Keeper, Lord Treasurer, eight white staves at the least, Captain of his Pensioners, Captain of his Guard, two Chaplains, who on *Sunday* last preached before him, and in the Pulpit made three low Legs to his Excellency before they began, which is much laughed at. My Lord Chamberlain [the Earl of Pembroke] lent him two fair Cloths of State, one hung up in the Hall under which he dines, the other in his Privy Chamber; he is served on the Knee, and all that come to see him kiss his Hand on their Knee.[40]

36. M. Axton, *The Queen's Two Bodies* (London, 1977), p. 7 and *passim*; M. C. Bradbrook, *The Rise of the Common Player* (Cambridge, Eng., 1962), pp. 259–61. I am very grateful to Dr. Axton for commenting on this paper.

37. J. Hutchinson, *Notable Middle Templars* (London, 1902), pp. 29, 131, 146–47, 159–60; *Publications of the Harleian Society*, XXXII, 264–65; LXXXVI, pp. 204–05. W. Davenant, *The Triumphs of the Prince d'Amour* (1635[=1636]), p. 17, lists the masquers.

38. *CSPD*, 1629–1631, pp. 362, 450; 1631–1633, pp. 34, 62, 439.

39. Knowler, *Strafford Letters*, I, 516; F. S. Boas, ed., *The Diary of Thomas Crosfield* (London, 1935), p. 83.

40. Knowler, *Strafford Letters*, I, 506–07. White staves were carried by the chief officers of the Crown.

The Earls of Salisbury and Holland and the Lord Mayor all sent him tributes, and like Charles he dubbed knights, kept a favorite and received petitions, including one from his "oppressed subjects in the Temple" about the interference of his vice-gerents in the alterations of costume.[41] In reply, he issued a series of edicts "to be observed & put in execution by all his loveinge Subjects" to repress the "present disorders which wee have observed within this our Realme."[42] As befitted a Prince d'Amour,[43] these concerned amorous affairs, and outlawed Platonic love, contumacious mistresses, and poetasters. But he also pretended to be reforming the court and made fun of those who make extravagant compliments, and of women who use no "conversation but only of perfum'd outsides"; he ordered his own courtiers, ironically, to maintain the "due state of magnificence of our Royal Court" by imitating the overbearing and confidence of other courtiers "& especially in the Court of great Brittaine." Burlesquing the political devices of the real king, he issued these commands "with the advise of our Privy Counsell only, not callinge at the time (the hast of our occasions pressinge us) our right trusty and wellbeloved the States of our Parliament."[44] Garrard commented, "I hear of no other Design but all this is done to make them fit to give to the Prince Elector."[45] These "great preparations" cost the mock prince alone £2000, but he was rewarded with a knighthood; the society's steward had arrears of over £250 as late as 1639.[46]

At some point, the mock prince presided over the debate of "Quaerees of State worthy the consideration of his Highnes & privy Councell" which "by way of jeast or giring were propounded" to him.[47] These continued the pretense of kingly rule by arguing such issues as the

---

41. HMC 3 (Bath MSS), p. 192.

42. L. Hotson, *Shakespeare's Sonnets Dated and Other Essays* (London, 1949), p. 239.

43. The traditional title of the Middle Temple Christmas Prince (Finkelpearl, *John Marston*, p. 35).

44. Hotson, *Shakespeare's Sonnets Dated*, pp. 239–44.

45. Knowler, *Strafford Letters*, I, 507.

46. Knowler, *Strafford Letters*, I, 525; HMC 55 (Various MSS) vii, p. 411; Martin, *Minutes of Parliament*, p. 880. Gervase Holles, who took the part of Comptroller to the mock prince, later claimed that the occasion had cost the society £20,000, of which Francis Vivian had contributed £6,000 (G. Holles, *Memorials of the Holles Family 1493–1656*, ed. A. C. Wood [London, 1937], p. 236). The poulterer's bill alone was £232 (Martin, *Minutes of Parliament*, p. 856).

47. Boas, *Diary of Crosfield*, p. 83. This may have been the occasion on which "the English nobility were treated by the Prince d'Amour," and Gervase Holles had difficulty in keeping order in the crowded Temple Hall. "This happened about a fortnight before the masque" of 24 February (Holles, *Memorials of the Holles Family*, p. 236).

constitution of the prince's court and power, but at several points the questions seem to have been intended to reflect on real matters of state. Particularly, the Prince d'Amour heard several questions concerning his status as an "elect Prince," ruler in name only and soon to find himself deposed from government. The court asked

> Whether it derogate not from ye power of an elected Prince to hold his estate of Soveraignty for any lesse time then terme of life
>
> Whether the Peeres that Elect, or a Prince y^t accepts a limited dignity for lesser time committs the greatest error
>
> Whether a man y^t hath ever commanded as an absolute Prince can ever after his deposall, or surrender, conforme him selfe to ye obedience of a subject.

Clearly, these queries mirror the situation of the Prince Elector himself very closely. Similarly, the Prince d'Amour was asked about his right to levy money from his subjects, the validity of the bonds he entered into with them, and whether

> it is not more honourable for ye subjects of an elect Prince to replenish his coffers by a generall contribution in Parliament then by their denyall to constrain him to raise money upon privy-sealls upon Persons in Particular.[48]

In order to finance his personal government without resorting to Parliament, Charles was using such unpopular fiscal devices as forced loans and Ship Money. In their Christmas game the lawyers skated on very thin ice indeed.

February 24, 1636, must have been particularly spectacular for the Palsgrave if, as seems likely, he saw the lost play *The Proxy* at St. James' before proceeding to his welcome at the Middle Temple.[49] This day the French party at court triumphed; the Prince was accompanied by the Queen and her leading courtiers, who joined in the revels by arriving in disguise: "Thither came the Queen with three of her ladies disguised, all clad in the attire of Citizens, Mrs. *Basset,* the great Lace woman of *Cheapside* went foremost and led the Queen by the Hand. My Lords of *Holland* and *Goring* with *Henry Percy* and Mr. *Henry Jermyn* waited on them somewhat disguised also."[50] By putting off majesty, the Queen deferred

48. Boas, *Diary of Crosfield,* pp. 83–84.

49. Bentley, *JCS,* VII, 102.

50. Knowler, *Strafford Letters,* I, 525. According to Holles, the Middle Temple masque was performed three times on successive days, the second performance being attended by Henrietta

to the Palsgrave, who thus took precedence of her; but her fancy dress also indicates her participation in the lawyers' game and her sanction of its significance.

Before Davenant's *Triumphs of the Prince d'Amour* was danced, the Prince sent an ambassador to Charles Louis, "to whom this Entertainment was onely directed" (p. 1), who declared the support he had among the lawyers:

> *Thus whisper'd by my feares, I must impart*
> *For Ceremony now, what is his heart,*
> *Though with content of Truth, I may report*
> *You have a num'rous Faction in his Court.*   (p. 2)

These "*feares*" were that the Prince's "*free love*" (p. 3) was so great that the ambassador, in expressing it, would be suspected of having defected in allegiance:

> *his Message moves so low, I feare,*
> *What sounds like tender Courtship in your eare,*
> *His jealous Barons will dislike, and say,*
> *I am perverted to disloyaltie;*
> *Urge my Commission false, then taxe me for*
> *An easie Traytor, no Embassadour*   (p. 2)

But the declaration does not detract from the Prince's dignity since "'*tis his Love decrees it, not his Fate*" (p. 2), and "*This Pallace where, by sword, then law maintain'd / His few, but mighty Ancestors have raign'd, / Is consecrated yours*" (p. 2). This prologue is a gesture of active support, and the ensuing masque pursues the theme of proper and effective action. The first antimasque showed a group of "swaggering Souldiers, and of the cheaper quallity, such as are said to roare, not fight" and an "old over-growne debaush'd Cavalier," rotten with riots (p. 3). These antitypes were displaced by the true prototypes, soldiers in rich costumes "neere the old Roman shape" (p. 8), who danced before a shrine of Mars and were intended to recollect the heroic past of the Temple: "These by their appearance and demeanour were devis'd to imitate those heroique Knights *Templers,* to which the Pallace of the Prince d'Amour was anciently Dedicated" (p. 8). The Priests of Mars sing of their overwhelming victories. Fate fights for them; so terrible are they that their enemies,

---

Maria, Charles Louis, and Rupert, "wth many of nobility and gentry, and most of the great ladies and prime beauties in or neare the towne" (Holles, *Memorials of the Holles Family,* p. 236).

"*ordain'd for a defeat*" (p. 6), fly at once in disorder, the knights even being saved from the effort of killing their foes.

A similar contrast was then repeated between the same masquers, as "a Troope of noble Lovers" (p. 13), and an antimasque of fantastic and affected lovers. Again, the knights were urged to be active:

> *Breath then each others breath, and kisse*
> *Your soules to union:*
> *And whilst they shall injoy this blisse,*
> *Your bodies too are one.*   (p. 12)

Although far from the rarefied platonism which Henrietta Maria usually sponsored, these lines compliment the woman who had already appeared as the Queen or Patroness of love in court plays and masques; entering love's warfare, the masquers implicitly enrolled under Henrietta Maria's own banner. Finally, before the Temple of Apollo, the blessings of this wise god were besought for the masquers. Instructed to "*Expresse your [thankfulnesse] in active pleasure*," the masquers anticipated a great harvest:

> *So much to strengthen and increase,*
> *As growth and verdure nere should cease.*
> *Come you industrious slaves of plenty, bring*
> *All that is hop'd for in an Eastern Spring:*
> *Or all that Autumne yields, when she doth pay*
> *Those promis'd hopes where 'tis perpetuall day.*   (pp. 14–15)

At this point, wild men set a banquet before the Prince Elector, "which did declare them Labourers in a Fruitfull Soyle; and what they carried did demonstrate a Fruitfull Season" (p. 15). In valediction, the blessings of Mars, Venus, and Apollo were again invoked, that he might be "render'd so Divine, / 'Twill be no Sin t'implore your Influence" (p. 16). The masque was printed by order of the Master of the Revels to the Prince d'Amour (sig. A2); the Queen told his real counterpart "that she liked it very well."[51]

IV

In the following months, during which the King failed to take the decisive action urged by the lawyers, his nephew was given at least three more dramatic entertainments. Six days after the Middle Temple masque, Lady Hatton presented him with a "huge *Entertainment*" of "rare

---

51. Bentley, *JCS*, III, 219.

Fireworks, two Masks, and a great Supper."[52] Unfortunately, no masque for Lady Hatton has survived, but she may well have employed the dramatic skills of Henry Glapthorne whose father had been in her household as bailiff.[53] Glapthorne did write at least one piece for the Palsgrave, since his *Poems* (1639) includes a single speech for an "Entertainment to the *Prince Elector* at Mr. *Osbalston's*" (p. 2), an effusive address by a speaker affecting to be rapt in a "sacred furie" by "A power inferiour scarce to Majestie [which] / Claimes my Prerogative." Describing his joy at the Prince's arrival, he asserts the place is "consecrate by vow" to him and warns him to distinguish "true zeale" from "fain'd Devotion" (pp. 2–3). The only prominent "Mr. Osbalston" of the time was Lambert Osbaldeston, headmaster of Westminster School. A "turbulent Medler . . . and a Jugler in the Affairs of State," he was an associate of the rebel bishop of Lincoln, John Williams, and unguarded words about Archbishop Laud in 1634 earned him in 1639 a savage Star Chamber sentence (mutilation and a huge fine), which he evaded by going into hiding until the Long Parliament was called.[54] If he was Glapthorne's "Osbalston," the rest of the entertainment was likely to have been heavily weighted towards the Protestant cause.

Glapthorne's *Albertus Wallenstein* (1639; staged at the Globe c. 1635?) provides more definite evidence about his views on foreign affairs.[55] The play luridly dramatizes the downfall of Ferdinand's great general, the Palsgrave's archenemy, at the hands of mercenaries in 1634, depicting him as a monstrous compound of ambition and cruelty, a Protestant propagandistic version of the historical figure ("Alas my Lord, your lookes / Are discompos'd with rage, your fiery eyes / Rowle with the accustom'd motion, they had wont / To dart upon your enemies" [sig.F4]). The height of his cruelty is his rage at his son's baseness for daring to love a mere gentlewoman ("Hell and furies, / Durst any mortall foole, but mine owne issue, / Venter to brave my fury thus" [sig.G1]); he murders both in the name of family honor. Thereafter melancholy for a violent life torments him. He impulsively kills his innocent page, and his wife concludes his "hands are purpled so in innocent blood, / Teares cannot wash the tincture of" (sig.G4). His final moments bring madness; his followers are killed in their cups.

52. Knowler, *Strafford Letters,* I, 506; many other letter writers mentioned this entertainment.
53. Bentley, *JCS,* IV, 473.
54. J. Rushworth, *Historical Collections,* II (1680), 806, 817.
55. See M. C. Heinemann, *Puritanism and Theatre* (Cambridge, Eng., 1980), pp. 229–31.

Albertus Wallenstein is an old-fashioned popular play, often distantly echoing Shakespeare and Marlowe, yet it was not the only play of the 1630s interested in continental affairs. Dekker's *Gustavus King of Swethland* (= Sweden) must have been written by 1632. Heywood and Brome had a play called "The Life & Death of S^r. Martyn Skink. wth y^e warres of y^e Low Countries" which no doubt concerned the siege of "Skink's Sconce" (Schenck's Sconce) in 1635–1636; this was probably another Globe play.[56] Perhaps the otherwise unknown *Play of the Netherlands*[57] also belongs with this group. These are all lost plays but were probably of the backward-looking type represented by *Albertus Wallenstein*. It would seem that the public stages were freely presenting a vigorous and aggressively Protestant drama designed to appeal to (and foster) the expectations and taste of an audience whose attitudes—political and artistic—were still substantially Elizabethan.

Much more refined was Lodowick Carlell's *Arviragus and Philicia* (1639), a two-part romance that enjoyed some vogue at court in 1636. Charles Louis saw it at least once and wrote home to promise his mother a copy, saying it was "hugely liked of every one."[58] A combination of standard romantic motifs, it has no single known source; however, Carlell's anachronism in naming his heroes (Arviragus and his friend Guiderius, who have no real place in a Pictish/Saxon setting) would not seem to be merely accidental. The chroniclers and the *Mirror for Magistrates* remembered Guiderius and Arviragus as British princes who resisted the Roman power. Guiderius refused tribute to Rome and was treacherously killed by the Romans in battle, but his brother Arviragus continued his resistance so stoutly that they were forced to buy peace with the hand of the Emperor's daughter (an incident Carlell perhaps recalls in Part 1, Act 5). Arviragus later revolted again, and a second peace was made; he died highly respected by Rome and was mentioned by Juvenal.[59] In *The Faerie Queene*, Arviragus is the "dred of *Romanes*" (2.10.52) and an ancestor of Elizabeth; alternatively, Carlell might have seen the brothers fighting the Romans on stage in the revival of *Cymbeline*

56. Bentley, *JCS*, III, 250; G. Edmundson, *History of Holland* (Cambridge, Eng., 1922), pp. 148–49.

57. Bentley, *JCS*, V, 1382.

58. Bentley, *JCS*, III, 113–14.

59. Geoffrey of Monmouth, *The History of the Kings of Britain*, trans. L. Thorpe (Harmondsworth, 1966), pp. 119–23; R. Hollinshed, *The First Volume of the Chronicles of England* (1577), pp. 47–52; L. B. Campbell, ed., *Parts Added to "The Mirror for Magistrates"* (Cambridge, Eng., 1946), pp. 311–12.

at court on January 1, 1634.[60] Romans are absent from *Arviragus and Philicia,* but the use of these names is functionless except to introduce the timely theme of opposition to the Roman Emperor.

Carlell's Arviragus is a Pictish prince dispossessed by the Saxon king, and Part 1 follows his rebellion to regain his crown; matters are complicated by his love for Philicia, the king's daughter, and by Guiderius' defection to the Saxons. Part 1 ends with the king's death, but in Part 2 the Danish queen Cartandes intervenes at the head of an army, captures Arviragus and Guiderius, and falls in love with Arviragus. Thereafter interest centers on her rivalry with Philicia. In this farrago there is no explicit reference to contemporary affairs, but several motifs do have distinct correspondences with the play's immediate political context. Arviragus is another exiled prince laying claim to his dominions against a usurper, alternately by seeking the king's goodwill and by armed resistance. The king matches the popular notion of Ferdinand, an atheistical, crafty, and base-minded tyrant who manipulates even his own supporters. Plotting and counterplotting, he is the complete antithesis to the noble, conscientious, and popular Arviragus. Especially interesting is the scene (Part 1, 5.5) in which the king deceitfully tempts Arviragus to accept his kingdom and Philicia in a dishonorable yet easy settlement: "if you will now lay down Arms, and fairely sue to be receaved my son in law, her Dowery shall be th'Principality of Pictland, in spite of . . . all that shall oppose it" (sig.D10). Arviragus is loath "to receave as dowry with a Wife, what I possesse both by a right of blood and conquest"; the king admits to the audience that he intends to disregard the agreement once Arviragus is in his power. At a time when King Charles was considering the Emperor's offer to reinstate Charles Louis if he would make a full submission to him, this scene would be particularly pointed.[61] Similarly, in Part 2 the presentation of Cartandes as a queen whose great beauty attracts immediate, devoted love from her (noble) subjects strongly recalls the self-image created for Henrietta Maria in court theatricals. The power Cartandes wields over the foreign princes, and their dependence on her, mirror at a distance the actual situation of Henrietta Maria and her dashing nephews. Although later elaborated in a wholly amorous direction, this plot begins by fancifully transposing the configurations of court politics into a fictional setting.

---

60. Bentley, *JCS*, I, 97.
61. Gardiner, *History of England,* VIII, 101.

Possibly there is here a cryptic commentary on current affairs. When discussing politics privately the Earl of Leicester, a serious diplomat, employed a cipher of romantic names, including "Arviragus" (used for the King).[62] But the play is not primarily political in the way in which *Albertus Wallenstein,* for example, obviously is. It does not strike a coherent political attitude but strives for a kaleidoscopic effect which sometimes provides analogies with contemporary politics, only to relinquish them shortly after. Such courtly drama is inherently playful, gratifying its audience with a series of romantic, heroic roles which reflect in a general manner the relationships existing within the court without pursuing them too closely, being everywhere suggestive without actually being anywhere definite. It heightens the intrinsic theatricality of court life, realizing, and making light of, the court's pretensions. Here politics is more than just the setting for a romantic action, but not so much as the subject. Carlell flirts with politics as a fund of patterns which can be manipulated into an essentially frivolous whole.

On May 5, 1636, the Queen took Charles Louis to a much more serious play at the Blackfriars, *Alphonsus, Emperor of Germany* (1654).[63] A specially revived Elizabethan tragedy remotely founded on historical fact, this showed the struggle for control of the Empire between the "Spanish tyrant" Alphonsus (p. 7) and the true heroic Englishmen, Earl Richard and Prince Edward.[64] Alphonsus is a monstrous villain beside whom Carlell's Saxon king pales into insignificance. He determines, in Marlovian fashion, to be "King, and Tyrant if I please; / For what is Empire but a Tyrannie?" (p. 1) and is instructed by his "Master," Lorenzo di Toledo, the popular Machiavellian stereotype, in the arts of poison and treachery, for to "keep an usurped Crown, a Prince must swear, forswear, poyson, murder, and commit all kinds of villanies, provided it be cunningly kept from the eye of the world" (p. 5): "To be an outward Saint, an inward Devill; / These are the lectures that my Master reads" (p. 2). Alphonsus' ambition involves the murders of three Electors and various outrages on the family of a fourth. His malice is deliberate and inexplicable; he delights in "manifold deceits, / Endless devices, bottomless conclusions"

62. Collins, *Letters and Memorials,* II, 387–88, 506–07.

63. Bentley, *JCS,* V, 1285–88. My discussion of court politics has shown why Bowers and Starck's arguments (cited by Bentley) against this being the "Alfonso" performed at court are unfounded.

64. The historical Alfonso never actually went to Germany (N. Denholm-Young, *Richard of Cornwall* [Oxford, 1947], pp. 86–89, 113–17).

for their own sake (pp. 22–23), desiring not just the domination of Germany but its destruction. He uses his religion—Catholicism, naturally—politicly, faking a miracle in Act 4 and requesting the canonization, for purposes of propaganda, of the foolish and vicious bishop of Maintz, whom he has just killed (p. 51)! However, Providence intervenes to cause him and his henchman to undo themselves by a coincidence ("O Heavens! justly have you tane revenge"[p. 69]), and he dies, like Nashe's Esdras, repudiating his salvation. This is melodrama of the most obvious kind, but to an audience wishing for Protestant intervention on the Continent, it must have been compelling to see a Spanish emperor advance from crime to crime until Providence cut him down.

The true German interest is represented by the English nobles who are romantic heroes in the manner of the 1590s, full of truth, valor, and honor, their plainness contrasted chauvinistically with the peculiar characteristics of the Spanish and Germans. The foreigners recognize their intrinsic superiority: "A most ingenuous countenance hath this Prince, / Worthy to be the King of England's Heir" (p. 16). Alphonsus has sown division among the German Electors, but the Palsgrave of the Rhine resolutely supports the Englishmen and, vowing a "pure sincere innated zeal / Unto my Country" (p. 7), he fiercely opposes the Emperor: "My hate is more than words can testifie, / Slave as he is he murdered my Father" (p. 9). In Act 3 he himself falls victim to Alphonsus, but Providence ultimately elevates the English into leaders of a new, purified Germany, the Electors choosing Earl Richard, to England's lasting honor, as the next Emperor:

> Was never Englishman yet Emperour,
> Therefore to honour *England* and your self,
> Let private sorrow yield to publike Fame,
> That once an Englishman bore *Caesar's* name . . .
> Let them expect from English Caesar's hands
> Peace, and abundance of all earthly Joys.   (pp. 70–71)

When *Alphonsus* was revived in October 1630, Henrietta Maria was involved in the opposition to Charles' negotiations with Spain for the Treaty of Madrid; the 1636 revival coincided with the joint diplomatic missions to Vienna and Paris. *Alphonsus,* with its attack on the "viperous blood-thirsty Spaniard" (p. 9) and its depiction of aggressive English leadership in Germany, exactly matched the needs of the French lobby at a crucial juncture, and the King's Men thought the play still worth protecting against pirated publication in 1641.[65] It exemplifies the way in which the Caroline theater, that in retrospect appears uniformly "Cavalier," was in practice continually modified by its program of revivals and by the freedom of speech still attainable on the non-courtly stages. Moreover, the continued relevance in the 1630s of this old-fashioned play, with its Senecanisms, broad humor, patriotism, and morality-play elements, testifies to the deeply held conservatism of the "opposition" to the government of Charles I and to the very radical nature of nostalgia for the greatness of England's cultural and political past. *Alphonsus* evokes an Elizabethan England faithful to its Protestant obligations and ruled by popular noblemen—high-minded yet fundamentally ordinary men—of a type to which King Charles did not conform. The fiction upheld Richard and Edward as princes to be loved, understood, and trusted. Like Prince Hal, they did not yet differ from the men over whom they ruled. The implications for King Charles of a performance of *Alphonsus* in 1636 went wider than the single issue of peace or war.

V

Through the summer, the Palsgrave's affairs dragged on fruitlessly as the anticipated alliances fell through. At Prague, Arundel saw a masque depicting Germany under Bellona's fury revived by the announcement that King Charles' ambassador was bringing Peace from England, whither she had fled; nevertheless his embassy made no headway whatever.[66] From England, Charles Louis reported "a perpetual hunting and changing of lodgings."[67] The court was visiting Oxford, where Laud had prepared a lavish welcome, including three plays spectacularly mounted with scenery. Several of the Prince's entourage took degrees,[68] but the festivities were intended principally in compliment to the King.

However, a fortnight later the returning court saw *The King and Queen's Entertainment at Richmond* (Oxford, 1636), danced by the Crown Prince. This was ordered by the Queen and probably arranged by her Chamberlain, the Earl of Dorset, whose children took part.[69] It was dedicated to the Queen and addressed her as principal spectator, the King being rather pointedly ignored.

---

65. Bentley, *JCS*, V, 1286; *CSPV*, 1632–1636, p. 557; Gardiner, *History of England*, VII, 176.
66. Springell, *Connoisseur and Diplomat*, pp. 74–75.
67. G. Bromley, *A Collection of Royal Letters* (1787), p. 81.
68. A. a Wood, *Fasti Oxonienses*, ed. P. Bliss (1815), pp. 490–96.
69. Bentley, *JCS*, V, 1359.

Its introduction is an act of homage to the Queen by a group of rustics, a country dance and a pastoral love-duet. Dorset's son directs the rustics to Henrietta Maria as to the platonic mistress of all her subjects' hearts:

> Dost thou not see a light outshine the rest,
> Two starrs that sparkle in a milky way,
> Dimming the shine of *Ariadnes* crowne,
> Or *Berenices* haire, and so serene,
> Their influence speak peace unto a kingdome   (p. 8)

However, this is not intended to be empty flattery. The rustics are dramatized as "real" countrymen, who bring comically prosaic tributes (a melon and a cabbage), make mistakes, and fail to maintain the decorum of the scene. Hence their behavior is unself-conscious and sincere, their homage an expression of their actual love. There are suggestions here of more symbolic overtones: of the "country" as a real entity (the people over whom Charles does indeed rule) or as a political unit representing a different set of interests from the "court" which at present looks to the Queen for leadership. In a rustic masque at Richmond, Henrietta Maria receives the unfeigned love of her devoted countrymen and subjects.

The Prince appeared as Britomart, seated on an *"arch Triumphant"* in a military camp with his *"Knights Adventurers"* dressed for war (p. 26). Spenser had created Britomart as the warrior maiden, progenitor and prototype of Queen Elizabeth, epitomizing the valor of the native race and fulfilling the purposes of the national destiny. In *The Faerie Queene* III. iii, Merlin narrates the history of her progeny as a long defense of the purity of the race and of holy church; the British are driven into Wales, whence they are finally restored to glorious rule in the mighty Tudor dynasty. Accordingly, the Richmond entertainment is a strongly archaeologizing piece. The antimasque has soldiers dressed *"after the old British fashion"* and are accompanied by a Druid (p. 17). The masquers, like Spenser's Redcrosse knight, have dwarf squires and are heralded by a Post who quotes a line from *The Faerie Queene* and demands to see the King and Queen in Welsh, *"which they say is the old British language."* His amazement that *"no body understands me, never a true Britaine amongst you"* is a clear rebuke to a court declining from the Elizabethan ideal (p. 23).

Like *The Triumphs of the Prince d'Amour,* this masque contrasts reprehensible and admirable soldiers. The Captain of the antimasque is a type of the soldier who only gapes for prey, his army ragged and savage:

> O thou God of warre,
> Great father *Mars,* the first Progenitor
> Of BRITOMART, inspire him with a courage
> That may extend his Armes, as farre as is
> Or earth, or sea, that he may think this kingdome
>   As *Alexander* did the worlds, too streight to breath in.
> Strike up a warlike sound, & you my Souldiers
> Come forth, and thinke of nothing but fresh booty   (p. 21)

The Druid, however, prays for war and peace to be balanced, that "this disordered route" may "learne some measure" (p. 21). In the ensuing song, the priests *"attribute the taming of the Souldiers fiercenesse to the* Queenes *presence"* (p. 22), and in a dance they *"lay downe their weapons at the* Queenes *feete,"* their wildness moderated into *"measure, and proportion"* (pp. 22–23). Before the main masque, the Welsh Post introduces a Spanish ambassador who is all absurd formality and whom he leaves "to your laughter" (p. 25); the Spaniard is then mocked in a series of burlesque dances. Finally, Britomart and the true knights appear and offer their devices to the Queen, another act of submission to her; the masque concludes with a song of lament for her imminent departure from Richmond: *"O then for pitty hast you to come hither / To keepe these parts alive, which else must wither"* (p. 30).

Thus the Queen was celebrated here as the patron of responsible and ordered soldiery, not reckless aggression. In fact, the Druid linked the violence of the unrestrained soldiers with the characteristics of Charles' government. The Captain offers to make the Prince secure by force:

> Let him advize with us, & we will shew him
> A neerer way how to be absolute;
> 'Tis but reserving a convenient Guard,
> Some certaine thousands of us 'bout his person
> The thing is done, give us but pay enough
> Weele warrant him, he shall do what he list.
>   *Druid.* This counsell fits a Souldier to give,
> Not him to take, if he heare us, weele tell him,
> A certaine truth, that he which rules ore slaves
> Is not so great as he that's king of freemen:
> O to command the wils of subjects, rather
> Then bodies, is an Empire truely sacred,
> And the next way to rule in heaven it selfe!   (p. 19)

The distinction drawn here, between a tyrant, ruling by compulsion, and a loving king, ruling by the free consent of his subjects, was one very familiar to the critics of Charles' absolutism. The puritan Simonds

D'Ewes, for example, asked, "What shall freemen differ from the ancient bondsmen and villains of England, if their estates be subject to arbitrary taxes, tillages and impositions?"[70] The Druid's speech, a "certaine truth," has a forcefulness to it which invites the listener almost to separate it out as a direct statement of advice or warning to the King. It is a measure of the willingness of the Queen, in her intrigues, to involve herself and the drama she sponsored with those areas of feeling which we normally term "puritan."

VI

The following month the Palsgrave described himself as "as far from his expectations as ever."[71] Nevertheless, the King had begun negotiating with France, and in January 1637 this developed into a scheme "that the Prince Elector shall have a good fleet fitted and paid, to concur with the whole league in any design for the common good."[72] The Palsgrave issued a *Manifest* and a *Protestation* setting out his wrongs, subscriptions were opened, and newsletters reported "a great preparation" in progress.[73] The prospect of a naval war against Spain was highly exciting to English Protestantism which had long desired such a project, and the puritan Earls of Essex and Warwick were among those widely known to have asked for captaincies.[74] Roe explained that the fleet would proceed to the West Indies, "so as to get means for future action, and to trouble the common enemy that he may be forced to give an honest peace."[75] The King, however, had no intention of allowing operations in the European sphere. The beauty of the scheme was that fighting would be sufficiently remote to avoid any more extensive commitment. George Garrard was cautious: "Anything they would do to get the *Palatinate* again; but I do not know whether this be the Way."[76]

Of course the scheme collapsed, but the plan for Prince Rupert to conquer Madagascar should be interpreted in relation to these designs. This idea was first advanced in 1636; Princess Elizabeth commented skeptically, "As for Rupert's romance of Madagascar, it sounds like one

70. *Autobiography*, II, 132.
71. *CSPD, 1636–1637*, p. 172.
72. *CSPD, 1636–1637*, pp. 162, 400; Gardiner, *History of England*, VIII, 204.
73. *Letters and Papers of the Verney Family*, ed. J. Bruce (London, 1853), p. 188.
74. Knowler, *Strafford Letters*, II, 56.
75. *CSPD, 1636–1637*, p. 504.
76. Knowler, *Strafford Letters*, II, 56.

of Don Quixote's conquests."[77] Nonetheless, it was taken up seriously by Arundel who, with the Earl of Holland, was still pressing Charles for a privateering campaign against Spain in June 1637; James Howell also linked it with other schemes to annoy Spain at sea.[78] Arundel was still organizing colonial plans for Madagascar as late as 1639.[79]

All that finally survived from the project was Davenant's courtly-heroic poem *Madagascar*, dedicated to Prince Rupert and prophesying his conquest of the island through the miraculous power of British kingship:

> So well these Ships could rule, where ev'ry Saile
> The subdu'd Winds court with so mild a gale,
> As if the spacious Navy lay *adrift*;
> Sayles swell'd to make them comely more than swift:
> And then I spi'd (as cause of this command)
> Thy mighty Uncles Trident in thy hand;
> By which mysterious figure I did call
> Thee chiefe, and universall Admirall!   (ll. 33–40)[80]

On Madagascar, Rupert does battle with a force of European interlopers, whom A. M. Gibbs suggests may be intended for Portuguese adventurers.[81] However, Davenant describes them as "ambitious Wanderers" who seek universal domination and proudly term the sun their *"Surveyor-Generall"* (ll. 106, 118), language which closely recalls the saying, *"The Sunne never sets in the Spanish Dominions, but ever shines, upon one part, or other of them,"* recorded by Bacon as a common aphorism.[82] Spain's imperial ambitions were widely suspected and feared, by none more so than England's puritans; Thomas Scott, the fierce opponent of the Spanish match, had an entire pamphlet on *The Spaniard's Perpetual Designs to an Universal Monarchy* (1624).[83] Davenant's Spaniards are opposed by two English champions, later identified as Endimion Porter and a Queen's courtier, Henry Jermyn. They are successors of that Elizabethan Protestant hero, Sir Philip Sidney:

> Of these the God-like *Sidney* was a Type,
> Whose fame still growes, and yet is ever ripe . . .

77. *CSPD*, 1636–1637, p. 559.

78. *Documents Relating to the Proceedings against William Prynne*, ed. S. R. Gardiner (London, 1877), p. 85; J. Howell, *Epistolae Ho-Elianae*, ed. J. Jacobs, II (London, 1892), p. 320.

79. Hervey, *The Life . . . of Arundel*, p. 508.

80. W. Davenant, *The Shorter Poems and Songs*, ed. A. M. Gibbs (Oxford, 1972), pp. 10–21.

81. Davenant, *The Shorter Poems and Songs*, p. 346.

82. F. Bacon, *Certain Miscellany Works* (1629), p. 102.

83. In any case, Portugal was under Spanish rule until 1640.

So whilst our judgement keepes unmix'd and pure,
Our *Sidney's* full-growne Fame will still endure:
Sidney, like whom these Champions strive to grace
The silenc'd remnants of poore *Orpheus* race.   (ll. 161–62, 168–71)

As in the victories of the Middle Temple masquers, the valiant English overcome their cowardly and faithless foes almost effortlessly:

straight (me thought) their perish'd Bodies lay
To soyle the Ground they conquer'd yesterday . . .
Thy selfe I saw, quite tir'd with victorie;
As weary growne to kill, as they to die:
Whilst some at least thy mercy did enjoy
'Cause 'twas lesse paines to pardon than destroy   (ll. 261–62, 321–24)

Rupert is left master of the isle and establishes a perfect rule over the natives, founded on devotion, not servitude ("Each then thou conquerst must a lover be, / The worst estate of their captivitie" [ll. 61–62; cf. ll. 328–30]). Davenant is left to hymn Madagascar's advantages, both as a paradise of wealth and fertility and as a strategic base:

An *Isle,* so seated for predominance,
Where Navall strength its power can so advance,
That it may tribute take, of what the East
Shall ever send in Traffique to the West.   (ll. 333–36)

His final hope is that Rupert may prove "the Wonder and discourse of Fame" (l. 438).

VII

The naval war, however, never materialized. The King became preoccupied by internal problems, the Queen fell increasingly under the influence of the Catholic faction at court, and the Princes returned to the Continent to pursue their fortunes by land. Davenant's poem was the last shot in the propaganda battle; but it significantly modifies our understanding of the literature of the Caroline court that such a campaign could have been waged at all. There was an important element within Whitehall that was seriously disillusioned with Charles' policies and which, in the confused conditions created by the Queen's political dabbling, was prepared to put pressure on the King to initiate policies favored by men of "country" or "puritan" leanings. One instrument of this pressure was the drama. It was not the "official" drama of masques and pastorals, but drama that occurred on the fringes of the court—at the Prince's or noblemen's residences, at the Inns of Court, at specially chartered performances at the Blackfriars. In these more relaxed environments, points of view could be expressed which are not normally associated with the Caroline court theater.[84]

This drama performed a decentralizing function, countering the imperialistic, standardizing tendencies of the culture which Charles himself sponsored. Its artistic retrospection, its continual use of Elizabethan literature as a point of departure or reference, matches its political retrospection. To his puritan critics, Charles had neglected those popular and godly forms of government which Elizabeth was believed to have established; ominously for him, plays like *Alphonsus* and *Albertus Wallenstein* would appeal to men who wished to overthrow the present in the name of the past. In these instances the Caroline stage was cooperating with those currents of thought and feeling which would eventually flow into the puritan "opposition" to Charles, rather than into the "Cavalier" clique. It is wrong to limit our conception of the Caroline theater to the "official" drama of Charles and the narrow world of the court; the mainstream was much broader, much more vigorous, and still highly conscious of its Elizabethan roots.

84. The entertainments for the Palsgrave were only one strand of the drama's involvement in the complicated political maneuvering around Henrietta Maria at the court in these years. I shall be considering some further aspects of this political theatre in a forthcoming volume, *Theatre and Crisis 1632–1642* (Cambridge, Eng., 1984).

85. Cf. A. Barton, "*The New Inn* and the Problem of Jonson's Late Style," *English Literary Renaissance* 9 (1979), 395–418 (406, 417–18) and Heinemann, *Puritanism and Theatre*, pp. 16–17, 102–04.

The Politics of Allusion: The Gentry and Shirley's The Triumph of Peace

LAWRENCE VENUTI

OPICAL allusions can be said to anchor a literary text in history, but they soon prove to be an unsteady mooring once we begin to investigate the textual operation by which they are transformed. References to historical figures and events ultimately put into question the naive assumption that literature can be a mirror reflection of reality; they rather show us that "the text takes as its object, not the real, but certain significations by which the real lives itself—significations which are themselves the product of its partial abolition."[1] These "significations" are social representations, values and beliefs that serve the interests of a particular class; they "abolish" the real because they are an ideological refraction of it. Since by definition topical allusions never announce their presence, they can easily lead us to think that the text gives us a knowledge of history which is free of ideologial mediation. The fact is, however, that the text so assimilates historical references as to transform them into an ideological signification of reality. A consideration of topical allusions can thus disclose a text's politics, its relation to a particular ideology, finally enabling us to arrive at a penetrating articulation of its place in history. For the literary historian, the crucial task is not only the accurate identification of such allusions, but a careful examination of how and to what end they are exploited.

When we approach the Stuart masque from this perspective, the matter grows more complicated. Critics have long regarded the masque

---

1. Terry Eagleton, *Criticism and Ideology* (London, 1976), p. 72. See also P. N. Medvedev / M. M. Bakhtin, *The Formal Method of Literary Scholarship: A Critical Introduction to Sociological Poetics*, trans. Albert J. Wehrle (Baltimore and London, 1978), pp. 21-23; Louis Althusser, "A Letter on Art in Reply to André Daspre," in *Lenin and Philosophy and Other Essays*, trans. Ben Brewster (London and New York, 1971), pp. 221-27; and Thomas E. Lewis, "Notes toward a Theory of the Referent," *PMLA* 94 (1979), 459-75.

as a politically significant genre, and there have already been important efforts to identify historical references in specific masques.[2] Indeed, following Jonson's suggestive mention of "present occasions" in the preface to *Hymenaei* (1606), Leah Sinanoglou Marcus has found that "the court masque was perhaps the most inherently topical of all seventeenth-century art forms. Masques were shaped by contemporary events and intended, in turn, to give shape to those events."[3] Without meaning to diminish the considerable value of this discovery, I would suggest that we revise our understanding of Jonson's remark: it is necessary to recognize that "present occasions" is an imprecise blanket term that may conceal more than it reveals; we can better illuminate the political dimension of court entertainments by distinguishing between true and proper occasions and topical allusions.[4] The Stuart masque is *occasional* in that it was designed to act as a festive celebration, usually of the Christmas season or an aristocratic wedding. But often it also *alludes* to royal policies and proclamations, to political theories and issues, to historical developments that actually lay beyond the immediate reason for its creation. This distinction is worth making because it can expose the different ideological determinants that operate on a given masque. In the case of the occasion, we can always discern the effects of the feudal ideology of degree, which subordinates the lower classes in English society by reserving for royalty and aristocracy the effusive praise of the songs and speeches and even the privilege of attending the performance. In the case of the topical allusion, more specific ideologies may be at work, and these may transform historical facts so as to legitimize a certain royal policy or, alternatively, question it and advocate the competing position of the dominated classes. Both the occasion and the topical allusion demon-

2. The seminal studies are Stephen Orgel, *The Jonsonian Masque* (Cambridge, Mass., 1965); Orgel and Roy Strong, *Inigo Jones: The Theater of the Stuart Court*, 2 vols. (Berkeley, 1973); Orgel, *The Illusion of Power* (Berkeley, 1975); and three articles by Leah Sinanoglou Marcus, "'Present Occasions' and the Shaping of Ben Jonson's Masques," *ELH* 45 (1978), 201-25, "The Occasion of Ben Jonson's *Pleasure Reconciled to Virtue*," *Studies in English Literature 1500–1900* 19 (1979), 271-93, and "Masquing Occasions and Masque Structure," *Research Opportunities in Renaissance Drama* 24 (1981), 7-16. Rhodes Dunlap has identified the many topical allusions in Carew's *Coelum Britannicum* (1634) in his edition of *The Poems of Thomas Carew* (Oxford, 1949).

3. Marcus, "'Present Occasions' and the Shaping of Ben Jonson's Masques," p. 201. Jonson's remark about court masques is that "though their voice be taught to sound to present occasions, their sense or doth or should always lay hold on more removed mysteries" (*Ben Jonson: The Complete Masques*, ed. Stephen Orgel [New Haven, Conn., 1969], p. 76).

4. Arthur Marotti has made a similar warning against relying too heavily on seventeenth-century critical concepts in his review of Richard S. Peterson's *Imitation and Praise in the Poems of Ben Jonson* (New Haven, Conn., 1981). See *Renaissance Quarterly* 35 (1982), 526-28.

strate that the masque has the capacity to maintain the feudal social hierarchy and justify the king's hegemony, but they do so in quite different ways. Clearly, it is the study of allusions, as Professor Marcus' work has persuasively shown, that will allow us to grasp the precise political function of a masque.

With this in mind, I want to examine a rather ingenious topical allusion in James Shirley's text for *The Triumph of Peace*. Thanks to the memoirs of Bulstrode Whitelocke, a lawyer who sat on the planning committee for the production, we have a reliable account of the occasion: performed during February of 1634, the masque was one of those court celebrations that traditionally took place during the Christmas season, but it was also intended to express the affectionate loyalty of the Inns of Court to the King and Queen and thereby voice their disagreement with the attack on theater recently published by their colleague William Prynne.[5] The masque contains several topical allusions, one of which, a glance at Caroline monopolies, has already received some attention.[6] My discussion will focus on another allusion to contemporary issues which shapes the entire antimasque: the interactions among the characters, the changes in scenery and the various dances all comprise a reference to Charles's prohibition of the gentry's residence in London.[7]

I

During the late sixteenth and early seventeenth centuries, members of the landowning classes increasingly visited the capital city for both business and pleasure. In their younger days many of them had attended one of the Inns of Court to acquire that basic knowledge of the law which was necessary to manage their estates and serve their counties as local officials or MPs. Yet since it was not unusual for them to be mired in some sort of litigation against tenants or neighbors, they occasionally returned to the city to be near the courts at Westminster where they made their depositions and inquired about the progress of their suits. As the center of commercial activity in England, London also offered the gentry the opportunity to borrow money from merchants, invest in

5. Bulstrode Whitelocke, *Memorials of the English Affairs* (London, 1682), p. 18.

6. Orgel and Strong, *Inigo Jones*, I, pp. 64-65.

7. James I was also disturbed by this development, and his criticisms of it in a speech delivered in Star Chamber became a source for Jonson's masque *The Vision of Delight* (1617). See Marcus, "'Present Occasions' and the Shaping of Ben Jonson's Masques," pp. 204-13.

trading companies and industrial monopolies, sell the products from their farms and procure those imported luxuries that did not reach the remote markets in their counties.[8] It was in the city, furthermore, that they could find a remedy for any dissatisfaction they may have felt with the routine and solitude of country life. By residing in London for much of the winter or spring, the country gentleman and his wife might indulge in the latest crazes from the Continent, see new plays and masques, enjoy the company of many friends and move in the most exclusive aristocratic circles. Perhaps the greatest attraction of the city was the dazzling range of things to do, for there was something to please every taste. Whether the visitor from the provinces was interested in learned sermons or dicing, news of foreign wars or court scandals, an audience with an ambassador or a frolic with a prostitute, he would not be disappointed.[9]

Under James I, the gentry's visits to the capital had begun to occur with some regularity, and by Charles's accession, it must have appeared that many were spending a great part of the year in London or even living there permanently. The early Stuart kings viewed this trend as a two-fold threat: it could weaken the ascendancy of the feudal ideology, which justified and reproduced the established social order, and ultimately affect their political power by limiting their control over local affairs. They believed that the gentry's residence in London inevitably meant a decay of rural hospitality and a loss of esteem for that medieval ideal of generosity (*largesse*), one of the "virtues" which set the gentleman above the commoner in the social hierarchy.[10] And they were concerned that this could have ominous effects: when gentlemen neglected housekeeping in the country and spent their wealth elsewhere, their customary relief of the poor languished, able workers went unemployed, and there might be a rise in crime as well as riots, if not rebellion. Similarly, the kings feared that when this landed wealth was consumed in prodigal spending on city pleasures, the result might be an increase in social

8. F. J. Fisher, "The Development of London as a Center of Conspicuous Consumption in the Sixteenth and Seventeenth Centuries," in *Essays in Economic History*, ed. E. M. Carus-Wilson (New York, 1962), II, pp. 197-207; Lawrence Stone, *The Crisis of the Aristocracy 1558-1641* (Oxford, 1965), pp. 386-87; Philip Lee Ralph, *Sir Humphrey Mildmay: Royalist Gentleman* (New Brunswick, N.J., 1947), pp. 17, 29, 53-57.

9. Stone, pp. 387-92; Ralph, pp. 25-26, 41, 44, 46-52.

10. Stone, pp. 41-44; Marc Bloch, *Feudal Society*, trans. L. A. Manyon (Chicago, 1961), p. 311; Ruth Kelso, *The Doctrine of the English Gentleman in the Sixteenth Century* (Urbana, Ill., 1929), pp. 88-91; L. A. Clarkson, *The Pre-Industrial Economy of England 1500-1750* (London, 1971), pp. 228-32.

mobility which would upset the traditional class structure.[11] Since the gentry were the backbone of local government, their frequent absences could also have a damaging effect on legal and political practice. Landowning gentlemen were the king's administrative officials in the country: it was they who were appointed directly by the king to fill such unpaid offices as justice of the peace and high sheriff.[12] Justices of the peace, for example, in addition to their essential role in law enforcement, "were responsible for providing poor relief, some pensions, trade regulations, food supplies, regulation of ale-houses and the collection of local taxes."[13] Anything that interfered with such duties would naturally hinder the implementation of royal policy.

In 1631, after two years of bad harvests had impoverished rural areas and threatened to cause uprisings, Charles and his Privy Council made an effort to increase the administrative efficiency of local government by issuing the Book of Orders, "for the better administration of justice and more perfect information of His Majesty, how and by whom the laws and statutes tending to the relief of the poor, the well-ordering and training up of youth in trades, and the reformation of disorders and disordered persons are executed throughout the kingdom."[14] The Book's directives apparently improved the operation and supervision of local government, at least in the beginning,[15] and on 20 June 1632 it was reinforced by a proclamation that commanded the landowning classes to maintain their country residences. The opening paragraph of the proclamation lists the adverse consequences which the King and his advisers feared would result from the gentry's extended visits to London; since the passage bears a striking resemblance to the antimasque of *The Triumph of Peace*, it is worth quoting in full:

11. Stone, pp. 392-93, 397-98; Christopher Hill, *The Century of Revolution 1603-1714* (New York, 1966), pp. 26-28.

12. Sidney and Beatrice Webb, *English Local Government* (London, 1906), I, pp. 287, 294; L. M. Hill, "County Government in Caroline England 1625-40," in *The Origins of the English Civil War*, ed. Conrad Russell (London, 1973), pp. 66-90.

13. L. M. Hill, p. 70.

14. "The Book of Orders, 5 January 1631," rpt. in *The Stuart Constitution 1603-1688: Documents and Commentary*, ed. J. P. Kenyon (Cambridge, 1966), p. 497.

15. Thomas G. Barnes, *Somerset 1625-1640: A County's Government during the "Personal Rule"* (Cambridge, Mass., 1961), pp. 196-202; L. M. Hill, pp. 77-83; Anthony Fletcher, *A County Community in Peace and War: Sussex 1600-1660* (London, 1975), pp. 224-26; Peter Clark, *English Provincial Society from the Reformation to the Revolution: Religion, Politics and Society in Kent 1500-1640* (Hassocks, Eng., 1977), pp. 350-53; Barry Coward, *The Stuart Age: A History of England 1603-1714* (London, 1980), pp. 145-46.

The Kings Most Excellent Majesty hath observed, That of late yeares a great number of the Nobility and Gentry, and abler sort of his People with their Families have resorted to the Citties of *London* and *Westminster*, and places adjoyning, and there made their Residence more then in former tymes, contrary to the ancient usage of the *English* Nation, which hath occasioned divers inconveniences, for where, by their Residence and Abiding in the severall Countries whence their Meanes ariseth, they served the King in severall places, according to their degrees and ranks in ayde of the Government; whereby their Housekeeping in those parts, the Realme was defended, and the meaner sort of People were guided, directed and relieved: but by their Residence in the said Citties and Parts adjoyning, they have not imployment but live without doing any Service to his *Majesty* or his People, a great part of their Money and Substance is drawn from the severall Countries whence it ariseth, and is spent in the Citty in excess of Apparell provided from forreigne parts, to the enrichment of other Nations and unnecessary consumption of a great part of the Treasure of this Realme, and in other vain Delights and Expences, even to the wasting of their Estates, which is not issued into the parts from whence it ariseth, nor are the People of them relieved therewith or by their Hospitality, nor yet set on work, as they might and would be, were it not for the absence of the principall Men out of their Countries, and the excessive use of forraigne Commodities; by this occasion also, and of the great Numbers of loose and idle People, that follow them and Live in and about the said Citties, the disorder there groweth so great and the Delinquents become so numerous, as those places are not easily governed by the ordinary Magistrates, as in former tymes; and the said Citties are not onely at excessive charge in relieving a great number of those idle and loose People, that growe to beggery and become diseased and infirm, but also are made more subject to Contagion and Infection; and the prizes of all kinds of Victualls, both in the said Citties are served, are exceedingly encreased, the poorer sort are unrelieved, and not guided or governed as they might be, in case those Persons of Quality and Respect resided among them.[16]

This proclamation is quite similar to those that James had repeatedly issued during his reign; in 1626, Charles himself had tried the same means, but to little effect. To insure the success of his latest effort, he ordered that any country gentleman in London who did not hold a court office and did not have legal business was to be prosecuted in Star Chamber, and in November of 1632, the Attorney General brought suits against more than two hundred offenders.[17]

The extensive instructions of the Book of Orders and the stringent enforcement of the proclamation suggest that they were intended to do much more than prevent riots in rural areas. In fact, the economic crisis

16. "A Proclamation Commaunding the Gentry to keep their Residence at their Mansions in the Country, and forbidding them to make their Habitations in *London* and places adjoining," rpt. in *Foedera, conventiones, literae et cuiuscunque generis acta publica*, ed. Thomas Rymer and Robert Sanderson (1704-32), XIX, 374.

17. Stone, p. 398.

that prompted these measures also offered Charles an excuse to consolidate his political power and strengthen the autocracy he had instituted with his dissolution of Parliament in 1629. Both the Book and the proclamation were attempts to bring about a radical reform of local government and counteract the perennial danger that county officials would discharge their duties as they themselves thought best, independent of the central administration and perhaps in opposition to royal policy.[18] Charles's interventions in local affairs can be regarded as political practice designed to realize his absolutist aspirations or, more specifically, the paternalistic ideology of Divine Right kingship.[19] This becomes more evident when we recognize that his proclamation against the gentry's residence in London seems to have exaggerated the actual situation. The local historian Alan Everitt has pointed out that whereas the nobility may have made a habit of visiting the city, the gentry were much more closely tied to their estates:

In the counties which I have studied most of the peers and a few of the baronets frequented the metropolis fairly regularly for part of the year. The great majority of the knights and virtually all the squires, on the other hand, rarely if ever visited it, except to attend an occasional lawsuit (not a circumstance likely to endear it to them), and virtually never possessed a town house at this date. As is well known there were many proclamations during the early seventeenth century banishing the gentry from London back to their native shires. But what these proclamations do not reveal is that in a large county, such as Suffolk or Kent, there might be 750–1,000 gentry, and that at least three-quarters of them were small parochial squires with an average income of less than £300 a year. Such families could obviously never have afforded a metropolitan establishment. They were essentially provincials, though not necessarily by any means the boozy squires of Whiggish legend.[20]

Everitt's remarks implicitly contain a warning that Marx made long ago in *The German Ideology*: we should not be uncritical in our acceptance of the dominant class's construction of contemporary events.[21] Since only a

18. Christopher Hill, pp. 71–72; *The Stuart Constitution*, p. 492; Fletcher, p. 224.

19. J. T. Cliffe, *The Yorkshire Gentry from the Reformation to the Civil War* (London, 1969), pp. 295–96; Stone, *The Causes of the English Revolution 1529–1642* (New York, 1972), p. 126; J. S. Morrill, *Chesire 1630–1660: County Government and Society during the English Revolution* (Oxford, 1974), p. 26.

20. Alan Everitt, *Change in the Provinces: The Seventeenth Century*, Leicester University Department of English Local History Occasional Papers, Second Series, No. 1 (Leicester, Eng., 1969), pp. 17–18. See also C. W. Chalkin, *Seventeenth-Century Kent* (London, 1961), p. 203; Barnes, p. 28; and Everitt, "The County Community," in *The English Revolution 1600–1660*, ed. E. W. Ives (London, 1968), pp. 48–63.

21. In *The German Ideology* Marx observes: "If now in considering the course of history we detach the ideas of the ruling class from the ruling class itself and attribute to them an independent existence, if we confine ourselves to saying that these or those ideas were dominant at a given

rather small proportion of the gentry travelled to London with any regularity, it appears unlikely that the administrative machinery of the provinces was markedly impaired at the beginning of the 1630s; on the contrary, the Book of Orders reinvigorated county government at this time and enabled a more strict supervision of local affairs. This clearly implies that Charles's proclamation is an alarmist document primarily designed to achieve a political goal: it constitutes a transformation of a real social trend into a "serious problem" that justifies royal intervention and therefore upholds the King's dominance in English society. The proclamation, like the Book of Orders, was inspired by the fear that the King was losing control over local government and by the ideological conviction that his power should be absolute and "thorough." In the end, however, the paternalism of Charles's policies seems to have produced the opposite result: it was instrumental in alienating those country gentlemen whose support he desperately needed in his constitutional struggle with the Long Parliament in 1640.[22]

II

Shirley's antimasque consists of the interactions of several allegorical characters, one of whom, Fancy, presents a number of dances and changes of scenery. The topical nature of this activity becomes apparent as soon as the characters meet and introduce themselves to one another in the urban setting of the first scene, "a large street with sumptuous palaces, lodges, porticos, and other noble pieces of architecture, with pleasant trees and grounds [which] opens itself into a spacious place, adorned with public and private buildings seen afar off" (p. 263).[23]

---

time, without bothering ourselves about the conditions of production and the producers of these ideas, if we thus ignore the individuals and world conditions which are the source of the ideas, we can say, for instance, that during the time that the aristocracy was dominant, the concepts honor, loyalty, etc., were dominant, during the dominance of the bourgeoisie the concepts freedom, equality, etc. The ruling class itself on the whole imagines this to be so" (*The Marx-Engels Reader*, ed. Robert C. Tucker, 2nd ed. [New York, 1978], p. 173).

22. Fisher, p. 207; Christopher Hill, p. 72; Stone, *The Causes of the English Revolution*, p. 124; Morrill, pp. 26-30; Coward, p. 146. Charles's proclamation may have also been intended to subdue the London merchants and financiers who opposed his fiscal expedients by driving away their most wealthy clients, the nobility and gentry. For the business community's growing opposition to the royal government, see Robert Ashton, *The City and the Court 1603-1643* (Cambridge, 1979).

23. All quotations of *The Triumph of Peace* follow *The Dramatic Works and Poems of James Shirley*, ed. William Gifford and Alexander Dyce (1833; rpt. New York, 1966), VI, 253-85. Page numbers will be given in the text.

Opinion, the first antimasquer we see, is a country gentleman visiting London with his wife Novelty and their daughter Admiration. It is Novelty who reveals that they belong to the gentry: she grows infuriated when Opinion calls her his wife, and her retort is, "they can but call / Us so i'th'country" (p. 264). Opinion's costume is another indication of his social status: as we might expect of a gentleman who hails from the country, he does not appear in the latest London styles. In contrast to Confidence, the fashionable man-about-town who wears "a slashed doublet parti-colored [and] a broad-brimmed hat, tied up on one side, banded with a feather," Opinion is dressed "in an old fashioned doublet of black velvet, and trunk hose, a short cloak of the same with an antique cape, a black velvet cap pinched up, with a white fall, and a staff in his hand" (p. 257).[24] The antimasque also contains allusions to some of the entertainments the gentry favored on their stays in the city. Opinion is fond of the theater, and he has come to court to see the masque. Later, when the scene is changed to a tavern, the gallant Confidence persuades the ladies to go inside and "accept the wine" (p. 268). Throughout the antimasque, Opinion and his family are accompanied by Jollity and Laughter, two characters whose names refer to the pursuit of pleasure which sometimes brought the landowning classes to London. Similarly, the names of Opinion's wife and daughter point to the gentry's desire for "novel" experiences that differ from their country routines and so are likely to elicit their wonder or "admiration." At one point, Opinion explicitly mentions the occasion for the masque and speaks favorably of the Inns of Court, saying,

> I am their friend against the crowd that envy 'em,
> And since they come with pure devotions
> To sacrifice their duties to the king
> And queen, I wish 'em prosper. (p. 266)

This gesture of camaraderie can be taken as yet another historical reference: apart from the glance at the disrepute in which lawyers were generally held during this period, Opinion's remark alludes to the fact that the gentry were closely associated with the legal profession, both because they customarily sent their sons to study at the Inns and because they were occasionally involved in litigation.

Two of the dances in the antimasque are pantomimes that dramatize

---

24. For the "old fashioned" quality of Opinion's clothing, see C. Willet and Phillis Cunnington, *Handbook of English Costume in the Seventeenth Century* (London, 1955), pp. 13-22, 41-54, 65-70.

specific details in Charles's proclamation. When most of the characters enter the tavern, Opinion stays behind with Fancy who presents "*a* Gentleman, *and four* Beggars" who walk on crutches: "*The* Gentleman *first danceth alone; to him the* Beggars; *he bestows his charity; the* Cripples, *upon his going off, throw away their legs, and dance*" (p. 268). This episode illustrates the "divers inconveniences" which the proclamation attributed to the gentry's residence in London. Since the term "gentleman" was virtually synonymous with landownership at this time, the victim of the confidence trick can be seen as a member of the gentry who has left his estate to spend his wealth in the city instead of the country "whence it ariseth," thereby neglecting his obligation to relieve the rural poor with his generosity. The thieves who pose as beggars, moreover, are apt examples of those "loose and idle People, that follow" country gentlemen to London and either become "Delinquents" or "growe to beggery." Another dance makes a similar use of the proclamation. Here the performers are dressed as "*a* Macquerelle, *two* Wenches, [and] *two wanton* Gamesters" (p. 268). After a brief dance in which they "*expressed their natures*," they leave the stage only to make a later entrance: "*The* Macquerelle, Wenches, Gentlemen, *return, as from the tavern; they dance together; the* Gallants *are cheated; and left to dance in, with a drunken repentance*" (p. 271). Once again we see the gentry attracting criminals in the city, but in this case, there is also the suggestion that the two gentlemen are squandering their wealth on gambling and prostitutes or, in the words of the proclamation, on "vain Delights and Expences, even to the wasting of their Estates."

The allusions I have identified make clear that Shirley's antimasque is hardly a transparent window onto Caroline England. There are indeed references to a real historical development—the gentry's occasional visits to London, the first signs of a fashionable "season"—but these are allied to a contemporary account of that development—the royal proclamation. As a result, the antimasque has that same inadequacy to the real which we found in the official document: both texts involve an essentially ideological operation that serves the King's interests by transforming a social trend into a cause for alarm which requires his intervention. The antimasque performs this ideological operation in its own way, with distinctively literary and dramatic materials, and consequently, it achieves a much more complex transformation of reality than the social commentary that opens the proclamation. The portrayal of Novelty, for example, suggests not only the gentry's interest in new experiences that cannot be had in the country, but also a questionable fascination with every passing fad, with newness for its own sake; the allusion simultaneously functions as a criticism.[25] Thus, when Confidence asks Novelty to drink with him, she replies that "It will be new for ladies / To go to th'tavern; but it may be a fashion" (p. 268). In accordance with the critical element in Novelty's characterization, she angers Opinion by returning drunk, and he reproaches her, "these are / Extremes indeed" (p. 273). The two dances we have considered also complicate the proclamation: they exploit a potential irony inherent in it, but never explicitly stated. The argument set forth in the official document is that when a country gentleman resides in London and fails to relieve the poor or employ able workers in his county, he drives these people to the city where they embark on a life of crime, among other things. The irony exposed by Shirley's text is that ultimately this same gentleman may become the victim of the people he has neglected. In this sense, those gentlemen swindled by the beggars and whores in the dances are themselves responsible for the crimes they suffer. For the gentry, the antimasque seems to be saying, living in London is self-destructive, and they have not the slightest awareness of this fact.

A similar lack of self-awareness underlies the interactions between Opinion and Fancy. As a country gentleman, Opinion represents the gentry's attitude toward Charles's personal rule. His somber clothing and the repeated references to him as the "most grave Opinion" who "will like nothing" (pp. 263, 266, 267) further suggest that he stands for the disgruntled Puritan segment of the landowning classes. Not unexpectedly, then, he is critical of the problems he sees in English society under Charles. When Fancy announces that he will present the effects of peace in the antimasque and the dances of urban crime are performed, Opinion launches into a tirade:

> *Opinion.* I am glad they are off:
> Are these effects of peace?
> Corruption rather.
> *Confidence.* Oh, the beggars shew
> The benefit of peace.
> *Opinion.* Their very breath
> Hath stifled all the candles, poison'd the
> Perfumes: beggars a fit presentment! how

25. This criticism was shared by conservative segments of the gentry. In *The English Gentle-woman* (London, 1631), for example, the royalist landowner Richard Brathwaite noted that in the city there are "some affecting nothing more than what is most nouell and phantasticke" (p. 11).

> They cleave still to my nostril! I must tell you,
> I do not like such base and sordid persons,
> And they become not here. (pp. 268–69)

Once again there is an irony in Shirley's text which derives from the proclamation. What Opinion does not perceive is that his very presence in London with his family may have caused the "corruption": as a rural landowner, he should be on his estate relieving the poor with his liberal gifts, not in London berating those people who may have turned to crime because of his own negligence. The fact that Fancy has presented the "corruption" sets up a psychological allegory that likewise disarms Opinion's social commentary. Because Fancy is "the sole presenter of the antimasques" (p. 257), Opinion's failure of perception is implicitly attributed to his faulty imagination, and his criticisms of Charles's reign are reduced to self-delusion. This also occurs when Opinion asks Fancy to create an antimasque of rare curiosities, "some other / Than human shapes" (p. 271). The scene is changed to "*a woody* Landscape," and we see

a Merchant *a'Horseback with his portmanteau; two* Thieves, *set upon him and rob him: these by a* Constable *and* Officers *are apprehended and carried off. Then four* Nymphs *enter dancing, with their javelins; three* Satyrs *spy them and attempt their persons; one of the nymphs escapeth; a noise of hunters and their horns within, as at the fall of a deer; then enter four* Huntsmen *and one* Nymph; *these drive away the* Satyrs, *and having rescued the* Nymphs, *dance with them.* (p. 272)

In these episodes, another criticism of Caroline society is undercut by an irony drawn from the proclamation and by the allegorical significance of Fancy. Because the constable's apprehension of the criminals is presented as a rarity, the suggestion is that law enforcement is not very effective in the provinces. The analogous scene with the nymphs and satyrs makes this problem even worse by hinting that rural crime is never solved in reality, only in pastoral romances! Since it was the gentry who were responsible for provincial government, Opinion's absence from his county means that he may share the blame for such administrative inefficiency. Opinion, of course, is entirely unaware that he or his class may be derelict in their duties, and the allegory associates his ignorance with Fancy's inventiveness. Thus an implied criticism of Charles's reign is again reduced to a misperception caused by an overactive imagination.

The antimasque of *The Triumph of Peace* is an especially shifty text, and we should not minimize its subtlety: on the one hand, it registers a criticism of the royal government through Opinion's comments on Caroline society; on the other, however, the interactions between Opinion and Fancy transform this criticism into an attack on that segment of the gentry which frequented London. The work of transformation relies both on the proclamation and Renaissance psychology. The use of Fancy to subvert Opinion's social commentary reveals the suspicion with which the imagination was often regarded during the Renaissance,[26] but the text also contains a brief portrait of "the sole presenter" which provides a more specific definition of his function. Significantly, it is Confidence who describes Fancy to Opinion, instilling in the country gentleman an unwise trust in the imagination:

> *Opinion.* is this gentleman, this Signor Fancy,
> So rare a thing, so subtle, as men speak him?
> *Confidence.* He's a great prince of th'air, believe it, sir,
> And yet a bird of night.
> *Opinion.* A bird!
> *Confidence.* Between
> An owl and bat, a quaint hermaphrodite,
> Begot of Mercury and Venus, Wit and Love:
> He's worth your entertainment.
> *Opinion.* I am most
> Ambitious to see him. . . . (p. 264)

As a "prince of th'air" with the characteristics of a "bat," Fancy is likely to create images that are not firmly grounded on an observation of reality. His resemblance to an "owl" increases his unreliability by giving it a political dimension: as we learn later in the masque, the owl symbolizes "faction" ("faction or owl's sight, / Whose trouble is the clearest light" [p. 278]), or what we may define as dissension resulting from a biased perception of the obvious. The inference to be drawn from this "quaint hermaphrodite" is that any product of the imagination which purports to be an accurate representation of society is highly suspect. A similar attitude toward the imagination is expressed in the text when the antimasquer Jollity hurries the other characters into the tavern by remarking, "let's leave Opinion behind us; / Fancy will make him drunk" (p. 268). Fancy's genealogy can be taken as another allusion

---

26. William Rossky, "The Imagination in the English Renaissance: Psychology and Poetic," *Studies in the Renaissance* 5 (1958), 49-73. Opinion was regarded with the same suspicion. In what became a source book for masque characters, Cesare Ripa's *Iconologia, overe descrittione di diverse imagini cavate dall'antichità, e di propria inventione* (1603; rpt. Hildesheim and New York, 1970), opinion is defined as follows: "Opinion is perhaps everything in the mind and imagination of man, or at least in the former alone, which is not evident through demonstration" ("Opinion è forse tutto quello che hà luogo nella mente, & nell'imaginazione dell'huomo, ò almeno quello solo, che non è per dimostratione apparente" [p. 369]).

to the Inns of Court, the producers of the masque who "begot" him and the other characters; it also indicates the reason why he should play so important a role despite his negative connotations. The "Wit and Love" belong to the Inns, who chose a sophisticated court entertainment to convey their devotion to Charles and Henrietta Maria. Fancy is the lawyers' offspring because the allegory he signifies allows them to display their loyalty by wittily exploding any criticism of the King's personal rule. Fancy's genealogy sets up what may be the greatest irony in the antimasque: as an anticipation of the later attack on the gentry, it shows the lawyers' Machiavellian strategy of criticizing a social group with whom they were closely associated in order to save face with the King.

III

The sheer elaborateness of the allegory can only remind us of the ideological operation at work in Shirley's text. Opinion and his family are not mirror images of the Caroline gentry; they rather constitute an ideologeme, a refraction of a real social class determined by another class's values.[27] Studying the portrayal of these characters cannot give us any historical knowledge of the gentry, but it can disclose the antimasque's relation to the King's ideology. This relation becomes quite apparent when we observe that the text represses the real conflict between Charles and the landowning classes: the social criticism assigned to Opinion does not have any resemblance to the gentry's actual complaints about his personal rule. In the years immediately before the performance of Shirley's masque, they were perhaps most annoyed by the King's fiscal expedients, the combination of forced loans, fines and taxes which he exploited to increase his revenue without the consent of their parliamentary representatives. In particular it was the gentry who were hardest hit by Charles's decision to revive distraint of knighthood, an ancient usage that permitted him to fine all gentlemen with an annual income of £40 or more who were not knighted at his coronation.[28] This was an unpopular measure that could only reinforce the landowners' growing alienation from the central government. The local commissioners who were appointed to compound with offenders faced the undesir-

27. I borrow the term "ideologeme" from Medvedev/Bakhtin, *The Formal Method of Literary Scholarship*, p. 21.

28. Frederick C. Dietz, *English Public Finance 1558–1641* (1932; rpt. London, 1964), pp. 262–63; Cliffe, p. 296; Stone, *The Causes of the English Revolution*, p. 122.

able task of pursuing their neighbors, and the fines could be quite stiff, some ranging as high as £70. Although largely successful in raising money for the Crown, the scheme of knighthood did encounter resistance in some counties. Sir David Foulis tried to persuade the Yorkshire gentry to refuse payment; in November of 1633, when the preparations for *The Triumph of Peace* were already underway, his efforts earned him a conviction in Star Chamber, and he was punished with a fine, imprisonment, and removal from all of his offices.[29] Elsewhere the commissioners might be deliberately lax in their collections, going so far as to omit names from their rosters.[30]

Shirley's text is strategically silent on such developments. The effect of its allusions to the proclamation is to displace a real reason for the gentry's opposition to the King with a criticism of Caroline society which is actually an ironic attack on them. This displacement reveals the operation of the absolutist ideology of Divine Right kingship: it shows that the entire thrust of the antimasque is to discredit the gentry as a political force and ratify the King's autocracy. Since Opinion and the other gentlemen are shown to be utterly incapable of recognizing the "divers inconveniences" which the proclamation imputes to their London visits, it would be imprudent if not pointless for Charles to summon Parliament and submit his policies for the consideration of the provincial MPs; indeed, according to the logic of the allegory, the best course would be for him to intervene solely on the basis of the royal prerogative and restore order in the kingdom. The lack of understanding which the allegory ascribes to the gentry in London is a key factor in the ideological operation of the antimasque: this was the very tactic that Charles himself had used in a proclamation issued in 1629 to explain his dissolution of Parliament:

we shall account it presumption for any to prescribe any time unto us for parliaments, the calling, continuing and dissolving of which is always in our own power; and we shall be more inclinable to meet in parliament again when our people shall see more clearly into our intentions and actions, when such as have bred this interruption shall have received their condign punishment, and those who are misled by them and by such ill reports as are raised upon this occasion shall come to a better understanding of us and themselves.[31]

29. Cliffe, pp. 299-301, 303. The preparations for *The Triumph of Peace* had begun in October of 1633: see G. E. Bentley, *The Jacobean and Caroline Stage* (Oxford, 1956), V, p. 1154.

30. Barnes, pp. 168-70. See also W. B. Willcox, *Gloucestershire: A Study in Local Government 1590–1640* (New Haven, Conn., 1940), pp. 121-22, and Morrill, p. 27.

31. "A proclamation for suppressing of false rumours touching parliaments, 27 March 1629," rpt. in *The Stuart Constitution*, p. 86.

Like this proclamation, the antimasque insists that the gentry who leave
their country estates are "misled," and thus justifies the King's exclusion
of them from the political process.

We can extend these observations by examining the antimasque of
projectors who seek royal patents of monopoly for their inventions.
During the late sixteenth and early seventeenth centuries, patents were
issued for a variety of reasons, most of which did not benefit the
commonwealth. They could be an effective means to promote industrial
expansion by protecting new technical processes and assuring fledgling
industries a market for their products. More often than not, however,
they were used to serve royal financial interests, reward favorites and
advance political power through economic centralization.[32] During
Charles's reign, patents were primarily a fiscal expedient designed to
raise money for the crown. Without a Parliament willing to vote him the
subsidies he needed to cover his expenses, the king and his ministers
developed independent sources of revenue by exploiting loopholes in the
Statute of Monopolies, a parliamentary bill which prohibited patents to
individuals in 1624. Since the Statute had excluded new inventions and
corporations from its provisions, Caroline monopolists pretended technical improvements and formed partnerships or companies, and in return
for the lucrative privileges which the patents granted them, they paid
into the Exchequer an annual rent or, in some cases, a fee for each
product sold.[33] The Company of Soapmakers of Westminster, for
instance, the most notorious monopoly under Charles, was incorporated
in 1632 to use a new manufacturing method and was gradually given the
exclusive right to produce soap in England. For their patent, the monopolists agreed to pay the King £20,000 per annum.[34]

Because patents were granted for such commonly used products as
soap, salt, wine and logwood, they were destined to have far-reaching
effects which ultimately alienated large segments of the population from
the crown. The interests of consumers were largely ignored. Monopolists knew that their privileges were unlawful and would doubtless be
revoked if Parliament ever met again, so they tried to get rich quick by
driving up prices for inferior goods. Merchants suffered because patents

32. William H. Price, *The English Patents of Monopoly* (Boston and New York, 1906), pp. 14-17,
31; Christopher Hill, pp. 31-32; Clarkson, pp. 112, 160-61.

33. Price, pp. 35-42.

34. Price, pp. 119-22; S. R. Gardiner, *The History of England 1603-1642* (1883-84; rpt. New
York, 1965), VIII, pp. 71-72.

frequently prohibited the import of certain materials long used in manu-facturing and gave the monopolists the right to search cargoes. Patents similarly disrupted established industries by forcing independent manu-facturers to use new materials and methods, to submit their products to tests conducted by the monopolists themselves, and to compound with them for infringements of their privileges.[35] Throughout the autocratic 1630s Charles "enacted" monopolies through proclamations, an effective strategy which enabled him to discourage infringers by bringing charges against them in Star Chamber for contempt of the royal prerogative. Late in 1632, for example, the government prosecuted several indepen-dent soapboilers for violating the patent of the Westminster Company. The offenders were prohibited from engaging in their trade, ordered to pay fines ranging from £500 to £1500 each, and committed to the Fleet. They were still in custody when *The Triumph of Peace* was first per-formed.[36]

Shirley's antimasque introduces six comic projectors. Three of the projectors refer, in their diverting way, to the customary practice of winning patents by pretending technical improvements in existing prod-ucts or methods: a "jockey" has developed "a rare and cunning bridle" that can so "cool and refresh a horse, he shall ne'er tire"; a "country fellow" has bought a "flail" which can thresh corn "without help of hands"; and a "physician" has contrived "a new way to fatten poultry / With scrapings of carrot" (pp. 269-70). Clearly these inventions are wildly improbable, and they appear to be nothing more than foolish get-rich-quick schemes devised by some rather incompetent projectors. Thus, the countryman "has sold his acres," giving up his living "to purchase him" the labor-saving flail, while the physician, who adheres to incompatible medical principles (he is "a Galenist, and parcel Paracel-sus"), once "thriv'd by diseases, but quite lost his practice" by devoting himself to his bizarre studies in animal husbandry. This note of ridicu-lousness is repeatedly sounded in the antimasque. We can hear it in the remaining projects which are equally implausible during this period of relatively slow technological development: they include a deep-sea diving suit described as "a case to walk you all day under water," a kind of double-boiler in which "the very steam / Of the first vessel shall alone be able / To make another pot above seethe over," and two nautical inventions, one to enable "a ship to sail against the winds," the other, "on

35. Christopher Hill, pp. 33-35; Ashton, pp. 141-47.
36. Price, pp. 43-44, 120; Gardiner, VIII, p. 73.

Goodwin sands, to melt huge rocks to jelly" (pp. 270-71).

The ideological operation at work in this antimasque becomes apparent if we consider the different responses it elicited. Whitelocke states that "by it an Information was covertly given to the King, of the unfitness and ridiculousness of these Projects against the Law."[37] The implication, of course, is that the antimasque is imputing illegalities to the King, the source of all patents, and this may well have been the intention of some of the lawyers who produced the entertainment. Yet Charles himself apparently did not perceive this implication; the evidence we have rather suggests that he was quite pleased with the entire masque: he ordered a second performance of it.[38] It seems likely, in fact, that the King viewed the antimasque as praise of his wisdom in selecting only those inventions worthy of monopolies. These opposed responses are possible because, once again, Shirley's text registers a potential criticism of the royal government, but so presents that criticism as to defuse it. Here the work of transformation is achieved by the convenient omission of any reference to the many adverse consequences of the monopolies and by the sheer absurdity of the inventions. The descriptions function as a comic displacement of serious issues, whereby the projectors can be seen not as threats to the social order, but as harmless fun. The antimasque does indeed satirize Caroline monopolies, yet in contrast to Whitelocke's statement, the emphasis is on their "ridiculousness" rather than their "unfitness . . . against the Law." Moreover, the gentry in London are implicated in the satire. Not only do we see a "country fellow" who has stupidly sold his land to invest in an absurd industrial venture, but Opinion shows his lack of judgment by praising the devices and their inventors with remarks like "A most scholastic project!" and "He will deserve a monument" (p. 270). Opinion's approval again raises doubts about whether Charles should rely on the provincial MPs for advice when he frames his economic policies, and thus its effect is to confirm the King's personal rule.

The final sequence of dances continues to discredit the offending gentry in a way that reflects the King's ideology. These too are pantomimes, and in keeping with the elaborateness that has so far distinguished the antimasque, they are rather indirect in their criticism:

A Landscape, *The scene; and enter three* Dotterels, *and three* Dotterel-Catchers. . . . *After the* Dotterels *are caught by several imitations, enter a* Windmill, *a fantastic* Knight *and his* Squire

37. Whitelock, p. 20.
38. Bentley, V, pp. 1158-59.

armed. The fantastic adventurer with his lance makes many attempts upon the windmill, which his squire imitates: to them enter a Country-Gentleman *and his* Servant. *These are assaulted by the* Knight *and his* Squire, *but are sent off lame for their folly. Then enter four* Bowlers, *who shew much variety of sport in their game and postures, and conclude the Antimasque.* (pp. 272-73)

These dances may be taken as references to diversions enjoyed by the gentry: bird-catching, reading chivalric romances like *Don Quixote*,[39] and bowling.[40] At the same time, however, each dance seems to satirize members of this class who are socially ambitious, who seek to elevate their status by imitating preoccupations associated with the nobility. This satire is first signified by the dotterels, a species of plover which, it was believed, allowed itself to be caught by mimicking the fowler's actions; accordingly, the term "dotterell" came to be used as a synonym for "silly person" (OED). The allusion to one of the more farcical episodes in Cervantes' work portrays the pretentious gentry as dotterels by showing two gentlemen in ridiculous imitations: a "fantastic" or irrational knight emulates the noble ideal of chivalry by jousting with a windmill, and his squire blindly follows him. These characters are so deluded by their imitations that they assault another country gentleman, perhaps the owner of the windmill who arrives to defend his property. Evidently the point of these dances is that certain gentry are similar to dotterels because they foolishly aspire to nobility but in the end are "caught" in adverse circumstances in which they endanger themselves and other members of their class. This would also explain the apparently unrelated entrance of the bowlers. Bowling was a sport on which noblemen gambled away large sums in early seventeenth-century England.[41] As John Earle noted, a bowling alley "is the place where there are three things throwne away besides Bowls, to wit, time, and money and curses."[42] The gentry also indulged in this sort of amusement when they came to London. A few months after the performance of *The Triumph of Peace*, Charles was responding to another consequence of their visits when he ordered that the bowling green in Spring Garden, a royal park attached to Whitehall, be closed to the public because it had become

39. See Louis B. Wright, *Middle-Class Culture in Elizabethan England* (1935; rpt. Ithaca, N.Y., 1958), pp. 375-94.

40. Cliffe, pp. 115, 126. See also Carl Bridenbaugh, *Vexed and Troubled Englishmen 1590-1642* (New York, 1968), pp. 154-55.

41. Stone, *The Crisis of the Aristocracy*, pp. 567-72.

42. John Earle, "A Bowle-Alley," in *Microcosmographie, Or, a peece of the world discovered; in essayes and characters* (London, 1628), p. 42.

"common" and disorderly.[43] Since the bowlers in Shirley's antimasque follow dances whose theme is social climbing through imitation, "their game and postures" can also be read as a criticism of the gentry who live above their station by participating in the leisure activities of the nobility and consuming their wealth on gambling. The bowlers are thus another illustration of those "vain Delights and Expences" which Charles cited in his proclamation against the gentry's residence in London.

My reading of these dances may appear dubious. After all, their extreme discontinuity seems to resist a neat interpretation, and the text does not provide a very detailed description of the dancers' performances. Yet as Professor Marcus has demonstrated with Jonson, if "we steep ourselves in the immediate political and social milieu of the masques, . . . incoherent passages will become recognizable as adroit commentary on events."[44] What needs to be emphasized about *The Triumph of Peace* is that the "adroit commentary on events" is the determinate product of the King's ideology. In the context of the entire antimasque, the concluding dances attribute the gentry's London visits to their social pretensions and so reveal the operation of the feudal ideology of degree which informed Charles's political practice. The fact that Charles was guided by this ideology is clear not just in his proclamation to keep the landowning classes in the country, but also in his efforts to strengthen the traditional social hierarchy by stopping the sale of titles and maintaining an overwhelming majority of peers on the Privy Council, among other things.[45] In view of such developments, the quixotic gentlemen and the bowlers who conclude Shirley's antimasque must be regarded as an ideological representation: in their suggestion of pretense and gambling losses, they express a concern that the gentry's pleasure trips to the city may ultimately blur class distinctions and cause undue social mobility.

IV

The main masque completes the ideological operation we have been examining. When the personifications of peace, law and justice (Irene, Eunomia and Diche respectively) descend from heaven "to wait upon the earth" where Charles and Henrietta Maria reign, the "profane"

43. Peter Cunningham and Henry B. Wheatley, *London Past and Present* (London, 1891), III, pp. 293-95; Fisher, pp. 204-05.

44. Marcus, "'Present Occasions' and the Shaping of Ben Jonson's Masques," p. 202.

45. Stone, *The Crisis of the Aristocracy*, pp. 34, 117-19, 397-98, 751; G. E. Aylmer, *The King's Servants: The Civil Service of Charles I 1625-1642* (New York, 1961), pp. 20-21.

antimasquers "go off fearfully" (p. 273), and the social problems for which they shared responsibility are magically solved. The heavenly emissaries refer to the monarchs as the gods "Jove and Themis" who are "the parents of us three," and their descent constitutes nothing more than a move to the earthly part of Charles's kingdom: "The triumph of Jove's upper part abated, / And all the deities translated" (p. 276). This image of the King and Queen expresses the ideology of Divine Right monarchy not only by deifying them, but also by characterizing their power as absolute: they are the sources of the law that "dost beautify increase, / And chain security with peace," and it is their justice that "giv'st perfection" to the orderly peacefulness which England is said to enjoy under them (p. 275). In this way, the actual grievances of the gentry and the business community are reduced to a mirage, and Charles's auto-cratic rule is legitimized.

It is important to notice, however, that like the antimasque of projec-tors, the allegory of the main masque may have elicited different responses from the royal couple and the lawyers who produced the entertainment. At one point, Irene and Eunomia sing, "The world shall give prerogative to neither; We cannot flourish but together" (p. 275), and this can easily be construed as a message from the legal profession to the King asserting that he must cooperate with them. As Stephen Orgel and Roy Strong put it,

Legally, British law is made by the King acting through Parliament, by Parliament acting with the assent of the King. But since Charles's dissolution of the Parliament of 1629, Irene, Peace, was the King's: peace had been maintained by the royal prerogative alone, and laws enacted without the consent of Parliament. Peace and Law sing explicitly of their joint prerogatives because the subject of the masque is prerogative rule; and they make the general point of which Bulstrode Whitelocke says the antimasque of projectors was a particular instance: there can be no peace without law.[46]

It is thus possible to see Eunomia, the personification of law, as a symbol of Parliament and read the song as an assertion that the King's peace (Irene) should not have prerogative over the MPs' contribution to the legislative process (Eunomia). Charles would no doubt have been enraged by this presumption, especially if it were boldly trumpeted in a court masque; given his enthusiasm with *The Triumph of Peace*, we are justified in assuming that his attention was focused on another, more flattering detail in the text: Eunomia's status as the divine offspring of Jove. Seen in this light, she symbolizes not Parliament's legislative

46. Orgel and Strong, *Inigo Jones*, I, pp. 65-66.

function, but an aspect of Charles's absolute power, his paternalistic control of political and legal practice in English society. Since the King is the divine "father" of peace, law and justice, he can freely exercise the royal prerogative without submitting his policies for parliamentary approval.

This is yet another example of the peculiar indeterminacy of Shirley's text. There are passages whose meaning seems to have been determined by the viewer's politics. Whitelocke's commentary shows that he and his colleagues considered the masque to be an important political statement: it would enable them both to profess their allegiance to Charles and advise him to curb the illegalities of his personal rule. Yet this intention is foiled because the allusions and allegory can occasionally support conflicting readings. The ideological force of this slippage of meaning becomes apparent when we realize that the criticism intended for the royal government is repeatedly deflected onto other social groups, primarily the gentry. Apparently, the merest suggestion that the text criticized the King was enough to give the lawyers the optimistic idea that their position would be heard, even though the dissolution of Parliament had left them without a political institution to represent their interests as well as those of the gentry and the business community. In the end, however, it becomes clear that the masque rather functioned as an apparatus of the absolutist state by presenting the contradictions in Caroline society and resolving them in a way that reinforces the King's domination.

The criticism of the gentry in *The Triumph of Peace* inevitably raises the question of how they responded to it or, more generally, whether it produced any concrete social effects. We know that the masque was a bestseller: even before it was performed, several thousand copies had been printed, and it went through several editions.[47] This popularity, however, may have been due not to any intrinsic qualities of the published text, but rather to the spectacular procession that travelled through the streets of London before the performance. The complex nature of the masque, furthermore, makes it seem unlikely that the gentry would have sufficiently grasped the satire on them to be irritated by it; no doubt the subtle allusions and intricate allegory were most fully appreciated by the King and the learned lawyers who created the entertainment. Thus, it is not surprising to find that Sir Humphrey Mildmay, an Essex landowner who violated the proclamation with his

47. Bentley, V, pp. 1160-62.

frequent visits to London, witnessed the first performance at Whitehall but felt it was little more than "stately."[48]

A more plausible hypothesis regarding the social reverberations of Shirley's masque is that like the other royal entertainments during Charles's reign, it widened the gap between the insular court and the provincial opposition to the central government. For the country at large, the elaborate procession and the lavish costumes and scenery probably nourished the growing suspicions of the court's frivolity and Popish decadence.[49] For Charles, the masque reproduced a questionable social representation that had already been disseminated in such official documents as the proclamation, and the sheer pleasure of viewing this theatrical reproduction could easily have encouraged the mistaken idea that his autocracy was more successful than it actually was.[50] Perhaps the most dangerous illusion fostered by the masque had to do with the loyalty of the legal profession. By attacking a group like the gentry who were already grumbling about Charles's government, the Inns of Court may have allayed his doubts about their political sympathies. If so, they also prevented him from foreseeing that lawyers like Bulstrode Whitelocke would figure prominently among the MPs who reversed his policies in the Long Parliament.

V

The foregoing consideration of *The Triumph of Peace* confirms the importance of distinguishing between occasions and topical allusions in our study of the Stuart masque. By investigating allusions, we can expose the complex textual process by which a masque works on history, as well as the ideological determinants which shape that process. Once we recognize that allusions do not give us history in an unmediated form, we are better able to define the precise sense in which a masque is a political intervention that advances the interests of a particular class. To my mind, the chief merit of this approach is that it can yield an incisive account of a masque's politics which does not oversimplify the manifold aspects of the production by reducing them to history; on the contrary, our investiga-

48. Ralph, *Sir Humphrey Mildmay*, pp. 50-51.

49. See P. W. Thomas, "Two Cultures? Court and Country under Charles I," in *The Origins of the English Civil War*, ed. Russell, pp. 168-93.

50. This reading of Caroline court literature was first put forth by C. W. Wedgwood, *Poetry and Politics under the Stuarts* (1960; rpt. Ann Arbor, Mich., 1964). See also Orgel, *The Illusion of Power*, pp. 88-89. In a similar vein, Stone has pointed out that Archbishop Laud's reports on religious dissent in the provinces involved misrepresentation: see *The Causes of The English Revolution*, p. 121.

tion respects the specificity of Shirley's antimasque, its unique literary and dramatic qualities, by indicating how these effect a transformation of historical events. Of course this approach is not in any way limited to the masque or even to topical allusions; it can profitably be applied to other literary and dramatic forms. Yet what remains unchanged in all its applications is a fundamental assumption about writing: the text is determined by the specific conjuncture of social forces in which it was created, and these forces enter it not directly, but through a series of dislocations produced by the text itself. For the literary historian, this seems to be an effective way to mediate between literature and history.[51]

51. I am pleased to acknowledge that my work on this article was supported in part by a Summer Research Fellowship from Temple University. An earlier version was presented to the Seminar on the Renaissance at Columbia University during the fall of 1984.

New Science and the Georgic Revolution in Seventeenth-Century English Literature

ANTHONY LOW

I F one were to believe historians of the georgic, Vergil's middle poem interested scarcely anyone between the Augustan age of Rome and that of England. A few scattered imitations have been found, not very like the original, while in England, scholars note, Renaissance schoolmasters sometimes set the *Georgics* as a text.[1] Of course, if at any time during this supposed hiatus a writer had occasion to speak of style, he would automatically cite the formula that assigned low style to pastoral, middle to georgic, and high to epic. Still, the trope might be thought little more than a reflex. Poets with Vergilian pretensions often leapt straight out of pastoral into epic, without troubling to serve out an apprenticeship at the georgic level. Therefore in English poetry the georgic is usually said to begin with Dryden's translation of Vergil's *Eclogues* and *Georgics,* which was published in 1697 along with Dryden's laudatory preface and Addison's influential essay on the georgic kind.[2] For the first time in the seventeenth century (save for a remarkable compliment by the iconoclastic Montaigne),[3] Dryden argued that the *Georgics* was Vergil's finest poem and that he wrote it "in the full strength and vigour of his Age, when his Judgment was at the height, and before his Fancy was declining." Addison agreed, calling the poem "the most Compleat, Elaborate, and finisht Piece of all Antiquity."[4] Three

1. On the history of georgic, see L. P. Wilkinson, *The Georgics of Virgil: A Critical Survey* (Cambridge, Eng., 1969), pp. 270–313.
2. For the georgic in England beginning with Dryden (1697), see Dwight L. Durling, *Georgic Tradition in English Poetry* (New York, 1935), and John Chalker, *The English Georgic: A Study in the Development of a Form* (London, 1969).
3. "Of Books," *Essays,* II.10: "I have always thought, that in Poesie, *Virgil, Lucretius, Catullus* and *Horace* do many degrees excel the rest; and signally, *Virgil* in his *Georgicks,* which I look upon for the most accomplished piece of Poetry"; *Essays of Michael Seignieur de Montaigne,* trans. Charles Cotton (1685), II, 134.
4. Dryden, *The Works of Vergil* (1697); see *The Poems of John Dryden,* ed. James Kingsley, II

earlier English translations of the *Georgics* had been published, the first by "A.F.," probably Abraham Fleming, in 1589.[5] Still it was Dryden's genius that enabled him, as so often, to discover and proclaim a new mode. Not even the appearance of his much-admired *Aeneid* the following year could prevent his *Georgics* from touching off a new fashion that was to last through much of the eighteenth century, reaching its acknowledged peak in Thomson's *Seasons* before it petered out among "The mob of gentlemen who wrote with ease."

Aside from frequent but usually perfunctory appeals to the "middle style" of the *Georgics,* the poem survived most obviously in seventeenth-century poetry in a few important but fragmented motifs and topoi. The omnipresent myth of Orpheus, symbol of the artist, of the harmonizer and civilizer, while it owes much to the *Metamorphoses,* achieved its most notable statement in *Georgics* IV. The myth of Proteus, so important to the age as a symbol for changeable matter in the phenomenal world, while it originates in the *Odyssey,* likewise takes vivid form in *Georgics* IV. A still more prominent topos, the idea or image of the Golden Age, although it owes much to Hesiod, Horace, Ovid, and Vergil's "Messianic" Eclogue, persistently echoes and alludes to the *Georgics*. Yet these Golden-Age allusions seldom adhere to the georgic spirit of the Vergilian original. Thus Montaigne's seminal essay "On Cannibals," which was to bear fruit in Rousseau's potent doctrine of primitive man, turns to the *Georgics* for its single supporting citation;[6] but the oppositions that Montaigne draws between labor and ease, property and community, invention and indolence, hierarchy and brotherhood, injustice and justice, employ the precise distinctions that Vergil draws in the *Georgics* to move away from a georgic world of work, invention, and civilization into a pastoral idyll of a kind Vergil had invoked mainly to provide a contrast to the hard and laborious world he delineates.

In the *Georgics,* Vergil suggests that the Golden Age of ease and communistic justice is gone forever. Instead, he proposes an alternative: the "happy husbandman." This figure Vergil associates with the past, but with a more recent and historical past, when Roman ancestors lived a

(Oxford, 1958), 913, and Joseph Addison, *Miscellaneous Works,* ed. A. C. Guthkelch (London, 1914), II, 11.

5. A. F., *The Buckolicks of Publius Vergilius Maro . . . together with his Georgicks* (1589); Thomas May, *Virgil's Georgicks* (1628); John Ogilby, *The Works of Publius Vergilius Maro* (1649; 1650, 1654, 1665, 1668, 1684).

6. *Essays* (I.30), trans. Cotton, I, 368–69.

simpler and nobler life as farmers before the city was cursed with luxury and civil war. The whole course of the *Georgics* suggests that this ideal, unlike the Golden Age, may actually be reattainable. Under the enlightened leadership of Octavius and by means of the exertions of individual citizens, typified by the husbandman, Rome may once more be entering a period of happiness and prosperity, which is characterized not by a miraculous transformation back to primal *otium,* as Vergil had earlier prophesied in *Eclogue* IV, but by the performance of equitable labor for the common welfare.[7] In such circumstances, work is transformed from a curse into a blessing.

Ironically, while Vergil's happy husbandman proved very popular throughout the seventeenth century, social conditions and assumptions were such in England that this figure was persistently transformed from a georgic ideal into what amounts to simply another variation on the theme of pastoral ease. When Christopher Johnson took his schoolboys at Winchester through the *Georgics* in 1563, he felt obliged to warn them not to despise agricultural labor, which the Romans obviously valued much more highly than the English.[8] But warnings of this kind had little effect on most schoolboys who grew up to be poets and writers. In a hierarchical society it was proper for a schoolboy or an agricultural laborer to work hard, but not for a full-grown man of the educated classes. "[G]oe chide / Late schoole boyes, and sowre prentices," Donne tells his intrusive taskmaster, the sun; "Call countrey ants to harvest offices." While an English gentleman might readily imagine himself sitting on a hillside at his ease, dressed in shepherd's garb, playing on his pipes or making love to the local shepherdesses, ordinarily he was unlikely to imagine himself a plowman.

Yet Dryden could scarcely have succeeded so strikingly in establishing a georgic vogue of such immediate universality if others had not prepared the ground for him. I am not referring simply to such minor poets as George Wither (see Plates I and II), Geffrey Whitney (Plate III), and Edward Benlowes, who had admitted genuinely georgic details into their work rather early in the century. Much more important was the role played by two major poets, Spenser and Milton, in the development of the new georgic consciousness in England. One cannot satisfactorily understand the work of either poet without some awareness of georgic,

7. See, e.g., Patricia A. Johnston, *Vergil's Agricultural Golden Age: A Study of the Georgics* (Leiden, 1980).

8. British Library MS. Add. 4379, fol. 79, cited by T. W. Baldwin, *William Shakspere's Small Latine and Lesse Greek* (Urbana, Ill., 1944), I, 327, and see 321–32.

its roots in Vergil, and its role in the developing culture of the period. William A. Sessions has written a powerful essay on Spenser and georgic; elsewhere I have discussed georgic in Milton.[9] To those two most significant names in the literary georgic a third should be added, that of a man only slightly less important in changing England's view of work: Ben Jonson. The intention of the present essay, however, is to examine the georgic background and especially to suggest how the New Science helped to dispel prevailing anti-georgic prejudices among the English and to replace them with a wholly new spirit. The New Science harnessed the old Vergilian vision, and this combination of pragmatic experiment with literary insight was remarkably fertile. In his *History of the Royal Society,* Thomas Sprat aptly remarks how moderns may use the ancients: "For methinks, that wisdom, which they fetch'd from the ashes of the dead, is something of the same nature, with Ashes themselves: which, if they are kept up in heaps together, will be useless: But if they are scattred upon Living ground, they will make it more fertile, in the bringing forth of various sorts of Fruits."[10] The result of this fruitful combination of poetic vision and New Science was what we may well call the georgic revolution of the seventeenth century, which preceded and was directly responsible for the agricultural revolution of the eighteenth.

II

The prejudices with which the age began, which were as much political and social as they were literary, are typically represented by Richard Barnfield. "The Shepherds Content, or The hapines of a harm-less life" (1594) begins, "Of all the kindes of common Countrey life, / Me thinkes a Shepheards life is most content" (ll. 1–2).[11] Not surprisingly, Barnfield's shepherd has few labors or duties to perform but is put into the world chiefly to enjoy himself. The only threats to his happiness are ambition, which might take him to court, and all-conquering love, which not even a shepherd can avoid (ll. 216–73). His only chore is to see that those sheep that contravene the rules of hierarchy are well "pounded" (ll. 155–61). A more idyllic life could scarcely be imagined:

9. Sessions, "Spenser's Georgics," *English Literary Renaissance,* 10 (1980), 202–38; Low, "Milton, *Paradise Regained,* and Georgic," *PMLA,* 98 (1983), 152–69. Sessions also has announced and mentioned to me an essay on "Bacon's Vergil" which I have not yet seen.

10. Facsimile ed. Jackson Cope and Harold Whitmore Jones (Saint Louis, 1958), pp. 24–25.

11. In *The Affectionate Shepheard* (1594); rpt. in *Poems, 1594–1598,* ed. Edward Arber (Westminster, 1896), pp. 25–33.

> He sits all Day lowd-piping on a Hill,
> The whilst his flocke about him daunce apace,
> His hart with joy, his eares with Musique fill:
> Anon a bleating Weather beares the Bace,
> A Lambe the Treble; and to his disgrace
>   Another answers like a middle Meane:
>   Thus every one to beare a Part are faine. (ll. 141–47)

Quite opposite to this pleasant *otium* is the lot of the husbandman, who is somewhat illogically lumped together with courtiers, scholars, merchants, and soldiers as an instance of how "low degree" (l. 107) as well as too much ambition can lead to trouble and unrest:

> The painful Plough-swaine, and the Husband-man
> Rise up each morning by the breake of day,
> Taking what toyle and drudging paines they can,
> And all is for to get a little stay;
> And yet they cannot put their care away:
>   When Night is come, their cares begin afresh,
>   Thinking upon their Morrowes busines. (ll. 99–105)

A realistic husbandman, unlike those pretended figures who are really courtly shepherds in disguise, is not a happy husbandman. How could he be, in the Elizabethan view, when he is base-born, poor, and condemned to endless labor?

What many poets really thought about rustics is documented by James Turner. Alexander Brome (1661) pretends to retire from polite society to country contentment, but he thinks very little of his real country neighbors:

> Here, if we mix with *company*, 'tis such
> As can say *nothing* though they talk too *much*.
> Here we learn *georgicks,* here the *Bucolicks,*
> Which buildings cheapest, *timber, stone,* or *bricks*.
> Here *Adams* natural Sons, all made of *Earth*—
> *Earth's* their *Religion,* their *discourse,* their *mirth*.

The unknown author of *Honoria and Mammon* (1659) provides us with an even more unsparing portrait, which indicates with full vividness how an aristocratic "shepherd" might view a real countryman who happened to cross his path:

>   thou horrid Lumpe
> Of leather, coarse wooll, ignorance, and husbandry,
> Most pitifully compounded, thou that
> Hast liv'd so long a dunghill, till the weeds

> Had over-grown thee, and but ten yards off
> Cosen'd a horse that came to graze upon thee.[12]

For the most part, however, poets preferred not to spoil their landscapes with such ugly objects; better to ignore the rural laborer entirely, keep him in the background, or transform him from a georgic into an acceptably pastoral figure.

Not too surprisingly, therefore, English poets who praised the happy husbandman preferred the milder and less laborious version of his life offered in Horace's second epode, *Beatus ille*. Notoriously, it turns out in the end that the body of this poem has been spoken by the usurer Alphius, who has just finished collecting his rents and is toying with the idea of retiring to a country villa. But in the closing stanza "avarice again gains the upper hand," and he decides to remain in Rome.[13] In other words, seductive as the poem is, it represents the vision of a city-dweller dreaming of the country life and reflects few of the nagging realities. It is also notorious that many of the English translators and paraphrasers of these popular lines dropped Horace's ironic stance along with his final stanza and thus essentially revealed themselves as gentleman amateurs. William Browne, whose pastorals Milton extensively annotated and who deserves credit for being more realistic than most, nevertheless can insert a leisured verse such as this into his paraphrase of Horace:

> By some sweet stream, clear as his thought,
> He seats him with his book and line;
> And though his hands have nothing caught,
> His mind hath whereupon to dine.[14]

Browne's "Happy Life" is not without labor, but it is labor well under control:

> His afternoon spent as the prime
> Inviting where he mirthful sups;
> Labour, or seasonable time,
> Brings him to bed and not his cups.

The vision is perhaps Stoic as well as Epicurean, yet there is nothing of Vergil's constant and even terrifying toil, which is better captured,

12. Brome, *Songs and Other Poems* (1661), p. 191; *Honoria and Mammon* (1659), p. 7; both cited by James Turner, *The Politics of Landscape* (Cambridge, Mass., 1979), p. 176; the book contains much similar illustrative material.

13. Maren-Sofie Røstvig, *The Happy Man* (Oslo: Akademisk Forlag, 1954), p. 71. Ben Jonson's version of the poem includes Alphius.

14. *Poems of William Browne of Tavistock*, ed. Gordon Goodwin (London, n.d.), II, 299–300.

although rejected, in Barnfield's portrait. To be truly georgic, a poem should come face to face with the realistic details of farming life, see them for what they are, yet accept them and even glorify them. Apparently most writers in England found such concepts impossible even to think about, and even in the eighteenth century poets seem to find it difficult not to sink back into the repose of the gentleman farmer, all of whose manual work was performed for him by his laborers.

Thus, as Raymond Williams aptly points out, Herrick is able to admire the sweaty laborers of "The Hock-cart," yet in the end he puts them firmly back into their proper social position:[15]

> Come Sons of Summer, by whose toile,
> We are the Lords of Wine and Oile:
> By whose tough labours, and rough hands,
> We rip up first, then reap our lands. . . .
> And, you must know, your Lords word's true,
> Feed him ye must, whose food fils you. (ll. 1–4, 51–52)

Although a modern reader, however conservative his views, may feel Herrick's politics sticking in his throat, he can still admire him for his poetic realism and the greater than usual openness with which he depicts country living as it was. A rather more typical Establishment attitude (taking the word mostly in its old Erastian sense) is expressed by Isaac Walton's Venator, after he has been tutored and converted by his master Piscator.[16] Sitting under a willow by a stream, he contemplates a farmer's meadow across the way and pities its lawsuit-ridden owner. Better to sit and look at such a field than to own or farm it. Better to be an angler than a farmer. His attitude is understandable; in 1653, when *The Compleat Angler* first appeared, Royalists had good reason to take the Stoic view. Land sequestrations and confiscations were at their height, and rural England was in turmoil. Still, fishing had always been a preferred activity for gentlemen who, with Venator, might sometimes find that the exertions of hunting came rather too close for comfort to hard work. As Henry Peacham confirms in *The Complete Gentleman* (1622), fishing is a proper gentlemanly accomplishment, a suitable "pastime for all men to recreate themselves at vacant hours."[17] At the height of Walton's vision, fishing rises to the dignity of religious contemplation; yet its roots are still to be found amid familiar English social and political prejudices.

15. *The Country and the City* (London, 1973), pp. 33–34.
16. *The Compleat Angler*, I.xvi.
17. *The Complete Gentleman*. ed. Virgil B. Heltzel (Ithaca, N.Y., 1962), p. 171 (Ch. XX).

For more extensive examples of the typical view that the country life is a leisured life, one can hardly do better than turn to Henry Vaughan. Vaughan's love of nature is of course well known. "Upon the Priorie Grove" and "To the River *Isca*" demonstrate what is obvious enough, that he liked to stroll about quietly and contemplate nature's beauties, and that he was a gentleman in retirement rather than a man with an interest in living off the land, or for that matter observing others living off it. His paraphrase of Boethius's "Metrum 5" celebrates, in the traditional terms, the Golden Age, which he calls "that first white age" (l. 1). Among his several paraphrases of Casimir Sarbiewski, the Polish Neolatinist, is "The Praise of a Religious Life . . . In Answer to that Ode of Horace," in which he dismisses even the modicum of work that Horace had allowed into *Beatus ille*:

> *Flaccus* not so; That worldly *He*
> Whom in the Countreys *shade* we see
> Ploughing his own *fields,* seldome can
> Be justly stil'd, *The Blessed man.*
>   That title only fits a *Saint,*
> Whose free thoughts far above restraint
> And weighty Cares, can gladly part
> With *house* and *lands* . . .
> Sits in some fair *shade,* and doth give
> To his *wild thoughts* rules how to live. (ll. 1–8, 19–20)

Vaughan's poem reflects two facts of English social life, the separation of the gentleman from close contact with the land and the separation of the contemplative "saint" from his original monastic foundation (where, according to the ancient Benedictine formula, prayer was to be balanced by work). The result is a rootless and etiolated rural spirituality, toward which not only the pleasure-seekers and the urban cynics of the day but even the most dedicated and ascetic of Englishmen seemed to be drawn. Vaughan certainly was not a lazy or an idle man. It was his habit, for one thing, to rise at midnight for his prayers. He can praise a country diet of "thin *beere,*" "*fresh berries,*" and "the *Bean* / By Curious *Pallats* never sought" (ll. 72–81). Nevertheless, he cannot seem to imagine himself doing the work of planting, gathering, or brewing these humble comestibles. This attitude comes partly from Casimir, yet it is perfectly consonant with Vaughan's thinking elsewhere.

The personal views of a translator like Vaughan are suggested by what he chooses to translate as well as by what he changes from his original. He clearly admired *The Praise and Happinesse of the Countrie-Life* (1651), translated from the Spanish of Antonio de Guevara, Bishop of Cartagena and adviser to Charles V, by "H. Vaughan *Silurist*." Vaughan takes the epigraph on his title-page from the opening of Vergil's praise of the happy husbandman in *Georgics* II, and a closing dash presumably signals the assumption that readers will recall the rest of this familiar passage. In the light of the present discussion, the interesting thing about this little treatise is the way it mingles and blurs the lives of the country gentleman and of the country laborer.

> In the Country the *Gentleman* as well as the *Ploughman* may live, to please himself, and is not bound to a chargeable Imitation of the *fashions* and *foppery* of others. . . . A *bill* to walk his grounds with, a *fish-basket,* an *angling-rod,* or *birding-piece* are his chiefest accoutrements. . . . Yea, more *blessed* is he, that living honestly in the *sweat of his face,* rides his own simple *Asse,* than a rich unconscionable *Tyrant* that furnisheth his great *stable* or *dairie* with the *Cattel* and *Horses* of an innocent, honest man. . . . (pp. 126–27)
>
> The Husbandman is alwaies up and drest with the morning, whose dawning light . . . chaseth away the darkness (which would hinder his early labours) from every *valley*. If his days task keep him late in the *fields,* yet *night* comes not so suddenly upon him, but he can returne home with the *Evening-star.* (p. 129)
>
> O who can ever fully expresse the pleasures and happinesse of the Country-life! with the various and delightful sports of *fishing, hunting,* and *fowling,* with *guns, Greyhounds, Spaniels,* and severall sorts of *Nets!* what oblectation and refreshment it is, to behold the *green shades,* the beauty and Majestie of the tall and antient *groves,* to be skill'd in *planting* and dressing of *Orchards, Flowres,* and *Pot-Herbs,* to temper and allay these harmlesse *imployments* with some innocent merry *song,* to ascend sometimes to the *fresh* and *healthful hils,* . . . to heare the *musick* of birds, the *murmurs* of Bees, the *falling* of *springs,* and the pleasant discourses of the *Old Plough-men,* where without any impediment or trouble a man may walk. (p. 130)
>
> [W]hen the *Sabbath-day* comes . . . The poorest *Country-labourer* honours that day with his best *habit*; their *families,* their *beasts,* and their *cattell* rest on that day, and every one in a decent and Christian *dresse* walks Religiously toward his *Parish Church.* (p. 131)
>
> Toward *sun setting,* the *nightingale* and other pleasant *birds* carroll to him out of the *wood,* his *dogs* like faithfull attendants walk about him; The *Rams* leap, the *kids* skip and his *Yard* abounds with *Pigeons, Turkeys, Capons, ducks* and all sorts of *Poultrie.* . . . Though he should rest no where else, but on *straw,* or the bare *Earth,* yet are his sleeps unbroken, and far more sweet, than those *naps* which are taken upon *silks,* and *beds* of *down.* (p. 134)[18]

I do not think I have misrepresented Vaughan's essay. There is much in his idyllic picture of the countryside that soothes and attracts a reader's imagination. It would have to be a very sour reader who did not recognize and sympathize with Vaughan's real love for the retired and

18. *The Works of Henry Vaughan,* ed. L. C. Martin (Oxford, 1957), pp. 123–36.

unambitious life of a country gentleman. When one recalls that this "Praise . . . of the Countrie-Life" was published in 1651, the year that Charles II lost the Battle of Worcester and became a fugitive, and also a year in which Royalist estates were being sequestered in increasing numbers, while the small tenants and laborers on those estates suffered heavy exactions from the new owners, local officials, and soldiers anxious for their pay, then Vaughan's nostalgic depiction of a harmonious and peaceful hierarchical society—even if it never existed in such a perfection of universal contentment—becomes more understandable. In the circumstances and given the chance, even the plowmen might have preferred Vaughan's ideal. Two years later a report on expropriated lands noted that "the tennants of those lands doe perfectly hate those who bought them, as possibly men can doe; for these men are the greatest tyrants every where as men can be; for they wrest the poore tennants of all former imunitys and freedoms they formerly enjoyed."[19]

Still, there is undoubtedly moral confusion and failure of vision in an idyll that turns its plowmen into pleasant fixtures of the landscape, making their discourses one with the singing of the birds and the murmuring of the bees, while the owner walks about his farm from task to task "without any impediment or trouble." The confusion between plowman and landowner obscures a never-quite-stated distinction between what is good for the laborer—to rise with the sun, work all day, sleep on straw, and rest (like the farm animals) on Sundays—and what is good for the owner—to read, contemplate, stroll about, enjoy the landscape and the rural sports, and turn even the supervision of chores into leisurely pleasures, secure in the illusion that his laborers are as content as he is and that he has successfully escaped the guilt of being a *"Caterpiller"* upon society (p. 136) by the simple act of fleeing the city for the country. I do not mean that Vaughan should necessarily have taken up a spade to join the laborers of Breconshire at their tasks—although two years earlier others had called upon Englishmen to do just that—but rather that his writings, like those of most of his fellow poets, are peculiarly blind to the moral and social value of labor of any kind. Vaughan and most of his fellow poets saw the countryside through the accustomed glasses of pastoral vision. Pastoral, whether it was concerned with shepherds suffering from the pangs of love or with hermits breath-

---

19. Letter of December 14, 1653, from "T. M." to the English merchant "Rider" in Paris, *Thurloe State Papers*, I, 633; see also Christopher Hill, "The Agrarian Legislation of the Revolution," *Puritanism and Revolution* (1958; New York, 1964), pp. 153–96; Hill cites this letter p. 187.

ing out their prayers in rural shades, was the almost universal preoccupation of writers, Puritan and Royalist alike. Georgic, by contrast, was usually ignored or silently converted by the alembic of imagination and prejudice back into pastoral.

III

If, as it seems at first, most poetry in England during the seventeenth century neglected the georgic mode, still other currents were at work. It is scarcely conceivable that georgic could have burst upon the literary world and the polite society of 1697 to quite such universal applause if there had not been some earlier, although unobtrusive, preparation of this fertile ground. When Dryden firmly established the mode for rhymed couplets during the Augustan Age, he had more than a century's worth of such verse (imperfect, to be sure) with which to work. It took criticism a considerable time to recognize the extent of that earlier history. Likewise when Dryden established the popularity of georgic his way had been made ready for him. One may trace through the course of the previous hundred years several intellectual developments, particularly in the fields of religion and science, which made his accomplishment easier.

One reason for the success that georgic was to enjoy in the eighteenth century was undoubtedly the coincidence of literary trends with social and economic changes. For it was in the eighteenth century that a long transformation in English agriculture finally reached its culmination in what was called the New Husbandry and, later, the Agricultural Revolution. Historians of agriculture have stressed the importance of certain mechanical inventions, such as the seed-drill and the horse-drawn hoe, which Jethro Tull developed near the turn of the century. Crop seeds, which had been hand-broadcast since the beginning of history, now could be planted in rows, producing a much greater yield per acre. But fifty years passed before these revolutionary devices came into common use. Arthur Young (the friend of Fanny Burney), who wrote extensively on agricultural theory, became Secretary to the Board of Agriculture (1793) and founded a periodical, *Annals of Agriculture* (1784–1809) in order to give farmers a place to record experiments, nevertheless wrote as late as 1770 that the new machines were worthless, since farm laborers might be expected to hitch them up and immediately bash them against a fencepost or a wall. Nevertheless, with his keenness for experimentation and innovation and his conviction that modern agriculture could enrich and transform the whole country, Young exemplifies the temper of his time. He urges the aristocracy and intellectual leaders to involve themselves in husbandry, to take an active part in directing the work—something that would not have been conceivable a century earlier. What would once have been a gentleman's shame has now become his civic duty:

> It is the business of the nobility and gentry who practise agriculture, and of authors who practise and write on it, to help forward the age; to try experiments on newly introduced vegetables, and if they are found good, to spread the knowledge of them as much as possible; to endeavour to quicken the motions of the vast but unwieldy body, the common farmers. But to omit this either in practice or in writing, is to reduce themselves to the level of those whom they ought to instruct; and to submit to that ignorance and backwardness, which left to themselves, cloud any country, in an enlightened age, with the darkness of many preceding centuries. Common farmers love to grope in the dark: it is the business of superior minds, in every branch of philosophy, to start beyond the age, and shine forth to dissipate the night that involves them.[20]

There still is class feeling here in plenty; but now it is the gentleman's duty not to scorn but to lead his laborers in their civilizing work. Indeed, to a large extent Young feels confident that he is preaching to the converted:

> Perhaps we might, without any great impropriety, call farming the reigning taste of the present times. There is scarce a nobleman without his farm: most of the country gentlemen are farmers; and that in a much greater extent of the word, than when all the country business was left to the management of the stewards, who governed, in matters of wheat and barley, as absolutely as in covenants of leases, and the merit of tenants; for now the master oversees all the operations of his farm, dictates the management, and often delights in setting the country a staring at the novelties he introduces. The practice gives a turn to conversation, and husbandry usurps something on the territories of the stable and the kennel; an acquisition which I believe, with reasonable people, will be voted legal conquest.
>
> But to speak in another strain: all parts of rural oeconomics are, at present, much studied, and no less practised. It is impossible but this admirable spirit, which does so much honour to the present age, must be attended with great effects. For men of education and parts cannot apply to any thing without diffusing a light around them; much more so when they give their attention to a business that hitherto has occupied few besides the most contracted and most ignorant set of people in the world. And facts, as far as they have been discovered, warrant this opinion; for, I apprehend, no one will dispute there having been more experiments, more discoveries, and more general good sense displayed, within these ten years, in the walk of agriculture, than in an hundred preceding ones. If this noble spirit continues, we shall soon see

20. *Rural Oeconomy; or, Essays on the Practical Parts of Husbandry* (1770), pp. 36–37.

husbandry in perfection, as well understood, and built upon as just and philosophic principles, as the art of medicine. (pp. 173–75)

By 1770 the English were in the forefront of European agricultural progress; still, they continued to trade ideas with the Continent. Bound up with Young's essays is a newly translated tract by a Swiss agriculturalist entitled *The Rural Socrates*. The engaging author of this work proposes the formation of a new society with a significant name: "a Georgical Society of men of character, whose inflexible integrity, and complete knowledge of every thing relative to husbandry, might secure universal confidence and approbation." The members of this Georgical Society would travel the countryside and awake "a noble emulation" in the breasts of peasants, in order "to bring agriculture to a state of perfection." They would keep a journal of discoveries and summon the most worthy peasants, "in testimony of the public approbation, presenting them with the destined prize! I would choose to have it a medal, representing a labourer driving his plough; in the air the genius of agriculture, placing a crown on his head, composed of ears of corn and vine leaves interwoven, with this motto, 'For the best cultivator'" (pp. 475–76). Somewhat patronizing, one may feel; yet surely the thought that a peasant could be stirred to "noble emulation" would have seemed strange to most people in the early seventeenth century. Such a georgic ideal of heroism would have been almost inconceivable; noble emulation was for budding Aeneases, not for plowmen. Nevertheless, a student of the seventeenth century who reads about these Enlightenment projects of the Rural Socrates and of Arthur Young may well recognize several familiar notes in this unfamiliar context: experiment, trial, dirtying of hands, working cooperatively, publishing the results. All of these progressive sentiments, including the awarding of honors to the contributors to, rather than the destroyers of, a fruitful society, go back to Francis Bacon.

The essence of the agricultural revolution belongs to innovations that were closely connected with well-known major social and economic transformations going all the way back to the Tudor accession. The basis of efficient farming is improvement of the soil, and that can only be accomplished by crop rotation and, as Young insistently argues, by what he calls "proportion"—the division of a farm into pasture and arable, so the livestock may be fed in summer and kept over in winter and may in turn help work and fertilize the fields.[21] New crops such as turnips, which

21. On soil husbandry, see also Edward Hyams, *Soil and Civilization* (1952; rpt. New York,

were popularized as an efficient winter fodder by Charles, Viscount Townsend (known to posterity as Turnip Townsend), came into general use. A second necessity was for the aristocracy as well as the rising middle class to change its views about what constitutes virtuous and public-spirited behavior—with the literary consequence that at least some attention was shifted from the martial ideal that is proper to feudalism to the georgic ideal that is proper to a newly centralized nation-state. A third necessity, or at least the only method available within the political possibilities, was enclosure, the process of converting land from commons to private use, for that was the chief method that permitted the improvement of the soil by means of "proportion" and rotation.

Ironically, as feudal England was slowly and painfully transformed into a nation-state, the way to agricultural progress and general prosperity lay directly through social injustice and widespread rural suffering. Although the process took at least two centuries—and is reflected in literature from *Utopia* to *The Deserted Village*—the decade that seems to have decisively tipped the balance from a basically feudal to a basically modern system of land use was that of the 1650s. Expropriations, forced and voluntary sales, enclosures, and expulsion of tenants so greatly accelerated as a result of the Civil War that economic pressures practically forced land- and rent-holders to increase the efficiency of their operations in order to survive. Forests were cut down, fields were plowed up, rents were doubled and doubled again, and out of this chaos emerged eventually the New Husbandry and the Augustan Age. By no coincidence remarkably similar historical processes underlay the composition of Vergil's *Georgics*: civil war, land expropriation, new capital formation, and the prospect of a period of national unity and peaceful prosperity somewhere just ahead.

Since the forces leading to change were well under way in the seventeenth century, one would expect to find in its literature more reflections of the georgic transformation than critics have spoken of. In any period the mass of writers may follow events, but ordinarily at least a few anticipate them. Indeed such proves to have been the case. To speak first of the minor writers and hacks, there were a few early, sometimes subliterary, writers on husbandry. Thomas Tusser published several editions of his abominable *Five Hundred Pointes of Good Husbandrie* in the late sixteenth century. His concern oscillated between making a quick

1976), esp. pp. 244–68.

Ere thou a fruitfull-Cropp shalt see;
Thy ground must plough'd and harro'wd be.

ILLVSTR. X.

Book.3

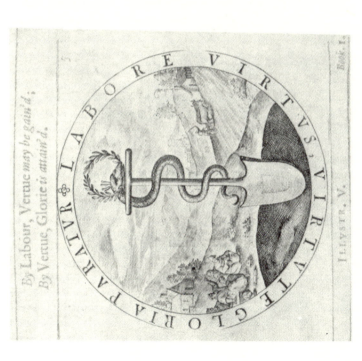

By Labour, Vertue may be gain'd;
By Vertue, Glorie is attain'd.

ILLVSTR. V.

Book. I.

PLATE I. George Wither, *A Collection of Emblems* (1635), p.5.

PLATE II. George Wither, *A Collection of Emblems* (1635), p. 144.

In vtrumque paratus.
To IOHN PAYTON *Esquier.*

2 Esd. cap. 4. WHEN SANABAL Hierusalem distrest,
With sharpe assaultes, in NEHEMIAS tyme:
To warre, and worke, the Iewes them selues addrest,
And did repaire theire walles, with stone, and lime:
One hande the sworde, against the foe did shake,
The other hande, the trowell vp did take.

Of valiant mindes, loe here, a worthie parte,
Ouid. 1. Pont. 4. *Nescio qua natale solū dulcedine cunctos Ducit, & immemores non sinit esse sui.* That quailed not, with ruine of theire wall:
But Captaines boulde, did prooue the masons arte,
Which doth inferre, this lesson vnto all:
That to defende, our countrie deare from harme,
For warre, or worke, wee eyther hande should arme.

Murus

PLATE III. Geffrey Whitney, *A Choice of Emblemes* (Leyden, 1586), p. 66.

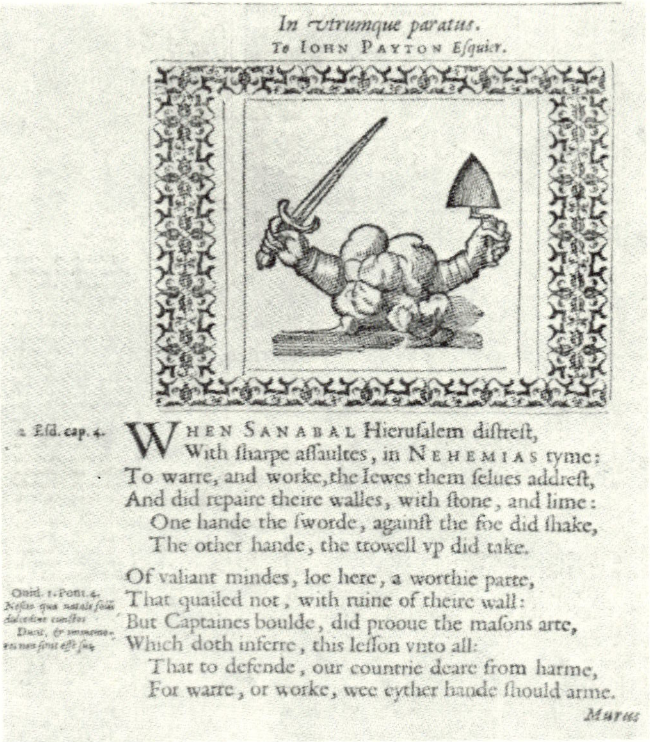

ADAM iubetur fodere & arare terram, eiectus è paradiso. Mulier sub viri potestate constituitur, & in dolore parit.

GENESIS III.

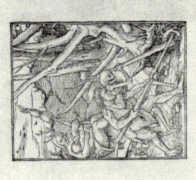

En grand labeur, & sueur de son corps
Le pere Adam a sa uie gaignée,
Heue tandis en doloreux effortz
Subiecte à l'Homme enfante sa lignée.

PLATE IV. Hans Holbein, *Icones Historiarum Veteris Testamenti* (Lyons, 1547).

profit and preserving the ancient hierarchies. Only once does he touch on anything like the georgic ideal, in a riddle poem that is quite Vergilian in theme if not in skill:

> I seeme but a drudge, yet I passe any King
> To such as can use me, great wealth do I bring.
> Since Adam first lived, I never did die,
> When Noe was shipman, there also was I.
> The earth to susteine me, the sea for my fish:
> Be readie to pleasure me, as I would wish.
> What hath any life, but I help to preserve,
> What wight without me, but is ready to sterve.
>
> In woodland, in Champion, Citie, or towne
> If long I be absent, what falleth not downe?
> If long I be present, what goodnes can want?
> Though things at my comming were never so scant.
> So many as loove me, and use me aright,
> With treasure and pleasure, I richly acquite.
> Great kings I doe succour, else wrong it would go,
> The King of al kings hath appointed it so.[22]

Tusser's conclusion suggests how easily the Vergilian vision of husbandry as a means for national prosperity, together with such related civilizing skills as fishing and the conquest of the sea (*Georgics* I. 141–45), can be given a Christian turn. Husbandry seems "but a drudge," yet it has the sanction of the King of kings and therefore is worthy of honor and respect even from those at the top of the social scale. One searches Tusser in vain, however, for any reappearance of this philosophic view. He quickly returns to his usual mixture of didacticism, forehead-knuckling, and greed, interspersed with characteristic moments of pastoral relaxation. His is generally the old view of husbandry, not the new.

In *Observations touching Trade and Commerce with the Hollander, and other Nations; Presented to King James* (posthumously published), Sir Walter Ralegh tries to persuade the King that his treasury would gain more by building up the nation's prosperity than by pillaging it with taxes. "Then how much more mighty things might we make," he asks the King, "where so great abundance and variety of homebred commodities and rich materials grow for your people to work upon, and other plentiful means to do that withal, which other nations neither have nor cannot

---

22. Tusser, *Five Hundred Pointes of Good Husbandrie (1580),* ed. W. Payne and Sidney J. Herrtage (London, 1878), pp. 15–16.

want, but of necessity must be furnished from hence?"[23] Ralegh succeeded no better than Bacon in persuading James to undertake such long-range, public-spirited projects; but his views, unlike Tusser's, represent the future.

In the early seventeenth century, Gervase Markham published a number of treatises on husbandry, although he tended to reprint the same work under different titles. An early title-page suggests the general idea: *The English Husbandman. The First Part: Contayning the Knowledge of the true Nature of every Soyle within this Kingdome: how to Plow it; and the manner of the Plough, and other Instruments belonging thereto. Together with the Art of Planting, Grafting, and Gardening after our latest and rarest fashion. A worke never written before by any Author: and now newly compiled for the benefit of this Kingdome* (1613). Although the conclusion of his title hints at altruistic patriotism, Markham was really a hack opportunist, not an innovator. His works are chiefly of interest as evidence that there was a market for various do-it-yourself publications. His "Second Booke" of husbandry, which appeared in 1614, contained practical advice on kitchen gardens and cattle as well as angling and the breeding of fighting cocks. Ambitious to be a Renaissance man of letters, Markham published works on a variety of other practical subjects: the breeding of race horses, archery, how to get wealth, country contentments or the husbandman's recreations, the grammar of soldiership, and the essentials of veterinary practice. Other writers in the period published manuals on hunting, fishing, horsebreeding, dog training, and the like. For the most part these manuals are concerned more with the sporting than with the practical side of country life, and they seem to be addressed to amateurs, to country gentlemen or would-be gentlemen, or to city-dwellers who dreamed of a change of occupation. Whatever pragmatic emphasis there may be is on traditional lore and on the theme of self-enrichment, usually couched in some variant of the perennial formula: Get rich quick! There is little interest in the sort of innovation and experiment that characterize the treatises of the following century. Moreover, however detailed and practical a given expert's advice may be, he is likely to portray the country against which that advice is set as a place for pleasant, essentially pastoral, relaxation—not for georgic improvement of the common good.

IV

The one writer before Dryden whom recent historians of the English

23. *The Works of Sir Walter Raleigh, Kt.*, VIII (1829; rpt. New York, n.d.), 375.

georgic cite is Abraham Cowley, although they commonly treat him as a kind of sport or exception, not as a connecting link to an earlier tradition. His *Several Discourses by Way of Essays* (1688) includes the century's fullest collection of verse translations from Vergil and Horace on husbandry and the country life.[24] Although Cowley's translations are skilled, they cannot be said to accomplish much more philosophically than to bring together in a crowning summary the fruits of the century-long practice of extracting happy-husbandman poems from the classics without offending the English taste for gentlemanly leisure.[25] Far more novel and significant is Cowley's introductory essay to the poems, "Of Agriculture." Cowley begins with an evocation of Vergil, perhaps in recognition that, while Horace had provided more country poems for imitation (as Cowley's own translations confirm), Vergil was the more serious advocate of husbandry. "The first wish of *Virgil* (as you will find anon by his Verses) was to be a good Philosopher; the second, a good Husbandman." Of husbandry, Cowley argues that "There is no other sort of life that affords so many branches of praise to a Panegyrist: the Utility of it to a mans self: The Usefulness, or rather Necessity of it to all the rest of Mankind: The Innocence, the Pleasure, the Antiquity, the Dignity" (pp. 400–01).

Cowley remarks directly on that crucial difference between Roman and English attitudes towards husbandry, which had earlier given trouble to English teachers of the *Georgics:*

[W]e have no men now fetcht from the Plow to be made Lords, as they were in *Rome* to be made Consuls and Dictators, the reason of which I conceive to be from an evil Custom, now grown as strong among us, as if it were a Law, which is, that no men put their Children to be bred up Apprentices in Agriculture, as in other Trades, but such who are so poor . . . [that they cannot farm efficiently]. Whilst they who are Proprietors of the Land, are either too proud, or, for want of that kind of Education, too ignorant to improve their Estates. (p. 401)

Cowley's words reveal that he knows very well that, while he may personally think that agriculture is the best of subjects for praise, his age did not; as any reader will realise, seventeenth-century panegyric chose for its commonest subject not farming but war.

24. Rpt. in *The English Writings of Abraham Cowley,* ed. A. R. Waller, I (Cambridge, Eng., 1906), 409–28.
25. For an overview of this tradition, see Røstvig, pp. 71–116.

Yet agriculture, Cowley goes on to argue, is the one necessary art, to which all others may be said to be "like Figures and Tropes of Speech which serve only to adorn it." The chief stumbling block to a recognition of this fact, and to a consequent acceptance of agricultural reform, is a deeply ingrained contempt, first for agriculture and second for manual labor, and therefore a double contempt for the combination. As Cowley ironically argues, the wrong accomplishments are valued and therefore honored:

> Behold the Original and Primitive Nobility of all those great Persons, who are too proud now, not onely to till the Ground, but almost to tread upon it. We may talke what we please of Lilies, and Lions Rampant, and Spread-Eagles in Fields d'Or, or d'Argent; but if Heraldry were guided by Reason, a Plough in a Field Arable, would be the most Noble and Antient Armes. . . .
>
> And yet, who is there among our Gentry, that does not entertain a Dancing Master for his Children as soon as they are able to walk? But, Did ever any Father provide a Tutor for his Son to instruct him betimes in the Nature and Improvements of that Land which he intended to leave him? (p. 404)

To remedy this unreasonable state of affairs, Cowley proposes the foundation of an agricultural college in each of the Universities. Four professors would preside over a body of scholars and fellows, and it is surely no coincidence that the four fields those professors would take for their specialties correspond almost exactly to the four books of Vergil's *Georgics*. "First, *Aration*. . . . Secondly, *Pasturage*. Thirdly, *Gardens, Orchards, Vineyards,* and *Woods*. Fourthly . . . the Government of *Bees*" (p. 405). Cowley departs from Vergil only by assigning to the fourth professor activities that Vergil had omitted, such as the care of swine and poultry, the study of decoys and ponds, and even the science of field sports, "which ought to be looked upon not onely as Pleasures, but as parts of Housekeeping."

Although Vergil might appropriately be named honorary founder of Cowley's proposed agricultural college, Cowley insists that there must be nothing backward-looking or theoretical about the projected course of study. His professors are not to read "Pompous and Superficial Lectures out of *Virgils Georgickes, Pliny, Varro,* or *Columella*" but should oversee a practical training program—so practical, indeed, as serendipitously to pay all the college's expenses out of resultant income. Cowley's caution almost certainly reveals that he was aware of complaints that the first holders of chairs in science and mathematics at the universities had disappointed their founders' hopes by their unenterprising pedantry.[26]

If one looks forward, he may recognize in Cowley's project the typical voice of the eighteenth-century agriculturalists and, beyond them, the eventual foundation of land-grant and agricultural colleges, the aims and programs of which are not very different from what Cowley suggests. If one looks back, he will recognize the voice of the man whom Cowley elsewhere calls the Moses of the scientific movement: Francis Bacon, with his emphasis on practice, experiment, and concern for the common welfare. The place of Bacon in Cowley's thinking about agriculture is even more evident in an earlier treatise on the founding of an all-purpose scientific college, *A Proposition For the Advancement of Experimental Philosophy,* which Cowley published in 1661, the year before the Royal Society received its charter. Among the facilities of the college are to be a "Garden, containing all sorts of Plants that our Soil will bear." Another garden is "destined only to the tryal of all manner of Experiments concerning Plants, as their Melioration, Acceleration, Retardation, Conservation, Composition, Transmutation, Coloration, or whatsoever else can be produced by Art either for use or curiosity" (p. 251). One of the sixteen resident professors will take agriculture for his specialty. Concerned that his project should not appear too visionary to be put into practice, Cowley misleadingly dissociates it from its obvious progenitor: "[W]e do not design this after the Model of *Solomons* House in my Lord *Bacon* (which is a Project for Experiments that can never be Experimented) but propose it within such bounds of Expence as have often been exceeded by the Buildings of private Citizens" (p. 251). At this point one might say that Cowley is speaking more as a fund-raiser than as a scientific historian.

Among the wonders of Solomon's House to which Cowley refers are Bacon's "large and various orchards and gardens, wherein we do not so much respect beauty, as variety of ground and soil."[27] There the fellows of the House practice experiments in grafting and innoculation. "And

26. The truth of the charge is much debated, but the existence of such criticism is admitted. See Christopher Hill, *Intellectual Origins of the English Revolution* (1965; rpt. London, 1972), pp. 14–84; Barbara Shapiro, *John Wilkins 1614–1672* (Berkeley, Cal., 1969), pp. 118–47; and further works cited by Shapiro, p. 253*n.*

27. *The Works of Francis Bacon,* eds. James Spedding, Robert Leslie Ellis, and Douglas Denon Heath (London, 1870), III, 158.

we make (by art) in the same orchards and gardens, trees and flowers to come earlier or later than their seasons; and to come up and bear more speedily than by their natural course they do. We make them also by art greater much than their nature; and their fruit greater and sweeter and of differing taste, smell, colour, and figure, from their nature. And many of them we so order, as they become of medicinal use" (III, 158).

Like Cowley, Bacon tries to redirect panegyric impulses from their usual subjects, such as war and conquest, to activities he considers to be more useful: innovation and invention. Bacon is taken by the idea of raising statues not to kings or generals but to inventors and similar benefactors of mankind. In Solomon's House are two long galleries: one a museum of notable discoveries, the other for statues of "all principal inventors." "For upon every invention of value, we erect a statua to the inventor, and give him a liberal and honourable reward" (III, 165–166). Elsewhere, the ingenious Bacon is able to find some time-honored precedents in support of his efforts to redirect human priorities. In *The Proficience and Advancement of Learning* (1605), he points out that, according to Dionysius, the highest orders of angels represent love and knowledge, while power and ministry are assigned to the lower orders. The Bible frequently honors invention and intellectual innovation. And, by taking a euhemeristic approach to the classical myths, Bacon is able to argue that even those militant heroes so often honored by humanity who performed the most constructive deeds, "founders and uniters of states and cities, lawgivers, extirpers of tyrants, fathers of the people, and other eminent persons of civil merit," could rise no higher than the rank of demigod. "[O]n the other side," Bacon claims, "such as were inventors and authors of new arts, endowments, and commodities towards man's life were ever consecrated amongst the gods themselves, as was Ceres, Bacchus, Mercurius, Apollo." At least two of these four gods were agricultural benefactors. They are rightly called gods, Bacon explains, because they benefited not the inhabitants of a single time or place, but all of humanity; and because their deeds were not violent but have "the true character of divine presence, coming in *aura leni,* without noise or agitation."[28]

In his efforts to overturn habitual attitudes, Bacon recognizes that the inherently different values of an aristocracy whose origins are feudal might impede his reforms. In his essay "Of Nobility" (*Essayes,* 1625), he

28. Bacon's "*aura leni*" or gentle breeze is from the Vulgate, 3 Kings 19.12, which corresponds to the "still small voice" of the Authorized Version, 1 Kings 19.12.

observes an important reactionary dynamic: "Nobility of birth commonly abateth industry; and he that is not industrious, envieth him that is" (VI, 406). In "Of the True Greatness of Kingdoms and Estates," he writes:"Let states that aim at greatness, take heed how their nobility and gentlemen do multiply too fast. For that maketh the common subject grow to be a peasant and base swain, driven out of heart, and in effect but the gentleman's labourer" (VI, 446). Roman moralists of Vergil's time and after frequently make the same point. That is the negative side of Bacon's view; the positive likewise echoes the Romans and expands on what Ralegh was trying to explain to King James:

> And herein the device of king Henry the Seventh (whereof I have spoken largely in the history of his life) was profound and admirable; in making farms and houses of husbandry of a standard; that is, maintained with such a proportion of land unto them, as may breed a subject to live in convenient plenty and no servile condition; and to keep the plough in the hands of the owners, and not mere hirelings. And thus indeed you shall attain to Virgil's character which he gives to ancient Italy:
> *Terra potens armis atque ubere glebae.*[29] (VI, 447)

The very basis of a nation, economically and culturally (including its ability to wage war should that be necessary), rests on the character and quality of its agriculture.

The convergence between Ralegh's views and Bacon's is evident in several of Bacon's other remarks in the *Essayes*. In "Of Plantations," Bacon recommends that a leader should choose, as the best sort of colonists, "gardeners, ploughmen, labourers, smiths, carpenters, joiners, fishermen, fowlers, with some few apothecaries, surgeons, cooks, and bakers" (VI, 457). Proper use of the soil is essential, and the colonists should develop such natural resources as timber, salt, soap, silkworms if the climate allows, pitch and tar from evergreens, drugs from plants, and the like. "But moil not too much under ground," he warns, "for the hope of mines is very uncertain, and useth to make the planters lazy in other things" (VI, 458). In Bacon's opinion, England should not seek too rapid enrichment (doubtless he has in mind the example of Spain, as well perhaps as the sad projects of Elizabeth and Ralegh) but should instead seek wealth that is more genuine, lasting, and beneficial to humanity. In "Of Riches," he argues that "The improvement of the ground is the most natural obtaining of riches; for it is our great mother's blessing, the earth's; but it is slow" (VI, 461). Nonetheless, it must be admitted that even the clear-sighted Bacon is not always prepared, in the *Essayes* at

---

29. *Aeneid*, I.531: A land strong in arms and in fertility of soil.

least, to put the georgic vision of peaceful national greatness first. In the passage quoted earlier from "Of the True Greatness of Kingdoms and Estates," which recommends the creation of a strong yeoman class in England, Bacon quotes not from the *Georgics* but a line of the *Aeneid* in which fertility of soil is balanced equally with strength of arms. So one need not be too surprised when Bacon concludes his discussion of how a nation's economy and social fabric may be strengthened by the pursuit of georgic values with an appeal to the epic sensibility of his audience: "But above all, for empire and greatness, it importeth most, that a nation do profess arms as their principal honour, study, and occupation. For the things which we formerly have spoken of are but habilitations towards arms; and what is habilitation without intention and act?" (VI, 449). Civil wars, Bacon subsequently remarks, are like a fever; but a good foreign war is like exercise; it warms and invigorates the body politic.

Benjamin Farrington credits Giordano Bruno with having brought to England and to Bacon's attention "a revolutionary conception of science as power." Farrington illustrates his thesis with a quotation from Bruno's *Lo Spaccio della Bestia Trionfante.* "The gods have given man intelligence and hands," Bruno argues, to enable him to work not only "in accordance with nature" but "beyond that and outside her laws," creating "other natures, other courses" and in the end making himself "god of the earth." But he must put his mind and hands to use. To prove his argument, Bruno adduces none other than the topos of the primitive development of human arts:[30]

> Thus, in the Golden Age, men, through idleness, were worth not much more than dumb beasts still are today, and were perhaps more stupid than many of them. But, when difficulties beset them or necessities reappeared, then through emulation of the actions of God and under the direction of spiritual impulses, they sharpened their wits, invented industries and discovered arts. And always, from day to day, by force of necessity, from the depths of the human mind rose new and wonderful inventions.[31]

The chief source of this particular and increasingly popular view of invention is the Jupiter theodicy of Vergil's *Georgics* (I.121–46), in which Vergil distills and transforms into his own more optimistic vision the

30. On the primitive invention of arts, see Arthur O. Lovejoy and George Boas, *Primitivism and Related Ideas in Antiquity* (Baltimore, 1935), and Erwin Panofsky, "The Early History of Man in Two Cycles of Painting by Piero de Cosimo," *Studies in Iconology* (1939; rpt. New York, 1972), pp. 33–68.

31. Trans. in Benjamin Farrington, *The Philosophy of Francis Bacon* (1964; rpt. Chicago, Ill., 1966), p. 27.

spirit of Lucretius' *De Rerum Natura*. At the heart of Vergil's theodicy is the idea that God wants man to struggle, to invent, and to improve his lot by his own efforts, and to that end that he has deprived man of the easy life and sent need (*egestas*) in order to drive him to invention and finally to civilization. Bacon could as well have found these ideas, which allowed a crucial reinterpretation of the development of the arts in Genesis, directly in the *Georgics* (from which he quotes four times in *The Proficience and Advancement of Learning*) as indirectly in the works of such intermediaries as Vitruvius or Bruno.

Taking into account the whole body of Bacon's writings, not just those moments when he talks specifically about agriculture, it should be obvious that his philosophy could not have been better calculated to lead a nation towards a georgic vision of its greatness. It is Bacon above all who was responsible for the tone of the eighteenth-century agricultural treatises. He emphasized hard practical work and experimentation, insisted that humanity (under God's benevolent but nonintervening eye) take its destiny into its own hands, stressed the material benefits and the fruitfulness of all useful endeavors, praised invention and discovery, and popularized an optimistic view of history that encouraged people to plan for the long term and to cooperate with one another for the benefit of humanity. Bacon supports these broad goals with relevant imagery, which includes recurrent georgic images of building, of path-cutting, of sea voyages and discovery, of planting and nourishing, and of bringing to fruition.[32] In the second book of *The Advancement*, Bacon poises the wisdom of Solomon against that of Vergil and clearly prefers the latter. He employs two telling quotations: "*Dicit piger, Leo est in via*" (The lazy man says there is a lion in the path; see Prov. 22.13); and "*Possunt quia posse videntur*" (They can because they think they can; *Aeneid*, V.231).

Contrary to Bacon's optimism was the traditional, pessimistic vision of many of his contemporaries, who were only capable of seeing agriculture socially as beneath contempt and theologically as little more than a manifestation of the continuing curse that God had laid on Adam at the fall. John Donne abruptly concludes his bleak tour of history in "The Progresse of the Soul" with a harsh and typical reminder:

> Who ere thou beest that read'st this sullen Writ,
> Which just so much courts thee, as thou dost it,
> Let me arrest thy thoughts; wonder with mee,
> Why plowing, building, ruling and the rest,

32. See Brian Vickers, *Francis Bacon and Renaissance Prose* (Cambridge, Eng., 1968), pp. 174–201.

Or most of those arts, whence our lives are blest,
By cursed *Cains* race invented be,
And blest *Seth* vext us with Astronomie.[33]

For Bacon, however, the fall was less a permanent curse than an opportunity: a chance for man, with God's approval, to take matters into his own hands and by his labors to regain the control over nature that he lost in Eden. Bacon concludes the "Plan" of *The Great Instauration* with a prayer that is virtually a distillation of all his aspirations:

> Therefore do thou, O Father, who gavest the visible light as the first fruits of creation, and didst breathe into the face of man the intellectual light as the crown and consummation thereof, guard and protect this work, which coming from thy goodness returneth to thy glory. Thou when thou turnedst to look upon the works which thy hands had made, sawest that all was very good, and didst rest from thy labours. But man, when he turned to look upon the work which his hands had made, saw that all was vanity and vexation of spirit, and could find no rest therein. Wherefore if we labour in thy works with the sweat of our brows thou wilt make us partakers of thy vision and thy sabbath. Humbly we pray that this mind may be steadfast in us, and that through these our hands, and the hands of others to whom thou shalt give the same spirit, thou wilt vouchsafe to endow the human family with new mercies. (IV, 33)

Later in this same volume, Bacon ends the second book of *The New Organon* with a similar hope: "[C]reation was not by the curse made altogether and for ever a rebel, but in virtue of that charter [in virtute illius diplomatis] 'In the sweat of thy face shalt thou eat bread,' it is now by various labours (not certainly by disputations or idle magical ceremonies, but by various labours) at length and in some measure subdued to the supplying of man with bread, that is, to the uses of human life" (IV, 248).

Given the religious beliefs of farmers and agricultural laborers in the seventeenth century, it is only natural that they too, as well as the intellectual leaders, should have had Genesis in mind when they considered their occupations (See Plate IV). As Edward Hyams suggests, such thoughts lingered in men's consciousness as late as the end of the nineteenth century, when American pioneers were settling Oklahoma. Those farmers, Hyams writes, "were simple and honorable men with a worthy purpose, that of keeping their families in bread and independence by the sweat of their faces—of religiously fulfilling the curse laid upon Adam and Eve."[34] What Bacon did was to reconsider the nature of that

---

33. *The Satires, Epigrams and Verse Letters of John Donne,* ed. W. Milgate (Oxford, 1967), p. 46.
34. Hyams, p. 140.

primal curse and, in the true spirit of Vergil's georgic theodicy, call it not a curse but a charter or, in Bacon's Latin, *diploma*: that is, a government document conferring privileges on the persons addressed, a grant of human liberty, a promise, should men fulfill the terms, of future prosperity and the return of Eden.

V

If Bacon was the originating, he was not the proximate source of Cowley's enthusiasm for a reformed agriculture. In "Of Agriculture," Cowley describes the sort of professor he wants for his proposed college and reveals, perhaps unintentionally, a good deal about the intellectual tradition to which he is indebted. His model professors "should be men not chosen for Ostentation of Critical Literature, but for solid and experimental Knowledge of the things they teach . . . ; so industrious and publick-spirited as I conceive Mr. *Hartlib* to be, if the Gentleman be yet alive" (p. 405).

Hartlib, Milton's compeer in the reform of education, represents the convergence in the middle seventeenth century of all those intellectual strains that were eventually to contribute to an English version of the georgic perspective on life, and thus at length to prepare a social nexus sufficiently firm to insure an enthusiastic response to georgic poetry. In Hartlib were combined an almost messianic commitment to religious reform, to educational reform, and to the advancement of science along Baconian lines for the benefit of humanity. Hartlib's "Experimental Academy," which opened briefly in 1630, took Bacon as its prime authority for a program that proposed to discard "emptie and barren Generalities, being but the very husks and shales of sciences,"[35] in favor of humanistic studies and training in various practical affairs. Among Hartlib's papers are notes on how much it might cost to found a "College of Tradesmen" such as one proposed by William Petty, and elsewhere there are suggestions for training students in such "mechanical" employments as navigation, surveying, and husbandry (pp. 45, 51).

Hartlib was also involved with writing prefaces for, encouraging, publishing, and sometimes begetting, during the crucial decade of the 1650s, a number of books on husbandry—books whose spirit contrasts sharply with that of Gervase Markham's. Hartlib transcribed and published Cressy Dymock's *An Essay for Advancement of Husbandry-Learning. Or Propositions for the Erecting a Colledge of Husbandry* (1651). The plan was to

---

35. G. H. Turnbull, *Hartlib, Dury, and Comenius* (London, 1947), p. 37. Further quotations from Hartlib's unpublished writings (except the letters to Boyle) are from this work.

apprentice students for seven years to a society of fellows, who were to perform agricultural experiments and to spread the knowledge and practice of good husbandry throughout the country (pp. 63, 96). Hartlib also directed to the Council of State a prefatory Epistle to Sir Richard Weston's *A discours of Husbandrie used in Brabant and Flanders* (1650), a book which proposed that the English might profitably imitate the Dutch and improve their land on a national scale. New editions appeared in 1652 and 1654. Still other treatises published between 1651 and 1655 in which Hartlib had a hand concerned farming, gardening, raising silkworms, and the natural history of Ireland "*with the several way[s] of Manuring and improoving the same.*" There is a similar scheme for draining the fens and improving the wastes of England, and a discourse on the grafting of fruit trees.

The cooperative spirit in which many of these treatises were conceived and written is suggested by one of Hartlib's notes, which refers to "The promised Observations of the Husbandry of Clover from Mr. Tho. Mackworth's friend" (p. 98). A similar group spirit is suggested by Hartlib's letter to Robert Boyle, in which Hartlib reports that he has "received a special commission from Sir Charles Culpepper" entreating him "most passionately to put you [Boyle] in mind of the promise you were pleased to make unto him, about the new invented plough of Dr. [John] *Wilkins* [of Wadham College, Oxford]."[36] In 1657 Hartlib again wrote Boyle, and some interesting names turn up among this circle of georgical correspondents:

> Here you have a vindication of the decaying clover-grass, written and sent unto me by Mr. *Wood* from *Dublin.* . . . I suppose you remember the great expectations I have of the Quaker of *Durham, Anthony Pierson,* his promises of husbandry. I have not yet obtained any thing from his hands, but major general *Lilburne* pretends to know his universal compost; and a friend of his was pleased to entrust me with it. . . . A greater quantity of lime, or laid in any other manner on the land, burns out the vegetable salt and spoils it, as is experienced in the West by colonel *Monck.* . . . Thus I have discovered unto you, that magnet of husbandry without any reserves.[37]

John Evelyn visited Hartlib at Charing Cross on November 27, 1655. He notes that the "honest & learned Mr. *Hartlib*" has "propagated many Useful things & Arts," and reports him to be "Master of innumerable

---

36. Shapiro, *John Wilkins,* p. 134.

37. *The Works of the Honourable Robert Boyle,* ed. Thomas Birch (1772; facsimile Hildesheim, Georg Olms, 1966), VI, 92–93. Although historians commonly think of Hartlib as a follower of Comenius, he took the lead in agriculture, a subject in which Comenius does not appear to have shared his interest.

Curiosities, & very communicative."[38] Evelyn also took an interest in agricultural reform; he reports that on the afternoon of April 11, 1656, a group that included Wilkins, Boyle, Lord George Berkeley, and Evelyn himself, called on Col. Thomas Blount after dinner, in order to have a look at his "new invented Plows" (III, 169–70). After the Reformation, John Wilkins, who turns up twice in these notices, became a member of the third most popular committee of the Royal Society (after Mechanical and Trade): the aptly named "Georgical" Committee.[39]

Clearly there were growing circles of people in England who shared Hartlib's interest in a Baconian reform of agriculture; one of his main achievements was to inspire others with the reforming fervor and to persuade them to publish in a similarly Baconian spirit of cooperation. The best-known result of this intellectual ferment (leaving aside the question of whether Hartlib had any part in founding the Royal Society) is Milton's open letter to Hartlib, *Of Education*. Milton, of course, was no man's follower; he represents another powerful center for the development of the georgic spirit during the period. Still, he presumably knew that Hartlib would approve when he urged that students be encouraged and taught how "to improve the tillage of their Country, to recover the bad Soil, and to remedy the waste that is made of good," or when he suggested that such men as "Hunters, Fowlers, Fishermen, Shepherds, Gardeners" be brought in to give a practical dimension to the teaching and to help clarify "the rural part of *Virgil*."[40]

The title of a treatise Hartlib published in 1652 summarizes the optimism, even the apocalyptic fervor, with which various experiments in husbandry were being urged: *Cornu Copia. A Miscellaneum of lucriferous and most fructiferous Experiments, Observations, and Discoveries, immethodically distributed; to be really demonstrated and communicated in all sincerity.* The proliferation of scientific and propagandistic treatises on agriculture between 1650 and 1655, quite different in tone from those of Markham and earlier writers, again reveals—as Walton and Vaughan revealed by their negative responses—that at the midpoint of the Interregnum fundamental changes in the way men viewed and practiced agriculture

38. John Evelyn, *Diary*, ed. E. S. de Beer (Oxford, 1955), III, 162–63.

39. Thomas Birch, *The History of the Royal Society of London* (1756–1757; facsimile New York, 1968), I, 406–07. The committees and their memberships were: Mechanical (67), Astronomical and Optical (15), Anatomical (3 named), Chemical (7 named), Georgical (31), Histories of Trade (35), collecting phenomena of nature and experiments (21), and Correspondence (20). Other familiar figures on the Georgical Committee were Aubrey, Boyle, Evelyn, Oldenberg, and Waller.

40. *The Works of John Milton*, eds. Frank A. Patterson, et al. (New York, 1931–1940), IV, 282, 284.

were well under way. Closely connected with those changes was the urge to put the theoretical agenda "really" and "in all sincerity" into practice. The perception that the majority of the English still resisted the new georgic vision accounts for the many proposals in the 1650s to found reformed schools and colleges, which would teach such practical arts as husbandry.

From the beginning, the New Science went hand-in-hand with religious reform, which in England (although not everywhere on the Continent) meant Protestant reform. The Puritan Revolution therefore seemed to be a heaven-sent opportunity for those with the right views to put their ideas about agriculture into practice and thus to develop still further ideas by experiment. At first it might seem odd that people wanted to publish and to read about farming in the midst of the turmoil of the second civil war, or that such men as Lilburne and Monck should concern themselves with fertilizer when they would seem to have had more important matters in hand; but in point of fact agricultural method—as Gerard Winstanley certainly knew—was close to the heart of the whole revolutionary movement. And while things did not always work out as the visionaries would have wished, the agricultural revolution was one of the most concrete results of the Civil War. In the 1650s, while private gain was scarcely forgotten, still there was a new and seemingly genuine sense that agriculture could be a civic and a public-spirited activity, and that its improvement might benefit the whole nation and at length all of humanity.

The title to a sequel to *A discours of Husbandrie* further reveals the new spirit: *Samuel Hartlib his Legacie: or An Enlargement of the Discourse of Husbandry used in Brabant and Flanders; wherin are bequeathed to the Common-Wealth of England more Outlandish and Domestick Experiments and Secrets in reference to Universall Husbandry* (1651; also 1652, 1655). The same spirit persisted through the Restoration; in a petition to Parliament, Hartlib claims to have benefited his adopted country with "The best experiments of industry practised in husbandry and manufactures and in other inventions and accommodations tending to the good . . . of this age and posterity" (p. 88). Thus Cowley, whose interest in agriculture goes back to this period, was one of the beneficiaries of Hartlib's "legacy"; and the audience for his essays had been well prepared by the agricultural reform movement of the 1650s, which Bacon did so much to inspire and over which Hartlib informally presided as coordinator and publicist.

By general agreement, Francis Bacon, hard as he tried, was not a successful experimenter. But before new inventions or new ways of doing things can come into general use, it is necessary to change people's minds. At that task, Bacon was the master; and Hartlib and Cowley were among his successors. The work of shifting the consciousness of a whole society is also, as Shelley claims, the responsibility of poets. When, at the very beginning of the georgic revolution, Spenser defied his time and spoke of himself as the plowman-poet of *The Faerie Queene*; when Jonson insisted, against the convention of aristocratic sprezzatura, that he who would "write a living line, must sweat"; when Milton gave his readers a Christ in *Paradise Regained* whose task is not to wage war against Satan but to turn him aside and *raise an Eden* "in the wast Wilderness"; then all three were in the forefront of the new movement. No one can say precisely how far the georgic spirit that pervades the work of Spenser, Jonson, and Milton helped to shift people's minds concerning the value of farming and of labor; but it is certain that the minor poets and trend-followers in the eighteenth century took to georgic quite as eagerly as their minor predecessors had ignored or scorned it. Doubtless Dryden's translation rode the crest of this transformation and helped to increase its momentum, but it did not solely account for it.

To summarize, critical inattention has blinded us to a powerful strain of georgic sensibility that runs through English writings of the seventeenth century, gradually displacing the age's prejudices against farming and manual labor. Over a considerable period, humanism, the impulse to religious and social reform, and (as we have been chiefly concerned to show here) the growth of the New Science all contributed to a georgic revolution of major proportions. The Vergilian dream of an alternative to war, of a realistic and fruitful goal for society, of a new kind of heroism for poetry to celebrate, was to issue at last in the Georgical Committee of the Royal Society, in the widespread practice of agricultural reform, and, oxymoronically, in the easy georgic of the eighteenth-century poets. Yet the early and middle seventeenth century witnessed the gathering of requisite mental energies and the transformation in modes of perception that made those later developments possible. As had been the case with Vergil, the best and most powerful poetry was written not by those who witnessed and responded to the agricultural revolution, with its inevitable compromises of generous ideals, but by those who dreamed and worked beforehand, and who participated in the task of bringing about a georgic revolution of the mind.

"Wee feaste in our Defense": Patrician Carnival in Early Modern England and Robert Herrick's "Hesperides"

PETER STALLYBRASS

I N February 1596 Thomas Platter observed the carnival processions in Avignon: "each group was masked and costumed in a different manner, as pilgrims, as peasants, as sailors, as Italians, as Spaniards, as Alsations etc. Others were dressed as women. In front of each group marched musicians, with cymbals." That was on Shrove Tuesday. The following day Platter watched "a large procession dressed as the Apostles, as the Evangelists, and as saints" which marched into the churches. The previous day's masquerades continued as before, but when they met this religious procession "they ceded the middle of the road to it." "Indeed," Platter continues, "they could do no less, for, I was assured, it was to obtain God's pardon for their folly that this procession was instituted."[1] The contrast between the processions is striking: the first broke into people's houses and danced to the noisy clashing of cymbals; the second, "some singing, some wailing," processed in orderly fashion around the churches. What Platter witnessed was the transformation of the unstable into the "inevitable" as the Christian calendar was reasserted and the shroving of carnival gave way to the shriving of Lent. Plebeian carnival was obliged to cede the middle of the road as it would be obliged henceforth to respect those laws and customs which subordinated plebeian to patrician.

The "inevitable" is, of course, implicit in the very notion of a festive *calendar*. And as E. P. Thompson notes, "to the degree that the ritual calendar year chimes in with the agrarian calendar, the authority of the Church is strengthened."[2] In pre-Reformation England, Hock-day and

---

1. *Journal of a Younger Brother: The Life of Thomas Platter*, trans. and intro. S. Jennett (London, 1963).
2. "Anthropology and the Discipline of Historical Context," *Midland History* 1 (1972), 51.

Michaelmas divided the rural year into its winter and summer halves. Hock-day (the second Tuesday after Easter Sunday) was an important marker in the agrarian calendar and it was commonly celebrated by the carnivalesque seizing and binding of men by women (usually on Hock Monday) and of women by men (usually on the following Tuesday). Release was dependent upon the paying of a fine, the money collected going to the parish.[3] Thus licensed misrule paid for ecclesiastical rule. But the church calendar could, in turn, be appropriated by the state. In Venice, the festivities to celebrate Candlemas (February 2, the Feast of the Purification of the Virgin) culminated in an elaborate procession by the Doge, the "political assertion of ducal pre-eminence."[4] In Florence the feast of the patron saint, John the Baptist, was prepared for months in advance and was supervised by a group of *festaioli* appointed by the government. The festival demonstrated the strength of "the male community of citizens" both to the subordinated groups of Florence and to admiring visitors.[5]

But ruling elites did not necessarily appeal to an already existing calendar. On the contrary, they could create new calendars so as to testify to their own power. Elias Canetti argues that "the regulation of time is the primary attribute of all government," that "a new power which wants to assert itself must also enforce a new chronology."[6] The Protestant England of Elizabeth I and James I, stripped of much of the Catholic calendar, witnessed the creation of new festivals: November 17, the accession day of Elizabeth I; November 5, the deliverance of James I from a Catholic plot. Elizabeth's accession day, for instance, became a major state festival, celebrated throughout the country: "Bells rang, bonfires blazed, guns were fired, open house was kept, festival mirth reigned."[7] If, as Natalie Z. Davis has argued, misrule could "decipher King and state,"[8] King and state could, in turn, harness and appropriate the forces of misrule. In 1602, John Howson preached a sermon in defense of the Accession Day festivities, in which he argued "God hath dealt with daies as with men." As God had blessed and exalted some ("Kinges and princes") so had He "cursed and brought lowe" others, putting them

3. E. K. Chambers, *The Medieval Stage*, 2 vols. (Oxford, 1903), I, 155.

4. E. Muir, *Civic Ritual in Renaissance Venice* (Princeton, N.J., 1981), p. 156.

5. R. C. Trexler, *Public Life in Renaissance Florence* (New York, 1980), pp. 247, 278.

6. *Crowds and Power*, trans. C. Stewart (Harmondsworth, Eng., 1973), p. 462.

7. Roy Strong, *The Cult of Elizabeth* (Wallop, 1977), p. 114.

8. *Society and Culture in Early Modern France* (Stanford, Cal., 1975), p. 97.

"in meane estate, and place of base calling."[9] The same was true of days, Howson argued, and the calendar had been adjusted accordingly to commemorate Elizabethan rule.

Mikhail Bakhtin believes that, from the beginning of the seventeenth century, one can observe "a narrowing down of the ritual, spectacle, and carnival forms of folk culture, which became small and trivial."[10] This process was consequent to the extension of the state which "encroached upon festive life and turned it into a parade." Y. M. Bercé similarly notes that, in France, urban festivals had become largely aristocratic affairs by the eighteenth century.[11] If state intervention in the festive calendar has a long history, that process, it would seem, quickened during the sixteenth and seventeenth centuries. Sir Henry Wotton, writing from Venice on 26 May 1606, observed: "Yesterday was the Feast of Corpus Christi, celebrated by express commandment of the State (which goeth farther than devotion), with the most sumptuous procession that ever had been seen here." Wotton thought that the main reason for "this extraordinary solemnity" was "to contain the people still in good order with superstition, the foolish band of obedience."[12] In Venice, as elsewhere in early modern Europe, the ruling elite attempted to direct the carnivalesque into the celebration of church and state.

I

"To give a distinctively ideological cast to social experiences outside of the workplace—to unite 'war veterans,' 'tax payers,' 'sports fans,' or 'national Citizens'—demanded the creation of a nationwide political culture that might persuade people that their shared goals transcended petty economic haggling, regional and ethnic disputes, or age-old social animosities":[13] so writes Vittoria de Grazia, describing the mass organization of leisure in twentieth-century Italy to produce a "culture of consent." It was precisely such a culture of consent which, at a radically different historical conjuncture, Elizabeth I and the early Stuarts attempted intermittently, and finally ineffectually, to construct. "Consent" was all the more necessary in a state which had no standing army and which was heavily dependent upon the unpaid work of the local gentry for law enforcement. To achieve that consent, it was necessary to maintain not

---

9. *A Sermon Preached at St. Maries in Oxford the 17 Day of November 1602* (1602), pp. 3, 4.
10. M. Bakhtin, *Rabelais and His World*, trans. Helene Iswolsky (Cambridge, Mass., 1968), p. 33.
11. Y. M. Bercé, *Fête et Révolte: des mentalités populaires du XVIe siècle* (Paris, 1976), passim.
12. *The Life and Letters of Sir Henry Wotton*, ed. Logan Pearsall Smith (Oxford, 1907), I, 350.
13. *The Culture of Consent: Mass Organization of Leisure in Fascist Italy* (Cambridge, 1981), p. 2.

only economic and political dominance but also ideological hegemony through which to structure, however incompletely, the consciousness of the subordinated classes. As the Duke of Newcastle put it, "Seremonye and order with force, Governes all both in Peace and warr, and keeps Everye man and Every thinge within the Circle of their own Conditions."[14]

One aspect of the hegemonic formation of "Seremonye and order" was the attempt to re-form popular festivities as a means of social contol. At its simplest, festivity could be organized to celebrate rule. A Maypole in Guildford in James I's reign, for instance, had the King's arms on it. The pole was pulled down, but the Earl of Nottingham defended it on the grounds that "the arms of his majesty, or any other arms of noblemen or gentlemen" were perfectly acceptable.[15] More subtly, Newcastle suggests how the gentry can usurp the role of saints in popular festivities: "all thy tennants shall at their owne charge make them selfes fine and march, like Cavaliers, with tyltinge feathers gaudy as *Agamemnons* in the playe after whom thou like a *St. George* on horseback, or the high Sheriffe, shalt make the Country people fall downe, in Adoration of thy crupper and silver stirrup."[16] These lines printed in 1649, the year of Charles I's execution, appeal to the rural idyll of the lord and his tenants at the same time that they imply the dependence of that idyll upon a monarch who defended both plays and St. George, a saint totally discredited in Puritan eyes.

Paternalist defenses of popular festivity usually claimed that it would reinforce "neighbourliness" and defuse social tensions. In 1637 the Bishop of Hereford defended church ales, a custom whereby parish churches raised money by selling alcohol, on the grounds that they helped to compose local differences, increased love and unity, and brought together the rich and the poor.[17] And the unknown author of *Pasquils Palinodia* (1619) justifies May games as "a signe / Of harmlesse mirth and honest neighbourhood, / Where all the Parish did in one combine / To mount the rod of peace, and none withstood." "Peevish, Puritan," "over-wise Church-warden" and "Capritious Constables" are alike upbraided for destroying these innocent pastimes which unite top and

14. "The Duke of Newcastle on Government" in S. A. Strong, *A Catalogue of Letters . . . at Welbeck* (London, 1903) p. 210.

15. Christopher Hill, *Society and Puritanism in Pre-Revolutionary England* (London, 1969), p. 179.

16. William Cavendish, *The Country Captains* (1649), p. 22.

17. Hill, p. 186.

bottom under the paternal eyes of "The Lord of Castles, Mannors, Townes, and Towers." Those lords are magically purified of legal powers and status which are, in the poem, concentrated in the middling sort who are blamed for the decay of "all good sports and merriments."[18] In Ben Jonson's "To Penshurst" we find the same amicable unity of top and bottom, rich and poor, but here it is the *nouveaux riches* who are accused of undermining neighborliness. It is only, Jonson suggests, in the "ancient pile" that the community of feasting happily coexists with the strict hierarchy of classes, family, and landscape.

The elite thus attempted to construct carnival as controlled misrule, aimed both at increasing the dependency of grateful "swains" upon their masters and at refreshing the work force. James I defended his *Book of Sports* (issued in 1618 in support of popular festivity) on the grounds that "poor men that labour hard all the week long" needed recreation, and Alexander Nowell in his *Catechism* (1570) suggested that it was "profitable" to masters "that servants should sometimes rest between their workings, that after respiting their work outside they may return more fresh and lusty to it again."[19] It was further argued that festivities could provide a harmless release for subversive energies. Thus Sir Henry Wotton commented on the Venetian carnival in 1622, "Never was there in the licensing of public masks a more indulgent decemvirate, never fewer mischiefs and acts of private revenge; as if the restrained passions were indeed the most dangerous." Not only were the passions permitted release, but they were also, Wotton noted, diverted away from political questions: "Now, after these anniversary follies have had their course, and perhaps their use likewise, in diverting men from talking of greater matters, we begin to discourse in every corner of our new league."[20]

If the governing classes feared the "restrained passions," they also feared those passions which they were unable to *survey*. After all, festivities had the advantage of being public and therefore open to surveillance and control. One alternative to festival was the alehouse, which in early modern England was a source of constant anxiety to the authorities. One of James's justifications for the *Book of Sports* was that if sports were not made legitimate the people would go to alehouses and make "idel and discontented speeches." And Bishop Pierce, the Laudian bishop of Bath and Wells, argued that men deprived of "their honest and lawful recreations . . . would go either into tippling houses, and there

18. Sig. B3.
19. Hill, pp. 190, 148–49.
20. *Sir Henry Wotton*, II, 265.

upon their ale-benches talk of matters of the church or state, or else into conventicles."[21] The French lawyer Claude de Rubys put forward a similar argument at the end of the sixteenth century: "It is sometimes expedient to allow the people to play the fool and make merry, lest by holding them in with too great a vigour, we put them in despair. . . . These gay sports abolished, the people go instead to taverns, drink up and begin to cackle, their feet dancing under the table, to decipher King, princes."[22] "Gay sports" are advocated not only as licensed release but also as a method of surveillance; in alehouses the people's feet dance "under the table," hidden from the scrutiny of authority.

The failure to initiate "honest Pastime, harmlesse mirth" with sufficient vigor was, according to Newcastle, one of the causes of the Civil War. He wrote to Charles II that "ther Shoulde be playes to Goe upp and downe the Counterye. . . . The devirtisementes will amuse the peoples thaughtes, and keepe them In harmless action which will free your Matie from faction and Rebellion."[23] Newcastle also encouraged the revival of the maypole, the hobbyhorse, the morris dance, the bagpipes, cakes and ale, Christmas festivities, Shrovetide and "all the olde Holedayes, with their Mirth, and rightes sett up agen; Feastinge dayleye will be in Merrye Englande, for Englande Is so plentifull off all provitions, that iff wee doe nott Eate them they will Eate Us, so wee feaste In our Defense."[24]

This vision of "Merrye Englande" revives the notion of the "emerald isle," the enclosed garden, the second Eden in which mirth will flourish as it did before the Fall. At the same time the jocular emphasis upon eating up the plentiful provisions so that they don't eat the English perhaps masks a more substantial threat. In the notion of feasting "in our Defense," the fear of an ungovernable people, controllable only by a conspicuous display of patrician "charity," is displaced by the more manageable fear of overwhelming fertility. "Feastinge dayleye" was indeed one of the ideological mechanisms by which social hierarchy was rearticulated as Christian communion. The culture of consent in early Stuart England required that the gentry feasted in their own defense.

And the "timeless" place of feasting was the country. So the establishment of "Seremonye and order" was often linked to the "ruralization" of an England which was already being transformed by agrarian capitalism, proto-industrialization, and the rapid growth of the metropo-

21. Hill, p. 189.
22. Davis, p. 97.
23. "The Duke of Newcastle on Government," p. 227.
24. "The Duke of Newcastle on Government," p. 226.

lis.[25] Victoria de Grazia defines ruralization as

an ideological defence of rurality that masked the real subordination of the countryside to the urban industrial world. Inevitably, it also involved far-reaching structural changes: above all, new institutions had to be established that were at once responsive to the national state, while reinforcing the "timeless," the "traditional," and the "harmonious" in rural social arrangements.[26]

For the English gentry, of course, the court, as much as a metropolis which sold both new commodities and new forms of entertainment (e.g., the theatre), acted as a magnet. At the same time, ruralization, in seventeenth-century England as in twentieth-century Italy, masked the growth of new institutions. Those country estates, so frequently celebrated in the seventeenth century as part of a timeless tradition, depended upon new shifts in power. As Raymond Williams has remarked, Sir Philip Sidney's *Arcadia* was written in a park made by enclosing a village and evicting the tenants; Saxham, celebrated by Thomas Carew, owed its importance to court connections——"it was a favourite stopping-place on the way to and from Newmarket"; Penshurst, celebrated by Jonson, only came into the possession of the Sidneys in the mid-sixteenth century when Edward VI presented it to his tutor William Sidney. But the neo-pastoral of Carew and Jonson, as Williams notes, transmutes "a quite precise and recent set of social relationships" into "a timeless order."[27]

It is precisely such a "timeless order" to which the Stuart proclamations, ordering the return of the gentry to the country, appeal. And it is notable that these proclamations were usually published before Christmas, a period of traditional festivity. Thus the Proclamation of 9 December 1615 laments "the decay of Hospitalitie" and claims that country "housekeeping" used to be a "mutuall comfort betweene the Nobles and Gentlemen, and the inferiour sort of Commons in this Our Kingdome."[28] The political purpose of this hospitality is made clear by a note which Francis Bacon wrote in the margin of the Proclamation of 24 October 1614: "done for the better government of the several counties of

25. See P. Kriedte, H. Medick, and J. Schlumbohm, *Industrialization before Industrialization*, trans. B. Schempp (Cambridge, 1981); I. Wallerstein, *The Modern World-System I: Capitalist Agriculture and the Origins of the European World-Economy in the Sixteenth Century* (New York, 1974); D. Levine, *Family Formation in an Age of Nascent Capitalism* (New York, 1977); Lawrence Stone, *The Crisis of the Aristocracy 1558–1641* (Oxford, 1965), pp. 385-504.

26. DeGrazia, p. 99.

27. Raymond Williams, *The Country and the City* (Oxford, 1975), pp. 22, 40, 41.

28. *Stuart Royal Proclamations*, ed. J. F. Larkin and P. L. Hughes (Oxford, 1973), I, 356-57.

your Kingdom and maintenance of hospitality and relief of the poor, especially now against Christmas."[29] "Better Government" would be founded upon a return to rural festivity, located in a festive calendar immune, at least at the level of pastoral myth, to the whirligig of time and its attendant turbulence.

Through ruralization, social relations which were crucially structured by court and city could be presented as part of a timeless country tradition. This paradox is exposed in the career of poets like Drayton and Jonson. Dependent upon London as a center of patronage and seeking (unsuccessfully in Drayton's case, successfully in Jonson's) favor at court, they nevertheless wrote of an harmonious rural order. Indeed, ruralization and the development of the center, seemingly opposed, were in fact interdependent. The English rural idyll, which focused increasingly in the 1620s and 1630s upon the defense of "popular" festivities and sports, was a strategy intended to consolidate the ideology of local paternalism while demonstrating the dependency of that paternalism on the central *pater familias*, the monarch.

II

We can examine the symbiotic relation between Court and Country, center and periphery, in the development of the Cotswold games. The games were organized by Robert Dover from about 1612, and were apparently presented as a simple continuation of rural tradition. But they were undoubtedly "modernized," which meant relating the sports "to classical mythology and Renaissance culture, whilst linking them with the throne and the King's Protestant Church."[30] The games, indeed, held during the traditional festival period of Whitsuntide, completely transformed *local* Whitsun-ales into a semi-professional, county (or even national) entertainment, organized, according to Anthony à Wood, "with leave from King James." Wood claims that the games were "frequented by the Nobility and Gentry (some of whom came 60 miles to see them)."[31] This rural festivity, then, was not only a neighborly festival but also a celebration of the national elite.

In 1633 Charles I reissued the *Book of Sports*, defending popular festivities; in 1636 *Annalia Dubrensia* was published, a collection of poems

29. *Stuart Royal Proclamations*, I, 323n.

30. *Robert Dover and the Cotswold Games: Annalia Dubrensia*, ed. C. Whitfield (Evesham, Eng., 1962), pg. 2. See also D. Brailsford, *Sport and Society: Elizabeth to Anne* (London, 1969), pp. 99–108.

31. Anthony à Wood, *Athenae et Fasti Oxonienses*, quoted in *Robert Dover*, p. 18.

by various writers celebrating Dover's games. The poems are inter-woven with the language of *The Book of Sports*: "honest mirth and recreation," "honest Pastime, harmless mirth." But the connection between the Cotswold games and the courts is made explicit by Nicholas Wallington, who wrote:

> Dover, strange Monarchs, and their force despiseth;
> Hee bowes to none, his Charles hee only prizeth:
> He is Invincible to all but one;
> To's King he yeelds, or els he yeelds to none! . . .
> Who durst assemble such a troope as hee,
> But might of insurrection charged bee?
> His souldiers, though they every one discent
> In minds and manners, yet his merriment
> Ones them: Lords, Knights, Swaines, Shepherds, Charles agree
> To crowne his sports: discords make harmony.[32]

"Merriment ones them." Wallington's poem is an essay in the politics of festivity, appealing to the discords which make harmony against the more troubling discords of what Jonson, in the same collection, calls "Hipocrites" (i.e., Puritans), "the worst of Subjects." The Cotswold games show the acceptable face of insurrection and dissent: they are the necessary irritants to be overcome in a "oneing" which, as in *Henry V*, suggests both an egalitarian community ("a band of brothers") and a paternal hierarchy in which all must yield to the King.[33]

At the same time the games served to exclude certain groups. If, at least in theory, knight and swain are brought together, the urban "middling sort" are conspicuous by their absence. Or perhaps they are subsumed under the heading of those opponents of the games who, according to John Trussel, should "like a Jew and heathen Turke" be "banished good societie." Puritans are elided with pagan and Jew as the demonized Other. The irony is that the Puritans objected to "countrie wake," "Carnivals," "Palme and rush-bearing," "Whitsum-ales," "May-games," and "general playes" on the grounds that they were "profane and heathenish," as Trussel himself notes.[34] The governing elite, royalist and Puritan, were at one in attempting to create national unity. Where the two factions differed was in their definition of the "forraine pastimes" to be avoided or censored.

---

32. *Robert Dover*, p. 150.

33. *Henry V*, 4.3.60. All quotations from Shakespeare are from the Riverside edition, ed. G. Blakemore Evans (Boston, 1974).

34. *Robert Dover*, pp. 106, 105.

And Dover's games, for all their appeal to the timeless and the traditional, did indeed savor of "forraine pastimes." In a period when "country" usually meant "county," Dover was a "foreigner," a Norfolk man who had only recently settled in the Cotswolds. From 1619 he was the agent of Endymion Porter, an important figure at court who had been educated in Spain and was probably a convert to Catholicism. Moreover, *Annalia Dubrensia* included not only the contribution of Dover's local friends and relatives but also of Dover's legal friends from London and of Jonson and Davenant, major figures in the development of the court masque. The very title of the collection suggests that Dover's games were a classicizing attempt to rival the festivals of pagan Rome. Given Dover's claim that he had been told "T'invent these sports,"[35] their appearance as timeless rural idyll seems largely fictional. Trussel, for instance, despite his rural rhetoric, was Mayor of Winchester in 1624 and 1633. The ruralization of the Cotswold games was, indeed, an ideological defense of country carnival that masked the real subordination of the rural periphery to the royal center; appropriately, the Robert Dover who listened to the "Jolly shepheards baggpipes" was dressed in the cast-off clothes of the king.[36]

But we should not dismiss rural rhetoric too lightly, for its function was complex. It provided a symbolic vehicle appropriate to the formation of a culture of consent by presenting the court and its clients as defenders of both rural freedom and rural harmony. Thus Randolph appropriates the term "ancient libertie" from those who would defend the rights of Parliament and reapplies it to the rural laborers: "O might I but their harmlesse Gambols see / Restor'd unto an ancient libertie." It is, Randolph implies, those who support "harmless May-poles" and "harmlesse Gambols" who are the true defenders of "libertie." "Harmless" is here a double-edged concept. It is both a religious term, legitimating sports against those "Who think there is no mirth but what is sin"[37] and a secular one, replacing Puritan "standings, lectures, exercises" with "harmless" (i.e., depoliticized) "Olimpicke exercise" which, Jonson claims in his epigram to Dover, will "advance true Love, and neighbourhood, / And doe both Church and Common-wealth the good."[38]

Rural rhetoric is one of the means by which social and political

35. *Robert Dover*, p. 224.

36. *Robert Dover*, p. 23.

37. "An Eclogue on the noble Assemblies revived on Cotswold Hills, by Mr. Robert Dover," *The Poems of Thomas Randolph*, ed. G. Thornbury (London, 1929), p. 121.

38. Ben Jonson, *Poems*, ed. Ian Donaldson (Oxford, 1975), p. 334.

struggle is reinscribed as the harmless insurrection of country sports. Such rhetoric, whether in praise of a country house banquet or of the Cotswold games, was the more politically eloquent for being depoliticized, appealing to the "disinterested," "gratuitous" relationships of "timeless" tradition. Dover's "generosity," his "conspicuous distribution," were, as Bourdieu says of gifts in general, operations "which tend to bring about the transmutation of economic capital into symbolic capital. Wastage of money, time . . . is the very essence of the social alchemy through which an interested relationship is transmuted into a disinterested, gratuitious relationship, overt domination into misrecognized, 'socially-recognized' domination, in other words, *legitimate authority*."[39]

III

A "timeless" past, structured only by the rhythms of the festive year, is central to the depoliticized politics of Robert Herrick's *Hesperides*, published in 1648. He writes:

> I sing of Brooks, of Blossomes, Birds, and Bowers:
> Of April, May, of June, and July-Flowers.
> I sing of May-poles, Hock-carts, Wassails, Wakes,
> Of Bride-grooms, Brides, and of their Bridall-cakes.[40]

"Times trans-shifting" is largely contained in the inevitability of aging and in the movements of a festive calendar which elides the profane and the religious. "Corinna's going a Maying," "The May-pole," and "The Hock-cart" rub sides with "Ceremonies for Christmas," "Ceremonies for Candlemas Eve," and "Julia's Churching." Pagan and Christian, classical, medieval and Caroline merge. As Leah Marcus observes, "*Hesperides* quite deliberately blurs historical distinctions."[41] This is not, of course, accidental. It is rather an essential part of a mythical genealogy which founds an "uncontroversial" Englishness in "custom," "rural life," "popular festivity."

Peter Heylyn, the biographer of Archbishop William Laud, began his *History of St. George* as follows:

> It is a sad complaint of Melchior Canus, that many of us in this more neate and

39. P. Bourdieu, *Outline of a Theory of Practise*, trans. R. Nice (Cambridge, 1977), p. 192.

40. "The Argument of his Book," *The Poetical Works of Robert Herrick*, ed. L. C. Martin (Oxford, 1956), p. 5.

41. Leah S. Marcus, "Herricks's *Hesperides* and the 'Proclamation for May'," *Studies in Philology*, 76 (1979), 64. I am indebted to Marcus' fine article throughtout this section.

curious Age, doe peevishly (to say no worse) reject those ancient Stories, which are commended to us in the best and gravest authors . . . . He spake it not at randome: but as a man which well fore-saw to what extremities, that restless humour of leaving nothing undiscussed, and not so onely, but leaving nothing in the state wee found it, at the last would bring us.[42]

Hesperides is implicitly directed against the "restless humour of leaving nothing undiscussed." Like Michael Drayton who wrote "Against those fooles that all Antiquitie defame,"[43] Herrick creates an idyll where everything remains "in the state wee found it." Herrick's pastoral enclosure is the more appealing since the "wolves" outside are scarcely referred to and therefore its justification appears to be pleasure rather than fear. In this enclosure, wantonness is encouraged for it remains a "cleanly-Wantonnesse,"[44] purged of the subversive power of restless humors.

Thus in "The Wake" (the patronal festival of a parish church), all "business" is transformed in "the sport" of morris dancing, pageants of Maid Marian, and plays performed by actors who, though "Base in action as in clothes," will be sufficient to please the "incurious Villages." Conflict is not absent, cudgel-play leading to a broken head:

> But the anger ends all here;
> Drencht in Ale, or drown'd in Beere.
> Happy Rusticks, best content
> With the cheapest Merriment:
> And possesse no other feare,
> Than to want the Wake next Yeare.[45]

"Ale," "Beere," "cheapest Merriment"—these are the opiates of "Happy Rusticks" whose lives are measured by the interval between one holiday and the next. But there is, perhaps, an implicit threat in these lines. At present the rural workers have "no feare" because they are contained within the inevitability of the festive calendar. We may recall, though, Newcastle's warning that the suppression of "harmless action" would lead to "faction and Rebellion."[46] In poem after poem Herrick

42. *The History of St. George of Cappadocia and the Institution of the Most Noble Order of St. George, named the Garter* (London, 1631), pp. 1-2.

43. "Poly-Olbion," Song VI, *The Works of Michael Drayton*, ed. J. W. Hebel (Oxford, 1941), p. 118.

44. "The Argument of his Book," *Robert Herrick*, p. 5.

45. *Robert Herrick*, p. 255. Cf. Ben Jonson, "To Sir Robert Wroth": "The jolly wassall walkes the often round, / And in their cups, their cares are drown'd."

46. "The Duke of Newcastle on Government," p. 227.

recreates that "harmless action." His fictive garden is defended by festivals as well as by feasts.

But *Hesperides* is curiously explicit about the role of festival within a patrician order. A. Van Gennep distinguished between the liminary stage of carnival, when the threshold is crossed into festive time, and the phase of reintegration into everyday time.[47] These stages correspond in *Hesperides* to the movement from the wantonness of licensed transgression to the re-entry into working life. Hence, Herrick's attention is not only to May-games but also to those festivals which mark the closing off of the carnivalesque. The wassailing of "Twelfe Night, or King and Queene" is balanced by "Saint Distaffs Day, or the Morrow after Twelfth Day," when women were supposed to resume their spinning and other employments after the Christmas celebrations. Saint Distaff's Day (January 7) holds, then, a liminal position between holiday and the everyday. Appropriately, Herrick's poem begins "Partly worke and partly play," and concludes: "Give St. Distaffe all the right, / Then bid Christmas sport good night; / And next morrow, every one / To his owne vocation."[48] Sport leads back inevitably into "vocation." Herrick has no less than four poems celebrating Candlemas Eve and Candlemas (February 2) which he seems to elide with St. Distaff's Day as the point of transition from Christmas revelry: "End now the White-loafe, and the Pye, / And let all sports with Christmas dye" ("Upon Candlemasse day"). And in "Ceremony upon Candlemas Eve" the taking down of Christmas decorations implies a return to the quotidian, fancifully embroidered by Herrick into the goblins who will afflict the maids who have not finished the task of clearing "the Christmas hall."[49]

Even in "The Hock-Cart, or Harvest Home," the expected "merry cheere" is partially closed off by the poem's ambivalent ending:

> And know, besides, ye must revoke
> The patient Oxe unto the Yoke,
> And all goe back unto the Plough
> And Harrow, (though they'r hang'd up now.)
> And, you must know, your Lords word's true,
> Feed him ye must, whose food fils you.
> And that this pleasure is like raine,

47. A. Van Gennep, *The Rites of Passage*, trans. M. B. Vizedom and G. L. Caffee (London, 1909), chapter 1.

48. *Robert Herrick*, p. 315.

49. *Robert Herrick*, pp. 285, 304.

Not sent ye for to drowne your paine.
But for to make it spring againe.[50]

The extent to which the "disinterested, gratuitous relationship" of the
lord to his workers is revealed as "overt domination" is surprising. For
the last three lines mark a strange *reversal* of that common ideological
maneuvre through which (contested) human history is transformed into
(uncontested) natural process. Here, the innocent "raine," which does
not drown (like the flood) but leads rather to "spring," must also be read
as the licensed "pleasure" which the lord provides only so as to make the
laborers' "paine" "spring againe." (The lines can mean either "this
pleasure is not sent for you, the labourers, to drown your pain, but to
restore spring" or "this pleasure is not sent to obliterate your pain but to
make your pain spring forth again.") The lines are so radically ambivalent that they threaten to subvert the ethic of "communal reciprocity"
which is central to the rural idyll.

But that ethic is not only challenged by internal contradictions.
Although, as we have already noted, *Hesperides* largely avoids the explicitly "political," within the presumed context of the writing of the poems
(mainly the 1620s to the 1640s) and of their first publication (1648), they
could not but have seemed a resolute defense of Charles I's policies. The
carnivalesque itself is used by Herrick, as it was by the Jacobean and
Caroline government in the *Book of Sports*, to produce a mythic unity of
prince, gentry and people which could be used as a weapon in a struggle
within the governing classes. Militant Protestants had been conducting a
prolonged campaign since Elizabeth's reign against popular festivities.
Stubbes's attack upon plays, pagan festivals and that "stinking Ydol" the
Maypole (1583) is greatly expanded by William Prynne in his massive
Histrio-mastix (1633) in which he denounces Christmas revelry as deriving
from the Roman Saturnalia "where fidlers and others acted lascivious
effeminate parts, and went about their Towns and Cities in womans
apparrell." Prynne also notes how the Catholic Church appointed a
counter-festival, like the patrician procession in Avignon, "to bewaile
those heathenish Enterludes, sports, and lewd idolatrous practises."[51]

Stubbes and Prynne were central figures in the ideological justification of new social regulations which were increasingly enforced by the

50. *Robert Herrick*, p. 102.
51. P. Stubbes, *Anatomie of Abuses*, ed. F. J. Furnivall (London, 1877-79), I, 149. W. Prynne,
Histrio-mastix (1633), pp. 755-56.

"better sort" in the localities. In Terling, an Essex village, dancing on the green in time of divine service was attacked in 1588, and pipers and dancers were prosecuted in 1594 and 1600. This seems to have had the precise effect which Bishop Pierce and Claude de Rubys feared: "These gay sports abolished, the people go instead to taverns."[52] Or rather, in Terling, the "gay sports," successfully removed from the green, continued *in* the taverns, for in 1616 Robert Melford was prosecuted for going "with a tabor and pipe from alehouse to alehouse upon the Sabothe dayes and often times he hath had a waringe of it."[53]

Of course, the royalist defense of sport was not intended to lift repression but to create an alliance between top and bottom against the growing power of the Puritans. Even Herrick's "Ceremonies for Candlemas" are partially aimed at forging that alliance. We have already stressed the importance of the concept of "Ceremony" to staunch royalists like the Duke of Newcastle. What we should now note is that the celebration of Candlemas, the Feast of the Purification of the Virgin, was a particularly contentious issue. According to L'Estrange, it had been celebrated at court "with more than ordinary solemnity," and in 1628 Peter Smart, preaching in Durham Cathedral, denounced the Laudian Bishop Cosins for "renuing that Popish ceremonie of burning candles to the honour of our Ladye."[54] Herrick's "Ceremonies" are not innocent. He wants ceremony for the sake of conformity. "Conformity," he writes, "gives comeliness to things." And in an epigram significantly entitled "Lawes," he claims: "Who violates the Customes, hurts the Health, / Not of one man, but all the Common-wealth."[55] Herrick wants to collapse laws into customs. But to do that, those customs must first be rewritten as the comeliness of conformity. Herrick would undoubtedly have agreed with the anonymous author of *Pasquila Palinodia* who, lamenting the decay of the Maypole, wrote:

> What should be the cause
> That you were almost banish't from the earth?
> You never were rebellious to the lawes,
> Your greatest crime was harmlesse honest mirth.[56]

52. Hill, p. 189 and Davis, p. 97.

53. K. Wrightson and D. Levine, *Poverty and Piety in an English Village: Terling 1525-1700* (New York, 1979), p. 157.

54. Sir R. L'Estrange, *Charles I*, quoted under "Candlemas" in OED; C. Hole, *A Dictionary of British Folk-Customs* (Frogmore, Eng., 1978), p. 58.

55. *Robert Herrick*, p. 318.

56. *Pasquila Palinodia*, Sig. B4.

The "harmlesse honest mirth" of a Maypole freed from the taint of subversion becomes a defense against "factious schismes."

We do well, though, to remember that laws are still necessary to reinforce a "culture of consent." The 1630s, in which Herrick wrote many of his lyrics, were the years of Charles's "personal rule." The emergency measures introduced in the dearth of 1630-31 to deal with public order and poor relief were not lifted in the following years, and the privy council ordered the assize judges to control carefully the work of the local J.P.s. Informers were used on a greater scale than ever before. The prerogative courts, and in particular Star Chamber, were notoriously active, and the pressure of central government "was probably stronger than it had been for at least a century."[57] As Newcastle argued, "Seremonye and order *with force*, Governes all." And force hovers on the margins of Herrick's rural idyll, which is framed by a series of epigrams on the absolute powers of the monarch:

> That Prince, who may doe nothing but what's just,
> Rules but by leave, and takes his Crowne on trust.
> ("A King and No King")

> The Gods to Kings the Judgement give to sway:
> The Subjects onely glory to obay.
> ("Obedience in Subjects")

> Twixt Kings and Subjects, ther's this mighty odds,
> Subjects are taught by Men; Kings by the Gods.
> ("The Difference betwixt Kings and
> Subjects")[58]

It is the King's authority which underpins Herrick's fiction of "harmless honest mirth," his culture of consent.

IV

Authority and consent were increasingly interrogated during the 1630s. Indeed, no rural idyll could fully counteract dearth and an economics of arbitrary taxation. It was, of course, a class fraction of the governing elite rather than a popular movement which initiated the breakdown of Charles's rule. But that breakdown exposed not only a

57. K. Wrightson, *English Society 1580-1680* (London, 1982), p. 154; M. Hawkins, "The Government: Its Role and Its Aims" in *The Origins of the English Civil War*, ed. C. Russell (London, 1975), p. 49; R. Ashton, *The English Civil War: Conservatism and Revolution 1603-49* (London, 1978), pp. 63, 45.

58. *Robert Herrick*, pp. 331, 109, 12.

failure of economic policy but also an ideological failure to merge court and country. Ruralization was, after all, only *one* of the policies pursued by the King's supporters, and it was a policy without a sufficiently firm basis in patronage. Indeed, the 1630s witnessed the development of a court culture whose "cosmopolitanism and baroque styles aroused little sympathy within a realm still suspicious of French and Italian culture on religious grounds, where a taste for Renaissance art had scarcely penetrated beyond the Court." It was arguably a culture "more detached from rural society than any that had previously existed in England."[59] If Newcastle advised Charles II to revive the great progresses of Elizabeth I and to "shewe your selfe Gloriouslye to your People Like a God,"[60] it was because royalist ceremony had been conspicuously unsuccessful as propaganda in the 1630s.

Prynne, branded as a seditious libeller, not the King, drew the crowds. When he and Burton returned to London in November 1640, after their imprisonment on the Channel Islands, "multitudes of people of several conditions, some on horseback, others on foot, met them some miles from the town, very many having been a day's journey; and so they were brought, about two of the clock in the afternoon, in at Charing Cross, and carried into the city by above ten thousand persons with boughs and flowers in their hands, the common people strewing flowers and herbs in their ways as they passed, making great noise and expressions of joy for their deliverance and return, and in those acclamations mingling loud and virulent exclamations against the bishops."[61] Three years before, Prynne, Burton and Bastwick had been publicly whipped and their ears had been cut off. But the marks of royal authority which had been inscribed upon these subjects' bodies had been transformed into the oppositional signs of a Puritan pageant.

Sir Kenelm Digby complained that fewer people would come to see the King and Queen than to see the victims of Archbishop Laud, who were held in "such veneration" that "the Puritans keep the bloody sponges and handkerchiefs that did the hangman service in the cutting off

---

59. M. Smuts, "The Political Failure of Stuart Cultural Patronage" in *Patronage in the Renaissance*, ed. G. F. Lytle and Stephen Orgel (Princeton, N.J., 1981), pp. 165, 186. Prynne claimed there was a plot "to seduce the King himself, with Pictures, Antiquities, Images, and other vanities brought from Rome" (Ashton, *The English Civil War*, p. 23; see generally pp. 21-42).

60. "The Duke of Newcastle on Government," p. 210.

61. E. Hyde, 1st Earl of Clarendon, *The History of the Rebellion and Civil Wars in England*, ed. W. D. Macray (Oxford, 1888), I, 268-69.

their ears."[62] "Concord," far from presiding over the whole land, was largely confined to court masques like *Salmacida Spolia* where, along with the "Good Genius of Great Britain," she incites "the beloved people to honest pleasures and recreations, which have ever been peculiar to this nation." Ruralization becomes no more than a courtly trope, a trope moreover which is undermined when, in the very next lines, "the beloved people" are transformed into the rabble of "a sullen age, / When it is harder far to cure / The People's folly than resist their rage."[63] Here, as in *Henry V*, we can see the contradiction between the "egalitarian" and the coercive modes. In the former mode, the people are already "a band of brothers"; in the latter, they are the many-headed monster, to be ruled by "awe and fear."[64]

As the Civil War progressed, the extent of "the People's folly" was revealed. That "Freedom," who, according to Gerrard Winstanley, "comes clothed in a clownish garment," is "the man who will turn the world upside down."[65] And, in Abiezer Coppe's words, the rulers "must bow before these poor, nasty, lousy, ragged wretches" for "The plague of God is in your purses, barns, houses, horses, murrain will take your hogs (O ye fat swine of the earth) who shall shortly go to the knife and be hung up in the roof, except ... you ... have ALL THINGS common." God himself is transformed from the authoritarian patriarch into "that mighty Leveller" who will "overturn, overturn, overturn."[66]

Nevertheless the myth of "Merrie England" was a powerful weapon in the containment of subversion by the "inevitable." The failure of that myth in the 1630s and 1640s should not blind us to the ways in which a myth can be adapted to new contexts. Witness one popular version of the Civil War, the basis for innumerable historical novels and films in which the kill-joy Puritan is opposed by the fun-loving Cavalier. That popular version is not without foundation, but its foundations are less in the conflicts of the 1640s than in the resurrection of patrician carnival at Charles II's restoration in 1660. On May 8, one of St. George's festival days, Charles was proclaimed King, "and his triumphal entry into London was timed to coincide with his birthday, May 29th." "In some areas," Leah Marcus continues, "Charles's effigy replaced the customary

62. W. M. Lamont, *Marginal Prynne 1600–1669* (London, 1963), p. 40.

63. *A Book of Masques in honour of Allardyce Nicoll* (Cambridge, 1967), p. 352.

64. *Henry V,* 4.2.60; 4.1.247.

65. Christopher Hill, *The World Turned Upside Down* (Harmondsworth, Eng., 1975), p. 107.

66. *The World Turned Upside Down,* pp. 211, 210.

figure of Flora, Queen of the May, and maygames re-enacted the English Civil War."[67] In Herrick's "A Pastorall upon the Birth of Prince Charles," the shepherds praise the "little Kingship" who "As he is Prince, he's Shepherd too."[68] That shepherd, born "Three dayes before the Shutting in of May," could also be transformed in the May King. Even today, the people of Castleton in Derbyshire celebrate on Oak Apple Day (May 29) Charles's restoration. Charles and May merge in the figure of the "Garland King," who with his train processes to the church wearing a wooden frame covered with flowers and greenery. The garland is then hauled up to crown the tower.[69] As at Avignon the procession leads back to the church; the carnivalesque is reinscribed as service to God and King.[70]

67. Marcus, p. 53.
68. *Robert Herrick*, p. 90.
69. Christine Hole, *A Dictionary of British Folk-Customs* (London, 1978), p. 114.
70. I am greatly indebted to Jonathan Dollimore, Ann Jones, Alan Sinfield and Allon White both for their support and criticism, and to the 1981 Renaissance Graduate Seminar at the University of Sussex, in particular to Paul Brown and Marea Mitchell. My debt to the work of Stephen Greenblatt, Leah Marcus and Louis Montrose is greater than can be recorded in the footnotes. I came across Steven Mullaney's fine work on early modern England (as yet unpublished) too late to use it.

Sir Thomas Browne's The Garden of Cyrus *and the Real Character*

JANET E. HALLEY

SIR Thomas Brown's *The Garden of Cyrus* begins with a diagram of the quincunx, "an arrangement or disposition of five objects so placed that four occupy the corners, and the fifth the centre, of a square or other rectangle."[1] The illustration bears an aesthetic gloss taken from Quintilian: "*Quid Quincunce speciosius, qui, in quam cunque partem spectaueris, rectus est.*"[2] Browne situates perfect form in the intelligible world of number and geometrical shape, making the abstract, geometrical and regular quincunx his standard of formal beauty. By juxtaposing this diagram with a five-chapter treatise about the quincuncial ordering of nature, Browne not only proposes that nature exhibits this aesthetic arrangement, but challenges his language to do so as well. He asks his own writing to meet the perfection of the visual image, to maintain its regularity and generality. But in fact his treatise bulges with digressions from its proposed argument, digressions which list empirical evidence that nature is not entirely ordered in fives.

It is possible to see in this peculiar phenomenon evidence of Browne's "dissociated sensibility." The opening passages of E. S. Merton's *Science and Imagination in Sir Thomas Browne* make it clear that the standard modern reading of Browne as a man whose literary and scientific faculties are divorced results in a condemnation of his works—and *The Garden of Cyrus* is a case in point—as "patchworks of digression."[3] Such a view certainly underlies Edmund Gosse's declaration that *The Garden of Cyrus* is a "radically bad book."[4] But this treatise rests on an assumption—which it

1. OED.
2. *The Works of Sir Thomas Browne,* ed. Geoffrey Keynes (Chicago, Ill., 1964), I, 178. Unless otherwise noted all subsequent quotations from Browne's works are from this volume of this edition, and page numbers are given in the text. For the convenience of those using other editions of Browne's works, section and chapter numbers are also given.
3. E. S. Merton, *Science and Imagination in Sir Thomas Browne* (New York, 1949), p. 1; pp. 51, 61–62. See also Basil Willey, *The Seventeenth-Century Background: The Thought of the Age in Relation to Religion and Poetry* (New York, 1953), pp. 50–51.
4. Edmund Gosse, *Sir Thomas Browne* (London, 1905) p. 128.

unwittingly helped to dismantle—that literary and scientific concerns are coherent. Its episodes of illogic and asymmetry need not be attributed to a self-divided, erratic, irresponsible, even glib author:[5] they are distinctive literary formulations of the relations between human knowledge and ignorance. The reading of Browne's work proposed here would result not in irritation at this text's deformations but in pleasure in their precise rendering of epistemological problems, and might help readers to accept Browne's offer of "garden delights" (Dedicatory Letter, p. 176).

According to Browne, the human artifact can be perfect only if its maker possesses certain knowledge of intelligible form in nature, and this power Browne disclaims in the dedicatory epistle: "Your discerning judgement . . . will expect herein no mathematicall truths, as well understanding how few generalities and *U finita's* [Browne's note: Rules without exceptions] there are in nature. How *Scaliger* hath found exceptions in most Universals of *Aristotle* and *Theophrastus.* How Botanicall Maximes must have fair allowance, and are tolerably currant, if not intolerably over-ballanced by exceptions" (p. 176). Before *The Garden of Cyrus* even begins its task of explicating the quincunx Browne defines a major stumbling block to human mental activity: its inability to discern "rules without exceptions," to create mental forms that contain natural diversity, to define genera that include all species. Although nature follows God, art cannot follow nature. As Browne deductively seeks in nature for the quincunx, which he calls the "fundamentall figure" (Ch. I, p. 181), he inevitably finds exceptions to the order he seeks, instances of other orders, even cases which seem to exhibit no order at all. Formally, Browne's imperfect knowledge results in distortion of the text's quincuncial regularity. Browne promises anomalies and digressions because he will prefer an encyclopedic rendering of nature in its irreducible plenitude to any specious accomplishment of his formal aims: "That in this Garden Discourse we range into extraneous things, and many parts of Art and Nature, we follow herein the example of old and new Plantations, wherein noble spirits contented not themselves with Trees, but by the attendance of Aviaries, Fish Ponds, and all variety of Animals, they made their gardens the Epitome of the earth, and some resemblance of the secular shows of old" (Dedicatory Letter, p. 176).

For Browne, order and certainty are univocal. When he observes that

5. See Gilbert Phelps, "The Prose of Donne and Browne," in *From Donne to Marvell,* ed. Boris Ford (Baltimore, Md., 1956), p. 120; Stanley E. Fish, *Self-Consuming Artifacts: The Experience of Seventeenth-Century Literature* (Berkeley and Los Angeles, Cal., 1972), pp. 353–64.

"the internodial parts of Vegetables, or spaces between the joints are contrived with more *uncertainty*; though the joints themselves in many plants maintain a regular number" (Ch. III, p. 208; emphasis mine), he implies not that the contriver was uncertain but that, given an irregular phenomenon, the human mind cannot *know*. A quincuncial physiological psychology underlies this epistemology: "Things entering upon the intellect by a Pyramid from without, and thence into the memory by another from within, the common decussation being in the understanding as is delivered by *Bovillus*. Whether the intellectual and phantastical lines be not thus rightly disposed, but magnified, diminished, distorted, and ill placed in the Mathematicks of some brains, whereby they have irregular apprehensions of things, perverted notions, conceptions, and incurable hallucinations, were no unpleasant speculation" (pp. 219–20). When the human mind operates in a diagrammatically regular way, following precisely the lines of the quincunx, it knows with certainty; but madness and delusion result from the least distortion of these lines. Certainty is allied, then, to formal regularity, doubt and ignorance to distortion of regular shapes.

Indeed, in a pivotal article on the close formal relationship of *Urn Burial* and *The Garden of Cyrus*, Frank L. Huntley has shown that the second treatise proposes its own certainty against the doubt and ignorance of the first.[6] This opposition is especially sharp in the two treatises' very different successes in recovering the historical past. In *The Garden of Cyrus* Browne is able to trace the archetypal form of the garden back to Eden itself. Of all human arts, Browne declares, "there is no rivality" for historical priority "with Garden contrivance and Herbary": "For if Paradise were planted the third day of the Creation, as wiser Divinity concludeth, the Nativity thereof was too early for Horoscopie; Gardens were before Gardiners, and but some hours after the earth" (Ch. I, p. 179). Browne marshalls considerable scholarship to prove Cyrus the elder the first such artificer, the first who "brought the treasures of the field into rule and circumscription": "All stories do look upon *Cyrus*, as the splendid and regular planter" (pp. 180, 181). After laboriously presenting evidence to prove that all subsequent gardens reproduced this original order, he concludes by grounding the garden of Solomon, all other gardens, and the order common to all of them, in Eden: "And since even in Paradise it self, the tree of knowledge was placed in the middle of

6. Frank L. Huntley, "Sir Thomas Browne: The Relationship of *Urn Burial* to *The Garden of Cyrus*," *Studies in Philology*, 52 (1956), 204–19.

the Garden, whatever was the ambient figure, there wanted not a centre and rule of decussation" (p. 185). The quincunx is, then, the certain and irreducible hieroglyph that all things paradisiacal imitate. Browne is finally able to conclude that the letter χ, with its absolute historical priority as the paradisiacal form, is "the Emphaticall decussation, or fundamentall figure" (p. 181).

This sure recovery of the primal episodes of Creation suggests that *The Garden of Cyrus* with its five chapters will render perfect knowledge in perfect form. But Chapter I, where this confident recovery of origins takes place, couches its findings in a language of probability. Nearly every paragraph rests at least one major assumption on a sound but unproven hypothesis. Moreover, Browne discovers in nature mere "hints and deliveries," findings "more then probable" and "not without probability of conjecture," ones that induce "no such Paralogicall doubt" and that "I could easily believe" or that "may favourably be doubted": he even invokes the authority of "witty Idolatry"! Far more than in *Urn Burial,* here Browne enjoys a gratifying aplomb in searching out truth, but a wobble of doubt remains. *The Garden of Cyrus* is something like an interim report, the performance of a seeker half-way to truth.

But the most important formal consequence of uncertainty in *The Garden of Cyrus* is its frequent recourse to digression. If *Urn Burial*'s characteristic transition is "meanwhile," *The Garden of Cyrus* begins new topics with "Where by the way" (Ch. I, p. 182; Ch. III, pp. 194 and 196). This locution, which invariably introduces a digression, suggests that the two passages on either side of it occupy not time but space, and that the treatise as a whole should not be followed through its duration but visualized as a shape. Browne's almost homonymous use of "where" in Chapter III virtually identifies this literary shape with places in the world of mass and extension: "*Where* by the way, we could with much inquiry never discover any transfiguration, in this abstemious insect, although we have kept them long in their proper houses, and boxes. *Where* some wrapt up in their webbs, have lived upon their own bowels, from September to July" (p. 194; emphasis mine). Digressive passages thus become almost visible protuberances on the regular quincuncial form of *The Garden of Cyrus.* The material they contain is therefore fundamentally important in defining the formal dilemma this work poses.

Digressions are so plentiful, especially in Chapters III and IV, that to catalogue them all would be redundant. Some detail instances of "strict rule, although not after this order," in which Browne lists dozens of specific phenomena that conform to another figure (Ch. III, p. 196). Not only do these epidodes deny the quincunx its pretended status as a *"U finita,"* but they also frequently give rise to a second sort of digression—the random list of unassimilable facts and questions not yet answered by science. The great digression on seeds in the middle of Chapter III (pp. 196–200) ends with a spectacular example of such a list. A later digression on the digestive mechanics of rumens introduces a wealth of unassimilable data:

As for those Rhomboidal Figures made by the Cartilagineous parts of the Wezon, in the Lungs of great Fishes, and other animals, as *Rondeletius* discovered, we have not found them so to answer our figure as to be drawn into illustration; Something we expected in the more discernable texture of the lungs of frogs, which notwithstanding being but two curious bladders not weighing above a grain, we found interwoven with veins not observing any just order. More orderly situated are those cretaceous and chalky concretions found sometimes in the bignesse of a small fech on either side their spine; which being not agreeable unto our order, nor yet observed by any, we shall not here discourse on. (Ch. III, pp. 205–06)

If the first kind of digressive episode invalidates Browne's deductive generalities as generalities, this sort releases the power of concrete particulars to mock any general rule at all. The basic formal issue—at once aesthetic and scientific—is the equivocal relationship of ideal or "Mathematicall truths" to the specific facts they should univocally order.

II

Chapter III of *The Garden of Cyrus* ends with an acutely poignant episode of this second kind of digression: "He that would behold a very anomalous motion, may observe it in the Tortile and tiring stroakes of Gnatworms" (p. 209). The context gives this odd line its power. Browne has presented eleven-and-a-half pages of painstaking natural history, mostly devoted to a businesslike muster of minute particulars, when he suddenly begins to incorporate natural detail with compelling cosmic metaphors. He finds the quincunx in the "linnen folds" of Egyptian mummies, then "in the figures of *Isis* and *Osyris,* and the Tutelary spirits in the Bembine Table"; these figures lead to the "Network covering" of *Orus,* the Hieroglyphick of the world. The next paragraph returns, in a rhapsodic progression, to the real source of wisdom, finding that "This Reticulate or Net-work . . . in the inward parts of man . . . . Emphatically extend[s] that Elegant expression of Scripture: Thou hast curiously embroydered me, thou hast wrought me up after the finest way of texture, and as it were with a Needle." Browne then achieves a crescendo of significance: "Nor is the same observable only in some parts, but in the whole body of man, which upon the extension of arms and legges, doth make out a square, whose intersection is at the genitals" (p. 204). This the the *homo universalis* made famous in the present century by the version in Leonardo da Vinci's notebooks; Browne and his contemporaries often employed it to epitomize certain neoplatonic and Hermetic microcosmic systems. The figure unites the quincunx, the universe, and the male body; and by decussating them all at the genitals it emphasizes the divine creative potency of this union. Immediately after this perfect alignment with full formal significance, though, Browne digresses to cows' stomachs, declining from there to the formless heap of facts about fish and frog lungs examined above, and then trailing off into an exhausted three-and-a-half-page meander in and out of digressions. The chapter's last sentence signals its loss of perfect form.

Browne does not present this failure as a purely scientific issue. By using the *homo universalis* to juxtapose ideal form with the digressive distortion that results from man's inability to make general form cohere perfectly with concrete particulars, he makes *The Garden of Cyrus* a problematical case in late-Renaissance aesthetics.

In fact, Browne owned almost every book he needed to trace the disintegration of the High Renaissance equation of *homo universalis* with ideal form: Vitruvius' *de Architectura* (in two Italian translations), Scamozzi's *Idea della Architectura Universale,* Leonardo da Vinci's *Trattato della Pittura,* and Albrecht Dürer's *Four Books of Human Proportion.*[7] The Vitruvian definition of symmetry was *the locus classicus* for the definition of ideal beauty in the High Renaissance: Alberti drew on it when he defined beauty as "the harmony and concord of all the parts achieved in such a manner that nothing could be added or taken away or altered except for the worse."[8] The formal, even Aristotelian emphasis of this passage was combined with mystical, cosmological, neoplatonic values through a

7. *Catalogue of the Libraries of the Learned Sir Thomas Brown, and of Dr. Edward Brown, his Son* (1711). Jeremiah S. Finch will soon publish his edition of this useful catalogue: see "Sir Thomas Browne's Library," *English Language Notes,* 19 (1982), 360–70. Keynes provides bibliographical information in his *Bibliography of Sir Thomas Browne,* 2nd ed. (Oxford, 1968), pp. 165–68; and Malcolm Letts lists many of the catalogue's entries in *Notes & Queries,* 11th Ser., 10 (1914), 321–23, 342–44, 361–62, 397.

8. *The Architecture of Leon Battista Alberti in Ten Books,* trans. James Leoni (1755), quoted in slightly modified form by Rudolf Wittkower, *Architectural Principles in the Age of Humanism* (London, 1949), p. 29.

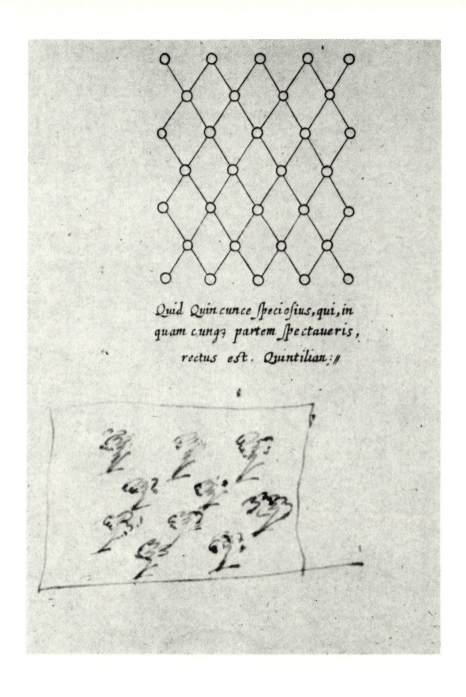

PLATE I. The quincunx, from Browne's *The Garden of Cyrus* (London, 1654), frontispiece. Reproduced by permission of The Henry E. Huntington Library and Art Gallery.

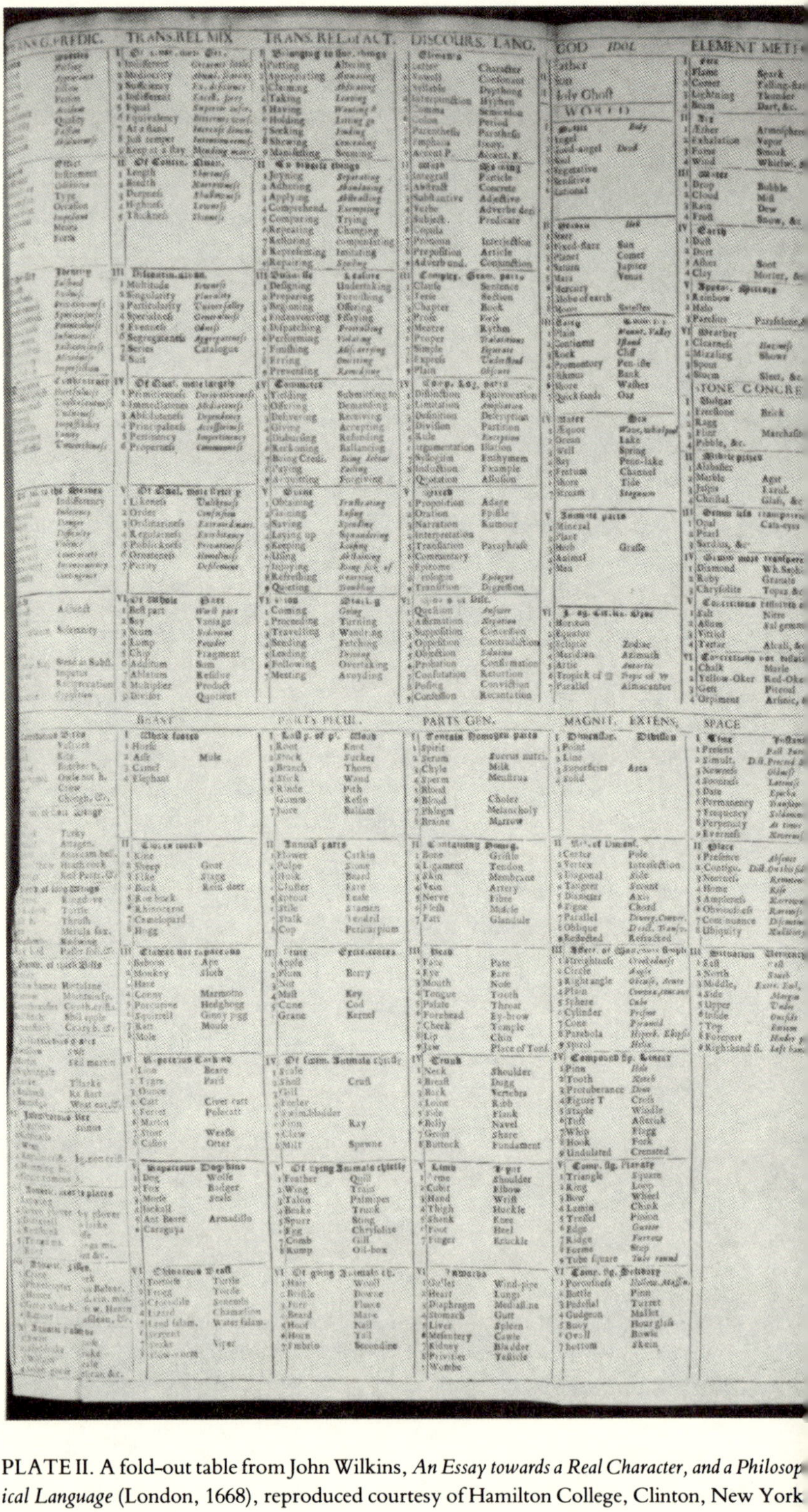

PLATE II. A fold-out table from John Wilkins, *An Essay towards a Real Character, and a Philosophical Language* (London, 1668), reproduced courtesy of Hamilton College, Clinton, New York

METTAL	HERB accor. to the Flow.	SHRUB	TREE	EXANG, INSECT.	FISH

MEASURE PROPOR.	N. POWER IMPOT.	HABIT DISPOS.	MANNERS CONVERS.	SENS. QUALITY	SICKNESS HEALTH

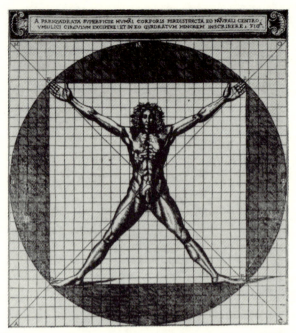

PLATE III. The *homo universalis,* from Cesariano, *De architectura* (Como, 1521), sig. G2. Reproduced by permission of the Huntington Library and Art Gallery.

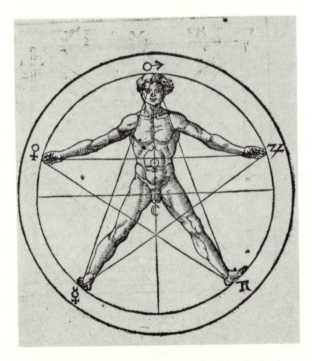

PLATE IV. The *homo universalis,* from Agrippa, *De occulta philosophia* (Cologne, 1533), sig. 04. Reproduced with permission from the Huntington Library and Art Gallery.

reading of the *homo universalis* in Vitruvius' third book on temples. There, Vitruvius observes that the human body with hands and feet extended describes the two most perfect geometrical figures, the circle and the square, and that human proportions reflect the universal proportions which the perfect temple must embody.[9] Subsequently, Alberti, Francesco Zorzi, Fra Giocondo and Cesariano (Vitruvius' two editors), Leonardo's friend Luca Pacioli, Bramante, Leonardo himself and Palladio all developed a cosmologized aesthetic of harmonic form using Vitruvius' *homo universalis* as their basic figure.[10] In his 1521 edition of Vitruvius, for instance, Cesariano wrote "Et in la supra data figura del corpo humano: per li quali symmetriati membri si po ut diximus sapere commensurare tute le cose che sono nel mundo[*sic*]."[11] And Luca Pacioli begins a treatise on architecture appended to his *Divina Proportione*: "First we shall talk of the proportions of man, because from the human body derive all measures and their denominations and in it is to be found all and every ratio and proportion by which God reveals the innermost secrets of nature."[12] As Rudolf Wittkower argues, this approach results in the Leonardesque centralized church, a self-contained form perfectly symmetrical from each vantage point, ramifying in every detail the mathematically proportioned relationships between the two basic figures of the square and the circle. No other shape finds a place, and no element lacks its symmetrical counterpart.[13] Not of course a simply "rational" architecture, this expresses a mystical harmony with the divine idea of a numerically disposed cosmos.

Erwin Panofsky has shown, however, that this High Renaissance conception of ideal form breaks down under pressures created by empirical observation. Both Alberti's efforts to establish a practical method and Leonardo's programmatic measurement of bodies in movement introduce the concept of a *subject* into the dominant aesthetic theory.

9. Vitruvius, *The Ten Books on Architecture,* trans. Morris Hicky Morgan (Cambridge, Mass., 1914), pp. 72–73. See Erwin Panofsky, "The History of the Theory of Human Proportions as a Reflection of the History of Styles," in *Meaning in the Visual Arts* (Garden City, N.Y., 1955), pp. 90–91. The figure appears in Agrippa's *De occulta philosophi* (Cologne, 1533), pp. 63–64, where astrological signs around the edge of the circumscribing square and circle emphasize the macrocosmic value of the human form: for reproductions of some of these figures, see plates, and S. K. Heninger, Jr., *The Cosmographical Glass: Renaissance Diagrams of the Universe* (San Marino, Cal., 1977), pp. 145–47.

10. Wittkower, pp. 13–20.

11. Cesariano, *Di Lucio Vitruvio Pollione de Architectura* (Como, 1521), f. 50v; see Wittkower, p. 14.

12. Wittkower, p. 14.

13. Wittkower, p. 16.

When the artist distorts perfect forms so that they will appear perfect (e.g., eurythmia), or systematically prepares for the beholder's perspectival organization of visual experience, a contradiction has entered the concept of ideal form.[14] Panofsky believes that Dürer's work on proportion, which Browne owned, finally shattered the univocal theory of proportions: "Firmly renouncing the ambition to discover one ideal canon of beauty, he undertook the infinitely more laborious task of setting up various 'characteristic' types which—each in its own way—should 'avoid crude ugliness.'... Not satisfied with even this"—a system of twenty-six general proportion formats, with special cases like the head, foot, hand, the infant, etc., treated separately—"he indicated ways and means of further varying these many types so as to capture even the abnormal and grotesque by strictly geometrical methods."[15] The empirical approach has required the establishment of incommensurate categories and has thereby fractured the concept of symmetry and proportion. When Browne strikes suddenly on the implosive metaphor of the *homo universalis,* finding a quincuncial figure that might indeed unify all reality, and then loses his own ideal form in a welter of inductive facts, he sets *The Garden of Cyrus* directly in this aesthetic predicament.

Once Borghini could say of bodily motions "Laqual cosa non si può insegnare; ma bisogna che l'artefice con giudicio dal naturale la imprende,"[16] the particular has replaced the general, and a gap opens between genius and rule, mind and nature. A crisis of authority divides the community of artists into a group of autonomous individuals, none with the authority to draw a "rule" from nature. The resultant "Mannerist" paintings, Panofsky shows, retain the ideal of symmetry and in practice abandon it[17]—precisely the formal strategy of *The Garden of Cyrus,* where an ideal form expressed in terms of the neoplatonic *homo universalis* is opposed by a bulging, digressive text. In both cases experience is willfully fractured into unrelated units, and the individual's lack of authority to impose order makes artistic or analytic form so problematical that deformation is the only honest means of rendering experience. For the Mannerist artist, this could result in the radically subjective image, the autonomous product of the artist's private motives,[18] but the

14. Panofsky, "Proportions," pp. 98–99.

15. Panofsky, "Proportions," pp. 101–02.

16. Borghini, *Il Riposo* (Florence, 1594), p. 150; see Panofsky, *Idea: A Concept in Art Theory,* trans. Joseph S. Peake (New York, 1968), p. 75.

17. Panofsky, *Idea,* pp. 75–83.

18. Walter Friedlaender, *Mannerism and Anti-Mannerism in Italian Painting* (New York, 1965), p. 10.

scientist exploits formal distortions, irregularities, and failures in an examination of his relationship with reality, with tradition, and with art itself. Bacon puts it this way: "Thus have I concluded this portion of learning touching civil knowledge; and with civil knowledge have concluded human philosophy; and with human philosophy, philosophy in general. And being now at some pause, looking back into that I have passed through, this writing seemeth to me, *si nunquam fallit imago,* as far as a man can judge of his own work, not much better than that noise or sound which musicians make while they are tuning their instruments: which is nothing pleasant to hear, but yet is a cause why the music is sweeter afterwards: so I have been content to tune the instruments of the Muses, that they may play that have better hands."[19] For science after Bacon the problems of natural and artistic order are determined by the scientist's historical circumstance or moment in the advancement of learning. The possibilities of significance are conditioned not so much by the subject's isolation as a perceiver as by his position in history.

III

The Baconian ideas that perfect literary form can emerge only from perfect knowledge, and that imperfect expression will therefore sharpen historical self-consciousness, shape the important debate about language in mid-seventeenth-century England. The specific form these issues take for Browne and his "Garden Discourse" is most concisely expressed in John Amos Comenius' concept of the Universal Language. This follower of Bacon and self-appointed apostle to the English nation was a neoplatonizing scientist with mystical intentions. In *The Way of Light,* translated into English in 1642[20] and dedicated much later to the Royal Society, Comenius condemns as sterile all explorations of material reality that do not recognize the apocalyptic power of science. The treatise thus places Bacon's alliance of literary disorder with imperfect knowledge at the initial stages of a progress toward apocalypse, and predicts an imminent state in which perfect human science will result in perfect form:

For the very nature of the synthetic method (which God follows in all his works) promises us the very highest light at the very end. For it is the very essence of his method to gather particular and individual things into a sum or end, and lesser ends into a greater, and finally all ends into the end of ends. So, when the blessing of God and the

19. Francis Bacon, *Of the Advancement of Learning* (New York, n.d.), Book 2, p. 208.
20. Benjamin DeMott, "The Sources and Development of John Wilkins' Philosophical Language," *Journal of English and Germanic Philology,* 57 (1958), 4.

inventions of men granted and produced upon scattered occasions have grown as we now see to their present multitude, why should we not now look for the crown of the whole process? Instances noted and collected make a rule; the assemblage of arts and sciences makes a system (of Philosophy, of Theology and so forth): what reason is there, then, to forbid us hope that an Art of Arts, a Science of Sciences, a Wisdom of Wisdoms, a Light of Light shall at length be possessed?[21]

Divine and human induction are crucial to Comenius, and he is at some pains in *The Way of Light* to assert that materialism is fundamental to any valid mystical ascent. He is convinced "that the supreme Light of the final age will shine forth from these things"—from created things—"as if from the torches of God,"[22] that the "restoration of the world for which we look will come from a better observation of the way of God's wisdom concerning his creatures."[23]

On this basis Comenius designs an educational theory that unites the most trivial study of concrete particulars with the attainment of "Panharmony," and stipulates as absolutely requisite a linguistic and literary form that not only provides students with new knowledge "in words however precise and carefully chosen, but present[s] the facts themselves to the senses directly as far as that is possible." He predicates the perfect attainment of Panharmony on a new universal language with "neither more nor fewer names than there are things."[24] Although Swift would later satirize Comenius and his followers by sending their benighted Laputan counterparts forth into discourse with huge sacks of objects on their backs, the universal language as Comenius conceives it is not concrete. It is a "language of thought," he insists, "and, what is more, [a language] of the truth of things themselves at the same time":[25] "a universal language ought to be a universal antidote to confusion of thought. And it can only be that if its course is parallel with the course of things, that is, if it contains neither more nor fewer names than there are things; and joins words to words with the utmost precision as things are joined to each other, by constantly expressing the nature of things with which it deals by the very sounds which it uses, and so presenting them to the mind."[26] The very words of the universal language will express not

21. John Amos Comenius, *The Way of Light,* trans. E. T. Campagnac (Liverpool and London, 1938), pp. 37–38.

22. Comenius, p. 117.

23. Comenius, p. 120.

24. Comenius, p. 183.

25. Comenius, p. 187.

26. Comenius, pp. 183–84.

merely "things themselves" but their precise position in a perfectly ordered cosmos. To borrow Michel Foucault's English title, they will perfectly express the order of things.

The perfect language cannot be framed without perfect knowledge of the material world. Comenius desires a perfect taxonomy of all creation, requiring that no one begin to establish the universal language until the most important volume of his universal books—Pansophia—"has been made complete at least in the correct definition of the kinds, the ideas and the qualities of things."[27] Pansophia will be a perfect encyclopedia, containing all matters "in their roots and sources, as the Universe of Things, in obedience to general ideas, and in consistency with itself in its own abstract comprehension, is held together by the bands of order and truth."[28] Perfect language thus relies wholly on the attainment of perfect literary form, perfect literary form relies on the attainment of perfect knowledge, and perfect knowledge is the full comprehension of the relation of every concrete particular to its general idea. Pansophia will be formally perfect, "of the strictest order, paying no need [*sic*] to conventional estimates and opinions, but concerning itself only with facts themselves, so that it may link and connect the concepts of the mind by . . . the laws of the same harmony by which the facts link themselves together."[29] And it will be total, an absolute encyclopedia, "so full and complete that beyond its limits there can be nothing, and nothing can be conceived to be."[30]

Bacon's preliminary formlessness and the final apocalyptic perfection of form predicted by Comenius frame *The Garden of Cyrus*: Browne's treatise takes up an intermediate position in the history of science and of the cosmos that this contrast implies. The quincunx is not only a potential universal hieroglyphic: Browne proposes it as a universal language made up of one entirely significant character, an abstract notation for the order of all things. *The Garden of Cyrus* gestures throughout toward the Pansophic encyclopedia.

What, then, did Browne's contemporaries think the crucial problems of linguistic significance were? Comenius departed from England in 1651, leaving a Latin manuscript copy of *The Way of Light* in the hands,

27. Comenius, p. 219.
28. Comenius, p. 144.
29. Comenius, p. 148.
30. Comenius, p. 150.

probably, of Samuel Hartlib and John Wilkins.[31] Benjamin DeMott has shown that before this date English thinking about language was primarily lexical[32]—Wilkins' essay of 1641, *Mercury, or the Secret and Swift Messenger,* for instance, argues that the perfect artificial language must be based on a lexicon of primitive words recovered from the oldest human language, probably Hebrew—whereas after 1651 the same thinkers unanimously aim for a universal language in which the very structure of letters, words and sentences expresses the order of nature.[33] The issues of scientific classification—and hence of syntax—have become crucial. This is not a shift, however, from a neoplatonic or mystical understanding of language to an opposed scientific one: instead, Comenian neoplatonism both consolidated and modified native neoplatonic traditions of the hieroglyph. Through his influence, the scientific treatment of language grows directly from Plotinus' definition of Egyptian hieroglyphics as "images not drawn, but real," each of which "was a kind of understanding and wisdom and substance given all at once."[34]

Mid-seventeenth-century linguists directly inherited mystical and occult traditions. Through the Hermetic philosophy of Giordano Bruno, universal language projectors received Raymond Lull's neoplatonizing system of memory, according to which the mind attains microcosmic powers to contain the universe by remembering divine names that actively function as "primordial causes" in the cosmos and thus contain

31. DeMott, "Comenius and the Real Character in England," *PMLA,* 70 (1955), 1069 and 1069n.

32. *Mercury, or the Secret and Swift Messenger,* p. 109; cited in DeMott, "Wilkins' Philosophical Language," p. 1.

33. DeMott, "Wilkins' Philosophical Language," pp. 1–3.

34. Plotinus, *Enneads,* V, 8. 5–6, translated from *Enneades,* trans. Émile Bréhier (Paris, 1954–56), by George Boas, in *The Hieroglyphics of Horapollo* (New York, 1950), p. 22. In *Sensible Words: Linguistic Practice in England, 1640–1785* (Baltimore, Md., 1977), Murray Cohen separates mystical from scientific-empirical linguists. Nevertheless, "the two groups make complementary practical contributions" and could blithely adopt their opponents' arguments (p. 21). The emergence of taxonomic thinking and the related syntactical understanding of language—phenomena that Cohen, following Michel Foucault, locates in the eighteenth century or the "Classical" age (pp. 4, 25ff.)—are implicit in mid-seventeenth-century English linguistic thought. Cohen concedes that "the more sophisticated identifying markers used by Dalgarno and Wilkins classify as they symbolize" (p. 4): it is important also to recognize that the latter, in a concern for order at once empirical and neoplatonic, aimed for an artificial language indistinguishable from a God-designed universal syntax. Similarly, the intimate relationship between Wilkins and Comenius belies R. F. Jones' influential argument that the theorists of universal language, and mid-century linguistic thought as a whole, express a value-free empiricism now generally taken to constitute modern science. The vast neoplatonic scope of Wilkins' system cannot be reconciled with Jones' contentions that it "represents the lowest state to which language was degraded" and that "barred from representing the creations of the imagination and stripped of all connotations from

all reality.[35] This tradition culminates in Wilkins' *Essay Towards a Real Character, and a Philosophical Language* (1668), an effort by the Royal Society to build Comenius' universal language. Wilkins' nonalphabetic character system refers, by the disposition of crossbars, circles, loops, dots, and accents, to precise locations on a tabular outline of all reality that is a preliminary draft of Pansophia.

Browne's abstract illustration of the quincunx belongs in this tradition: in its form as a right-lined circle the quincunx appears as one of Bruno's astral memory "seals."[36] For Browne as for his contemporaries "neoplatonic" and "scientific" aspects of language are indistinguishable. The preferential treatment one critic will give to Browne's neoplatonism and another to his science introduces an anachronistic distinction. An accurate reading of *The Garden of Cyrus* in particular depends on correcting this mistake. The text's mystical analogies and its scholarly rationalism, for instance, interpenetrate so completely that any tension between them is the extrinsic product of the twentieth-century reader's concerns. In Chapter I, for example, Browne declines to discover a mystical adumbration of Christ in the X-shaped gestures of Jewish ceremony because the cross analogy is based on Greek not Hebrew, but he suggests that accurate linguistic scholarship would find a "typical thought of Christ" anyway: "yet being the conceit is Hebrew, we should rather expect its verification from Analogy in that language" (p. 183). Repeatedly Browne applies rational analysis to the garden of Solomon and the Canticles—the exhortation "Arise O North-winde, and blow thou South upon my garden, that the spices thereof may flow out" becomes a botanically astute plan for precipitating the "Aromatical gummes" of trees (Ch. IV, p. 212)—and these are performances not of the author's amphibious powers but of the subject's complete coherence.

---

past usage, language was to become nothing more than the dead symbols of mathematical equations" (R. F. Jones, "Science and Language in England of the Mid-Seventeenth Century," *Journal of English and Germanic Philology*, 31 [1932], 315–31; in Fish, ed., *Seventeenth-Century Prose: Modern Essays in Criticism* [New York, 1971], p. 104). In Browne's understanding mystical and empirical knowledge, and lexical and syntactic linguistics cohere: "Certainly of all men that suffered from the confusion of Babel, the Aegyptians found the best evasion; for, though words were confounded, they invented a language of things, and spake unto each other by common notions in Nature. Whereby they discoursed in silence, and were intuitively understood from the theory of their Expresses. For they assumed the shapes of animals common unto all eyes; and by their conjunctions and compositions were able to communicate their conceptions, unto any that coapprehended the Syntaxes of their Natures" (*Pseudodoxia Epidemica*, V. 20, in *Works*, II, p. 379).

35. Frances A. Yates, *The Art of Memory* (Chicago, Ill., 1966), pp. 174–78.
36. Yates, p. 250 and plate 14.

Later in Chapter IV, Browne finds that the cypress is "in its Essentials of affinity unto this order," and concludes that "this we rather think to be the Tree mentioned in the Canticles, which stricter Botanology will hardly allow to be Camphire" (Ch. IV, p. 215): rational analysis has intensified the mystical inclusiveness of the "fundamentall figure." The botanical expertise Browne displays throughout *The Garden of Cyrus* is an intrinsic element of his literary investigation of neoplatonic significance.

From a seventeenth-century point of view, in fact, two of Browne's most basic decisions—to write of "Garden Delights" and to predicate meaning on the presence of order—are equally central to the current concern of linguistic significance. Prior to the vogue of the universal language, herbals follow the incommensurate categories of use: where nourishing, medicinal and magical properties distinguish some plants, toxic powers and even magnitude others, it is easy to imagine the duplicated and haphazard classifications that would result. Platonizing motives seem to lie behind efforts of the late sixteenth century to correct this disorder: Mathias de L'Obel (namer of the lobelia) endeavors to establish a methodical classification that will reflect an *"ordo universalis"* in which "things which are far and widely different become, as it were, one thing."[37] The full transformation of the herbal from a pharmacopeia into an encyclopedia did not occur, however, until the Comenian campaign for perfect signification reached England. In the earliest response to *The Way of Light* for which we have a record, Hartlib's friend Cyprian Kinner undertook, as a pilot project, to construct a universal language limited to botanical names, the different syllables of which were to indicate the appropriate categories under which plants belonged.[38] Although Kinner's language never got off the drawing table, his immediate resort to the botanical kingdom as the first testing ground for the new linguistic ideas reveals a basic affinity with Browne's efforts in *The Garden of Cyrus.*

Developments in this field after 1658, when Browne published his treatise, demonstrate exactly what he and his contemporaries understood their scientific and literary position to be. Wilkins engaged John Ray, already known for his precise, alphabetically arranged catalogue of Cambridgeshire plants, to construct botanical tables for the real character. As this letter to Martin Lister shows, Ray was disgusted with what he produced:

37. Mathias de l'Obel, *Stirpium Adversaria Nova* (1570–1571); cited in *Renaissance Books of Science from the Collection of Albert E. Lownes,* n.d., n.p., p. 36.
38. DeMott, "Wilkins' Philosophical Language," pp. 5–7.

I was constrained in arranging the Tables not to follow the lead of nature, but to accommodate the plants to the author's prescribed system. This demanded that I should divide herbs into three squadrons or kinds as nearly equal as possible; then that I should split up each squadron into nine "differences" as he called them, that is subordinate kinds, in such wise that the plants ordered under each "difference" should not exceed a fixed number; finally that I should join pairs of plants together or arrange them in couples.

What possible hope was there that a method of that sort would be satisfactory, and not manifestly imperfect and ridiculous? I frankly and openly admit that it was; for I care for truth more than for my own reputation.[39]

The encounter was not fruitless, though: the tables' deficiencies seem to have focused Ray's attention on the problem of plant taxonomy. His biographer Charles E. Raven informs us that "Immediately after the compilation of the tables Ray had begun a series of investigations which gave him a deeper insight into the principles which determine taxonomy. The work for Wilkins had proved that he realised the need to take the whole structure of the plant into account rather than to fasten, as Cesalpino and Morison did, upon a single character."[40] As the resulting work, the *Methodus Plantarum Nova,* neared completion, Ray felt that his *Real Character* tables would be of positive use to him, and wrote to John Aubrey asking for the Latin manuscript.[41]

The Comenian project, then, not only raised taxonomic issues that stimulated Ray to what Raven calls his "first serious essay in classification;"[42] it also provided useful material for that system. We should remember that the *Methodus* was a genuine breakthrough: it was the first system to insist on taking the whole plant's structure as the criterion for classification, and the first to observe the basic division of monocotyledons from dicotyledons.[43] And perhaps it was the first to contain such a warning as this one: "I would not have my readers expect something perfect or complete; something which would divide all plants so exactly as to include every species without leaving any in positions anomalous or peculiar; something which would so define each genus by its own characteristics that no species be left, so to speak, homeless or be found common to many genera. Nature does not permit anything of the sort."[44]

39. Charles E. Raven, *John Ray, Naturalist: His Life and Works* (Cambridge, 1942), p. 182; Raven translates the Latin letter, found in *The Correspondence of John Ray,* ed. Edwin Lankester (1848), pp. 41–42.
40. Raven, p. 186.
41. Raven, p. 192.
42. Raven, p. 186.
43. Raven, pp. 195–96.
44. John Ray, *Methodus Plantarum Nova* (1682), sig. A2v; trans. by Raven, p. 193.

Of course Browne did not reach these conclusions—before completing the *Methodus* in 1682 Ray hadn't reached them either—but he did struggle with the same taxonomic difficulties that led to them. The tables in the *Real Character* and *The Garden of Cyrus* occupy a single stage in intellectual history, a time when nature was assumed to be a perfect order that human systems of classification manifestly fail to reproduce.[45] Wilkins himself admits his project's failure, confessing that his inability to classify "all the particular species of things" renders his character arbitrary, not real:

For the accurate effecting of this [a real character], it would be necessary, that the *Theory* it self, upon which such a design were to be founded, should be exactly *suted to the nature of things*. But, upon supposal that this Theory is defective, either as to the *Fulness* or the *Order* of it, this must needs add much *perplexity* to any such Attempt, and render it *imperfect*. And that this is the case with that common Theory already received, need not much be doubted; which may afford some excuse as to several of those things which may seem to be less conveniently disposed of in the following Tables, or Schemes, proposed in the next part.[46]

The provisional, intermediary position Wilkins assigns his project belongs to *The Garden of Cyrus* as well. Although Browne's dedicatory epistle declares that "we write no Herball" and that "We pretend not to multiply vegetable divisions by Quincuncial and Reticulate plants; or erect a new Phytology" (p. 175), his search for a fundamental figure in the species of nature is taxonomic, and his failures, as we have seen, bear directly on the surrounding epistemological and linguistic problems. The real difference between Wilkins' and Browne's schemes, after all, is that Wilkins expected to reach his goal while Browne did not: Browne expected perfect order, perfect significance, and perfect knowledge only on the Last Day.[47]

45. Although the surviving evidence does not prove that Browne played any active role in the development of Ray's taxonomic ideas, we do know that Ray valued and respected him as a colleague during the time he was inventing his method. Ray probably visited "the famous Mr. Th. Brown M.D.," as he twice calls him, in 1660, when Browne showed him two plant species unknown to him before, and the two men corresponded frequently on ornithological topics for many years, perhaps as early as 1664 and as late as 1682. Raven believes that Ray's discovery of monocotyledons and dicotyledons, the critical element in his new taxonomy of plants, was first sparked by the digression on seeds in *The Garden of Cyrus,* Chapter III. (See Raven, pp. 100–01, 116, and 337–39.)

46. John Wilkins, *An Essay Towards a Real Character, and a Philosophical Language,* ed. R. C. Alston (1668; facsimile rpt. Menston, Eng., 1968), p.78.

47. In *Religio Medici,* Browne finds that angels already have this perfect knowledge, and describes it with characteristic terminology (L. C. Martin glosses "numericall" as "particular": *Religio Medici and Other Works* [Oxford, 1964], p. 302): "I beleeve they have an extemporary

IV

The Garden of Cyrus begins with the abstract, geometrical diagram of the quincunx, and thus poses the taxonomic problem in terms of the visual image. So did the projectors of a universal language. The Comenian real character was intended not only to engage in a fully universal order, but also to express this truth by its visual appearance: it had to make "visible sense."[48] This goal comes straight from older neoplatonic traditions of the hieroglyphic. Samuel Botley's *Maximum in Minimo* (1674), for instance, presents a shorthand system allied with occult memory systems and Egyptian hieroglyphics: its "Simbolicall Characters . . . teach the art of Memory more exact than the Egyption Hyerogliphicks."[49] As the theorists of a universal language encountered the problems of taxonomy, however, the idea of a visual sign with universal significance became less tenable. The important introduction of tabulation into books on language[50]—reaching the delightful extravagance of Wilkins' great fold-out epitomes of all knowledge—was intended both to render the world's order visually and to articulate the visual signs of the universal language themselves. In effect, however, it incorporated *into* the visual system the awareness of representational inadequacy, the failure of taxonomy perfectly to rationalize genus and species.[51] Significantly, Comenius' own use of visual signs is thoroughly preliminary, in frank recognition that, until Pansophia was ready, no hieroglyphically implosive real character was possible. His last publications were among the first picture schoolbooks, designed to teach children Latin words by juxtaposing them with pictures of actual objects in the material world.[52] In direct contradistinction to the generalizing

---

knowledge, and upon the first motion of their reason doe what we cannot without study or deliberation; that they know things by their formes, and define by specificall difference, what we describe by accidents and properties; and therefore probabilities to us may bee demonstrations unto them; that they have knowledge not onely of the specificall, but [of the] numericall formes of individuals, and understand by what reserved difference each *Hypostasis* (besides the relation to its species) becomes its numericall selfe" (Part I, Section 33, pp. 43–44; the brackets are Keynes'.).

48. Cohen, p. 5.

49. Samuel Botley, *Maximum in Minimo* (1647?), sig. B2.

50. See Walter J. Ong, *Ramus, Method, and the Decay of Dialogue* (Cambridge, Mass., 1958); "System, Space and Intellect in Renaissance Symbolism," *Bibliothéque d'humanisme et renaissance,* 18 (1956), rpt. in *The Barbarian Within* (New York, 1962), pp. 68–87; and "From Allegory to Diagram in the Renaissance Mind," *Journal of Aesthetics and Art Criticism,* 17 (1959), 423–40.

51. For another view, see Cohen, p. 140.

52. Comenius, *Orbis Sensualism Pictus,* trans. Charles Hoole, ed. R. C. Alston (1659; facsimile rpt. Menston, Eng., 1970).

and ordering power of the real character, these pictures recognize the primitive state of knowledge by allying the visual image exclusively with concrete particulars and so denying it any power of broader signification.

Browne engages the visual sign's problematical relations to genus and species not only by confronting the diagram of the quincunx with the text itself but also by writing verbal still life. For example:

> Mechanicks make use hereof [that is, of "this decussation"] in forcipall Organs, and Instruments of Incision; wherein who can but magnifie the power of decussation, inservient to contrary ends, solution and consolidation, union, and divisions, illustrable from *Aristotle* in the old *Nucifragium* or Nut-cracker, and the Instruments of Evulsion, compression, or incision; which consisting of two *Vectes* or armes, converted towards each other, the innitency and stresse being made upon the *hypomochlion* or fulciment in the decussation, the greater compression is made by the union of two impulsors. (Ch. II, p. 189)

The household nutcracker is described here with a ponderous precision that overwhelms it: the passage creates a gap rather than a link between abstract and concrete, between language and visual referent. It is an exercise in the impossibility of encapsulating visual reality in a verbal image.

Rosalie Colie points out that the Greeks recognized an etymological kinship, at least, between painted still life and the mock encomium of the rhetorical tradition: they both chose "insignificant objects, . . . odds and ends" as their subject matter.[53] From Isocrates to Thomas Nashe, the mock encomium is understood to rely almost exclusively on the originality or invention of its creator:[54] as Browne notes in the dedicatory epistle to *The Garden of Cyrus,* "In this multiplicity of writing, bye and barren Themes are best fitted for invention; Subjects so often discoursed confine the Imagination, and fix our conceptions unto the notions of fore–writers" (p. 175). When the depiction so clearly fails, then, we will refer the failure to its maker. E. H. Gombrich's term *vanitas* is appropriate to painted still life not only because the genre analyzes the difference between "semblance and reality," then, but also because it scrutinizes the artist's vanity.[55] As Colie tells us, "the illusionism that all still-life painters strive to achieve brings to a focus the illusion of all painting and

---

53. Rosalie L. Colie, *Paradoxia Epidemica: The Renaissance Tradition of Paradox* (Princeton, N.J., 1966), p. 276.

54. See Henry Knight Miller, "The Paradoxical Encomium with Special Reference to Its Vogue in England, 1600–1800," *Modern Philology,* 53 (1950), 146–47.

55. E. H. Gombrich, "Tradition and Expression in Western Still Life," in *Meditations on a Hobby Horse* (London and New York, 1963), p. 104.

all art. . . . [T]he illusion involved in the still life risks the painter's art by drawing attention to the artifice."[56]

This much, clearly, the *"Nucifragium"* passage does. But Browne sets these ironies in the context of a radical challenge to the very grounds for associating still life with mock encomium: the notion that the depiction of "insignificant objects, of odds and ends" need mock the objects themselves. *The Garden of Cyrus* owes a direct debt to Bacon's argument in the *Novum Organum:* "And for things that are mean or even filthy— things which (as Pliny says) must be introduced with an apology,—such things, no less than the most spendid and costly, must be admitted to natural history. . . . For whatever deserves to exist deserves also to be known, for knowledge is the image of existence, and things mean and splendid exist alike."[57] Browne introduces painstaking observation of natural objects, and especially the discovery of order in the miniscule and even infinitesimal creatures, as intrinsically *aesthetic* projects. To borrow Colie's term, he "risks" the writer's art in order to redefine it.

Bacon's injunction that knowledge include the smallest, most negligible things into its visual "image of existence" lies behind Browne's apparently uncontrolled particularization. Passages like these embody the aesthetic motto from Quintilian with which the treatise begins:

The Spongy leaves of some Sea-wracks, Fucus, Oaks, in their several kindes, found about the shoar, with ejectments of the Sea, are over-wrought with Net-work elegantly containing this order, which plainly declareth the naturality of this texture; And how the needle of nature delighteth to work, even in low and doubtful vegetations. (Ch. III, p. 193)

And no mean Observations hereof there is in the Mathematicks of the neatest Retiary spider, which concluding in fourty four Circles, from five Semidiameters beginneth that elegant texture. (Ch. III, p. 201)

And some resemblance there is of this order in the Egges of some Butterflies and moths, as they stick upon leaves, and other substances; which being dropped from behinde, nor directed by the eye, do neatly declare how nature Geometrizeth, and observeth order in all things. (Ch. III, p. 203)

The minute descriptions of more minute particulars that can be found on every page of *The Garden of Cyrus* have been a stumbling-block to the literary enjoyment of this work. But they are intrinsic to the work's viability as an encyclopedia and as a genuinely Baconian "image of

56. Colie, p. 273.
57. Bacon, *Novum Organum,* Book I, Aphorism CXX, in *The Works of Francis Bacon,* ed. James Spedding, Robert Leslie Ellis, and Douglas Denon Heath (1858), IV, 106–07.

existence": they pose a direct challenge to aesthetic assumptions that would deny them literary value.

The famous digression on seeds provides the treatise's sharpest illumination of the pleasures and problems raised by Browne's literary strategy. This section is structurally crucial: a self-described digression (p. 200) is ironically the centerpiece of the central chapter, a formal paradox uniting disorder with decussation. And, since it constitutes one of Browne's genuinely important contributions to contemporary science, this digression asks us to see that his literary and scientific methods work together to constitute the seed as the perfect sign. Finally, by pursuing infinitesimal orderliness directly to the vanishing point, to an ordered but unknown locus in the seed from which life and speciation itself emerge, it articulates a relation between literary disorder and natural order, human and divine creativity.

Browne's importance in the history of embryology rests largely on this passage, but as we would expect, the most important modern studies of early embryological science, concluding that he "uses his amassed details of scientific knowledge most effectively in support of nonscientific propositions,"[58] strike the neoplatonist from the rolls of science.[59] Yet science was defined differently then, and Browne's contemporaries took his discovery that the seed is the absolutely concentrated hieroglyphic and the perfect shorthand of *maximum in minimo* as serious science. Browne argues, "Where by the way, he that observeth the rudimental spring of seeds, shall finde strict rule, although not after this order. How little is required unto effectual generation, and in what diminutives the plastick principle lodgeth, is exemplified in seeds, wherein the greater mass affords so little comproduction" (Ch. III, p. 196). This is the second occurrence in English of the term "plastic principle" to indicate a vital power derived from God but resident within matter. The concept and the term were to enjoy a half-century's vogue as a preferred argument against the materialism of Hobbes and Descartes and the revival of atomism:[60] the digression on seeds is clearly a significant part of an

58. Charles W. Bodemer, "Embryological Thought in Seventeenth Century England," in *Medical Investigation in Seventeenth Century England,* ed. Bodemer and Lester S. King (Los Angeles, Cal., 1968), p. 18.

59. Bodemer, "Materialistic and Neoplatonic Influences in Embryology," in *Medicine in Seventeenth Century England,* ed. Allen G. Debus (Berkeley and Los Angeles, Cal., 1974), pp. 197–99.

60. William B. Hunter, Jr., "The Seventeenth-Century Doctrine of Plastic Nature," *Harvard Theological Review,* 43 (1950), 197–200.

ongoing scientific debate. Browne understands the plastic principle to be the "little nebbe or fructifying principle," "the generative particle," the "seminal nebbe"—an infinitesimally small entity (his terms leave open the question of its possession of matter and extension) that determines speciation. Browne insists that "Beside the open and visible Testicles of plants, the seminall powers lie in great part invisible" (p. 197), so small that the scientist cannot perceive or "know" them. Nevertheless, Browne tells us, "From such undiscernable seminalities arise spontaneous productions" (p. 199). "The Aequivocall production of things under undiscerned principles, makes a large part of generation, though they seem to hold a wide univocacy in their set and certain Originals, while almost every plant breeds its peculiar insect" (pp. 198–99). Later, Locke would object strenuously to a theory that proposes to "explain" speciation by "the supposition of essences that cannot be known,"[61] and Newton would deliver it a final blow in his *Opticks*: "To tell us that every Species of Things is endow'd with an occult specifick Quality by which it acts and produces manifest Effects is to tell us nothing."[62] But the concept was not "unscientific" when Browne proposed it. For him, "undiscerned principles" constituted a perfectly valid scientific explanation of speciation, of the mysterious way "grapes under ground make a Fly with some difference" (p. 199).

So the seed becomes the sign around which the literary problems raised by *The Garden of Cyrus* as a whole find articulation. It is a single and central sign capable of generating all intelligible order, and yet finally it is unknowable. As a result it possesses a perfect univocal relationship with things at precisely the point where Wilkins' real character and the quincunx itself have failed—at the level of individual species. And yet at precisely that point it is also unintelligible: "The exiguity and smallnesse of some seeds extending to large productions is one of the magnalities of nature, somewhat illustrating the work of the Creation, and vast production from nothing" (p. 199). At the center of *The Garden of Cyrus,* Browne places a sign that not only repeats its companion piece, *Urn Burial,* by including everything in nothing, but reverses the first treatise by making that sign the promise of a new birth. The seed has replaced the urn. This is what Browne promised in the prefatory letter to *The Garden of Cyrus*: "Since the delightfull World comes after death, and Paradise succeeds

61. John Locke, *Essay of Human Understanding,* in *Works of John Locke* (1794), I, 450–51, cited in Hunter, p. 211.

62. Isaac Newton, *Opticks,* rpt. of 1730 ed. (London, 1931), p. 401.

the Grave. Since the verdant state of things is the Symbole of the Resurrection, and to flourish in the state of Glory, we must first be sown in corruption" (p. 178). The mystery of this seed is the corollary of its incomplete germination—or to say the same thing another way, of the author's position in providential history. And the strange generic character of *The Garden of Cyrus* as a whole, with its formal unevenness and modest subject matter, is exactly fitted to an imperfect moment in history. In this only apparently "minor" treatise, Browne inscribes his conviction that great power will emerge from small things.

I extend thanks to Professor Christopher W. Grose for reading drafts, to Professor Jonathan F. S. Post for generous bibliographical help, to Hamilton College for the Research Stipend on which this essay was revised, and to the staff of the Huntington Library for unflagging assistance. In addition, I acknowledge with thanks the aid of Hamilton College and the Huntington Library in making the illustrations available.

Notes on Contributors

PHILIP J. AYRES is Senior Lecturer in English Literature at Monash University, Victoria, Australia, where he also teaches courses on political history. His works include books on Elizabethan recusant history and on Jacobean drama and essays on Renaissance history and literature in several American and British journals. He is the editor of the forthcoming Revels edition of Ben Jonson's *Sejanus* and the author of *Malcolm Fraser: A Political Biography,* the authorized biography of the former Australian Liberal prime minister.

MARTIN BUTLER is a lecturer in English at the University of Leeds. He is the author of *Theatre and Crisis 1632–1642* (1984) and has edited Volume II of *The Selected Plays of Ben Jonson* for Cambridge University Press. His current projects include an edition of *Cymbeline* and work on the political dimensions of Jacobean masques and theater.

DAN S. COLLINS in 1987 retired as Professor of English at the University of Massachusetts, Amherst. An editor of *English Literary Renaissance* since its inception, he was co-editor of the special issue on "Renaissance Historicism" published in 1986. He has published essays and notes on Milton and Donne and is the author of *Andrew Marvell: A Reference Guide* (1980).

JONATHAN V. CREWE is Associate Professor of English at The Johns Hopkins University. The author of *Hidden Designs: The Critical Profession and Renaissance Literature* (1986) and *Unredeemed Rhetoric: Thomas Nashe and the Scandal of Authorship* (1982), he presently is working on discovery in the Renaissance with special reference to Bacon and Shakespeare.

PHILIP J. FINKELPEARL is Anne Pierce Rogers Professor of English at Wellesley College. His work includes a book on John Marston and the Inns of Court and he presently is completing a book on Beaumont and Fletcher.

SUZANNE GOSSETT is Professor of English and Director of the Women's Studies Program at Loyola University of Chicago. She has edited and written about Shakespeare and Jacobean drama and is co-author of a forthcoming volume for the Malone Society; in addition, she has published on nineteenth-century American literature. Her recent work includes an essay on Ralegh's *Notes on the Navy* for *Modern Philology* and an essay on women in masques for *English Literary Renaissance*.

JANET E. HALLEY, who has taught at the University of California at Los Angeles and at Hamilton College, is the author of "Versions of the Self and the Politics of Privacy in Vaughan's *Silex Scintillans*," published in the special Henry Vaughan issue of *The George Herbert Journal*. She is presently at work on Donne's "A Litanie" and the politics of private devotion; on heresy, orthodoxy, and the politics of discourse in the Family of Love; and on women and fiction in Milton's early verse.

EUGENE D. HILL is Associate Professor of English at Mount Holyoke College. He has published essays on Donne, Milton, and other Renaissance authors. His first book, *Edward, Lord Herbert of Cherbury*, was published in 1986.

JEAN E. HOWARD teaches Renaissance literature and critical theory at Syracuse University. She is the author of *Shakespeare's Art of Orchestration* (1984) and co-editor with Marion O'Connor of *Shakespeare Reproduced: The Text in History and Ideology* to be published in late 1987.

ARTHUR F. KINNEY, Thomas W. Copeland Professor of Literary History at the University of Massachusetts, Amherst, is the founding editor of *English Literary Renaissance* and editor of the Twayne English Authors Series in the Renaissance. He recently has published *Humanist Poetics* (1986) and *John Skelton, Priest as Poet* (1987); *Continental Humanist Poetics* and *The Birds and Beasts of Shakespeare*, with the artist Alan James Robinson, are forthcoming.

F. J. LEVY is Professor of History at the University of Washington, Seattle. He currently is engaged on a study of the political and social background of the literature of the 1590s in England.

DAVID LINDLEY is Senior Lecturer in the School of English, University of Leeds. His most recent publications are *Thomas Campion* (1986) and an edition of Campion's unpublished poem *De Puluerea Coniuratione* (1987). He currently is working on a study of Frances Howard.

ANTHONY LOW, Professor of English at New York University, has written *The Blaze of Noon: A Reading of "Samson Agonistes"* (1974) and *Love's Architecture: Devotional Modes in Seventeenth-Century English Poetry* (1978). His recent book, *The Georgic Revolution* (1985), expands on the historicist concerns of "New Science and the Georgic Revolution." Currently he is writing a book on politics and the English love lyric, 1550–1700.

LOUIS ADRIAN MONTROSE is Professor of English Literature at the University of California, San Diego. He is presently completing a book entitled *The Sub-*

ject of Elizabeth: Relations of Power and Cultural Practices in Elizabethan England. His essay "Shaping Fantasies: Representation of Gender and Power in Elizabethan Culture" will soon be reprinted in *Representing the Renaissance,* a collection of essays edited by Stephen Greenblatt.

KAREN NEWMAN, Associate Professor of Comparative Literature and English at Brown University, is author of *Shakespeare's Rhetoric of Comic Character* (1985) and various essays on classical and Renaissance topics. She currently is working on the problem of social history, gender, and representation in English drama.

ANNABEL PATTERSON has recently moved to Duke University where she holds joint positions in the Department of English and the interdisciplinary Graduate Program in Literature. Her essay on Spenser and Marot is incorporated in a larger study of the cultural history of pastoral, *Pastoral and Ideology,* which is forthcoming.

MARY BETH ROSE is Director of the Center for Renaissance Studies at the Newberry Library. She is editor of *Women in the Middle Ages and the Renaissance: Literary and Historical Perspectives,* and she has contributed essays on Renaissance drama and Renaissance women to *Renaissance Drama, Review,* and *Journal of British Studies,* as well as to *English Literary Renaissance.* Her second book, *The Expense of Spirit: Love and Sexuality in English Renaisssance Drama,* is forthcoming.

PETER STALLYBRASS, who taught for years at the University of Sussex, is presently Associate Professor of English at Dartmouth College. He has published widely on Shakespeare, Sidney, and Renaissance popular culture and is co-author with Allon White of *The Politics and Poetics of Transgression* (1986). He is presently working on enclosures and transgression in the Renaissance.

LAWRENCE VENUTI is Associate Professor of English at Temple University. His essays on Renaissance poetry, prose, and drama have appeared in the *Journal of Medieval and Renaissance Studies, Assays: Critical Approaches to Medieval and Renaissance Texts,* and *English Literary Renaissance.* His book *Our Halcyon Dayes: Marxist Critical Theory and English Literature in the Pre-Revolutionary Period* will be published shortly.

Index

Titled persons are listed by title and cross-referenced by family name. Significant critical terms used throughout are indexed as well as significant collections of documents and major scholarly, theoretical, and critical books using all the methodologies employed in this volume. Anonymous works are listed by title; others are listed under the name of the author or editor.

Adams, Thomas, *Mystical Bedlam* (1615), 226 n
Addison, Joseph, 317
Aesop, 79, 119
A.F. (Abraham Fleming?), *The Buckolickes of Publius Vergilius Maro* (1589), 318
Agricultural Revolution, 327–34
Agrippa, *De occulta philosophia* (1533), 376, 377 n
Akrigg, G. P. V., *Jacobean Pageant* (1967), 168
Alberti, Leon Battista, 372, 377; *Architecture* (trans. 1755), 372
Albright, Evelyn M., *Dramatic Publication in England, 1580–1640* (1927), 201 n
Alençon, Francis, duke of, 78
Alphonus, Emperor of Germany (1654), 284–86, 292
Althusser, Louis, x, 17–18, 133–34; *Lenin and Philosophy and Other Essays* (1971), 18 n, 293 n; *Réponse à John Lewis* (1973), 133
Amyot, Jacques (trans. Sir Thomas North, 1579), vii
Andreson-Thom, Martha, 139 n
androgyny, 243–44
Annalia Dubrensia (1636), 355–57
Antonio, King of Portugal, 120 n
appropriation, 11, 39, 106–07, 137, 349, 351, 354–58, 361–66
Ardolino, Frank, 127–28
Aristotle, xiv, 221, 368, 372
Armstrong, Archie, 203
Arundel, Countess of, 268

Arundel, Thomas Howard, earl of, 267, 268, 290
Ashley, Robert, *A Comparison of the English and Spanish Nations* (1589), 113 n
Ashton, Robert: *The City and the Court, 1603–1643* (1979), 300 n, 309; *The English Civil War* (1978), 363
Aubigné, Agrippa d', 66–67
Aubrey, John, 345 n, 385
authority, xiv, 21–28, 38, 44, 98, 101, 133, 191–206, 238, 275, 297–300, 307–09, 313–14, 349, 351–58, 361–66
autonomy, 104
Axton, Marie, *The Queen's Two Bodies* (1977), 276 n
Aylmer, G. E., *The King's Servants* (1961), 312

Bacon, Anthony, 153, 157, 159
Bacon, Sir Francis, xii–xiii, 19, 91, 146–49, 151–67, 205, 253, 290, 329, 334, 337–38, 338 n, 339, 341–43, 345–47, 354–55, 379, 381, 389–90; *Colours of Good and Evil* (n.d.), 157, 159, 165–66; *Essayes,* 146, 156; (1597 ed.), 156–62, 165–67, 339; *The Great Instauration* (1620), 342; *New Atlantis* (n.d.), 337–38; *New Organon I* (n.d.), 389; *New Organon II* (n.d.), 342; "Of Ceremonies and Respectes," 163; "Of Counsels," 66; "Of Discourse," 162–63; "Of Expense," 165; "Of Faction," 163; "Of Followers and Friends," 164; "Of Honour and Reputation," 165; "Of Negociating," 164; "Of

Bacon, Sir Francis (cont.)
Nobility," 338–39; "Of Plantations," 339;
"Of Riches," 339; "Of Studies," 163, 167;
"Of Sutes," 164; *Of the Proficience and Advancement of Learning* (1605), 338, 341, 379;
"Of the True Greatness of Kingdoms and
Estates," 339–40; *Promus of Formularies*
(1594–95), 156, 166
Bacon, Sir Nicholas, 152, 158
Baker, Howard, 108, 110; *Induction to Tragedy*
(1939), 180 n
Bakhtin, Mikhail, xi, 20; *The Dialogic Imagination* (trans. 1981), 20 n; *The Formal Method of
Literary Scholarship* (with P. N. Medvedev;
trans. 1978), 293 n, 306 n; *Rabelais and His
World* (trans. 1968), 350
Baldwin, T. W., *William Shakespere's Small
Latine and Lesse Greek* (1944), 319 n
Bancroft, Richard, bishop of London, 204
Barish, Jonas, 208; *The Anti-Theatrical Prejudice* (1981), 10, 10 n, 11
Barnavelt, Jan van Olden, 199
Barnes, Thomas G., *Somerset, 1625–1640*
(1964), 297, 307 n
Barnfield, Richard, "The Shepherds Content," 320–21, 323
Baron, Hans, 147 n; *The Crisis of the Early Italian Renaissance* (1966), 147 n
Barthes, Roland, 10 n
Bastwick, John, 364
Bean, John, 142
Beaumont, Sir Francis, 178, 204–05; *The
Woman Hater* (1607), 204–05
Beaumont, Sir Francis, and John Fletcher, 178
Bedford, Francis Russell, earl of, 267
Benjamin, Walter, 13 n
Benlowes, Edward, 319
Bennett, Josephine Waters, *"Measure for Measure" as Royal Entertainment* (1966), 8 n
Bennett, Tony, 19; *Formalism and Marxism*
(1979), 19 n
Bentley, Gerald Eades, 193, 194; *Jacobean and
Caroline Stage* (1941–68), 201 n, 269 n,
274 n, 278 n, 280 n, 281 n, 282 n, 283 n,
284 n, 286 n, 307 n, 310, 314; *The Profession of Dramatist in Shakespeare's Time*
(1971), 193 n, 205–6
Bercé, Y. M., 350; *Fête et Révolte: des mentalités populaires du XVIe siècle* (1976), 350
Berkeley, Lord George, 345
Birch, Thomas: *The History of the Royal Society
of London* (1756–57), 345 n; *Memoirs of the
Reign of Queen Elizabeth* (1754), 155
Blackfriars Theatre, 292. *See also* children of
Blackfriars; childrens' companies
Bloch, Marc, *Feudal Society* (1961), 296 n
Boas, Frederick S., 108, 115 n
Boas, George. *See* Lovejoy, Arthur O.
Boccaccio, Giovanni, 84
Boethius, 324; "Metrum 5," 324
Book of Common Prayer, 44–45
Book of Orders, 297–300, 302–03, 305, 307,
312, 314
Book of Sports, 355–56, 361. *See also* James VI
and I
Borghini, Raffaello, *Il Riposo* (1594), 378
Botley, Samuel, *Maximum in Minimo* (1674),
387
Bourdieu, P.: *Outline of a Theory of Practise*
(1977), 358; *Reproduction in Education, Society and Culture* (with Jean-Claude Passeron;
1977), 25 n
Bowden, Peter J., *The Wool Trade in Tudor and
Stuart England* (1962), 53 n
Boyle, Robert, 344–45
Bradbrook, M. C., *The Rise of the Common
Player* (1962), 276 n
Bradford, Alan T., 152 n
Brailsford, D., *Sport and Society* (1969), 355 n
Bramante (Donato d'Agnolo), 377
Bramston, John, 276
Brant, Sebastian, 82
Bridenbaugh, Carl, *Vexed and Troubled Englishmen* (1968), 174, 311
Bridgewater, Thomas Egerton, lord Ellesmere, earl of (Lord Chancellor), 176, 192
Bristol, Michael D., xi
Brome, Alexander, 321; *Songs and Other Poems*
(1661), 321
Brome, Richard. *See* Heywood, Thomas
Broude, Ronald, 127 n
Browne, Sir Thomas, 368, 370, 372, 378–79,
383, 383 n, 384, 386, 386 n, 388–91, 392;
The Garden of Cyrus (1658), 367–73, 378–79,
381, 383–84, 386, 386 n, 387, 388–92; *Pseudodoxia Epidemica* (1646), 383 n; *Religio Medici* (1643), 386–87 n; *Urn Burial* (1658), 369,
370, 391
Browne, William, 322; "Happy Life," 322
Bruno, Giordano, 340, 341, 382, 383; *Lo Spaccio della Bestia Trionfonte,* 340
Brydges, Giles. *See* Chandos

Buc, Sir George, Master of the Revels, 198. *See also* Herbert, Sir Henry; Master of the Revels; Segar, Sir George; Wilson

Buckingham, George Villiers, duke of, 168, 175–76, 203

Burckhardt, Jacob, xiv, 5, 5 n, 6, 7

Burghill, Philbert, 176

Burghleigh. *See* Burghley, William Cecil

Burghley, William Cecil, lord, 117, 148–49, 151, 152–53, 154, 204

Burke, Kenneth, 36

Burton, Henry, 364

Calder, W. M., 111

Camden, Carroll, *The Elizabethan Woman* (1952), 224 n

Camden, William, xiii, 225 n; *Annales* (1615), 40; *Britannia* (1586), viii

Campion, Thomas, 251, 251 n, 253–54, 263; *The Somerset Masque,* 252, 262

Canetti, Elias, *Crowds and Power* (1973), 349

Carew, Thomas, "To Saxham," 354

Carlell, Lodowick, *Arviragus and Philicia* (1639), 282–84

carnival, 348–57, 360, 361, 365–66

Carr, Robert, 251–52 nn, 252, 253. *See also* Somerset, Robert Carl

Carroll, David, 10 n

Castiglione, Baldesar, *Book of the Courtier* (trans. 1561), 148, 166–67

Castlehaven, James Tuchet, earl of, 176–77

Catherine de Medici, 78

Cavalier poetry, viii–ix

Cavendish, William, *The Country Captains* (1649), 351

Cecil, Sir Robert, 151, 152, 154, 155. *See also* Salisbury, Robert Cecil

Cecil, William. *See* Burghley, William Cecil

Certain Sermons or Homilies (1559), 224–25, 225 n. *See also* homily on obedience

Cervantes Saavedra, Miguel de: *Don Quixote,* 290, 311; *La Fuerza de la Sangue,* 184, 184 n

Cesariano, 377; *Di Lucio Vitrvio Pollione de Architectura* (1521), 376, 377

Chalker, John, *The English Georgic* (1939), 317 n

Chalkin, C. W., *Seventeenth-Century Kent* (1961), 299

Chamberlain, John, 175, 227–28, 233 n, 252, 253, 260

Chambers, E. K., 193–94, 197; *The Elizabethan Stage* (1923), 194 n; *The Medieval Stage* (1903), 349

Chambers, R. W., *Thomas More* (1935), 6 n

Chandos, Giles Brydges, lord, 58–59

Chapman, George, 196, 202, 205, 251, 253, 254; *Andromeda Liberata* (1614), 251 n; *Eastward Hoe* (1605), 196, 202

Charlemagne, 271

Charles I (of England), 168, 190, 205, 219, 248, 265–92 passim, 295, 296, 297–300, 300 n, 302–04, 306–15, 355–56, 361, 363, 364

Charles II (of England), 326, 353, 364, 365–66; restoration of, 365–66

Charles IX (of France), 78

Charles, Prince of Wales, 195

Chaucer, Geoffrey, 81

Chester Nativity Play, 43

Chichester, Sir Arthur, 256–57

children of Blackfriars, 197, 203

childrens' companies, 195, 202. *See also* children of Blackfriars

Chodorow, Nancy, *The Reproduction of Mothering* (1978), 10 n

Cicero, xiv, 147–48, 151

Clarendon, Edward Hyde, earl of, *The History of the Rebellion and Civil Wars in England* (1702–04), 364

Clark, Alice, xi

Clark, Peter, *English Provincial Society from the Reformation to the Revolution* (1977), 297

Clarke, Aidan, 257

Clarkson, L. A., *The Pre-Industrial Economy of England, 1500–1750* (1971), 296 n, 308

class, 133, 136, 138, 230, 236–42, 294–99, 300–04, 311–12, 315, 321–30, 333–36, 338–39, 340–46, 351, 352–63, 365; dominant class, 299, 299–300 n

Cliffe, J. T., *The Yorkshire Gentry from the Reformation to the Civil War* (1969), 299, 306, 307, 311

Cockburn, J. S., 174

Cohen, Abner, *Two-Dimensional Man* (1974), 34 n, 46–47, 50–51, 60

Cohen, Murray, *Sensible Words* (1977), 382–83 n, 387

Coke, Edward, 173, 205

Coke, Frances, 175

Coleman, D. C., *The Economy of England 1450–1750* (1977), 53 n

Coleridge, Samuel Taylor, 219

Colie, Rosalie L., xii, 388–89; *Paradoxica Epidemica* (1966), 388–89
Columella, 336
Comenius, John Amos, 344 n, 379–82, 382 n, 383, 384, 385; and Panharmony, 380; and Pansophia, 381, 383, 387; and universal language, 379–81, 383–84, 387–88; *Orbis Sensualism Pictus* (1659), 387; *The Way of Light* (trans. 1642), 379–81, 384
Commynes, Philippe de, *Mémoires* (n.d.), 126 n
contestation, 25, 27, 31, 104, 107, 361
Cooper, Helen, *Pastoral: Medieval into Renaissance* (n.d.), 80 n
Coppe, Abiezer, 365
Cornu Copia (1652), 345
Cornwallis, J., 265–66, 266 n
Cornwallis, William, 217; *Essayes of Certaine Paradoxes* (1616), 213, 217
Cosin, John, bishop, 362
Cotswold games, 355–58
Coward, Barry, *The Stuart Age* (1980), 297
Cowell, Dr. John, 204; *The Interpreter* (1607), 204
Cowley, Abraham, 335–38, 343, 346–47; "Of Agriculture," 343; *A Proposition for the Advancement of Experimental Philosophy* (1661), 337; *Several Discourses by Way of Essays* (1688), 355–36
Crashaw, William, 195, 203
Craven, William, earl of, 268
Croll, Morris W., *Style, Rhetoric, and Rhythm* (1966), 152 n
Crosfield, Thomas, *The Diary* (1935), 276 n, 278
Culler, Jonathan, 5 n
Cunningham, Peter, and Henry B. Wheatley, *London Past and Present* (1891), 312

Daniel, Samuel, 261; *Vision of Twelve Goddesses* (1604), 261
Davenant, William, 357; *Madagascar* (1638), 290–91; *The Triumphs of the Prince d'Amour* (1635), 276 n, 279–80, 287
Davies, Sir John, 256, 257–58; *A Discovery of the True Causes why Ireland was never entirely Subdued* (1612), 257–58, 258 n, 260
Davis, Natalie Zemon, xi, 132 n, 137 n; *Society and Culture in Early Modern France* (1975), 349, 353, 362
Day, John, 196–97; *The Isle of Gulls* (1606), 196–97; *Lust's Dominion* (with Thomas Dekker and William Haughton; 1600), 169 n, 205
deconstruction, x, 4–5, 20, 32, 132, 145
Dee, John, 122
deGrazia, Vittoria, 350, 354; *The Culture of Consent* (1981), 350
Dekker, Thomas, *Gustavus King of Swethland* (by 1632), 282. *See also* Day, John; Middleton, Thomas
de L'Obel, Mathias, 384; *Stirpium Adversaria Nova* (1570–71), 384
DeMan, Paul, ix
deMedici, Catherine, 78
DeMott, Benjamin, 379 n, 382, 384
demystification, 32, 103, 104
Derby, Anne Stanley, countess dowager of, 177
Derrida, Jacques, 20
Descartes, René, 390
Devereux, Robert. *See* Essex, Robert, second earl of; Essex, Robert, third earl of
D'Ewes, Sir Simonds, *Autobiography*, 252 n, 268 n, 288–89
dialectic, x, 49, 52, 74, 83, 126
Dietz, Frederick C., *English Public Finance, 1558–1641* (1932), 306 n
Digby, Sir Kenelm, 364–65
Dionysius the Areopagite, 338
Divine Right kingship, 299, 307, 313
Dollimore, Jonathan, 3, 5–7, 11, 18; *Radical Tragedy* (1984), 3 n, 107 n
Donne, John, 251, 341; "The Progresse of the Soule," 341–42; "The Sunne Rising," 319
Dorset, earl of, 286
Drake, Sir Francis, 120 n
Drayton, Michael, 41, 42, 62, 355, 359; "Against those fooles that all Antiquitie defame," 359; *Poly-Olbion* (1612), 359
Drummond, William of Hawthornden, 196
Dryden, John, 317–18, 327, 334, 347; *Eclogues and Georgics of Vergil,* 317
Dudley, Robert. *See* Leicester, Robert Dudley; Warwick, Sir Robert Dudley
dumb show, 125–26, 195. *See also* metadrama
Dürer, Albrecht, 31; *Four Books of Human Proportion,* 372, 378
Durling, Dwight L., *Georgic Tradition in English Poetry* (1935), 317 n
Dusinberre, Juliet, *Shakespeare and the Nature of Women* (1975), 224 n, 229, 233 n

Dymock, Cressy, *An Essay for Advancement of Husbandry-Learning* (1651), 343–44

Eagleton, Terry: *Criticism and Ideology* (1976), 293; *Literary Theory* (1983), 5 n, 19 n; *Walter Benjamin* (1981), 13 n
Earle, John, 311; *Microcosmographie* (1628), 311
Eden, Kathy, *Poetic and Legal Fictions in the Aristotelian Tradition* (1986), xiv
Edward VI (of England), 354
Edwards, Philip, 263; *Threshold of a Nation* (1979), 8 n, 251, 259
effacement, 102
Egerton, Thomas, 58. *See also* Bridgewater, Thomas Egerton
Elizabeth (Stuart), Princess, 263, 266, 268, 270, 289–90
Elizabeth (Tudor), Queen, xi, 21, 22, 34–63, 78–79, 80, 81, 83, 84, 87, 91–92, 117–18, 122, 126, 132, 136, 147–55, 166, 191, 192, 193, 194, 205, 206, 266, 270, 273, 274, 282, 287, 292, 339, 349, 350, 361, 364; speech of, to Parliament (1576), 37
Elizabethan world picture, xi
Elton, G. R., viii
Elyot, Sir Thomas: *The Boke Named the Gouvernour* (1531), 94 n, 157; *Defence of Good Women* (1545), 141 n
Emmison, F. G., *Elizabethan Life* (1973), 174–75, 175 n
Empson, William, 112; *Some Versions of Pastoral* (1936), 38
Englands Helicon (1600), 42
English Gentlewoman, The (1631), 303 n
epistemology, 367–92
Erasmus, Desiderius, 147
Esler, Anthony, *The Aspiring Mind of the Elizabethan Younger Generation* (1966), 146 n
Essex, Robert Devereux, second earl of, 146, 150–56, 166, 175, 204
Essex, Robert Devereux, third earl of, 250–52, 255, 267, 269, 289
eurythmia, 378–79
Eusebius, 122
Eutropius, 213
Evans, Margery, 176
Evelyn, John, 344–45
Everitt, Alan, 299; *Change in the Provinces* (1969), 299

Farrington, Benjamin, *The Philosophy of*

Francis Bacon (1964), 340
Fatal Marriage or a Second Lucretia, The (1594?), 169 n
Ferdinand II, 265, 273, 274 n, 281
Ferguson, Arthur B., *The Articulate Citizen and the English Renaissance* (1965), 147 n
Field, Nathaniel, 178 n. *See also* Fletcher, John
Fineman, Joel, 143, 144 n
Fish, Stanley E., *Self-Consuming Artifacts* (1972), 162 n, 368 n
Fisher, F. J., 296 n, 312
Fitz, Linda T. *See* Woodbridge, Linda Fitz
Fitzgeffrey, Henry, *Notes from Black-fryers* (1617), 226 n
Fletcher, Anthony, *A County Community in Peace and War* (1975), 297, 299
Fletcher, John: *Bonduca* (1611–14), 169 n, 172, 177, 178, 179; *The Maid in the Mill* (with William Rowley), 184; *The Queen of Corinth* (with Philip Massinger and Nathaniel Field), 169 n, 172, 177–81, 183, 184, 186–87, 188; *Sir John van Olden Barnavelt* (with Philip Massinger ?1619), 199; *The Tragedy of Valentinian* (with Philip Massinger and Nathaniel Field), 169, 169 n, 170, 170 n, 171–72
Florimène. See Henrietta-Maria, Queen
Florio, John, 159
Ford, John, 184 n
formalism, 4, 7, 31, 366–72, 377–78, 381
Forman, Simon, 132
Foucault, Michel, x, xi, xiii, 12, 12 n, 13 n, 16, 29, 381, 382 n; episteme, x, 6, 12; *The Order of Things* (1966), 10 n, 12 n, 38 n; *Surveiller et Punir (Discipline and Punish;* 1975), 137 n
Foulis, Sir David, 307
Foxe, John, 122, 270; *Book of Martyrs,* 270
Francis I (of France), 64, 67, 69, 70, 72, 73, 91
Fraser, Russell, 193; *The War Against Poetry* (1970), 193 n
Freud, Sigmund, 141–42, 143, 144
Friedlaender, Walter, *Mannerism and Anti-Mannerism in Italian Painting* (1965), 378
Frith, Mary (Moll), 234, 234 n, 235, 235 n, 245
Frubach, V. a, *The Evaporation of the Apple of Palestine* (1637), 264 n
Frye, Northrop, 244–45; *A Natural Perspective* (1965), 244–45
Fulbecke, William, 212, 213, 217, 218; *An His-*

Fulbecke, William (cont.)
torical Collection of the Continuall Factions, Tumults, and Massacres of the Romans and Italians . . . (1601), 212 n, 213–14, 217, 218

Gadamer, Hans–Georg, xiii; *Truth and Method* (1975), xiii
Galen, viii, 309
Garber, Marjorie, xiii
Gardiner, Samuel, *History of England from the Accession of James I to the Outbreak of the Civil War 1603–1642* (1895), 192 n, 267, 283 n, 308–09
Garrard, George, 276, 289
Gascoigne, George, *The Steele Glas* (1576), 226
Geertz, Clifford, xi, 24
gender, xi–xii, xiv, 17, 20, 30, 61, 130–45, 168–90, 223–47, 349
Geoffrey of Monmouth, 282 n
Gibbs, A. M., 290
Gibson, Charles, ed., *The Black Legend* (1971), 119 n
Giocondo, Fra, 377
Glapthorne, Henry, 281; *Albertus Wallenstein* (1639), 274 n, 281–82, 284, 290; *Poems* (1639), 281
Goldberg, Jonathan, ix, xi, 3; *James I and the Politics of Literature* (1983), 3 n; *Voice Terminal Echo* (1986), ix
Golden Age, 318–19, 324, 340
Goldsmith, Oliver, *The Deserted Village* (1770), 330
Gombrich, E. H., 388; *Meditations on a Hobby Horse* (1963), 388
Gorboduc, 106
Gordon, D. J., 249; *The Renaissance Imagination* (1975), 249 n
Gramsci, Antonio, 94, 107
Greenblatt, Stephen, xii, 3, 4 n, 7, 7 n, 9, 21–22, 27–32, 366 n; *Allegory and Representation* (1981), ix; *The Forms of Power and the Power of Forms in the Renaissance* (1982), 3 n; *Renaissance Self-Fashioning* (1980), ix, 3 n, 27, 157
Greene, Robert, *Penelopes Web* (1587), 135 n
Greville, Fulke, 118, 151–52, 153, 200, 204; *Life of Sidney* (1612? pub. 1652), 118, 204; *Mustapha* (1608), 200

Griffin, Robert, *Clément Marot and the Inflections of Poetic Voice* (1974), 68–69 n
Grindal, Edmund, archbishop of Canterbury, 84–87
Guevara, Antonio de, bishop of Carthagena, 324–25
Guicciardini, Francesco, *Ricordi* (n.d.,), 160
Gustavus Adolphus, 274

Haec-Vir: Or the Womanish Man (1620), 224, 227 n, 228, 228 n, 229 n, 231–36, 240–41, 246–47
Hakluyt, Richard, 118–20, 120 n, 121; *A Discourse on Western Planting* (1584), 118–21
Hall, Edward, xiii
Harbage, Alfred, 202; *Shakespeare and the Rival Traditions* (1952), 202
Harrison, William, *A Description of England* (1587), 225 n, 243 n
Harsnett, Samuel, 30
Hartlib, Samuel, 343–44, 344 n, 345–47, 382, 384. See also *Samuel Hartlib his Legacie*
Hatton, Lady, 280–81
Haughton, William. *See* Day, John
Haward, N., *A Briefe Chronicle* (1616), 213
Hawkins, M., 363 n
Hayward, Sir John, 61, 151; Annals (n.d.), 61; *History of Henry IV* (1599), 61
hegemony, viii, 84, 94–107, 139, 295, 350–51, 361–66
Heilbrun, Carolyn G., *Toward a Recognition of Androgyny* (1973), 241
Heilman, Robert, 109
Heinemann, Margot, *Puritanism and Theatre* (1980), 281 n, 292 n
Helgerson, Richard, ix
Heninger, S. K., Jr., *The Cosmographical Glass* (1977), 377 n
Henrietta-Maria, Queen, 62, 190, 268–69, 273, 278–79 n, 278–79, 280, 283, 284, 285–91, 292 n, 295, 306, 312–13; *Florimène,* 62, 269
Henriques, Julian, et al., *Changing the Subject* (1984), 10 n
Henry VI (of England), 57–58
Henry VIII (of England), 48, 122, 200
Henry, Prince of Wales, 168, 170 n, 203, 286, 287
Henslowe, Philip, 194; *Diary,* 194
Herbert, Sir Henry, Master of the Revels, 194,

199–200, 202; *Office Book,* 194. *See also* Buc, Sir George; Master of the Revels; Tilney, Edmund

Herbert, Philip. *See* Pembroke, Philip Herbert

Herington, C. J., 110–11

hermeneutics, 88

Herrick, Robert, 323, 360; "Ceremonies for Candlemas," 362; "Ceremony upon Candlemas Eve," 360; "The Difference betwixt Kings and Subjects," 363; *Hesperides* (1648), 358–61; "The Hock-Cart," 323, 360–61; "A King and No King," 363; "Lawes," 362; "Obedience in Subjects," 363; "A Pastorall upon the Birth of Prince Charles," 366; "Saint Distaffs Day," 360; "Twelfe Night," 360; "Upon Candlemas day," 360; "The Wake," 359

Hesiod, 318

Heylyn, Peter, 358; *History of St. George* (1630), 358–59

Heywood, Thomas: *An Apology for Actors* (1612), viii, 194–95; *England's Eliza* (1631), 270; *If You Know Not Me* (1605), 274 n; *The Life and Death of Sir Martyn Skink* (with Richard Brome; n.d.), 282; *Love's Mistress, or the Queen's Masque* (1634), 273; *Pleasant Dialogues and Dramas* (1637), 270–73; *The Rape of Lucrece* (1608), 169–70, 270, 273–74; *A Woman Killed with Kindness* (1607), 30

Hic Mulier, or the Man-Woman (1620), 135, 223–24, 227 n, 228, 228 n, 229–33, 233 n, 234–36, 238, 239–43, 243 n, 246–47

hierarchy, 133, 230, 234, 236, 246, 295–98, 303–04, 318, 320–26, 330–33, 338, 349, 351, 352, 353, 356, 361–66

Hill, Christopher, viii, 26, 61; *The Century of Revolution 1603–1714* (1966), 297, 299, 300, 308, 309; *Intellectual Origins of the English Revolution* (1965), 205 n, 337 n; *Puritanism and Revolution* (1958), 266, 266 n, 326 n, 351, 352, 353, 362; *Reformation to Industrial Revolution* (rev. 1969), 53 n, 60; *The World Turned Upside Down* (1975), 365

Hill, L. M., 297

Hobbes, Thomas, 390

Hoffman, Nancy Jo, *Spenser's Pastorals* (1977), 65 n

Holbein, Hans, *Icones Historianum Veteris, Testamenti* (1547), 332

Holdsworth, W. S., *A History of English Law* (1923), 173–74

Hole, Christine, *A Dictionary of British Folk-Customs* (1978), 362 n, 366

Holinshed, Raphael, xiii; *Chronicles of England, Scotland, and Ireland* (1579 ed.), 282 n; (1587 ed.), 36 n

Holland, Henry Rich, earl of, 268, 269–70 n, 277, 290; "Poem of Joy" (?), 269–70

Holles, Gervase, 277 n, 278–79 n

Holloway, Wendy, et al., *Changing the Subject* (1984), 10 n

Homer, *Odyssey,* 318

homily on obedience (1559), 21, 43

Honoria and Mammon (1659), 321–22

Hooker, Richard, 219 n, 220; *Of the Laws of Ecclesiastical Polity* (1597), 219 n

Horace, 318, 335; *Epode II,* 322, 324

Howard, Charles. *See* Nottingham, Charles Lord Harold

Howard, Frances, 175, 250–51, 251 n, 252 n, 253–56, 263

Howard, Thomas. *See* Arundel, Thomas Howard; Suffolk, Thomas Howard

Howard family, 252, 254–55, 263

Howell, James, 201, 201 n, 276, 290, 290 n

Howson, John, 349–50

Hughes, P. L. *See* Larkin, J. F.

Huizinga, Johan, 93; *Homo Ludens,* 93

Hull, Suzanne, *Chaste, Silent, and Obedient* (1982), 135 n, 229 n

humanism, vii–viii, ix, 5–6, 27, 62, 65, 69, 70, 79, 95, 142, 147–49, 151, 152, 154, 157–58, 166–67, 317–20, 335–36, 338, 341, 343, 347, 372, 388; humanist poetics, 96; "political humanism," 147–52, 154, 166–67

Hunter, G. K., 109, 205; *John Lyly* (1962), 148 n

Hunter, William B., Jr., 390

Huntley, Frank L., 369

Hurstfield, Joel, *Freedom, Corruption, and Government in Elizabethan England* (1973), 60 n, 150

Hyams, Edward, *Soil and Civilization* (1952), 329 n, 342

Hyde, Edward (later earl of Clarendon), 276. *See also* Clarendon, Edward Hyde

Hyde, Nicholas, 276; as Lord Chief Justice, 275

identity formation, 27, 133–35, 157, 159–60
ideologeme. *See* ideology
ideology, xiv, 7, 18–20, 23–26, 29–32, 43, 45,
    49, 72, 83, 91, 105, 138, 142, 144, 145, 149,
    152, 249, 265–92, 293–94, 298–99, 302, 306,
    310, 312–15, 318–19, 321–30, 333–36,
    338–40, 350, 353–57, 361–66; ideologeme,
    306
imagination, 305–06
Inns of Court, 274, 301, 306, 315; revels,
    275–79, 291–92, 295
intertextuality, xiii–xiv, 15, 17, 64–92,
    108–16, 317–20, 335–36, 341, 343
Irigaray, Luce, 143, 144; *Ce sexe qui n'en est pas
    un* (1977), 143; *Speculum de l'autre femme*
    (1974), 137 n, 143
Isocrates, 388

James VI and I (of England), xi, 8, 14, 21,
    61–62, 150, 168, 174, 191–206 passim, 219,
    227–28, 233, 249, 251, 253, 255–66 passim,
    270, 273, 295, 296, 298, 333–34, 339, 349,
    351, 355; *Basilikon Doron* (1599), 203;
    Book of Sports (1618), 352
Jameson, Frederic, 133–34, 144–45; *The
    Political Unconscious* (1981), 133–34
Jardine, Lisa, 3; *Still Harping on Daughters*
    (1983), 3 n, 135 n
Javitch, Daniel, *Poetry and Courtliness in Ren-
    aissance England* (1978), 146 n, 147 n, 148 n
Jermyn, Henry, 290
Johnson, S. F., 127 n
Jones, Inigo, 269
Jones, R. G., 382–83 n
Jonson, Ben, 15, 18, 196, 202, 205–22 passim,
    248–64 passim, 294, 312, 320, 347, 354,
    355–57; and Roman history, 208–10; on
    Thomas Kyd, 109; *The Alchemist* (1612),
    15; *Bartholomew Fair* (1631), 15; *Catiline*
    (1611), 188, 207–17 passim, 220, 222; *A
    Challenge at Tilt,* 252–54; *Discoveries,* 214,
    216; *Eastward Ho,* 196, 202; *Epigrams* (1640),
    216–17; "Epistle to John Selden," 263;
    Hymenaei (1606), 249, 255, 263, 294; *Irish
    Masque at Court,* 252–53, 255, 257–63; *Love
    Restored,* 261; *Love's Triumph Through
    Callipolis* (1630), 250; *The New Inn* (1629),
    248; "Ode to Himself," 169; *Poetaster*
    (1601), 218; *Sejanus* (1605), 207–11, 215–22,
    "To Penshurst," 352, 354; "To Sir Robert

Wroth," 359 n; *The Vision of Delight* (1617),
    295 n; *Volpone* (1606), 169 n
Jordan, Constance, 141 n
Juvenal, 205, 282

Kahn, Coppélia, 170 n
Kautsky, Karl, *Thomas More and His Utopia*
    (1888), 6 n
Kelly-Gadol, Joan, xi
Kelso, Ruth, *Doctrine for the Lady of the Ren-
    aissance* (1956), 135 n, 296 n
Kenyon, J. P., ed., *The Stuart Constitution
    1603–1688* (1966), 297–98, 307
Kermode, Frank, *The Classic* (1975), 122
*King and Queen's Entertainment at Richmond,
    The* (1636), 286
King's Men, 202, 285–86
Kinner, Cyprian, 384
Kinney, Arthur F., ed., *Elizabethan Back-
    grounds* (1975), 43 n
Koebner, Richard, 122
Kolve, V. A., *The Play Called Corpus Christi*
    (1966), 43–44
Kriedte, P., H. Medick, and J. Schlumbohm,
    Industrialization before Industrialization
    (1981), 354
Kyd, Thomas, 108–16, 120 n, 121–24; *The
    Spanish Tragedy* (1589?), 108–16, 120 n,
    121, 122, 123–29

Lacan, Jacques, 27, 143
LaCapra, Dominick, 13, 13 n, 20, 20 n
Lake, Sir Thomas, 197
Lambe, Dr., 175–76
Lane, John, *Elegie upon the death of the high
    renowned Princesse, our late Souveraigne Eliza-
    beth* (1603), 80 n
Larkin, J. F., and P. L. Hughes, ed., *Stuart
    Royal Proclamations* (1973), 354
Laud, William, archbishop of Canterbury,
    281, 286, 315 n, 358, 364
LeFèvre, Jacques, 69, 71
Leicester, Robert Dudley, earl of, 80, 84, 117,
    150–51, 284
Lemaire, Jean de Belges, 74–75
Lentricchia, Frank, *After the New Criticism*
    (1980), 5 n
L'Estrange, H., *The Reign of King Charles*
    (1656), 275 n

L'Estrange, Sir R., *Charles I* (n.d.), 362

Levin, Richard, *New Readings vs. Old Plays* (1979), 9, 123

Levine, D., *Family Formation in an Age of Nascent Capitalism* (1977), 354

Lévi-Strauss, Claude, xii

Levy, F. J., *Tudor Historical Thought* (1967), 160 n

Lewis, Thomas E., 293 n

libel, 191–206

Life and Death of Mrs. Mary Frith, The (1662), 234 n

Lilburne, John, 344, 346

Lisle, John, 276

Livermore, H. V., *A New History of Portugal* (1966), 120 n

Locke, John, 391; *Essay of Human Understanding* (1794 ed.), 391

Lodge, Thomas, 214–15; *The Wounds of Civil War* (1594), 210, 214–15

Longhurst, Peter, 4 n

Louis XIII (of France), 271–72

Louis, Charles, Count Palatine of the Rhine and Prince Elector of the Holy Roman Empire, 265–92 passim

Louis, Frederick, 265

Louis, Rupert, 268, 271–72, 279 n, 289–91

Louise of Savoy (Queen Mother of France), 68, 70, 71, 72, 80

Lovejoy, Arthur O., and George Boas, *Primitivism and Related Ideas in Antiquity* (1935), 340 n

Low, Anthony, 320 n

Lucretius, *De Rerum Natura*, 341

Lull, Raymond, 382

Luttrell, Thomas, 257, 261

Lytle, G. F. *See* Orgel, Stephen

MacCaffrey, Wallace T., viii, 147 n; *Queen Elizabeth and the Making of Policy 1572–1588* (1981), 117 n

Macfarlane, Alan, *Witchcraft in Tudor and Stuart England* (1970), 137 n

Machery, Pierre, 19; *A Theory of Literary Production* (trans. 1978), 19 n

Machiavelli, Niccolò, 151, 161–62, 163, 208, 215, 284, 306; *Discourses on Livy*, 160–62; *The Prince*, 162

McLane, Paul, 80; *Spenser's Shepheardes Calender* (1961), 80 n

Maltby, William S., *The Black Legend in England* (1971), 119 n

Mannerism, 378–79

Manners, Roger. *See* Rutland, Roger Manners

Mantuan, 74, 84; *Eclogue 6*, 74

Marcus, Leah, 3, 249 n, 294, 294 n, 295, 297 n, 312, 358, 365–66, 366 n; *Childhood and Cultural Despair* (1978), 3 n

Margaret of Angoulème, Queen of Navarre, 67–70

Markham, Gervase, 334, 343, 345; *The English Husbandman* (1613), 334; *Second Booke* (1614), 334

Marlowe, Christopher, 106, 282, 284; *The Jew of Malta*, 214; *Tamburlaine* (1590), 28

Marot, Clément, 64–92 passim; *Adolescence Clementine* (1532), 69, 71, 72; "Colin d'Anjou Thenot de Poictou" (and English paraphrase), 70, 77, 78; *La Complaincte d'un Pastoureau Chrestien* (1549), 75–76, 92; *Eglogue au roy soubz les noms de Pan et Robin*, 64, 67, 73–78, 81–82; *L'Enfer*, 68, 69, 70, 76; *Epistre au Roy, du temps de son exil a Ferrare*, 72–73; *Oeuvres* (1539), 77; *Trente Pseaulmes* (1542), 65, 76

Marotti, Arthur, 3, 4 n, 294 n

Marston, John, 196, 205; *Eastward Ho*, 196, 197; *The Fawn*, 205; *The Scourge of Villany* (1598), 205; *The Wonder of Women or the Tragedy of Sophonisba* (1605), 169 n

Martines, Lauro, *Power and Imagination* (1979), 148 n; *The Social World of the Florentine Humanists* (1963), 147 n

Marvell, Andrew, 90; "The Garden," 90

Marx, Karl, *The German Ideology*, 18 n, 299, 299–300 n

Marxism, x, 17–20, 22, 32, 91

Mary Tudor (Queen of England), 36, 37, 56, 122, 270

Masque of Flowers, 253

Massinger, Philip, 168, 169, 178 n, 180, 187, 188, 189; *The Bondman* (1623), 188; *The Unnatural Combat*, 187, 188–90. *See also* Fletcher, John

master narrative, 133, 145

Master of the Revels, 192–206 passim

Mathew, D., *The Age of Charles* (1951), 268

matriarchy, 54

maximum in minimo, 390

May, Sir Humphrey, 276
May, Thomas, *Virgil's Georgicks* (1628), 318 n
Mayer, C. A., 68, 71; *Clément Marot* (1972), 68 n
Medick, H. *See* Kriedte, P.
Medvedev, P. N. *See* Bakhtin, Mikhail
Melton, John, 195
"Merrie England" myth, 348–66
Merton, E. S., *Science and Imagination in Sir Thomas Browne* (1949), 367
metadrama, 133, 138, 195. *See also* dumb show
Mexia, Pedro, *The Historie of all the Romane Emperors* (trans. W. Traheron; 1604), 217
Middleton, Thomas, 183, 187, 205, 235; *The Changeling* (with William Rowley), 189; *A Game at Chess* (1625), 196, 200–201, 201 n, 202; *Masque of Cupid* (lost), 253; *The Roaring Girl* (with Thomas Dekker; 1608–11), 135, 223–24, 228 n, 230, 234–47; *The Spanish Gypsy,* 169 n, 172, 184–87, 188
Mildmay, Sir Humphrey, 314–15
Miller, Edwin H., 200; *The Professional Writer in Elizabethan England* (1959), 200
Miller, Nancy K., 141 n, 143
Milton, John, 266, 319–20, 322, 343, 345, 347; and Vergil, 345; *Eikonoklastes* (1649), 46; *Lycidas* (1638), 62; "Of Education," 345; "On the Morning of Christ's Nativity" (1629), 62–63; *Paradise Regained,* 347; *Poems of Mr. John Milton* (1645), 62
Miner, Earl, viii–ix
modernism, 89, 91, 92
Monck, George, 344, 346
monopolies, 308–10
Montaigne, Michel de: on Vergil, 317, 317 n; *Essaies,* 159–60; "Of Books," 317 n; "On Cannibals," 318
Montemayor, Jorge de, 90
Montgomery, earl of. *See* Pembroke, Philip Herbert
Montrose, Louis Adrian, 3, 3 n, 7, 7 n, 9, 21–27, 32, 65, 91–92, 93 n, 132, 134, 134 n, 136–37, 366 n
More, John, 252
More, Sir Thomas, 6 n, 28; *Utopia,* 148, 157, 330
Moretti, Franco, *Signs Taken for Wonders* (1983), 102 n
Morrill, J. S., *Cheshire 1630–1660* (1974), 299–300

Mucedorus, 195
Muir, E., *Civic Ritual in Renaissance Venice* (1981), 349
Mulde Sacke: Or The Apologie of Hic Mulier: To the late Declamation against her (1620), 227 n
Mullaney, Steven, 3, 3–4 n, 366 n
Mulvey, Laura, 137 n

narrativization. *See* Althusser, Louis; Jameson, Frederic; White, Hayden
Nashe, Thomas, 388; *Christs Teares over Jerusalem* (1590), 225 n, 243 n; *Lenten Stuffe* (1599), 388; *The Unfortunate Traveller* (1594), 285
Nativity pageant (Chester cycle), 43
Neale, Sir John, 51; *Elizabeth I and Her Parliaments 1558–1581* (1958), 37 n, 38 n; *Essays in Elizabethan History* (1958), 46 n, 51 n, 147 n
neoclassicism, 106
Newcastle, Duke of, 351, 353, 359, 362, 363, 364
New Criticism, 4
New Husbandry, 327–34
New Science, 317–47 passim
Newton, Sir Isaac, 391; *Opticks,* 391
Newton, Thomas, 111; *Seneca His Tenne Tragedies* (1581), 111
Niccoles, Alexander, *A Discourse of Marriage and Wiving* (1620 ed.), 226 n
Nichols, John, *The Progresses and Public Processions of Queen Elizabeth* (1823), 40 n
Noot, Jan van der, *A Theatre for Worldlings* (1569), 78, 78 n
Norbrook, David, *Poetry and Politics* (1984), 263 n
North, Sir Thomas, *Lives of Noble Greeks and Romans* (trans. Plutarch, 1579), vii
Northampton, Henry Howard, earl of, 251–52 n
Northumberland, Henry Percy, earl of, 204, 268, 278
Notestein, Wallace, *The House of Commons 1604–1610* (1971), 204 n
Nottingham, Charles Lord Howard of Effingham, earl of, 351
Novy, Marianne, 138 n, 139 n
Nowell, Alexander, 352; *Catechism* (1570), 352

Ogilby, John, *The Works of Publius Vergilius Maro* (1649), 318 n

Ong, Walter J.: *The Barbarian Within* (1962), 387 n; *Ramus, Method, and the Decay of Dialogue* (1958), 387 n

Orgel, Stephen, 3; *The Illusion of Power* (1975), 3 n, 107 n, 315; *Inigo Jones* (with Roy Strong; 1973), 294 n, 295 n, 313; *The Jonsonian Masque* (1965), 294 n; *Patronage in the Renaissance* (with G. F. Lytle; 1981), 364 n

Orpheus, 318

Osbalston, Lambert, 281

Overbury, Sir Thomas, 175, 251, 253, 263; *Characters* (1614), 253

Ovid, 47, 53–55, 69 n, 96, 139, 318; *Metamorphoses*, 53–54, 318

Pacioli, Luce, 377; *Divina Proportione*, 377

Palladio, Andrea, 377

Panharmony, 380

Panofsky, Erwin: *Idea: A Concept in Art Theory* (trans. 1968), 378; *Meaning in the Visual Arts* (1955), 377–78; *Studies in Iconology* (1939), 340 n

Pansophia, 381, 383, 387

Parker, Patricia, viii

Pasquils Palinodia (1619), 351–52, 362–63

Passeron, Jean-Claude. *See* Bourdieu, P.

paternalism, 351–52, 355–56

patriarchy, 30, 133–45, 170–71, 187, 355, 356

patronage, 146, 146–47 n, 151, 152–56, 166, 364

Patterson, Annabel, *Censorship and Interpretation* (1984), 206 n

Peacham, Edmund, 191–92, 197

Peacham, Henry, *The Complete Gentleman* (1622), 323

Peele, George, 23 n, 38–40; *Descensus Astraea* (1591), 38; "An Eclogue Gratulatorie . . . " (1589), 39

Pembroke, Philip Herbert, earl of Pembroke and Montgomery and Lord Chamberlain, 196, 202, 252, 252 n, 254, 276

Percy, Henry. *See* Northumberland, Henry Percy

perspective, 378–79

Peterson, Joyce E., *Curs'd Example: "The Duchess of Malfi" and Commonwealth Tragedy* (1978), 104 n

Petrarch (Francesco Petrarca), 55, 77, 84; *Canzoniere*, 55; *Trionfi*, 55

phenomenology, 367–92

Philip of Spain, 117–19, 150

Phillips, John, *The Reformation of Images 1535–1600* (1973), 46 n

Pickering, 191, 197

Pierce, bishop of Bath and Wells, 352–53, 362

Plato, xiv

Platter, Thomas, 348

Play of the Netherlands, 282

Pliny, 336, 389

Plotinus, *Enneads V*, 382

Plutarch, xiv, 212, 214; *Lives of Noble Greeks and Romans* (trans. 1579), vii

Pocock, J. G. A., *The Machiavellian Moment* (1975), 148 n

Polybius, 210

Porter, Endimion, 290, 357

Poster, Mark, 12 n

postmodernism, x, 65

poststructuralism, 9, 32

Prescott, Anne Lake, *French Poets and the English Renaissance* (1978), 65 n

Price, William H., *The English Patents of Monopoly* (1906), 308–09

Prima Pastorum, 42

Privy Council, 194, 271, 277, 297, 312. See also *Book of Orders*

Proteus, 318

Proxy, The, 278

Prynne, William, 205, 295, 361, 364, 364 n; *Histrio-mastix* (1633), 361

psychology, Renaissance, 305

Ptolemy, viii

Puckering, Sir John, 154, 155

Puttenham, George, 93–107; *The Arte of English Poesie* (1589), vii–viii, 21, 34–35, 88–89, 91, 93

Queens Entertainment at Richmond (1636), 286–89

Queen's Men, 273

Quinn, David Beers, *The Elizabethans and the Irish* (1966), 258 n

Quintilian, xiv, 367, 389

Rabelais, François, *Gargantua* (1532), 66

Ralegh, Sir Walter, xiii, 58, 118, 118 n, 127 n, 204; *History of the World* (1614), ix; *Observations touching Trade and Commerce with the Hollander, and other Nations* (n.d.), 333–34, 339

Randolph, Thomas, 357

Rankins, William, *A Mirrour of Monsters* (1589), 100 n, 105 n
Ray, John, 384–86, 386 n; *Methodus Plantarum Nova,* 385–86
reader-response criticism, 8, 11, 89, 90, 161–62, 165
Renaissance imagination, 305–06
Renaissance psychology, 305
representation, xii, 18–20, 28, 32, 64, 84, 90, 95, 98–101, 104, 105, 132, 137–38, 142, 144, 145, 305, 312, 387
Reynolds, John, *Votivae Angliae,* 266
Reynolds, Richard, *A Chronicle of all the noble Emperours of the Romaines from Julius Caesar* (1571), 217
rhetoric, ix-x, xiv, 38, 110, 146, 148, 165–66, 183–84, 230–31, 357–58, 388
Riceour, Paul, ix
Rich, Barnabe, 257; *The Honestie of this Age* (1614), 226 n; *A New Description of Ireland* (1610), 257, 259
Rich, Henry. *See* Holland, Henry Rich
Righter, Anne, 161
Rigolot, Francois, *Poétique et Onomastique* (1977), 68–69
Rilke, Rainer Maria, "Sonnets to Orpheus," 96
Ripa, Cesare, *Iconologia* (1603), 305 n
Riviere, Joan, 141 n
Roe, Sir Thomas, 268, 289
Roos, 175
Rosenmeyer, Thomas, *The Green Cabinet* (1969), 65, 89, 90
Rossky, William, 305 n
Røstvig, Maren-Sofie, *The Happy Man* (1954), 322, 335 n
Rousseau, Jean-Jacques, 318
Rowley, William, 187; *All's Lost by Lust* (1633), 169 n, 172, 180–82, 184, 187, 188; *The Changeling* (with Thomas Middleton; n.d.), 189; *The Maid in the Mill* (with John Fletcher; n.d.), 184; *The Spanish Gypsy* (with Thomas Middleton; n.d.), 184–87, 188
Roy, Louis le, *De la vicissitude ou variéte des choses en L'univers* (1575), 126 n
Royal Society, 337, 345, 347, 379, 383. *See also* Birch, Thomas; Sprat, Thomas
Rubys, Claude de, 353, 362
ruralization, 354–58, 364–66

Rural Socrates, The, 329
Rushworth, J., *Historical Collections* (1980), 281 n
Russell, Francis. *See* Bedford, Francis Russell
Rutland, Roger Manners, earl of, 157–58
Ryan, Kiernan, 3, 3 n

Sackville, Thomas, 58, 108; *The Mirrour of Magistrates* (1559), 94 n, 108, 217, 282
Salisbury, Robert Cecil, earl of, 168, 277
Sallust, 209, 214
Salmacida Spolia (n.d.), 365
Samaha, Joel, *Law and Order in Historical Perspective* (1974), 174 n
Samuel Hartlib his Legacie (1651), 346
Sannazaro, Jacopo, 77
Sarbrewski, Casimir, 324
Saussure, René de, 8, 69
Savile, Henry, 151
Scaliger, Julius Caesar, 368
Scamozzi, Vincenzo, *Idea della Architectura Universale* (1616), 372
Scandalum Magnatum, 191, 194, 195, 200
Schellhase, Kenneth C., *Tacitus in Renaissance Political Thought* (1976), 152 n
Schelling, Felix E., *Foreign Influences in Elizabethan Plays* (1923), 122
Schlumbohn, J., *See* Kriedte, P.
"Scots' Mine" (play), 197, 201
Scott, Thomas, *The Spaniard's Perpetual Designs to an Universal Monarchy* (1624), 290
Sebillet, Thomas, *L'Art poétique francoys* (1932), 88 n
Second Maiden's Tragedy, The (1611), 169 n
Second Shepherds Play, The, xii; as *Secunda Pastorum* (Wakefield), 59
Segar, Sir George (assistant to the Master of the Revels), 199. *See also* Buc, Sir George; Herbert, Sir Henry; Master of the Revels; Tilney, Edmund; Wilson
Selden, John, 207, 263
semiotics, x, 8, 68–69
Seneca, 108–12, 115–16, 123–25, 127, 129, 151, 177–78, 286; *Hippolytus,* 127, 129; "The Man Who Raped Two Women," 177–78; *Medea,* 129; *Oedipus,* 110; *Thyestes,* 109–10
Senilis Amor, 274
Servius (Maurus Servius Honoratus), 65, 65 n, 81, 111–12, 116

Sessions, William A., 320

Shakespeare, William, 4, 4 n, 16, 23–24, 28, 31, 106, 129, 133, 137, 144, 209, 243, 282; *Antony and Cleopatra*, 197–98, 210; *As You Like It*, 23–24, 144, 187, 243–45; *The Comedy of Errors*, xii; *Coriolanus*, 210; *Cymbeline*, 169 n, 282–83; *Hamlet*, 195; *Henry V*, 356, 365; *Julius Caesar*, 210; *King Lear*, 30–31; *Measure for Measure*, 14, 180; *The Merchant of Venice*, 143, 144; *A Midsummer Night's Dream*, 26 n, 203, 244–45; *Othello*, 28, 182; *Pericles*, 169 n; *The Taming of the Shrew*, 132–35, 137–45; *Titus Andronicus*, 169–70, 180; *Twelfth Night*, 144, 243–45

Shapiro, Barbara, *John Wilkins 1614–1672* (1969), 337 n, 344

Sharpham, 205

Shelley, Percy Bysshe, 347

Shepherd's Paradise, The (1630), 62

Shirley, James, *The Triumph of Peace* (1633), 275, 295, 300–307, 307 n, 309–16

Sidney, Sir Philip, 22, 39, 78–79, 80, 88, 90, 94, 103, 106, 118, 150–52, 166, 213, 221–22, 290–91, 354; *An Apology for Poetry* (1595), 88, 103–04, 130, 213, 221–22; *Arcadia* (1590), 31, 39, 354; *The Lady of May* (c. 1578), 22; *Letter to Queen Elizabeth* (1580), 78–79, 84

Sidney, Robert, 151

Sidney, William, 354

Siebert, Frederick S., *Freedom of the Press in England, 1476–1776* (1952), 191 n, 192, 193

Sinfield, Alan, 3; *Literature in Protestant England 1560–1660* (1982), 3 n

Singleton, Hugh, 79

Skelton, John, 64, 79, 79 n

Smith, Hallett, *Elizabethan Poetry* (1952), 34

Smith, Henry, *Preparative to Marriage* (1951), 143 n

Smuts, M., 364

Somerset, Robert Carr, earl of, 168, 175, 203, 250–51

sophistry, xiv

Speed, John, 207

Spelman, Sir Henry, 276

Spenser, Edmund, 22, 26–27, 28, 62, 64–66, 77–92, 121, 122, 126, 130, 221, 258 n, 259, 287, 319–20, 347; *The Faerie Queene* (1590; 1596), 66, 221, 282, 287–88, 347; *The Shepheardes Calender* (1579), 47–49, 54 n, 64–66, 77–90, 92; *A Theatre (for) Worldlings* (with Jan van der Noot; 1569), 78; *A View of the Present State of Ireland* (pub. 1633), 259

Sprat, Thomas, 320; *History of the Royal Society*, 320

Springell, F.C., *Connisseur and Diplomat* (1963), 265, 265 n, 267, 286 n

Stanley, Anne. *See* Derby, Anne Stanley

Star Chamber, 191–92, 202, 257, 276, 281, 295, 298, 307, 309, 363

Stationers' Company, 192

Statute of Monopolies (1624), 308–10

Stimpson, Catharine R., 170 n

Stone, Lawrence, viii, 9, 16, 26, 58–59; *The Causes of the English Revolution 1529–1642* (1972), 299, 300, 306, 315 n; *The Crisis of the Aristocracy* (1965), 58–59, 135 n, 175, 296 n, 297 n, 298, 299, 311, 312, 354

Stow, John, xiii

Strong, Roy: *The Cult of Elizabeth* (1977), 46, 349; *Portraits of Queen Elizabeth* (1963), 46 n; *Splendour at Court* (1973), 44. *See also* Orgel, Stephen

structuralism, 4–5

Strype, John, 87 n

Stubbes, Philip, 361; *Anatomy of Abuses* (1583), 225 n, 226, 361

Stubbs, John, 79, 205; *The Gaping Gulf* (1579), 79, 87

subversion, xi, 19, 20, 24–25, 27–31, 89, 107, 137–38, 144, 145, 162–65, 275, 348–59, 361–66

Sudeley Entertainment (1591), 52–57, 58, 59, 60, 91

Suffolk, Thomas Howard, earl of, 252, 261; as Lord Chamberlain, 261

Swetnam, Joseph, *Arraignment of lewd, idle, froward and inconstant women* (1615–16), 135, 227 n

Swetnam, the Woman-hater, Arraigned by Women (1620), 227 n

Swift, Jonathan, *Gulliver's Travels* (1726), 380

Tacitus, 151, 208, 209, 214, 219–20; *Works* (trans. H. Savile; 1591), 146 n

Talbot, Sir William, 257, 261

Taylor, T., *Christ's Victory over the Dragon* (1633), 266

Tenison, E. M., *Elizabethan England* (1933), 117 n

Tennenhouse, Leonard, 3, 4 n
Terence, *Hecyra, or The Mother-in-Law,* 172 n
textualization, 133–34
Theocritus, 77, 90
Theophrastus, 368
Thirsk, Joan, ed., *The Agrarian History of England and Wales 1500–1600* (1967), 53 n
Thomas, Keith, 9, 24, 26; "The Place of Laughter in Tudor and Stuart England," 240; *Religion and the Decline of Magic* (1971), 137 n
Thomas, P. W., 62, 315
Thompson, E. P., 348
Thompson, James, *The Seasons* (1726–30), 318
Tillyard, E. M. W., viii, xiv, 4, 4 n, 8; *The Elizabethan World Picture* (1943), viii
Tilney, Edmund, Master of the Revels, 198. *See also* Master of the Revels; Segar, Sir George; Wilson
Todorov, Tzvetan, 12; *The Conquest of America* (1984), 12 n
Touerner, Cyril: *The Atheist's Tragedy* (1609), 169 n; *The Revenger's Tragedy* (1607), 169–70, 172
Townsend, Charles, Viscount ("Turnip Townsend"), 330
transvestism, xii, 131–34, 145, 223–47, 361
Trexler, R. C., *Public Life in Renaissance Florence* (1980), 349
Trompf, G. W., *The Idea of Historical Recurrence in Western Thought* (1979), 126 n
Trussel, John, 356–57
Tuchet, James. *See* Castlehaven, James Tuchet
Tudor myth, xi, 122, 312
Turner, James, *The Politics of Landscape* (1979), 321, 322 n
Turner, Victor, 24, 25
Tusser, Thomas, *Five Hundred Pointes of Good Husbandrie* (1580), 330–34
Two Angry Women of Abington (1598), 135

Underdown, David, 132 n, 136–38
universal language, 379–81, 383–84, 387–88
Urwin, Cathy, et al., *Changing the Subject* (1984), 10 n

Van Gennep, A., 360; *The Rites of Passage* (trans. 1909), 360
Varro, 336
Vaughan, Henry, 324–26, 345; *The Praise and*

Happinesse of the Countrie-Life (1651), 324–26; "The Praise of a Religious Life," 324; "To the River *Isca,*" 324; "Upon the Priorie Grove," 324
Vellius, Paterculus, 221
Venn, Couze, et al., *Changing the Subject* (1984), 10 n
Vergil, 41, 47, 49, 54, 55, 62, 64–69, 69 n, 71, 74–92 passim, 108, 110, 112, 122, 124, 125, 126, 129, 130, 317, 333–47 passim; *Aeneid,* 100 n, 108, 110–16, 123–24, 126, 129, 318, 319, 339, 340, 341; *Eclogue 1,* 64, 69, 70, 71, 73, 83, 88; *Eclogue 2,* 73; *Eclogue 4,* 41, 42, 54, 77, 83, 91, 318; *Eclogue 5,* 83; *Eclogues,* 92; *Georgic 1,* 81, 333, 340; *Georgic 2,* 325; *Georgics,* 317–20, 330, 340. *See also* Dryden, John
Villiers, George. *See* Buckingham, George Villiers
Vinci, Leonardo da, 377; *Notebooks,* 372; *Trattato della Pittura,* 372
Vitruvius, 341, 372, 376, 377; *The Ten Books on Architecture* (trans. 1914), 377
Vives, Juan Luis, 147; *Instruction of a Christian Woman* (c. 1529), 225–26, 225–26 n
Vivian, Sir Francis, 276, 277 n

Waith, Eugene, 177–78
Walkerdine, Valerie, et al., *Changing the Subject* (1984), 10 n
Waller, Edmund, 345 n
Wallerstein, I., *The Modern World-System* (1974), 354
Wallington, Nicholas, 356
Walsingham, Frances, 151
Walsingham, Sir Francis, 80, 117, 118, 151
Walton, Izaak, 323, 345; *The Compleat Angler* (1653), 323
Warwick, Sir Robert Dudley, earl of, 268, 289
Wayne, Don E., viii, 3, 4 n, 15–16, 18; *Penshurst* (1984), 4 n
Webb, Sidney and Beatrice, *English Local Government* (1906), 297
Wedgwood, C. V.: *Poetry and Politics under the Stuarts* (1960), 315; *The Thirty Years' War* (1938), 265 n
Wernham, R. B., *The Making of Elizabethan Foreign Policy 1558–1603* (1980), 117, 117 n
Weston, Sir Richard, *A discours of Husbandrie used in Brabant and Flanders* (1650), 344. See also *Samuel Hartlib his Legacie* (a sequel)
Wheatley, Henry B. *See* Cunningham, Peter

Whigham, Frank, viii

White, Hayden, *Tropics of Discourse* (1978), 11–12, 11 n, 14. *See also* master narrative

Whitelocke, Bulstrode, 295, 310, 313–14, 316; *Memorials of the English Affairs* (1682), 295

Whitgift, John, archbishop of Canterbury, 191, 204

Whitney, Geffrey, 319, 332

Wickham, Glynn, 192–93, 206

Wilkins, John, 344–45, 382, 382 n, 384, 385–87, 391; *An Essay towards a Real Character, and a Philosophical Language* (1668), 374–75, 383, 385–86, 391; *Mercury, or the Secret and Swift Messenger* (1641), 382

Wilkinson, L. P., *The Georgics of Virgil,* (1969), 317 n

Willcox, W. B., *Gloucestershire* (1940), 307 n

Willet, C., and Phillis Cunnington, *Handbook of English Costume in the Seventeenth Century* (1955), 301 n

Willey, Basil, *The Seventeenth-Century Background* (1953), 367

Williams, John, bishop of London, 281

Williams, Raymond, x, 26, 91; *The Country and the City* (1973), 91, 323, 354

Williamson, George, *The Senecan Amble* (1951), 152 n

William "the Silent" (Prince of Orange), 117

Wilson (assistant to the Master of the Revels), 199. *See also* Buc, Sir George; Herbert, Sir Henry; Master of the Revels; Tilney, Edmund

Wilson, Elikin Calhoun, *England's Eliza* (1939), 35 n, 55 n

Wilson, John Dover, *Life in Shakespeare's England* (1920), 225 n

Wilson, Thomas, *The Arte of Rhetorike* (1560), 97

Wingfield, Antony, attrib., *A true coppie of a discourse written by a gentleman, employed in the late voyage of Spaine and Portingale* (1589), 120 n

Winstanley, Gerard, 346, 365

Wither, George, 319, 331

Wittkower, Rudolf, *Architectural Principles in the Age of Humanism* (1949), 372, 377

Wood, Anthony à, 355; *Athenae et Fasti Oxonienses,* 355

Woodbridge, Linda Fitz, *Women and the English Renaissance* (1984), 224 n, 225 n, 227 n, 229, 229 n, 231, 238

Wotton, Sir Henry, 350, 352

Wright, Louis B., *Middle-Class Culture in Elizabethan England* (1935), 224 n, 226–27, 227 n, 228–29, 231 n, 311

Wrightson, Keith, *English Society 1580–1680* (1982), 135 n, 363

Wrightson, Keith, and D. Levine, *Poverty and Piety in an English Village* (1979), 362

Yates, Frances A., 121; *The Art of Memory* (1966), 382–83; *Astraea* (1975), 46, 54–55, 57, 59, 121–22

Young, Arthur, 327, 329; *Annals of Agriculture* (1784–1809), 327; *Rural Oeconomy* (1770), 327–28

Zorzi, Francesco, 377